They Say There Was a War

Sad Sack made his debut in the May 1942 issue of *Yank Magazine*. The character became enormously popular among servicemen and the public and lived long after the war in his own cartoon strip. Sad Sack was the protagonist in many Army training films. *Courtesy Latrobe Historical Society.*

They Say There Was a War

General Editors:

Richard David Wissolik
David Wilmes
Eric Greisinger
John DePaul

Editors:

Katie Killen
Srdan Smailbegovich
Rick Claypool
Gary E. J. Smith
Michael Cerce
Barbara J. Wissolik
Erica Wissolik

*Publications of the Saint Vincent College
Center for Northern Appalachian Studies
Richard David Wissolik (Director and General Editor)
Latrobe Pennsylvania
2005
Second Printing 2006*

©PUBLICATIONS OF THE SAINT VINCENT COLLEGE
CENTER FOR NORTHERN APPALACHIAN STUDIES

Richard David Wissolik, Director and General Editor

Saint Vincent College
300 Fraser Purchase Road
Latrobe, PA 15650

All rights reserved. No portion of this publication may be reproduced, stored in a retrieval system, or transmitted, in any form or by any means, electronic, mechanical, or otherwise, without prior written permission of the Saint Vincent College Center for Northern Appalachian Studies.

They Say There Was A War

General Editors:
Richard David Wissolik, Fellow of the Center
David Wilmes, Fellow of the Center
Eric Greisinger, Fellow of the Center
John DePaul, Fellow of the Center

Editors:
Katie Killen (Fellow of the Center)
Srdan Smailbegovich (Fellow of the Center)
Rick Claypool (Fellow of the Center)
Gary E. J. Smith (Fellow of the Center)
Michael Cerce (Fellow of the Center)
Barbara J. Wissolik (Fellow of the Center)
Erica Wissolik (Fellow of the Center)

Introductory essays:
Mark Gruber, O.S.B., Ph.D. (Fellow of the Center); David J. Wilmes;
John DePaul; Eric Greisinger; David Zauhar

Original Illustrations and Cover Design:
J. Scott Downs and Associates
Michael Cerce
Michael Wilkey
Henry "Hank" Stairs

With Financial Assistance from:
John Elliott, Esq.
Chapter 14 (Western Pennsylvania) Veterans of the Battle of the Bulge

Printed in the United States of America by Sheridan Books,
Ann Arbor, Michigan
ISBN: 1-885851-51-0

Library of Congress Cataloging-in-Publication Data

They say there was a war / general editors, Richard David Wissolik ... [et al.] ;
Editors, Katie Killen ... [et al.].
p. cm. – (Publications of the Saint Vincent College Center for Northern Appalachian Studies)
Includes bibliographical references and glossary.
ISBN 1-885851-51-0 (alk. Paper)
1. World War, 1939-1945 – Pennsylvania. 2. World War, 1939-1945 – Biography—Dictionaries.
3. World War, 1939-1945 – Personal narratives, American. 4. Pennsylvania—Biography—Dictionaries
5. United States—Armed Forces—Biography—Dictionaries. 6. Soldiers—Pennsylvania—Biography.
7. Sailors—Pennsylvania—Biography. 8. Oral History. I. Wissolik, Richard David, 1938- II.
Killen, Katie. III. Series.

D769.85.P4T54.2005
940.54'8173'0922748—dc22   2005046463

The Editors Proudly Dedicate This Book to the Veterans of the Battle of the Bulge Chapter 14 (Western Pennsylvania)

Peter J. Angelo
Carl Barney
Stephen Blasco
Everett A. Brewer
Elroy C. Byers
William C. Burd
Paul Chemski
Walter R. Christopher
Gus College
John DiBattista
Jay Downs
John Dudek
Joe Folino
William F. Frischolz
Michael Giannini
Charles Greenwood
Kenneth F. Haydon
Wallace Heath
Jim Herrington
Mark G. Hoffman
Frank M. Hornack
William P. Hughes
Robert E. Jenkins
Eugene Jones
Thomas Katana
Frank Kulik
Karl Landis
Francis Langham
Chester Lapa
Charles Lewis
Dick Lukehart

Paul Luther
Paul Mance
Frank McClelland
Harry McCracken
Paul G. McKelvey, Jr.
Harry McWilliams
Paul T. Minno
Archie Mullaert
Harold Musnug
Cliff Naugle
Francis Neighly
Paul Neighly
Paul Noel
Peter Palmintera
Albert Pellish
Richard Raddock
Dan Restauri
Michael Rudy
Leroy D. "Whitey" Schaller
Lou Skelly
William R. Smith
Henry "Hank" Stairs
Edward Steck
Peter Talarovich
Mrs. Marjorie Taylor *(Leonard Sharbough, KIA)*
John Tuskan
Harvey Waugaman
Harvey Weber
Charles Wilcher

Table of Contents

Remembrance and Obligation (David J. Wilmes) xi
As Time Goes By (John DePaul) xiii
Each One is Different (Eric Greisinger) xvii
Without Varnish or Excuse (Mark Gruber, O.S.B.) xix
It Wasn't Like That (David Zauhar) xxiii
About the General Editors and Artists xxiii
Angelo Barone, *80th Infantry Division, POW* 1
Clarence Brockman, *80th Infantry Division* 7
Ben Byrer, *3rd Marine Division* 13
Dale Allen Bullock, *USN (Medical Corps)* 23
Martin Burke, *94th Infantry Division* 31
Thomas R. Cable, *Fifteenth Airforce, 456th Bomb Group* 37
George Clark, *366th Fighter Group (P-47 Thunderbolts)* 49
Ronald Colflesh, *83rd Infantry Division* 55
Sante "Sandy" DeMarino, *4th Marine Division* 59
Thomas Dix, *USN (Destroyer Escort/Mine Sweeping)* 69
Thomas J. Evans, *4th Armored Division, 704th Tank Destroyer Battalion* 75
B.J. Fleckenstein, *4th Marine Division* 93
James Foley, *4th Marine Division* 97
Joseph Folino, *691st Tank Destroyer Battalion* 107
James Forster, *2nd Infantry Division* 115
Michael Gates, *4th Marine Division* 119
Hubert "Butch" Gower, *5th Marine Division* 125
Robert M. Johnston, *340th Bombardment Group (B-25 Mitchells)* 137
Clarence Kindl, *Seventh Airforce, 15th Pursuit Group* 145
Robert Knorr, *5th Marine Division* 157
Chester Lapa, *63rd/90th Infantry Divisions* 163
Joseph LaValle, *17th Field Artillery, POW* 173
David Locke, M.D., *63rd Infantry Division* 181
John Martino, *81st Chemical Mortar Battalion* 185
Nicholas P. Matro, *Twentieth Air Force, 6th Bomb Group* 193
Harold "Hal" Mayforth, *4th Armored Division, 25th Cavalry Recon* 205
Harry McCracken, *99th Infantry Division, 395th Regiment, Medics* 211
Peter Messer, *17th Airborne Division* 225
Alexander Robert Nelson, *Fifteenth Air Force, 449th Bomb Group, POW* 231
Fielder N. Newton, *Eighth Air Force, 389th Bomb Group* 253
Orlando Pietropaoli, *629th Engineers, Light Equipment* 263
Antonio "Tony" Priolette, *24th Infantry Division* 271
John Paul Priolette, *USN, Northern Carrier Group, USS Monterey* 287

Table of Contents (Continued)

Paul Danks, *USN, Northern Carrier Group, USS Monterey* 293
Michael Rudy, *83rd Infantry Division* 295
Ross Saunders, *66th Infantry Division* 301
Leroy "Whitey" Schaller, *28th Infantry Division, POW* 315
Joseph "Sam" Seanor, *106th Infantry Division, POW* 331
John S. Slaney, *Royal Air Force, POW* 341
William R. Smith, *28th/63rd Infantry Divisions* 369
Antonio Spanish, *Merchant Marines* 375
Marvin R. Spencer, *80th Infantry Division* 381
Ralph Sperber, *10th Mountain Division* 385
Henry M. "Hank" Stairs, *66th/30th/28th Infantry Divisions* 389
Lewis Jacob Steck, *2nd Marine Division* 407
Earl Vincent Stratton, *63rd Infantry Division* 423
Jim Takitch, *USN, USS Kidd (Destroyer)* 429
Peter Talarovich, *26th Infantry Division* 441
Steven Vincent Vella, *101st Airborne Division* 455
William Wachter, *Eighth Air Force, 452nd Bomb Group* 461
Robert Wasson, *34th Combat Engineers* 467
Harvey Waugaman, *87th Infantry Division* 471
Terance Arthur John Wickham, *M.D., RAMC, POW, Thai/Burma Railroad* ..477
Robert "Boomer" Woomer, Jr., *23rd Constuction Battalion ("Seabees")*. 494
Robert C. Yowan, *Eighth Air Force, 487th Bomb Group* 499
John M. Zubay, *803rd Engineers, POW, Bataan Death March* 507
Vintage Maps 517
Glossary 525
Autographs and Notes 541

Editors' Note and Acknowledgments

THE STAFF OF THE SAINT VINCENT COLLEGE CENTER FOR NORTHERN APPALACHIAN STUDIES prepared the accounts in this book from taped interviews, diaries, letters and other appropriate materials from the personal collections of the interviewees. While the interviewees shared many common experiences concerning basic training, overseas journeys, weaponry, briefings before bombing missions, return trips to the United States, and other topics, the editors chose to preserve only unique details. General descriptions of these topics appear in the glossary.

The narratives which follow are not merely stories of combat. Center staff questioned the interviewees about their families, their childhood, their work and educational experiences, as well as their military and post-military experiences. Their stories, though edited and arranged into narrative form, remain unadorned, and the editors present them without editorial interpretation or interpolation. Specific comments on the socio-historical circumstances the veterans witnessed may be found in the introductory materials. The Center has made every attempt to help the reader come to know the person as well as what the person did.

The Center's continuing oral history program and process is an arduous, yet rewarding, one. Typically, Center staff screen interviewees concerning the experiences they had before, during, and after the war so that interviewers can conduct in-depth research into the campaigns, theaters of operation, weapons, tactics and units of each oral history candidate. This process enables interviewers to prepare appropriate questions and to anticipate some of the experiences of each veteran. Experience has shown that when the interviewer can demonstrate a working knowledge of the material in question, the veteran tends to "open up" and provide more expansive answers to questions. Interview sessions might last as long as two hours, and there may be up to six or more sessions per veteran. Often the most difficult part of the interview process is seeing the pain in the veterans' eyes and hearing the anguish in their voices as they relive some terrible event, perhaps for the first time in sixty years.

Each interviewee completed a general set of questions on forms provided by the Military History Institute at Carlisle, Pennsylvania. The Institute's aims and questions reflected and supported those of the Center.

Center staff conducted several interviews with each interviewee over the period 1993–2005. Each veteran assisted in reviewing and editing transcripts. The wives and families of interviewees who died during the interviewing/editing process were of great assistance in providing photographs and other materials. They also assisted in editing final transcripts. The Center returned all tapes, rough transcripts, and other materials to the interviewees and their families, leaving them to decide whether to preserve them in family archives or donate them to appropriate entities.

The Saint Vincent College Center for Northern Appalachian Studies wishes to thank the following: Saint Vincent College: Mr. John Elliott, Esq. and Chapter XIV (Western Pennsylvania) Veterans of the Battle of the Bulge for their generosity in assisting the Center in the publication of *They Say There Was a War*.

The Center also thanks Thomas Mans, Vice-President for Academic Affairs for his continuing guidance and support; Mrs. Patricia Dellinger, Mrs. Gina Nalevanko, Ms. Michele Pennesi, Ms. Julie D'Anna Parsons, Mrs. Carol McDowell, Ms Barbara Pushic, Mrs. Connie Philips, and Mrs. Evelyn Santone of the Saint Vincent College Business Office for their efficiency and patience in handling the accounts of the Center; Mr. Don Orlando and Ms. Theresa Schwab of the Saint Vincent College Public Relations Office for arranging timely publicity for the Center's projects; Ms. Shirley Skander, Faculty Secretary and Ms. Lee Ann Ross, Mailing and Duplicating, for their prompt and uncomplaining assistance during the preparation of the manuscript; Mr. Joseph Strazzera and Mr. George DePalma of the Saint Vincent College Facilities Management Department; Donna Werner of the Saint Vincent College Post Office; Anthony Grossi, O.S.B. of the Saint Vincent College Bookstore; Steve Brown and the staff of Saint Vincent College Campus Security; Rob Best and all of the people who run the Saint Vincent College Food Service; Patty Babusci, Missy Ellis, Lori Rebosky, Roger Wilson, Jeff Klocek and Cindy Hoffman of Information Services for making sure the Center's computers are always up and running; Dave Safin and Jeff Zidek of the Saint Vincent College Communications Department; the staff of the Saint Vincent College Library who are always ready to help; Fran Zauhar, Wufstan Clough, O.S.B., Denny McDaniel, Bill Snyder and Beth Martinelli of the Saint Vincent College English department; to them, especially, many thanks for this and that.

The Center is most grateful to the veterans for their willingness to tell their stories, not only for this volume, but to continue to do so for Saint Vincent College students in class visits, a generosity that continues to enrich the educational milieu of the campus.

Remembrance and Obligation

Now be witness again, paint the mightiest armies of earth,
Of those armies so rapid so wondrous what saw you to tell us?
What stays with you latest and deepest? Of curious panics
Of hard-fought engagements or sieges tremendous what deepest remains?

- Walt Whitman

As the events of World War II retreat further into our national past, an opportunity and an obligation presents itself to preserve the stories of that generation of Americans who lived through those times. In response, the Saint Vincent College Center for Northern Appalachian Studies has been interviewing, archiving and publishing oral histories of World War II veterans since 1991, years before it had become so fashionable to do so, and years before such projects were mandated by an act of Congress. The Center is also involved in collecting the stories of veterans of the Korean War (the "Forgotten War"), the Vietnam War, and the more recent of our nation's conflicts.

The farsightedness of people like Professor Richard Wissolik, Director of the Center, and, with Ronald E. Tranquilla and Warren Murrman, O.S.B., one of the Center's founders, led to the formation of this unique organization. Beginning with a skeleton crew of students, alumni and professors from Saint Vincent College, the Center began collecting the stories of World War II veterans from Western Pennsylvania and the surrounding areas. Over the next few years, the scope of the project grew immensely.

I became involved with the Center in 1995, my senior year at Saint Vincent College. I learned the finer points of interviewing veterans from Professor Wissolik and Gary Smith, an alumnus of the college. Smith laid the foundation for interview techniques, which I found to be extremely successful. Some of Gary's interviews dating back to 1991 (John Slaney, Hubert Gower, Clarence Kindl, Tom Evans) appear in this book. Over the years I honed my interview skills, and discovered that I could get incredible stories out of these men by lending a compassionate, non-judgmental ear to their tales. Since that time, I have conducted hundreds of interviews with World War II veterans, including several Britishers and Germans who are now United States citizens.

As the Center's archive continues to grow so does our desire to share our work with the public. We received several grants from the Pennsylvania Museum and Historical Commission, the Commonwealth of Pennsylvania's Department of Community and Economic Development, and from Dr. Richard Buchanan of Wilmington, Ohio, who was the Medical Officer for the 704th Tank Destroyer Battalion. With these monies and through book sales, the Center was able to collect and publish its materials. Also, the Carlisle Military History Institute archived some of the interviews we collected and provided us with detailed questionnaires that we still use.

From 1999 to 2002, under the Center's auspices, I conducted a series of lectures in cooperation with Westmoreland County Community College Continuing Education Program, The Adams Memorial Library in Latrobe, Pennsylvania, Pennsylvania historical societies, public libraries, and high schools on the oral history process. Veterans who had given interviews also appeared in these public programs.

By invitation, the Center helped develop a program with the Pennsylvania Historical and Museum Commission in York, Pennsylvania, that concentrated on the oral history process. I delivered an address on the Center's World War II, Korean War and Vietnam War oral history collection. In 2002, the Center became one of the first partners in the Library of Congress's Veteran's History Project that was mandated by the United States Congress. In May of that year, I represented the Center at the Library's first gathering of partners.

During the course of our research into the process of oral history, the Center came upon many collections of tapes, military or otherwise, deteriorating in storage in various libraries and historical societies. To us, these tapes represented hard but essentially useless work, mainly because for years no one had bothered with them. We also discovered that collecting oral histories was fun work, but transcribing them, arranging them into viable narratives, and then allowing the informants to participate in the editorial process was not so much fun. It involved patience, scholarly discipline, continuing research, the uncovering of corroborative evidence, and additional cost. But we knew we needed to do all of these things if the stories were truly to be told.

Many of the stories in *They Say There was a War* are the realization of my own experiences interviewing veterans from 1995 to the present. Unfortunately, a number of these veterans have since passed away. One, Bob Nelson, especially stands out in my mind. My interview of him was my first, and it led to a profound change in my life. His story of surviving thirty-plus missions over Germany and then a year as a prisoner of war has, to a great measure, shaped my existence. Even today I think of the deprivation and danger he experienced, and I try and lead my own life in a way that is exemplary and worthy of the sacrifices he made.

Today, each person I interview affects me on some level. All have given me an appreciation of the World War II generation. But more so, they have revealed to me, and to others, a great understanding about what it means to be in a war. Patriotism was certainly a reason for them going to war, but once the fighting started, the stakes were raised. Personal survival and the survival of their comrades became their paramount reasons. Greed and the desire for power, the instigators of wars, were surmounted by the nobility and quiet courage of the common man at war.

The stories contained within *They Say There was a War* are merely a token of the millions of untold stories from the World War II generation. They act as representative pieces to a vast collective memory of the events between 1941 and 1945. The rest of that memory may quietly fade with time, but the honesty and courage of these men live now within these pages and we all have an obligation to learn from them.

David J. Wilmes
Hackettsown, New Jersey
Winter 2005

As Time Goes By

THOSE WHO SURVIVED ARE OCTOGENARIANS NOW, their gait slowed by the passage of time, their voices less robust than they once were. It has, after all, been nearly six decades since the end of World War II. Sadly, of the sixteen million Americans who served in our armed forces in that frightening epoch, the elderly survivors of that generation are passing from this world at the rate of a thousand per day.

With the passage of time, opportunities to collect first-hand historical accounts from the men who were there diminish by the day. As such, it was imperative that the stories in this book, told by the men who lived the experiences of military service in WWII, should have been preserved for scholars and generations yet unborn.

Thousands of books have already been written about the Second World War's great battles, grand designs, larger-than-life leaders, and military strategies and tactics. But little has been published about the experiences of the soldiers and sailors who languished in foxholes, shot the bullets, fired the big guns, flew the planes, dropped the bombs, manned the ships and, in the bargain, earned a chance of death or sufferance of severe wounds under ghastly conditions. Until oral history became an important adjunct to the traditional methodologies of history, what was published about the personal experiences of ordinary soldiers during World War II was mainly in the realm of fiction; most notably by writers such as Norman Mailer in *The Naked and the Dead*, and Willi Heinrich in *Cross of Iron*. Much to the benefit of the existing historical record of World War II, *They Say There Was a War* has been published.

To gain a better appreciation for the stories in this book, one must first understand the context in which these extraordinary experiences occurred. The genesis of the titanic struggle of the 1940s had its roots in battles fought decades before. From 1914 to its conclusion through armistice in 1918, Europe was locked in a deadly struggle of arms costing millions of European lives, and those of 126,000 Americans. To mark the armistice signed on "the eleventh hour of the eleventh day of the eleventh month" in 1918, world leaders proclaimed that the Great War — the War to End All Wars — had mercifully come to a close. They were wrong.

Just a scant twenty-one years later, in September 1939, Nazi Germany attacked Poland, shattering an uneasy peace and igniting a tinderbox of torturous alliances and treaties in the process. The failure of diplomacy and the ill-fated efforts of the League of Nations came home to roost. Within days, what came to be known as the Second World War had erupted into global conflict as those alliances and treaties were called to account. Before World War II ended in August 1945, nearly fifty-five million civilians and military had died in a horrible war that threatened the very existence of the free and open societies of Western Civilization. Many of the great cities of Europe and others in the Far East had been destroyed or heavily damaged. The world economy was in shambles. But the armed forces of totalitarian governments in Germany, Italy and Japan had been subdued, and those young Americans who played a major role in their defeat came home to an appreciative nation.

At the onset of America's entry into the conflict our future soldiers were young boys, many of them recent high school graduates or members of their junior and senior classes when Japan attacked Pearl Harbor on 7 December 1941. By mid-1943, those American boys had been molded into the most powerful military force the world had ever known, or has known since. From the farms and factories of America, from its coalmines and small businesses, from its large cities and small towns, these "citizen soldiers" had left their homes and loved ones to serve their country.

They slogged through the sands of North Africa, and through the mountains of Italy. They crossed the English Channel to invade France, and pushed the vaunted German Wehrmacht back through the star-crossed battlefields of the Great War (known by then as World War I) into the heart of the Third Reich itself. In the Pacific, they fought terrible, bloody battles on land and sea against an enemy willing to fight to the last man. The army and marines invaded island fortress after island fortress, evicting their Japanese garrisons one after the other, moving across the vast ocean in thousand-mile leaps ever closer to the home islands of the Empire of Japan itself.

Sailors and naval aviators successfully fought the German U-boat menace in the Atlantic, and rendered nearly helpless the powerful Japanese Navy in little more than a year after the infamous sneak attack on Pearl Harbor. Fliers of the army air corps flew thousands of dangerous missions over enemy territory in continental Europe, suffering appalling losses while systematically destroying communications, transportation and manufacturing facilities vital to the enemy's war effort.

A newly famous corps of journalists recorded their exploits; men like Gabriel Heatter, Lowell Thomas, Edward R. Murrow, Ernie Pyle and Eric Severeid. A young soldier by the name of Andy Rooney served as a reporter for Stars and Stripes, and Bill Mauldin, a cartoonist for the same armed forces newspaper, created Willie and Joe, a cartoon series that captured the ethos of military life and was much beloved by the troops. Aided by extensive coverage in newspapers and magazines and by the magic of radio, battles fought in far-away places became part of the American consciousness: Kasserine Pass, Anzio, Montecassino, Omaha Beach, Utah Beach, Point du Hoc, St. Mère-Eglise, Normandy, St. Lô, The Siegfried Line, Huertgen Forest, Bastogne, Elsenborn Ridge, Bataan, Corregidor, Midway, New Guinea, Phillipine Sea, Guadalcanal, Bougainville, Coral Sea, Tarawa, Iwo Jima, Okinawa and many others too numerous to mention here.

So too did the popular music of the era capture the mood of the nation. There were many poignant ballads of love and hope, when both were in short supply in a war weary world. GIs and their loves, often oceans apart, listened and yearned for the end of hostilities to songs like "I Left My Heart at the Stage Door Canteen," "When Johnny Comes Marching Home," "I'll be Seeing You," "When the Lights Go On Again All Over the World," "You're in the Army Mr. Jones," and "As Time Goes By," the hit song from the hit movie of 1942, *Casablanca*.

When the war ended with Japan's capitulation in August 1945, over 405,000 of

America's fine young men had lost their lives in defense of world freedom. Another 79,000 were missing in action. Millions more were wounded, many severely. Among them are some of the men whose stories appear in these pages.

Several Saint Vincent College students and alumni, all now Fellows of the college's Center for Northern Appalachian Studies, have done yeoman service to obtain these important oral histories, arrange them into narratives, and then put them into print format, in the form of this book and its predecessor volume *The Long Road*. My brother, Mario, contributed one of the stories in *The Long Road*. What I read in that book about his experiences in combat was all-new to me; he simply never talked about it. The stories in this book as in the first volume are just as revealing of inner secrets locked away in the minds of men who for years would choose to forget rather than glorify. To many of the veterans, the process of relating their stories in scholarly fashion served as a cathartic release of experiences once held back from public or even family view.

Readers of these stories will no doubt cringe at the horrors perpetrated not only by the enemies of our country in that distant past, but also by some of our own combatants. There are those who will see these recollections only as testimony to our nation's greatness. Still others will see only the negative aspects of those personal experiences. But all who read these stories, even though presented to us by old soldiers through the foggy filter of time, must agree that civilization's very survival rests in the avoidance of another global war at virtually any cost, short of a last act of appeasement to forces dedicated to the destruction of our world. Somewhere between the horrors of worldwide nuclear and biological warfare and appeasement lies the answer to achieving the civilized world's most cherished prize, a peaceful co-existence of conflicting cultures, religions and ideologies

The veterans of World War II won the war, and came home to win the peace. The generation of warriors became a generation of builders: of homes, roads, schools and factories, of bridges, and office buildings and hospitals, of corporations and small businesses, and of industrial and military might unparalleled in the human experience, a powerful combination which history shows was the major deterrent in preventing yet another conflict on the scale of World Wars I and II. On their watch, America assumed the role of leader of the free world, and became the bulwark against communist aggression.

There is a remarkable presence about these men that transcends any thought of rank or demographic standing in society, even as they now enter the twilight of their lives. It derives from a quiet, yet clearly visible sense of pride in what they have accomplished in their lifetimes, a pride that has no doubt evolved out of fulfillment of the cherished military traditions of Duty, Honor, Country.

Only the eloquence of Winston Churchill can adequately express the sentiment these veterans of World War II so richly deserve from Americans of all ages. To celebrate the RAF's defeat of the German air blitz on London, Churchill said, "Never have so many owed so much to so few."

John DePaul
Jeannette, Pennsylvania
Winter 2005

"Each One is Different"

EACH ONE IS AN INDIVIDUAL. As different as they are, they share a common bond that separates them from us. There is something in their walk, something in the softening of their voices when they speak of friends who never made it, there is something of young men's eyes in old men's faces when someone asks them about the war, a war that remains with them, for better or for worse, a war that returned them to us as fathers, nation builders, teachers, and quiet heroes.

From earliest days of my childhood, these veterans of World War II have been my heroes. At night my father would read me accounts of Guadalcanal and Iwo Jima, Bastogne and Normandy. The first pictures I remember seeing were of men with haunted eyes, faces darkened by smoke and helmets, young men turned old by war. The first television show I saw was *GI Diary*. I liked it because of the slow, black and white picture of a scruffy soldier, with a dogleg smoke in his lips, his rifle slung, wading through the mud that began the show. That tired boy was to me what a hero should be. Not the fastball pitcher, not the video game champion, but the simple, tired soldier. There was an aspect of greatness in that that image of a boy thrown into hell.

The veterans of World War II came home and went on with the business of daily living, working, raising families, remembering and reminding us, through their reunions and parades, of what they had done. I have had the privilege of knowing and speaking with many of the men in this book, men whom I hold in awe, men whom I count among my closest friends. They are common men, but what they did was so uncommon that it seems almost impossible. By going to a war they didn't start, they saved a world that was in flames, a world we wouldn't have known had it not been for them. Of all of these men, one stands out in my mind. His name is Colonel Robert Johnston.

When I first met Bob, I knew he was a pilot. He had that special swagger, that special aura of command. After we spoke for a while, I knew he was a man straight out of real history, of myth and legend. He was a warrior poet, an artist, and a bulldog of a man. Whenever I visited him in his home we talked about everything that time would allow, but most of the time we talked about war and current events.

It wasn't hard to see that Bob was a proud veteran, even though his medals were quietly framed on a black background and hung on in a corner above his pool table. If their placement was meant to intimidate, it worked. I always lost the games, but I didn't care because we always discussed the war while we played.

Bob got into the war early. He piloted B–25's out of Africa and Sicily, and then, after the war, he stayed in the Reserves to train other pilots. Bob was the grandfather I never knew, and the face of the young man that went to fight the war long ago.

Though we talked many times, I never recorded his words. After he became ill, I knew his time on earth would be short. So, one August day I took my tape recorder with me and interviewed him. The interview was hard for him. He was on Oxygen and his breath came with difficulty, but true to the spirit of his generation, he went on until the job was finished. He gave me one of the best interviews I ever had with a veteran. I knew his take would be a unique one — the war seen through the eyes of an artist. He told me that when he flew into combat toward potential death, he let the co-pilot take the reins while he gazed at the blue of the sky and the blue of the water. He saw the beauty of the world even when flying into the world's most ugly expression.

It was wonderful, yet sad. I knew Bob was going to die, and that I would never again hear his stories. As he spoke into the microphone, my thoughts raced back to our many meetings. I remembered the day he gave me a letter opener fashioned from one of the struts of the first trainer in which he flew. I remembered the day that he told me that I should become a writer. He said it just that way, "You should become a writer." I remembered walking toward the gym on my college graduation day and hearing his Colonel's voice calling out to me. He took a picture of me that day, and I think is the finest portrait I have of myself. The same day, he gave me a pen. I carried it often, but I never used it because I wanted to save it for something important. And I did.

Bob knew about my book, and I wanted him to see it more than anyone. He was tough, but not immortal. In the spring, Bob died. I had just gotten my first shipment of complimentary copies when a message on my answering machine told me Bob was gone. I became the writer he wanted me to be, but he never got to see that. I took a book to his widow, took out the pen Bob had given me, and signed A *World Away, but Close to Home* for her. I looked around at the emptiness of the room that this great man's presence had filled for so long.

Bob was one of many, and a breed apart from us. His was a generation who had witnessed first hand the horrors of war, and who had participated in our century's defining moment. They are the simple men among us, these silent heroes. We need to know them.

Eric Greisinger
Bakerstown, Pennsylvania
Winter 2005

"Without Varnish or Excuse..."

IN THE LANGUAGE OF ANCIENT CHRISTIAN WORSHIP the *anamnesis* was the act of communal recollection that made the assembly of one mind. But the matter that they recollected inevitably concerned one messianic but bloody sacrificial act, which saved them from death.

In *They Say There Was a War*, the first sequel to its 1999 publication *The Long Road*, the Saint Vincent College Center for Northern Appalachian Studies again provides an enormously important service to the larger reading community: it recollects the bloody acts of battlefield sacrifice by which a nation — and indeed, a whole civilization — was once saved from the original culture of death in the age of the Axis. Without the effort *anamnesis*, all that remains is amnesia, or the forgetfulness of the sacrifices made by those who preserved our future.

This volume is a gallant effort at *anamnesis*, and contributes to our collective purpose and inspiration. But let the reader be aware that herein are not the stories of foreign wars our grandfathers once told us of in former times. In the last few years, the genre of war telling has shifted from the glories of soldierly discipline and heroism to the graphic depictions of young lives cruelly tortured and ruined in the fray. Nineteen ninety-eight's *Saving Private Ryan* is a far, far different war movie from 1949's *Sands of Iwo Jima*, as Gibson's *Passion of the Christ* is from 1965's *The Greatest Story Ever Told*.

Apparently, the further removed we are from the acts remembered, the greater courage we have in remembering them more graphically, or the more we need to do so if we would not forget their real value. The value of these stories is that the reader is made privy to a layer of human drama rarely afforded in more traditional war story productions. There is much less of the self-serving narrative here and much more of the truth-telling reflection in which the storyteller and the reader are purified. Here are confessions almost sacramentally poured out in the deepest catharses of compunctions for violence done and compromise made. Without varnish or excuse, the policies of war making are exposed by which unforgivable deeds of indiscriminate reprisal and no-hostage-taking hardness are regularly done without a second thought.

Undoubtedly, the enemy one fights becomes the dark lower standard by which one excuses his own mode of violent contest. Has America ever come to moral grips with her war machine of massive fire-bombings of civilian cities or her policy of dropping residual payloads on any target at all behind enemy lines? The veterans who tell these stories reveal the personal side of institutionalized treacheries and troubles as they saw them and participated in them. They are too old now and we are too tired to prosecute the crimes they lay bare before us. This book needs a hygienic disclaimer. The readers must realize that in a moment they will be covered in literary scabs, lice, booze, blood and feces, the humors described in the stories told. Only so baptized will readers begin to appreciate the world of moral options and social opportunities afforded the veterans who inform them.

In the year this volume was compiled, two presidential candidates ran on or ran from their own military records. Scandals rock the modern military from prison tortures at Abu Ghraib to misinformation about WMD (Weapons of Mass Destruction). The arrogance of national political leaders, generals and parties is translated into the moral ambivalence of soldiers in the proverbial trenches. In the Great War of 1914–1918, it turned out to be little different. World War II is a war our media have always loved to romanticize. Seldom could a cause seem more just and a drama seem more profound. But the veterans who have lived long enough to assess it all cannot forget the darker sides of that war; the sides by which all the combatants were reduced into something other than the propaganda and good intentions by which they were commissioned. We no longer need a justification for our war policies in the Pacific or on the European stage; that time is passing. But the very meaning of war itself always needs to be plumbed if we are to avoid it as much as we ought. The intense suffering and tragedies of the lives revealed by these stories transcend the theater of that midcentury conflict, and place us both in the timeless quandary of all violence itself. And this is the deepest service of story remembering and truth telling in any generation.

Rev. Mark Gruber, Ph.D., O.S.B.
Department of Sociology and Anthropology
Saint Vincent College, Latrobe, Pennsylvania
January 2005

"It Wasn't Like That."

My father, who died in 1982, kept silent about his experiences during WWII. We knew he participated in D-Day, of course. June 6th, 1944 never passed without my mother mentioning the anniversary to us, though not within earshot of my father.

Most of his friends who had similar experiences during the war also kept quiet about these things, at least around us kids. In fact, they all tended to look down on people who told "war stories," implying, I believe in retrospect, that those who told stories didn't really experience the war.

Judging by the stories he did tell, we kids could conclude his war consisted of waiting around in England for a couple of years, bored enough to get in minor trouble frequently. Lots of card playing. Lots of drinking. Alternating between the ranks of private and corporal for awhile, eventually making sergeant, then shuttling back and forth between that rank and corporal a few times due to various infractions that he never fully detailed.

Then came June 6th, 1944. We know nothing of what happened between 6 June and 9 June, when a piece of shrapnel took off half his foot.

Every time the movie *The Longest Day* came on TV, he watched it, silently. He spoke only to tell us when "it wasn't like that."

In the years since he died, however, I've learned that he did talk about what happened. My mother knows a lot more than I do, and I suspect more than I ever will know, about what he went through. So did some of his closest friends.

There is no way I can fault him for not telling us about those events and experiences that most shaped his life. What child, what teenager, could even begin to understand what it would be like for his father to have participated in, and to have endured, those things that soldiers endured?

Now that I'm older, though, I am grateful to hear the stories of my father's fellow soldiers, no matter how horrifying they are at times. They are definitely not *his* stories, of course. Each soldier's experience is his own, a burden that he will have to bear. Typically, combat veterans tend to be ordinary, decent people who lived through the most hellish experiences, and as ordinary, decent people, they tend to not want to inflict those horrible stories on the people closest to them.

I am grateful, however, that these ordinary men, the men like those whom I remember from my childhood getting up early, going to work, mowing lawns on weekends, teaching us how to play baseball and to camp and generally giving us good ways to deal with life, are telling their stories. And have been for quite some time now, thankfully.

We'll never know exactly what it was like for them. But thanks to stories told in this book and others like it, we'll have a much better idea than we would from reading the standard histories.

I thank all these soldiers.

David Zauhar
Greensburg, Pennsylvania
Winter 2005

U.S. Government Printing Office/ Northwestern University Library (http://www.library.northwestern.edu)

About the General Editors and Artists

DICK WISSOLIK IS A PROFESSOR OF ENGLISH at Saint Vincent College. He is a Fellow of the Center for Medieval and Renaissance Studies at California State University, Long Beach, California, a recipient of the General Arthur St.Clair Award for Historical Preservation, and a co-founder of the Saint Vincent College Center for Northern Appalachian Studies and General Editor of its publications that include *Listen to Our Words: The Oral Histories of the Jewish Community of Southwestern Pennsylvania; Out of the Kitchen: Oral Histories of Women in World War II; The Long Road: From Oran to Pilsen; A Place in the Sky: A Spoken and Pictorial History of the Arnold Palmer Regional Airport; and Ice Cream Joe: The Valley Dairy Story and America's Love Affair with Ice Cream.* Dick has published studies on The Bayeux Tapestry and the Norman Conquest of England in *The American Benedictine Review, Medium Aevum, and Annuale Medievale.* His other publications include *Bob Dylan: American Poet and Singer* and *Bob Dylan's Words: A Critical Dictionary and Commentary.* He has edited and published, through Eadmer Press, works on Martin Heidegger, John Donne and G.M. Hopkins, and the poems of Will Stubbs and Rina Ferrarelli. At Saint Vincent College, Dick teaches courses in Myth, African Studies, Satire, Epic, Medieval Studies, and Short Fiction. For over thirty years he has taught a course called Faces of Battle: War and Peace in History, Literature, and the Arts, a course which he created with the late Roy Mills. Over the years veterans of World War II (several of whom appear in this volume) the Korean War and the Vietnam War have participated in the class as guest speakers. Before coming to Saint Vincent College, Dick was a Program Director for Catholic Relief Services in East Africa.

JOHN DEPAUL IS A GRADUATE OF CARNEGIE MELLON UNIVERSITY, Class of 1959. Upon graduation, John began a forty-one year career in the advertising agency business. First in the Pittsburgh office of Batten, Barton, Durstine & Osborne, then as a partner with Dudreck, DePaul, Ficco & Morgan until his retirement in 2000. He is a veteran of the Korean War, with service in the U.S. Navy from 1951-1955. John's writing credits include articles for *U.S. Trade* magazine, *The Pittsburgh Business Times* and various advertising journals. Foreign credits include articles in *Millimetri*, a regional magazine published in the Molise region of Italy, and *Il Sole 24 Ore,* the Italian equivalent of the *Wall Street Journal.* John has been very active in economic development efforts to build trade relations with Italy and France, and to bring European investment to southwestern Pennsylvania. He was appointed to the Western Pennsylvania District Export Council by Secretaries of Commerce in both the George H.W. Bush and Clinton administrations. John was a founding director of the Italy-America Chamber of Commerce of Pittsburgh and served as its first president. He was also one of the early members of the French-American Chamber of Commerce of

Pittsburgh. Both chambers were active in organizing trade missions, which brought together small-to-medium size European enterprises with their American counterparts in the Pittsburgh area. The most important of these activities was the World-Wide Energy Conference held in Pittsburgh in 1992, which was organized by the French and Italian chambers in conjunction with the United Nations Energy Commission headquartered in Geneva. In recognition of his volunteer work in trade relations, John holds numerous citations and awards from regional governmental bodies in Italy, France and Spain. In addition, he was honored by the Columbus 500 Committee of Western Pennsylvania in 1992 for distinguished service on the occasion of the 500th anniversary of the discovery of America.

DAVID WILMES IS A GRADUATE OF SAINT VINCENT COLLEGE with a BA in English, and has worked with the Center for Northern Appalachian Studies since 1995. He worked as an editor for the Center publications *Reluctant Valor, The Flag is Passing By, Listen to Our Words, Mission Number Three: Missing in Action, The Men of the 704th, The Long Road, Waiting for Jacob,* and *A Place in the Sky*. He has given talks on World War II and oral history at libraries, high schools, and veterans' organizations. He has also presented lectures on World War II and the Center's oral history projects for the Westmoreland County Community College, the Westmoreland County Historical Society, the Pennsylvania Historical and Museum Commission, the Pennsylvania Humanities Council and the Library of Congress' Veterans History Project. He is currently completing a Master's degree in American history at East Stroudsburg University. He resides in New Jersey with his wife Cathleen.

ERIC GREISINGER HAS BEEN LECTURING in grade schools, high schools, and colleges for over ten years on World War II and the Civil War. He was a Civil War Infantry Living Historian for fifteen years with two Pennsylvania based units. He has been a volunteer guide and historical interpreter at the Gettysburg, Antietam and Harper's Ferry National Parks. Eric also formed and commands the 36th Infantry Division Living History Group. During his freshman and sophomore years at Saint Vincent College, he was a member of Indiana University of Pennsylvania's Army ROTC Warrior Battalion. While working on, and upon completion of his M.A. in History at the University of Wisconsin and Indiana University of Pennsylvania, he was a historical consultant to the Somerset Historical Center, Pennsylvania, where he developed for publication materials pertaining to their World War II veteran oral history project. Eric published his work in *A World Away but Close to Home* in May 2004. Eric is an avid collector of military memorabila and weapons, and his private collection rivals many that are to be found in museums.

MICHAEL WILKEY LIVED AND WORKED IN NAIROBI, Kenya before Uhuru. His teaching position at the Prince of Wales School was 'Africanised' shortly after Independence in 1964. He stayed on and worked at a variety of jobs until he was obliged to leave the country. He went to Uganda but once again political changes there forced former 'colonials' to leave the country. He went to live in the Bahamas and saw British colonial rule come to an end there, too. He eventually made a new life in Western Canada teaching in various schools, colleges and finally at the University of Victoria in British Columbia. He writes columns and feature articles for many internationally published magazines. Michael has written many feature articles on subjects as varied as automobiles, aviation, travel, wildlife conservation, and, of course Africa. An aviation buff, Michael has written and illustrated *Pillars of Faith* and *They Never Gave Up*, both of which were published in Canada. *They Never Gave Up* was nominated for the Red Cedar Award in 1999. His *Going Straight Up*, a fully illustrated history of helicopters, is forthcoming. He has just completed a collection of short stories about his life in Africa, and is presently working on an extensive historical novel *Ivory Candlesticks*, about colonial times in Kenya. He is an enthusiastic ultralight aircraft pilot and aircraft builder and is one of the founding members of the British Columbia Aviation Museum. He has a Bachelor of Arts in Education from Sheffield University in the UK and a Masters degree in Educational Administration and Curriculum Development from Gonzaga Jesuit University in Spokane, Washington. Currently, Michael lives on an island off the west coast of Canada, but because of his love of the people and the country, he returns to Africa as often as he is able to spend time with special friends and visit special places.

AN AVID MOTORCYCLE ENTHUSIAST AND TRAVELER, Mike Cerce is a graduate of the Indiana University of Pennsylvania, with a BA in Marketing. He has been with J.S. Downs and Associates for the past ten years as a designer, senior designer and currently is employed as the Art Director. He has worked with Dick Wissolik and the Center for Northern Appalachian Studies on a variety of projects over the past eight years. He contributed design for *The Long Road* and *Mission Number Three: Missing in Action*. Mike is responsible for the design and layout of several other projects including: *The Gold Standard, Waiting for Jacob, Men of the 704, A Place in the Sky* and *Ice Cream Joe: Valley Dairy Story*. *They Say There Was A War* will be the sixth collaboration with Dick and the Center for Northern Appalachian Studies. Currently, Mike and his wife Jen reside in Greensburg along with their dog, Shane.

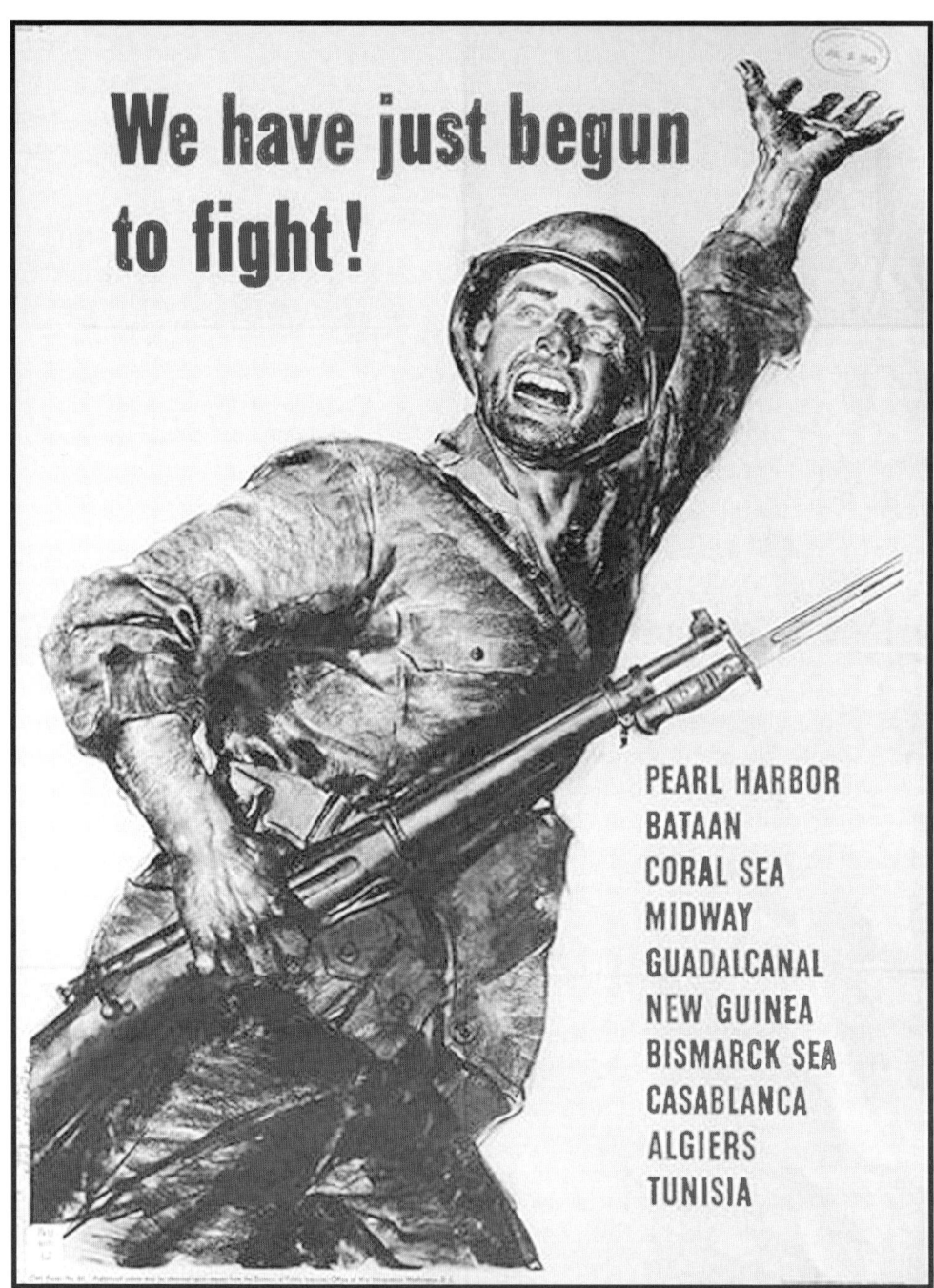

U.S. Government Printing Office/ Northwestern University Library (http://www.library.northwestern.edu)

"I Got My Ass Shot Off!"

Angelo Barone
80th Division, 317th Infantry Regiment, Company L;
Pottsville, Pennsylvania

"Lieutenant Ferguson asked the German who was questioning him to get us out of the barn because American artillery was going to hit it. The German said, 'No, the Americans aren't that good a shot. They'll never hit the barn.' He said, 'Well the next shell is going to hit in front of the barn, get us out of here.' No sooner said that than the next shell did hit in front of the barn. He said, 'Get us the hell out of here! They're going to hit the barn! This is a hell of a way to die!' No sooner he said that than a shell hit the barn, killed the lieutenant, the German, and quite a few of the other guys. I dove under the cow before the shell hit, and shrapnel killed the cow. I was covered with blood. I looked a mess. They said they didn't know if I was alive or dead. They carried me out of the barn. Twenty-nine of us were wounded, nineteen seriously."

I WAS DRAFTED IN JULY 1942. Two uncles were at my going away party. "Good luck, but don't get in the infantry. It's the worst place in the service," they told me.

I wound up in Camp Forrest, Tennessee. "Welcome to the 80th Infantry Division, Tullahoma, Tennessee," a big sign said. That about killed me. I was only twenty-years old, and I wound up in Company L of the 317th Infantry Regiment with guys that were older than me, like twenty-five or twenty-eight. I didn't have a care in the world, but most of those guys were married and had obligations. I told them, "Well, don't worry about me. One of these days I'm going overseas and get my ass shot off."

That became a favorite phrase of mine. Whenever I went home for a visit, I told them, "Don't worry about me. One of these days I'm going overseas and get my ass shot off."

I ended up in Camp Laguna in Yuma, Arizona, for desert training. We were supposed to go to North Africa, but things turned out for the best there, so they changed our orders. On 7 July 1944, I found myself in Greenock, Firth of Clyde, Scotland. We couldn't get all the way into port, so we had to crawl down off the ship on five-story rope ladders into smaller boats. I did it with a full field pack and a machinegun. I must have weighed four hundred pounds going down that ladder. We wound up at a big estate that had stone walls all around it. We lived there in tents. Actually, we had our first combat experience there. V–2 rockets came over, and when their engines stopped, we'd run like hell for the wall. When they dropped, they'd come straight down.

On 2 August, we landed on Utah Beach in Normandy. The first thing they told us was, "Make sure you wear your gas masks, and take no prisoners."

We marched about five miles that first day and stopped at St-Jores. There was a Free French guy there who came over to our captain and said that there were two

Germans in a shack above, and he wanted a couple volunteers to help get them. My machinegun sergeant went up with two guys. But he brought the Germans back alive. One of them was wounded. I opened my big mouth and said, "Bring them back alive, Frank? We're supposed to not take prisoners."

Well, he got me and another fellow to take these two prisoners back, and I guess we were supposed to kill them. I was scared to death. While we were marching back, a group of women came out of the town and started to curse these Germans. They wanted them to themselves. Crowfoot, my assistant gunner, said, "We're not supposed to give them up. We're supposed to kill them."

I said, "Well, let the women kill them, then."

They took the two German prisoners into town. Inside the town were two lampposts, one on each side of the street, and on them were hanging two French women. Their heads were shaved. They had helped the Germans during the war. Collaborators, they called them. The French took those two German prisoners, and shot them. Then they hanged them up on the lampposts, right alongside the dead women.

From the hedgerows we fought in the Argentan-Falaise-Gap and from there we went to St. Mihiel. From there, our company went into a little town, Florise, where we stayed all day. Then they loaded us onto trucks. Our objective was Pont-A-Mousson on the Moselle River. They drove us within about three miles of the city. By two o'clock in the afternoon, the Germans were out of town and across the river. About four o'clock in the afternoon, the Germans blew up the bridge.

Our squad set up a machinegun outpost by the river. Around four or five o'clock in the morning we got an order to cross the river. The engineers were supposed to bring up boats, but they didn't have enough gas, and they were afraid that if they came into the city with the boats, they wouldn't be able to get back out. So we took a couple men from each squad and they carried the boats up to the river. We started crossing in the dark. Halfway across, some guy cracked up and started firing. The Germans didn't know we were there until that happened, and all hell broke loose. They threw mortars and artillery shells at us like mad. Some of the boats never made it across, but ours did. I had just gotten out of the boat and up the bank when shrapnel from air bursts hit two of my squad. I went to pick one of them up, but he was dead, so I just let him lay there. About an hour or two later, I got hit, and I started to laugh.

Somebody hollered, "The poor bastard must have got hit in the head."

That shook me up.

I said, "No, I didn't get hit in the head, but I got my ass shot off!"

Then everybody started to laugh. We lay there all night under heavy fire, ran out of ammunition, and the next morning a squad or more of Germans came over and rounded us up. There was a barn about 800 or 900 yards from this riverbank and they put us in this barn. I lay down on the floor. There were a couple of cows there in the corner, and we thought maybe we could milk them, but all at once a shell went over the barn. Lieutenant Ferguson asked the German who was questioning him to get us out of the barn because American artillery was going to hit it.

The German said, "No, the Americans aren't that good a shot. They'll never hit the barn."

He said, "The next shell is going to hit the barn, get us out of here. This is a hell of a way to die!"

No sooner he said that than a shell hit the barn killing the lieutenant, the German, and quite a few of the other guys. I dove under the cow before the shell hit, and shrapnel killed the cow. I was covered with blood. I looked a mess. They said they didn't know if I was alive or dead. They carried me out of the barn. Twenty-nine of us were wounded, nineteen seriously. They dropped us off in a few houses that were half way up Mousson Hill. They interrogated us there. I had on a new pair of combat boots, and the first thing the German that was searching me took was my boots. I figured my boots wouldn't be the last thing they took, so later I took off my socks, took off a ring my great-grandfather had given me, put the ring on one of my toes, and then put my socks back on. I was right. They took everything of value that we had, but they didn't get my ring.

We were there the rest of the day and night. In the morning, they put the nineteen of us in a horse wagon and took us to a barn in Metz. We were hungry. I was lying in the hay, turning around, trying to get comfortable, when I saw three eggs. I said, "Anybody want an egg."

Nobody did, so I ate them myself, raw. That night they put us in a wagon and took us to a railroad station outside of Metz. We rode a train for two or three days, and then wound up in a hospital in Frankfurt, Germany, where they operated on us.

They took two of us in at a time. They cut an arm off one guy, and a leg off another. They threw me on the table, opened me up, and took a piece of shrapnel out of me about three inches square. They didn't sew me up. They just put a bandage on me, operated on the rest of the guys, then took us all to the 4th floor. I was there seven weeks. They came around every three or four days and changed the bandage. It stunk like mad. Tissues were growing across the wound, and they would just tear them out and put a new bandage on. I thought, "These sonsofbitches don't want me to heal. They just like to tear those tissues off."

After I healed, the Germans put me on a train. Three days later I came to Stalag XIIA, in Limburg, Germany where they separated the officers from the enlisted men. I was in the hospital there for two weeks, and then I was shipped out to Moosberg, Stalag VII A. I wasn't with my friends anymore, and my wound had gotten infected. They kept me in the hospital there for three weeks.

The living conditions in the camp were terrible. They had one building, which served as a latrine, and one water spigot outside, for 1,000 men. They kept the water on for only three hours a day. By the time some guys got around to it, they were lucky to get a cupful. The latrine facilities were terrible. They had no commode, just holes in the floor. We were lucky if we managed to hit the hole. Once a day, they'd come in and squirt the place down. Funny we didn't all die of some disease.

Finally, I was put in the regular barracks with the other guys, and sent out on work detail. There were ten of us in my group. We got up at daybreak, got on a train for Landshut, a main rail center. There were also Russian prisoners there, and they were good workers. We "gold-bricked" as much as we could. After a week or so, the guards found out we weren't working too much, so they took us by train to a wooded area and put us to work cutting wood. I guess we didn't cut enough to keep them happy, so they got the ten of us again and put us to work keeping the road between Munich and the Dachau concentration camp clear after bombing raids. We kept hearing rumors that they were burning bodies in Dachau, but we never believed it until we smelled odors coming from the camp.

The Americans bombed the Munich area by day and the British bombed it at night. There wasn't much time between bombings. Whenever the air-raid sirens sounded, we ran a half-mile or so to a cave to get shelter. One day, for some reason, the British didn't arrive until much later in the morning. When we got back to work, the Americans came over. Three of us decided we weren't going back in the cave. The Germans did run for shelter, and weren't watching us too closely. We jumped into a bombed out building, and stayed there for three days eating turnips that were stored in there. It was a feast! All they gave us in camp, even in the hospital, was a cup of soup that we put into the canteen cups they let us keep. The soup was water and some kind of green stuff, probably peas. We called it "Grass Soup."

When we came out at the end of the third day we had a new guard, an older German. He told me to do something, and I cursed him back in Italian, figuring he wouldn't understand me. The guy came over to me like he was going to nail me. Instead, we got to be pretty friendly. He had been stationed in Italy for a couple of years and had learned a little of the language. Every once in a while, he sneaked us a loaf of bread and a hunk of cheese. One day, my guard friend got a letter from a friend of his who was a POW in the States, up near Indiantown Gap, Pennsylvania. The guard's friend told him how well the Americans were treating him, and the guard couldn't believe it. After that, he brought us even more food.

After I got home from the war, I got a letter from Germany, and when I opened it, a baby picture fell out. At first, I thought it was a buddy of mine playing a joke. I know he slept with a German woman, and the first thing I thought was he had given her my address, and she was writing me thinking I was the father of her kid. Scared the hell out of me. I started reading the letter, and, here, it was the German guard writing to me. To tell you the truth, he wrote three letters and I answered three times. I still have the letters. Then the Berlin Wall went up, and he must have been on the wrong side of it, because I never heard from him after that.

About the beginning of April 1945, my guard friend came and told me that he was going to leave us some place. I asked him, "Leave us to die?"

He said, "No."

About the middle of April, we started to march, and we marched a whole day. Finally, we told them to go to hell, and that we weren't going to march anymore. We lay down and fell asleep. When we woke up, the guards were gone, like they said they would be. My friend had gotten into civilian clothing and told us to walk in one direction toward the American lines. He also said that the guys coming to relieve him would shoot us.

That next day we were in an open field with a couple hundred others. Nobody had anything to eat, and none of us had eaten for a couple days. One of the guys in my group was sick, so the nine of us decided to take off, right between the German and American lines.

A week later, we ran into the 80th Division Headquarters Company. They wanted to feed us, but we were so sick we couldn't eat anything. They took us back in a Jeep, put us on a plane, and flew us to Camp Lucky Strike in Le Havre, France. They dropped us off in front of three tents, told us to strip, and then threw us clippers. We had to take every hair off our bodies, armpits, heads, and everywhere else. They wouldn't get near us; we stunk too bad. They picked our clothes up with pitchforks, put them in a pile, and burned them. Then they sprayed us with DDT powder. After that, they sprayed us with water, gave us bars of soap and washrags, and we washed ourselves down. After we were done with that, the sent us to another tent where we got uniforms. They didn't bother to measure us. Nothing fit, anyway. I said, "Boy, the goddamn Germans treated us better than these Americans."

A second lieutenant there said, "What did you say?"

I said, "If you want me to repeat it, you probably heard what I said."

He didn't know we were POWs. Boy, we got the royal treatment after that.

They put us in the hospital in Le Havre, where we stayed for about a week. On 7 May 1945, we boarded a hospital ship. It was on board where we learned the Germans had surrendered. On 13 May, Mother's Day, we shipped out in a convoy for the states. We ended up at Camp Miles Standish in Boston.

We were there for three days, and they were going to ship us down to Fort Dix for discharge. I got a sore throat, so they were going to admit me to the hospital.

I said, "No way I'm going to the hospital. I'm not getting separated from you guys again."

So this one doctor sat me on the chair he said, "Open your mouth."

He got a big swab, dipped it in this big bottle of Iodine and swabbed my throat up. I thought my toenails were coming out of my mouth, but the Iodine did the trick. We went to New York and from New York we went to Fort Dix. We didn't get discharged. Instead, we got furloughs.

Before I finally got home, I ended up in a hospital in Asheville, North Carolina, with a reinfected throat. From there they shipped me up to a hospital at Fort Meade. I was supposed to get discharged from there. So, here I was in this big hall with three or four hundred other guys. They called right past the Bs down to the Zs, and I was still there. No discharge. They had no records on me! They reassigned me to a company, on Kitchen Police (KP). I kept arguing with the first sergeant. Somebody from Regimental Headquarters heard me, and took me there. The next day, a couple of officers listened to my troubles. They gave me a thirty-day furlough, or until my records could catch up with me. I was home fifteen days, when I had to go back into the hospital. I got out of the hospital in February of 1946, when my records finally showed up. I got discharged the same month.

A typical guard tower and its ever-present guard who manned a machine-gun. This tower was one at Stalag Luft I in Barth, Germany. *Courtesy of Pat Seanor.*

A German propaganda leaflet the Germans scattered from aircraft in an attempt to induce Allied troops to surrender. The Allies dropped similar leaflets. *Courtesy of Mrs. Thomas J. Evans.*

German guard at Stalag Luft I in Barth, Germany. His name was Fritz, but they called him "Fred." *Courtesy of Pat Seanor.*

"Where's the Booze?"

Clarence Brockman
80th Division, 317th Regiment, Headquarters Company
26 June 1920

"He put them on the front of the Jeep, and they're holding on to that freezing steel with their bare hands. He drove that Jeep as fast as it would go. Down at the PW camp there was a barnyard where we kept prisoners of war. The barnyard was surrounded with a stone wall. Instead of going through the gate, this Wyoming guy headed straight for the wall, and slammed on the brakes. Both Germans flew off. The private went over the wall, and the SS man hit it square"

LIFE ALL STARTED for me on 26 June 1920, at 5:30 on a Friday morning. Twenty years later, a buddy and I went into Pittsburgh to join the Army. The sergeant at the Old Post Office Building looked at me and said, "Come here. Take off your glasses and read that sign."

I said, "What sign?"

That was it for me and the military, or so I thought.

My buddy got in and became a cryptographer. After the war he worked for the State Department. He was a brilliant guy.

When the war started I was drafted. I spent my first four days at Fort Meade. For those four days we played a game called "In the Bag." What that meant was that we were given a bag and we put two of everything in it, socks, underwear, all the uniform parts. Then we got on a train. I spend most of my time in the dining car. I knew enough about train routes, so when we hit Cincinnati, I figured we were headed straight south. I was right. I ended up in Louisiana, the "Hell Hole of the Nation," where they had the Louisiana maneuvers.

When we pulled into Nashville and changed train crews, a first lieutenant came into our car. I asked him, "Where are we going. Lieutenant?"

He said, "Sit down, and I'll tell you."

He pulled out some papers, took a look at them, and said, "You're all members of the 80th Infantry Division."

Everybody's heart just sank.

After we finished training, we crossed the Atlantic on the *Queen Mary*. We landed at the Firth of Forth in Scotland. There we got on a train and went down to near Manchester, England, to a place called Ashton on Makerfield. England had double daylight savings at the time. When we arrived at Ashton it was midnight and still light out. They set us up at a place called Gordon Park.

I had trouble finding my land legs again. When I got to my tent I said, "Corporal, I got the strangest feeling."

I went over to the center pole and held on to it. For three days, everything just kept spinning around. Then I got acclimated.

Soon, we got over to the Continent. A few of us got captured on the Moselle River, but we got away. There was a German guard watching five of us in a house. Our artillery started a barrage, and then our troops made a counterattack. As soon as the shelling started, the German hit the dirt. He never got back up because one of the guys took a knife to his throat. After that, we sneaked back to our own lines. It was harder to get through our lines than it was to get the other way. We had to know the password or else. We knew how to cuss in American, so the sentries knew we were okay.

During the Battle of the Bulge, we slept on the top floor of a town hall where they had a big Christmas tree set up. We had a guy from Maine, a Frenchman, who didn't learn English until he got into the service. He would say, "Let's go heat, instead of, let's go eat."

Anyway, he and I got to rooting around in the basements of some houses. People had left them in a hurry, but they left a lot of booze behind. We found some Schnapps, drank it all, and ended up in an interesting sleeping arrangement. He slept up in the tree, and I slept under it.

The Army was kind of slow telling us where we were going and what we were going to do. They usually told us that stuff after we did it. We didn't find out until the next morning that the Germans had broken through, and from then on out we were in the middle of the Battle of the Bulge. I froze my hands, but I wouldn't go back to the medical station. I had been born and raised in the snow, so I treated myself. Another reason I didn't go was because as soon as you got into an ambulance, they took everything off of you, and I didn't what them to find and take away all of my loot.

They had a story about me in the *Stars and Stripes* magazine once. We were getting hit with tree bursts. They were wicked anytime, but this time they had direct observation on us so it was worse. At the time we had two battalions up on line and one battalion back in reserve. They were trying to hit the men, and they had zeroed in on our vehicles.

The Captain said "Brock, you're a driver, take that truck out of there, take it around and put in on the other side of the hill where it can't get direct fire."

I drove that truck but it was going along kind of slow. Something wasn't working too well. I thought I saw steam coming out of the front, but when I opened the hood, I found out it wasn't steam but smoke. I checked things out and found a piece of shrapnel that had taken out a spark plug and the carburetor drain plug. While I waited to get the thing fixed, I saw two Germans about seventy-five yards away go into some scrub oak trees. We had a couple companies around there, and they started firing blindly in to the trees.

I hollered, "Wait a minute. You got another battalion on the other side of these woods. You want to kill them as well as the Germans?"

So I went into the woods and captured these two guys. One was an SS man, and the other was just a common private. The Germans told us, "If you come on back tomorrow, down the woods, you'll get seven more of us"

In the meantime, one of the guys came up. He said, "What are you going to do with them Brock?"

I said, "Well, I don't want to take them back to PW camp."

I'd have been in charge of them until I got back to the PW camp, and that was a fairly long walk. I said, "The only thing to do is shoot them. Let's get rid of them because I don't want to walk back there."

"We can't do that."

"Why?"

Just then a Jeep carrying four war correspondents came by. They took down our story. There was a soldier from Wyoming with them, and he put the Germans on the Jeep. He hated Germans, and killed any of them he saw. I was worried he would kill those two, especially with the correspondents present.

I said, "Don't do anything because you got correspondents there. You can't do anything to them."

He put them on the front of the Jeep, and they're holding on to that freezing steel with their bare hands. He drove that Jeep as fast as it would go. Down at the PW camp there was a barnyard where we kept prisoners of war. A stone wall surrounded the barnyard. Instead of going through the gate, this Wyoming guy headed straight for the wall, and then slammed on the brakes. Both Germans flew off. The private went over the wall, and the SS man hit it square. I saw the German private again in Luxembourg in 1988 at a ceremony. I was standing in front of a statue when a guy came up to me and said, "Do you remember me?"

I said, "No."

"You took me prisoner."

"Yeah, now I remember. There were two of you, what happened to the other guy?"

"He didn't live."

This guy's name was Warner Stanke. I visited him after that. He lived in a beautiful apartment and he entertained us for the day. We corresponded until two years ago, when he passed away. He was my age.

After the Battle of the Bulge we went east into Germany, and got into Kaiserslautern, in the Rhineland. Kaiserslautern was a big town and it was there that I liberated a pistol off a Colonel who was sitting in the Mayor's office. That was one of my best war souvenirs. After Kaiserslautern we crossed over a river at Mainz. Mainz was a fairly well bombed-out city but it happens to be a wine export center. Well, we helped them "export" a lot of Champagne.

It was there that one of those funny coincidences in war you hear about took place. They had long buildings in that town, and you could be on one end, someone at the other, and never know it. We set up the outpost at one end of this building, and when I got home from the service, my cousin, who was in the 90th Division, said he had been at the other end of that same building.

I got to snoop around that building, and an old German there didn't look too happy, and I found out why.

I said, "Where's the booze?"

He said, "Come."

He took me down about twenty steps. He opened a door to a big room. Inside were big A-frames, ten feet high, with row after row of booze. Everything you could imagine, Champagne, Schnapps, just anything we could want. We got a two-and-a-half-ton truck, and put everything on there. Case after case of champagne, magnum bottles, and everything. This was as when were getting ready to go over the Rhine, and they were taking the trucks over on LCI's.

They Navy guys on the LCI told the driver of our truck, "When you get over there, that bank, its mud, you will have to gun it to get up that bank, its about five feet high. Its kind of steep, they didn't level it off for the trucks to get off."

So we crossed and the guy said, "Ok, gun it."

He gunned it, hit the bank, we took about three bounces, getting up there and all that champagne went pow, pow, pow. All those bottles broke apart. It was a sad day.

After the Rhine crossing we went to the town of Wiesbaden, a resort area. We captured a German general there. He and his staff were using the hospital as their headquarters. After we captured them, we rode up a hill on the end of the main street, and, as we went around a bend, we looked over and this German Officer was looking out of a window. Right away we went to check it out. I forget how many German soldiers were with that officer, but we got about 600 overall. Three days later we got orders to move out to the north. We got out on the autobahn and we could see in the distance the I.G. Farben works in Frankfurt. Why we never bombed that factory, I'll never know.

We met some resistance when we got to the town of Kassel, a German tank production center. The Germans threw about twenty tanks at us. The paint on them wasn't even dry. We knocked out the first five, and the rest of them headed back toward the factory.

After Kassel, we headed east again, toward Gotha and Weimar. Twelve kilometers out from Weimar was Buchenwald. We found the camp by accident while we were out scouting around for booze. One of the citizens in town told us to go to a certain farm. He said, "You go out this road, this farmer, he makes the good Schnapps."

Well we got up there, four of us, with a three-quarter ton truck. About twenty-five yards from where we stopped was the farmer. He started talking about the booze, but he was kind of shaking in his boots because, we thought, we were the first Americans he had seen. Then, out of the barn steps this blue-eyed, blonde farm boy. All four of us turned our heads, and we all thought the same thing. He looked suspiciously like one of those Nazi supermen.

The farmer said, "Oh, go to the next farmer. He's got better booze."

We started down the road, and we saw something up in the trees, black figures in the branches.

I said, "They don't have monkeys over here, do they?"

They weren't monkeys. They were people! They saw us first and hid up in the trees. Then they saw who we were and they wanted us to come down to the camp, so we went with them. Nobody liberated that camp; the prisoners liberated Buchenwald after the Germans left.

From Buchenwald we went to Chemnitz. When we got there, we were halted and let the Russians take the town. Instead, we went south to the northern part of Nuremberg, to the railroad yards. Then we got orders to go east to Regensburg and then down to Dingolfing, Edeberg, and Simbach. In Braunau, where Hitler was born, they had a brewery. The guys started rolling barrels of beer out of it, and one guy from Cleveland started taking sniper fire. The sniper fire hit the barrels of beer instead of hitting him. That made the guys madder than if they got shot, so they got the sniper pretty quick.

From Braunau we went down to the town where the Christmas song, "Silent Night," was composed, right outside of the Salzburg area. Then we went into Lake Gemünden, that's where the Germans hid a lot of loot in the salt mines. They had millions and millions of dollars worth of stuff hidden there. They even had U.S. dollar bills, paintings, everything. Of course that place was off limits to us.

From Gemünden we ended up just outside Spital. That's where the war ended for us. When we arrived there, the Hungarian army came out to meet us. They wanted us to stay at the church and guard it along with the bank, where the entire wealth of the Bank of Hungary was stored, along with Saint Stephen's Cross, the Hungarian Royal Crown, everything. The Germans and the Austrians knew about that, but they didn't tell us. Not long after we got there, the 3rd Army MP's came in and seized it all. They brought the cross back over to the United States along with the money, and Truman gave the cross back later.

After it was all over, I came home with the 10th Armored through Camp Lucky Strike. We left in September from Marseilles on the troopship *S.S. Breckenridge*. We landed at Newport News and went to Camp Patrick Henry. Then we got on a train and came up to Indiantown Gap. They couldn't take us in there, there were too many of us, so they sent us home for a week and told us to come back. Instead, ten of us went down to Harrisburg and hit the saloons.

We all came back and we got discharged out of the chapel at Indiantown Gap. The Chaplain shook hands with us and gave us our papers. We walked down the street and there was a place for reenlistment and to join the reserves. We didn't feel too good because we were looped yet from drinking all night. To get into the re enlistment center you had to go up six steps that I didn't want to climb. I came home the next day, and got a job in the mine. If it wouldn't have been for the booze and those steps, I would have been in Korea.

THE STARS AND STRIPES

WAR ENDS

Truman Announces Total Surrender

WASHINGTON, Aug. 15 (AP)—The United States, Britain, Russia and China announced today that Japan had surrendered unconditionally.

The job of disarming millions of Japanese soldiers still had to be accomplished, but it seemed that peace had returned to the world for the first time since 1937, when Japan invaded central China.

President Truman, who announced the surrender for the U. S. at 7 p. m., EWT (1. a. m., Central European Time), revealed that Gen. Douglas MacArthur had been named Supreme Commander in charge of occupation forces and would receive the surrender. Mr. Truman started his dramatic announcement by saying that he had received "full acceptance of the Potsdam Declaration, which specifies unconditional surrender of Japan." He said that arrangements had been made for the formal signing of the surrender at "the earliest possible moment."

In the meantime, he continued, the terrible atomic bomb attacks, the Superfortress raids and the fleet bombardment that had brought Japan to her knees had been ordered suspended.

The President said this note had been received from Japan through the Swiss legation:

"The Emperor is prepared to authorize and insure the signature by his government and Imperial Headquarters of the necessary terms for carrying out the provisions of the Potsdam Declaration.

"His Majesty is also prepared to issue his commands to all military, naval and air forces under their control, wherever located, to cease active resistance and to surrender their arms."

About the same time, Prime Minister Clement R. Attlee of Great Britain and representatives of the Soviet and Chinese governments—the powers that had signed the Potsdam Declaration—were announcing the surrender.

Radio Tokyo alerted the U. S. and the world on a celebration yesterday by announcing at 1:49 a. m., EWT (7:49 a. m., Central European Time) that "The text of an imperial message accepting the proclamation will be forthcoming soon."

At 6:35 a. m., EWT, Charles G. Ross, White House secretary, announced that the Japanese reply was "in the hands of the Swiss."

This was quickly denied by Berne. The misunderstanding seemingly arose from the receipt by the Japanese diplomats in Berne of other communications from Tokyo. The Swiss legation here issued a memorandum that "the Japanese legation reports that code cables it received this morning do not contain the answer which was awaited by the whole world." Ross then made public this memorandum without further comment.

Ross had said that when the official reply arrives here it would be delivered first to Secretary of State James F. Byrnes and then to the President.

Radio Tokyo's announcement was heard by monitors on both the East and West Coasts. But as the hours wore by, it failed to read the proclamation that it had advertised would be forthcoming "immediately."

An earlier broadcast appealed for loyalty to the Emperor, now that "the worst has come to the worst," saying:

"It is fortunate—most fortunate—that his majesty's decision on the leader is final and loud. Even if the imperial command should not be in line with our individual desires, the only thing left us to do is to obey."

Domei transmitted in scripted dots an imperial statement which expressed Hirohito's "extreme concern" for "the calamity caused by the U.S." government machines reported, but added that it is "held for release"

(Continued on Page 4)

Adm. Halsey's 3rd Fleet men may be first to enter Japan

"Let's Go Join the Marine Corps."

Ben Byrer
3rd Marine Division

"Once we got off the beach, we went into the high country. There wasn't much opposition. I got up on a mountain and saw green fields, and little houses below. It was a beautiful farm scene. It was a place we had passed before we climbed. In fact, the whole island was beautiful. When we were going through the jungle, I saw a shaft of sunlight coming down through the trees and shining on a beautiful, orange flower. I made a painting of it, years later."

I WAS A CRANE OPERATOR at Republic Steel in Canton, Ohio, when war broke out, I became a Civil Defense Warden, but that didn't seem to be quite enough. So, one day after work, a couple good friends of mine and I stopped for a beer on the way home. I said, "Let's go join the Marine Corps."

I was twenty-one. I didn't think of my responsibilities at home, and what I really should have done. My folks were dead and I had siblings to support. I had an uncle who was head of the local Draft Board. When I got back from the war, he told me I never should have gone and left my brothers and sisters. We were making eighteen-dollar-a-month mortgage payments on the house. But my older sister was getting old enough to work, and then the second sister started working. My brother, who got killed in the war, worked after school, when he could. But, even so, while I was gone, they burned up most of the house furniture to keep warm in the winter. They couldn't afford to buy coal. All the while I was gone, I sent my entire pay home except for fifteen dollars.

The Marines told us to return in a week, at which time they would have a new program in place. When we went back, they swore us in, and then put us on a train for Cleveland. Paris Island was filled, so we had a choice of going home for a month until there was an opening, or we could go to a boot camp in San Diego, California. Since I had never been more than fifty miles from Canton, I said, "Oh, man I'll take this San Diego deal."

Several hundred of us from Ohio and Western Pennsylvania went out on a troop train. I fell in love with the Marine Corps in San Diego. It was that simple. I loved the buildings, I loved the regimentation, I loved the food, but the clothing left a lot to be desired. This was early in the war, and we didn't have enough uniforms. Instead of hats, they gave us these little overseas caps, just little things that sat on one side of your head. We stayed in San Diego for about eight weeks. All of us had scabs on our heads from when they shaved our hair off. Fluid kept running out of these scabs, and down our cheeks.

President Roosevelt made a tour of San Diego base one day. We were out on the parade ground around ten o'clock in the morning, all lined up, at ease, but in formation. We were like that until two o'clock in the afternoon, in the hot sun. Guys passed out from the heat. Finally, Roosevelt arrived in a big limousine, rode down through the parade ground, and went out the other side! In one gate and out the other! He wasn't' there more than half a minute. We let loose some bitter feelings in his direction!

We went to Scout and Sniper School. We called it "Snoop and Droop. We learned camouflage, and how to move quietly in the jungle. Then we went to the rifle range. I shot expert. I'll never forget shooting from the prone position at 500 yards. I can hardly see 500 yards now, but my first shot was in the four-ring at four o'clock just out of the bull's eye. I set the sight and the next nine shots went right into the bull. It was an awesome thing; it was really neat!

We didn't' get a furlough. Instead, around Christmas 1942, we headed for Auckland, New Zealand, aboard the *Mount Vernon*, a converted cruise ship. I believe we had three battalions on board, all crammed down in the lower decks, three bunks high. Once in awhile we got a chance to go topside for working parties. The officers' area was really neat, and had walnut banisters on the staircases. It was a beautiful ride. It was the first time I ever saw a flying fish. We had no escort because the ship was supposed to be faster than any submarine and faster than any torpedo, but we did zigzag all the way across the Pacific Ocean. When we landed in early February, the New Zealanders gave us a glorious reception. They were glad to see us because the Japanese were already in Guadalcanal, and their next stop might have been New Zealand. Most of the New Zealand guys were away at war.

Once we were out on drill for three days. They gave us a sock full of rice and a sock full of raisins and a handful of heat tabs, sort of like an Alka-Seltzer. The idea was to light the heat tabs, cook the rice in our canteen cups, and then put in the raisins. We were supposed to live on that for three days. It was a fiasco! In the first place, the heat tabs never made enough heat to get the water warm, let alone to the boiling point. Frustrated, we threw the rice away and ate the raisins. After New Zealand, they shipped us out to Guadalcanal.

The main campaign on Guadalcanal was over, but there was still a lot of enemy back in the jungles and mountains. It rained all the time and it was always muddy. We trained in a coconut grove, and it was a hot, terrible, effort, but I realized why they trained us so hard. They wanted to get us used to the heat and the discomfort. Eventually, we went into the interior to find Japanese stragglers. Every night we were bombed because the enemy still had air and sea superiority. Their warships also shelled us. It wasn't very pleasant.

After several months at Guadalcanal, we headed for Bougainville, our first real landing. The navy ships and planes had been shelling and bombing the place for quite a while, so our landing was more or less unopposed, except for the mortars and artillery shells that tried to hit the Higgins boats.

We had just hit the beach when three planes came up the beach strafing. The first one flew by. The second one flew by. Our machinegunners got the third one. They thought all three planes were Japs, but the third one wasn't. It was an Australian chasing the Japs. He crash-landed in the ocean, and when they got to him, he was furious with our gunners. Plus he had taken a fifty caliber round through the leg.

Once we got off the beach, we went into the high country. There wasn't much opposition. I got up on a mountain and saw green fields, and little houses below. It was a beautiful farm scene. It was a place we had passed before we climbed. In fact, the whole island was beautiful. When we were going through the jungle, I saw a shaft of sunlight coming down through the trees and shining on a beautiful, orange flower. I made a painting of it, years later.

It rained every day on Bougainville. One night, we slept on the roots of a Banyan tree; the ground was like a swamp. Those Banyan trees dropped branches, and the branches rooted and became big gnarly roots. There were about twelve of us, and we all got a big knob to sleep on. We were the patrols, and we kept the line moving forward. Often, we had to wait for the Army and supply to catch up with us, and that left an opening for Japs to get through. Our job was to try and keep the line closed.

After about three weeks of patrolling, they sent us clean socks. None of us had taken our shoes for all the time we were plodding around in water and mud. When I took off my shoes and socks, my feet swelled like a football. I looked at them, and got sick to my stomach. My flesh was eaten away, and I could see the bones and the tendons of my feet. We called it "Jungle Rot." I went to sickbay, where they told me they didn't have a cure. They experimented on me. I'd soak my feet in five-gallon cans filled with hot water. One day I'd soak them in potassium permanganate, the next day in something purple, another day in something red. They made me walk in the surf, and the saltwater seemed to help. My feet itched like crazy, and I could feel things moving under the skin. I think it was bacteria. Even today, I think the bacteria are still in there. I have the same feeling when I go to the beach and stand in the surf. I wore white socks for twenty-five years after I got out of the Marine Corps. It took that long for that stuff to heal over. I still have gray scars on my feet.

I healed enough for them to send me back to the front line. Then they relieved us for a couple days for shore duty, unloading ships, and bringing the stuff back to the line. Of course, we'd accidentally drop a box or two, and everyone grabbed something. We buried canned pineapples, baked beans, and all the stuff that looked really good to us. We collected quite a cache, and planned our own Thanksgiving dinner. Then we found out that they were going to give us a good Thanksgiving dinner of turkey and potatoes, anyway.

I carried the Browning Automatic Rifle (BAR) most of the time, and I was good with it. When we first landed on Guam, they gave me a flamethrower to carry. They were a weird implement. When we started moving ahead, we took some fire from a kind of a shack, a tropical type thing up on stilts. They told me to go up and take care of it, so I snooped and drooped up to it as close as I could get and I gave a blast and set that thing on fire. Boy! There was screaming in there, but not much. When flames from that flamethrower hit someone, they tried to scream, but when they inhaled they just sucked that heat into their lungs and burned from the inside out.

On the afternoon before Thanksgiving, they sent us up to a hill Marine Raiders had been trying to take. There went our Thanksgiving dinner! They had already relieved one battalion of Raiders with another one, but I guess they couldn't take the hill, either. We made our way through the swamps, and up to the hill. All of a sudden a machinegun opened fire, and the rounds kicked up the dirt in front of me. I held on to my weapon, and hit the deck. As I was going down, I bent over a sapling. Every time that sapling shook, this Jap on the hill would open up again. The Japs didn't move their guns around like we did. Each of their gunners had their own fire lane, a machinegun here, a machinegun there. The rounds were landing just in front of my head. I thought, "Why doesn't that sonofabitch move his gun." It got almost hysterical. He could have had me if he had moved his gun just half an inch. Finally, one of our guys on our left flank from our company got close enough to lob a couple grenades. That took care of that!

We started on up the hill. There was a big, tree, about three feet in diameter, fallen across the path. I had gotten fairly close to the tree, when a Jap jumped up and started running. He was wearing something like a tan trench coat. I raised my BAR and hit him maybe five times in the back. I saw every shot hit. That guy was the first man I shot. I dreamed about shooting that guy for forty years, every night. Finally, I called a priest, a Capuchin, who had been in New Guinea during the war and who lived nearby. I said, "Father, I would like to come over and go to confession."

We didn't go inside, but sat in the yard while I told him about the shooting. He made me realize that what I had done wasn't a sin. It was my duty. I didn't dream about that incident after that talk.

We got as far on Bougainville as we were going to go. We built foxholes, and laid coconut logs over them. The Japs still had air superiority, and they bombed us every night. They'd come in at about twenty or twenty-five feet and drop their bombs. We could hear the click of the bomb release, and see these things come down. Twenty or thirty seconds later, the bombs would explode. They must have been delayed action. If that wasn't enough, the volcano on Bougainville erupted, shaking the ground and caving in a couple of our emplacements. A couple guys got their legs smashed when the logs fell into the holes.

After a time, the Army came in to mop up, and we went back to Guadalcanal to refit and train. We never knew where we were going next. Tinian? Rabaul? Truk? Where? MacArthur finally decided to bypass many of the islands, and let the enemy starve out. Then we found out that the Marine 1st Division was going to land on Saipan, and we were to land a couple days later on Guam. The resistance the 1st met was so great, though, that the brass thought they might have to call on us to reinforce them. We stayed on our ship for two months and fifty-nine days, just waiting to see what was going to happen. The officers decided at some point that we needed a little exercise. We went to a dinky, little island, about twice as big as a football field, and covered with sand and scrub grass. We all got in a row and smoothed this little sand heap into a ball field. Crazy! Eventually, they got control of Saipan, and we went to Guam.

Before we landed, everybody went up on deck and waited at the bulkhead, ready to board Higgins boats. Then we started down the landing nets with 100 pounds of equipment on our backs. The landing nets were like rope lattice, and we held the rope going one way, and put our feet on the rope going the other way, stretching our arms so that the guys above us wouldn't step on our hands. We felt like turkeys before a Thanksgiving slaughter, except the turkeys probably had a better idea of what was going to happen to them. We were excited and exhilarated. Would I be man enough to do my part, to do what I was supposed to do, to do what I was trained to do?

The Higgins boats jostled back and forth in the waves in the waves. Once in awhile, a guy got knocked off the landing net, and with all that equipment on him, went straight to the bottom. Once we got on the move, we hoped the driver would get us in safely, and we hoped we wouldn't get hit by the shellfire coming from the island. After we hit the beach and the ramp of the Higgins boat dropped, we hoped small arms fire wouldn't hit us. We questioned whether we would get off the beach, and up the bank. Everything was a question, one question after another. We were trained to think teamwork. We didn't think how we felt. Here's Dale, and here's Jesus Madero. I'm watching them; they're watching me. We just went on, across the beach, up the bank, up the hill. That was war!

The Navy and Air Force, as usual, softened up the island before we got there, and, as usual, it didn't do much good. Then there was a big coral reef. We also had to fight our way through barbed wire. The beach was short, and we had to climb up a twenty-foot high bank of sand. On top of the sand hill was a rice paddy laid out like a checkerboard that must have gone on for almost a mile. We had to cross that to reach the highlands. We got over one paddy, sloshed through water, got up and down another one, then another one, one after the other, all the time under machinegun, mortar, and artillery fire.

Finally we got up into the high ground. It was a little quieter there, and we weren't sitting ducks. It took a little while to get everybody pulled together. Then we started our push farther inland. We made good ground in the first day. On the second day, we started up a hill, but came under heavy fire. We had to withdraw a couple hundred yards or so. We threw away our packs, but kept our rifles. We sat out the shelling.

The temperature was 110 or 115 degrees. Water was precious to us. We got one canteen of water a day, if we could, and it had to last us all day. I found that if I could go to two o'clock in the afternoon without touching the water, then I could make it to evening, but if I started at ten o'clock, in the morning, I would only crave more. When it rained, we spread our ponchos out into a trough and let the water run into our helmets. We'd rather take the risk of having our helmets off, than to miss getting water. When we dropped our packs during our withdrawal, one guy stayed behind with the packs. He was actually a friend of mine from Missouri. I could see him. He was taking my canteen of water. I raised my BAR. I was going to knock him off. One of my other friends talked me out of it. That's how precious water was!

We moved out again, and retrieved our packs. A corporal from our platoon got hit in the groin. He screamed and cried in terrible pain. He screamed for two or three minutes, his blood pouring out of him, and then he stopped. He was such a nice man. He was from Utah, and his name was Gerald Rich.

As Gerald died, I thought about Sabby, from Wauwatosa, Wisconsin. He was like our mascot. I don't know how he got into the Marines, because he wasn't much over five-feet tall. Sabby was a beautiful little boy, but he was a real Marine. Everybody watched out for Sabby. When we were back on Guadalcanal, we had to cross the Tenaru River. The water was getting deeper and deeper, up to the chin. Sabby was right in front of me. I grabbed him by his pack and lifted him up until we got to the other side. Then Sabby went down on one knee. I went over and touched him on the shoulder and said, "Come on Sabby its time to go."

When I touched him, he fell over. I looked and saw that he had been shot in the neck. He must have been killed so fast that he died like that on one knee.

On Guam we had quite a few Banzai chárges. In the night the Japs attacked in waves. They just came and came and came, and we just fired and fired and fired. Most of the time we couldn't see who we were shooting at, but in the morning we would find piles of dead Japs. When I would be in a hole by myself because the line was spread out, I had to be on watch all night long. I might grab a few winks, but I was tense the whole time. If the line was tight, then there would be two of us in a foxhole, and one of us could sleep a couple hours while the other kept watch. I don't know if sleep is the word, really. None of us were ever really sure the other guy wouldn't fall asleep, too. Sometimes, when we had three guys to a foxhole, we could get more "sleep," but that didn't happen too often.

Guam was rainy, and we dug our holes in the red clay, and our clothes got dyed red. When it rained the foxholes filled with water. One night, when it was raining, our foxhole filled. Another night, three of us were sitting on the upper side of the hole, a big mud puddle in front of us, when the Japs Banzai-ed us. We just jumped to the bottom, water or not. When it rained the clay mud made it hard to walk. We slipped all over the place when we were on patrol. The heat was terrible. It got so that I couldn't eat some of the meals, especially the meat. I could eat the dehydrated potatoes, I could eat the dehydrated eggs, I could drink the coffee, and, if they made pancakes, I could eat those. One bite of meat, and my stomach would turn. I ate as much jelly and bread as I could.

One time we were sitting around in circle on top of a hill. A Jap mortar round came in and landed in the middle of us. It was a dud. The twelve of us scattered like roaches when the lights come on. Another time, we were stopped for a break. A Jap came running out of the jungle and started chasing one of the guys with a big sword. The guy had on his pack, and the Jap is slashing at him. The Marine ran around in circles, yelling for help. The Jap's right behind him, cutting his pack to pieces. Stuff's hanging out of the pack. We're dying from laughter. Finally, one of the guys shot the Jap.

One evening, as we dug our foxholes, a guy comes walking by about twenty feet away from me. Marines are all over the place digging foxholes. Someone yelled, "Hey, he's a Nip!"

I picked up my BAR and started shooting. Everybody started shooting. Nobody hit that guy. He just kept walking. He must have been in some sort of daze. I was an expert with a BAR, and I didn't hit him! Something was protecting him, I guess. It's funny how things happened.

One night, maybe the last night I was in combat on Guam, there were three of us in a foxhole. One of them was a guy who had taken my helmet during a Banzai charge. He didn't use his because it was full of water, and I went through that whole Banzai charge without a helmet. The other guy, Dale, our squad leader, was a lumberjack from California. Our foxhole was right beside a trail that led through the jungle. Everything was fine during the night, but toward morning when the sky was just starting to lighten a little bit, one of the guys started to light a cigarette. I told him not to light one because it was still too dark and the Japs might see the light. As it got lighter, I saw a bunch of Japs coming down the trail. I woke Dale up, and we stayed down until the Japs were pretty close. I don't know why they didn't see us, because we had fresh dirt piled on the outside of the foxhole. Dale and I jumped up when the Japs were about twenty feet away. The other guy didn't get up. Dale and I started shooting. I don't know what happens when soldiers do that, but it happens so many times. It was like a fog. I remember taking the first shot, and then all of a sudden everything was fogged out. I know I was standing there shooting, but I don't remember seeing anything. Whether God puts a spell on you, or your guardian angel holds a veil in front of your face, I don't know. The only thing I remember is that just before we moved out, there were bodies out there in front of us. I don't know if they were close or far, or how many there were, or in what position they were. I just knew that there were bodies lying out in front of us. It must have been an hour before that spell passed.

We were fighting through the jungle, fighting, fighting, fighting, shooting and pushing, pushing. We came to an airstrip. The Japs were supposed to be on the far side, about a hundred yards away. The Japs didn't shoot. Nobody shot! The Captain told me to take two of the guys and go across to see what's happening. We had to cross a hundred yards of flat airstrip, and there was nothing to hide behind. I expected to get shot any second. When we got there, there was nobody. It was funny that the Japs didn't leave anyone there, someone to shoot a little bit, anyway. I hollered for the rest to come over.

We kept on. I was walking in front of a tank with two of my buddies. We got to this hump, sort of like a hilltop, and it was barren. All the trees were either on the ground, or there were bare trunks standing up. All of a sudden, there was this big flash. It was like a scene in a comic book, when you see nuts and bolts and springs and curly things. I actually saw little things like that flying in this big, white cloud. Something must have hit that tank. I got hit in the head, but I don't remember that. My buddies later told me that I staggered and fell down. I woke up a week later in the field hospital, but I thought it was just the next day. The doctor came in and told me it was all right for me to go back to my company. I got back to where the company was, but none of the guys were there. They had gone on another sweep of the island, looking for stragglers.

On another occasion, the Japs had a roadblock set up and we were to go and knock it out. Again, I was leading a tank with two other guys. We were pushing through the jungle, and couldn't see through the vegetation. We got to the roadblock, and we didn't even know it. Suddenly, one of their tanks shot at our tank, and my two buddies and me were in between. The two tanks were maybe fifty yards apart, having this duel. I ended up with two ruptured eardrums. Today, I get disability. I still can't hear anything. Finally, our tank got in a fatal hit on their tank. We went on up the road. The tank ran over quite a few of the Japs. They just wouldn't get up. The tank just pushed them right down into the mud.

A short time after I came back to the company, I got yellow jaundice. I wasn't feeling too good with that. Besides that, over the months I had several malaria attacks, the jungle rot, and dengue fever. When the company came back after their sweep, we all got a couple cans of beer. While we sat around drinking, somebody came around with a list with my name and a couple other guys' names on it. We were going back to the States. By next morning, we were packed. Tom Chambers, a real good friend of mine from Chicago, begged, borrowed, and stole quite a few cans of beer. He got pretty popped up, and he wouldn't believe we were going, "You're just kidding me! You're not going back, are you? I'm never going to go back. I've forgotten what my mother looks like. I'll never see home again."

We packed Tom's stuff for him, because he staggered into a foxhole. We let him be. In November 1944, we were taken aboard a Dutch merchant ship bound for Hawaii. When we got there, they quarantined the ship and examined us for infectious diseases. I was six-four and weighed 135 pounds. I could see why the doctors wanted to keep us on the ship for a while. The Dutch gave us steak and potatoes, to fatten us up. We had lots of butterscotch pudding. I think the Navy had a contract with somebody who manufactured butterscotch pudding. After awhile we got sick of the pudding. We had a bunch of Jap prisoners we were bringing back to the States. They loved the stuff. They put it on their potatoes, their meat, and their bread. They really went for that butterscotch pudding!

When I finally got to San Francisco, I weighed 180 pounds. We had nothing to do there, except wait for the troop train that would take us home. Tom Chambers and I rode the same train. In Arizona we were pulled off to a siding. The door opened, and we were like a covey of quail. We all spread out to find a liquor store. All we could find was Tequila, so we ended up with practically a trainload of it. When we got to Chicago, Tom asked me to come and meet his mom and his family. I had three lost days in Chicago. I don't know if we slept or drank. I left Chicago and made for Cleveland, where I had a three-hour layover, waiting for a bus to Canton. I went into a bar and ordered a beer at the bar. There was a young man and an attractive woman sitting next to me. He was much older than she. She told me to put a nickel in the jukebox so we could dance. I went over to do that. I didn't know any of the songs, so I turned around to ask her what to play, and I noticed her putting something white in my beer. I went back over, and I sat down. I toyed with my beer, and sat there, talking. She got up to go to the restroom, and I took the chance and switched glasses. I drank her beer, and when she came back I told her I had to go, that it was time for my bus. I don't know what happened to her. There were lots of people back then who knew that we had money on us for time served. I had $300.00 for being overseas for two-and-a-half years.

I finally got home. My brother and his wife came to the bus station to meet me, and I broke down in tears when I saw him because they had given up all hope. I was home for thirty days, and then I went to Yorktown, Virginia for guard duty at the Navy Mine Depot. That's where I first found out I was going to have a problem. The barracks were full, and some of us were set up in the attic of one of them. There were no windows, and they turned out the lights at night. If there had been a fire, none of us in the attic would have gotten out. At night I couldn't see. I'd lie in bed, and it was like I was back in the jungle on one of those nights when I couldn't see my hand in front of my face, keyed up, listening for any sound. It was all I could do in that attic to keep from screaming. It really got to me. It's something that happens. Once something gets into your brain, it won't come out. It's buried deep, but it surfaces every once in a while.

Today, when I go into Pittsburgh, and I get behind a big bus or truck and smell those diesel fumes, I'm back on a Higgins boat. A couple of years ago, my wife and I went to Heinz Hall to hear the Duquesne University Choral Group. They sang one song where they just hummed, continually. One group would start, and then another would start. Then one would stop and another would begin. No breaks. It went on for minutes. For a while I thought it was one of the most beautiful sounds I ever heard. Then, suddenly, the sound was Jap bombers! I told my wife that I had to get the hell out of there. I get goose bumps when I even talk about it. I could see the stage and the singers, but in my mind Jap bombers were attacking, like they did, every night, night after night, when I was over there.

My time in the attic lasted only a couple days, until I was transferred over to the Mine Warfare School, which was a smaller contingent, only twenty-eight Marines and a sergeant. We had our own kitchen, but if we didn't want to cook we'd go eat the Navy food. We had our own place, we did the guard duty, and that was nice. In fact, that's where I met my wife, Vi. She was in the Navy, and she was stationed there. I was discharged the October after the war was over, but she was still in the Navy. Right after we got married, she got a discharge.

When I got discharged, I got my pre-war job back. Vi and I talked it over, and I decided I wanted to go the Art Institute in Pittsburgh. I went there, then to the Melbourne School of Art, then the Dietz Industrial Art School. I got work right after art school. I was the staff artist for the Buhl Planetarium on the North Side of Pittsburgh for thirty-five years. When they showed the scenes around in the sky, that was all my artwork. So were all the murals, the Hall of the Universe. I did displays for

United States Steel, Gulf Oil, mining and medical companies. I also illustrated a history book for Middlesex Township, and the *2 Score 10* for the Third Marine Division.

We still get together for our Marine reunions. We have some real glorious times, and its great to get together with the guys. The sad part is, every time we meet these days, there are one or two less of us.

This 1942 Marine recruitment poster was painted by Haddon H. Sundblom. Recruit posters in general and for all services accounted for the enlistment of millions of American men and women in World War II. Nearly 700,000 young men enlisted in the Marine Corps. *National Archives.*

"We Had Visions of High Adventure"

Dale Allen Bullock

United States Navy, Chief Pharmacist Mate (Ret.), U.S.S. *Rotanin* ("Named After a Star"); Jeannette, Pennsylvania, 20 August 1922

"Of course, with all the monotony on board ship, a sailor starts thinking about getting liberty in the next port. It had been a long time since we had liberty. Well, that's how the famous Fiji Islands incident occurred. The Rotanin docked there and the captain granted the crew liberty. This of course was one of the stories that developed into Tom Heggen's screenplay for the movie Mr. Roberts. Tom Heggen was an assistant communications officer on the Rotanin. His experiences on the Rotanin and another ship he was assigned to became the inspiration for the book and later the movie. The character of Mr. Roberts was in many ways modeled after many men on the ship. But more than anyone else Don House was our ship's Mr. Roberts."

MY FATHER, HENRY, was gassed in Word War I, and he had stomach problems the rest of his life. I think the gas worked on him internally all that time. He was only fifty-nine when he died. He served in the 80th Infantry Division, 313th Machinegun Battalion, Company B. He was in four out of the five major campaigns in France. He used to tell me, "After I die I would be happy if the American Legion puts an American flag on my grave."

I graduated high school in 1941, after which I got a job at the Pennsylvania Rubber Company in Jeannette, where I had been working toward the end of my high school career. I sprayed rubber play balls with two other guys. In the summer of 1941, well before the war started for America, we got it into our heads that we might join the Navy. We had visions of high adventure. When the war did start, I knew that sooner or later I'd be drafted. In those days, most men my age were very anxious to go to war. For them, it was the right thing to do. None of my family wanted me to go, and, on top of that, I had a good job. My father told me, "If you have to go don't join the Army. It's a pretty rough life."

I joined the Navy in November 1942, in Greensburg, Pennsylvania. A bunch of us went to Pittsburgh, and marched through the city to the train station. My mother said goodbye to me there. We went to Newport, Rhode Island for boot camp, and I was put in Company B. They called Newport, "The Island." We drilled in the cold wind that came off the bay. They taught us to wash and fold our clothes in a way appropriate to life on a ship, and we learned to sleep in hammocks. Toward the end of Boot Camp, they told me, "Bullock, you're assigned to Hospital Corps School"

I didn't know much about medicine, but I guess they thought enough of me to

"Tell Uncle Russ Hello"

send me there. I came home for a while, and then left for Portsmouth, Virginia, and a naval hospital that dated back to the Civil War. I did twelve weeks of training there. We took care of a lot of sick servicemen at Portsmouth. Many of them had pneumonia and other illnesses. Most were later reassigned. This is where they really gave us intensive training in the medical field. We learned how to give shots, general care of the patient, anatomy, pharmacy and a little on how to do a tracheotomy. We had thirty days of night duty, with no time off. My shift went from nine o'clock at night to seven in the morning.

Eventually we had to view an autopsy. It was on a Sunday afternoon, right after they had given us a big chicken dinner. The guy doing the autopsy would every once in a while pull something out of the body and show it to us. That's where we learned a great deal of our anatomy. After a couple hours of that, however, I just wanted to get out of there.

Instead of becoming a field medic I was assigned to a ship in San Pedro, California (Port of Los Angeles). In August 1943 they assigned me to the *William Kelly*, a ship that was still under construction. It was commissioned the *U.S.S. Rotanin* (AK–108) 23 November 1943. The ship was a Liberty ship converted by the Navy to serve as a Crater class troop and cargo ship. It was a little over 441-feet long, had a crew of about 200, and could carry one thousand troops. After awhile, we got to calling her "Rotten Annie." Then we called her just plain "Annie." After she was commissioned, we took a "shakedown cruise" off the California coast. Then we went up to Port Hueneme, which is north of Los Angeles. It was a big Seabee base. We loaded up about one thousand Seabees and cargo. We didn't know where we were going, but we knew it was somewhere in the South Pacific. Eventually we ended up, via Samoa, in Noumea, New Caledonia, a big staging area for the South Pacific offensive. We unloaded the Seabees and picked up cargo for our first run.

Going over to New Caledonia we had four or five cargo ships in our convoy. We didn't have escorts because this was 1944, and things were a lot safer by then. Of course you were always alert for submarine attacks, but we didn't have any, and we were not especially armed to deal with submarines, but we did have one five-inch gun and a three-inch gun as well as anti-aircraft guns. We did not have sonar, but we had radar with a twenty-five-mile range, and we could detect surface vessels and airplanes. Later on, when we made our runs between the islands, we had a small sub-chaser with us. One time we were alongside a tanker when we went to general quarters. The sub-chaser reported picking up soundings on what the sonar operator thought might have been a submarine. That could have been a disaster with us being that close to a tanker full of fuel! We had to break away from the tanker and start zigzagging. Nothing came of that, though. It turned out to be a whale!

We were ten days out when a crewman came down with scarlet fever. Here we had one thousand men on a medium-sized ship, cramped conditions, with the chances of the disease spreading very easily. We had to put him into our two-bunk isolation ward back in our sick bay, which we changed into a pharmacy and a laboratory. We wore masks and gowns while we took care of this man. The medication we gave him helped him to recover. One of the great benefits we had was the raw penicillin that was coming in to use at that time. The military had supplied us with it before we went over. To replenish our need for the drug, they mailed containers of it to us. We could use raw penicillin right on a bandage. It seemed to be very effective.

We had a good medical staff on board that consisted of a doctor, a chief-pharmacist mate, and myself. One man, the chief pharmacist mate, was named Theodore Lessel White from Arizona. Another one of our corpsmen was Charles Vinyard. He had already had a lot of experience serving with the 1st Marine Division on Guadalcanal. Chief White was an excellent pharmacist mate. The motto of the hospital corps was to keep as many men and, thus, as many guns in operation as many days as possible. In other words if you were on a combat ship and a man had a gash above his head, you would treat that wound to keep the blood out of his eyes so that he could get back to his battle station.

We had an operating room on our ship. One of the crazy things that went on was some of the men wanted to be circumcised. So the doctor did that for them. Then some of the crew liked to look through the portholes to see these operations taking place. Afterwards the guy who got circumcised would be lying in the sick bay recovering from the painful operation. I don't know why men wanted to do that, but they did.

We had 210 officers and men on board. We had a plan of action every day. The men stood their watches down in the Ends Room. Our communications and deck crew had their own jobs to do such as chipping, painting, or standing on the bridge as lookouts. Men were assigned to engineering, system engineering, and communications. Basically those were the jobs that kept the ship going.

Our first runs between the islands were from New Caledonia to Guadalcanal and Bougainville, a safe and routine run by 1944. We'd unload and go to our next destination for more cargo. The bright point was receiving mail at an island, or from another ship. We would also exchange movies, all of which were a great morale boost.

I could write home anytime I wanted to although an officer censored it so that it would not reveal our location. I remember one time when I cheated a little bit. We were nearby Russell Island around Guadalcanal. I wrote to my folks, "Tell Uncle Russ 'Hello.'"

Some people tend to think the Navy is all coral beach and palm trees. Most of the time we were on the ship, and it was very hot! I don't know how those men stood it down in the engine rooms, where it was well over 100 degrees. Some of the men there worked in their underwear. It was hot even topside. Many men developed groin rashes as a result of the heat. As a precaution against dehydration, we encouraged the crew to take salt tablets.

Occasionally, we rescued Japanese from the water, probably ones who came from one of the islands the Army and Marines had bypassed. One Japanese soldier apparently was trying to desert his garrison. He still had part of his uniform on. He was half-drowned when they brought him down to sickbay. He died soon after. One of the men painted a Japanese flag on the hatch going into the sick bay to signify this victory. We wrapped him up in a camel sack and buried him at sea. The other Japanese we picked up out of the water became a prisoner. I was kind of leery about that, because they were fanatics. We kept him under guard while we transported him.

We did have a couple American sailors die, also. Sailors always like a good drink. Some of them took it too seriously, though. Some of the men would sneak on board wood or ethyl alcohol that they had gotten from other ships from one of the islands. These kinds of alcohol were for medical purposes only, and it took only a small dose to kill a man, and men did die after they drank it. We didn't bury them at sea, but took them ashore someplace for burial.

Our duties were carried out in very confining spaces. We slept in these five cargo holds, which go down about forty feet inside the ship. The crew really didn't have any luxuries. They'd sleep on cots that were stacked five high, suspended from wall chains. There were only eighteen inches between each cot. The officers lived a better life, altogether. They were quartered in the main deck located above us, and could catch the breezes.

Life was also very monotonous. Every division had its routine duties. I worked aft, in the sick bay from morning until late at night. I didn't have to stand watch, but others did. Some ships made crew stand watch between duty shifts. A man's job ran from 8:00 a.m. to 4:00 p.m., then he would stand watch from 4:00 to 8:00 p.m. After that, he would "hit the sack" until his next duty shift. That went on day and night. The Navy would spread the medical people around so that if we got hit we wouldn't lose all of them. There was a constant threat of fire from the engine rooms, and we would have frequent fire drills. We in the medical department would check all the lifeboats for First Aid and fishing equipment.

An especially dangerous cargo run we had was when we went to Okinawa, an island only 350 miles from Japan. The *Rotanin* was to take the Army Sixth Station Hospital and all of its personnel and equipment there. We had no female personnel on board. Our objective was to go into Buckner Bay, named after General Buckner, who was killed in action at the end of the battle for Okinawa. We went in there with extreme caution because the enemy was using Kamikaze attacks at that time. We were also on the lookout for suicide motorboats. We remained in the bay in relative safety, however, because the Kamikazes flew out to where our picket ships were protecting the Marines and soldiers who were engaged in the fighting on the island. The ships on the outside ring really took a beating. I saw the terrible damage they caused on some of the ships. The attacks killed hundreds of men. One time I walked past this chief who was smoking up a storm. He asked me, "Hey, Dale, do you want this cigarette?"

I didn't smoke, so I said, "No, it won't do me any good."

He thought for sure we were going to get hit. I thought if a Kamikaze was going to hit, then it was going to hit, and there wasn't much I could do about it.

On 31 May 1944, we got out of Okinawa without a scratch and went to Ulithi, in the Caroline Islands. It was there that I saw the carrier *Bunker Hill* covered in fire and smoke after a Kamikaze attack. It made me cry, because I knew that men were dying on that ship. The sky was black with flak. While we were in Ulithi, they brought in the *USS Kidd*, a destroyer now at the memorial in Baton Rouge. The *Kidd* had been hit on the port side by a Kamikaze off Okinawa. The attack had killed thirty-eight men.

After twenty-two months at sea, our ship had had it. We sailed back to Pearl Harbor to replenish and refuel, then we set sail for San Francisco. Three days out from San Francisco we got the word that the war had ended. Don House broke out some five-inch ammo, made sure there was nothing around us, no ships of any sort, and fired a twenty-one-gun Presidential Salute to the moon.

San Francisco was the greatest sight I had ever seen! It was very foggy in the morning when we went in. Then as we got close, we looked up and saw the Golden Gate Bridge, and, as we sailed under it, the weather cleared, and the city just opened up for us! When we go off the ship, everything was quiet. The city's three-day celebration was over, but we felt pretty good about ourselves, slapping each other on the back, and I know that more than one hidden bottle was brought out for our celebration.

After twenty-two months at sea, there were only five officers left on the *Rotanin*. Some of them got transferred, but we still had most of the original crew, the "Plank Owners" as we called them

We set sail again in September or October to the Philippines, on what the Navy called a "Magic-Carpet Run." Our objective was to bring back troops, and we did, about one thousand of them. We could tell who the men were who had been in combat. They never complained, because they were glad to be away from the awful conditions. Other men, who had not seen combat, complained about everything.

"We commandeered a Jeep, then hoisted it aboard as 'cargo.'"

Our ship could only go about eleven knots, and it was slow going into Midway Island. We stopped there for a short time and then came home. After that, we went to the southern part of Korea, picked up more troops, and brought them back. We made two "Magic-Carpet Runs" in six months. We finished in January 1946. I was transferred back to New York, to the Finger Lakes, where I was discharged. I could have gone to work, but I was unhappy with civilian life. Neither work nor college appealed to me, not the way that the Navy did.

One day, I said to Dad, "I'm gonna go back into the Navy."

He said, "Well, if you want to, Son, go ahead. It's all right with me."

I spent twenty-six years in the Navy and finished with the rank of Chief Hospital Corpsman, an E–7. In the Navy, I had my ups and downs. I was on three different ships in the Korean War. I traveled over most of the Far East. I married late in life, when I was thirty-nine. I always had an adventurous spirit, one that attracted me to the Navy, in the first place. That spirit made we ask for overseas duty during the Korean War, and, later, to become a member of the "Pineapple Navy" in Pearl Harbor where you spend six months at sea, six months on land.

When I got married and had a son, my adventurous spirit started to wind down, and I tired of the military. After twenty-five years, I decided to retire. I applied for a discharge, but I didn't move fast enough. The Navy assigned me to the 1st Marine Division in Vietnam. I was forty-four years old, a little old to be doing that kind of thing, I thought. My wife was quite shook up about it. I was stationed with my family at Guantanamo Bay. Betty had to bring both of our sons home to the States. I thought she should have gotten a medal for that, coming back to the States and living alone while I was off for at least a year to Vietnam.

In all my years in the military, I had never been assigned to a Marine detachment as a corpsman. Now I was. They sent me down to Field Medical School at Camp Lejeune. I was finally doing what my buddy did all those years during World War II. I ran and exercised and crawled under barbed wire while live machinegun rounds passed over me. Forty-four-years old! Here I was, training with kids. I almost couldn't keep up, but some of them got more exhausted than me! When they first saw me, they asked, "Who's the old man?"

While I was in Vietnam, I experienced more out-going artillery than incoming. I once had a scary night in a jungle camp while the VC sent rockets over our heads into the Da Nang airfield. In Vietnam, I was assigned to a MASH unit, the 1st Medical Battalion. They brought wounded in by helicopter, and lay them off to one side. The dead would be in body bags. They would put the dead beside the wounded, then take the wounded in directly to operate on them. The dead would just lay there. I offered my services in the operating room as a technician, but they told me that they had enough people to give that kind of care.

Coming home from Vietnam, my plane stopped to refuel in Okinawa. I thought of the Kamikaze attacks many years before. I landed at Travis Air Force base right outside of San Francisco. I was in uniform, but it was kind of a cold reception. It was a far, far different San Francisco at that time than in World War II. It made you feel what the war in Vietnam was all about. Things had changed so much over the years. It has been such a wonderful feeling in 1945–46. Everybody treated you well. I remember one time being on a bus sitting across from a nun. She had one of the most beautiful faces I think I ever saw. She looked down at my campaign bars and nodded and smiled but did not say a word to me. I can still see that angelic face and just a little bit of a thin smile. It seemed like she was very appreciative of me. I remembered a day many years before to 1943, when I was on a train bound for the west coast. Across Iowa, people waved to us because they knew we were on a military train. We waved back. Old farmers in their fields waved to us. They had a great love of their country. I don't feel that all of our people feel the same thing today.

I ended up with two battle stars on my campaign ribbons, one for Okinawa, and the other for the Northern Solomons. Nothing extraordinary, really.

I have a saying that I often use, "Old men start wars and young men die in them." And I think it's a shame!

As I said, when we were aboard ship, things could get monotonous. Sailors started thinking about getting liberty in the next port, and it could be a long time before we got liberty. One of our liberties took place on the Fiji Islands. The sailors, quite naturally, went out and got drunk. Four officers, among which were our Assistant Gunnery Officer, Don House, and our Communications Officer, Tom Heggen, stole a Jeep and went joy riding. The four men went out looking for girls. They got to one place and it turned out to be colonel's residence where there was a party going on. They crashed the party, and danced with the women until they were discovered and thrown out. The crazy things you do when you are young! Also, an islander informed some sailors that there was a "house for girls" nearby, and that he would take them there for fee. It turned out to be the French Embassy. They broke in, put furniture out on the front lawn, and stole a globe of the world. When the officers who stole the Jeep came back, they were afraid that the Shore Patrol would pick them up, so they abandoned the Jeep. Some of the other men came back to the ship so drunk they couldn't negotiate the gangway. We hoisted them aboard in a cargo net. That night, I bandaged the ones who got injured in fights and falls. We got the drunken ones into bunks and tried to keep them on their sides so, in case they vomited, they wouldn't choke on it. I watched them most of the night. I kept thinking of the words of the old song, "What do you do with a drunken sailor? Put him in the brig 'til he gets sober." We didn't have a brig on our ship, so we stuck them in their bunks.

The commandant of the island was not happy with us, and he ordered us to leave the port. There were also to be some courts martial. Don House was also our Legal Officer, and he used his skills to keep us from getting punished. He went to the captain and pleaded, "Captain, we need these men in the engine room, on the bridge. They are valuable men."

While the men were coming back to the ship, Don said, "Boy somebody ought to write a story about this!"

He was just talking, though. He didn't realize at the time that he would become the famous "Mr. Roberts" in Tom Heggen's play and movie *Mr. Roberts*. Heggen portrayed some of the Fiji Island incidents, and others, and our crewmates, but the model for Mr. Roberts was definitely Don House.

Tom Heggen changed the names of everyone in his story except for Ensign Pulver. We had a *real* Ensign Pulver on the *Rotanin*. He was a tall, nice looking man on the quiet side. He was the complete opposite of Jack Lemmon, who played him in the movies. He wasn't a crazy hijinx, who always tried to be funny.

"My Mother Didn't Know a Thing."

Martin Burke
94th Infantry Division, 301st Regiment, Company G
Pittsburgh, Pennsylvania, 25 December 1925

"One tank passed very close to my hole. The tread seemed as close as six inches. Anyway, part of it ran over my rifle. After that it was useless. After the tanks passed, I got out of my foxhole. The foxhole in front of me and off a little to the left had two soldiers in it. One of the guys was our radioman. He had a hole in his back you could have put a soft ball through. The other guy had half his face blown off. They were both dead. Today, I still think about that situation and how our sergeant probably should have had me with the two others in the same foxhole."

WHEN I CAME HOME from the war, I still had a year of high school to do. Actually, I had a deferment to finish high school. I was a year behind everyone else, because I spent the worst years of my life in first grade. It seemed I wasn't ready for school, and I just was too immature. They didn't have kindergarten. They just put us directly in the first grade. I was in a Catholic school, and we had an old nun. She was cranky, and I just sat there terrified day in and day out. I didn't do well, so they kept me in first grade for another year.

So, I was eighteen in my senior year in Catholic high school, and eligible for the draft. I had a deferment to finish school, but all summer people I knew were going into the Army, and I felt guilty. I didn't give a thought to where I would go. I wasn't smart enough to realize this was a couple months after D-Day, and almost all the people taken in that time were taken in as infantry replacements. As I was to find out, infantry replacements didn't last very long in combat. So, I went down to the draft board where my cousin worked. I told her that I didn't want the deferment any longer. "Does your mother know about this?" she asked.

"Oh, yeah," I answered. "She knows."

My mother didn't know a thing, of course.

The next thing I know, I get my "Greetings."

My mother said, "But you had a deferment!"

I never told her what I had done. I just told her that a lot of guys got their deferments canceled right after D-Day.

A week later I started to feel that I had done the wrong thing, but it was too late. I found out that they had an accelerated program where I would be deferred until around January. I could have finished high school by just taking the basic subjects.

I went into the Army 2 August 1944. I went to Camp Blanding, Florida, for basic training in the IRTC, the Infantry Replacement Training Command. From Camp Blanding we went to Camp Shanks in New York. We had a ten-day delay en route, so I was able to go home and visit. It was around Christmas time and my birthday.

After a couple days at Shanks, we boarded a ship and sailed to Le Havre, France. We stayed in a tent city there. Then we got on those old World War I boxcars, the Forty & Eights (forty men or eight horses), and went up to the line at Metz, France, on the Luxembourg/German border, where they put me in the 94th Infantry Division. Finally, I met my company in a German town called Butzdorf. There was a lot of incoming shell fire there, so we slept in basements. We also did guard duty in foxholes on the edge of town. Fortunately, the Germans didn't attack.

I saw my first combat at Sinz, Germany. This was an important town because one of the few asphalt roads went through Sinz. Most of the other roads were dirt roads. This was January, there was deep snow, and the dirt roads were muddy. It was difficult for the tanks and trucks to travel on them, so it was essential that we controlled the asphalt road. This was our third attempt to take Sinz.

After being in the town for a few days, we were sent up to a plateau on the edge of a wooded area. We were ordered to go through the woods with the guys in line about ten paces apart. It was dark, and the idea of ten paces apart didn't work. We ended up in single file with each soldier holding on to the soldier in front of him. None of us wanted to feel alone in the dark.

What they didn't tell us was that we were going to go through these woods, and then come back and dig a line of foxholes on the edge of the woods. We were to have two men to a foxhole. Unfortunately we had an odd number to our squad. There were thirteen men in the squad and I ended up being number thirteen. I was the odd one because I was the last replacement in a group that had been serving since they came to Europe.

Thirteen turned out to be a lucky number for me. Our foxholes were about thirty feet apart, not in line, but staggered. I ended up digging my foxhole alone. Everyone else had a helper, so they were able to finish their holes faster. I was down about six inches when I ran into hard clay that wouldn't break up. It just sort of powdered. Maybe in a thousand years it would have become rock, but at the time it was difficult to dig.

I got down to about a foot, when three, huge German tanks came around the edge of the woods. I just hunkered down in my hole as best I could. There wasn't even room for my rifle, so I laid it outside the hole. I prayed that the German tankers would think I was dead. The tanks stopped and fired a couple rounds. They hung around for about twenty minutes and then moved on. A piece of shrapnel landed on my back, but not with much force. It sort of dropped on, but it was hot. It burned through my jacket and underwear and gave me a burn, but it wasn't anything serious. One tank passed very close to my hole. The tread seemed as close as six inches. Anyway, part of it ran over my rifle. After that it was useless. After the tanks passed, I got out of my foxhole. The foxhole in front of me and off a little to the left had two soldiers in it. One of the guys was our radioman. He had a hole in his back you could have put a soft ball through. The other guy had half his face blown off. They were both dead. Today, I still think about that situation and how our sergeant probably should have had me with the two others in the same foxhole. If that had been the case, I would probably have been with those two who were killed. One of the guys was also a replacement who came to the outfit a week before I did.

After the tanks had passed, I headed back through the woods to Sinz, but in the dark I got confused. Someone in a foxhole said "Where you going?"

"I'm going back to Sinz."

"Well, Sinz is the other way."

I turned and went in the right direction, and could just make out Sinz down in the valley. A German came out of the woods carrying gun, and I ran back to my foxhole.

"*Nicht Schiessen, Nicht Schiessen*!" he kept saying. I wasn't sure if he was telling me not to shoot or that he was not going to shoot me. I didn't have my rifle, anyway. When I got back to my hole, I told two guys in a hole nearby that there was a German coming out of the woods. They weren't about to get out of their hole.

I said, "Look. Here he comes. He's about eleven o'clock from where you are."

One of the guys was a BAR man. I said, "Come up with your weapon. Spray some rounds. He'll probably turn and run, or maybe you'll hit him." He wouldn't do it.

"Hey, I've got a wife and kids at home."

I said, "Well, I want to get home, too!"

One of them said, "He just wants to take you prisoner. Go ahead. The war isn't going to last long. They'll just take you prisoner."

"I don't want to be taken prisoner. I'm not taking any chances. All you have to do is come up with that BAR, come up spraying the BAR. He doesn't know you are there. He'll turn and run. Either that or you'll hit him."

They wouldn't do it. The German got closer, and then he came toward my hole. I remembered that I had a hand grenade in one of my pockets, the only one I did have. I pulled the pin but held the lever down. The thing was supposed to explode in five seconds or so, and I didn't want him to have time to throw it back at me, like I had seen a Japanese soldier do in a John Wayne movie. I figured I'd count to three, then throw the grenade. One, two, three, and I threw it. He must have seen it coming, so he turned and ran. It exploded, and he cried out. He must have been hit, but how bad, I didn't know.

After that, I decided again to get back to Sinz. The other two, cowards if you want to call them that, went with me. They were veterans, and I felt like kind of a tag-along-guy. After all, I was a replacement, and some of the veterans didn't give us much worth. They were going to let that German either shoot me or capture me. I often think that if I had been through it all with them, it would have been different. They probably thought I was more of a detriment than an asset. Back in Sinz we found out that out of our company there were only thirty-seven of us left.

Those of us who were left were sent back to a rest area. It was the first time that

I could take off my winter boots. The next morning I couldn't get them back on. My feet were so swollen that I had to remove the felt packing of the boots to get my feet in. They were also frostbitten. I got sent to a hospital in Paris, where I stayed for about two weeks. Then I went back to my outfit. The guys were stationed in a town called Trier. They had been sent to cross the Saar River, and there were a lot of casualties. I guess I was lucky again. My frozen feet saved me.

At that point, the Germans were pretty much in flight. We got to Dusseldorf in the Ruhr Valley. The Army called it the Ruhr Pocket. The area was famous for steel mills and other industry, and for the making of steel for tanks and other weapons. The valley was very important to the Germans. Our division was ordered to surround the pocket. The allied forces decided rather than fight through the Ruhr, which the Germans had fortified rather strongly because of the big manufacturing area, the Big Brass decided better to just surround that area and just keep it in a "pocket." At the time, the Germans made no effort to fight out of there. They seemed to know things were kind of hopeless for them, and they were just waiting for it all to end. The Germans surrendered in May 1945, but there was still fighting in the Pacific.

They broke up our division, and started sending guys home. I got sent to a town near Dusseldorf to an outfit called the War Crimes Bureau assisting an officer who made photostats of evidence of war crimes. They were also choosing people to be guards at the Nuremberg Trials. I was considered because I was tall, and they wanted tall soldiers, but after spending some time checking me out, they decided they didn't need any more guards. They discharged me in April 1946.

I finished my high school. The day I finished, a friend stopped by the house. He told my mother he was going to go and register at Duquesne University. My mother looked at me and said, "Aren't you going to go with him?"

"No," I answered, "I wasn't planning on going to college. I figured I'd join the police or the fire department."

My friend said, "Tell him to go, Mrs. Burke. It won't cost anything. We have the GI Bill. Tell him to go."

Sure enough, she told me to go. Duquesne was overloaded with GI's and understaffed with teachers, so we got rejected. My mother wasn't the type to accept something like that. She got on the phone and talked to the Director of Admissions and told him how I was such a good Catholic boy, and how I could go to Pitt University, but how I didn't want to go to a Protestant School. So the Director of Admissions, Father Sal Federici, told her to send me down. So I did, and got accepted. My friend never did get to go to college.

I decided I would do best to be a teacher. I took the education courses at Duquesne. I taught for thirty-five years, most of that time in the Baldwin-Whitehall school district in Pittsburgh.

All those years after I got discharged I still had trouble with my feet, especially in winter when I would shovel snow. I didn't make any connection to that problem and the time my feet got frozen in Europe. About five years ago I ran into an old friend who told me he had run into another friend of ours named Bobby Conroy. He was driving in Pittsburgh when he saw Bobby. Bobby was on his way to the Veterans' Administration to a meeting of the Purple Heart Organization. Bobby had found out that some Purple Heart winners were eligible for compensation. My friend told Bobby that I had frozen feet in the war, and Bobby said that I should go to one of the meetings and see the "Purple Heart Guy."

Well, I didn't have a Purple Heart, and, the funny thing is, I was supposed to have one. When I got that burn on my back, the medic told me, "See me when we get out of here. I'll write you up for a Purple Heart."

I thought you had to have your arm blown off or something. After it was all over, I didn't see the medic again. I didn't worry much about it then, because all I wanted to do was get home.

Anyway, I took Bobby's advice and went to the Veterans' Administration to see the "Purple Heart Guy." I told him about the shrapnel and my frozen feet. He sent me to the Veterans' Hospital at Leech Farms, where they examined me. They found out that some of the arteries in my feet weren't working properly, and that some were destroyed. So, they gave me forty percent disability for my feet. I told my wife. She said, "You should have thought about that forty years ago."

Today, I get about $490.00 from the government.

A B-24 Liberator of the Fifteenth Air Force releases its bombs on the railyards at Muhldorf, Germany on 19 March 1945. *U.S. Air Force photo*

An Eighth Air Force Boeing B-17 Flying Fortress climbs into the morning sky over the English Channel in 1944. *Courtesy Simon Obarto.*

"Get This Thing on the Ground!"

Thomas R. Cable
Fifteenth Air Force, 456th Bomb Group, 744th Squadron
Pitcairn, Pennsylvania, 28 January 1922.

"One fighter was boring right in on my window. He had a set of cannons mounted on the front. Of course, he had a better range, and I couldn't touch him with my .50 calibers. I saw his guns firing alternately, boom, boom, boom. I saw the rounds exploding just like anti-aircraft rounds, coming closer and closer, and all I could do was stand there. It was the oddest feeling in the world. I wasn't scared, but I knew I couldn't do anything about it. Then he veered off. All he had to do was fire one more shot, and that would've been the end of us."

WHEN I WAS GROWING UP, I used to visit a little repair shop down the street from us. I'd fool around in there, and got to learn quite a bit about mechanics. I built engines before I even had a driver's license. That suited me very well for my life in the Air Force. I was always interested in flying. As a matter of fact, I signed up to go to the Pittsburgh Institute of Aeronautics at the Allegheny County Airport, and it was there I got my first flying lessons. I was going to try and get into the airplane mechanics at the time the war started.

I had just come home from church the morning of 7 December 1941. I gathered up my Ink Spots records and was going to take them over to this girl's house when it came over the radio that the Japanese had bombed a place called Pearl Harbor. I knew then what I had to do.

I knew I wanted to fly, and I also knew that if I enlisted before I got drafted I would stand a better chance of getting what I wanted. I went down to the Induction Center. I almost didn't pass my physical because I had a heart murmur, but they let me go through.

Then I went in to talk to them. They needed people on the railroads, and they knew that I had worked on the railroad, so they said, "We've got just the job for you. Railroader."

I said, "No thank you. I don't want any part of it."

Since I had ridden down on a motorcycle, they said, "How about Motorcycle Scout?"

I said, "I don't want Motorcycle Scouts."

They asked me what I wanted, and I said I wanted to be an aerial gunner.

They said, "Do you know that the life of an aerial gunner in combat is less then a minute, maybe somewhere in seconds?"

I said, "Well . . ."

They said I could be a glider pilot. That way I wouldn't have to worry about engines. I said that I didn't mind worrying about engines. So I ended up at Mechanic School at Keesler Field, Mississippi. It was a brand-new field, but it was a stinking place. One famous newscaster called it the "Hell Hole of the Air Force." They had a cooking school there, and they were teaching people to cook horsemeat. You could smell it when it was cooking. At Keesler, I learned the basics of the whole airplane, from the engines to the fuselage. I graduated at the top of my class, and they wanted me to stay on as an instructor. I said no to that.

From Keesler, I went to the gunnery school in Laredo, Texas. Once again, I came out on the top of the class, because I knew how to use a gun. We practiced out in the desert, and some guys did some destruction by shooting cattle. The ranchers got kind of upset about that. It cost the government some money, and the boys quit doing that. We fired on targets that were pulled behind planes. We also did ground strafing. I flew in AT–6s and AT–11s. We had turret practice and open gunnery where there was a second cockpit with a ring-mounted gun. We practiced with twin 12-gauge shotguns mounted in turrets. And we had BB machineguns. Those were fun.

In training, they'd drive around in a pickup truck, on a track that had little sheds on it. They'd release skeet from those sheds, and, when we saw them we had to lead them and shoot. It was like the real thing, bouncing around, trying to reload, allowing for a lead. It was all very educational.

I also got parachute training in a big auditorium. A master sergeant told us, "We've got three types of chutes here. This is a chest chute. You hook it on like this. This is a seat chute that the pilots and copilots use. This is a back chute. This is the kind ball-turret gunners use."

The back chute was a little, thin thing. The sergeant started to walk off the stage. Someone yelled, "Hey, how do you open that thing?"

"Oh, yeah! You count to ten and pull this."

That was my parachute training. They didn't figure you were going to use the parachute, anyway. Of all the airplanes I would see go down, I'd see very few parachutes. One of the times I did see a guy use a chute he must have panicked and opened his chute too soon. He baled out and flew right into the propeller of another plane. He got chopped up just like he had flown into a meat grinder.

We got our full crew in Salt Lake City. Our pilot, Desperock, was from Reading, Pennsylvania. Our navigator, Victory J. Peytral, came from New Orleans. He was one of the most accurate navigators I ever flew with. The nose gunner was William B. Mills, from New York. Alexander Chernak, the tail gunner, was from New England. The ball-turret gunner was from West Virginia, and we just called him "Country Boy." The guy opposite me on the waist gun was Clifford E. Adams from Dayton, Ohio. We were from all over the country.

I might have gotten my position as flight engineer through the pilot. He liked what I did. I knew my airplane very well. As the engineer, I had my choice of position, so I took the waist gun because I could move freely in the plane if I had to. If I had to leave it to take care of an in-flight problem, the top turret gunner could take care of my side, the three-o'clock side. A lot of the engineers chose the top turret, but if they had to leave for a problem there would be no one to cover for them.

The Army held us up from shipping out because they hadn't built bases for our planes where we were supposed to go. In the meantime, I got pneumonia. I was so damn sick I couldn't stand up. The major came in, and he was madder than hell; he thought I was trying to get out of going overseas. He raised cane with me, but then he took my temperature. I almost blew up the thermometer! In the hospital, they gave me seven pills. We left the day I got out of the hospital.

We went to Texas first. Before we landed, I had raised a huge boil. I went to the Medics. A medic took a can of something, like dry ice, and froze the boil. Then he took a scalpel, made a big "X" on the boil, and all that frozen blood came out.

From Texas, we went to Memphis. We hit an overcast, and it lasted a week. The overcast finally cleared, and we took off the next day. Talk about learning to fly blind! We took off as a group of several airplanes, which was stupid. Once you're inside stuff like that, it's just like in the water: you don't know if you're going up or down. That's when you have to depend on your instruments. I couldn't help the pilot. I was just standing there, and he kept up as much as he could on the instruments. We finally came out of that thing, and it was just flat on top. Planes were just coming out over here, coming out over there, just coming out. It was funny some of them didn't run into each other. We never saw the ground till we got down past the Everglades in Florida.

We landed in Palm Springs, stayed overnight, and then flew down to Puerto Rico. We were supposed to leave from there at midnight. We stuffed as much as we could, including candy bars, into duffle bags. It was up to me to make sure the plane was balanced. I started to push on the duffle bags and other stuff to spread them around. While I was doing that, something pierced my hand. Someone had put a stiletto in a duffle bag. It had come out of its sheath and ran right into my hand. When I pulled the knife out, I bled like a stuck pig. I went to the Medics, and they wrapped up my hand. After awhile, I felt my hand get warm. It had started to bleed again, and they couldn't get the bleeding to stop. Because of that, I wasn't able to fly, so we didn't take off until the next night, 31 December 1943. While we were ready to take off, the B-24 ahead of us crashed into the woods. We took off and had to fly over that burning plane. We had fuel tanks in the bomb bay because it was a twelve-hour flight to our destination, which was going to be Dakar, Senegal, West Africa. But we didn't know that until we were well out into the Atlantic. Then they told us we were going to be part of the Fifteenth Air Force in Italy.

On the way over, everyone else was asleep. The plane was on automatic pilot. I was sitting with my back to the console drawing a picture of Bugs Bunny eating a carrot. Suddenly, all four engines shut off. I knew you could lose one engine, maybe two, but four was pretty tough to take. The only thing I could think of that could have caused it was the crash bar over the magnetos. When it was brought down, all the electricity would be shut off. The pilot was up front fighting the controls. I looked over at the copilot position and saw that the crash bar was down. In his sleep, he must have thrown his arms over and hit that thing. I had to crawl over top of the copilot, reach out, and flip that bar up. The engines were still rotating in the air stream, so they all started up again, just like in the movies. Nobody slept for the rest of the flight. It's a good thing I had been awake, or we would've been just another statistic.

When we got close to our destination, we were supposed to be able to see the coast of Africa, but we didn't. All we saw was ocean. Our navigator was a great navigator, so I knew something was wrong. He wouldn't have made a mistake. This is what happened. On our first briefing, the night we were supposed to take off, but were delayed because of my hand wound, they told us that we would have a tailwind the whole way. We never got briefed the second time, so what we had was a headwind, not a tailwind. The navigator had done everything he needed to do, but didn't know to account for the headwind. I figured we must have been flying on fumes, because those engines used up fifty gallons of gas an hour, each. Finally, the coast came into view. We set up for a landing, but a P–38 cut us off. We had to make an extra loop. I was scared to death because I didn't know how much fuel we had left. We made it in, and I took a fuel measure. Fifty gallons left. Enough for a couple minutes flying!

After a couple days, we went off on a mail run. I went along with the pilot, the copilot, and two officers. The other guys stayed behind. On the way I looked up and saw oil flying out of number three engine, the most important engine on the plane because it generated all the electrical equipment we needed for flying. If it gave out, our instruments wouldn't work. When we landed, I checked things out, and saw that the oil cap had not been put back on. I fired up the engines and told the pilot to go out and watch. At first, he gave me the "OK" sign, than suddenly the sign to cut the engines.

I went out, and there was oil everyplace. I unbuckled the cowl and cleaned up the engine. One of the hoses was burned clean through and there was some damage to other parts. I knew what kind of an engine it was, so I went down to where they worked on planes, and there was a DC–3 there. The mechanics were working on one of the plane's R–18–30 engines. When they went to lunch, the pilot and I stole the parts we needed to fix our engine. It took me three days to finish the job. When we got back to our own base, the ground chief said, "What did you do with my airplane? Where the hell have you been for three days?"

He gave me holy hell. He was a little redheaded guy from Detroit who used to run booze out of Canada during Prohibition. He was a tough guy. He calmed down and checked out the engine. "Hey, good job!" he said.

I thought it was a great compliment.

Most of the time in Africa I was out doing maintenance in the airplane. When the ground crew was trying to do something, a lot of them had no idea what they were doing. I used to go down and help them. They'd come up, "Hey Sarge, how about coming down? I've got a new alternator or something to put in there."

I lived in a tent, with mud and dirt floors. For heat, we'd take a fifty-five-gallon drum and get Maintenance to cut it in half. Then we turned it upside-down, got a coffee can, and put that in the middle. The only fuel we had was 100-octane gas. What we did was take another drum and fill it with 100-octane gasoline, and then we got a hose from the airplane, put a spigot in the end of that thing, and ran that down and put it into the top of this can. We just let it drip. We took a projectile from a 50-caliber bullet, and we got a hose clamp; that's how we regulated the amount of fuel in it. Sometimes guys would have it running too fast, it would spill over, and they'd burn their tents down. We had to make do, you know.

We had nothing to wash with. I hadn't taken a bath for a long time; my clothes were so stiff you could stand them up. I took a .50-caliber ammunition can and filled it with water, more water than I could have gotten into my helmet. I put the can on the fire, and first thing I knew, it melted! Somebody came and put the fire out.

Another time in Africa, I woke up one morning and I heard someone yelling, "Comrade, Sahib! Comrade, Sahib!"

I looked at Country Boy, my ball gunner. He had his .45 pointed right at this Arab's head. The Arab was leaning over top of me.

"Comrade, Sahib!"

I said, "What the hell's going on?"

Country Boy said, "This guy came in the tent."

The Arab was scared to death. The crew that had been there ahead of us had given him their clothes to wash, and he was returning them. He didn't know who we were. If I hadn't woken up, I think Country Boy would have shot him. The Arab was only bringing clothes back.

Our final destination was Cerignola, near Foggia, in Italy. There was no facility, just a farm field and olive grove. The headquarters was a farmhouse. There was no barracks. Our latrine was a box with a hole in it, placed over a ditch. That was it. And it rained a lot. As a matter of fact, it rained so badly that when they put the runway in, the planes would get stuck in it. We had to put down steel mats. The mud would suck your shoes right off your feet.

Our B–24 was supposed to be named *Miss I Hope*, and on it was a picture of a girl coming out of a shower with a towel hanging out in front of her. They called that "nose art." One plane was called *Preg Peg*. She was naked, just standing there with everything showing. The chaplain made the guys put a dress on her. So the guys gave her a cellophane dress, and in the proper place they put black fuzz that was supposed to be the back of her skirt. We had some really nice nose art. Our picture never got finished though, so we ended up calling our plane *Tally Whacker*.

Our first mission was kind of a washout. We had bad weather. I didn't get to do anything except go up there and run into a few fighters. We had to go twice before we got to drop bombs. We were in the Balkans quite a bit. Bulgaria, Vienna, Yugoslavia, and places like that. I never knew where we were going until we got there because when the officers were getting briefed, I was out making sure the plane was ready to go.

One time a fighter bore right in on my window. He had a set of cannons mounted on the front. Of course, he had a better range, and I couldn't touch him with my .50 calibers. I saw his guns firing alternately, boom, boom, boom. I saw the rounds exploding just like anti-aircraft rounds, coming closer and closer, and all I could do was stand there. It was the oddest feeling in the world. I wasn't scared, but I knew I couldn't do anything about it. Then he veered off. All he had to do was fire one more shot, and that would've been the end of us.

When we were on a mission, we wore flak vests. Our electric flight suits had three pieces, gloves, boots, and something like long underwear. The vests were made with layers like Venetian blinds. One day our captain said, "I'll show you how good these things are."

He hung up a vest, took a .45, and fired a round at it. The bullet went right through. It didn't go through the armor part, but through the folds made by the "Venetian" blinds. The pilot's vest didn't have a back in it because he sat in an armored seat. Come to think of it, neither did mine nor the radio operator's, for the same reason. When we manned the waist guns, we backed up against each other's back. We figured the flak couldn't go through both of us.

On our last mission, we were going up to northern Italy to bomb an airbase. Our ship that day was "Leap Year Lady." We flew up over the Adriatic coast, an area heavily concentrated with flak. A burst knocked out our number three engine and buggered up the ship. We started to straggle, then decided to head back to base. We stayed twelve feet off the surface of the water, trying to stay under German radar.

The pilot wanted some pictures. I got the camera out of the waist, and took a picture of the feathered engine racing above the water. After that, I gave the camera to the bombardier and told him he could take some pictures. Then I went back to the flight deck and gave the pilot our air speed. The copilot saw some boats and decided to buzz them. I didn't need my parachute harness anymore so I started to take it off. I turned to check the air speed again, and that's when it happened. It felt like the tail got sucked down, and then thrown into the air. Then the nose hit the water. The top turret fell and struck me in the back and the right buttocks, and then I was thrown in the air, through the pilot's compartment, and through the greenhouse. I hit the water at a terrible rate of speed. I went under.

I was still wearing my flight jacket and parachute harness. There must have been enough buoyancy in them that I just floated up. I thought, "So this is what it is like to be dead."

Everything above me was bright. When I broke through the surface, I realized I was still alive. I pulled the releases on my Mae West. There were oxygen bottles floating all around us, so I grabbed one in case my Mae West gave out.

I had come up about twenty feet from the ship. It was broken in the middle, and hydraulic fluid was pouring out from somewhere. It looked like an animal bleeding to death. I heard someone hollering for help. It was Adams. He told me later that he was trapped inside the flight deck and could not get the escape hatch open. He saved himself by swimming out through the hole I had made in the greenhouse. The pilot popped up by the wreckage, hollered something at Adams, and then went back under.

He never came up again. The ship started to sink. I thought, "Oh, my God. I'm going to be sucked down by that thing!"

Someone was hollering about fifty feet away. I hollered back, but then realized that I was only answering myself. Whoever it was, was no longer there. I had no idea who it might have been. Eventually, I found the radio operator and the copilot. I took my leg straps and hooked up to them. It would be easier to find the three of us. None of us knew where we were.

We were in shock. My throat was cut, but whatever cut it missed my jugular vein. My hands were all stripped with glass, and my hip, where the turret had hit me (I didn't know this until I got into the hospital) was as big as my head. I could move my hands and head, and I started feeling around, checking myself out. Somehow, my foot got caught up on something behind me, and as I felt around I couldn't find my right leg. I thought, "God, I only have one leg!"

Suddenly, a big wave washed over and my leg came back down straight. The copilot looked at me, and looked at my neck, and he said, "Boy, you look terrible."

I was out there bleeding in the middle of the water, and he said I looked terrible. That's a nice thing to tell somebody. But that's the kind of guy he was. He had no sense at all. I never did like him.

I started yelling in Italian, what little I knew. I didn't much care who picked us up. Germans, Italians, whatever. I wanted to get the hell out of that water. After a while, it seemed like hours, some Italian fishermen in a fair-sized boat came around. There were three guys in it. They pulled me in, and tried to make me stand, but I fell right back down.

Once they got us on board, they made us strip down to our underpants. We had escape kits in little pouches. Inside were maps, appropriate currency, and an "Asshole Compass." We were supposed to stick those up our asses to hide them. I got all of those escape kits and I tore them open. I took the money out of mine and I gave it to the Italian captain. I took the money from the copilot and gave it to the captain. I gave the captain a pop-open pocket compass that I had. He was tickled pink. He looked me over and got a bottle of wine. He poured some wine into the palm of his hand and used the wine as an antiseptic. Then he poured some wine into a bowl and soaked some hard bread crusts in it and gave that to us to eat. I thought that that was a pretty versatile wine!

I asked the captain to circle the area and look for the other guys. He did, and he found Koski, but Koski was dead. Later, someone found the other guys. They are buried in Florence, except for the radioman. His family brought him home and buried him in the States.

The fishermen made us lie down. Then they put all their fishnets on top of us. When German planes flew over, the crew waved at them! The Germans would dip in low to check us out, but we were pretty well hidden. I found out later that my feet were sticking out!

When we finally got to the shore, the British picked us up.

The Italian captain showed a British officer the money I gave him, and the officer said, "I'll take care of that."

I said, "Like hell you will. That's our escape money. I gave it to him, and it's his."

I couldn't walk, of course, but the other two guys could. I didn't go to a hospital right away, because the Germans were still shelling the place around it. The road was all pockmarked. I was on a stretcher, and I kept bouncing off. They all had Cockney accents, and I had a hard time understanding them. One guy leaned over to the driver and said, "Slow down! He's lived this long. He'll live until we get him to safety."

The British took me to an old farmhouse. As I lay inside, a British officer came over. He had a little notebook, and he asked me all kinds of questions. Then a black guy sewed me up. I think he was from Senegal. He couldn't speak English. Every time I looked like I was going to pass out, another little guy threw water on me. They sewed me up with horsehair, and they didn't cut the ends off. Later, another British officer came in to ask me questions. When I told him another officer had been in to ask me the same questions, all he said was, "Oh! My God!"

There had been German spies in the area posing as British officers!

I wasn't a tea drinker at that time, but they gave us tea and these little hard biscuits. I didn't like them. What they were going to do was put us on a troop train the next day and take us down to a British hospital in Barletta. I didn't want to do that, but what choice did I have?

Finally, the captain from our outfit came up. He had driven all the way from the airbase. "Sarge, what do you want to do? They're gonna take you down to Barletta. Do you want to go back with me?"

I said, "All they do is feed me this damn tea and those damn biscuits—I want to go with you."

That's what I did. They had two ambulances, and they put me in one with him. They took me into a hospital in Foggia. I couldn't figure out why my feet hurt, and they started laughing. I didn't see anything funny about it. My feet were all blistered from the sun. One of the British, I can't remember who it was, he put purple stuff on my hands and my face. When I got down to our hospital, they put Mercurochrome on it. It turned gold and I looked like a goldfish. A priest came in to see me one night. He said, "Boy, you look just like a goldfish."

He made me laugh. He didn't come in like some of those guys, "Oh, you poor soldier…"

The guy next to me had part of his leg blown off, and they had to cut it off below the ankle. They patched him up, brought him in the bed, and laid him there. The ward boys were trying to dress him. He was trying to stand up. He had been knocked out, and he was trying to stand on that stump. I went over to help them undress him.

Then I went to the restroom; I was sick from looking at all that kind of stuff. The smell of disinfectant was making me sick. A nurse came in there, and she started giving me hell. I said, "Listen. I just helped get that guy undressed. I'm not one of your ward boys. I'm a patient."

One of the guys I made good friends with had been hit in his leg. They unwrapped it a day or so before I left. They were going to fix him up. His wound went through the bone, and it got infected. I could see clean through to the other side of his leg. It dripped with infection.

The kid across from me had been hit in the knee, and they put a long pin in there. He lay there for twenty-some days. They gave him so much Morphine that he got used to it, and it wasn't helping him any more. He was just a young kid. Hell, we were all young kids. They found this out, and they took him off Morphine. So they finally pulled that pin off. They were going to cut up his leg, and his foot had turned purple. It looked terrible. He had gangrene. But they finally had to take his leg off down below the knee. All that suffering, and they took it off anyhow.

They brought a colored boy in and they put him in the bed next to me (the other guy had been moved out). The nurse came over. She had a big long needle, and she said, "This is what we're gonna give you." He buried himself in the covers. He had been playing ball and got hurt, and that's how he ended up in the hospital.

One of the other guys was telling me about one of the guys in his crew who had his leg blown off during a mission. They wrapped it up. His foot was still in his shoe, and they threw it out the window. They didn't try to put it back on again. That's one of the things about flying like that: if you get hurt, you're on your own. You were lucky if you had a guy up there that could, maybe, if he had time, patch you up to stop the bleeding. There wasn't much else anyone could do about it. The first aid kits that we had contained a little bit of sulfur, some bandages, and stuff like that. But what could you do? You couldn't leave your gun. But that's what they did; they tied him up, bandaged him, and threw his foot out the window.

When I got back to the squadron, they asked, "What are you doing back here?"

I said, "I came back to finish my missions."

"You can't do that."

"Why not?"

"You went down in enemy territory. The Italians picked you up. They were still our enemies. If you get picked up again, you can be shot as a spy, because you're an evadee."

That meant no more flying. I got other duty. I was sergeant of the guard for a while. I'd go out and pick up guys who were in the town jail, then put them out to guard the perimeter. In the mornings, it was my job to wake guys up at reveille. It thought it would be nicer to wake up to something other than that bugle call. I hated that damn bugle call. I got a record player and played "Sunrise Serenade" on that instead. That went over big! The guys came up to me and told me that they thought they had died and gone to heaven. I got away with that for two days. On the third day, the major came up to me and said, "You play that record player one more time, buddy, and you're done."

I lost my stripes twice over that, but the guys liked what I did. What the hell did it hurt? They had all gotten up.

They didn't just let us come back home. They always made us do something. When I got shipped back, they made us guard prisoners. We had some Italians aboard, and I made friends with them. I made a few trades, got a hat, and a few other things. I could get along pretty well with what little bit of Italian that I knew. We were talking one time, and I found that they had operated antiaircraft batteries. I told them about getting shot down, and then they didn't want to talk to me anymore. I told them I wasn't mad at them. They were just doing their jobs, just like I was doing mine. But, for some reason, that conversation ended the friendliness.

Then I had a compartment full of German soldiers. What a hell of a difference between them and the Italians! The Germans ran on a caste system; there were the officers, the noncoms, and then the little guys. I had to sit at the top of the stairway with my rifle to guard them. They needed some water, and I told this German to go get it. He appointed somebody else to get it. I told him I didn't want somebody else to get it. I wanted him to get it. Well, push came to shove, and word got back to my captain. He told me not to do that. The German was an officer, and officers didn't do manual labor. I said to my guys, "What're you going to do? Let those Krauts run the ship?" I was really pissed about that.

When I got back to the States, I volunteered for the Pacific. Well for that I had to do more training. I went back to gunnery school, then I took parachute training. They had towers, and they had pulleys hooked on there, and they'd hook you on the harness on that thing. You went up this tower, and then you went zipping down, and there was some idiot down there to pull the trip rope like we used to have on the farm, when you used to haul hay out and trip it down. When you least expected it, they would trip it. You never knew how the hell you would land on that stuff. They delighted in having you land on your head, or backwards, or stuff like that. But that was real good training.

I took some of those refresher courses at Keesler Field. Once again, they wanted me to stay on. "No way," I said, "I don't want to be an instructor."

I got a fifteen-day furlough. Instead of going home, I headed for Minnesota to meet a friend. There was a layover in Chicago. In Chicago, people were dancing in the streets, but I didn't know why. Then someone told me Japan had surrendered. We didn't get news on the train.

Things were getting wild, and the MP's were picking up everyone they could. The town was littered with paper. Everyone was kissing and hugging. I just wanted to go home. There was a guy from Greensburg, Pennsylvania, on the train with me, so we went over to the Pennsylvania Station. The damned MP's were there. The train was just ready to pull out. The MP's started for us. Some guy saw us coming for the train, and held the gate open for us. We jumped on the train just as it started to pull out. The MP's were left standing. Just like the movies!

I didn't know if I had accumulated enough points to get out of the military. The Army sent me to study jet engines. Then I was asked to go down to Texas and help a young cadet take care of some B–24s. I got there, and the cadet didn't do a damn thing! He didn't know a damned thing! Then they wanted to put me on B–29s. I told them no, that I liked B–24s.

I finally got out. When I got home, I couldn't eat. I think I had lost thirty pounds. My neighbor was Italian. She had me over for a big spaghetti dinner. My aunt had me over for a big chicken dinner. Aside from those two meals, I couldn't eat anything.

You don't just forget about your military experience. It comes back to you. I had horrible nightmares. Every now and then I think about it. At night, when I say my prayers, I ask God to bless my crew. After sixty years, I still have a Mass said for them.

Bursts of black flak greet the Fifteenth Air Forces 744th Bomb Squadron on a mission over the Adriatic coast. *Courtesy of Tom Cable.*

Tom Cable in his high-altitude flight suit. *Courtesy of Tom Cable*

Tom Cable's B-24H "Talley Wacker" Serial Number 42-52212 parked at the New Box Airfield, Foggia, Italy.

Tom Cable's crew (left to right): tail gunner Al Chernak; nose gunner Billy Mills; left waist gunner, Cliff Adams; ball turret gunner "Country Boy" Caudill; right waist gunner, Tom Cable. Top row, left to right: navigator Pete Peytral, copilot Hoffman; first pilot "Pop" Desperock; bombardier Les Carlson.
Courtesy of Tom Cable.

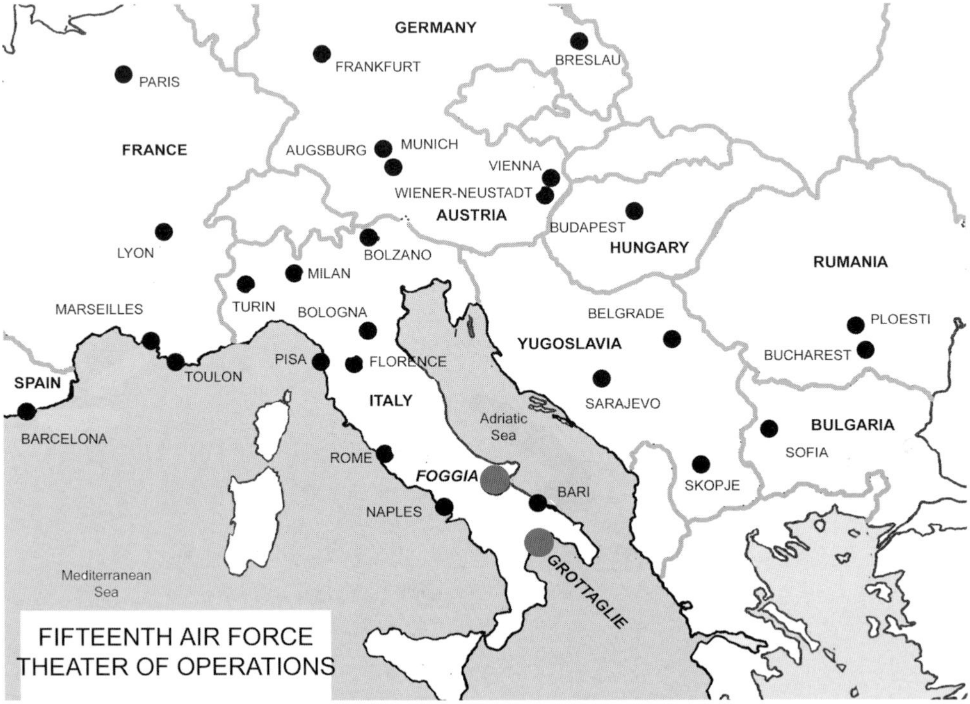

FIFTEENTH AIR FORCE THEATER OF OPERATIONS

"You Shot What Sucker Down?"
George Clark
United States Army Air Force, 366th Fighter Group,
(Republic P47 "Thunderbolt"); Saint Marys, Pennsylvania
3 January 1922

"We carried rockets, as well. We were especially interested in train movements. Those locomotives would just about disappear in huge clouds of steam and smoke. Every now and then a guy would see a farmhouse or some other building that looked suspicious we'd go in and strafe it. Sometimes there were very big explosions. They were probably ammunition stores."

THEY CALLED ME "BUZZ" AND "ROGER" when I was in the service. They called me some other things, too, but you don't want to record that. Before the war, I had a job at a carbon company, a dirty but "good-paying" job. It was hard to get a job anywhere, but my dad, who was a dentist, knew the owners of the plant, and he helped me get the job. I worked in the black end where they packed these carbon things up in boxes and sent them to Europe. I worked there twelve hours a day six days a week for ten dollars a day. After a while, a little powdered metal company by the name of National Molder offered me a job as a traffic manager. I was nothing more than a glorified shipping clerk, and I got sixty dollars a month for doing that. Anyway, my ego got boosted because I was Traffic Manager.

When the war came along, I took the Air Corps exam and physical at Erie, Pennsylvania. I flunked the physical because they said I had stigmatism. In the meantime, a friend and I volunteered for the Marine Corps. We were ready to depart for Paris Island, but I gave it one last shot with the Air Corps. I went to my eye doctor and told him they wouldn't pass me because my stigmatism was too severe. The doctor said, "Oh, I don't think so."

Then he wrote something down on a piece of paper and said, "Here you take this back and you show it to them and it should get you in."

His note, whatever it said, worked. I was sworn in on 3 July 1942.

Then I went to San Antonio, Texas, for primary training, plus a lot of examinations. Psychological examinations were the big thing. Everybody was afraid they were going to flunk those. I should have graduated in October or November of 1943, but halfway through the course, my father died, and I went home on compassionate leave. I didn't graduate until 5 December 1943. I started for home on leave, but got lost somewhere along the way. They were hunting all over Hell for me, because I was supposed to be married on a Saturday, and by Thursday they still hadn't located me. I was hitchhiking across the country in various airplanes when, finally, General Gimble of Philadelphia flew me on his plane to Dayton, Ohio. From Dayton I got to Pittsburgh, and finally to Ridgeway, Pennsylvania, near home. I had to do all this pre-nuptial crap so that I could get married that Saturday. Now, it was Advent and St. Marys was a bastion of Catholicism, and that pre-nuptial stuff was very important. The priest announced in front of the congregation that because of special services, he would suspend the rules and permit the Clark-Gregory marriage. It was on 11 December that Ann and I got married, at seven o'clock in the morning. It was twenty-below outside.

While I was in San Antonio I got my finger cut off in a car door. The doctor who treated it sewed it back on, but told me he didn't know if it would stay on or not. I told him I was afraid of being washed out if the brass found out I had lost a finger. The doctor put the finger in an aluminum splint. The finger did stay on.

While I was healing, I got sent off to Oklahoma, then to Garden City, Kansas for basic training. We got there just after a big dust storm had cleared away a grasshopper plague. We'd get out of bed in the morning and scrunch, scrunch, scrunch, crickets everywhere, getting crushed under out bare feet. Then another dust storm came along and chased the crickets away. After that, when we got out of bed, we stepped into dust drifts, and, when we ate, we could feel our teeth getting worn down because all that dust was in the food. It was like sandpaper. We even got to fly in some of those dust storms and tornados.

One day I was on the down-wind leg on approach, and I saw this tornado coming across the plains. I had the canopy open. Just as I was paying attention to the wind shift, the tornado was almost on me. There was a 180 degree wind shift, and off come my goggles and helmet. Everything! Goggles, earpieces, helmet, and radio, right out the cockpit. I got the plane back on the ground in a hell of a hurry. You didn't mess around with a tornado. But those things were awesome, especially the dust storms. All you saw was a wall of dust in the distance, thousands of feet high.

From Garden City I went to Texas, down on the Rio Grande, about as far south as you can get in Texas without being a Mexican. I did some advanced training there in AT–6s and P–40 fighters. After basic training they divided us up to fly single or multi-engine planes. I knew I was going into single engines, because I was a little more aggressive in my flying. More conservative types got the multi-engine planes. I also did well firing at the air targets. Some guys washed out, and some of them got to be glider pilots. To be a glider pilot was a fate worse than death to someone who really wanted to fly.

I got into flying the P–40 for about ten or fifteen hours. That was a thrill. The plane had a real heavy nose, and a little, skinny landing gear. It was difficult to control, and one had better know what he was doing. It was a good transition for me. After Texas, they sent me to Dover, Delaware for beginning and advanced operational training, and P–47 Thunderbolts. People were afraid of that plane. They called it the "Jug." It had eight machineguns, provisions for bombs, and they hung all kinds of other crap on it. It was a monster plane for a fighter.

To put everyone's mind at ease, Charles Lindbergh came down and demonstrated what a versatile airplane this P–47 was. Lindbergh was tremendous. He was the best pilot I had ever seen. He flew that P–47 like it was a Piper Cub. After his demonstration we went out and did some strafing and smoke practice missions. We practiced navigation. Then, my ears got screwed up in an air pressure chamber, and they put me on to flying shuttles down to Norfolk, Virginia.

After six months of that, I was reassigned to operational training again in the P–47's. It was near election time, 1944. We were assigned to a secret mission at Camp Kilmer, New York. When we got there, armed guards took us out into the middle of a field where there was a little shack. We sat around in the shack for a while, then in came this General. He walked over to a table and spread out some papers. He told us to gather around. Then he said, "Gentlemen, these are German buzz bombs, propelled by rockets. A German submarine captain a few days ago avoided British patrols and he's got one of these buzz bombs on board his boat. We presume he is going to fire it at New York City at the height of the election business."

Then we got our orders. We were to fly in circles out over the Atlantic, twenty-four hours a day. Great! It was November, cold, and we were flying these single-engine planes over the ocean. And those planes were big buggers, at that!

Our segment was around from Fort Kilmer, out to Fire Island, and back. We were out there three and four hours at a stretch. Fortunately, we had GCA on the plane (Ground Control Approach). The ground people would just talk us to the ground. You listened, watched your instruments, and didn't rubberneck. Sometimes you were in the soup (fog). No matter how bad the weather was, they'd get you right in. They'd get us to within fifty feet of the ground and say, "If you can see the runway, you're OK!"

We did that for ten days. Then, all of a sudden, they said, "OK. You can go home, now."

I went to Bradley field, and finished my operational training. I never heard another word about the buzz bombs until I got to England. While I was there waiting to get assigned a squadron, I got to talking to another pilot.

"Oh, yeah," he said. "We were flying a segment right above yours, and we shot the sucker down."

"You shot what sucker down?"

"That buzz bomb that they fired from a sub."

I never saw a thing in the news about it. Before we flew the segments they told us that the way to bring down a buzz bomb was to fly underneath, tip the wing, disorient the bombs gyro, and send it into the ocean. Anyway, my friend confirmed the General's suspicions, and those guys flying the segment out of Suffolk, New York, saved New York City from being bombed. Was that a good thing, or a bad thing. I don't know. Had the sub captain been successful, maybe the people would have been awakened to the realities and dangers of war. They weren't being affected much by it, not like the Europeans were. They were more concerned about the cigarettes and booze and gasoline rationing, and the fact that their loved ones weren't with them. How tough! Nobody could get a decent pack of cigarettes, had to drink cheap booze, had to ration their meat and butter, and all the while, London was getting bombed every night.

The assigned me to the 366th Fighter Group. We went over to Paris and from Paris up to Belgium. Everyday the enemy buzz bombs flew over us, through the anti-aircraft barrier, then on toward Antwerp and Brussels and London. We used to go out and watch them fly over. You knew any time you heard them cutoff, it was too early for them to do so. Then you knew they were coming down in your area. We mostly dive-bombed and strafed enemy units, or we provided close ground support for the Allied troops. One of our pilots would be down on the ground in a lead tank. He would throw colored smoke. We would fly in and make contact with one of our pilots who was in one of the lead tanks up in the front, and they would throw colored smoke and things over on targets and we would dive-bomb them.

We carried rockets, as well. We were especially interested in train movements. Those locomotives would just about disappear in huge clouds of steam and smoke. Every now and then a guy would see a farmhouse or some other building that looked suspicious and we'd go in and strafe it. Sometimes there were very big explosions. They were probably ammunition stores.

After the Allies crossed the Rhine and we got into Germany, we got assigned to operate out of a big German air base in Muenster. We flew the rest of the war out of there. We had them bottled up in the Ruhr Valley, what we called the Ruhr Pocket. I got shot up there and had to make an emergency landing in a field were there were over 10,000 Russians in a German POW camp. Poor buggers. They looked like walking skeletons. Some of them sent a delegation to me asking for food. I went to the doctors and nurses and said, "These poor guys need something to eat."

They said, "Listen, we know what they want, and if we gave them what they want to eat, they would die! We have to be very careful with their diet until we get them to hospitals."

The Germans had been driving them toward the East from the Ruhr where the Russians had been used as slave labor. They had been surviving on the raw meat from dead horses. There were American prisoners there as well. One guy, believe it or not, was from Pittsburgh. He looked like the living dead, like a Zombie. He was nothing but skin, bones, and eyeballs. I still see him in my mind. Some of the Russians got loose in the countryside and started scavenging. They weren't too gentlemanly about it, either. The German women were scared to death of them. I went out armed, looking for the scavengers. I didn't shoot any of them, but we fired off enough rounds to scare them away if we saw them.

Finally, I got back to my squadron, and had some R&R. I flew guys from their outfits to their R&R facilities. It was a cushy job. I got to Paris. As a plus, they made me Operations Officer, and I drove around looking for nice spots where the guys could relax by fishing, getting to a library, or playing some sport or other. I had a Lithuanian pilot who was my driver and translator, a pad of requisition slips, and a guide. I was still just a kid, but I was Officer in Charge with a .45 on my hip. I'd go marching in someplace and say, "I want tablecloths, wine and food." Then I'd just write out a requisition slip.

When the war ended, we went back to dressing for dinner. We had to have uniforms, waitresses, wine, linen, and all that stuff. Our CO was a West Pointer, and he wanted everything spit and polish. He was a real "go by the book" character. I managed to gather six horses for the guys to ride. I kept them in a stable at a brewery. I told the CO. He said, "OK, but they're your horses."

"My horses?"

"Yeah! We're not Cavalry, so we don't have regulations that say we can have horses."

I didn't know how to ride a horse. I had a German captain taking care of the horses, and he knew I couldn't ride. One day we took two out for exercise, and he got them to galloping. Suddenly, my horse stopped, but I didn't. I flew over his head, hit the ground, and broke my elbow. They took me to the field hospital, and fixed me up.

When I was ready to ship out they said, "Well, the horses are yours. You can take them along."

They were serious.

I said, "How about one of those Opel automobiles we requisitioned.?"

They said, "In either case, you will need to go down to Marseilles and take a boat home. "Otherwise, you can go home on the hospital plane and be at Mitchell Field tomorrow."

I took the "otherwise." They put me on a hospital plane for the States. That was the end of my military career.

We had to wait in Paris for a full plane. While I waited, I did the dumbest thing I ever did in my life. I had a chance to stay for a month or two for recuperation. I didn't. I went home right away to St. Marys.

Eventually, I got a job with the Civil Aeronautics people. After six months, I was offered a job to travel all over the world as a pilot, while they evaluated Air Force facilities. By this time, I had been away from home almost seven years, off and on. We had three kids, and I turned the job down. I would have started as a GS–14, a good government rank with good pay. Occasionally, I still regret turning that job down, but after one has been away from home for a long, long time, without a family around, one begins to wonder what is really important in life.

A montage of D-Day landings at Normandy. Images are from the collection of the late Richard "Doc" Buchanan, M.D., the 704th Tank Destroyer Battalion's historian. *Reprinted from Men of the 704 (CNAS/Buchanan).*

"We Didn't Dig No Foxholes"

Ronald Colflesh
83rd Infantry Division, 736th Tank Battalion
Confluence, Pennsylvania, 22 February 1921

"Everybody was scared. You were so nervous at times that you could've just cracked up. I never did, but I tell you, my nerves were in pretty bad shape. Once I stuck my head out of the tank, and a sniper shot at me. The bullet hit the turret and there was some splash off of it. The bullet more or less just went to pieces and I got hit with some of that splash. Wasn't enough to put me out of commission, though."

WORLD WAR II TAUGHT ME that this is the greatest country in the world, and it still is. I knew a great bunch of guys in the service. We more or less depended on ourselves, but you had to have your buddies, too. We had a really strict officer, strict but goodhearted. Captain Rodgers was his name. He wouldn't ask you to do anything he wouldn't do himself. When we were training in the desert, he took us out to a steak dinner. He drove the truck himself, and he paid for everything. There weren't too many officers like that.

I was born and reared in Somerset County, Pennsylvania, in a little town called Confluence. I was the first of eight kids. I had three brothers. They all went into the service, too. My brother Vick was in the Air Force, and my brother Paul was in the infantry and my brother Dale, the youngest, was in the Air Force in Korea.

My first job was in the Clairton steel mills, and it was an awful place. I stayed there a week, and then went to work on a farm, for two bucks a day. When I got out of high school, I went to work with Westinghouse Air Brake.

I got drafted into the Army in September 1942. They lined us up in front of the Wilmerding High School. A guy came out and said to us, "Are there any of you guys that don't think you're ready to go yet?"

There was no argument from me. Not long after, I was in Fort Knox.

I trained in armor and armored infantry training at Fort Knox for thirteen weeks. I got appendicitis while I was there. I was in the mess hall, and I just dropped to the ground. They thought I was faking, but when they took me to the hospital they knew what I had and operated on me right away. In the meantime, the guys I was supposed to ship out with left, and, as far as I know, they all got killed in North Africa.

Then I went down to the Arizona desert to train a bunch of kids. I was a kid, myself! It was in Arizona where they formed the 736th Tank Battalion. We practiced on a British invention there, a tank with a big searchlight on it that was supposed to blind the enemy.

They sent us over on the *Queen Elizabeth* in March 1944. There were 16,000 troops going on that ship, including the heavyweight champion, Joe Louis. We landed in Scotland, and from there went on to Wales, where we did more training with the searchlight tank. After all that, the Army decided to not use them, so they gave us regular Sherman tanks. A couple months after D-Day, in August 1944, they sent us into combat.

We crossed the Channel to Utah Beach. The stench of death was still heavy. Our first job was clearing mines. The first guy to die in our battalion was blown up when he tripped a wire. That was it for him. We didn't move with our tanks very much, and we dug foxholes just like regular infantry. We named our tank "The Cleaver." Later we got another tank and we painted the name "The Mad Hunky" on it.

We spent some time keeping the Germans pinned down in Lorient, where they had submarine bases. We bivouacked in a place called the "Apple Orchard." The French made a lot of apple cider there; only it was a lot more potent than our apple cider. We stayed there until it got pretty cold. Then we moved up into Holland. It was in Holland where I saw the biggest piece of steel in my life. It was a burned out German Tiger tank. There was a terrible stink of dead men coming out of it. It made me wonder about my own death, and it if I'd live through the war.

We were still in Holland in December. Word came down that the Germans had broken through the Ardennes Forest. It was the beginning of the Battle of the Bulge. They attached us to the 78th Division, and then to the 83rd Infantry Division. I stayed with the 83rd until the end of the war. The 83rd used us like mobile artillery. We'd take counter fire from the Germans, but because we could move at will, they rarely did us any damage.

Everybody was scared. I got so nervous at times that I wanted to just crack up. Once, I stuck my head out of the tank, and a sniper took a shot at me. The bullet hit the turret, and I got hit with some metal splash. It wasn't enough to put me out of commission. The lieutenant we had in the Bulge cracked up. He shot himself in the foot to get out of the war. We didn't like him too much, anyway.

It was so cold we couldn't sleep in the tanks because of the steel. It was warmer to sleep out in the snow. We just took a tarp, spread it out on the ground, and went to sleep. This time, we didn't dig no foxholes, like the infantry did. In March 1945, we crossed the Rhine River. We got quite a bit of resistance on the other side, but we just shot up the towns until the Germans surrendered. The Burgermeister would usually come out and tell us that the town was ours. We slept wherever we wanted to. Then it was on to the next town to do the same thing all over again.

Sometimes we'd get harassed by what was left of the Luftwaffe. On Easter Sunday, at dinner, they bombed the place where we were eating. I got glass all over my meal, and I had to throw it out. That was a shame. Hot meals were hard to come by.

There were a lot of German-Americans in our army. The German civilians all said they had relatives living in America. We were supposed to be the conquerors, but I didn't feel like one. We had a no-fraternization rule, but no one paid any attention to it. If we stayed in a German home, all the women wanted to come back home with us! We weren't supposed to loot, either, but we did. I took Nazi daggers and pistols, officers' caps. I also took a camera. When I came home, I put it in the American Legion, but someone broke in and stole it. I even kept my .45 GI-issued pistol.

Toward the end of the war, we were only thirty-seven kilometers from Berlin, but we were in Russian "territory." We had to turn around. Some of the boys wanted to go right on to Berlin, but our lieutenant talked them out of it. From there, we just waited for the war to end.

After the war, I was part of the Army of Occupation. I came home in November 1945 with the 8th Armored Division. I left on a Liberty ship from LeHavre. I had Thanksgiving dinner on that ship. We docked in New York, and I went to Camp Shanks, then to Indiantown Gap. I ended up with five Battle Stars, the Victory Medal, the Good Conduct Medal, and the Army of Occupation Medal. I had been overseas for two years. It was good to be home.

When I got home, I told my dad about what it was like over there.

He said to me, "Wouldn't you rather have been there than shoveling horse shit in Louisiana?"

My dad was always mouthing off like that!

I loafed around for a while, and then I went back to work. If I had the chance to do it over again, I would have gone to college and become a history teacher. But I went back to Westinghouse Air Brake and made a good living. I got married a year after I got home. I've been married nearly fifty-eight years.

My son went into the service. He put four years in the Navy. He used to go out on the Mediterranean every six months, and then he'd come back. He took us out on his ship, and he was complaining about the Navy.

I said, "You didn't see nothing! You ought to see what we had!"

A page from the scrapbook of Thomas J. Evans.
Courtesy of Mrs. Thomas J. Evans. Reprinted from CNAS/Buchanan Men of the 704.

"Just Because They're Marines, Don't Mean They're Not Human!"

Sante "Sandy" DeMarino

4th Marine Division, 24th Marine Regiment, 3rd Battalion, L Company
Greensburg, Pennsylvania, 23 December 1921

"Well, I've seen guys crack up and charge pillboxes. They just got machine-gunned down. They'd charge a pillbox with only their M-1. They really cracked all together! Then there were the guys who would crack and would eventually come back to the outfit. They'd be taken off the line and given treatment. Where they treated them, I don't know. I've heard of guys giving themselves self-inflicted wounds, but I never saw that happen. Then there were stories of guys who cracked up and killed themselves. We heard about that on Saipan. Just because they're Marines don't mean they're not human! People think Marines are made out of steel. That's bullshit!"

SANDY IS A NICKNAME that I got in school. When I was in the first grade my mother called me Sanduce, because we talked in Italian at home. The teacher said, "Your name's not Sanduce."

"Yes, it is."

"No, it's not."

The other kids said, "Yeah, his name's Sanduce!"

She said, "Your name is Sandy."

So I went straight through life as Sandy. My honorable discharge papers say, "Sandy." My social security pension, "Sandy." No matter what I get, anything at all, it's "Sandy." Nobody knows me by Sante! Imagine! The only thing it's on is my baptism paper at Our Lady of Grace in Greensburg. But all the rest is "Sandy." Imagine drawing social security on your nickname! And being honorably discharged with your nickname!

My father's name was Vincent DeMarino. He was born in Italy around Togale, near Rome. He came over here when he was thirteen years old and worked in the mines and the steel mills. My mother's name was Agatha Piccola. My dad knew her from Italy but they got married over here. She came to this country about five years after my dad. I have four brothers and three sisters. Two others passed away at birth. The names of my brothers and sisters from oldest to youngest are: Rosemary and then Angeline DeMarino. Then there's Larry or Lawrence. Tony or Anthony DeMarino. After Tony there was me. Then there's James Vincent DeMarino. And my sister Agatha lives up in Detroit. Rosemary, Angeline, Larry and James have all passed away.

All four boys were in the Marine Corps at the same time. We were all in battle at the same time. I often wonder who fought the war, my mother or us! I would say my mother. Can you imagine having four sons in the service and all in battle at the same time? I know a lot of the Italian families in Greensburg had four or five brothers in the service at the same time. The battles were bad, too. Two of us were on Saipan. One was on Guam. But we all pulled through.

People have asked me, "I'm surprised that all of you were in combat at the same time."

I respond, "Well, it was war time, and we were all in the Marine Corps."

I started selling papers with my older brother when I was five years old. It was for survival because of the Depression. I did that until I was about eleven, then I went to work in a baker's shop. My pay was two loaves of bread and a pastry. Sometimes they'd give me fifteen cents. So we didn't starve. We had gardens, too. My mother canned our vegetables. We kids didn't understand hardship because we were young.

I got a job when I was in high school at Walworth's where my dad worked. I worked right next to him at the foundry. I started out at thirty-two cents an hour. After nine months working there, I joined the service.

I heard about Pearl Harbor the day after it happened. I was down on the corner and somebody said, "They bombed Pearl Harbor!"

What the Hell did we know about Pearl Harbor?

Then they said, "The consequences will be they'll come over here!"

They said that the Japanese are going to do this and do that, and they tried to stir everybody up with patriotic feelings. Of course, being young, I got all stirred up. I just wanted to defend the country, I guess. I didn't know any better. I thought they were going to come over here and kill us. Everybody was patriotic at the time, not like it was in Vietnam. Nobody wanted to go there. I can't blame them.

Then kids started joining up. It was nothing to be seventeen or eighteen and go into the service. I was nineteen when I joined. When I was in the Marine Corps there were kids who were sixteen years old who lied about their age. The Marines didn't care. They wanted all they could get! I was small then but they took me right away. You had to weigh 121 pounds and you had to be five-four and a quarter. I was five-four and a quarter and I weighed exactly 121!

When I told my parents that I joined the Marines my dad said, "You do whatever you think is right, because if I tell you to go and something happens, then I'll think it's my fault. So you do whatever you think is right."

So all of my brothers volunteered, too! Actually Tony was in since 1937. I volunteered in May of 1942. My other brothers went in 1943.

I never was out of Greensburg before I went into the service. All I did was work in stores, sell papers, and work in baker shops and Walworth's. I didn't go anyplace. Then all of a sudden I was in Parris Island, South Carolina for Boot Camp! I got all this tough drilling. I couldn't believe what was happening to me!

The drill instructors were tough on you! At the time you didn't appreciate it but after you're out of boot camp you realized they taught you something! You dare not look cross-eyed at a drill sergeant because they'd boot you or hit you. And you didn't raise your hand to them because you'd go to jail. If they'd give you a kick in the fanny today, they might get a dishonorable discharge, but back then, that was common.

Boot camp lasted about three months. After that, I was a drill instructor for about two or three months. They picked me to do that because I guess they thought I was young and nuts! I went to school for about a month and they told me how to treat the new recruits. I had to be tough on them. After all, I had to make Marines out of them. But I didn't join the Marines to be a drill instructor. So I put in for the Paramarines. Those guys jumped from planes behind enemy lines. I had to be nuts! I went up to North Carolina with the Paramarines for about three months, but then they disbanded the program. I never did get to fly in a plane. They said, "Now you guys are just gonna stay in the infantry."

We stayed in tents up there for about two months and then they shipped us to Camp Pendleton when they started the 4th Marine Division.

At that time we were training on the 1903 Springfield. That was a bolt action rifle. When we landed on the Marshall Islands we still had the 1903. Then the M–1 came out and we used that. Those damn things would jam. We trained with .30 caliber machineguns, too, and BARs. We trained on everything, so we would be able to use any weapon for any situation. I had to know all the stuff, especially because I was a squad leader, with fourteen men under me. We were trained for jungle fighting, and we learned a lot about that from the guys who had fought for five months on Guadalcanal. After that, they ended up in the 4th Marines as officers. Captain Stips was our company commander. Lieutenant Knoll and Lieutenant Purcic were in our company, too. These are the names that stick with me. They were good officers and good leaders!

But it's the buddies you went into battle with who were like brothers! They stuck with you! I had a friend named Lamont Bernelli. Me, him and another guy by the name of Marchessi made a vow that if one of us got killed, we'd have to go to the father of the one who got killed and tell him how it happened. Bernelli was killed on Roi-Namur and I didn't get a chance to go up and see his dad. I wrote to him while I was in the hospital in Philadelphia recovering from my wounds. But Marchessi had been killed too. When I heard Marchessi's father lived up in New Jersey I decided I better at least go see him. I kept my promise. I went up to Marchessi's and knocked at the door.

They said, "Oh, my God! Come on in!"

They recognized me. They had my picture.

The father said, "My son's missing in action."

All the family came over and I thought to myself, "How am I gonna put this across to them?"

I knew he got killed. I saw it!

They said, "He's missing in action. What happened? Maybe you can tell us something."

I said, "Your son's not missing. Your son got killed."

Oh, my God! Marchessi's dad wanted to kill himself! Oh, they had to stop him, and the neighbors came from all over town. You know how Italian neighborhoods are! But they settled him down and I talked to him.

He said, "Are you sure?"

"I'm positive."

I told him about the vow we made and this and that. I saw his body. You never think you're going to get killed. It's going to be the next guy. You think like that and you make deals with each other like we did.

I guess, what they drilled into was, "You're a Marine! You can do anything!"

We couldn't wait till we got in battle! We couldn't wait! They got you so pepped up that we thought we were indestructible in a battle! What did we know? We were just kids. We didn't know what danger was. All we knew was we were going to go over there and kill Japs!

Then one day they just said, "We're shipping out!"

Nothing else. They couldn't tell us where until we got on the ship about four or five days later. Then they told us we were bound for Honolulu, and, after that, the Marshall Islands. The ship we went over on was a cattle transport, and we were crammed in there. Everything kept falling out of the bunks, onto the floor; guys were getting seasick, including me. What a mess! We stopped in Honolulu, but we didn't get off. We stayed out on the ocean two or three days, and, from there, sent straight into battle. We were on that ship almost a month, counting the time it took to cross the ocean to Hawaii. In all that time, we all got great sun tans from playing cards on deck, just like nothing was ever going to happen. After we left Hawaii, we seemed to go all over the Pacific while joining up with other ships. We also did that to confuse the Japanese about where we were going. We were supposed to hit Roi-Namur, one of two adjacent islands. Believe it or not, my brother was going to be on one of them, while I was on the other.

They had Mass on the ship a couple of days before we landed. They always had that before an invasion. Anybody who wanted to take Communion, could. There were guys who stayed away from it, not because they didn't have religion, but because they were playing cards on the other side of the ship. There are no atheists in the foxhole! At the time, I thought going to church would help me survive. I always had that thought.

Some guys would carry a rabbit's foot. I'm sure loved-ones gave them something, too. "Put this around your neck," or "Carry this with you." That doesn't stop a bullet!

Before we went ashore they bombed the hell out of that place! After those blockbusters went off, we went ashore on Higgins boats really Gung-Ho.

We thought, "No problem now!"

When we hit the beach, we found out that all that bombardment didn't give the Japs a scratch. They were dug in their caves really deep, and they were raining artillery, mortars, and small arms down on us, trying to push us off the beach. But we kept pushing forward. There was explosion after explosion. All this stuff was going on. Planes fighting in the air, and ships firing over our heads into the caves. It was noise all over. When we encountered close resistance, there was a lot of grenade throwing. I saw Marines jump on grenades to save their buddies. Common sense should have told them to run away from a grenade, but they were really psyched up and maybe didn't realize what they were doing. When I saw something like that, I put it out of my mind. At first I was glad it wasn't me, and then if I thought about too much, I might get it next. We were all scared, but we were only kids with no brains! Now when I think of it, I realize why they want kids! If we had had brains, we would have all got killed. I'm sure of that!

Bernelli was my BAR man. Before we hit the beach he said, "We're gonna stick together."

I said, "Yeah, and don't forget it."

When we hit the beach, he was about twenty feet away from me. We looked at one another across that beach. I motioned to him, waved my arm, and yelled, "Come on!"

We were gonna fight together, but he shook his head. He was pinned down in a shell hole.

I moved forward without him.

Afterwards someone told me, "Bernelli got it."

I went looking for him. He was still in that shell hole. The top of his head was gone. Artillery had gotten him. I got his rifle, put it right by his head like a marker, and then I covered him up.

On Roi-Namur, and, later on Saipan, we used a lot of flamethrowers. We'd go as close as we could, shoot the flame into a cave or pillbox. At the same time, other guys were inching up behind us. When the Japanese came out, we'd shoot them. They'd be maybe two or three feet away. We would use anything to get them out of their holes. And the Japanese knew what we were up to. Sometimes they'd come out with their hands up, but some Marines would have none of that. Guys would be psyched up. They'd yell things like, "This is for my buddy," or "You dirty bastard!" Then they'd shoot. If we shot them, we really didn't give a shit about it. Even after we shot them, some of us wanted to stab them with bayonets. It didn't mean anything, at least at the time. I remember one crazy bastard who went up to a bunch of sick and wounded Japs on Saipan. He sprayed them with his BAR while they lay in their bunks. Somebody finally grabbed him, but it was too late.

When we were in boot camp, we didn't know what killing was all about. Today, I feel sorry for the Japanese I killed. They were somebody's loved ones, somebody's husband, somebody's son, somebody's boyfriend. Back then, we had a good propaganda machine, as good as anybody's. They taught us to hate the Japanese. Hell, I got so brainwashed I could have taken a Jap's heart out and eaten it, and think nothing of it. If you found a picture of an enemy's family, you threw it away. You couldn't go soft on them. I had that hatred for years after the war, but then I started to change, especially after I had my own kids.

A lot of guys cracked up in combat. I've seen guys crack up and charge pillboxes. They just got machine-gunned down. They'd charge a pillbox with only their M–1. They really cracked all together! Then there were the guys who would crack and would eventually come back to the outfit. They'd be taken off the line and given treatment. Where they got treated, I never knew. I heard of guys giving themselves

"There were some kids of sixteen who lied to get in!"

wounds, but I never saw that happen. Then there were stories of guys who cracked up and killed themselves. Just because they were Marines didn't mean they weren't human! People think Marines are made out of steel. That's bullshit! In the movies you see guys running into battle, looking really tough. That's bullshit! We got down in the dirt and crawled most of the time. Those guys I saw charge a pillbox weren't in a John Wayne movie. There's other stuff they don't show you in the movies. You'd be surprised what guys took off the dead Japs! Even off our own men! Wrist watches! Rings! That's crazy! As far as the Japs went, some guys would take anything they could get from them. They didn't give a shit about anything. Those guys were animals! I saw guys digging out gold teeth from the dead! Rings, wristwatches and gold teeth were worth money. If you came out alive then you'd have some money, but maybe you'd get killed two days later! And someone takes it from you! Tit for tat! Right? The best thing to do was leave them alone. I did none of that! I never heard about any of that stuff in the papers during the war. Who was going to write about that? Everything went through a censor. It wasn't like today's media.

When we hit Saipan it was raining Jap artillery. We never expected that. Just like we never expected it on Roi-Namur. On my first day on Saipan, I got into hand-to-hand combat. We were advancing, and some bypassed Japs came out of their holes. One of my guys got bayoneted, and I shot the Jap who was standing over him. I ran to my buddy who was still alive and he yelled, "There's one right behind you!"

This Jap came running at me with his bayonet in his hand but my bayonet stopped him just in time. That wasn't the only one I had to do that to.

The first three or four days on Saipan were the worst. That's when we really got a lot of casualties. After that it was mostly getting snipers and pillboxes.

There were a couple of Banzai attacks on Saipan. They just come right at you. They were committing suicide. They didn't give a shit! They'd just keep coming even though we were shooting them. They overwhelmed us a couple times, just by weight of numbers. It was like getting into a fistfight, except it was him or me. Anything went!

The Japanese weren't the only ones committing suicide. The natives of the island were committing suicide. They knew the end was near. They knew the Japs were losing even when the battle was a week away from being finished. There were these cliffs, and the natives were jumping off. If they didn't, the Japs would shoot them. Then the Japs would jump off. We'd try to shoot them as they were coming down. We couldn't trust anybody. Some Japs would come over to surrender, but they would have grenades in their hands. They'd jump into a bunch of our guys. Even women from the island would do that. Anybody that came near us, we shot.

I was a sergeant and still squad leader when I was on Saipan. On a typical advance the lieutenant would say, "Squad one, Sandy. Get your squad and head to the right."

Then he would tell the next squad, "Get to the right of Sandy."

Then the platoon would advance, followed by the company or the battalion. So you had the responsibility of not only your men but the men who would be coming behind you. I was a sergeant, but who cared about rank in something like that. You just did what you had to do!

There were always some enemy positions that had to be taken on Saipan. They were everywhere. My squad had a big fight about the seventeenth day on Saipan. Some Jap snipers were holding up the advance of the company. So my squad went forward to meet their resistance while the company stayed back. The whole company couldn't come forward because we didn't know what was ahead of us, and we all could have gotten wiped out. Maybe they might have had a machinegun and the Japs could have gotten all of us.

We attacked these Jap positions, which were made up of mostly snipers and Japanese riflemen in holes. We killed as many of them as we could. During the fighting a Japanese grenade rolled by me and exploded. I got a little bit of shrapnel in my left side, my left hand and leg, and my pinky got blown off. We had to hold our position until reinforcements arrived. I kept fighting with the remnants of my squad for another four or five hours, even though I was wounded. I couldn't go anywhere, anyway! The Japs counterattacked many times but we wiped them all out. That's what I got my Silver Star for. A couple of my buddies got killed in that fight, though. After we wiped them out, the company moved up and took over for us. A corpsman came up to me and immediately gave me a shot of morphine to numb me. Then I went back to the rear to an aid station. They took care of me and all the casualties from this fight at this aid station. Then I went on a hospital ship. There they bandaged me up, did what they had to do, and then they took me back to Pearl Harbor.

There were some terrible sights on that hospital ship. You see them, but you're numb. I was all doped up, anyway. They could have cut my leg off and I wouldn't have known it!

After all these years I think that if I had to see all that again I would cry. I was glad, anyway, that I was on that ship. I didn't care what I saw. I was just glad it was over. Nobody wanted to die, but I think I would have rather been dead than to have both legs gone, or both arms gone. Still, there's nothing like living. When you're dead, you're gone a long time.

Once I got to Hawaii, to Maui, I went to a hospital where they examined me. I was there a couple of months. That's where everyone who got wounded recuperated, after which they'd be sent back into battle. Not me. Once someone got it like I did, the war was over for him.

From Hawaii, I went to San Francisco, and from there, to Philadelphia. It was beautiful being back in the United States, even though I was still in the hospital, and even had to do a little guard duty there.

In 1945, I was discharged. My division ended up going to Iwo Jima, where it really got sacked. I wrote to guys I knew, but I never got answers. Then I wrote to their families, and they would tell me that my friends had either been killed or wounded.

When I finally got home Mom was happy! She got one of her sons back. Now that I have children I can see how she felt. But she still had three more over there! Soon, another brother came back from Guam. We had a nice big dinner at home. That was nice! Especially the way the Italians cook it! I got invited out, people were glad to see me, but everybody had sons over there still.

I was glad when the war was over. We wouldn't have any of the kids killed or wounded any more. It's a different life. As long as the war was going on I wasn't myself, because I still had brothers and cousins and friends over there. I would think, "Gee Whiz! My buddy. What did he get out of it? What happened to him?"

My dad wanted me to come back to Walworth's, but I told him I wanted to look for something else. I didn't loaf too long. I didn't want to stay idle. I joined the 52/20 club and lived off that for a while. Then I went to Westinghouse and got a job there. I worked there about eight months putting welding-rod motors together. They were ready to send me to school to learn the new technology, but then they went on strike.

I waited about three or four weeks and a friend of mine said, "Why don't you go on the road selling."

I always did like to talk to people. I went on the road down to Louisiana selling portrait pictures and I was doing well selling house to house. Back then, you could do that successfully because people trusted you.

My mother called me and said, "Westinghouse came back."

I said, "Naw. No more factories. I'm gonna stick to business."

I did that for a couple of years, and then I got married. Then I got off the road and stayed around the house and sold that way.

I met my wife before the war. We were dancing. I started dating her and we'd write to each other when I was in the service. Then after the war we started dating again and we got married. Her name was Ann Zevata. We had our fiftieth anniversary here a while ago.

I have a son in Pittsburgh. He's a surgeon. His wife's a doctor. I have a daughter in South Greensburg. Her husband is in the insurance business. She helps him out with that. I have a daughter in Philadelphia, too.

The first five years after the war I had a lot of bad dreams, but then it eased off. Even today I think of some of the guys and things that went on. I think of it more as an angry person. What benefit was it? The kids who got killed? For what? All those poor kids. I think of LaMont Bernelli. He had just come out of high school. He was an A student. His father was Lowell Thomas's right-hand-man.

Lamont told me, "Sandy, when I go back, I'm gonna go to college and if you don't get a job I'll take care of you."

I think of LaMont because he had so much to live for. He said he was going to go into journalism like his dad. Maybe there was a reason for his death, but I don't care. For what? Wars are always the same. "This is the last one! This is the last one!"

But there is no such thing as a last war. That's what gets me.

You hear these senators and bleeding-hearts in Congress crying over American dead and saying they want peace and that they don't want any more casualties. Bring the boys home! That's bullshit! Those are crocodile tears. They're not crying for you, and never will. The only true tears anyone will ever shed for you are the ones your mother sheds.

"Our War Had Just Started."

Thomas Dix

United States Navy, U.S.S. *Minivette*, U.S.S *Heminger*,
U.S.S. *Panament*; Davistown, Pennsylvania, 26 December 1924

"The water was cold, and the air was cold, too. I think the air was worse than anything else. I held onto a piece of floating debris that was about ten-feet long. There were other guys holding onto this piece of the ship. There was one fellow who crawled on this debris. He hollered for me to help this other fellow. He had blood all over his face. I swam out and helped him up on this piece of wreckage. One of the officers was there, and he said, 'Who is that? Get away from me!' He was a little crazed. He didn't want any of the enlisted men near him. Another fellow said to him, 'We're all the same out here now!'"

I AM ONE OF EIGHT CHILDREN. There were five boys and three girls. My oldest brother died when I was six months old, so I never got to know him.

My father, Robert, got his first job in a bakeshop in Scottdale. Then he went to work as a baker at what was called the "County Home"; today they call it Westmoreland Manor. That's where he met my mother, Helva Witt, who was a seamstress there. She was Pennsylvania Dutch. They were married in January 1914, and moved to Morgantown, West Virginia, where they bought a bakery. After about five years in Morgantown, they came to Indianhead, Pennsylvania, where they also bought a bakery. We never went hungry. We at least had bread when we needed it.

A neighbor across the street told me about Pearl Harbor the Sunday it happened. I thought it was foolish of the Japanese, being from such a little country, to attack the United States. I was sixteen and never thought I would be involved in the war, a war I thought would be over in a week. I was very wrong. Nineteen months later, I found myself in uniform.

My draft number came up in April 1942. I got a deferment to finish high school, and on 20 July 1943, I entered the United States Navy. My mother didn't want me to go into the Navy because her brother had been, and was killed in World War I. She wanted me to go into the Army. I think my being lost at sea was too much for her. She never saw her brother's body. I wanted to follow her wishes, and when I went for my physical I told them that I didn't want the Navy. As it turned out, I had a hernia and flunked the physical. They said, "Since you have a hernia, we'll put you in the Navy."

"But, I don't want to go."

"If you want to go into the Army, go home and get the hernia fixed up at your own expense."

"Well, I don't have the money for that."

They stamped "Navy Only" on my paper. So I was drafted into the Navy with a hernia. They said they'd take care of me there.

My mother cried when she learned I was going into the Navy, but since I got several furloughs, she changed her mind.

Being in the service was just a big change from civilian life, though. I think they kept us so occupied that we didn't even have time to think about how training was changing us. In boot camp, they showed us lots of movies, the only entertainment we had, but the movies they showed us were all about how horrible the Germans and Japanese were.

I had another physical after boot camp, and another hernia kept me from being shipped out. They operated on me, and I spent six weeks in the hospital after the operation. After that I left the Naval Training Station in Samson, New York and headed to Diesel Training School in Richmond, Virginia, for an eight-week mechanical course. From Richmond, they sent me to the Navy Pier in Chicago for advanced diesel training. I did that for six weeks. Then I went to Norfolk, Virginia, for training on the specific type of diesel engine that would be on my assigned ship, which turned out to be the *USS Heminger*, under construction at the time in San Pedro, California. The *Heminger* was Destroyer Escort 746, 312-feet long, armed with 20mm and 40mm anti-aircraft guns, one three-inch gun, torpedoes, antisubmarine hedgehogs and depth charges, and a crew of 200.

We went on a shakedown cruise from San Pedro to San Diego, and I got seasick! I just sat down in the engine room with a five-gallon can between my legs. I was so sick I didn't care if I lived or died. I got over it, but some guys couldn't even get out of bed. One guy even had to be sent back to the States. He just couldn't hack it.

After our shakedown cruise, we went to San Francisco, and from there to Pearl Harbor. The harbor was pretty well cleaned up, but we could still see partially sunken ships, remnants of the Japanese attack. We were assigned duty with the submarines, our job being to escort a submarine so far out to sea, then drop depth charges a safe distance from them, while they were submerged. The purpose of that was to test the subs' stability, check for water leaks that might occur with shock or vibration. The sub crews were also training to get used to depth charging. I'm sure it was a frightening experience for them, the first time they heard a depth charge go off.

Then, in the summer of 1944, we were assigned to what they called a "killer squadron," a group made up of the aircraft carrier *USS Corregidor*, and five destroyer escorts. We patrolled the North Pacific, up close to Alaska, checking for enemy submarines. The pilots from the carrier looked for them from the air, and we tried detecting them with sonar equipment. We were called to battle stations several times, released depth charges, but, to my knowledge, never sank a Japanese sub.

The weather was always cold in the North Pacific, and we ran into rough seas up there. When that carrier was right beside us sometimes, we couldn't even see it, because we were down in a valley between waves. Our biggest list was sixty-six degrees, pretty far for a destroyer escort, but we made it through.

Around Christmas 1944, we arrived in the Marshall Islands, which was back in American hands. I spent Christmas there, swimming in the Pacific Ocean! We were there only a short time, when one day, we looked out, and there were ships as far as we could see. This was around February 1945. We were sent back to Pearl Harbor, but the fleet we had seen was gathering for the invasion of Iwo Jima. That's how close we were to being in that invasion.

When we got back to Pearl Harbor, there was still a chance to get back to the States, to be transferred off of the ship. I was a third-class petty officer at the time. I was given the option to transfer. I didn't know what to do. Some of my shipmates said I was foolish if I didn't go back and take a chance on getting duty at home for the rest of the war. Finally, I agreed with them, and went back to the states, on a troopship. In San Francisco, I was given twenty-three days delayed orders to get to Philadelphia. I spent most of that time at home. Then I loafed around Philadelphia for two weeks. Finally, my name came up on the assignment bulletin board. Next to my name was "MCTC, Little Creek, Virginia."

All I could think was this stood for Marine Corps Training Center. A lot of the other guys thought the same way. We thought they were going to put us into the Marine Corps! When we got to Little Creek, however, we found out that MCTC meant "Mine Craft Training Center." We were going to learn mine warfare, about contact mines and magnetic mines and acoustical mines, about mines that had a disc inside that dissolved when a ship passed over it. Actually, there were six discs inside. One would dissolve as a ship passed over, the theory being that the sixth ship in a convoy would likely be an ammunition ship or troop ship, or any ship more important than the first couple ships, ships that were likely escorts. The contact mine had prongs sticking out of it. When a ship hit one of the prongs, a vial broke and set off the explosion. The acoustical mine exploded when the sound of the ship's propellers came near. Some of our ships had devices that made vibrations go out well in front. The magnetic mine exploded in contact with the ship, and was attracted by the ship's metal hull. That's why many minesweepers were made of wood. The one I would be assigned to, however, wasn't. It was made of steel.

After training, I was assigned to a brand-new minesweeper, the *USS Minivette*, commissioned 29 May 1945. We put up in dry dock to be degaussed. They wrapped cables around the ship and created an electrical current that was supposed to demagnetize the steel. We had to remove the ship's gyroscope and take off our watches because they would have been affected by the degaussing.

By the time our shakedown cruise was over, the war ended in Germany. So did the U-Boat menace in the Atlantic. They stripped off our antisubmarine and mine equipment, and re-equipped the ship for anti-aircraft defense. The war was still on with Japan, and the Kamikazes were sinking a lot of our ships. By the time we got to the Pacific, the war with Japan was over. But my war wasn't. We had to sweep the ocean of mines.

We escorted some LSTs to Japan. Then we went to Pusan, Korea. It was a mess. There must have been a million people there. All the Koreans that had been in Japan were going home, and all the Japanese that had been in Korea were going the other way. We did escort duty until we got assigned to mine sweeping.

Our base of operations was Sasebo, Japan, and we got there around Christmas

1945. One of the other mine sweepers had broken down, and we went out on 29 December in her place. It was strange! The ship was commissioned on the 29th day of the month, we went through the Panama Canal headed for the Pacific on 29 August, and we got our first mine sweeping duty on the 29th.

We were in the Tushima Straits. At the time, Japanese ships were doing the sweeping and we were just marking where they swept. We knew we were in dangerous waters. Mines were floating around us. Some of our gunners were destroying the mines by shooting holes in them so they'd fill up with water and sink. I wasn't a gunner, but they told me they were hard to hit whenever they're bobbing up and down and the ship is listing from one side to another. We had some gunners that were pretty good. Some of the mines exploded, but so long as you were far enough away from them, they didn't do any damage to the ship.

I was on the main deck at eleven o'clock in the morning one day, working on a whaleboat, one that we used to carry fellows ship to shore. Someone had bent a propeller the day before, and I was helping straighten it out. There was a sudden, huge explosion. A submerged mine had struck one of the screws. We were ordered to abandon ship. Four minutes after the explosion, the *Minivette* started to sink.

There was confusion. Debris was flying up in the air. We watched it so we wouldn't get hit with it when it came back down. Some of the ammunition was going off, boom-boom-boom! When the mine exploded, I grabbed my life jacket that I had taken off and laid beside me. It was too difficult to work while wearing it. I was wearing foul-weather gear, because it was cold, and we had blizzards the day before. I ran to the main deck, and got port side where I tried to release a lifeboat. I was too excited and fumbled around so much, I couldn't get it released. Water was up to my knees, and I thought it time to get going. I stepped over the railing, and started swimming away from the ship, all the while remembering what I had been taught. Get away from a sinking ship as fast as you can, because a sinking ship causes suction, and the suction might draw you under. The ship started to list over, and it seemed like it was going to fall over on top of us, but, at the last minute, it stopped, and fell back the other way. The aft end of the ship sank in the water first, and then it just settled with the bow sticking out of the water. Two of our officers, one was our captain, crawled up the bow of the ship. The one officer jumped off. I saw our captain, the last man off the ship, take his hat off and swan dive into the ocean. It was approximately twenty minutes from the time we were hit till the ship was out of sight.

The water was cold and the air was cold, too. I think the air was worse than anything else. I held onto a piece of floating debris that was about ten-feet long. There were other guys holding onto this piece of the ship. There was one fellow who crawled on this debris. He hollered for me to help this other fellow. He had blood all over his face. I swam out and helped him up on this piece of wreckage.

One of the officers was there, and he said, "Who is that? Get away from me!"

He was a little crazed. He didn't want any of the enlisted men near him.

Another fellow said to him, "We're all the same out here now!"

I was in the water almost an hour before I was picked up by a Japanese boat. The crew threw me a rope. I kept twisting it around my arm as much as I could so it would have a good hold on me, and they pulled me up the side the ship. When they pulled me up, the ship was hanging over on the left side. I would say it took about five or six fellows to pull me out. With my own weight, the weight of the water in my coat, the way it was soaked, I don't think I'd be exaggerating to say I weighed maybe 300 or 400 pounds. That's a lot of dead weight to pull over the side of a ship!

After I got aboard the ship, they immediately took knives and cut the strings on our foul weather jackets, and took all our clothes off of us and put us in a bunk. There were five of us. Then they wrapped us in blankets, and gave us cigarettes, Japanese cigarettes. They were terrible! It was funny getting rescued by the Japanese Navy, when just a few months before we were trying to kill each other. More than that, they put dry clothes on us, uniforms of the Imperial Japanese Navy. When they transferred us back to an American ship, we were still wearing those Japanese uniforms!

We had ninety-one men aboard the *Minivette*. Only sixty-five survived. They took us back to Sasebo. One of the worst ordeals that I remember was roll call on the ship going back and hearing all the names of our shipmates who didn't make it.

We were posted to a communications ship, The *USS Panament*, HEC 13. We were there for several months, from the end of December 1945 to 1 March 1946. Then they had an inquiry into the sinking of the *Minivette*. I was one of the ones that were called in. They asked me several questions.

One of the officers asked me, "Was the water cold?"

I felt like telling him why doesn't he jump in and find out for himself! I didn't think that was too bright of a question. It was December! Of course it was cold! But, I guess they were trying to find out just exactly what happened. To my knowledge there was never any negligence found in the case. I do know that one of the fellows tried to get some information about it from Washington just a year or two ago, but it was still classified. One of the officers, a man I visited after the war, won't come to any of our reunions. The official inquiry tried to pin the whole episode on him. What it was they thought he did wrong, I don't know.

M-18 Tank Destroyer No.13, the first one lost by the 704th Tank Destroyer Battalion near Rennes, France, July 1944. The vehicle was lead vehicle when it came under fire from a German 88mm cannon. Three of the crew were killed, but Sergeant Turcan (Company A, First Platoon) continued to fire the gun until he neutralized the enemy. Turcan was awarded the Silver Star. *Reprinted from CNAS/Buchanan Men of the 704.*

German troops firing the dreaded 88mm. Though developed as a Fliegerabwehrkanone (anti-aircraft gun - FLAK), the weapon proved to be deadly against Allied tanks and infantry. "Doc" Buchanan developed the photo from film found in a camera "liberated" from a German soldier. *Reprinted from CNAS/Buchanan Men of the 704.*

"That War I Was in Was An Ugly Thing!"

Thomas J. Evans
United States Third Army, 4th Armored Division, 704th Tank Destroyer Battalion; Greensburg, Pennsylvania
11 March 1920 - 14 July 1998

"That evening, Patton came with Colonel Clarke and they stood up on that hillside. Looking down at the carnage from my CP, Colonel Clarke said, 'Captain Evans was in charge of this shootout.' Patton asked me what kind of ammunition we were using, and if we had enough of it. I said, 'We had plenty of ammunition, we're in good shape.' Patton said to me, 'This is the kind of thing that's going to end the war quicker than anybody had hoped.' And he turned around, walked to his Jeep and took off."

I WAS DRAFTED IN MARCH 1941. I was twenty-one years old. In October 1941, I got a notice to report on 11 November. I was sent to New Cumberland and from there to Fort Knox. When war broke out on 7 December, I was getting ready to come home for Christmas holidays and all leaves were canceled. I stayed at Fort Knox, finished my basic training and became a sergeant in charge of seventeen men. For six weeks we demonstrated the proper procedure for gunnery on the 75mm howitzer. Then I got a notification that I could apply for Officer Candidate School (OCS), which I did. I was accepted and went into OCS 1 May 1942 at Fort Knox. I was what they called a "Ninety-Day Wonder." In the fall of 1942 I was assigned to Pine Camp, New York.

Eventually, I was assigned to the 704th Tank Destroyer Battalion, attached to the 4th Armored Division at Pine Camp, New York. I stayed with the 704th for all of my training and went overseas with them and stayed with them the entire war.

The 4th Armored was one of the four or five armored divisions that were formed into "triangular" divisions. The Army reduced the number of men and increased the number of tanks, decreasing the size of the divisions. They were regiments at one time, and I think they cut them down to what they called "combat battalions." The division fought three combat commands. They would assign, depending on the situation, which of the combat commands would lead the attack and which of the battalions in the division were assigned to the combat command.

About every third week we would have field problems and fight as a tactical unit to an objective. These exercises brought out a lot of flaws. At the same time, they taught a lot, too. A lot of it was set up for actual combat conditions. We trained probably for two, maybe two-and-a-half years as a division, and as a battalion within the division. We were well trained and well prepared. In combat, I was glad that we had the variety of training that we had. Of course, at times I wished that we'd had more.

Our original tank destroyer was a halftrack with a 75mm gun mounted on it. It was big and bulky and it was a fair terrain vehicle, but it couldn't maneuver in mud and snow and ice. They talked about developing a new tank destroyer which would be fast, low in silhouette, and would pack as large an artillery piece as it could handle. Anyway, they talked more and more about it and when we were in the desert in California, the Army decided to develop a new tank destroyer. Each tank destroyer battalion assigned two men to attend classes for the development of this tank destroyer at General Motors in Detroit and Flint, Michigan. I was one of the ones who got to go.

The first night in Detroit, after dinner, they had a meeting. I would say there were roughly thirty to thirty-five officers there from various tank destroyer and tank outfits, people from different camps all over the United States. Two of the engineers and two of the artists from the Buick Division of General Motors were at this meeting. They asked everybody's opinion as to what they thought this tank destroyer should look like. As we talked to them, these artists would actually draw our ideas on a blackboard. If we wanted a lower silhouette, or a different shape, we would make suggestions, and they would change the drawing accordingly. When they finished they had quite a machine drawn on this blackboard. And everybody agreed to the new adaptations. From there, the engineering people went to work. They had the actual chassis of this tank built. The engineers intended to use a Sherman tank chassis, which was not suitable. It was too heavy, too bulky and not maneuverable enough.

The next day, they went on with this tank idea. Overnight, they built an actual mock-up of the new design, a life-size model of wood and clay. They had olive drab paint on it and a white star on the front and all the markings. Everyone agreed that it would be quite a machine if it could be built. This was in April 1943.

In December 1943, this tank was completed. They had a "T" number on it at first, which meant "experimental." They called it a "Hellcat." Then it became the M–18. The previous type was the M–10. The 4th Armored Division was sent to maneuvers in Louisiana. From there, we went to Camp Hood, Texas, came back to California, and went from there to Camp Maxey, where they gave us the first two of these M–18s.

We operated the M–18s at maximum to discover flaws and work the bugs out. They had an engineer from Buick Division who came along with the tanks. He stayed with us about six weeks. We ran those things day in and day out, night and day, just to see what they would do, what kind of performance we'd get out of them. This engineer kept a complete log of everything that was done on them. He went back to Detroit, and Flint, Michigan, where they actually built the tanks, to make the modifications that we suggested. They made these modifications and we received thirty-six M–18s at Maxey. We trained in these during January and early February 1944. Thirty-six vehicles were a full complement for a battalion.

We were very much pleased with it. It had a Wright Whirlwind 400–horsepower airplane engine. The back armor plate door opened down and had tracks built right on it, so with four bolts you could take that engine and slide it right out on those tracks, and pick it up with the crane on the back of the "draggin' wagon," as we called it. It was easy to work with. There was nothing to it. It had fully automatic transmission, what they called a "torquematic transmission," which Buick later used in their automobiles. It had three forward speeds and one reverse. You'd pull a lever down and put it into gear just like you'd do a modern automobile. It had two steering levers. You pull back on the one to the right, it would lock the right tracks and it'd spin to the right. Visa-versa on the left. And to stop it, you just pull back on both steering levers. It had torsion bars instead of volute springs like there are on a tank track. It had a torsion bar that would turn and twist and take the shock out of the tank bouncing over rough terrain. It was a Christie-type suspension, where all the bogey wheels were all the same size and interlocked with one another. The final drives that drove the track on the front were hooked to the automatic transmission so there was no secret to running it. You just get in and turn it on. It could go as fast as sixty-five or seventy mph on a straight highway. Even cross-country it could traverse ditches and bumps and obstacles at high speeds. It could ford a three-foot deep stream, move in reverse at forty mph and change direction on a dime.

The tank had a force-taper, high-velocity 76mm gun, with a muzzle velocity of 4,000 feet-per-second. It could penetrate German armor on anything under 2,000 yards, except a Tiger tank. And I was hoping and praying I would never run into one of those straight on. A Tiger had anywhere from nine to eleven inches of armor plate on the glacis plate of their tank. When we would hit it at a thousand yards, which we did a few times, it was like throwing a snowball at it. We'd see our projectile bounce off!

The M–18 had a .50 caliber machinegun on the race where the tank commander stood. They had intercom systems throughout the tank, a machinegun, and a bow gun mounted coaxially with the 76mm. It was very thinly armored for a tank. It had an inch-an-a-half of armor on the side and two inches on the front. It had an open turret. You could not close the turret and be completely safe. You would be exposed to all kinds of small arms fire. If we were hit, it would do a lot of damage to the tank. Our success and part of our expertise was to outmaneuver the enemy, and with our speed and the maneuverability, we did. We practiced many times and we knew what that tank would do and what it wouldn't do. We had excellent people. My company was as fine an outfit as I'd ever want to be around. And they proved themselves in combat. We were highly trained and that was to our benefit.

We had five men in each tank. The tank commander was up in the turret. We had a driver, assistant driver, radioman, and the loader/gunner. Of course everybody would interchange jobs. We later on eliminated the assistant driver, as he had no duties. Many times we'd send him to scout when we were stopped or taking up a position.

We also used the gun for indirect fire. The executive officer was trained, as well as I, to be able to line the guns "parallel," for indirect firing. But, the gun had a low trajectory, and was not good for indirect fire. We came up with the idea to have a tank with a bulldozer come over and build a ramp, so we could elevate the gun.

Our indirect fire was good for about 8,000 yards. One time we had the whole battalion lined up to fire around Reims, France. And we couldn't get the guns elevated enough to fire over the tree line, so we wrapped some primacord around forty or fifty trees to cut them down and get a field of fire. The Germans picked up the blast and we got a hell of a counter battery down on us. That was the end of that! We didn't do too much more of that around there!

On 19 February 1944, we went from Camp Maxey to the staging area at Camp Miles Standish, Massachusetts. We sailed out of Boston Harbor for England on 27 February 1944 on the British ship, *Britannic*, which was at one time a cruise ship. We were "double-loaded," which means that we were in a bunk for eight hours, then somebody else had the bunk for eight hours while you were up on deck. A lot of the guys below deck got sick as dogs! The water was rough and the ship bobbed up and down like a cork.

We landed in Liverpool, England on 11 March 1944. The 4th Armored Division gradually came, unit by unit, until we were all assembled within a thirty or forty-mile radius of each other. We trained there during March, April and May. We were out every day with the tanks, moving, cleaning, and taking 76mm gunnery practice. Of course, everyone was expecting D-Day at that time. We went into a staging area around Trowbridge. And on D-Day, we were on the road at 5:30 in the morning, heading for Bournemouth and Southampton, which was where the armored divisions would await their channel crossing. We were on the road, lined up vehicle to vehicle, until 6:00 that night. In the meantime, they had told us to just shut the motors off and sit there a while. They weren't ready to load the armor yet. We were in that position for several days. And all the time this stuff is sitting row after row on every road in England. Our planes were back and forth overhead, for air cover, which was a great feeling. I don't know how many different areas they took off from along the coast to go across the channel.

In the meantime, the situation changed. There was a violent storm that came up that destroyed a lot of the landing facilities in Normandy. As a result, it was three weeks before the armored divisions moved across the channel. But, three days after arriving at Bournemouth, I went to recon an area for C Company's position near Sainte-Mère-Eglise. I sat there for ten days with nothing to do because we couldn't get our troops over.

I had to go back to Cardiff, Wales, which was probably ninety or 100 miles away from where we were, to pick up twelve more of our tanks. I took two Jeeps and a six-by-six truck with the drivers to bring this equipment back. The tanks that we picked up came equipped with metal tracks, which we were not accustomed to. Most of the tanks we practiced with had rubber grommets built into the tracks, which gave them a little more traction.

A steel track was much better in the field. It would last longer. In this little town right outside of Cardiff, with narrow cobblestone streets and houses built right up close to the streets, one of the tanks slid going down a hill and had turned sideways over the curb. The gun barrel knocked the front door out of this house. I was up ahead in the Jeep when I was notified of the accident. So I turned the Jeep around and went back to the house.

A woman standing in front of the house with her hands on her hips was giving me a nasty stare. I walked over to her and said, "I'm Captain Evans."

"Evans? Oh, we have Evans' across the street, we have Evans' down here and there are probably sixty other Evans families in our town. Come on in and have some tea."

So I went in and had a cup of tea and some biscuits and we talked about the war and things. I said, "I'll have somebody from the Army come back and fix the door."

"Oh, just forget about it. I'll have my man fix the door. It's my contribution, since your name is Evans."

I landed at Utah Beach. There were troops all over the beachhead. As we landed, English beach masters would keep the men and equipment moving inland. Everywhere you looked there were tanks and trucks and Jeeps just stuck off the road.

Different beaches were assigned to different outfits. They had brought a portable docking facility that they had floated into the Channel area a day or two after D-Day, when they saw that we were going to be entrenched there. It was floated in sections and then the engineers put it together. It was going to prevent having to get everybody off of a ship in the deep water and onto a smaller craft to get into shore.

They were going to load them right onto this dock and drive them right onto the beach. It was in operation and then this tremendous storm came up from the sea and just wrecked it. Sections of it were all mangled and upset, some sunk. From then on, they brought everything in the old fashioned way, on landing craft. They'd just come in as far as they could and let the door down and the guys were up to their necks in water. We got on some six-by-six trucks that drove us to an area about where we were going to be.

Sainte-Mère-Eglise was probably three or four miles inland from the beach. There were a good many other American units there in an old apple orchard, our designated area. I scouted around, then I had to go back and report as to how much area I thought we would need in addition to what we already had. Maybe one of the companies would have fit in this orchard.

When they finally did bring our tanks in, it was a couple weeks after D-Day. We were scheduled to come in a lot sooner, but fighting in the hedgerows slowed us down.

We were pretty much entrenched at that time. We were there to stay. We held enough area and there were infantry and airborne out ahead of us. The front line at that time was, maybe, three miles from Sainte-Mère-Eglise. They were well established and pushing inland to get more and more area to get room to bring more people in. And that was a gigantic buildup. They were just bringing stuff in just as fast as they could unload it.

I went back down to the loading dock, to see about a supply of food, and they had many LCIs that they were cleaning out, getting ready to take the wounded back. I'll tell you, part of that bay was actually red with blood. They'd bring in the wounded by the hundreds, loaded them in head and foot, head and foot, laying them down and taking them back out to the hospital ships.

The hedgerows were terrible. Over the years, the farmers that had a couple acre piece of ground planted thick shrubs to mark their boundaries. The farms were all enclosed with tree lines, and the roots went down in and had formed an almost impenetrable wall. A tank could get over it, but as soon as it did, the thinly armored underside would be exposed to fire. Later on, one of the men from one of the tank outfits came up with the "hedge-buster." All it was three or four spiked teeth welded on the front of each tank. They would bust into this hedgerow and it would be enough penetration to allow the tank to push the wall down. Every day we'd get through three of four of those hedgerows. We would move enough troops forward to push the Germans back far enough to make room for a few more. It was quite a buildup. When we finally did get our outfit in France, we got everybody assembled and got them into a fighting force.

We had three positions that the infantry and the airborne had pointed out and decided if the Germans break through in a certain area, then I was to move my company from in the woods down a rocky road to a forward position. It was probably about a four-thousand-yard move. Sure enough, about the second or third night we got orders that the Germans had counterattacked and they wanted me to move my company down into this position we had picked out. So I led them down a little narrow road and the tanks snagged all the infantry's communications wire that had been laying beside the road! We must have had fifty commanders out there raising hell!

A colonel came up to me, and inch from my face and yelled, "Get these tanks off the road."

"Where do you want me to put them?"

He said, "You pick out the first field that you see and get them off of the road."

It's pitch dark. I couldn't see the hand in front of my face. The first field we went in, the lead tank hit a mine. Boom! Blew the tracks off and stalled everything. The next morning I could hear these tanks starting up. They weren't ours. It was the sound of what I called German "one-lungers." They didn't hit like American engines when you revved them.

We were on the high ground overlooking maybe three or 4,000 yards of valley. It was fog-covered and you couldn't see a thing, but you could hear all this activity. So I got the tanks lined up and we waited. When that fog lifted or if somebody started up across there, we were just gonna have to take them on. We waited and waited while these tanks started up. They grew loud for a while, then the noise would die down. The fog was starting to lift. By ten o'clock that morning, it cleared off and you couldn't see a thing, you couldn't hear a thing. They'd evidently moved off in another direction. You talk about being scared. My first day in combat and I couldn't tell whether it was my knees knocking or my heart pounding!

We stayed in that position till around noontime, and battalion headquarters called and said that the attack was canceled. So we returned to our original positions. I took the Jeep back up the road, and saw all those infantry guys out fixing their communication wires! They should have had that wire buried. It was something they learned and something we learned. I'll bet we took fifty miles of wire off of those tank tracks. I reported to my colonel.

"Yeah, I know all about it," he said, "it's one of the things that we're going to have to remember in the future."

I said, "The only thing to remember in the future is, tell the infantry that if they want our support, make sure those wires are buried."

And they wanted our support, believe me. To the infantry, a tank is the great savior.

We stayed in that hedgerow country, probably three or four weeks, till the breakout from Carentan to St. Lô. We patrolled the highway running between Carentan and St. Lô.

I got caught out on the Carentan Highway in a Jeep one night. They told me to try and find a position toward St. Lô where I could move my company. It's starting to get dark and the only way we could get back was on that highway. I wasn't about to go cross-country. As we started up the highway, all was blacked out, so I sat out on the hood, just to the right of the wire cutter, to direct the driver. There were four of us in the Jeep. And it started to rain. The highway was all pockmarked from the shelling and bombing.

We were dodging the holes, trying to get up the road. We had gone about half a mile when we heard a "click-click," the sound of a bolt coming back.

I hollered, "Stop, stop!"

The blackout headlights were all we could see by.

This guy yells, "Halt!"

"I'm already halted."

"What outfit are you with?"

"4th Armored."

"Never heard of ya!"

"Well, we've got to get up to St. Lô."

"Well, you'll never make it up this way."

I asked him where he was, and he said he was down in the ditch that ran along both sides of the road.

I walked over and here was a .30 caliber machinegun about six inches from my face. It was a paratrooper.

He said, "We're dug in all along here. How far are you going?"

I told him and he said, "You'll not get through here. Who sent you up this way?"

"It's the only way I know to get to St. Lô."

"Well, the best thing for you to do is go back and wait for daylight."

I guessed that was the only thing I could do. We had radio contact with battalion. I called back and they said to stay where we were until daylight. Which we did. When it got light, I looked up ahead and all I could see were dead cows, machinery and equipment all over that highway. We couldn't have gotten through there if we wanted to. There must have been 200 paratroopers who came out of those ditches.

They had on their helmets with leaves and camouflage netting stuck in them so you couldn't see them. It was the 101st Airborne. They'd been there for six weeks, since the invasion. Shortly after that, they pulled them back and they moved the 1st Infantry into their positions. This airborne outfit was pretty slick. They really moved around and you never knew they were there. I had no idea there were that many of them dug in like that.

In Normandy, we had an outpost of two tanks at a crossroads for the night. During the night I got a call on the radio back to my command post that something was coming down the road. I said, "Well, if they don't stop, shoot them."

About five minutes later I heard a main gun fire. I walked up. I was about 300 yards back from where the outpost was. They had shot a horse. Blew him all apart!

Everything quieted down and I said, "If anything else comes down the road, shoot it. That's what you're out here for."

The next thing I know, they've shot again. And then I heard the other tank shoot. I went back up and this time they had hit three German vehicles. One tank shot and the shell went through all three vehicles. It set the first one on fire and the third one was burning. The first vehicle had eight or ten German soldiers in it. We killed a couple of them and captured the others.

The second vehicle was a paymaster's truck, which was full of boxes of French Francs. They were going to pay the German troops at the front line. So we confiscated a lot of the French francs. We were not at that time allowed to use French francs, because we had what they called "invasion money." For the next couple of days, as we drove through towns, we'd reach into this box and throw out hundreds of francs to the natives! About two or three weeks later they had put out an order that we could use French money as our exchange. But we had already given away about two or three million dollars worth!

The third truck, incidentally, was an artificer's truck. They'd do repairs to small arms. They had several boxes of Lugers, German pistols, still packed in the Cosmoline. We took a couple boxes of those for souvenirs, which we later used.

The breakout in Normandy started on 25 July. It began with the six-mile saturation bombing, Operation COBRA. They blew out everything for the length of six miles and about two miles wide. We stood up on the tanks and watched as thousands of planes dropped their bombs. We were told that there were 5,000 planes in the attack. As far as you could see in the sky were American planes coming. You could hear them and then see them. They started probably three-quarters-of-a-mile from where we were.

The first plane dropped red flares to show the front line. As the planes passed over that point, they unloaded all that they had. I stood up on top of the tank and could feel the concussion pulling my combat pants back. This went on I would say, for a good hour or two. Fighters were zigging in and out. Every once in a while you'd a plane get hit, and it would spin and drop down out of the formation. After the bombing, we moved out of St. Lô and started across France.

After that breakout, we were hitting into German outfits that were trying to get out of that area. We had several major conflicts, but they were short skirmishes, none lasting for any length of time.

The 4th Armored was pretty close to Patton. I got to see him many times. When I moved from C Company commander up to Battalion S–2, one of my jobs was to go up to Third Army Headquarters to get the situation maps updated. Many times Patton was around, with that little dog, Willie, that white mutt of his, named after William the Conqueror. I always thought the dog's name was "Son of a Bitch," because that's what Patton called it. It would be laying somewhere and he'd say, "Get out of the way, Son of a Bitch."

Patton never missed an opportunity to talk about history. I'd go in there lots of times to get the information and there'd be eight or ten people around, talking about history. One day there was this general and he was talking about an attack by this division. He had his hand on the map, and said, "We're going to attack, in force, through this area."

Patton was back behind him and he said, "General, do you realize how much space you're talking about from your thumb to your little finger?"

"Yes, sir," he said, "about 2,000 yards."

"Well, you look at it again, because you're covering about five miles."

The general had the wrong scale map! But that's the kind of a man Patton was. He'd be talking to you and listening to three other people at the same time. At the drop of a hat he'd talk about battles that happened a thousand years ago, about who commanded what legion, about how long the battles were, what weapons they used, about anything and everything.

When he was made Third Army Commander, he walked up on this tremendously big platform, and from where he was standing in the center he couldn't look down to see the first eight or ten rows, where all these nurses and WACs were seated. He's up there talking about "grabbing those sons of bitches by the throat," and a couple other remarks. Then he said, "You see all these," slapping at his chest full of medals. He had medals all over him. If you gave him a medal for drinking water, he'd have it on there. He believed that was a show of what you were as a soldier. Anyway, he made some remark about all the skin he could get with these medals. His aide walked over to him and whispered something to him. Patton took about three steps forward and looked down at these nurses. "Oh, sorry ladies," he said. "But, oh, what the hell, you know what I'm talking about anyhow."

We did a lot of Patton's dirty work. We were up front a good bit of the time. I think he thought a lot of the 4th Armored, and rightly so. It was a good outfit. The 101st Airborne was one of his pets. After the breakout from the Peninsula, we were with Third Army the whole time, the whole way through to Czechoslovakia.

Our good friends were the P–47 pilots. We called on them for help many times. We had luminous plastic panels that we'd drape over the back or the turret of the tank to make sure they would see us. Usually, if we had a target, we'd call for the planes, then fire a smoke round into the target area to indicate where it was. We got very good at it. The air to ground communication was well coordinated. Lots of times, on their days off, these fliers would come up to visit us, to get to know who they were talking to on the radio. They wanted rides in the tanks and souvenirs.

We had a "good" time at Troyes. We had three-quarters surrounded Troyes with tanks, artillery and infantry. They sent a mission to the mayor of Troyes to give them an hour to surrender, or we'd attack the town. Of course, there was no answer. All three tank battalions attacked the town, with artillery blowing the town apart.

The German soldiers waited until we were within 100 yards of them before they opened up from basements and buildings. They had two or three artillery spotters up in a church steeple. I brought one of my M-18s around and told him to blow the top of the church off. We did that and the German artillery stopped. Then we got into the town, which is something we rarely did. In a three-or-four-block area there were a lot of German infantry and mortars. We spotted another likely spot where they had forward observers, and we knocked that out. That stopped their mortar fire. After that, their fire wasn't as accurate.

One of my tanks got hit and I got on the machinegun and machine-gunned a few of the German infantry. Well, not a few of them, a lot. They just kept coming at us. I just stayed there and fired until the tank was destroyed. That was it.

They were all infantry, and they had some airborne troops there. And they were all SS. They weren't fly-by-night troops. I can truthfully say that any time we fought head to head with the German army they were well-trained, disciplined and competent troops. We just overwhelmed them, that's all. They were just getting thin and didn't have enough replacement equipment. They would send a few tanks here and a few there, to try and plug the holes. We just wore them down. We had so damn much stuff that they'd destroy it and we'd replace it, while they couldn't.

In an attack like Troyes, the M–18s we would back up the tanks. The tanks would move in, the forward elements, and we would be a secondary line in case of a breakthrough or if the German tanks would counterattack. We'd just protect the ones that were going in, give them supporting fire. Lots of times we were in position where we'd just fire at any targets that were available. Many times the company would be divided up. The platoons would fight with different units. One platoon would be with one of the infantry outfits, one would be guarding the supply units, and another would be up with the tank command. So lots of times we'd sub-divide the company. But always in supporting fire. We were never really the front line.

Our first German casualty got hit in the head. His brains were splattered all over the tank. Everybody was kind of stupefied. They didn't know quite what to do. "Doc" Buchanan, our Medical Officer, came over and threw a shirt over the man's head. He said, "C'mon, let's get him out of there. He's not going to hurt anybody now."

Around 1 September it started to rain. The ground was just soaked. It rained for two or three weeks. All the time we were in this area. We moved to attack Lunéville. I had one platoon with Combat Command B, and Combat Command A was attacking toward Feterange. The Germans came through and attacked Arracourt. Colonel Clarke was the head of Combat Command A. I had two platoons on a little hillside at Arracourt. There was nobody—nobody—through there but us.

We were in a pretty good position. It was kind of foggy on 19 September down where we were. We could hear the German tanks starting up. That's how we got a warning. I was shaving, beside a tank, when a shell came right down between the tank I was standing near and another. It plowed up the ground. Colonel s came over, and had a captain from the 37th Tank Battalion, Captain William A. Dwight with him. He said he wanted one of my platoons right away and he wanted me to place the rest of the company in position to stop the German attack.

Third Platoon was the one that went with Clarke. They moved to Rechicourt and Coincourt on what they thought would be a routine assignment. They ran smack into sixty Mark IV and Tiger tanks. They knocked out two German tanks before one of the tank destroyers was hit. Private Richard Graham was killed and Sergeant Emilio Stasi received slight wounds. Stasi was one of my gun commanders. First Lieutenant Edwin T. Leiper was the platoon leader. I left him there and I moved down with the other platoon to try and stop them, because where we were on the side of this hill, the Germans were going to try to come around between the two hills.

Well, we got them from both sides. Before the day was over, we knocked out twenty-nine German tanks. And we turned them back. In the meantime, the 3rd Platoon that was down in Lunéville was supporting B Company. They really got the hell beat out of them down there. We had three or four of our officers killed. 3rd Platoon came back and took up position along with us. We were there for ten days. But this was our big day.

One of the M–18s was hit. It had its track knocked off, and I could see these German tanks out in front of me. I just got in and emptied the gun. I guess I was more mad than anything else. It might have been foolhardy. I saw this perfectly good gun and thought I might as well fire it. The tank destroyer right beside it was burning and evidently the Germans thought that both tanks were burning because there was a lot of smoke from the other tank. They didn't put another shell into it. After I fired the gun and fired the machinegun at them I did get some return fire. I got out and got down on the ground and crawled away. They eventually burned that tank, too. But, it's just one of those things that happen so quick that you figure you can take on the whole German Army.

I liked to fire that big gun. It had a nice sight on it. It was like pointing your finger. It would go out 1,000–2,000 yards just as accurate as any rifle. It would take on any tank, I would say, at under 1,000 yards, except the bigger tanks, the Tiger and the Tiger Royal. I only saw five or six Tiger tanks in this whole battle. The Tigers were a formidable weapon. The one I know that we hit, was probably 1,000–1,500 yards away. A gunner put at least three shells into that tank. It was coming at us up a hill, and I watched in the binoculars. At least two of them bounced off like it was nothing. And they were 76mm armor-piercing shells. The third round took his track off, which was what we tried to do, disable them and get them to stop or turn. Then you could really pour everything into them.

On top of the hill I had a little command post set up. Down in the valley we could see burned vehicles, ours and theirs. The 37th Tank Battalion moved in and the

Germans knocked twenty of their tanks out before they knew what the hell had hit them. We hit one tank. This German got out of the top of the tank. It was burning and he was on fire. He had his hands up and he started walking toward us. We were 500 or 600 yards away, looking right down on him. He walked to within 100 yards of us and finally fell over. We couldn't go out after him because the Germans were firing. Nobody could go after him. The poor sonofabitch burned up right there in front of our eyes. But there was nothing we could do.

That evening, Patton came with Colonel Clarke and they stood up on that hillside. Looking down at the carnage from my CP, Colonel Clarke said, "Captain Evans was in charge of this shootout."

Patton asked me what kind of ammunition we were using, and if we had enough of it.

I said, "We had plenty of ammunition, we're in good shape."

Patton said to me, "This is the kind of thing that's going to end the war quicker than anybody had hoped."

And he turned around, walked to his Jeep and took off.

We moved up into Bastogne with the 4th Armored, Christmas Eve, 1944. We had moved from around Sarreguemines, where we were engaged, and came back and got into Longwy, which was maybe twenty miles from Bastogne. It was about twenty degrees below zero. There was maybe ten inches of snow on the ground. It took us all night to move from Sarreguemines. They had MP stops every twenty miles. They had these big cans and logs burning so we could get out and warm our hands up. But we were only allowed to stay for two minutes!

Eisenhower had promised that every GI was going to have turkey dinner for Christmas. Supply came along in a Jeep with frozen turkeys that were as hard as wood. They were hollering "Merry Christmas" and throwing us frozen turkeys. Each tank crew got a turkey. We gathered them up and had them later, around 15 January, after we pulled out of Bastogne.

The whole division was lined up bumper to bumper going up that road to Bastogne, with steam coming off of everything. They said that Combat Command A was to attack Bastogne on Christmas morning, which they did. The Combat Command got orders to attack Bastogne at three o'clock Christmas morning. We started out across what was a cornfield that went up hill into a wooded area. We moved probably a half a mile when we were pinned down by German artillery and tank fire coming from the vicinity of Bastogne. They had completely surrounded Bastogne by that time. They had moved in reserve troops. The Americans were trying to move more troops into the area to surround them, which eventually they did. There was some very, very fierce, heavy fighting almost completely around Bastogne, in the fields and the town.

My headquarters pulled back to Chaumont, which is about a mile or so to the east of Bastogne. In the meantime, Colonel Clarke sent Colonel Abrams to attack Bastogne. He eventually broke through and got into Bastogne and relieved the siege. Then he had to turn around and fight his way back out, because the Germans had

Major Tom Evans dressed in a captured German colonel's uniform. Lieutenant Marion Taake stands guard over this "fine-looking Kraut," as a caption to the original photo reads.
Courtesy of Richard Buchanan, M.D.

closed in behind him. So they fought their way back out and got down the highway, this was the main road that ran from Longwy directly into Bastogne. We were up and down that highway, going in and out of Bastogne several times before they finally got the Germans backed off enough to say that the siege was lifted. In the meantime, the skies cleared and the Air Force sent in bomber after bomber, fighter-bombers strafed and bombed them, plus our artillery. I don't know how many divisions were in that area, but before that battle was over, I think it was the largest concentration of American troops in any battle area in Europe at that time. We left there around 14 January, and went to a rest area in the vicinity of Luxembourg City. On 19 January, we were on the march again. The whole 704th Tank Destroyer battalion was assigned a mission along with the 94th Infantry Division. Our joint task was to clear what was called the Saar-Moselle Triangle, or the "Siegfried Switch."

There we engaged the remnants of the 14th Panzer Division and three infantry divisions. There was more infantry there than tanks. Their tank battalions were pretty well shot up, and they couldn't replace them. They were fighting with five or six tanks, when they should have had twenty or thirty.

It was hazy, overcast, cold and snowing. We couldn't get any air cover in for weeks. It was somewhat like the weather up around Bastogne, although not as cold. It was a mess. And there weren't any roadways to travel through that whole area. We traveled mostly overland against fortifications. The worst obstacles were dragon's teeth, pillboxes, mine fields and artillery fire. We would pick out an area and the engineers would blow four or five of the teeth out. Most of the areas we had picked to move through had artillery fire, both direct and indirect, covering them, as well as small arms, mortar fire and some anti-tank weapons. We tried to pick an area we could get through without much harassment. But, they had it pretty well engineered. All the low spots were covered with small arms fire and the higher spots were covered with artillery fire. If you were attacking one position, another position would be able to hit you with direct fire from the woods or up on a hill. A lot of them were camouflaged. You couldn't see them. That Siegfried Line was pretty well set up. After we got through it, they had no resistance. It was one of their last lines of defense. We fought through that for the next six weeks, with the 94th Infantry. Our command post was just outside of Bouzonville.

My brother, Jack, who was a Master Sergeant in the 94th Infantry Division, stopped to visit. I had persuaded him to stay with us overnight, then go back to his outfit the next day. During the night a 280mm railroad gun shelled us. One of these shells hit just down the street. It completely obliterated the building and left a crater thirty-feet deep. When my brother saw that, he started packing up and said he was going back with the infantry, where it was safe.

We rejoined the 4th Armored Division at Bitburg. We had fought through the Siegfried as a full battalion, but after that the companies of the 704th were parceled out to the Combat Commands. We fought through Kroft and Leubach, Meisenheim, Kobern, Seirsenheld, toward the Rhine River. We crossed on 24 March 1945. We had minor engagements in all these little towns. We just overran everything.

We cleared out Darmstadt then crossed the Main River at Hanau. We traveled on the Reichsautobahn, which was copied after the Turnpike in Pennsylvania. We went on it for many miles, towards Hersfeld, Creuzburg, Gotha, and into Ohrdruf. The light tanks from the Combat Command had come onto this concentration camp quite by surprise. Nobody said that there was a concentration camp in the area. In fact, it was the first one I ever heard about. I didn't know that they had anything like that.

The German guards were still there early that morning. They didn't expect us to come up on them that quickly. The tanks actually knocked the front gates down and got into the camp itself. The German guards went out the back. They were captured later. We shot a lot of them. I was with the advance party of Combat Command A. A driveway went in through barbed wire fencing on both sides, maybe 200 yards till we got into the main camp. The prisoners realized that something was going on, because they started to walk down this driveway toward us. They were emaciated, their faces were sunken, and their eyes were bulged out. They just staggered down toward us when they realized that we were Americans. Then they had big tears coming down their faces. More of them started coming out. Tears were streaming down their faces and they were chattering and crying. They had gray-striped uniforms on with a big Star of David on them.

The next day, Georgie Patton came up and went through the camp. Then he went down to the town, which was two miles away. He brought the Burgermeister and all his council, anybody who had anything to do with operating this little town. Patton made them go through the camp. Of course, they all denied knowing it was there or what went on there. After viewing the camp, they went back. That night the mayor killed himself. Patton brought many different generals, photographers, newsmen and others to view the camp.

We stayed there for two days, then we moved on. All the guys were required to walk through it, but we weren't to touch anything or move anything. We could see the bodies in the ovens. It was the damndest thing I ever saw. In some of the buildings there were bins filled with clothing. There was one that must have had 10,000 pairs of glasses. Then there was the gas chamber. There was a 400-foot-long building. The Nazis had piled bodies in there, two rows, head to foot, right to the roof. At the far end of this building they had a conveyor belt that went into the ovens. It went around in a semi-circle into six ovens. They would move on around to each next oven. They did this continually, twenty-four hours a day. But they were killing faster than they could burn.

Most of the camp inmates I spoke with were Polish. The others were German, from Upper Silesia. There were all nationalities there. If we didn't understand them, we'd get somebody to interpret for them. I had German, French, Polish, and Russian interpreters. Nobody that was fluent, but enough to find out what was going on. One Polish fellow said that his whole family had been picked up in Poland. He never saw them again. He had just been trying to survive, and he couldn't believe that he'd made it.

We went on from there to Erfurt and Chemnitz. There, we were told that the Russians were within thirty miles of us, coming from the opposite direction. So the Division started to move south, through Bayreuth to the Danube River.

We'd got into one plant near Bayreuth. We had heard through the grapevine that it was a munitions manufacturing plant for artillery shells. I went over with my translator and talked with the manager of the plant. It was a four-story building. On the first floor they made leather-goods. Jackets, belts, really nice ankle-length leather coats, like the German officers wore. I picked one up for a nice souvenir.

We went up to the second floor and it was nothing but machines: lathes, presses and such. All made in Cincinnati, Ohio! Must have been fifty machines. On the top two floors, they had stored, end on end, heavy artillery shells that they had made. The leather shop was just a front for the munitions plant. So we arrested the manager and had the MP'S surround the plant. I don't know whether the building was destroyed or whether they got all the shells out of it.

I took that leather coat out with me. We were riding in a Jeep on the autobahn and it was cold and rainy. So I put that coat on and somebody took a shot at me! That coat came off in a hurry! The bullet went right into the hinge where the windshield folds down onto the hood. But that coat was all fur-lined. It was nice and warm.

We crossed the Danube, turned northeast into Czechoslovakia and took up positions in various locations just south of Pilsen. We were there when the war ended. I was with S–2 by then.

With S–2, my biggest job was to make sure that everybody got information, as far as maps, to bring them up to date as to what the division was doing, what the battalion was doing, what our goals were for the day, what our targets were, make sure everybody had ammunition, make sure they had food, make sure the supply trains were in order. Also, I coordinated the attacks. By that I mean whatever the S–3 and the battalion commander would decide as far as the orders for the day, I would make sure everyone understood what their job was for the day, what their target was, all the lines of egress, where the ambulance flow would be, where the ammunition supply was if they ran out. Many times I'd go out to the platoons and talk to the tankers and they'd thought they were all alone, that was nobody to tell them exactly what the situation was. As much as I could, I would disseminate the information to them, give them the "big picture."

In S–2, we also interrogated prisoners, then turn them over to division. There was a route set up just for that purpose, if we picked up anybody important or any news or maps, it all went back to division

We were still fighting ten days after the war ended. Some of the German SS had tanks and some infantry in an area up near Pilsen. They refused to surrender. Several attempts to try to get them to come out failed. They finally came out, but they had tied children and women from the area onto their tanks.

I stayed in and around Susice for two or three weeks, then we moved back to an occupation area around Landshut, Germany, which was south and west of Czechoslovakia. At that time my job was to screen prisoners. There were several large POW camps there. I had an office set up and had German, Polish and Russian interpreters. We screened probably 500 to 1,000 prisoners a day. We had to check them to make sure that they were not SS. We did this by having them remove their shirt and hold their hands above their heads. All SS troops had their blood types tattooed on their upper left underarm. Anybody who was connected with the SS was automatically put back in the cages.

Other people, we checked them, and if they had no connection with the government or the SS, we released them. We told them to pack up and go back to their homes.

One day I was bringing back a couple prisoners, SS. I made them sit on the hood of the Jeep. I rode past some infantry and they shot them right off the front of my Jeep. I went back and asked who the wise guy was, but nobody would admit to it. And I didn't blame them. Towards the end of the war, it got pretty hairy.

One morning there were five men in German uniforms. They were traveling with the German Army. They called themselves "White Russians." That term dates back to the Czarist days before World War I, when the Red Russians and the White Russians clashed. The White Russians fled and took up residence in Germany, where they stayed until World War II. Then they fought as a unit with the German Army Group South.

They had this treasure with them that had been in the bank in Berlin. As the Russians started to overrun Germany and were pushing towards Berlin, the White

Russians took the treasure, put it on these horse-drawn carriages and traveled south and west out of Berlin to get away from the Russians. In the meantime, they were captured by the Americans and sent to my compound for interrogation.

The five came in and I checked them and told them they were free to go. They wanted to know about their belongings. At that time, they were allowed to take any personal belongings, but nothing else.

One of them was a kind of spokesman, and he told me their story, and the story about the treasure. They traveled with General Vlasak, who was wanted by the Russians. I guess they had been after him for some time. The Americans had taken Vlasak away from this group and left this Colonel in charge of the treasure. I notified G–5, the bunch dedicated to POW matters, at Division about the treasure. They informed me to inventory the stuff and get back to them with a dollar value. I opened the boxes, which were full of mostly church articles, icons and church artwork, chalices and gold pieces. There were some paintings and glasswork, some coins. We put a value of between four and six million dollars on it. We inventoried this stuff and sent the list back to Division. They came and confiscated the treasure along with the five men. Division took the stuff. I don't know what happened to it after that. The *Armored News* in 1945, valued the treasure at ten million dollars. I don't know where they got that figure. What those Russians had intended to do with this treasure was to restart the White Russian government. They hoped to one day return to Russia to overthrow the Communists.

This POW camp also had a group of German nurses that had gotten out of Berlin somehow. There were sixty or seventy of them. They had just come back from the Russian front. A nurse officer came and talked to us. She was very fluent in English. She had gone to school in Texas when she was a little girl. She told us about the conditions in Russia. She said she had been there when the winter came in 1941. She said that the Russian soldiers didn't win that campaign, the weather did. She said they had thousands of amputations. Men were eating horses because there was no food. Men were freezing to death. She said that conditions were so terrible there was nothing they could do.

She said there was one artillery outfit that she knew of, of which her boyfriend was a captain. He told her it was so cold that it would freeze the recoil mechanisms on the artillery pieces, which were hydro-recoil. Whatever fluid they had in the recoil system would freeze. She said they would fire the gun once and it would blow apart, because it couldn't recoil. It was really something, the picture she painted of what went on there.

The Army had developed the point system for discharge, the Green Project, where you could get points for every year in service or overseas, for every medal or award that you got. I took advantage of it. I flew from Susice to Paris and stayed there for four days. Then we had to go down to Marseilles, which was a return-staging area. We were there for three days, got some shots and got all of our papers in order, turned in our supplies and went to Casablanca, North Africa. We flew in a converted B–29 bomber. They had taken the guns and the bomb bays out. We had thirty or so men on each plane. We were there for about three days, then we flew Brazil. The reason they took this round about route was so that the planes could fly mostly over land, rather than be out over the water. We stayed in Brazil for three days then flew from there to Miami, Florida. We got there ten days after leaving Marseilles, in September 1945.

From Miami, I got on a train to Fort Indiantown Gap, Pennsylvania. I had probably three or four months of leave accumulated, so I checked in and came home from there. I had to report back in January 1946. Before that, I had gone to Fort Sam Houston, Texas. I taught tank tactics for about six weeks and that's when I decided to get out of the army. I stayed in the reserves for a while. Right before the Korean War, they said I was either in or out. So, I got out!

Jesus! I'll tell you. That war I was in was an ugly thing!

The M-18 Tank Destroyer, the "Hellcat." In 1941, The United States Army began the development of armored vehicles to be used as tank destroyers. The M-18 was first designated as the T-70 in January 1943, and was standardized as the M-18 in February 1944. *CNAS/Buchanan.*

The German "Panther" tank, a major adversary of the M-18 Tank Destroyer. *Courtesy of Mrs. Thomas J. Evans.*

"You Yellow Sonofabitch! Take These Guys Back In."

B.J. Fleckenstein
4th Marine Division, 3rd Battalion, 25th Regiment
South Pittsburgh, Pennsylvania, 24 1925

"No one will ever know what war is like, unless he fights one. Take every July 4th fireworks show you ever saw and multiply it by cannons going off at your rear, and things exploding over you head, and your buddy holding his guts in his hand. That's war. That's not the fun part."

The Marine Corps had all this publicity out, and that's what caught my eye. I joined them and ended up at Camp Lejeune, North Carolina, where they were toughening up little boys. From Camp Lejeune we went to Maui. They really trained us there. If anyone gave them an argument, they beat the shit out of him. I you cooperated, they still might beat the shit out of you, but you'd get a little time off, a candy bar once in a while, and maybe a beer. They took no mercy on us, and we hated them by the end of the day. Not until we got into combat did we realize what the training was all about.

We on Maui for about a year, then we boarded a boat and went to Saipan. They didn't tell us where we were going, but we knew were going to get into a fight. On Saipan, I said to my buddy Leo, from Pittsburgh, "Hey Leo, how about me being in the foxhole with you?"

Leo had been in the Marines longer than me, and I wanted to be with somebody that knew what he was doing. Leo said, "Ok, you can be in my foxhole, but at night there's no guard duty. When it gets dark, you're supposed to go to sleep, when it gets light you're supposed to get up. If they come down at night and we're all asleep it's tough beans."

One night a Jap crawled in the foxhole of one of the guys in our unit and he used a shovel on him. That was a good weapon. It was a good tool for swinging, and he beat that Jap to death with it.

After we left Saipan, they told us we were going to an island called Iwo Jima. Well that didn't make any difference to any of us; we didn't know where it was or what it was like. So they showed us maps of it and it was pretty close to Japan. We went to Iwo Jima on 19 February 1945, and turned out to be one of the turning points of the war. I was supposed to be in the first wave, but we had to turn around, and I actually went it with the second wave. Most Marines who were in the first wave at Iwo think they have bragging rights, but it was the second wave that took all the shit.

Our AMTRAC pulled up to the beach to drop its ramp, but the Coast Guard driver turned yellow, and he turned the damned boat around, stepped on the gas, and headed for open water. The Coast Guard guy that was in the back with us called him every name possible, "You yellow sonofabitch! "Turn this damn thing around. Take these guys back in!"

The Japs let the first wave in, figuring to open fire after our boys made twenty-five yards or so. Our lieutenant was a new guy, and he knew a private and me by our names. He told us to follow him. We jumped off. The others didn't move as quickly, and they got it with a mortar round or artillery shell. One of our guys went down to the shore late that afternoon after it happened; thousands of Marines had landed by that time. He looked at our landing craft and said everyone was still there but they were all dead. The bodies were intact because the guys had been killed by concussion. He said they looked like they were just frozen in the same position without a scratch on them, like wax figures. I don't know if that was better than being shot or worse.

I almost didn't get off the landing craft. I had a shovel on the back of my belt and that sonofabitching shovel was hanging down and got stuck. I rode the craft sitting on the hood of the Jeep. The other guys were lined along the side. The driver pulled the landing craft up fifteen feet from the shore. He stepped on the gas a couple times and choked it up and this damned Jeep moved forward and over to the side and caught a bunch of our guys that were standing there. It pinned them up against the wall and my shovel was caught, I was trying to get off, thinking what the hell is the matter. So I took my belt off, lost my water canteen, my ammunition. I got thirsty after we had been on shore for a while, so I went over and took a canteen off a body; he wouldn't mind I figured.

Once we got on shore, the three of us we worked our way in to try and find our outfit. The Japs were up on a big hill to the right of the beach, and they had a full view of the whole damned beach. They could pick their spot, so the shit was really flying, guts all over the beach and dead guys everywhere

On the second day one of our lieutenants told me that the 3rd and the 5th came in on the southern part of the island, and he need to get a message to them. He told me, "Go over and find the officer in charge and give him this message."

I don't know why the hell he didn't use the radio, but he wanted his message to be hand-carried. I didn't know where I was going, and the shit was still flying. I finally found a captain who was attached to the colonel's headquarters and the message to him. Then I had to go back through all that stuff again. Back up on the beach, there were a lot of guns going off at once on the shore and from the ships out at sea. I asked a guy what the matter was and he said, "Look up there on Suribachi. Our flag is up!"

I looked up at the flag and said, "Sonofabitch, we couldn't move ten yards and those guys went up that damned hill and put a flag on it."

That flag looked like it was a mile high. The guys had gotten up there without anyone getting hit. When they came down a little later to get some gear, they ran into some Japs in caves, and that's when they took casualties.

We stayed on Iwo for twenty-six days; by that time our whole outfit was in shreds. It was bad to be a second lieutenant in the Marine Corps because he was always in front taking all the crap. It was better for privates. They could find a hole and crawl into it.

A friend of mine, a kid from Washington, D.C., came up to me all excited. He pointed out into the ocean and said, "There's my dad's ship. I'm going to go out to see him somehow."

He went down to the beach and he got someone to take him out to his dad's ship on a supply boat. I don't think he had permission; he just went. A couple hours later he came back with some peanuts. "Here, I stole these off the ship."

He was so proud that he had brought us a delight, but I didn't have the heart to tell him they were stale. The next day, we were in a concrete pillbox on a little hill to the north of Suribachi. The guy kid who gave us the peanuts went out the back and tripped a wire, a booby trap. He lost both legs. He didn't survive, and, I found out later, when the officers came to tell his mother, she asked, "Which one?" She didn't know right away if it was her husband or son.

I learned to hate the Japanese, because of the dirty tricks they pulled. They'd cut a guy's dick off and let it hang out the side of his mouth. We started doing the same. We never really took prisoners, even if they came up to us with their hands up, especially if they came in three or four at a time. One of them might have a grenade hung somehow on his back, and when they would get close enough to some Marines, they'd detonate the grenade, sacrificing themselves and killing as many Marines as they could. I still have a hatred for them. They killed a lot of my friends like that. They didn't mind dying for Hirohito, but we didn't particularly want to die for the President.

Looking back, the war was quite an experience. Actually, if you take out the bad parts, it was sometimes fun. One thing I never wanted to do was turn yellow and run away in front of my buddies. Some guys did, but I never wanted that to happen to me. Some guys just broke down and cried like babies. No one will ever know what war is like, unless he fights one. Take every July 4th fireworks show you ever saw and multiply it by cannons going off at your rear, and things exploding over you head, and your buddy holding his guts in his hand. That's war. That's not the fun part.

"What Did I Get Into Now?"

James Foley
4th Marine Division, 24th Marine Regiment, 2nd Battalion
E Company
Pittsburgh, Pennsylvania, 13 May 1926
(Lower Burrell, Pennsylvania)

"There was a new and awful odor that mixed in with the sulfur and cordite. The closer we got to the front, the worse the smell got. The smell made me sick to my stomach, but chewing gum helped a little. When I lifted my head and looked up the path, I found out what the smell was. It was coming from dead Marines lying on stretchers. They hadn't had time to bury them. "

PEOPLE CALLED ME "RED" because of my bright red hair. I got called "carrot top" too but I didn't like that much. I was the youngest, and I used to hate being introduced as the baby of the family. One Sunday after church, while my mother prepared dinner, I was listening to some classical music on the radio. Just as I was about to turn it off, there was a news flash that Pearl Harbor had been attacked. I didn't wait for dinner. Instead, I went up to the corner store where I hung out with my buddies. They were all up there and I told them about the announcement. They went home and listened for themselves. Finally, we found out where Pearl Harbor was. Everything they were reporting was vague. The next day, at school, they played Roosevelt's speech during lunch. I thought about going in, but I wasn't Gung-Ho about it. I knew if the war continued I'd eventually get called.

I stayed in school until my senior year, and then I dropped out. I worked for a while, and then I joined the Marines. I was seventeen when I signed up. That was April 1944.

The day I left, my dad and brother took me down to the B&O Railroad station. We had to wait for a while for the train. There was a beer garden nearby, so my dad and brother decided to get a beer. My big brother wanted to get me a beer, but my dad said, "No! He'll learn that quick enough when he gets in."

There were about twenty-five of us on that train, heading for the San Diego Recruiting Depot. We stopped at different stations to pick up and drop off passengers. In Chicago the Red Cross had coffee and donuts for us. At another place we got Christian cards. Someone gave me a Rosary that I lost later on Iwo Jima. It slipped out of my hands while I was in the foxhole one night. I guess it's still there. We got off the train in San Diego and faced this six-foot-two Marine Master Sergeant who had chicken pox marks on his face and looked like he was fifty years old. He shouted, "FALL IN!"

I thought, "What did I get into now?"

That's the first time I had a negative thought about the whole thing. He counted everybody to make sure that we were all there. After that he marched us over to a bus, and that was the last we saw of him. Once we got to the recruiting depot no one screamed at us. We gave our names and serial numbers. Then we went into a room where we had to empty out our pockets of all unnecessary items such as dirty pictures. The only thing that we were allowed to keep was pictures of girlfriends or parents. We weren't allowed to have any money so they made us buy War Bonds. That's a trick they pulled on us, but I had twenty dollars in my wallet that they never saw. The thing was that if we had no money then we couldn't run away.

We remained at Camp Pendleton during the time of our advanced training. Around that time we found out we were shipping out. We were in the 24th Regiment Replacement Draft of the 4th Marine Division The 4th Division had already been through some battles in the Pacific like Roi-Namur, Saipan and Tinian. We went to Maui where we joined the 4th Division, which was recuperating after their last campaign. I actually didn't get assigned to a unit until we got to Iwo Jima.

When we sailed for Iwo Jima, we didn't know exactly where we were going, except that we were going into combat. Iwo Jima looked like a sinister place the first time I saw it rising up out of the ocean. It smoked and it smelled of sulfur. We were spared the first onslaught. We knew we were replacements, so we were waiting for the division to go in. We were just marking time until they needed us.

In the meantime, we helped to unload 100-gallon drums of gasoline to ships that came alongside ours. We did this for a few days, and then it came over the loudspeaker that our flag was flying over Mt. Suribachi. All the whistles on the ships started blowing and we were cheering. I thought the fighting was over, but it wasn't.

We could see how ferocious the fighting was even from the ship. There was so much firing from the island that we could hear bullets hitting the side of the ship. A guy next to me said, "My foot is hot." When he looked down he saw this spent bullet wedged between the sole and the leather of his boot. We also saw a gun battle between a destroyer escort and a hidden Jap gun position. The escort went in real close and fired its .50 cal guns and 40mm guns at the position. The Japs fired back. We could see the water splashing around all around the boat. Finally, the ship must have knocked out that gun because they didn't get any more fire from the Japs. The lieutenant let us look at the fight through his binoculars.

They used our ship as a hospital ship after it had unloaded its supplies. Once I came up on deck in the evening, and the sun was shining through a foggy haze. They were playing taps as four Marines slid out from under flags into the ocean. It was heartbreaking. Those guys would never go home. There was no one else to watch them go to their rest but the sailors and the marines.

On 23 February, we learned we were going in. Before we went I attended Mass. The priests came around and blessed us. They transferred us to an LST and we went to shore on Yellow Beach. They had us moving supplies around on the beach for a

few hours and then sent us up to Air Field #1. Around suppertime, they had 10-in-1 rations brought up — ten meals in one package. We stayed there that night. Every once in a while a shell would hit a few hundred feet away. Everyone took cover.

At two o'clock in the morning they woke us up and moved us to Hill 382 on the front line. We moved in single file with a scout looking ahead. I was nervous because I was the second to last man in the line. In a way I was glad because I knew that as long as I could see him behind me then everything was all right. I kept looking over my shoulders to make sure that guy was still a Marine and not a Jap.

There was a new and awful odor that mixed in with the sulfur and cordite. The closer we got to the front, the worse the smell got. The smell made me sick to my stomach, but chewing gum helped a little. When I lifted my head and looked up the path, I found out what the smell was. It was coming from dead Marines lying on stretchers. They hadn't had time to bury them.

They gave me this fellow named Roy "Pinky" Jiles. He was about six feet tall. This was his second battle. They were trying to give all the greenhorns somebody with experience. When I heard that he was in battle before that gave me a lot of security. He was a BAR man, and I was his ammunition carrier. I was armed with an M–1, six bandoleers, four hand grenades, a cartridge belt, two canteens of water, and a backpack. Pinky told me that he would take the second watch until daybreak, and then he'd wake me up. I slept well. He woke me up just a little before daybreak. It was still foggy. As time went on the fog started lifting some and we could see into the distance. There was a big radar screen on top of Hill 382. I couldn't see it the night before. Now as the fog lifted I could.

I asked Pinky, "Why do they have a baseball backstop up there?"

He laughed and said, "That's a radar screen."

On the front line we organized, and then went forward. Our platoon went to the left of Hill 382. We circled half way around, and then turned east. I was the last man on our platoon's flank. As the assistant BAR man, I was the first to move out. I can see why they wanted young guys there, because they didn't question anything. I got up to a small ridge where we got mortar fire. Pinky gave me the signal to hold up. Then we heard a machinegun burst. Sergeant Gentry got hit in the nose and eye, but he kept shooting. When the Japs finally ran out of ammo, the corpsmen were able to get to the sergeant.

We kept moving up. I saw a Jap in a spider hole, but he didn't see me. The Jap did see the guys to my right and a little ahead of me. I threw a hand grenade into the spider hole and yelled, "Fire in the hole!"

The grenade exploded, and I'm sure that Jap died in there, but we had to keep moving, so I didn't get a chance check for sure. We continued moving up the hill, and then Japs throwing grenades and firing machineguns stopped us. Some of us found a shell hole and dove in. We huddled in there while some guys to our right engaged in a hand grenade duel with the Japs. Finally, one of our men yelled, "You three guys shoot at the top of that hill."

We released a steady fire toward the Japs. They had one of their tanks dug in, and were using it as a pillbox. Guys with satchel charges got up there and destroyed the tank and the Japs.

There were a lot of dead Japs laying around while we moved up the hill. We had to watch them to make sure they were dead. Most of the ones I saw must have been there for days, because they were all bloated. I went over to a dead officer who had beautiful boots and a shiny sword, but we had to move. Even though he was dead, taking a souvenir could be fatal. The Japs sometimes booby-trapped bodies.

The next day we continued the attack, but were stopped by mortar fire when we came into a little ravine. Our radioman, Adam was trying to get into a shell hole. I saw him grab his face. There was blood gushing from it. He screamed, "They got me! They got me!"

A corpsman got to him. The tip of his nose had gotten hit, and grabbing his face only made the wound seem worse, especially with the blood running through his fingers. The corpsman told him, "Keep quiet! It's only a scratch!"

After that the fighting settled down for the rest of the day. One thing we always watched out for were huge rocket mortars. We called them "ash cans" because that's what they looked like wobbling through the air. One day I went to fill canteens for some guys and me. I went back to the water tank that was towed by a Jeep, waited my turn, filled my canteen, and then left. I had gotten about two hundred feet when, suddenly, one of those ash cans came down. I was too far away to get hurt by it. Then a second one came in, and when I turned, the Jeep was gone, together with the driver and his assistant. A Marine hollered to me to come into a Jap pillbox our guys had taken. I squeezed myself in there. The Japs dropped two or three more ash cans. After that, we got shelled for a while with mortar rounds.

Nights on Iwo Jima were always unnerving. One night, Pinky and I found ourselves at the bottom of a ravine about sixty feet wide. We had a machinegunner on our left at the top of the ravine. It was about three o'clock in the morning, and it was my turn to watch. One of the machinegunners said, "They're sneaking up!"

I woke up Pinky and told him that Japs were coming. Then we heard some shots. Later we found out that a Jap officer and two of his men had been sneaking along the side of the cliff. The Marine killed them with his rifle and a Jap Nambu pistol he got somewhere. He told us, "I let them get to about seventy-five feet. I killed them with their own gun."

At night we put our ponchos into our holes. The heat from the sulfurous ground warmed the ponchos and kept us warm. The ponchos also kept the fumes out. It cold get very cold at night on Iwo, even though I wore a sweatshirt, a wool shirt, and a jacket. One night, in the rain, a corpsman came around with some brandy. He saw me shivering and said, "Drink this."

I said, "I don't drink."

He said, "Drink this, now!"

I did, and, boy, it warmed me up!

On one rainy night, one of our tanks stopped by my foxhole. The tank commander told me to watch out for Japs who would come up on the blind side of the tanks and stick magnetic mines on them, committing suicide in the process. Then he hollered out from the tank, "I'm going to shoot the .50"

He shot about three or four bursts, which wasn't too bad. Then he shot that 75mm gun and I nearly jumped out of my foxhole. I wasn't expecting him to shoot that thing! He must have let five rounds off. After that he backed up, and that's the last we saw of him.

All of this happened around the east side of Hill 382. Next, my company moved to the south side. I got wounded there, on 26 February. We came up to a ravine that had a little bridge about the width of a Jeep, and we had to go across. Another Marine and I crossed the bridge to watch for Japs who might try and get us in a cross fire. We got up on a ledge about twenty-feet high and fifteen feet wide. Suddenly, my buddy got hit in the left thigh. I cut open his pant leg to see where he was shot, but I didn't know exactly what to do. I hollered for a corpsman. In the meantime, the Japs started throwing hand grenades at us. Eventually one of them hit on top of this ledge and started rolling down. I dove towards it. That put me between the grenade and the wounded Marine. I put my hand my hand over my eyes just as the grenade exploded. I got hit. Three pieces of shrapnel went through my helmet and gave me slight wounds on my head. I was also hit in the hand. I started to say the Hail Mary. A corpsman came running across that bridge. He looked at me and then sent me back over to the battalion aid station. On my way back, I ran into four demolition guys. They told me to stay with them that night.

The sergeant said, "I don't want you in there because it's filled already. There's a shell hole over there."

I said, "Okay."

I went and got into that hole. Shortly afterwards a shell came into the hole I had just left, which was about thirty feet away. It killed two guys and wounded two, one of them in the neck. The next morning I got patched up and went back to my outfit. They had had a counterattack that night. Pinky told me a guy that I came up to the front lines with that first night, John Hall, had been killed during the counterattack.

That day we occupied a lot of open ground filled with shell holes. There was very little digging of foxholes for us. Three of us, a corporal, another rifleman, and myself got in a hole and the lieutenant came over and told us to stay there. We were getting some rifle fire from the Japs. This rifleman with us takes his helmet off and sticks it up where the Japs can see it.

I told him, "You better not fool around. Wherever that guy is, he has a good bead on us. Stay face down here."

The rifleman stuck his helmet up again. Apparently, the Jap had a scope, so he could see that there was nothing underneath the helmet. He must have known that the guy was playing around. The rifleman then stuck his head out and the Jap hit him right between the eyes. Boy, the blood came out thick. I felt sorry for him, but I told him that the Jap had a bead on us. They always told us the Japs couldn't see anything. That was just propaganda.

One day I was helping a machinegunner settle in by bringing up ammo and keeping watch for them. I was on a small ridge and saw a Jap come out from somewhere and head towards a road. He was running when I fired at him. The bullet went between his legs. I brought the rifle up a little and fired again. Again, right between his legs. I fired four rounds at him, but missed. Finally, he dove into a spider hole. I fired at others, and I know I hit them. I never saw them go down, though. They probably jumped into one of the many spider holes that were around.

We came upon a cave and a Marine looked down and could see the Japs. "It looks like they are going to kill themselves."

Then there was an explosion in the cave. A big chunk of human flesh flew in the air and landed beside me. The blast was tremendous. They must have killed themselves with some kind of demolition charge. Just a few minutes before a dud Japanese shell landed near me. I thought if that shell didn't kill me, then that body part could have.

Pinky and I got into a rough situation the day before I got my second wound. We were moving up, and we came upon a Jap pillbox. In front of it were steel reinforcement bars and a small Japanese flag. Jiles said, "I'm getting that flag."

I covered him as he came up on the left of the pillbox with a hand grenade. He threw the grenade but it hit the bars and bounced back. I hollered "The grenade! The grenade!"

He dove for cover and I dove into the nearest depression. The grenade went off but we were all right. He almost got it from his own grenade, trying to get that flag.

I told him, "That was a dumb trick!"

The next day Pinky was not so lucky. He received three letters from home on this day. He was married and had three children. I didn't know how old his children were. He opened two letters and said, "I'm saving this third one for this evening."

He got killed about at eleven o'clock that morning. We started to go back down from the high ground around Hill 382 towards more open, level ground. That morning we found a big rock that offered front and side cover. I had just gotten got up to the rock and Pinky came beside me and said, "No, I want you over there."

I looked at the spot I thought, "You have to be crazy."

He usually had me out further from him, but this place was close to his position. When I got there, mortar rounds came down on us. I got hit in the neck. I looked around, but didn't see anybody. I thought I was the only one who survived. Then I saw Pinky. His left arm was gone, and so was part of his chest. A corpsman came running over. He went to Pinky first, saw that there was nothing he could do, and then he came to me. Blood was running down my chest. He asked, "Are you all right?"

I said, "My back."

He cut through the back of my shirt and said, "There's nothing wrong with your back. You must have fallen on something."

Then he cut down through the front of my jacket and patched me up. Then he called over his walkie-talkie, "I don't care if it is the general, you get that damn stretcher up here!"

I couldn't see Pinky any more because the corpsman stood between me and his body, probably intentionally. I heard someone tell a friend of Pinky's that he had been killed. The friend cracked up, and they had to calm him down and take him to the rear. They gave me morphine to relax me. Finally, the stretchers came up. They put me on one, and then I passed out. When I came to, I saw the stretcher-bearers changing hands. Just as they finished, I heard bullets snapping across me. One of the corpsmen said, "Let's get the hell out of here!"

They ran so fast I thought they were going to drop me out of that stretcher. I passed out again and woke up while they were taking me off of a Jeep at Air Field #2. From there they took me to a field hospital. I saw shining lights and a big opening in a tent. It was the operating room. After the doctors worked on me, they took me out to a DUKW that took the wounded out to a hospital ship. There was a steep, narrow gangway going up to the ship's deck. I thought, "How are they going to get me up there?"

Two sailors carried me up. I was held tightly to my stretcher hoping they wouldn't drop me in the ocean. Then a corpsman came and cut right down my pants, coat, and everything, and then flipped me out onto another stretcher. Then the priest came over, made the Sign of the Cross over, and gave me Absolution and Communion. He must have seen the information on my card, and knew I was Catholic.

They put me in a nice, clean bed. The guy next to me, a husky Italian fellow, started to act up. They had him tied down, but he had free use of his arms. The guy had been hit in the face with grenade fragments, and his face was completely bandaged. It was probably such a bad wound that they had to keep changing the bandages. This guy kept yelling for the police. They had a railing, about an inch wide that went around the top part of the bed and across that was a leather strap, and he managed to break that strap. One of the sailors, a 200-pound nurse, did everything that he could do, but he had to holler for help. They gave the guy a shot. After that they took me to the X-ray section. The doctor told me one of my neck wounds was a sixteenth of an inch from my jugular vein.

They transferred me to another hospital ship, the *Good Samaritan*. I ran into some bad cases there as well. There were soldiers moaning and crying. A lot of then were still in their uniforms, and they hadn't been washed. I learned that the *Good Samaritan* had already made a trip to Guam. That's how I found out I was headed for Guam. My time in battle was over. I felt bad for the other guys who were still fighting, but I was glad to be out of it.

I was on Guam for about three weeks in Hospital 111. They put a tube in my neck, which kept the wound open so that it would heal from the inside out. They asked me to tell them if I spit any blood. If I did, that might mean that some shrapnel had gotten into my lungs. Luckily, none had.

They had a sort of triage system where those with the most severe wounds were taken care of first. I was in the middle of a long ward. As I got better, they moved me down to make room for the badly wounded guys. They wouldn't moan unless they were really bad, and the morphine wasn't enough to ease their pain. I could take only so much of that ward. If they put you in a private room it meant that you were ready to die. One guy moaned all night long in one of those rooms, and then he died in the morning.

My wound was serious enough that they sent me all the way to Pearl Harbor. By then, I could walk around a bit, but I couldn't lift my self up. I had to put my hand behind my head, while someone else lifted me. I had to do the same if I wanted to lie down. I stayed in Pearl Harbor from April until the middle of June before they sent me back to the 4th Division. A lot of guys didn't get to return to there outfits. Fortunately, I did.

When I reported for duty, the Division was back on Maui running training exercises. I looked a little scrawny because I had lost forty pounds. On my first day there, a Ninety-Day-Wonder lieutenant, replacement came to me and said, "If you ever got in battle, you would be the first one killed."

I laughed to myself. He didn't say any more to me. Later, his attitude changed. He must have looked up my record.

Then we shipped out for Okinawa where we trained for the invasion of Japan. The island had been taken at the end of June. They had a mock Japanese set up because they figured we would be fighting in little villages throughout Japan. We never invaded. The Atomic Bomb ended the war. It was like someone lifted a heavy weight from my shoulders.

Back in the States, a couple of us decided that we were going to stay in the Marines. We went to chow and when we came back there was a trailer that had our sea bags on it. An officer came up to us and said, "Get your sea bags! You're getting discharged!"

I said, "If that's the way they want it, then so be it."

I didn't bother seeing whoever was in charge to sign up. I came home on 12 May 1946, Mother's Day, by train and bus. The bus pulled in at a gas station about five houses from where I lived. I looked at my watch and it was ten minutes to midnight. The next day, 13 May, was my birthday, so I walked very slowly to make sure it would be after midnight when I got to the house.

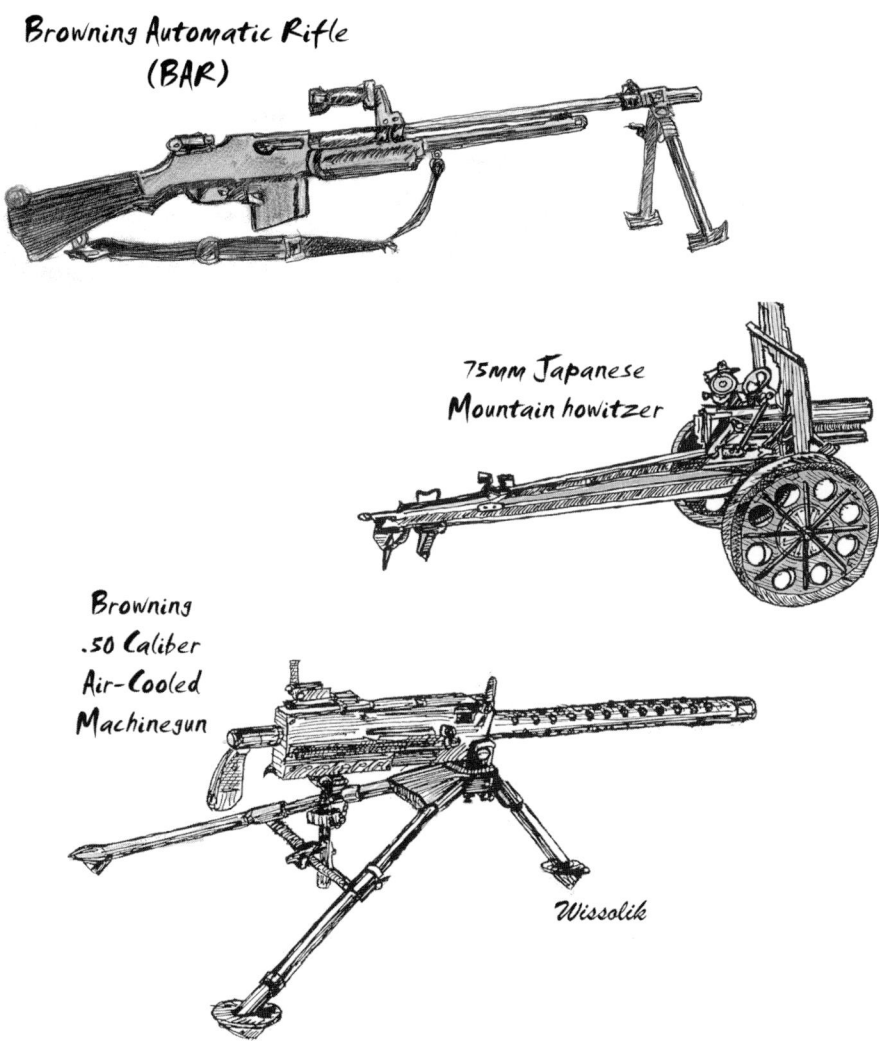

December 1941 Marine Corps recruitment poster. *National Archives.*

"Maggie's Drawers"

Joseph Folino
691st Tank Destroyer Battalion
Wall, Pennsylvania, 1 April 1922

"Many Italians condemned me when I came into contact with them. They said, 'You're Italian! How can you fight your own people?' I replied, 'I am an American soldier, you started the war I didn't, I was sent here.'"

I CALL THE WAR my big adventure, my life's adventure. We had some bad times and we had some good times, too. I am glad I went through it, just to see what it was about, and thank God that I came back. I lost a lot of buddies and they're still buried over there in Luxembourg Cemetery. Some were killed in the Battle of the Bulge, and some in other places. We were all so young then. That's what makes me feel bad. They never came back, all those young men.

I was drafted in April of 1942. I was sent to Fort Meade, Maryland where I was assigned to the First Calvary Division at Fort Riley, Kansas. Fort Riley was a horse cavalry and horse-drawn artillery training camp. That soon changed because we saw that the Germans in North Africa were using horse-drawn artillery and were at a loss after the horses were killed. Soon after we mechanized. The horses remained for ceremonial duties. I was assigned to a new branch in the armored forces, the tank destroyers. We got that idea from the Germans, who employed that kind of weapon with great success.

From Fort Riley, Kansas we were sent to Fort Bliss, Texas as the cadre for the formation of the 691st Tank Destroyer Battalion. From there we were sent to Camp Hood, Texas where we were brought up to full strength. From Camp Hood we were sent to Camp Bowie and from Camp Bowie we were sent to Camp Claiborne, Louisiana. We did most of our training at Camp Claiborne and we took part in the Louisiana maneuvers. After that, we were sent to the California/Arizona maneuvers. Since we were going to go to North Africa, we did some training in the Mojave Desert.

The tank destroyers' motto was, "Seek, Strike, Destroy." Our unit comprised a headquarters company, a recon company, and three line companies, A, B, and C. Each line company had twelve tank destroyers and the recon company had six light tanks. Our job was to destroy, and that's what we did. We destroyed everything, roadblocks, bridges, and any obstacle that could stop the army. We normally weren't attached to any divisions like the other armored units were; anybody that needed tank destroyer support would call on us. We supported the 28th, the 26th, the 80th and the 83rd Infantry Divisions.

My position was gunner. I sighted the gun, so I was the one who did all the damage. In combat, we had artillery observers at high points, and they gave us all the target information. We all used call signs for our tanks, so after you got your gun sighted, you would call in under your call sign. Our call sign was "Con-Tiger 2." We'd radio, "Con-Tiger 2, ready to fire." After we fired, the observer radioed back where our shell hit, then we made adjustments based on his information. We never put the shell in, until we called back to the artillery observer. We did that just in case we might not need to fire. If that was the case, then we didn't want a shell in the gun. Once we locked the breech block it would be hard to remove. We had to pry it out with a bar, and that was dangerous work.

We used different kinds of shells. HVAP (High Velocity Armor Piercing) shells were about ten or twelve inches long. Once it got inside a tank, it exploded. We also had incendiary and phosphorus shells. Once we got those inside buildings, the oxygen in the air ignited the phosphorous. The phosphorous shell could melt steel. It could melt anything. Once we fired on a German tank with a phosphorous round that we had mistakenly loaded into the gun. That was the best thing that could have happened. That phosphorous just spread all over the tank and made it so hot inside the crew couldn't stand it, and they surrendered right away.

We also used a lot of anti-personnel shells, called canister rounds. They were about the size of a juice can and filled with steel balls. We would explode those over enemy troops. The canister rounds had timers. If we wanted a tree burst, we'd set them to explode in the trees. That brought down pieces of wood and the steel balls. If we wanted them to explode on the ground we set the timer for delayed action. A few seconds after they hit, they went off.

We're lucky because we were a little crazy with all those shells. They told us to never put a timer in the shell unless we were going to use it. There was a plug inside them that you took out, then put your timer in. We put the timers in anyway, and the shells would be rolling around on the steel floor. The good Lord must have been with us.

When we went overseas, we landed first in England, and in March 1943, they sent us to North Africa. We got there at the tail end of the fighting in the Sahara Desert, just in time for the battles at the Kasserine Pass and El Alamein. As it turned out, we weren't really prepared for desert fighting. Thank God we had the British to back us up, because they had the experience of desert warfare. The heat was hard on us, and the sand was hard on our equipment.

In the desert water was at a premium, and we had to bring it in tankers. We had no fresh food, just K-Rations. They were terrible, but we had to eat them to survive. We also had some potted meat to eat, and that was really terrible, especially in the 120-degree heat. When you opened the can, you had to press the lid down and turn it over to get the grease out. It was awful! We also drew British rations. The British were great for mutton, because of Australia and New Zealand. It came in a little can and they boiled it before they canned it. The way it smelled they must have cooked it with the hide on! It smelled like kidney, and it was like eating rubber balls. You could eat the stuff once you got it past your nose. The only good ration the British had was tea, and we used to trade them for it. As far as food was concerned, there was one high spot, my twenty-first birthday, when I got cookies from home. My mother made Toll House cookies, wrapped each one in wax paper, and put them in a three-pound coffee can. Then my father soldered the can all the way around. It took a month for the cookies to get to me, and then I had a heck of a time getting the can open. I finally did, and, boy, those cookies were great. They weren't spoiled, at all. I had quite a birthday celebration. I wrote my mother and told her how good those cookies were.

After most of the fighting in North Africa was over, the Army sent us to Libya where we captured a big German air and supply base there. We needed the place as depot for the upcoming Sicilian and Italian invasions. After we took it over it was renamed Wheelus Air Force Base.

When the fight in Africa ended we went on to Sicily. We thought as long as we had the Germans and the Italians on the run that we should keep them on the run. Our unit landed in Agrigento, and from there we took Ragusa, Syracuse and Palermo. We didn't meet much resistance because the Italian Army was fed up with war and a lot of them didn't like Mussolini. Whenever a lot of them had a chance to surrender, they did. Many of them wanted to join the American Army, but weren't allowed to because of something in the Geneva Convention. They helped us out, anyway, by surrendering. The Germans were diehards. One Italian I had dealings with, however, was a real hard case, a fanatic. I learned to speak Italian at home, so I got really good at it. The Army made me an interpreter. I asked this Italian the usual, "name, rank, serial number."

Most of the Italian prisoners would tell me anything I wanted to know, but not this guy. He was a Fascist, and he would say a word, and he started to give me a rough time. I told the captain, "I'm going to make him talk."

"What are you going to do?"

"You leave it to me."

"Okay, Folino!"

I told the MP's, "Put him against the wall and handcuff him."

I had a .45 pistol; I put it on the table. He looked at it and thought I was going to shoot him. I said, "Now are you going to give me your name, rank and serial number."

He nodded, and I put my gun away. He gave me his name rank and serial number. You could see he was a little bit leery, talking about it because he was a Colonel, so he was fairly high up in the ranks and knew a lot. I said in Italian, "Everything is lost, everything you fought for. We're going to help you. We're not going to hurt you."

I kept telling him different things. Finally, he started giving me information. There were some cigarettes on a table, and he asked me if he could have one. I gave him one.

Many Italians condemned me when I first came into contact with them.

They'd say things like, "You're Italian! How can you fight your own people?"

I'd reply, "I am an American soldier. You started the war I didn't. I was sent here."

Even in North Africa where we captured a lot of Italian prisoners, they got mad. "How can you fight your brothers?" Well, it was war, and they were the enemy.

The Sicilian campaign lasted a total of seven weeks. We were spread out pretty thin, trying to cut the Germans off from escaping back into Italy. A lot of them got through, and we knew there would be a big fight there, but not for my unit. Even though we had enough combat points to go home, they sent us to Wales, where we trained new tank destroyer outfits sent from the States. Those new units brought over the M–18 Tank Destroyer. It was on a Sherman chassis, but the top was flat and the sides were beveled so that a shell would bounce off.

Our training in Wales was also in preparation for the invasion of Normandy. At the end of our training as the invasion date neared, we moved to our embarkation point. There they loaded us on the LSTs and we crossed the Channel with the invasion fleet. We didn't go in the battle until six days later, at Utah Beach where it was more level. Even there, the water was high enough to stall the tank engines. The LSTs could get in only so far. The Combat Engineers built Bailey Bridges out to the LSTs, and that's how we got in.

Our orders after we landed were to keep moving until we met resistance, and we didn't have to go too far. The Germans were holed up in hedgerows that surrounded Normandy, and we just couldn't get through. We used flamethrowers on them, but the hedgerows were impenetrable. When we did get past the hedgerows, we ran into the Germans around St. Lô. We had to carpet bomb the place, but before we did, we dropped leaflets advising the civilians to leave. We leveled the place. All that was left standing were a few chimneys. That bombing was called Operation Cobra. Some of the bombs dropped into our own lines and killed a lot of our guys. Even a general, McNair, got killed.

In September 1944 we were on a bivouac in a wooded area outside Nancy, without much to do. The captain allowed us to go into town, but only two at a time. Two guys on each tank had to stay behind in case the vehicles needed attention. I went in with Earl Brenner, a farm boy from Kansas. We never "took" anything. We "liberated" it. Cattle were running loose all over the place, so we "liberated" a cow, and brought her back with us so we could have fresh milk, something we hadn't had all the way across Europe.

The captain asked, "What are you going to do with that cow?"

"We're going to get fresh milk off her."

"You can't do that! You don't know if that cow is sick, or what."

Brenner, the farm boy, said, "It's OK, Captain, as long as you boil the milk."

The captain said, "Well, we better check with the medics."

The medics said it was all right, as long as the milk was boiled.

There was a stream nearby, and we washed that cow in it, got her looking pretty good. We kept her really well groomed. Then we decided we were going to take the cow with us. We had different kinds of trailers, so we started to fix one up for the cow.

The captain said, "You can't do that. We're a combat outfit. What would it look like if we were seen with a cow in one of our trailers? Take her and find a herd you can leave her with."

The captain left. We were out on guard with the cow, thinking about where to take her, when a Jeep pulled up. There was a general in it, but not just any general. It was George S. Patton.

We saluted, and all that, and Patton asked, "What's that cow doing here, soldier? Where did it come from?"

We told the general that the cow just wandered in from somewhere. He asked us where our Command Post was, and we told him. We did the salute stuff again, Patton left, and we radioed to the CP that he was on his way in. In the meantime, we herded the cow down the road and left it loose with some other cows.

While we were gone (this we found out when we got back), Patton said to the captain, "It looks like you are in the cattle business, Captain. Where did that cow back there come from?"

The captain told the general the same thing we did, that it had just wandered into the area. The guys told us that the two talked about something for a few minutes, and Patton started to leave. Suddenly, the driver reversed the Jeep and came back. Patton looked at the captain and said, "Captain, that cow was the cleanest stray cow I ever saw in my life!"

We didn't come back right away, and we learned later that the captain was really worried that our story about the cow didn't jibe with his.

After we got rid of the cow, we made a few stops on the way back. We got back to the bivouac carrying two sacks. Benner's was full of chickens, and mine was full of wine. The captain called us in and said, "What did you say to the general?"

"We told him that the cow had just wandered in."

The captain broke into a big smile. He was relieved that our stories matched up. Then he asked us, "What do you have in the sacks?"

I told him, "Benner has chickens and I have wine. We're going to have fried chicken with wine for our dinner!"

And we did. The Coleman stoves and utensils we had on the vehicles came in handy.

On 9 November 1944, I'll never forget the date, Franklin Roosevelt was elected for a fourth term. Immediately after that election, we were ordered to the Saar River on the boundary of France and Germany and the town of Metz. In those border areas, many French were pro-German and we didn't trust them much. We were moving so fast that we got ahead of our supplies, a lot of which had gone to the British a couple months earlier when Montgomery launched Operation MARKET GARDEN. We were held up at a little town on the French side. We didn't have much to do, so I headed into town with my crew.

One of the guys was Mexican, "Pancho" we called him, a really mischievous type. Pancho looked inside this barbershop and said to us, "Look at those dead Germans in there."

We said, "Yeah. So what?"

It wasn't like we hadn't seen dead Germans before.

"Look," Pancho said. "Let's set them up like they're getting a haircut!"

I said, "How are we going to do that. They're as stiff as a board."

We didn't see a mark on them. They must have been killed by concussion from an artillery shell. The Germans must have dragged them into the barbershop when they left the town.

Anyway, Pancho must have had some experience with dead bodies. He went over to one, stepped on the guy's legs behind the knees, and bent the legs. All we could hear were bones cracking. Then we put the guy in the chair, stood on the tops of his thighs while Pancho straightened up the guy's back. We got a barber's apron, and put that around the guy. Then we stood one German up. He was the "barber." We got the other two, got them into chairs, like they were waiting customers, then put cigarettes in their mouths.

We didn't think much about it at the time. Dead bodies didn't mean much to us, then, I guess. When I think back, I guess that, with all the stress of combat, a soldier's sense of humor gets a little strange.

We finally crossed into Germany. It was a Sunday afternoon in a town called Bitche. We saw people coming, refugees, carrying their belongings on carts and horses. We asked them, "Why are you moving? What's going on?"

They said, "The Boche are coming,"

Immediately that afternoon, we got orders to move out and we kept on the move all night until we got back to the outskirts of Rheims, France, where we got the whole outfit back together. We had been scattered since we were re-supplied the previous September. The next day was 16 December, the day of the Bulge.

Our first mission was to get back to the front immediately. It was snowing, and it was very cold in our open-top tank destroyers. The elements were against us. We had to get trucks and Jeeps to hook cables to us and keep tension on them so we could guide the vehicle in the mud and ice. It was a mess.

We were to go to St. Vith where Company B of the 110th Infantry Regiment was pinned down. Our troops there were in a pocket and the German lines were ahead of that pocket. If they had circled around and encircled our troops they would have cut them off. We went in there and stopped that from happening.

In order to support the 99th Infantry Division, we moved to the town of Elsen and the Elsenborn Ridge. If the Germans had taken that it would have been a straight shot for them into Bastogne. If they'd have come into Bastogne then they would have gone up to Antwerp that would have cut our supplies off so, we were told to save the Elsenborn Ridge at all costs. While we were there, American reinforcements got up to Bastogne. Until then Bastogne was encircled by the Germans. If they wouldn't have sent the reinforcements up, we would have been in deep trouble. Finally, things started to straighten out about 20 December.

Soon after that Patton, ordered a prayer asking God for good weather. Well God must have heard us because Christmas morning was a beautiful day with a blue sky and everything. That morning, in the distance, we heard airplanes. As they came closer, we could tell the sounds were our fighters so, we put out our panels. We had panels, about two feet wide and about six feet long. They were red, blue, green and yellow and we would be told each day which one to fly. We started waving them and the planes tipped their wings. The fighters came first then, the B–26s and A–26s, then the B–17s came in. They bombed the front line continuously, one after the other, the ground just shook from it. That's the thing that broke the German's resistance. Soon after, they pulled back to the Rhine River.

From the Battle of the Bulge we were sent to Luxembourg because we had casualties and we needed equipment. At a little town outside of Luxembourg City we got reinforcements and that's when we were issued new M–36 Tank Destroyers. It was built on the same chassis as the M–18, but it had a 90mm anti-aircraft gun that the Navy used.

After we got our reinforcements and our new tanks, we started to head back into Germany toward the Rhine River. From there we headed into Frankfurt, after we got up to Frankfurt we could see the war was settling down. The Germans had lost a lot of their men and they were using kids as troops. They weren't trained and they would just surrender. They didn't know what else to do. They were just demoralized and scared. We jumped on the Autobahn and headed south.

We were always after German uniforms and other loot. One day we went in this warehouse and we saw these big bales. We cut them open and we were surprised to find American Flags, but not the usual kind. Where the stars should have been, there were white Swastikas. We all took some, but when the officers found out we had them they made us give them up because of morale, and the effect it would have had at home. They put out a general order that if anyone got caught with one of those flags he would face general court martial. We guessed Hitler was so sure he was going to win the war that he had those flags made up. I must have had a dozen of them in my duffle bag, but I burned them. I wasn't about to get a general court martial over a lousy flag.

One day we came upon Buchenwald, hidden behind the trees on the Autobahn. When we got there, we couldn't get in because of big iron gates locked with chains. We broke the chain and got inside, and what we saw sickened us. Inside were sick, pathetic people. When Patton came up, he sent some troops into the town to get the townspeople and bring them to the camp. We made the townspeople bury the bodies.

Even after the fighting ended, there were problems. There were still a lot of diehard Nazis left, and they didn't want to give in. We were fired on by some of them one day. We soon found out where the shots came from. Our company commander dealt with it. He didn't fool around with anyone or anything. We used to get 100-octane gasoline in five-gallon cans for the tanks.

He said, "Go down to the motor pool and get about six or eight cans of gasoline."

When we came back with the gas he said, "Be very careful. Start from the top and douse that place. I'll take care of the rest."

He got some hand grenades and lobbed them in this building, and the place went up in flames. The Burgermeister, the mayor, he came down hollering mad.

Our Commander said, "I am here. I'm running this town, and if some of my men get shot, I'll burn the whole town. These boys have come through the war, and they're not going to get hurt now!"

The Burgermeister got the message real quick. So did any snipers that were still around.

We were in that town until the first week in August, and then we were pulled back to France. We were supposed to go on to the CBI, China, Burma, India Theater because the war in the Pacific was still going. We were sent to Le Havre and got on the train to Marseilles, that's where we were supposed to get a ship to go to India. In the meantime the war ended and they changed our orders and they sent us down to the Riviera; Nice, Toulon, those areas. We didn't care, we were single, young, you know, still full of mischief, that was okay with us. Some of the old timers that had been in since North Africa wanted to go home though. They were getting letters from guys that came in after them, and were sent home before them.

They said, "How come everyone's going home, and we're not going home?" We, the young guys, were living in the lap of luxury, but the old timers wanted to get home to their families. They went and said something to the battalion commander about it, and by Thanksgiving they sent us all home. I landed in Staten Island, New York, and was discharged 19 December 1945.

I brought a lot of stuff home with me. I got a big Swastika flag in Kaiserslauten, Germany, that I took from a Nazi headquarters in a train station. It was hung up outside the building, so I got them to bring the tank in close. I got up on the gun, and the guys elevated it so I could reach the flag. I couldn't pull it off, so I took out my combat knife and cut it down. The flag has a jagged edge because of that. I got a lot of German loot, like helmets. I gave all of that to my son, who is in the insurance business. He has what he calls "The War Room" in one of the conference rooms at his business, and he has my medals, one of my shells, and pictures. I gave him what we called "Maggie's Drawers." They look like a four-foot-wide pair of red underpants. When we were training on the firing range, and if we missed the target, they would wave "Maggie's Drawers." Even if the target would get hit, they'd still wave "Maggie's Drawers," and the guys would fire at it. It's full of holes. When my daughter was in high school, she took "Maggie's Drawers" in for a sewing project. She put lace on the edges, and stitched "Maggie's Drawers" across it. That's also hanging in my son's conference room. He tells everyone that they belonged to an old girl friend of mine.

"All I Got was Some Aspirin."

James A. Forster
2nd Infantry Division
Died October 1990

On 16 December, the Germans broke through the Ardennes Forest, and the Battle of the Bulge began. We were sent to Elsenborn. During our battle there, several men came walking toward us with the heavy olive-drab coats and helmets our troops wore. The one man had a cigarette hanging out of his mouth and he came up to me, never said a word and motioned with his hand, to light his cigarette. I lit his cigarette, and that was it. He and his buddy and maybe four or five others passed going in the opposite direction. I remember asking a buddy of mine, "Why are these guys going in the opposite direction? The fighting's the other way!" After we were told that there were English-speaking Germans posing as American soldiers all through the area, I started to wonder who those guys really were.

THE 2ND INFANTRY DIVISION is the "Indian Head" Division and its nickname is "Second to None." It had a great battle record dating back to World War I, so fighting in France in World War II was not new to them. The 2nd was responsible for the drill song, "Cadence." It went something like, "I had a good home when I left, your right. Sound off, one, two, three, four, cadence count." Of course, the troops made up a lot of verses to it like, "I know a girl who lives on the hill. She won't go but her sister will. Sound off...."

The 2nd Division story started on D+1, 7 June 1944, at Omaha Beach. I arrived there a week later on a British Corvette (Destroyer), and was immediately taken to a hospital that was set up on top of a hill. I had left from England in LST 75–4. I'll never forget those numbers. I had my gear stowed below, but somebody robbed me of my place to sleep. I took my gear up to the bridge and was pretty well along the way of falling asleep. The Channel was calm, and the night was warm. Then the LST was either torpedoed or it hit a mine. Most of the boys in the hold where I was supposed to sleep were killed. I flew down the deck, and my head went through a wooden door up to my shoulder. People say I haven't been right since, but that's a matter of opinion. When I got to a hospital in Brest, I tried to finagle a Purple Heart, but no dice. I hadn't lost any blood, so all I got was some aspirin.

The 2nd got to Paris, but they didn't liberate the city. They stayed on the outskirts while the French went in. We went in later. I was walking down a side street and saw a store that sold pastries. I ran inside, grabbed a berry pie, and wolfed it down. A couple days later, I discovered a warehouse full of German hats and coats lined with bunny fur. They were supposed to be used on the Russian front, but they never got there. I took six hats and six coats and sent them home. I still have one, and I wear it every winter.

We entered Germany on 4 October, crossing the border at the Schnee-Eiffel ten miles west of St. Vith in Belgium. Sixty-eight days passed between October 4 and December 11, and the fighting was heavy. General Eisenhower visited us on 8 November and presented Silver Stars at the forward command post at St. Vith.

On 16 December, the Germans broke through the Ardennes Forest, and the Battle of the Bulge began. We were sent to Elsenborn. During our battle there, several men came walking toward us with the heavy olive-drab coats and helmets our troops wore. The one man had a cigarette hanging out of his mouth and he came up to me, never said a word and motioned with his hand, to light his cigarette. I lit his cigarette, and that was it. He and his buddy and maybe four or five others passed going in the opposite direction. I remember asking a buddy of mine, "Why are these guys going in the opposite direction? The fighting's the other way!" After we were told that there were English-speaking Germans posing as American soldiers all through the area, I started to wonder who those guys really were.

On Christmas Day, we got a hot meal, a turkey dinner, with all the trimmings, but most important, good, hot, strong GI coffee. We knew the Jerries were on the other side of the next hill. They must have known we were being fed. They waited until we all got comfortable, and then they sent some artillery rounds over. I went one way, and the turkey dinner went the other. That was Christmas dinner.

We were on the front line for two months there in the area of the Ardennes, then we were sent back to a staging area in a place called Krinkelt. When I got there, my name was James Arthur Cochran. When they gave us new dog tags, mine said James Arthur Forster. How they got my name wrong, I never found out. Anyway, I just decided to keep the new name. That's how I got to be James Arthur Forster.

We crossed the Rhine River at Remagen. The Ludendorf Bridge was still intact, so all we had to do was walk across. It later collapsed, and the engineers had to construct a new pontoon bridge. As we crossed, what was left of the German air force kept trying to bomb the bridge. I was surprised because they used one of their new jet bombers in the process. What really scared me, though, was their dive-bomber, the Stuka. That thing had a siren on it and it screamed as the plane dove. The engineers put up barrage balloons that were held in place with steel cables. Some of the German planes hit those cables and got demolished.

After we crossed, I got my first good souvenir, a German pistol. We weren't supposed to loot, but most of us did. We billeted in some very expensive chalets along the river. Five of us were in one of them, and we found a floor safe in the living room. We cracked the safe, and I got a solid-gold expansion bracelet and some diamonds, one of which was about a karat and a half. The other was two karats. I got rid of that stuff when I came home. They got twenty-seven hundred dollars on the fence in Houston.

I got leave to the Riviera for a week. I didn't take much money with me, just cigarettes, because they were worth up to $200.00 a carton. If somebody threw a butt onto the sidewalk, ten Frenchmen would dive for it. Those cigarettes paid for a week's room and board. I stayed in a place that had a bath, a living room and a bedroom. I had my breakfast served in my room. It consisted of French fries and horsemeat, and a young lady served it. A carton of cigarettes paid for female companionship and beach equipment for twenty-four hours.

I tried my hand at the roulette table. I went to the cashier's window with cigarettes, and they would give me chips. Within three hours I lost five thousand dollars. I won fifteen hundred at Blackjack, but lost it at another table. Within a period of seven days I had gone through forty-seven cartons of cigarettes.

When I returned I took part in the Weser River crossing. The Germans waited until our boats were in the middle of the river, and then opened up on us. Many didn't make it across. If gunfire didn't kill them, they drowned.

I was wounded in Pilsen, Czechoslovakia. Since I was attached to the Intelligence and Reconnaissance Squad, it was my job to locate the enemy, and then report back to Headquarters. On one of our patrols, somebody up front tripped a "Bouncing Betty mine." I took some shrapnel in my right leg and foot. A Jewish kid carried me back to our lines, a distance of two miles. When we got back, they put me in the hospital.

By the time I got back, the infantry had cleaned out most of the snipers. I ran into a lady who must have weighed four hundred pounds. She gave me a sixty-four-ounce container of beer. I took it from her, sat down on a street corner, and drank the beer. When I finished, I gave her a kiss, and then she went and got me another beer. We stayed in Pilsen another couple weeks, billeted with the local families. They were most interesting, they had beautiful girls, and they had awfully good whisky. I got a chance to go to Prague, the capital of Czechoslovakia. It was there that I saw a Russian soldier whose wrists were tied to a pair of posts, being whipped with something that looked like a cat-o-nine tails. I watched him take six lashes. Every time he got hit, he body made a huge curve. That was one of the more gory things I saw in the war.

I came home on the *Queen Elizabeth*. There were twenty-two thousand passengers on board this boat, twenty thousand were men and two thousand were 2nd Infantry nurses. The Army, of course, had taken every precaution by separating the nurses from the troops with a wall of barbed wire. On the way back, my buddy and I took three-hour turns playing Hearts for a dollar a point. We each cleared over a thousand dollars each. I had thirteen thousand dollars stuffed in my duffle bag, money I had raised by different "business" dealings in Europe. At Fort Meade, the bag got lost in the shuffle, and there I was looking for it in a pile of fifty thousand other bags.

Greeting us in New York Harbor was Marlene Dietrich. She had one leg propped up on the dock exposing a lot of skin. Everyone on that side of the boat had his head sticking out of a porthole. She's waving, and they're waving. The Salvation Army was also waiting for us. Each one of us got a quart of white or chocolate milk.

I spent thirty days at home, and then was forwarded to Camp Swift, Texas, as a

USAFI German instructor. I also interpreted for German POWs who were returning to their homes in Europe. Then the 2nd got transferred to Fort Lewis, Washington. We passed through San Francisco for the Army Day parade on Armed Forces Day. While we were there, there was a riot at the prison on Alcatraz Island. They called the 2nd in to fire several rounds of 105mm howitzer into the prison compound. There was a big spiel in the papers about it. People in San Francisco thought it was terrible that the Army should be shelling Alcatraz because people could get killed!

Eventually, we got to Fort Lewis. One night, a black MP asked a white sergeant to show his weekend pass, which he didn't have. He had his wife with him and was trying to get off the post illegally. The two got into a fight, and the black MP pulled his .45 and shot the sergeant dead. In those days a colored man that did something like that to a white man wasn't around long enough to tell what happened. Within several days three black soldiers were found head down in three GI trashcans behind the major PX.

I was discharged from an Army post near San Francisco. I had travel money, but I decided to hitchhike home. I got on the 52/20 roll for a week, and then got a job at the National Transit Pump Company, on the assembly floor. I went to school at the same time. I don't know how I ended up in a God-forsaken part of Pennsylvania called Fayette County and Green County, but I've been here a long time. I married a local girl and she's been pretty good to me. I've grown several inches around the waist since then which means she's not a half bad cook.

"If I'm Gonna Get Killed, I'm Gonna Get Killed!"

Michael Gates
4th Marine Division, 1st Battalion, 23rd Regiment
Yukon, Pennsylvania, 25 September 1923

"One time we were to clean out a pocket of resistance. Our Lieutenant Walker got wounded in the advance and got pinned down in this big crater that was about twice the size of a house. The Japs were coming up over the crater. I got to the top of the crater with my BAR and I just kept shooting the whole way around it. Some of the Japs I shot fell into the crater. Others were in the crater coming out from holes, or tunnels they had built for protection. I killed everybody that was in that crater. It was like a nest of them. My buddies said I must have been crazy for standing on top of that crater with those Japs. Next to some of the dead Japs you'd find empty bottles of Saki. They were drunk when they got killed. I got the Silver Star for that crater battle."

MIKE BABICH AND I were best friends when we were kids. The day before we joined the service we went to a town picnic and got into a fight with some other guys. I didn't want to go home to my folks because my old man would have given me hell. Mike went to his home, and I slept on my grandmother's front porch.

Mike came by in the morning and said, "Let's go join the Marines!" I was eager to go even though I was only seventeen. A buddy of ours had already joined and we didn't want to be left out of it. So we both started hitch hiking for Connellsville, Pennsylvania, where there was a recruiter. We had a dollar between us. We were able to get two cups of coffee and two donuts with that dollar. I don't know what we were thinking of doing for money once we spent that buck! When we got to the recruiter, we argued about who was going in first. Mike went first, and flunked.

He came out and said, "I didn't pass."

"What are you gonna do?"

"You go in and see if you make it. I'll try joining later on."

I passed, but he never did get into the Marines. He went into the Navy.

When I got home from the recruiter, I told my folks I joined the Marines. My old man was so mad he kicked me in the hind-end, and this and that! My parents had to sign papers so I could get in because I was only seventeen. The old man was really mad at me. But he finally agreed to sign for me.

Before I went into the service, the only job I ever had was on a farm. I was too young to get a job any place else. I guess I wasn't too young for the Marines, though!

I left for the service on 23 July 1942. Someone took me to Greensburg and I got on the train there. We went to boot camp to Parris Island for six to eight weeks. We had a DI who was from Ohio and had played football. He was a rough sonofabitch!

I never shaved before going into the service. I had that peach fuzz. But I caught hell for that when we had inspection.

The DI got in my face and said, "Gates! You didn't shave!"

"No, I just got peach fuzz, sir!"

"Tonight, at five o'clock, be in my office!"

So, I went to his office and he gave me a tooth brush. He said, "At ten o'clock, when the lights go out, you go in the head and I want you to scrub the head with this tooth brush."

Jesus! I scrubbed all night long. Didn't sleep. Five o'clock was reveille and I was still in there scrubbing! He came in there and said, "Are you done, Gates?"

"I don't think so, sir!"

"Drop what you're doing, and fall out with the rest of your platoon!"

So I had to fall out, and I drilled all day without any sleep. He pulled me aside during the day and said, "Tonight, after lights out, you finish that job!"

So I finished it. It took me two days to do that! I started shaving after that! Every morning! I never missed a day!

Training was rough! When I went to Parris Island in 1942 it was all sand. When we'd drill, we'd walk through the sand, and it might be six-inches deep. They'd tell us to stack rifles. We would, and that sonofabitch DI would come up to them and knock those stacks over.

He'd say, "Pick your guns up!"

Then he'd inspect them and say, "Your guns are dirty!"

I said to my buddy, "That sonofabitch!"

There was nothing but sand in the barrels. We had to take them apart, clean them, then he inspected them again. He was something else!

I was always getting into fights. I'll tell you the truth. I'd get drunk and then start fighting someone. I was a private all my life in the Marines. I was a sergeant for a couple of weeks, but then I got drunk and started a fight and they busted me down again. One night I got into a fight with this kid, Ed Lukas. The DI said, "After chow tonight, Gates, you and Lukas come behind the barracks!"

He had a pair of boxing gloves. He made me and Lukas fight. I don't know who won! We fought till we couldn't even move. He wouldn't let us quit. We kept beating each other, beating each other! Oh, Jesus jumps! That night I slept like a log! I'll tell you we got good training. Our DI was a sonofabitch but he was a good trainer. He trained us like we should have been trained for what we would have to face on the islands.

After Parris Island we went to Camp Lejeune in North Carolina, where they were forming regiments for the 4th Marine Division. We had a good captain, Captain Weinstein. He was between twenty-six and thirty years old. He was an old man compared to some of us. Most of us were only seventeen and eighteen. He was a prince, a good officer. He had been a criminal lawyer in Detroit. He taught us how to fight, how to kill or be killed.

We left Camp Lejeune and went to Camp Pendleton to go on maneuvers. They were showing us how to throw hand grenades one day. This one kid pulled the pin to a grenade and went to throw it and that thing blew him apart! He didn't even throw it. He kept it in his hand. When I saw that, Jesus! That's when I started thinking, "Hey, this is gonna happen to me." But when you're young like that and Gung-Ho you don't give a hoot for nothing!

After Camp Pendleton we went to Maui. That was our base camp. We had a good bit of training there, too. Everything's going through your mind at this point. You had guys every night in their bunk with their prayer books. Everybody praying, what's gonna happen? I figured what the heck, if I'm gonna get killed, I'm gonna get killed.

The first island we hit was Roi-Namur. That was nothing. We secured that in a couple of days. I can remember we got off the Higgins boat and ran onto the beach and everything was burning from our ship bombardment and air bombardment. I didn't see one live Japanese when I was there. I only saw dead ones. I didn't even shoot one round! We were only there a week and we boarded ship and went back to Maui where we got replacements. They didn't have nearly the training we had. Hurry up and shove them off, that's what the Marines were doing. We explained a lot of things to those kids. I couldn't tell them much about combat. We hadn't seen much yet, ourselves. These kids were young, we were young, but at least we had more training.

Saipan was our next invasion. Saipan was a bitch! I thought it was worse than Iwo Jima. It took us a long time to secure the island. It took us a week to get to the O1 line, one-thousand yards from the beach. We got hung up fighting in Garapan, a big town on the island. There was a sugar mill in the town that had a big water tower. There was a Japanese observer in it ordering fire down on us. He was radioing up into the mountains where they had their artillery. It took awhile before somebody noticed he was up there and then they blew the tank up. There wasn't much fire after that.

We were stuck around Garapan for over a week. There was street fighting, house to house. It was a pretty nice town. The sidewalks were built out of marble. At night we'd be set up in our holes, and that's when a lot of guys got killed. Japanese would sneak up on them. Once we got to the O1 line, there were Japs all over the place.

I was never thinking about anything, just going straight ahead. Move out! I remember seeing a couple of guys who just froze in their holes when it was time to attack. You couldn't move them, no way, no how! They were that scared. My squad leader was married and had two kids. He was always praying. He got shell shock on Saipan. Finally he went berserk. He started screaming and hollering. We had to knock him down to calm him. I never saw him after that.

One time we were to clean out a pocket of resistance. Our Lieutenant Walker got wounded in the advance and got pinned down in this big crater that was about twice the size of a house. The Japs were coming up over the crater. I got to the top of the crater with my BAR and I just kept shooting the whole way around it. Some of the Japs I shot fell into the crater. Others were in the crater coming out from holes, or tunnels they had built for protection. I killed everybody that was in that crater. It was like a nest of them. My buddies said I must have been crazy for standing on top of that crater with those Japs. Next to some of the dead Japs you'd find empty bottles of Saki. They were drunk when they got killed. I got the Silver Star for that crater battle.

There was a little baby in that crater that was still alive. I picked it up and saw it must have been a couple of weeks old. I don't know where it came from. I took it out and took it to the sick bay. I told the doctor that I wanted to keep it!

There were a lot of civilians on Saipan. Toward the end of the battle a lot of them committed suicide by jumping off this cliff. I saw their bodies splattered all over the place at the bottom of that cliff. That was terrible! We were able to convince some of them not to jump. Some Japanese soldiers committed suicide by jumping off that cliff. Others we were able to capture. We put them in a prison camp next to this lake.

They called us back for a short rest. The army was taking over our positions. We caught a pig and a chicken and started roasting them.

The captain came around and said, "Okay, boys we got to move up. The army's losing ground."

So we left our pig and chicken. I don't know what happened to them. Someone ate pretty good!

On our way up to the line we caught a Japanese hiding in a cave. He spoke a little English, too.

He said, "Me don't want to die! Me truck driver!"

We got a hold of a wooden ox cart, put our extra ammo in it and made him lug that cart up after us. At night we would tie him to the cart so he wouldn't try to sneak away. We called him, "Ox." I don't know what happened to him.

We got to the top of this mountain and these villagers came out and they were happy to see us, not like the others who killed themselves. They said that the Japanese took everything from them.

During lulls in the fighting, guys always collected souvenirs. I got two Jap swords. I strapped them on my back. I sold one to a Marine Corsair pilot.

He asked, "How much do you want for it?"

"What good is money here?"

"How about some whiskey?"

"Okay!"

He came back later with five fifths of whiskey, so I gave him the sword.

I picked up everything along the way. Swords, money, bayonets, pistols, wrist watches. There was one guy in my outfit who carried a pair of pliers with him. Every dead Jap he'd see who had gold teeth he'd pull them out!

There was a strait between Saipan and Tinian. We went straight from the battle for Saipan to take Tinian. We went in on the Higgins boats and ran into this coral reef. We got off the coral reef, and hit the beach. They said the Japs were gonna counterattack that night. We got ready. We set up machineguns, BARs, artillery. Sure enough they attacked at three in the morning. Out of the dark you heard this singing and hollering and screaming. You heard cries of, "Banzai!" There were flares in the sky that we sent up to light up the area. And there they were all lined up for us. They kept coming. I fired my BAR a lot that night. Twenty rounds a clip. I think we killed every one of them. I still don't feel bad for having killed them, because if I hadn't I would have been dead. That's the way they taught us. Kill or be killed. I saw a lot of Japs falling in front of my fire. Maybe twenty, maybe fifty or more. You don't have time to count. The BAR was good for massed fire like that. It wasn't a single-shot weapon. There were only two guys in my company that could fire a single round from a BAR, me and this other kid, Johnny Weeks. That thing had a bipod on it that weighed nearly as much as the gun. I threw that bipod away on Roi-Namur!

There was a kid with us named Ozbourne, from Illinois. He went to throw a grenade into a cave when there was an explosion. The blast hurt a couple of guys. Ozbourne couldn't throw the grenade, so he just fell on it. It blew him apart, but he saved the rest of the guys. He got a Medal of Honor for that.

That was the worst time we had on Tinian. After that we didn't have any trouble securing the island. It only took about ten days after that.

While I was on Tinian, me and this goofy guy from California, Pettit, stole two bicycles. We were riding around one day through this area where there were a lot of shattered trees, cut down because of all the firing from the battle. All of a sudden some Japs started shooting at us from some place in those trees! They were leftovers from the battle. We got the hell outta there!

After we secured Tinian, they had showers set up for us on the island, big barrels full of water. Everybody got the crabs after we showered. They gave us clean clothes and hot chow. Beef stew in these big garbage cans. That's how they cooked it up.

They sent us back to Maui, and we got more replacements. We needed them because we started out with 240 guys, and I think by that point we only had eighty left. I had gone through those three campaigns without a scratch, too. Iwo Jima would be a different story for me.

The 23rd Regiment went in on Yellow Beach at Iwo Jima on 19 February 1945, at eight in the morning. I was one of the first men off the Higgins boat. The guys with the BAR usually are. We got on to the beach and the sand was so deep you couldn't run. They were firing at us the whole way. There were no pill boxes on the beach, but we were getting all this fire from Mount Suribachi. Guys were getting killed left and right. The Japs were using this huge rocket-mortar. We called them ashcan because that's what the round looked like when it was in the air. They'd come flopping in and make giant craters.

I remember running up the beach, and I ran past this crater. It had ten or eleven guys in it. A large artillery shell landed right in there and every one of those guys was blown to bits. You saw what was left of them flying into the air. I believe a company commander was in that hole with those guys. We lost a lot of officers.

Iwo Jima was made up of sulfur ash because the island was volcanic. When we dug foxholes, they would be warm. It was cold at night, and it was nice getting into those holes we dug. The Japs fired on us all night long. Flares were popping up in the sky. It was weird. We weren't allowed to fire at night because it could give our position away.

The 01 line on Iwo was Airfield Number One. It was real rough till we got up there. The Japs had spider holes. You'd walk past those holes and they'd climb out and shoot you from behind. We had to check every cave or hole in the ground. I was wounded at the airfield. A buddy and I had our foxhole set up, and I had just gone to get some water in a five-gallon can, but the water was black with filth. A little while later, a Marine truck came by. It had cases of juice on it. I told my buddy, "I'm gonna get a whole goddamn case of that!"

The truck started to take off, but I ran up behind it, jumped on, got a case of it up on my shoulder and jumped off again. I was running back to the fox hole when a Jap sniper took a shot at me. The bullet creased my cheek and pierced my left ear. It knocked me cold! A fraction more, and that would have been it for me! The scars are still there. Al Pettit, the medic, came by, and he wrapped my head in bandages, then gave me two shots of brandy. I got sent down to the aid station, and from there they sent me out to a hospital ship. The doctor on the ship asked me where I was from.

I said, "Pennsylvania."

"What part of Pennsylvania."

When you're from western Pennsylvania, it was easy to just say Pittsburgh.

I said, "Pittsburgh."

"What part of Pittsburgh."

"You ever hear of Greensburg?"

"Hell, yeah, I'm from Jeannette!"

"I'm from Yukon!"

Then he asked, "What's your name?"

So I told him. Then he put "Stateside" on my jacket. I was on that ship for a day or two. My section of the ship was filled with guys who had been burned up in their tanks, burned from their heads to their toes, legs off, arms off. Jesus! That's why they took us walking wounded off the hospital ship onto a transport. They shipped us to Pearl Harbor, but there was no room in their hospital. So they shipped us to Oak Knoll, California. Then they made an announcement, "All the men from the east coast will be shipped to Chelsea, Massachusetts."

They put us on a train, and it took us five days to get there. It took a good while for my wound to heal. They took good care of us there. The doctors and nurses were great. I was in the eye, ear and nose section of Chelsea. There were guys there that were shot up pretty bad. There was one guy who had been shot through his jaw. He had pins in his jaw holding everything together. A lot of guys said if you ever find me all shot up, just finish me off. I don't know if I could have done that. I know I would have wanted to die, too, if I was like that. My wound wasn't as bad as some of those guys. I had some hearing loss from my wound. And for a while I'd get headaches really bad. I had to buy hearing aids, and I never got a pension for that.

I was in the hospital when the war with Japan ended. There was a big parade in Boston, which wasn't too far from Chelsea. Horns were blowing, people were cheering, everybody was happy. The war's over!

I was in the hospital from March to 6 September 1945, the day I got discharged. I got a big pay out of that, and I couldn't wait to get home. I got off the train in Greensburg. The only one who had a phone in Yukon at that time was a local garage. I called the owner and he came and got me. Before he hung up, he asked me if I could walk, because my parents wanted to know. Jesus! Before he came to get me, he told my parents that I could walk and talk. They were waiting for me when I got home. When I got back, I kissed the ground.

"Butch! Where Are You?"

Hubert "Butch" Gower
5th Marine Division; Greensburg, Pennsylvania, 23 November 1923

"My real introduction to the Marine Corps happened on the parade ground. We were lined up and the DI came up. He was all man. He tapered exactly four inches from his shoulders to his waist. Under his arm was his swagger stick, two thirds of a billiard cue. He walked up to us and said, 'Ha, I never saw a more ragged-assed bunch of ragged-assed militia in my life. You people are feather merchants, yard birds. I can whip any one of you, any one of you I can whip. If you think I can't, and if I can't, I got a friend down the way that can help me out. Sell your soul to God because your ass belongs to me. You're going to do what I want you to and you're going to do it, so you may as well do it and like it.'"

I WENT TO THE SERVICE on 1 June 1944. It was peculiar. I was working at the Elliot Company making Navy lighting equipment for the lights aboard ship and the company told me they could only keep me another six months in order to keep me out of the Draft. Even though I was twenty, married and the father of two sons, I was still cannon fodder. I figured I might as well enlist and get the branch of service I wanted. I went to the Latrobe induction center and told them I would like voluntary enlistment in the Navy.

I went to Pittsburgh to be examined by the Navy prior to induction. I passed all the tests, and I was standing in the hall with 149 other young men. Around two in the afternoon, three Marine Corps sergeants, recruiting officers, came in and one of them said, "We are authorized to take 10% of you and we want fifteen volunteers for the Marine Corps."

Only one of us stepped forward. The recruiter said, 'Okay, then, I'll pick the other fourteen. You, you, you..." I was a sturdy-looking chap about 210 pounds, five-feet-ten-and-a-half inches, and he picked me.

I said, "Sir, I voluntarily enlisted in the Navy."

He said, "Keep you bowels open, and your mouth shut."

Then he said, "Okay, the young man who volunteered, then the big mouth, then the other thirteen of you, step forward!"

I remember that I hated him, instantly.

They marched us down the hall, enlisted us into the Marine Corps, then discharged us from the Navy, so we wouldn't be free in between and said, "Be back here at ten o'clock tonight. You're on your way to the San Diego Recruit Depot, San Diego, California."

I didn't get home to see my dad or my kiddies. Right at ten o'clock I caught the train at the Pennsylvania Station in Pittsburgh and I was on my way. The train already had some men on it, and we picked up more along the way. There were 500 of us by the time we got to San Diego. It was eight o'clock at night, and it was raining. I saw a sergeant. I never saw so many stripes in my life. It looked like he had stripes from his shoulder to his knee.

They put us in cattle cars that had slotted sides and hauled us down to the recruit depot in San Diego and found us a place to sleep. They told us, "Tomorrow morning, we get to work."

The next morning they got us up quite early and gave us some chow. Then they took down our personal history and gave us our clothing issue — two pair of dungarees, two dungaree shirts, six pairs of green under shorts, six green T-shirts, six pair of green socks, two pair of combat shoes, one pair of dress shoes, two pair of suntans, two shirts, two field scarves or neckties, pith helmets, a ten-quart bucket, a brush, cake of laundry soap, face soap, shaving cream, and this all came out of our first pay! The bucket and brush were to be used to launder our clothes. After that, they marched us over to a barber. He said to me, "How do you like your hair."

I told him.

He said, "Okay. Hold out your hands."

I did, and, zip! I was bald!

The next day we got sea bags, a couple of sheets and blankets. Then we started to train. I was lucky. I had been in the National Guard, so I became a squad leader.

My real introduction to the Marine Corps happened on the parade ground. We were lined up and the DI came up. He was all man. He tapered exactly four inches from his shoulders to his waist. Under his arm was his swagger stick, two thirds of a billiard cue. He walked up to us and said, "Ha, I never saw a more ragged-assed bunch of ragged-assed militia in my life. You people are feather merchants, yard birds. I can whip any one of you, any one of you I can whip. If you think I can't, and if I can't, I got a friend down the way that can help me out. Sell your soul to God because your ass belongs to me. You're going to do what I want you to and you're *going* to do it, so you may as well do it and like it."

The next day, he started teaching us how to march, and it wasn't easy. We had one recruit we called "Colonel Doom." The guys who knew him swore he had been a cook in a logging camp in the Arkansas mountains. They said the only way they got him was that he came down from the mountain twice a year to get clothes and stuff. On one of those occasions they got him and packed him off to the Corps. He wouldn't bathe, wouldn't wash his clothes, and he couldn't march. Everyday after work we had to take a shower. The DI stood at the door with a clipboard and checked off our names. One time we gave him a wink and told him to disappear for awhile. He did. We got a bucket half full of sand and water, took a scrub brush, pinned Colonel Doom down, and gave him a bath. We took all the hide off his back and legs. He got put in the hospital for three days, but he smelled better! He just wasn't with it. Eventually he got a Section Eight, and went home. Maybe he was smarter than we thought he was!

The rest of us learned to march. The parade ground in San Diego was a mile and a quarter. Part of it was asphalt, the other part was sand. Hot! There was a poem:

> *He was trained at San Diego,*
> *The land that God forgot,*
> *Where the sand is fourteen-inches deep,*
> *And the sun is always hot.*
> *When I get to heaven,*
> *To Saint Peter I will tell:*
> *"Another Marine reporting, Sir,*
> *I've done my time in hell."*

We came down to the parade ground one morning. Sergeant Wylie was being a special bastard. He gave us the manual of the rifle, left shoulder, right shoulder, port, so forth. They were supposed to make a slapping sound. Wylie said, "You people are a little bit weak this morning, so we'll have to get you squared away. Platoon halt, left face, open ranks, stack rifles."

So we stacked them up, four together. There were stacking clips up on the ends. You hooked them together so they wouldn't fall. Wylie said, "All right, gentlemen, down on your knees, pound the asphalt with your hands."

So we pounded that asphalt with our hands until we drew blood.

Wylie said, "Do you think you can hit 'em now."

"Yes, Sir!"

"I can't hear you."

"YES, SIR!."

"Okay, Gentlemen, on your feet, close ranks, secure weapons, right shoulder arms.

WAP! WAP! I mean we really hit them.

He said, "That's getting a little better gentlemen."

Everybody graduated, and then we went to different outfits. Some went to Sea School, some went to Air School, and so on. The majority went to "Grunt School," which were the "Ground Pounders," the "Sand Stompers," in other words, the infantry. I went to a casual company because I was in the National Guard and the National Guard was dragging its feet about giving me my discharge. Until I got that I was a "casual." They knew I was something, but they didn't know what. I became a "Butt Sniper" for a couple days, and it was degrading as hell. I got laughed at. Butt snipers picked up cigarette butts, paper, and cleaned ditches and latrines.

Finally, I got lucky. I got a job as the company colonel's orderly. He liked me for some reason. I chauffeured him around for a while, or drove his wife and daughter shopping. What an enviable task. He had a daughter that was ugly as sin. You'd have to have two sacks to cover her head. She must have been born ugly, and gotten progressively worse. His wife was nice enough.

When the Guard discharged me, I went to Tent Camp Two at Rancho Santa Margaretta in Oceanside, California, which was the base of Camp Joseph H. Pendleton. Pendleton Camp was created out of a working ranch, the Tommy O'Neill Ranch. It was nearly seventy-thousand acres, and it had a tank-training area, an artillery range, two airfields, and a hospital.

We went to rifle range at La Jolla, California. I had a lot of fun there. I liked shooting. I came back and they said, "Well, boys, you're going overseas. They're forming the Fifth Marine Division in Hawaii. They have a plan for you. We can't tell you where, but they have something in mind for you."

On 23 November 1944, my twenty-first birthday, we were on board a Dutch ship, ready to cast off. The ship was carrying a Navy gun crew, the Army ran it, and it was carrying nurses and marines. If that wasn't messed up! It was great fun. I ate salt crackers because a guy told me they would keep my stomach dry and I wouldn't get seasick. It worked. But a lot of guys did, mostly because of me. I'd go down to the mess hall, get a big piece of fat bacon, tie it on a string, and drag it around on deck. As soon as guys saw the bacon, BRAWWW!, they'd puke. I was evil.

They had secured the nurses behind a wire fence to protect them, or us, I didn't know which. Around five o'clock in the afternoon, the nurses would go to the showers, and they were very inconsiderate in their dress. In fact, they were mostly naked, with only their essential parts covered, and I saw many a naked fanny down the hallway to their rooms.

I went to shore at Iwo Jima as a 27th Replacement with the 5th Shore Party Battalion. Our job was to unload ammunition, and then load the wounded that were lying on the shore for transfer to a hospital ship. Medics (corpsmen) were busy with their stretchers, getting the wounded down to the beach. The ships lay anywhere from one to two miles out in the ocean, outside the range of enemy artillery. Iwo was volcanic sand, and it was like being in a steam bath. The sand was ankle deep, and you couldn't dig a foxhole without supporting it with sandbags. The hole would quickly fill in with sand. It rained every day.

We put down porous planking, pieces of steel about an eighth-of-an-inch thick, ten or twelve feet long, and got tanks in over those. We also got our flamethrowers, rocket trucks and other heavy equipment ashore the same way. The Japs hated our flame-thrower guys, and they hated the rockets. We used them anyway.

We got ready for the night by digging in around five o'clock in the evening. We made our holes long enough so that we could sit down and stretch our legs, and wide enough so that a guy could sit at each end. The guy in the rear watched while the other guy slept, if he could. I went for days without sleeping. The stench from human excrement and rotting bodies was terrible. We were hungry, we were thirsty, we were exhausted, and we were filthy. We never got out of our holes after dark, never, never. It wasn't because we feared the Japs so much, but anybody outside his hole at night would automatically be considered an infiltrating enemy, and he would get shot. It was as simple as that. If we had to relieve ourselves, we used our holes.

There was no natural water. We filled our canteens out of a barrel that might have been sitting there for ninety days. Each evening we got two boxes of C-Rations, a quart of water out of the barrel. Most evenings we got a can of some kind of fruit juice that we split with our buddies. We got as much ammunition as we wanted.

I was a BAR man. I carried nine clips, and my buddy carried eighteen. Each clip held twenty rounds. My BAR was a particular bitch. It wouldn't fire with twenty rounds in it, so I had to load only nineteen. I found that out real quick. I lay in that hole at night watching artillery fall. I thought, "Good Lord, distribute that stuff like you do Marine pay. Give the officers the most. Lord, if you can't help me, please don't help the Japs."

The Jap soldier was a good soldier. He was brave, and he was a good rifleman. But he was stupid a lot of the time, and he seemed to have had poor leadership. He also seemed to lack imagination, especially when groups of them would be on their own without an officer. We had frontal attacks at night. They'd come in all drunked-up on Saki, yelling "*Banzai, Banzai!*" We'd cut them down. Their bodies would pile up like you wouldn't believe, and then they'd fall back and reorganize, and come right up again over their own dead. We'd always be ready. I couldn't miss. I'd be blazing away like crazy. They would do that two or three times before they got the message. We dug trenches and pushed the Jap dead in with bulldozers and covered them up. We didn't want to risk disease from decaying flesh.

On Iwo at night they kept the lines straight across the island for a purpose. All our outlying ships knew where the lines were, and their gunners would fire illumination flares into the island based on coordinates.. At night they'd use a one minute flare. They looked like Fourth of July fireworks. They'd fire them every forty-five seconds so that there would be a fifteen-second overlap. We could see the enemy in the light, but they couldn't see us. All night long there was this unnatural light from the flares. It never got really dark. If the Japs attacked, word would go to the ships to double the flares, then the place would light up like downtown in a city. Then the rockets would come in, CHOO, CHOO, CHOO! Then the artillery. We'd let go with rifles, grenades, flame-throwers. Noise, noise, noise, stink, dirt, filth. You can't imagine! I wouldn't change the experience for a million bucks, but I wouldn't do it again. I don't think so, anyway.

Of course, even if they couldn't see us at night, they knew where we were because they watched us digging in. Occasionally, infiltrators came in, and we'd use our knives on them. We weren't supposed to use our rifles on them.

In the morning, we'd get out of our holes, stand up, take two steps, and then dive and roll. We knew that he knew where we were, and there were snipers. Before we went into the line, we got a shot of Green River whiskey that we were supposed to drink in case of shock. I always thought, "God, I might be killed and not get a chance to drink that." Everyone else probably thought the same. Within the first mile toward combat, everybody drank his whiskey. We also got gas masks, and all of us threw them away. Guys in a truck usually followed to pick up the discarded masks.

For the Japs, death was an honorable thing. They died for their Emperor, but I think he could've cared less. We gave a lot of them the chance to be honorable. Our skipper told us, "You know, there's no use of you taking a prisoner because invariably he'll have went to USC (University of Southern California). He can probably speak better English than you can. The only thing he knows is clean clothes and hot food. You've got to risk your life taking him, and you've got to risk your life getting him back here. He won't talk. You're left out in the wet, and he's in the dry, and, sooner or later, you're going to get ticked off and shoot him anyhow, so you might as well shoot him when you see him."

I never saw the Jap who shot me. There was a ravine with a platoon of Japs hiding in holes dug into the sides. We didn't have any more grenades, and my sergeant said, "Butch, you know where the stockpile is. How about going back and getting some more grenades."

I got to the stockpile. There was an empty sack there, and I put about thirty grenades in that, and stuffed another fifteen or so inside my shirt. I had just gotten back to the company when, BANG, I got hit. The guys spotted him, eventually. He had gone over to the reverse slope, and dug himself a hole then covered it, leaving just enough of an opening to shoot through. He didn't have much traverse, and just waited there until someone came into his line of sight. He had already killed one of our guys, and wounded another.

When I got hit, I rolled down into the ravine and crawled back in a hole. I heard someone holler, "Butch! Where are you?"

"Over here," I managed to answer.

"Come on out here where I can take a look at you."

Imagine what I looked like. Forty-two days without a bath. Forty-two days of beard. Blood squirted across my face from a hole in my shoulder. My arm just hung there. It was a corpsman that called. He came to me and cut away my shirt, and taped my arm.

"Hold still," he said, and gave me a shot of Morphine. He drew an "M" on my forehead and said, "You're going home! You're going to make it!"

"How do you know?"

"I just know."

"That's great!" I said.

He said, "Can you find the aid station?"

"I think so. I know where it's at."

"Well, we got a man here who was creased along the head, and he can't see. Will you help him?"

"Yeah. We'll make it."

My buddy came up and said, "We got the Jap who shot you, Butch. We fired a rifle grenade at him. He's still in there, in chunks!"

I got back to the first aid station. We had a Roman Catholic priest with our outfit and everybody called him "Holy Joe" or "Padre" or whatever name they could think of. He was a nice enough guy. "Are you Catholic, Son," he asked.

"No. Why, do I have to be?"

"No. Do you mind if I say a few words?"

"I don't mind. I can use all the help I can get."

So he flipped some kind of purple thing around his neck and gave me the whole ball of wax in Latin. I didn't understand, but he was trying to do me some good. I was thankful for that. I started shivering and he said, "Are you cold?"

"Yeah, I am cold."

"I've got something for that."

He went into his bag and came out with a fifth of Green River whiskey, the same kind the Marines gave us. "Here take a belt of this."

I wasn't supposed to drink alcohol because of the Morphine, but I took a healthy belt, anyway.

Our colonel came up in a Jeep. "How you men doing?" he asked.

I answered, "I'm doing pretty good. My buddy here, I think he's going to make it. I think we're a couple of lucky boys."

The corpsman said,, "Sir. would you give these two men a ride back to Division?"

He said, "Absolutely!"

I started to get in the back seat. The colonel said, "You only have one good hand there, Jar Head. You just sit still. I'll ride in back. You ride in the cat-bird seat, today. Tomorrow, I ride there, and you don't ride you walk. But today you ride in the cat-bird seat."

I said, "Aye, Aye, Sir!"

Back at Division, Captain Sharpe said, "We're sending you out to the hospital ship *USS Solace*."

They put me on a DUKW. The driver was a black guy, the first I had seen in combat. The rest served in the mess. The driver said, "Y'all lay still."

Hell! I couldn't move, anyway. They had me strapped to the stretcher and the stretcher to the "Duck." The ship was about a mile-and-a-half away. We pulled alongside. They dropped a cable with four leather straps with loops on the ends. They put a loop over each corner of the stretcher and up I went. When I got topside, they put me on a gurney.

The hospital ship was a converted pleasure liner, and there were fifteen hundred wounded aboard. It was a huge ship, painted white, and it had a green band painted around it and an illuminated green cross on the side. It was a complete hospital. They wheeled me into a room. A nurse came up and said, "Okay, Marine, I have to give you a bath."

After forty-two days on the island, I had to stink. The nurse took off my shoes, and my socks fell apart in little pieces. Then she cut off my pants. I lay there stark naked, like a newborn baby. She washed me fore and aft, athwart ships, all decks and ladders!

Her name was Miss Bianci, from San Francisco. She was an awfully nice person. When I would be in the head (toilet), she'd knock on the door and say, "All right boy, pull' em up. I'm coming in."

She'd come in with her needle. Jab, jab, jab. I got it in the rump every three hours.

There was a guy in my ward who had lost his right arm. He was a musician in civilian life, and I figured his career was over. He kept moaning and groaning, moaning and groaning. There was another guy there who had lost an arm and both legs. He said to the musician, "Why the hell don't you shut up! You're not hurt that bad."

On our way to Guam and the hospital, I walked the decks at night and worry.

All I could see was water from horizon to horizon. I worried about Jap submarines. They weren't going to give a damn about the green cross on the ship. I wasn't much of a swimmer, even though the Marines tried to teach me, and I made sure that I had a life preserver with me at all times.

We got to Guam, and I remained in the hospital there for around fifteen days. They found a piece of metal in my shoulder, and sent me to the OR. I had to wait. There were more serious cases. They told me that they left another piece in.

The dear old Red Cross gave us each a razor, and then they took the cost of it out of our pay!

It was April, and one day an announcement came over the loudspeaker, "Now hear this, Mate, now hear this. Franklin Delano Roosevelt passes away today in Hot Springs, Georgia. All hands turn to for a moment of silence for our Commander in Chief."

The announcement crushed me. I couldn't talk. Most of us cried.

They sent us on to Honolulu on a converted freighter. We were supposed to sleep in the hold deck, but we couldn't. We were up on deck for all hours of the night. I made friends with a Turk ("Harry" we called him, but his name was something like "Hairtoon") who was reputed to be the best fudge maker in the whole Navy. He was always asking for sugar so he could make fudge.

We had a sub scare one night, and they tied the safety valves down. We could only do seven knots. We couldn't have outrun a rowboat. We got back to Pearl Harbor safely, and went to the hospital. After a while I got a week, free, at the Royal Hawaiian Hotel.

At the rest camp at Kokokahia, I got a job cleaning up mangoes that had fallen from the trees near the library. In addition to that, I had to straighten up the cushions and magazines in the library. I had to do that in the morning and the afternoon. Then I was on my own. We were on the honor system and they didn't do much roll call, except for spot checks. Only a couple guys went AWOL. They brought in nurses from the Army, Navy and Marines for dances on Saturday nights. We called the Marine nurses BAMS, or "Broad-Assed Marines." They called us HAMS, or "Hairy-Assed Marines." The chow was great. We had a cook who had worked at the Waldorf-Astoria.

We salvaged an old car, and repaired it with stolen parts. We had to have a seven-digit registration number, and we stole that as well. We went into town and took the last number from each of seven Navy Jeeps. We got caught, and they took the numbers away. We went downtown again and stole seven more

They sent me back to Pearl where they put me on temporary duty as a Military Policeman. I got the worst neighborhood in Honolulu — North King, Canyon Canal, and Water Street. There was a canal that came right down the middle of the city, and we found dead people in there every day. There would be fights in the bars, people got stabbed and then thrown into the canal.

I got healed, and then got ready to invade Japan with the 5th Division. In the meantime, mother had a stroke, and I came home instead. After that, they sent me to Treasure Island in San Francisco, where I ran into a sergeant major I knew.

"Butch! Where are you going?"

"I'm going back to the Pacific."

"Why?"

"Because that's what my orders say."

"Butch, you have more than enough points for discharge."

"I know that. You know that. Other people know that. But there's men with more points than me and they have priority."

A guy had to have 105 points, so many for combat, so many for marriage, so many for each child. I had 120. The sergeant major said, "Butch, I'll see what I can do."

While I waited for transportation back to Honolulu, they put me in a casual company. They gave me a rifle and ten Italian POWs to guard. I had them mowing grass, sniping butts, things like that. I had orders to shoot to kill if any of them tried to escape. None of them did. They had a better life as POWS on the West Coast than they ever had in Mussolini's army.

One day the sergeant major called me in and said, "Hey, Butch! You're not going back to the Pacific."

"How'd you manage that?"

"I wrote a letter, made a phone call or two, and I know a person or two, and you're on the list and I'm going to send you back to Maryland, to a Naval Air Station there. That's where they are discharging people from the East Coast. You're the senior man so I'm going to send about eight men with you. You and eight men, and they'll give you train tickets, vouchers for eats, transfers and whatever you need."

In Maryland, in December 1945, I went to see the captain. I knocked on his door.

"Hit the hatch," he yelled.

"Private First Class Gower has a request for the captain. Requesting ten days furlough, Sir. I have thirty-five days on the books, Sir, and would like to have ten of them, Sir."

"Why do you want a furlough?"

"Sir, I'd like to go hunting with my dad and brothers."

"Don't you know there's a war on?"

"Sir, the war's over, Sir."

"Get out of here. Goodnight. About face."

"Aye, aye, Sir."

So I left his office. There was a sergeant major there named Olds. "What's the matter, Butch?" he asked.

"The captain turned me down."

"Do you really want that furlough?"

"I sure do!"

"Okay. Go down and see this lady at the Red Cross. She doesn't like that captain worth a damn. She'll get you the furlough."

I did. In the afternoon, the guy who sat outside the captain's door and ran his errands for him, came up to me and told me the captain wanted to see me, and that I should look sharp. I hurried up and shined my shoes, made sure that all the seams were straight and sharp, made sure I was shaved, and went up. I knocked on the door. When I got into his office, the captain inspected me. He made me lift my feet and checked for dirt. He took a match out of his pocket and put it against my head to make sure my hair didn't cover it.

He stepped back, looked at me, and said, "You had to be a smart-ass? O.K. I'm going to give you your furlough. I don't have much choice. Ten days! Not ten days, one hour; not ten days and a half hour; not ten days and five minutes: not ten days and one minute. TEN DAYS!"

"Aye, Sir, thank you."

"Don't thank me. Thank that f—ing Red Cross lady."

"Yes, Sir!"

"About face. Hit the hatch!"

This all happened on a Friday. I find the sergeant major. He said, "Hey, Butch, I'm dating this furlough starting Monday morning."

"What'll I do? Run around here?"

"No, no, no, no! Get the hell out of here. You're entitled to a three-day pass. I'll make you a pass from four o'clock this afternoon until seven o'clock Monday morning, and I'm giving you a duplicate. Monday morning at seven o'clock you eat this thing. I don't want any trace of it. I'll file the original when I come in Monday morning to show that you came back."

I left late Friday afternoon and came home. I hitch-hiked and got home at noon on Saturday. I got back to base on time. I expected the captain to call me in. I got really sharp-looking, went to his office and knocked on the door.

"Hit the hatch. Stand at attention. Well, you didn't improve much, did you. Did you get a deer?"

"Begging your pardon, but why would the captain want to know?"

"Oh, you're still a smart-ass Marine, huh? Okay. Your furlough is over, back to work."

He managed to nail me, anyway. Later, he gave me six days "piss and punk." What we'd do is put our belts on a rope and drag them behind a ship until the salt water turned them white. One day, I'm wearing my white belt. I never gave it a second thought. He saw me coming across to the mess hall one day. He stopped me and asked, "Where did you get that belt, Marine?"

"It was issued, Sir."

"We do not issue white belts in the Marine Corps."

"It's first issue, Sir, and I've washed it so many times it turned white."

"I know what you did — you salted it. I'll see you at one o'clock."

"Aye, aye, Sir."

Then he gave me the six days piss and puck. That was one full meal in four. The other meals consisted of a full cup of water and two slices of bread.

Finally, I got processed for discharge. On discharge day, the captain would hand out the discharges and shake hands with the guys. One guy wouldn't shake his hand. The captain gave him ten days in the brig. A week before that, another guy got seven days for not shaking hands. When my day came, the captain asked me, "Are you going to reenlist?"

"No, Sir."

"Are you going to shake my hand?"

"Sir, I'll kiss your ass if you want me to, just to get the hell out of here."

I shook hands with him, but I hated it. HATED IT! I still get mad when I think about it.

I got home for good in January 1946.

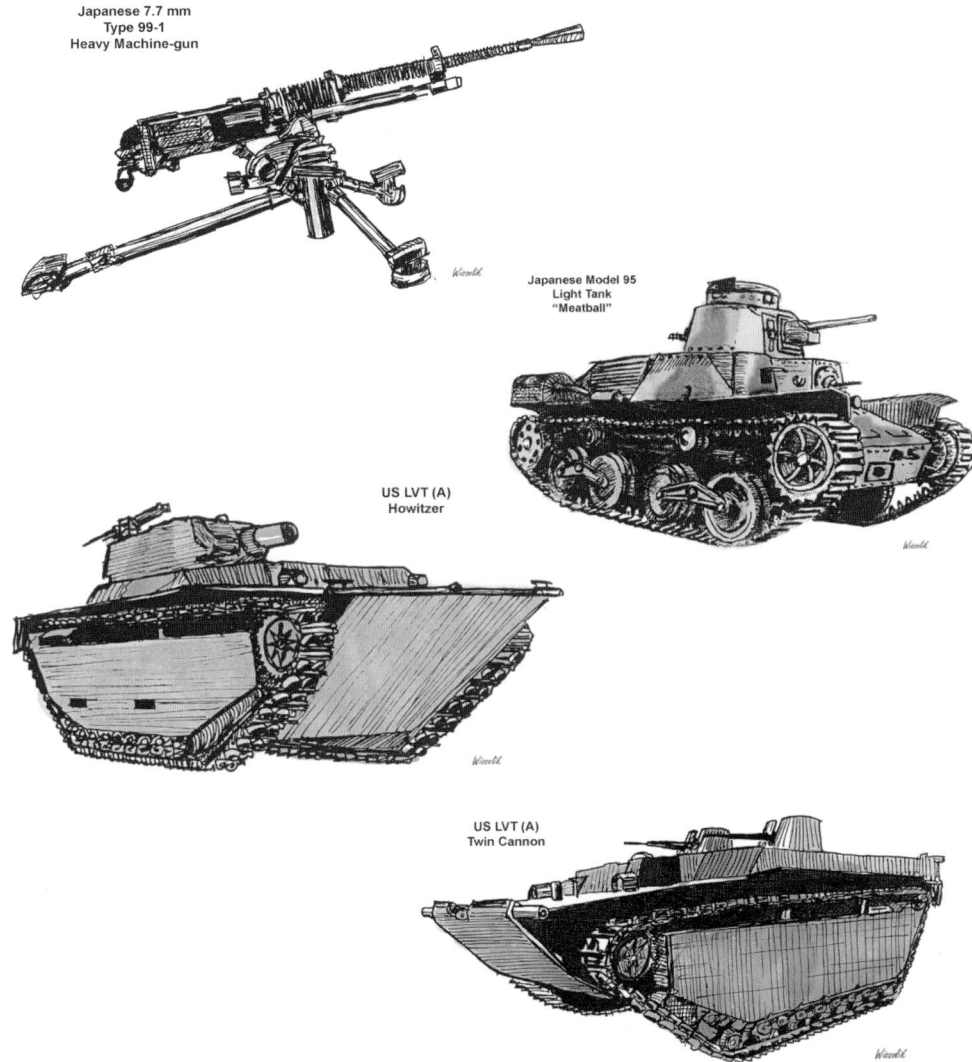

"After a Time It's All Just Hell."

Robert M. Johnston
Colonel, U.S.A.F., Ret. 488th Squadron
340th Bombardment Group (Medium)
March 15, 1919

"I had a little guy in the tail gunner position that day. I had handled that plane so violently that I ruptured his kidney and spleen. When we landed, they rushed him right to the hospital where I had always thought he died. Forty years later, my wife, Elaine, and I were at a reunion. She got talking to a guy whose story sounded like the tail gunner's. She said, 'Who was the pilot?' He said, 'R.M.' R.M. is what everyone called me. She said, 'He thought you died.' She came and got me, and we met up again after forty years. They had done surgery and rebuilt everything that had ruptured. For forty years I thought that I had killed him."

FROM THE VERY START of the war in Europe I knew that it was just a matter of time before the U.S. would be involved. I was in college at the time and I knew that I would be number one on the draft list because of it. I thought if I volunteered and got in early, I would be in better shape than the guys that were going to get drafted. I left New York where I was in school and came home to tell my family that I had decided to volunteer. This was 1940 I told my father, "I am going to enlist in the Army."

He said, "Don't do anything drastic. Give me one day to contact my friend."

He called his friend downtown, Colonel Fry, who proceeded to lecture me on the Air Corps. I really didn't need the pep talk because I loved everything about flying.

The Colonel asked me if I was finished with school, which I wasn't. He said to get into the Air Corps Cadet program you had to have two years of college. I didn't want to fool around with the cadets; I wanted to get in as soon as I could and I told him that. The Colonel told me that a new program was being created called the Enlisted Pilots Program and told me that I might be qualified. In the meantime he told me to sign up for the Cadets so that's what I did.

I enlisted at the rank of private and was sent to Sheppard, Texas for basic training. After basic training I went to mechanics school and near the end of that training I got a call that I had been selected for the brand new Enlisted Pilot Training Program. I thought I had died and gone to heaven, but I found out that it was a tad short of heaven.

We went to Kelly Field, Texas for training. There were twenty-eight of us in that group, and we were trained exactly like the cadets were trained. The difference was that when we graduated we were given the rank of Staff Sergeant, and the cadets were commissioned as Second Lieutenants. We became known as the "Flying Sergeants." Everyone else thought that was terrible that we were a lower rank, but I thought it was great because we didn't have to do all the extra duties the officers had to do. We just had to fly.

After we got our wings, we went onto advanced training where we were told that were to be P–38 pilots. Like everything else in the Army, that also changed. When we graduated from advanced flight training, they sent us to Columbia, South Carolina where we were assigned to a B–25 Squadron. It was a sad day for all of us; we wanted the fighters and they gave us bombers.

The worst part of it was the B–25s we trained on. They were the planes that Doolittle's men had trained with for their raid on Japan in April 1942. They were tired aircraft when we got them and should have been scraped. That's all they had though, so we used them until we were issued new planes right before we went overseas.

I grew to like the B–25. Unlike some other planes, a pilot needed a bit of muscle to jockey it. It could also take a lot of punishment and carry a heavy load of bombs. The B–25 was a medium bomber, and because it was much smaller than the B–17s and the B–24s, we could fly tighter formations. The formation we flew in training and demonstration was called a "four in, four out." What that meant was that we flew four feet out from and four feet behind the plane next to us. That changed when we got into combat because flak and fighters made everyone a bit nervous, and we wanted the extra room to get away if we had to. Even in combat, though, we weren't more than fifteen or twenty feet apart.

While training at Columbia, new crews were arriving to fill out the squadrons. When that was finished, we were sent to Walterboro, South Carolina where we practiced tactical join-ups, bombing and night navigation.

When all our training had been completed, we were sent by train to pick up our new planes. It was funny because they put us on a train after dark with all the shades drawn so nobody would know where we were going. It didn't make a damn bit of difference. Anyone that wanted to know where we were going could find out.

The train took us to Battle Creek, Michigan where we boarded buses for the airfield. The first thing we saw was row after row of pink airplanes. Pink was desert camouflage, and we knew immediately where we were going to go. We took each plane up and tested it out. We checked every single part of the plane and if it did everything it was supposed to we brought it back and told the operations officer. Our CO signed off on all of them and we were ready to go overseas.

We left from Battle Creek and flew to West Palm Beach, Florida. When we left Michigan it was freezing, but it warmed along the way. By the time we hit Florida it was ninety-eight. When we landed, all we were wearing were our skivvies. From Florida, we flew to Puerto Rico then onto Trinidad, Georgetown and finally far back into the swamps of Belem. On the way we lost a plane. One of the guys (I guess you could say chickened out) ditched. We hit a front and it was one of the worst storms

I ever saw. We circled and tried to figure out whether to go above or below it. We decided finally to go above because below us were hills and an island.

I radioed this guy and said, "Get on our wing and follow us."

He called back and said, "There's a big field below. I'm going to put down there."

He went down and wiped out one B–25. Eventually he caught up with us in a new plane. That was our first downed plane, so to speak.

When we got to Belem, we stripped the planes of all their cold weather equipment because it wouldn't be needed in North Africa. We took off from there and made a few more stops before reaching Kabrit, on the Suez Canal.

On the way to Kabrit our plane developed mechanical problems, and we had to make an emergency landing. Sand had gotten into the harnesses and fouled all the spark plugs, making the engines run rough. The mechanics had to pull every plug and change them. Once that was done and everything checked out, we caught up with the rest of the group at Kabrit.

Kabrit was a British base. We had never been exposed to the Limeys before and we were as curious about them as they were about Yanks. Since they had already seen many months of desert combat, they were given the job of helping us to get organized.

That first base and all the other bases we were at in Africa were barren desert. A week after we abandoned a base the sand covered it over, and no one could tell that there had ever been anything there. When we moved into a new base, we dug three-foot-deep holes and put our tents over them. That way, we would be below ground and safe from low shrapnel, or "daisy cutters," as we called it. We had to constantly dig the sand out of the hole. After twenty-four hours, it would fill up with sand. So that we had something to dive into for protection during an attack, we put slit trenches a couple feet from the tents.

Robert M. Johnston in the desert of North Africa with "Patches," the plane he piloted with the 488th Squadron. *Courtesy of the Johnston family.*

For Nature's calls, we built our own urinals out of a piece of pipe. We'd bury one end in the sand, and put a funnel over the other end, and then we covered the funnel with wire mesh to keep out the flies. For other matters we just took a shovel, made a hole, did what we had to do, and then covered up the hole. It was all primitive at best.

There were no buildings, just tents, planes and sand. The runway was sand, reasonably flat and level, marked off on either end by fifty-five gallon drums. The crew chief and his crew stayed right next to the plane. They did the best they could under the conditions to keep the plane in good shape. They tried to seal the planes off from the sand but it was impossible. The sand was as fine as talcum and the ground crews couldn't stop it from saturating everything. I had a waterproof watch when I went overseas. Before too long in the desert, it stopped. I took the back off and it was just packed tight with sand so that none of the gears would move. That was a watch that was supposed to keep out water. That's how fine that sand was.

Taking a plane off in the desert was a challenge. We set everything up so that we took off in the crosswind. We taxied up, turned, and then fire walled the throttles so that the dust blew away from the plane. If the sand hit the engines, that was it; they would just seize up.

One day we had twelve planes in the air and twelve waiting to take off. We were in a hurry to break up a tank battle, and nobody gave a thought to the wind direction. We started to run up our engines and a sandstorm hit us. That was it! We had to shut down the engines and scrap the mission. Mother Nature was as much an enemy as the Germans.

Before we started to fly missions as a group, after we got set up at Kabrit, my tent mate and I flew six missions with the 12th Group. We had answered the call for volunteers to fly scouting missions and get an idea of how missions were flown. When we got back, we were immediately made flight leaders. I flew a few missions in that role until I saw what happened to a guy in the number four spot when he got hit. He tried to get out of formation, but didn't quite make it. When I saw that happen I wanted the hell out of lead. I told the operations officer, "That's not for me. If someone else wants the glory, fine. I want to fly wing. If someone gets hit, I want the hell out of there right away."

That's how I got to fly wingman.

We flew our earlier missions over the Mareth line in support of the British Eighth Army. They didn't have enough of their own air support and they'd get in a bind and call on us. Usually it was a tank battle they wanted us to break up.

We followed the Germans and Italians as the British pushed them out of Tunisia. We flew some missions up toward the Italian peninsula over a tiny island called Pantelleria. That was a scary little place. As we neared the island, the Germans always set up a box of flak. It was odd because the Jerries or the Italians would get all charged up, fire everything they had into that box until just before the planes hit, and then stop. Once we were through that area they would start firing again. They shot round after round but it was either ahead of or behind us.

It's hard to describe getting hit with flak shrapnel, but if you throw a handful of gravel at a sheet of tin, that's what it sounds like. The enemy gunners fired in line, four guns per battery, with a total of three batteries. They set the time fuses on the shells to explode at our altitude, and they were very good at figuring out an altitude. We could never be sure if anyone would take a direct hit, but we did know that we would get hit with pieces of shrapnel. It was a very high pucker factor. Our group operations officer was piloting a plane that took a direct hit in the cockpit. It blew him all over the cockpit. Everything was just a bloody mess. The explosion just made mincemeat out of him. Luckily the copilot was able to get control of the plane and bring it back safely.

We had a trick to throw the gunners off. We came in hot and high at first. Then, after we hit the IP, we dove to increase airspeed. Right before the target we dropped airspeed. By the time we hit the bomb release point, we slowed down to 150 knots, which was pretty slow. Then we dropped our bombs, ran the throttles all the way forward, and got the hell out of there.

My worst day was the day when I got the Distinguished Flying Cross. The plane in front of ours took a direct hit. My copilot was flying the plane while I kept an eye on flak and what was happening below. Suddenly I heard an explosion in front of us. As soon as I heard that, I looked up and yelled, "I'll take it!" A plane in front of us had been hit in the left wing, and parts were coming off it and flying back toward us. In the split second it took me to take over the controls, we were caught in the flames coming of that plane. A wing flew by, and I don't know how the hell it missed us. I pulled up and put the plane into a split S. At nine thousand feet a split S in a B–25 was not an easy thing to recover from. I had to ease the plane out of the maneuver; otherwise the tail would have come off. By the time I pulled the plane out, we were pretty damned low. I had it under control, but I couldn't stop the vibration. I needed more power from the engines, but the plane was pretty beaten up. One prop was running cockeyed, and the vertical stabilizer was bent.

Finally, I got full control. Suddenly fighters appeared at six o'clock low. I thought how surreal it would be to have come out alive after the split S, and then get shot down. The fighters came alongside, and one tipped up to show me his wingtips. I knew right away that it was a British Spitfire. There were no other wings in anyone's air force like those on the Spitfire. One fighter went above us to give us protection, and the other went below to check out our damage. He got so close I could have touched him. I had never seen a bastard fly closer. He checked out every inch of the plane, and then came up beside us with a thumbs up. Then he joined his buddy, and they escorted us out over the Mediterranean and halfway to Africa. Then they peeled off and went home.

I had a little guy in the tail gunner position that day. I had handled that plane so violently that I ruptured his kidney and spleen. When we landed, they rushed him right to the hospital where I had always thought he died. Forty years later, my wife, Elaine, and I were at a reunion. She got talking to a guy whose story sounded like the tail gunner's.

She said, "Who was the pilot?"
He said, "R.M."
R.M. is what everyone called me.
She said, "He thought you died."

She came and got me, and we met up again after forty years. They had done surgery and rebuilt everything that had ruptured. For forty years I thought that I had killed him.

After a tough mission, everybody counted the holes in their planes. On a bad run some would come back holed in a hundred places. The crews repaired the holes with flattened-out C-ration cans. The skins of tin cans were all we had between the flak and us. Some of those planes looked like they had silver measles.

In between the daily fear was gallows humor. One time, one of our planes was coming in from the wrong end of the runway on a single engine. That's the only engine he had, so he was trying to get on the ground a fast as possible. Another plane was landing on the correct end of the runway, and, at the last second, the pilot powered up, pulled back the controls, and leapfrogged the one-engine plane. He caught its tail and cut it right off. Fortunately, the plane was close enough to landing so it came in safely. Just before it stopped, the gunner jumped out and pulled the ripcord on his parachute. It opened and damned near smothered him.

Another time, I was waiting for one of our flights to come back. We all had dysentery, and I was sitting over a slit trench on a long board that had eight holes in it. There was no back on the board. The planes started to come in as I sat there. I saw a couple flares go up, a sure sign of trouble. By the third flare, one plane had landed and was rolling down the runway. As it rolled past, I saw that it had a 250-pound bomb hung up on its rear shackles. At the time, we were using British bombs with daisy-cutter fuses, and the damn things would go off just for the hell of it. The plane was in real trouble. Just as it passed me, the bomb released. I threw myself backward, and tried to bury myself in the sand. The bomb went off and sent a fireball rolling down the runway. People jumped out of the way all the way down the line. It could have been tragic, and it wasn't really funny at the time, but I guess we laughed at them anyway because when we had close calls with death there wasn't much else to do but laugh. We laughed at fate to release out tension. We made fun of anything. In a way we were saying, "Hey you missed me. Want to try again?"

Boredom is number one in any war. It's not the moments of intense fear. It's the hours and hours between moments of fear that gets you. War is moments of panic and long periods of nothing. One of the ways we killed boredom was to torture the flies that constantly tortured us. They landed on anything that carried moisture, especially sweating human bodies. They swarmed around us and landed on our mouths, our eyes, and our ears. They were just hell. We'd catch them, make lassos out of thread, and then put the lassos on them. Then we'd tie the thread around our belts, and our pet flies would fly along with us wherever we went. We weren't exactly crazy. We were just on the edge of it.

Eventually, we left the sand of North Africa for the mud of Italy. We got there in the middle of winter, and it was miserably cold and rainy. We were stationed at Foggia. Foggia had no runway so the engineers laid down a runway using Marston Mat. I'll never forget that stuff. I hated it because when the plane's wheels touched down it would send a ripple over the whole mat, and if I hit the brakes the plane just skidded along it. It worked in a pinch but I didn't like it at all. It was from Foggia that we flew three missions over Monte Cassino. Along with the infantry's artillery, we managed to level the place. Until then we had been flying missions against the Germans on the Volturno River. When orders came down for Monte Cassino, everyone griped because they didn't want to bomb a sacred place.

We were supposed to pulverize it and that's what we did. We blew the hell out of it. There wasn't much flak over the target. It was more or less a milk run. Everyone had a run at it, B–17s, A–20s, B–26s, B–25s, dive bombers, every kind of plane we could think of. In the end it made the situation worse for the infantry because the Germans had better cover from the rubble than they did from the buildings.

The last run on Monte Cassino was my fifty-sixth mission. I had a chance to come home, and I took it. I had some real fun when I came home. They sent me to be an instructor on the A–20. That was a lovely little aircraft, the sports car of airplanes. It was light, fast on the controls, easy to fly, lots of power, just great all around. It couldn't carry the bomb load of a B–25, so the military used it as a strafer. I taught mainly low level flying, but I never understood why they used the A–20 for low-level support because there were other planes designed for that role. It was a hell of a challenge and a pilot had to be a damned good to use the plane in that way. We flew so low we were pulling up all the time trying not to pull up fence posts. I flew the A–20 for a year until the A26 came out. That was a great plane; you could lose an engine and not even know it. I used it once to buzz my house when I was home on leave. It was Easter and all my brothers were home. I came over the house at rooftop level. I must have been doing almost 400 knots. I pulled up quickly before anyone could identify the plane. It someone had, I would have caught all kinds of hell.

When the war ended, they sent me to a transportation group. There were so many pilots coming home that the army didn't know what to do with us. As a second lieutenant, I was very low on the totem pole. I knew I would have to start officer's school in order to make it anywhere in the Army. I was separated from the service in 1947 or 1948, and I went back in 1950. I put in a total of thirty years in both active duty and reserve duty. I retired at the rank of full colonel.

When I think about the war, I think about the drama, the power, and the terrific force involved, even the beauty of it. When I wasn't involved in a fight, I just sat in my aircraft and enjoyed the view, the time of day, the way the sun played on the plane next to you, the changing light in the clouds. It was always beautiful, and it was the best part. Once, while I was flying to
Trinidad, the sky was the color of lead, and it was rainy and cloudy. It was sort of somber. There was a hole in the clouds right over the city, and the sun shone down on it. It's a picture I will never forget. I think I saw it all from an artist's point of view, and the picture is still in my mind's eye.

Really, I think you have to experience war before you can talk about it. One word sums it up — hell. We were like ducks in a shooting gallery. Each day, when the sun came up and we took to the air, we know there were those below us who were going to try and kill us. In that situation you're nothing more than a number on a chart somewhere. Your days are so many days and then your time is up. Despite that you get up, you go to the briefing, they tell you where the batteries of guns are, and where the fighters are likely to intercept you, and you say to yourself, "I am going in there again, and I am coming back again." Every day you do the same thing and think the same thing. You do it again and again and again.

How the hell a person can do that and stay sane over a period of time, I don't know. I know soldiers and airman often hoped that they would get hit, not badly, but just enough to take them home, or at least out of the mud or the flying or the artillery for a while.

There is no glory. After a time it's all just hell. That's war in a nutshell.

"War Was the Farthest Thing From Our Minds"

Clarence Kindl
Seventh Air Force, 46th Pursuit Squadron, 15th Pursuit Group,
Pearl Harbor 7 December 1941, Wheeler Field, Oahu, Hawaii
Loyalhanna, Pennsylvania, June 17, 1916

"We were at church on December 7, 1941. After church, three buddies and I went to the mess hall to see if we could scrounge up some late breakfast. When we got there, they were cleaning the place up. The mess hall was an old, one story, wooden building. We sat down at a table. The guy on KP asked us, "Would you all mind moving over one table?" We moved, and because of that we owed that guy our lives. As soon as we moved, there was a big explosion outside. I said, "What the hell was that? There's no flying today. Maybe something happened out on the line, a gas explosion or something." Then there was another explosion, then another, then another. I walked over to the door and looked out. I saw a plane go by that had big, red balls on it. 'Christ,' I said. 'There are Jap planes out there!'"

MY FRIEND AND I WERE HITCHHIKING around the country looking for work. It was the Depression and work was hard to come by. One day we found ourselves in Washington, D.C. I saw a big recruiting flag hanging outside a building. I said to my friend, "Hey, let's join the Army!" We enlisted in the Army Air Corps in July 1940. The only openings they had in the Air Corps were in the Hawaiian Department, Unassigned. In other words, we'd go where they told us to go. From Washington, D.C. we were sent up to New Rochelle, New York. There, we got our uniforms and spent a month going through physicals. In August, we were sent to Fort Jay, on Governor's Island, off of Lower Manhattan. At the time, Fort Jay was the home of the 16th Infantry Regiment of the *Big Red One*, the 1st Infantry Division. While we waited for a boat to take us to Hawaii, we trained with the infantry.

We left Brooklyn Army Base in Lower Manhattan, went up the Hudson River and got on the Army transport, *Fort Leonard Wood*. That was the first time I was ever on a large ship. The ship had been named after an Army hero who had been with Teddy Roosevelt on San Juan Hill during the Spanish-American War. Our first stop was Charleston, South Carolina. Then we went down through the Panama Canal to Hawaii.

In Hawaii, as we walked down the gangplank, an officer was there counting us. He sent one person to the right, and another person to the left, and so on. One group went to Hickham Field, the bomber field, and the others to Wheeler Field, the fighter field. I wanted the bomber field, but I had to go where I was told. They sent me to Wheeler.

Sergeant Clarence Kindl, 46th Squadron Clerk, Hawaii, 1941.
Courtesy of the Kindl family.

I really enjoyed the military. I felt sorry for the fellows who counted the days, you know, who wanted to get out. I told them they were going to be in for three years, and they should make the best of it. I watched the guys who had it easy, and they all had stripes on their sleeves. I was determined to get me some stripes, too.

The Army had picked old timers from Hickham and Wheeler Fields to be supply, mess, and first sergeants. They came into my tent one day and told me they wanted me in the orderly room. Orderly room! It was just another tent. When I got there a colonel wearing a Sam Browne belt and leggings beckoned me over. He scared the hell out of me. He said, "From now on, you're the squadron clerk."

I told him I didn't know anything about being a clerk.

He said, "Well, we've gone over all the service records and you've had some clerical duties. You're the clerk."

I tried to remember where the hell I had gotten clerical duties, but I couldn't. They sent me to correspondence school for four hours every morning for six months. At the end of that time, I was wearing my stripes. I was a sergeant with an assistant, a corporal. We did all the work. Then our first sergeant got transferred, and they brought a guy down from infantry to take his place. All he wanted to do was dress up and sit. He didn't know how to fill out a report or make up a duty roster. He couldn't type. He didn't know our correspondence procedures. It wasn't that he didn't know anything, but he was a line infantryman. After six months, he got sick and went back to the States. What did they do? They sent down another infantry first sergeant. He was as bad as the one before him.

When I got to be staff sergeant, the second infantry first sergeant got sick. They sent him back to the States. After that, some of the officers and line chiefs held a meeting in the operations room to decide on a new first sergeant. One of the line chiefs wondered why the hell we were always going to the infantry for first sergeants when we'd had a man who'd been running the squadron by himself for a year. Why didn't they make him first sergeant, the line chief wanted to know? Then the commanding officer said, "Hell, I never thought of that. Clarence, cut yourself orders promoting you from staff to first sergeant!" That was early 1943. Now I had more stripes.

Throughout 1940 and 1941, it was business as usual in Hawaii. Every once in a while there would be a sabotage alert. Then we'd set up extra guards around the airplanes and send out patrols. Once a month, the squadrons went out to an isolated grass field and took gunnery practice. War was the farthest thing from our minds, and there was not much talk of it. Of course, the war was going on in Europe, and we figured that some day we might get involved in it, but no one ever thought the Japanese

Hawaii 1941. Lieutenant Bill Southerland, Athletic Officer (top row left) and the 46th Pursuit Squadron champion basketball team. *Courtesy of the Kindl family.*

were going to bomb Hawaii.

Our squadron was issued second-hand Curtiss P–36 fighter planes from Mitchell Field in Long Island, New York. We also had two, old Boeing P–26 fighters. A Sikorsky OA–8 rounded out our "strength." Sometime during the middle of 1940, Curtiss P–40's started coming over, but most of them went to other squadrons. It wasn't until late in the war that we got the great fighters, P–38s, P–39s, P–47 Thunderbolts, and the "Paper Doll," the P–51 Mustang.

Ray Ohlues from Custer Park, Illinois. He and Clarence Kindl flew rented planes from Rogers Field, Honolulu. Despite poor eyesight, Ohlues was finally accepted into the Army as a B-25 pilot. *Courtesy of the Kindl family.*

In the early days, we had a lot of leisure time. For fifty cents each, six of us would take a taxi down to Honolulu, and then hit the bars and restaurants. When we got three-day passes, we'd rent a cottage on the beach. On paydays, they'd set up Chuck-a-Luck wheels, pool tables, and card tables. One of us would play poker, another would play Blackjack, and so on. If we won any money, we'd put that toward the rent of the cabin. The cottage wasn't much, but it was better than some of the places in town. It was hard to get a nice place there, anyway. There were only two good hotels neither of which we could afford, and the YMCA filled up fast with ship crews. On ordinary days, most work stopped at noon.

Clarence Kindl at Rogers Field, Honolulu, with the plane he and Ray Ohlues rented and flew on weekends.
Courtesy of the Kindl family.

It was like siesta time in Mexico. We weren't allowed to leave the base then, but we could play ball, sleep, or do whatever.

I had a buddy, Ray Ohlues, from Custer Park, Illinois, who had a private pilot's license. We would go down to the Rogers Civilian Airport; it was just a grassy field where they kept small planes. That guy, he loved to fly, and he had to maintain his license. I'd go with him every chance I got, every weekend, almost. For five dollars we could rent a plane for an hour. He would be in his glory. Most of the planes had two control sticks for teaching purposes. The grounds man always took one stick out so we couldn't fool around once we were in the air. After we got to know him, he just said, "Well, go ahead and take that plane down there," and he didn't take the stick out. Ray tried damned hard to take the military pilot school, but his eyesight kept him out. I told him, "Ray, don't give up. You'll make it yet."

He kept trying, and he kept getting rejected. Then when the war came, they grabbed him just like that, eyesight be damned. Ray wanted to be a fighter pilot, but he was too tall to get into the cockpits they had. They put him in B–25 bombers, and he flew missions all over North Africa and Italy.

We were at church on December 7, 1941. After church, three of my buddies and me went to the mess hall to see if we could scrounge up some late breakfast. When we got there they were cleaning the place up. The mess hall was an old, one storey, wooden building. We sat down at a table. The guy on KP asked us, "Would you all mind moving over one table?" We moved, and because of that we owed that guy our lives. As soon as we moved, there was a big explosion outside. I said, "What the hell was that? There's no flying today. Maybe something happened out on the line, a gas explosion or something."

Then there was another explosion, then another, then another. I walked over to the door and looked out. I saw a plane go by that had big, red balls on it. "Christ," I said. "There are Jap planes out there!"

The mess hall was in a crossroad area between the shoe shop and the tailor shop. A bomb came down and hit almost in the center of that crossroads and blew half the mess hall apart. Then a plane came in strafing right through the area where we were originally sitting. Had we not moved, we would have been killed.

We ran out through the kitchen and out the back door. Years later I read an article in the Pearl Harbor Survivors *Newsletter* that was written by the same kid who asked us to move. [*Mr. Kindl reads from the article*: I was on KP. I was working in the kitchen.

There were four or five other guys in there eating late chow. When that bomb fell, they all ran out the back door, through the kitchen. There were stacks of milk crates, with glass bottles in them at that time. They knocked that over. Knocked it down on me. I'm laying on the floor. Not one of them stopped to pick me up. They all ran out the back]. When I read that, I laughed and laughed like hell. I wrote a letter to that guy saying I was one of those guys who ran out the back door.

We ran across the street to the officers' quarters where there was shrubbery all around. A couple of us lay down under those bushes. And, oh, Christ, we could see smoke coming up from the burning hangars. After things settled down a little bit, we started down to the hangar line. When we got to the hangars we looked in and I said, "Jesus, we can't do anything in here."

The hangar roofs were completely gone, and there was nothing inside but clumps of metal and engines. The fuselage skins were made out of aluminum and they melted. The hangars were bent in every direction. There was a tent area across from the hanger line. The tents in them could sleep ten or twenty guys. They belonged to the 72nd Squadron. There were bunkers outside the tents. Lying dead in a bunker was a sergeant who had helped us start our outfit. He had a hole right in the middle of his forehead. The tents were half burned. There were mattresses and springs laying everywhere. A guy was sitting on a bunk trying to hold in his guts. I said, "Hell, he isn't gonna make it."

We got to Wheeler field. This other kid and I started to work our way down the sides of the runway. We ran into an officer and he said, "We don't need you down here. You get back to the orderly room!"

We didn't have much to do. We set up our orderly room as a point. The CO set up his command post out where the planes were. We would shift information back and forth. We'd have to go to him sometimes at night. Every ten feet was, "Halt. What's the password?" It was like that for days. Then we were sent down to the Marine base in Pearl City. They had lost quite a few planes down there. They were quite happy to see us. We went down there with six operable fighter-planes, a couple P–40s and about three P–36s. We stayed there a few weeks. We slept in the gymnasium, and had a nice dinner on Christmas Day. The Marines let us go to the head of the chow line because they knew we were doing them a big favor. *[Editors' note: The following is a Tokyo radio broadcast intercepted by United States Intelligence personnel on 1 January 1942 and distributed to the Command Post of the 18th Pursuit Group on 2 January 1942: "Intell Memo No. 10. Intercepted broadcast from Tokyo on bombing of Oahu. Radio Tokyo. Flight Commanders report on the glorious bombing of Oahu. Early that fateful morning we sighted the island of Oahu after leaving our carrier out to sea. Certain units had certain tasks to perform and if successful we would leave Oahu a mass of smoldering ruins. Over Pearl Harbor we proceeded to bomb the much over-rated American Pacific Fleet. In hardly no time at all, rising columns of smoke began to emerge from many ships in the harbor, including a battleship. Our pilots had already made short work of Wheeler Field where the American pursuit ships were stationed. They bombed hangars and airplanes on the ground, destroying them in great numbers. Hangars were completely set afire and were destroyed due to their poor construction. At no time did the personnel attempt to fight back during the raid. After the major operations were complete, the anti-aircraft batteries began to* go into action. Then, I thought to myself, "All right, if you want more I'll give it to you." We returned to get into the fray once more. The ground troops, obviously badly frightened, displayed a poor degree of marksmanship and were freely wasting ammunition. We had nothing to worry about from them. From an altitude of about ten thousand feet, we reorganized our dive-bombers and were off again. Down, down, down we went. At eight thousand feet we released our deadly cargo and prayed to our Guiding Force that our pilots would find their mark. Then, far below us, it happened. The harbor was a blazing inferno. We made a direct hit on a large battleship of the Arizona class, and it literally cracked in half, sprouting into the air and down again. Another large warship was seen to have been listing in the water at a forty-two degree angle. The anti-aircraft were now beginning to get the range and one of our ships had a large hole in the wing, and we all prayed that he would make it back to our carrier. "Banzai," we all shouted as we returned. Another flight was taking off from the deck of the carrier to complete mopping-up operations. There was Oahu behind us, Oahu in flames. A task we thought so great that none of us would return, but all we suffered was a large hole in a wing tip. The hand of Providence was with us.... END. (The U.S. dispatcher signed the memo: "Remember Wheeler Field"].

In the months after Pearl Harbor we remained stationed on Oahu. We got ready eleven SBD dive-bombers for Midway Island. We put wing-tanks on them. It was the first time such a long, over-water mission on single-engine planes would be flown. Enlisted men flew those planes. They were all volunteers. It just showed that enlisted men had some smarts too, and that a guy didn't have to be an officer to fly a plane. We really sweated it out in the radio room waiting for word about those guys from Midway. Then we heard that all eleven made it to the island. We were happy about that, but we couldn't have known that they would all be killed a short time later in the Battle of Midway.

We stayed on Oahu until 1944. Then we went to Canton Island about 1,850 miles southeast of Hawaii. The British had a weather station there, and Pan American Airways had one of their Clipper stops there. There was nothing there but coral. The place was a stepping-stone to some of the atolls that were occupied by the Japanese. Our planes made patrols every morning and sometimes in the afternoon. The salt air was so bad that the rivets on the planes got corroded and were ready to pop out. But we had some darn good men. They could tear an engine apart and put it back together right there. It was nothing for those guys to change an engine. Our armament people, the radio guys and the guys who specialized in hydraulics and propellers were all good. We had a good outfit. A lot of them worked as a machinist or a mechanic or something like that in civilian life. When they got in the service, all they had to do was learn how to do it the Army way.

Canton could be a lonely place. We were there nine months. The isolation was tough for some of these guys. If you stayed there long enough, you'd go nuts because there's no grass, no trees, and no fresh water, just coral. We did have two guys take their lives. One guy hung himself, and one guy walked out into the ocean and just kept on walking until he went under and drowned. I felt sorry for him. He used to talk to me. He'd get these letters from home, so we thought that maybe his girlfriend had given him the hi-ho. Some girls back home just picked up and they were gone. These guys on the islands got a lot of Dear John letters.

This one kid, Larry, from Cincinnati, he'd come to me and say, "I got a letter from my girlfriend. We're saving money. When I get out, we're gonna get married." One day he came, and I could see something was wrong. I asked him, "Larry, what's wrong?"

He answered, "My girlfriend took all the money and she married somebody else."

He talked to me about committing suicide. I kept an eye on him for a few days. After I left the squadron, Larry was still in it. Maybe three or four years ago I got a letter from him. In it he told me that he had seen my name in our Pearl Harbor survivors newsletter, and that he was writing to tell me that he would never forget me for practically saving his life after this girlfriend jilted him. It kind of made me feel good that I did some good for somebody along the way, even if it was just talking.

After what seemed like an eternity on Canton, we went back to Wheeler and got new planes. Then we went down to Makin Island in the Gilberts. Makin was another small island in the middle of the Pacific, but at least it had trees. Still there was not much else there except the natives and missionaries making Christians out of them. Once in a great while we'd get a ration of beer, but we weren't allowed whiskey. That was reserved for officers. On Makin, the natives would crawl up into the coconut trees and get the green ones and drink the coconut milk before it turned white. That gave us a kind of buzz. Of course, guys made alcohol out of anything they could get their hands on, prunes, vanilla extract; I saw guys drink straight Aqua-Velva with grape juice in it. They called it "Purple Passion."

We didn't get the big USO shows out where we were. I read all these stories about all these guys going to USO shows here and there. Hell, we never had any. We used to hang a sheet between two trees for a movie screen and run a projector. That was our entertainment. Let's face it, who's gonna come to Makin Island. Who's gonna come to Canton Island? Or who's gonna come to any of those smaller islands? It's understandable. We didn't even have a USO show in Hawaii. All we had there was an over-the-hill Hawaiian dancer.

One time, while we were on Makin, we had to go back to Wheeler. We were on the escort carrier, *Kalinin Bay*. I got to feeling a little hot. A corpsman took my temperature and immediately put me in sickbay. When we got to Pearl, they put me in the hospital at Schofield Barracks. I was in this ward all by myself. They couldn't figure out what I had so they had me quarantined. The room had a glass door. The doctors and nurses would look through it at me. It was warm outside but I was crying for more blankets I was shivering so much. My lips were split. My eyeballs burned. My joints ached. I was dizzy. I didn't care if I croaked right then, that's what it felt like. One doctor said, "Well, if he has what we think he has, his body should be covered with hives."

The nurse says, "I can't see any hives. That young man is so suntanned that you couldn't see a hive if he did have one."

Another doctor said, "Pull his britches down and look at his backside."

The nurse said, "I already did, and he's just as dark there as he is everywhere else!"

I stayed in there for twenty-one days until they found out what was wrong with me. I had dengue fever. After they found out I had dengue fever, I started feeling better feeling better. They sent me back to Makin Island after that and then I came back to Wheeler again, where we got transferred out of the 15th and into the 21st Fighter Group. We'd load up, and then our orders would get canceled. We'd get ready to go again, and again orders would get canceled. Guys were starting to get a little pissed off. Finally, we got on a carrier with P–51's, and headed off to Iwo Jima. We landed on the south end of the island around 24 April 1945. Everything was blasted all to hell, holes all over the place. We pitched our tents among all this junk laying around. It was a terrible looking place. It was evening so we didn't bother cleaning anything up. We just went to sleep.

The next morning there was a hell of a row! "Banzai! Banzai!" Here comes a couple hundred Japs with fixed bayonets. One of them sliced open the tent and threw in a grenade. Our CO, Kip Pyle, got plastered with shrapnel. I thought, "I joined the Air Force, but I sure as hell didn't expect to get into this kind of mess!" Our guys killed every damned one of them.

As it turned out I had enough time in the military for them to send me stateside. I was the only one left in the squadron out of the original thirty-five men who started back in 1940. All the rest of them had either transferred or gone on to different assignments. So they sent me to Florida for a while for R&R. And then they sent me to Scott Field, Illinois. I didn't have anything to do there so they sent me to Langley Field, Virginia. They put me in with Squadron H. It was made up of all B–24 pilots that came from a place in the Dakotas. They came to Langley Field for the final phase of training. They would finish up their gunnery and their night/celestial flying. Then they would be sent to England. I was only there a short time when they sent me to Indiantown Gap where I was discharged on 13 July 1945. It was my lucky day, Friday the Thirteenth!

On the fiftieth anniversary of Pearl Harbor we went back to Hawaii and Wheeler Field. The old gang was together again, civilians who had been there at the time of the attack and the military. A lot of the guys were already gone, though. But it was good to get together and say, "Remember this, remember that?" We're all getting older now. At one of the conventions we were trying to figure what was going to happen when everybody was gone. I mean, who will be left to remember?

A postcard photo of the Leonard Wood, a liner converted to an Army troop ship. Clarence Kindl arrived in Hawaii on this ship.
Courtesy of the Kindl family.

Clarence Kindl with the landscape of Canton Island in the background, 1944. *Courtesy of the Kindl family.*

Members of 46th Squadron relax on Canton Island, 1944. *Courtesy of the Kindl family.*

The PX on Canton Island. *Courtesy of the Kindl family.*

Clarence Kindl (right) outside the club on Canton Island, 1944. *Courtesy of the Kindl family.*

Clarence Kindl (center) at a beach beer party. Members of the 46th Squadron often rented a cottage at this site because rooms in downtown Honolulu were too expensive or too difficult to obtain. *Courtesy of the Kindl family.*

Dec. 1941

United States Marine Corps
Marine Aircraft Group Twenty-one
Second Marine Aircraft Wing, Fleet Marine Force
EWA, OAHU, T. H.

Christmas Dinner

Cream of Tomato Soup — Crackers

COUNTRY FRIED CHICKEN

Oyster Dressing   Giblet Gravy

VIRGINIA BAKED HAM

Snowflaked Potatoes   Scalloped Corn

Asparagus Tips — Russian Dressing

Stuffed Celery   Lettuce — Mayonnaise Dressing

Ripe Olives   Sweet Pickles   Stuffed Green Olives

Apple Pie   Fruit Cake   Mincemeat Pie

Candy   Butter   Ice Cream   Mixed Nuts

Oranges   Cigars   Cigarettes   Lemonade

MESS SGT. J. B. PARKER (IN CHARGE)
MESS SGT. R. C. HARRIS (BUTCHER)
MESS SGT. R. L. YOUNGBLOOD (IN CHARGE OF MESS HALLS)

CCK. W. H. SHUMAKER   FLD. CK. A. A. GRUENKE
CCK. P. P. SHOWS   FLD CK. P. A. HAGSTROM
CCK. S. A. GOEDERT (BAKER)   FLD. CK. R. F. KONECNY (BAKER)
CCK. W. J. YOUNG   CORP. W. R. MILLER (BUTCHER)
CCK. J. DEEN   ASST. CK. N. H. LAYMON

J. ROELLER   W. J. WALLACE
C.M.G. U.S.M.C.   LT. COL. U.S.M.C.
MESS OFFICER   EXECUTIVE OFFICER

CLAUDE A. LARKIN
LT. COL. U.S.M.C.
COMMANDING

The Christmas dinner that never was, December 1941. *Courtesy of the Kindl family.*

Clarence Kindl and a buddy check out a Curtiss P-36 fighter plane at Wheeler Field, ca. 1941. *Courtesy of the Kindl family.*

A Mitchell B-25 light bomber ready for action somewhere in the Pacific, ca. 1944. *Courtesy of the Kindl family.*

Somewhere in the Pacific, ca. 1943-1944. "L'il Nell," an obviously successful, but battle weary B-17, ready for servicing by Seventy Air Force ground crew. *Courtesy of the Kindl family.*

Curtiss A-12 "Shrike" attack bomber at Wheeler Field, Hawaii, 1940. *Courtesy of the Kindl family.*

A North American O-47A reconnasiannce plane at Hickham Field, Hawaii. It had a production total of 239 and held a crew of three. It is a rare aircraft, and probably a rare photo as well.
Courtesy of the Kindl family.

Pan American trans-Pacific "Clipper" ship at Hawaii, ca. early 1941. Pan American also had a stopover on Canton Island.
Courtesy of the Kindl family.

46th Squadron's Sikorsky OA-8 Observation/Reconnaissance plane in its hanger at Wheeler Field, ca. 1941. *Courtesy of the Kindl family.*

"We Were Treated Like Dirt"

Robert Knorr

5th Marine Division, Fleet Marine Force

Bethel Park, Pennsylvania

"After the war was over, I joined the Marine Corps League. Three years ago, we took a trip down to the Iwo Jima memorial. We were wearing our uniforms. It looked just like the real thing I had seen on Iwo. I stood there looking at that like a kid looking at a candy store. All of a sudden a voice from behind me said, 'That's quite a thing, isn't it?' I said, 'It certainly is!' I turned around, and there were two Marines in their blues. One was a major, and one was a lieutenant colonel. I guess they were in their late thirties. I said, 'Yes, Sir. I was there the day it went up.' They took two steps back, gave me a salute, and then shook my hand."

It was harsh training, but I was seventeen. What the hell did I care? We were treated like dirt, we were nothing, but that was because they were getting us ready for whatever we were going to get into. I don't know what the hell I'd do, but I'd go in again.

I enlisted in the Marines June 1942. I saw some pictures of them, and I talked to some fellows who were already in. I had to have my parents' permission because I was seventeen. My dad was sort of reluctant to sign for me.

He said, "Why don't you wait till you're eighteen. They're gonna draft you anyhow."

I said, "That's just it. I don't want to be drafted. I want to go to the Marine Corps."

When they drafted you they could put you anywhere they wanted too. My dad finally caved in and signed for me and I went down and enlisted.

My first day in Boot Camp was 4 July. Boot Camp consisted of nine weeks of combat training. Most of it was pretty basic, up early, calisthenics, chow, rifle drill, marching drill, and obstacle courses. We did what they called the "Infiltration Course." For that we had to crawl under barbed wire, just barely. On the other end, guys fired live rounds from machineguns. Some of the guys had their ass up too high, and they got a bullet in the ass. We learned how to swim, in case we had to abandon ship. They put us in thirty-foot towers, and we were supposed to step off. Of course, some fellows had to be pushed off. They'd get to the edge and freeze. A DI would come up behind and say, "Are you going? Yeah, you're going!"

On graduation day, the DI came over and shook our hands. Now he was our buddy. We were Marines!

After graduation, we were transferred to different outfits. I asked for Marine Aviation, so they put me in an amphibious tank outfit at New River, North Carolina.

When we were down New River, we had Sundays off. Three of us sergeants went to see the officer of the day, the main man on the post, to see if we could go down the shed and take three tanks [Amtracs] out and go through the woods and clear some of the trees out. So that's what we did, one goes to one tree, the other one moves over a little bit, takes the other one down. Then we came across two farmhouses that were empty; they had been there for years and years.

I said "I'm gonna take that farm house out."

One guy went right through the middle of it. We waited till he came out the other end, and then we took care of the other parts of it. When we hit the second one, we waited. He didn't come out. The place had a cellar, and that tank broke through the floor and dropped. The driver ended up with a fractured skull. That ended our days playing with tanks, except for the winter, when Courthouse Bay, the inlet there, froze over. The tanks had three shaped paddles that were supposed to cup water. We'd get at one end of the inlet, get the vehicle up to about forty, and then pull back on the brakes. Talk about ice-ball shavers! Those paddles went along for five or ten minutes, and ice flew all over the place. We weren't worried about the vehicles breaking through the ice and going down because they were amphibious.

We were at New River about five or six months, after which we went to Camp Pendleton, California, for advanced training. We used called the fellows at Camp Pendleton "Hollywood Marines." They didn't like that. They had sun all the time. We had heat and swamps at Parris Island.

In August 1944 we went to Saipan, a big, well-vegetated island. We were in there three or four days before we even saw the Japs. The only trouble would be a few Jap planes flew over. You had to watch out, that was all. After we secured the island, they made a B–29 base out of it, from which we could bomb Japan. We went back to Hawaii, our home base, for more training and equipment.

After Saipan, we hit Iwo Jima. It was bombed so much before with B–24s and B–29s, by the time we got there, there was nothing standing. For seventy-two days we bombed it. The island was nothing but volcanic ash. The Navy sent Frogmen in two days before we landed. They cleared the mines on the flat side of the island.

The morning of D-Day, we got up on the ship decks. There were 900 ships in the sea, aircraft carriers, battlewagons, destroyers, troop ships, anything you could think of. It was quite a sight to see. On 19 February 1945 at 9 o'clock in the morning, we hit the beach. The 3rd, 4th, and 5th Marines all went in together. On 23 February, we were still on the beach. We couldn't get off. We wouldn't have the island in our hands until thirty-five days later. It was supposed to be a three-day operation, but we found out that there were 30,000 Japs on Iwo Jima, or should I say, "in Iwo Jima." In other words, it was honeycombed with caves and tunnels, and the Japs hid inside them.

I was in charge of nine AMTRACS. After we hit the beach, I had six left. Three were blown out of the water on the way in from mortar fire coming from Suribachi. Landing craft were mixed with waves of AMTRACS. I was in the second wave, and there were five or six waves after me. We lost many vehicles in the water. The volcanic ash was like snow, and our tracks spun. The Japs hit them, right away.

The island was seven miles long and two-and-a half- miles wide at its widest point. Battlewagons would come in as close as they could without beaching. They would fire sixteen-inch shells on top of Mount Suribachi, to quiet it down. We had quite a few guys killed from short rounds. Thirty-minutes after the battlewagons let up, the Japs would roll out artillery on rails from their caves, and they would start shooting at us again.

The generals and admirals must have thought of us getting the hell off the island. All of our equipment was jamming the beach, and they couldn't bring anything else in. My outfit was just below Mount Suribachi, but some 5th Marine guys had gotten up the hill. I looked, and saw our colors going up. Five guys from the 5th had raised our flag on the peak.

After the colors went up, we got off the beach and started moving inland. Out of the 30,000 Japs, we took 100 prisoners. The rest are still laying there today. 60,000 Marines hit that island, and it was pretty crowded. We rubbed shoulders with the enemy a lot of times. I never did hand-to-hand combat with any of them, but I popped a lot of them. That's what we were there for.

They used the AMTRACS whenever we had trouble at pillboxes. The troops would line up behind the tanks for protection, and we'd go. You could hear the shells hitting the armor like a ball-peen hammer. When we got close, we gave it the gas and shut the viewing slots so the Jap machinegunners couldn't fire rounds into them. As soon as we did that, the troops in back came to the front with their flame-throwers. Then we'd back away, and they'd let loose with the flame. You could hear screaming and yelling from inside the pillboxes.

One evening, one fellow was getting low on gas, so he pulled up to where we had our fuel drums stored on the beach. He had a flashlight but he put a poncho over it so it wasn't too much light on him. And he starts pumping.

I said, "Come on. Let's go."

Once you were on the beach or anywhere on that island, if you didn't keep moving you were in trouble. I mean the enemy got after you.

He said, "This is tough to pump."

I went over, put the light on the drum, and looked. I said, "Oh, my God! Get off the damn thing and leave it there."

He was trying to pump what he thought was gasoline, but it wasn't. It was the thick Naphtha mix that was for the flamethrowers. We got out of there. Not long after, the whole thing went up.

The Marines didn't take many prisoners, except for the ones our Intelligence needed for questioning. We had a Doberman Pinscher unit with us. They'd send those dogs into the caves. The next thing, thirty or forty Japs would come running out. Of course, our machinegunners would be waiting for them. As they came out of the caves, the gunners just mowed them down. We used the tanks to take the wounded down to the beach and out to the hospital ships. Sometimes we'd load a guy, and someone would say, "Why'd you bring him. He's dead!"

"Hell," we'd answer, "He was alive when we picked him up!"

Thirty-nine days I was on that island. During that time, we lost 7,000 Marines dead, and had 23,000 wounded. They passed out 30,000 Purple Hearts. The Seabees put a beautiful cemetery up for the 5th Marine Division.

We wanted Iwo Jima and Ichi Jima as bases for our B–29s, and they started to land them there even before we had the island secure. The islands acted as emergency landing fields for those planes that were low on fuel or were so badly shot up that they couldn't make it back to their home base. I guess it was all worth it. Four or five months after we secured the island, the number of Air Force guys whose lives were saved, were triple the number of Marines killed there.

We were supposed to be the floating reserves for the 1st, 2nd, and 6th Marines and their campaign on Okinawa, but we were shot up so bad they sent us back to Hawaii. We left the ship on 19 February, and we went back to it the 30th of March. We were still wearing the same clothes. We came up the gangplank. Sailors were there with hoses. We took all our clothes off, and they disinfected us. Before we hit Iwo, we were allowed to have salt-water showers. When we got back, the captain came over and said, "All those Marines that just came aboard, give them fresh-water showers for as long as they want."

And, boy, we had a hell of a meal!

We got back to Hawaii, where we were issued all new tanks and clothing. After Okinawa was secured, word came through that we would be hitting the homeland of Japan. We were expecting hundreds of thousands of casualties. Then we got word that President Truman had ordered the dropping of two new kinds of bombs, Atomic Bombs. The bombs wiped out two cities, Hiroshima and Nagasaki. Truman's decision ended the war. Today, people look back and say that it was a terrible thing that we dropped those bombs, but don't say that to anybody who was going to be in on the invasion of Japan. We all thought it was great! When the surrender finally came, I think we fired more ammunition than we did during the whole war. We just lay on the beach with machineguns and fired into the ocean. I had about five months to go for my four years so I stayed over in Hawaii. We got rid of all our new tanks. We'd go out in the ocean with two tanks, and scuttle one. When it started to fill with water, we'd jump on to the other tank. Down in the drink the first one would go. We did that with everything, Jeeps, ammunition, small arms. Anything you can think of went down in the Pacific Ocean. When my time was up, I went in the Captain's office and he gave me my discharge papers. He said, "Well, sergeant, you've got six months to decide if you want to come back. If you do, you can have the same rating. Do twenty years. You have four in now, and you only have sixteen more to go. Keep that in mind"

I said, "OK, Sir, I will."

Sometimes I could kick myself for not doing it, but I had been away for so long, I wanted to see my family again. I was home a little over a year, and I got married. That shot any chance for reenlistment. That was sixty-two years ago. Sixteen years back then, when I was young, seemed like such a long time, but here it is, almost tripled. But then, like my wife says, I could be laying dead in Korea or Vietnam.

After the war was over, I joined the Marine Corps League. Three years ago, we took a trip down to the Iwo Jima memorial. We were wearing our uniforms. It looked just like the real thing I had seen on Iwo. I stood there looking at that like a kid looking at a candy store. All of a sudden a voice from behind me said, "That's quite a thing, isn't it?"

I said, "It certainly is!" I turned around, and there were two Marines in their blues. One was a major, and one was a lieutenant colonel. I guess they were in their late thirties.

I said, "Yes, Sir. I was there the day it went up."

They took two steps back, gave me a salute, and then shook my hand. I have a picture of the flag raising in my living room. I'll never forget it. Never! I'll be seventy-nine in May, and if I lived to be a 100, I'll still think about it.

Into the Snow, And on to Bastogne December 1944

Illustration by Katie Plows, Saint Vincent College, 1997

Reprinted from *Men of the 704* CNAS and Richard "Doc" Buchanan

"We're Just Rookies."

Chester Lapa
63rd Infantry Division, 90th Infantry Division, 357th Regiment
Claytonia, Pennsylvania, 13 November 1925

"After they took Mooney back, I came across a dead GI. He was laying on his back. On his chest was an open wallet. There was a picture of his wife and little girl inside. We wanted to take the wallet for the address so that we could write to the wife back in Ohio and tell her how her husband had died. We decided against it, because we didn't want someone to think that we stole his wallet. We hoped that Graves' Registration would do the job for us. We marked where he lay by sticking the rifle in the ground, bayonet first, and putting his helmet over the butt stock."

MY MOTHER DIED three months after I was born, and my maternal grandmother raised me. My brother and my uncles all lived in the same house with my grandmother. I spent my first fifteen years in a mining town where my Dad, an Italian immigrant, worked. When I went into the service, my paternal grandmother, and several uncles and aunts still lived in Italy. My grandmother had four of us in the service at one time, but I was the only one to see combat. At one point, we moved to Slippery Rock, Pennsylvania, where I finished high school, and where I got my first real job mowing the lawn for a church. Then I worked at Stoughton Beach, a resort there, painting and cleaning the pool. I started there at thirty-five cents an hour, and eventually got a raise to fifty cents. After that I worked at a grocery store and made three dollars a day. That was a lot of money back then.

I heard about Pearl Harbor on the radio on a Sunday afternoon. Of course, we were very shocked. My grandmother and father were worried about my uncles and my brother having to go to the service. I was only sixteen at the time so no one thought much about me going. I was seventeen when I graduated from high school, and between June and November of 1943, when I turned eighteen, I took courses at Slippery Rock College. Slippery Rock was a small town, and every time I walked down the street people would ask me why I wasn't in the service. I really couldn't wait to get in, and when I was drafted in January 1944, I wanted to pass the physical so much that the anxiety raised my blood pressure and I had to sit around for a while until it got back to normal. I didn't want to come back and tell everyone that I had gotten a 4-F rating. I dreaded the thought of being called unfit for duty. Anyway, I passed the physical, and got a three-week furlough, during which time I had to get everything in order. On 8 February 1944, I went to Fort Meade, Maryland.

I was at Fort Meade with my uncle, who was twice my age, and a few guys from my high school, so I wasn't alone. I took the Air Force test with one of those guys, but we flunked. We finally ended up in the infantry. That's where they needed us, and that's where they sent us, to the 94th Division at Camp McCain, Mississippi. When I got there, the troops were getting ready to go overseas. I had to stand guard duty around the motor pool. They gave me a rifle, but since I wasn't as yet qualified to shoot it, they gave me no ammunition. I wrote home and told my grandmother and dad that I was only two weeks in the service, had no training, but was going to get shipped overseas anyway. But then they put us on a train and sent us down to Camp van Dorn, Mississippi, with the 63rd Division. So, in less than a month, I was with two different infantry divisions. I got my basic training at Camp van Dorn.

After regular basic training, I went into field training. The Infiltration Course was scary. The Army had permanent foxholes there. We would get in the foxholes while tanks ran over them. They wanted to show us that we could survive that. By the time that course was over, my foxhole was practically flat. I had the advantage of being short, so I made out alright. Other guys weren't so lucky. A tank rolled over one hole, and everything caved in on a GI. Whenever a tank passed over me, I could smell oil and fuel.

The heat in Mississippi was terrible. I got heat exhaustion twice. The first time was after training in the field, just as we got close to finishing the march back to camp. They laid down smoke and started yelling, "Gas, gas!"

At the time, I was on a machinegun crew, and I was carrying part of a machine-gun. In the heat and with the extra weight, it was already hard for me to breath, plus I had to put on my gas mask, and that made things worse. I had trouble keeping up, but I did. Everything caught up with me at retreat, right after we got back. The last thing I heard was my helmet and gun hitting the ground. I woke up behind the barracks where the sergeant had taken me. They fed me ice cream to cool me down. The second time it happened we were on a march. So many guys passed out from heat exhaustion that they did away with daytime forced marches. Any march over twenty miles had to be done from sun down to sun up.

After training, I got sent to Camp Shanks, New York. We all got passes and I got a chance to visit some cousins there. Some of my buddies and I went to the USO Stage Door Canteen for dancing and entertainment. It was November, my birthday month, and the MC announced that anybody had a birthday within three days, he could have a chance to call home. I got up on stage with two other guys, and we drew straws. I got the shortest straw, and I lost. The winner said, " I live in the area, so I can call home anytime I want to. Give the prize to someone else."

The second guy said, "I'm from New Zealand. I can't call home."

So they gave the prize to me. They took me back stage, and I called home, and talked to everyone I could. Finally I said, "I better hang up they're probably waiting on me outside."

I went out and there was nobody there. I could have probably talked as long as I wanted to.

The Army made us take off all of our identifying marks, patches and so forth. The idea was to keep everything secret from the enemy, but nothing was a secret. The hostess at the Stage Door Canteen asked us, "Why don't you guys have any markings on you?"

We said, "Well, we're just rookies."

She said, "You're not rookies."

She had a husband overseas, and she said that they made him do the same thing when he left. When we went on pass they had specially-marked buses that we would take back to camp. While we waited in line to board the buses, cabbies would come by and say, "Why wait in line? We'll take you right to Camp Shanks."

Everybody knew what was going on.

We went overseas in a small Liberty ship in a large convoy. The seas were rough. As we ate standing up, our mess kits would move down the table with the waves. You never knew if it was your mess kit you were eating out of. The seasickness was terrible. There was vomit all over the place, and the commodes would back up and wash over everything, making things worse. I was seasick the first three days out. We were at sea for thirteen days, long enough that we thought we might be headed to the Pacific, but we weren't. We landed in Marseilles, France, on 8 December 1944. When we landed, our morale sank. American troops had invaded southern France in August, but we could still see the destruction and all of the smoke stacks of the ships that had been sunk.

They marched us quickly up into the hills around Marseilles where we set up camp. It was strange because for the first few days, after being on the ship so long, everything still seemed like it was moving under your feet. About the third night we were there, we had big campfires going. We heard the sound of distant bombing. All of a sudden, we had to do everything to get those fires out, no matter what, because those enemy planes could have spotted us. Everything was supposed to be such a secret, but the Germans knew we were there. Somebody said they dropped leaflets that said, "Welcome 63rd Division."

We stayed in the area about five days while they repaired bomb damage to the railroad tracks. Finally, we boarded 40&8 rail cars that were left over from World War I. We traveled by rail for a couple days. There were times when we partially opened the doors on the rail cars. As we got closer to Alsace-Lorraine, we saw bomb and artillery craters and dead bodies, Germans. That's when reality started to set in. We asked each other who was scared. A few said "no," but they had to be lying or crazy.

When we got off the train, there were big trucks waiting for us. They had only so many trucks, and they packed us in like sardines. We had to stand, and were packed so tight that we couldn't move even enough to get our rifles ready to defend ourselves, if we had to.

We got up into some mountains. At midnight, our truck blew a fan belt. Military convoys don't stop. They just keep on going, so we were left on our own. After someone fixed the truck, we got under way again, but we were lost. I can still hear the roar of that truck going through towns at night as fast as it could go. When we got to a point where we heard small arms fire, we'd turn around and try another road. All I could think of was running into Germans and getting captured. I imagined a telegram reaching home saying "Your son is missing in action." I worried about that telegram, especially on account of my Grandmother. Finally, around two o'clock in the morning, we caught up to our unit. They were in a holding position on one side of a river, and the Germans were in pillboxes on the other side. We'd take potshots at the Germans, and they'd take potshots at us.

On 23 December 1944, I was sent to the 90th Division as a replacement. We didn't know what was happening. They just put us on trucks, and we did what we were told. We didn't even know we were being sent to another division. It was the first clear day in a couple weeks. Our planes were in the sky as far as we could see. It was some sight! We thought the war would soon end, but we soon found out differently. I trained with the 90th around the French Maginot line. I stayed there until early January 1945. I was glad to go to the 90th division because they were experienced soldiers who had been fighting since D-Day + 1. The officers and non-coms knew what they were doing, and we learned a lot from them about surviving in combat.

When we did finally move out for combat, we hiked for many miles in the cold and the snow. Burning, knocked-out vehicles were all over the place. A cow came running up on three legs. A bullet or shrapnel had hit its fourth. Right after the cow went past, there was a commotion behind me. I turned and saw a family running and yelling. I went back to see what they wanted. They had a boy of about twelve with them. His right arm was in a sling, and he was trying to make it up a small embankment. When I tried to help him his mother yelled at me, "*Boche! Boche!*" She was trying to tell me that the Germans had shot the boy. Two GI's took the family back to Battalion for processing.

We moved on across a field, some guys on top of a ledge, and others beneath it. I was in some tall, brown grass that stood out in the snow. A German machinegun opened up. I dove into the snow, and lay there watching bullets tear through the grass right over my head. That was my introduction to combat, and that's when I started talking to God, promising him if I ever got out alive I'd say a Rosary every day. And I did, every day for the last fifty-nine years.

A minute later, I felt a tapping on my foot. I thought I was going to be captured, but it was only the sergeant trying to get my attention. He motioned us to follow him. We went backwards in the snow, and down into a gully. To me, it was just like the Infiltration Course all over again, what with the bullets whizzing overhead. Then I saw my first wounded GI. Most of his hand was gone. It had been hit by a burst. Then things got quiet. Someone must have knocked off the German machinegun position, and we were able to move on.

We moved to a wooded area where we spent the night. The wind was up, and it was bitter cold. We stood guard two hours on, and two hours off, listening to the artillery shells going over, ours one way, and the Germans' the other way, all night long. The shells made a fluttering sound, and I hoped that the fluttering sound didn't stop. If it did, there was a good chance that the shell was going to come in on me.

The next day we got into heavy combat. There was a lot of mortar and artillery fire, and we went from tree to tree pushing the Germans back. That's when my friend Mooney came to me shaking. He dropped his rifle. Mooney was Regular Army, almost twice my age, and he was a good guy. I thought he had combat fatigue, and called the medics. They took him back. I didn't hear of him again until I got out of the service, when the Veterans' Administration sent me an inquiry. Mooney had not been suffering from combat fatigue, after all. The concussion from an artillery round had separated his skull. The VA wanted me to swear that a shell had caused his wound. I swore to it, easily, because we were under heavy artillery fire when Mooney came up to me. Mooney died not long after the war, in North Carolina.

After they took Mooney back, I came across a dead GI. He was laying on his back. On his chest was an open wallet. There was a picture of his wife and little girl inside. We wanted to take the wallet for the address so that we could write to the wife back in Ohio and tell her how her husband had died. We decided against it, because we didn't want someone to think that we stole his wallet. We hoped that Graves' Registration would do the job for us. We marked where he lay by sticking his rifle in the ground, bayonet first, and putting his helmet over the butt stock.

We left the dead GI, and soon after came to a clearing. We stopped to regroup. The Germans had been pushed back far enough, and we needed a rest. While we were there, someone beyond the clearing kept crying, "I'm hurt, I'm wounded, please help me."

None of us went to help, because the lieutenant said, "You don't know who that is. It might be Germans, and they want to lure you out into the open."

The cries kept coming, and we wondered if it was really one of our guys, but there was nothing we could do. Even today, I can still hear those cries and wonder.

We moved out again, and eventually came to an old barn on a small hill that overlooked an orchard. The orchard had trees to the right, then an opening, and then more trees. It was a bitter, cold night. We set up our position there and slept in the barn. We had our machineguns set up so we could cover the orchards clearly, and we had to spend one hour each on guard to watch for a German counterattack. One guy got behind the machinegun ready to fire it, the other one beside him ready to feed the ammunition. That was a dangerous position to be in, because if the Germans were counterattacking, they'd be the first to get it. When it was my turn to guard, I swore I saw things moving. I'd turn to my buddy and ask him if he saw the same thing, and vice-versa. It was mostly fear and imagination. We got through the night without incident.

Most of our fighting in the Ardennes was in hills and forests. As we pushed forward, we bypassed some of the Germans in the hills. They were left there until they ran out of ammunition and food. At times, we took several prisoners. One afternoon there was a prisoner on our truck who could speak English as well as we could. He told us the war was over for him and he might get to America before we did. I asked him where he learned how to speak such good English and he told me he raced bicycles in Cleveland, and that he had been all over different parts of the United States.

It was one of the oddities of my war.

From 5–9 January the combat was light, but it was bitter cold. On the ninth, we advanced into Luxembourg and took Berle. Then we fought in the surrounding hills and woods. The Germans had units of the 2nd SS Panzer Division dug in. Tanks couldn't get traction on the ice. On the night of 11 January, we stayed in a wooded area, hidden from the Germans. They fired tracers all night, trying to find our position. We couldn't dig foxholes because of the frozen ground. We just scraped away the heavy snow, and lay down, two of us, sharing blankets, one blanket on the ground, and one for cover. I always thought I would freeze in the night. The cold was terrible on the feet. I woke up next morning, and had no feeling in them. I told the captain that I thought my feet were frozen. He answered that several men had told him the same thing. He told us we could try to make it back to Battalion, past the bypassed Germans, or try to make it to the next town with our unit. I decided to stay with the unit. The next town was Doncols.

We had to cross an open field, then go into the town. Our artillery started about fifteen minutes before we jumped off from a wooded area. There was artillery and rifle fire all around us when we went, and the officers tried to keep us moving because if we had stopped in that open field we'd be either killed or wounded. We came to a hedgerow just outside of town, and, as our Lieutenant went to step over top, he got hit in the leg with a bullet. Many guys were also wounded. I dove under the hedgerow. The Germans had crossfire directed on the hedgerow, and anyone trying to go over was either killed or wounded. I called for medics, but the lieutenant said it was no use because most of them seemed to be hit, too. He told me to see how bad he was bleeding, and if he wasn't bleeding much, then to go and check some of the other guys out. He was lucky, because the cold had slowed down the flow of blood. It was the same with the other wounded, which was most of the company. All I could do was put sulfa powder on the wounds. We stayed pinned down at the hedgerow from about ten in the morning until late afternoon. At about four o'clock, the artillery from both sides really picked up, and some of the soldiers who were already wounded got hit again, including the captain, who took some shrapnel in his shoulder.

We heard tanks coming, and we prayed that they were ours. Our prayers were answered! One brave sergeant pulled up in the lead tank, and asked us to point out where the cross fire was coming from. About four of us directed him to the windows of buildings to the left and right. The tanks pulled right up to those building and blew them apart. We all moved to a big tree outside of the town and ran, one by one, into town. One man had to be helped in because he had been hit on the back of the neck, and had gone blind.

When it was my turn, I got about half way between the hedge and the tree, and a shell exploded not far from me. I fell down, dazed, and when I came to I was on my knees, bullets were digging into the ground all around me. I moved to the tree, then into the basement of a ruined house. There was straw on the floor because the house had had a barn attached to it. About the only thing left standing was the basement.

By that time, one of the other companies or regiments had secured the rest of the town. The medics came around and started to evacuate the most seriously wounded. A boy about my age cried for his mother. He had a bad stomach wound, and his boots were frozen to his feet. I tried to cut his boots off. The medics put him on a Jeep and took him away. I doubt that he made it.

We stayed in the building the rest of the night. The next morning one of our guys got killed by a sniper. I was able to take my boots off, but I had no feeling in my feet. By noon the next day my feet were badly swollen. I could only get my boots halfway on. The battalion medics took my boots from me and put me on a stretcher. They tried to weed out the guys who were faking. They had no doubt about me. A nurse asked me if there was anything I wanted, and I told her we'd been eating snow for three days, and that I'd really like to have a drink of water. She gave me a canteen full, and said I had to take six big sulfa pills with it. Then they checked me out, and discovered that I had shrapnel in both knees. After that shell hit near me, I noticed that my rifle stock was all nicked and gouged. I figured the stock must have saved me. They treated and bandaged my knees. I had cuts on my hands and fingers, and they bandaged those, as well. They were ready to put me on a train for Paris, when the captain came over. He said, "I see by your tag that you are entitled to the Purple Heart."

The captain put the Purple Heart on my chest. Then the medics picked up the stretcher and carried me to an ambulance. We were given strict orders not to aggravate our wounds. Some guys actually did that to keep from going back to the front lines, and they got court martialed for it. We weren't allowed to dangle our feet over the bed, or anything like that. All we were allowed to do was lie there and keep our feet elevated. My feet went from pure white, to cherry red, then to black and blue. Penicillin was a life saver. They gave me a shot every four hours for the first three or four days.

I was taken to a hospital that had been shelled the night before. The shelling had killed two nurses and wounded two others. I stayed there over night, and then I was put on a hospital train to Paris. A Red Cross worker assisting the nurses on the train asked me if I needed anything. I asked her if she thought the War Department would send a telegram to my dad stating that I was wounded. She told me she didn't know. I had her write a letter to my family stating that I was alright, and I was sending the Purple Heart home. My family received the letter in the morning mail the same day they got the telegram saying that I had been wounded.

While I was in the hospital in Paris, a boy in the bed next to me made his way over to my bed and looked at my tag. He told me I was going to England. I asked him how he knew that. He had been trying to get the UK on his tag, he told me.

He said, "Your tag says UK on it."

He was right. From Paris I was put on a train for Cherbourg where they put me on a hospital ship. I ended up in Cardiff, South Wales, where I stayed in the hospital there for almost three months. There were all types of wounded men there. They had a special room for the most serious ones. Not many made it out of that room, we soon found out. It was a long time before patients like me were permitted to walk. The worst part was when the feeling started to come back into my feet. The blood would enter the veins, and my feet would just throb.

Other than the phone call that I made from the canteen in New York, I didn't hear from my family or receive any mail until I was in the hospital in Cardiff. We were moving so much that it took a long time for mail to catch up with me. That first delivery I got had sixteen letters and two packages in it. I just opened them according to the date.

Before we were released from the hospital, the Lord Mayor of Cardiff had a tea for us. They took pictures and sent them to our families and the local papers. After I got well, I spent a couple days in London, and then I was shipped back across the Channel. That was April 1945. During the crossing, some of us were playing cards. For some reason I had left my life jacket back on my bunk. A big explosion rocked our ship. The lights went out for a couple minutes. Guys got knocked out of their bunks, and I had to step over them to get my life jacket. I just lay in my bunk the rest of the night with my life jacket on listening to the distant explosions that took place every so often throughout the night. The next morning we learned that a German submarine was in the area, and our destroyers had dropped depth charges too close to our ship.

We landed in Le Havre France. Even a year after the invasion it was still hard to drive a Jeep up the streets because of all the rubble. I was sent to a replacement depot and from there to the 22nd Finance Dispersing Section in Rheims as an enlisted man's pay clerk. My building was right across the street from General Eisenhower's headquarters. Every afternoon the electricity was turned off for a couple of hours because they wanted to save the electricity. We had to work on the payroll by candle light.

Working in the finance section wasn't an easy job because we had to figure out a GI's pay for a month. That meant we had to take into consideration his length of service, time overseas, rank, combat time, if he had the combat infantry badge or not, all sorts of things. Then came all the deductions for insurance, allotments, and deductions for being AWOL and other infractions.

When we moved to the field, we had the responsibility of guarding the money, about a million dollars kept in four field safes. Besides having combinations, the safes were locked together with heavy chains. We converted American money to French francs and other European currency. When we had a surplus of dollars, we sent it back to the States.

Soon after I started to work on the payroll and got promoted to Technician 4th grade, the Germans signed surrendered. We moved to a new building, worked there in the day, and slept in tents at night. That was a step down for us. In August, I took a leave to Switzerland. While I was there, the Japanese surrendered. So, instead of having to go to Japan, I ended up in Chamonix, France, at a winter resort in the Alps. I gave the soldiers going on leave a partial pay. Finally, I got orders to go back to the States. I was discharged from Fort Dix, New Jersey. I got home about two o'clock in the morning on 11 May 1946, Mother's Day, and my grandmother was so tickled to see me. That morning we went to church.

Chester Lapa in Belgium on the anniversary of the Battle of the Bulge, December 2004

December 2004. Chester Lapa poses in front of the Luxembourg hedgerow where his unit became pinned down by enemy fire in 1944.

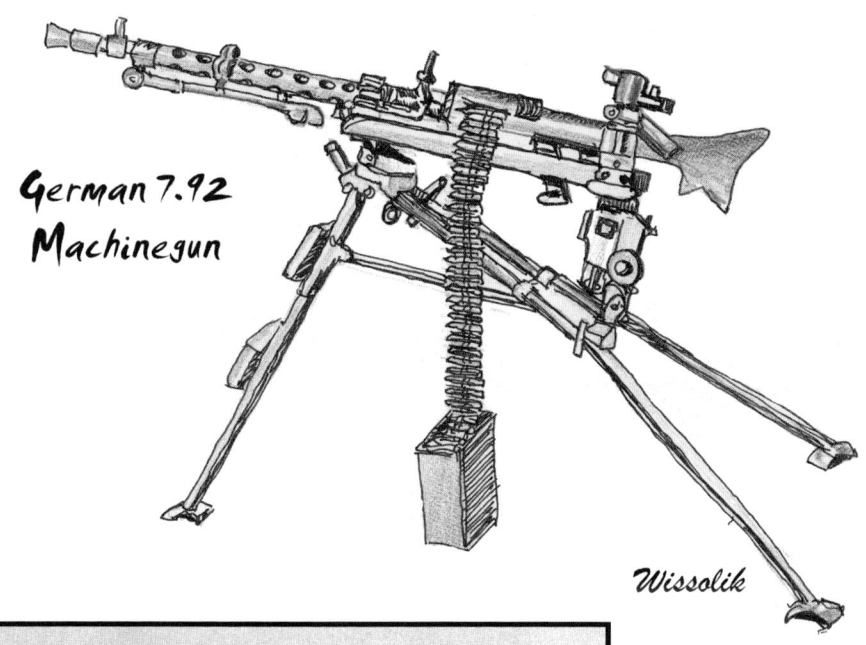

German 7.92 Machinegun

Wissolik

NEBELWERFER - "SCREAMING MEEMIE"

Hank Stairs

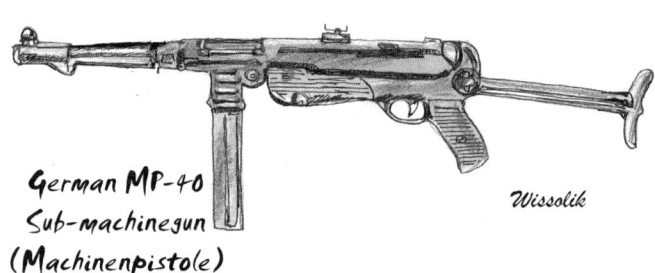

German MP-40 Sub-machinegun (Machinenpistole)

Wissolik

"It Was Enemy Territory. It Was Awful."

Joseph LaValle
United States Third Army, 17th Field Artillery, POW
South Greensburg, Pennsylvania, 21 June 1913
11 June 2003

"We started walking. We walked all night, and we walked right into an ambush. Boom, boom, boom, the Germans started shooting, and all hell broke loose. Our guys were dropping like flies! God was with me, because when they opened up and oh my God, I just hit the dirt and all I got was a little flesh wound. Every time I think of it, it hurts. It really hurts. Seeing all my buddies, laying there dead and wounded, nobody doing anything for them. It was enemy territory. It was awful."

MY FATHER WAS BORN IN SICILY, in a little village called Villarosa. My mother was born in Calabria, across the Straits of Messina. We had a big family. I'm one of five brothers, and four sisters. I was the only son who went into the service. My father got real sick with Black Lung, which he got from the coal mines. He never got a dime for it. Dad was killed in an auto accident in Jamestown, New York, where he had two sisters. My brother, Nick, was driving the car. He backed out right into the path of a streetcar, and BOOM! That was it. About a month later, a streetcar also killed my little brother while he walked the track going to the store.

My mother and father always talked to me about life in Italy. My dad was a policeman over there, a Carabiniere. He had also been in the army, in the cavalry. I went back to Sicily in 1978 to try and find some of my relatives, but they had all moved, some to the island of Corsica, and some to Rome. When I was in Sicily during the war, I got to talk to one of my relatives on the telephone. I could do that because my parents always spoke Italian at home, and I knew the language, and the dialect. I didn't get to see my cousin because my unit had to move out.

It wasn't easy growing up during the Great Depression. When the government people gave out food they put all the Italians, Poles, and Slavs (people called us "Dagos," "Polacks," and "Hunkies") in back of the room. We got what was left, and that's the truth. If you were one of those groups and Catholic too, that was two strikes against you. When I went to church, I used to have to cut through the field, because if I went down the street some people would call me "Little Dago." If you weren't Protestant in South Greensburg back then, you couldn't even join the Fire Department. My mother sewed, she took in washing, she made doilies, and she made handkerchiefs. That's how she supported the family when my dad went back to Italy to have his Miner's Asthma taken care of. He was over there for about a year. I had a job at a little restaurant called the Sugar Bowl. The people there also made candy on the side. I got nine dollars a week, and I helped support my whole family on that. That paid the rent, and that bought us groceries. Nine dollars a week! That was when the dollar was worth a dollar. All in all, though, we lived a good life. We stuck together.

The Draft was reinstated just before we got into the war, and there was a stipulation that whoever got drafted would only have to serve for one year. A friend said to me, "Let's go down to the Draft Board and jump our numbers up."

So, in March 1941, we went up to Greensburg and enlisted, thinking that we would serve our year and be out. We got examined in Greensburg, and, later, they sent us to Pittsburgh, where they examined us again. First thing I knew, a couple of sergeants came in and said, "We have too many guys. Anybody who wants to go home can go."

Hardly anyone raised a hand. Finally, this sergeant said, "OK. You, you, you, and you. You go home."

I was one of the guys to go. Then, on 8 July, I got called back. I was in for seven or eight months, until my twenty-seventh birthday. Then they said that anyone who was twenty-six or older could go home. I gave all my clothes away to my buddies, and, the night before I was to go home, I went to the movies. In the morning they said, "Joe, you can't go home."

"Why not?"

"Pearl Harbor got bombed!"

I had no idea where Pearl Harbor was.

Next thing I knew, I was out doing maneuvers back at Camp Blanding, where we had just come from. We lived there in tents for a month or so, until they put us on a train to New York, then on a boat. Away we went! That was August 1942.

We landed in Liverpool, England, and from there, after a couple weeks, we went to a little community called Hanover for more maneuvers. In November 1942, as part of Operation TORCH, the invasion of North Africa, we were supposed to hit the beach at Oran, Morocco. The lead ships got in. But when we got out to sea, we got into a terrible storm. Boy, that boat was going up and down! By the time we got in, Oran was fairly well taken care of, hardly any Germans, and the Vichy French had put up a very light resistance.

Then we went up on the front lines. We were up there for maybe a week or so, and then they relieved us. I don't know how many artillery units there were. I was up on the border as an observer, and I gave all the information as to where the enemy was. We were there day and night. As a matter of fact, it was kind of dangerous out there. I was laying there at night, and Germans on patrol would walk right by me. They had those German police dogs. They would come over and smell me; I must have smelled bad, because they left. I knew they were German, because they definitely weren't speaking English.

When somebody tells you they were never scared over there, they're lying. I was scared plenty of times, especially up on the borders, close to the enemy. As a matter of fact, one time we pulled up and I looked through the scope, and I bet the German's were 100 yards away—we had pulled up too far. So I called back down and we moved back. I could see the Germans playing soccer. Imagine, they were kicking a soccer ball around!

At one point, German General Rommel's *Afrika Korps* had us surrounded. We were up on this mountain right between the Faid Pass and the Kasserine Pass. My lieutenant said that he had to do something or other, and he just took off. After he left, the captain called me and told me that we were on our own. Then he told me to keep the phone open and wait for more orders. Then a little plane, a Piper Cub artillery spotter, went over and dropped a kind of can that had a note in it. The note said for us to walk to such and such a place where we would get support from our troops. We started walking. We walked all night, right into an ambush. BAM, BAM, BAM! The Germans started shooting, and all hell broke loose. Guys were dropping like flies! God was with me, because when they opened up I just hit the dirt. All I got was a little flesh wound. Every time I think of it, it hurts, it really hurts, seeing all my buddies laying there dead and wounded, nobody doing anything for them. It was enemy territory. It was awful.

Then German tanks came in. A young German lieutenant jumped off and said, "You are all prisoners of war." A couple guys and I tried to get away, but they stopped us and put us on a tank. There were other GI's who wouldn't give up, and they started shooting at the tank we were on. We jumped off, then got captured again. We were surrounded. There was no place for us to go. But we tried. Before we got over there, and we talked about what would happen if we ever got captured, some guys said, "If you get captured, you're supposed to try to escape. Give the Germans some trouble, you know."

So the Germans got us all together, thousands of us, and we started walking. We had to walk clear up to an airport. I don't know how many miles, but we just walked, day and night. Nothing to eat, no water. At least I had a canteen with me. Guys were laying down; they just quit. We slept out at night, no blankets, just our little jackets. If you think it's not cold in North Africa at night, you've got another think coming. It's freezing.

"What is your unit?"
"99th Underground Bloomer Corps."
"What is your occupation?"
"I work at the Gin Mill."
"How many in your family?"
"Twelve or Thirteen."

I'd tell them anything but the truth, except for what I was trained to say; name, rank, serial number.

We went through a lot of little towns. Bizerte was one of them. All of them were in German hands. Finally, we made it to the airport. They put us on these Junker 52 transport planes, and they flew us over to Naples. We waited in the open until a

German officer came around and picked the ones who were to go on the next train, to the next place, wherever that was. There we built some billets for POWs. We stayed in Italy for three months, working. The Germans had us burying fifty-gallon drums of gasoline to hide them. When the guard wasn't looking, we'd fix them so they would leak a little.

I talked to Italian civilians, but they were mostly Mussolini Fascists, and they hated Americans, at least until the war took a turn for the worse for them. Then they got scared, and wanted us to put in a good word for them. One of those Germans had a team of white horses, and a big whip, and boy he'd crack that goddamn thing. I got dysentery so bad, I couldn't walk. That Kraut came by on a horse, and yelled, *"Aufstehen! Aufstehen! Macht Schnell!"*

I couldn't get up, or hurry up, so he pulled out his pistol, and pointed it right at my head. Then he said, "Bah! *Amerikanner Schwein.*"

He let me lay there until someone came by with a horse and wagon and picked up a lot of other sick GI's and me. They took us to another camp. It was a filthy place. I couldn't believe my eyes. There was human waste all over the place. You had to sidestep to get around it. "What the heck kind of camp is this?" I said.

While we were there, an Italian priest, Father Diagnol, smuggled stuff to us under his robe, stuff like toothpaste, toothbrushes. After I came home, I don't remember how long afterwards, he visited me in South Greensburg. He came all the way from Italy just to see me!

When our troops invaded Italy and started pushing the Germans out, the Germans moved us up to Germany. By comparison with the German camps, the camp we first had in Naples wasn't all that bad. In Naples, some guys would make rings out of coins. They would take a pen knife and keep tapping them and tapping them, making a finger hole. We worked every day, but along with whatever little they gave us to eat, we got Red Cross parcels.

In Germany, they put us in Stalag 7–A, in Moosburg, near Munich. We worked in Munich in the old car barns. It was bombed flat. Then they had us working in some kind of factory, and we complained. We told them that that was against the Geneva Convention. They said, "The Geneva Convention was just a piece of paper. You know what you do with a piece of paper, don't you?"

Well, we had guns at our backs, and we did what we were told. If you had the will to come home, to see mothers and fathers and brothers and sisters, you did anything they told you. Some guys didn't think the Germans would shoot them, but they were soon dead. Even at that, I escaped three times, but it didn't do me any good. As a matter of fact, when we were first being interrogated, the German major said, "Do not try to escape! It's a long swim from here to America!"

Most of the prisoners in the camps I was in were Army. We had a couple Air Force guys, but they moved them out. Our officers had their own camp, and they seemed to have gotten pretty good treatment. Most of the prisoners were Americans, but there was one Englishman who didn't want to go back to England. He wanted to go to the States. Another kid, an Italian-American, when he first got captured, they put him in a camp right in his hometown in Italy. His mother and dad were still there, and he got to see them! Angelo Santangelo was his name. There wasn't much food around in those camps. I'll tell you, when we were working over there on the farms, they gave us a loaf of bread. That was for eight guys, and the bread was half sawdust. We got maybe two potatoes, a spoonful of sugar, and a spoonful of oleo, a kind of colored lard that was made to look like butter. They gave us *ersatz* coffee. I don't know what the hell it was made of. That's all we lived on, unless we got Red Cross parcels.

I saw a couple prisoners get killed. This one kid and I were working in potato fields, and the guard, who had been wounded in Italy, didn't like Americans. This kid let him have it with an Italian insult, and the guard understood it. He took his rifle off his shoulder and shot that kid with a wooden bullet that the Germans used. Then he spit on him. The kid was warned I don't know how many times not to agitate this guy, because he was bad.

Sometimes you got a good guard, and sometimes you got a bad one. Most of the time we had a bad one. We had signals. Like when the guard was coming, we'd holler, "Air raid!" Then we'd hide. If they found a knife on you, they'd confiscate everything. If somebody tried to escape, they'd search everything.

We slept in bunks, on the wood. They had no mattresses or anything. They gave us something like a burlap sack to sleep on and one blanket. We had to keep ourselves clean. I still had the toothbrush Father Diagnol had given me, but I didn't have toothpaste. I used salt. I washed myself and my clothes whenever I could. A lot of the GI's didn't wash, and their pants were stiffer than boards. If we didn't keep clean, we got all kinds of problems. They gave us clothes. Somehow they got American trousers and shirts, and we'd trade with different guys. Some guys would have two or three different pairs of pants. I don't know how they got them. But if you watched yourself, your clothes would last a long time. You had to wash them yourself, every week. To take a bath, there were four or five guys in the same tub of water.

A lot of the farmers over there, they weren't bad people. A lot of them said, "I'm not mad at you. Why should we fight?"

I would answer, "Well, I got a letter that said I had to go."

Then they would say, "Yeah, that's what my son did. He got a letter, and he was supposed to go."

In Munich, though, the civilians weren't so nice, maybe because we were bombing the shit out of the place. The young people there would throw stones at us and jab us with sticks, and the guard wouldn't do anything. He'd just laugh. They called us all sorts of names. Once, after they had shot down a plane full of colored guys, the local paper headline was "*Oncle* Sambo."

We worked hard. Yeah, when we worked on the farms, we had to dig up potatoes. They had a machine that dug them, but we had to pick them up. In the wintertime, we had to go out and work when it was fifty below zero. Rain or shine, six days a week. Sometimes on Sunday, we had to exercise the horses. I had to get my team of horses and run them and ride them.

Every camp, every farm that the GI's worked on, had an escape roster. The first time I tried to escape, it was from a farm. I took off with another kid. We slept in a barn. With the guards being around, though, the farmer got scared and reported us. The Germans came and put is in "The Hole." We lived there for three days, on nothing but bread and water.

The next time I escaped with a kid named Hank Perner. We got onto the second floor of the barracks. Perner crawled out the window and down a rope. I went next. First thing we knew, they started shooting. Perner made it to the ground, but I got back in, took off my clothes, and jumped into bed. The guards came running up the stairs. In the end, nobody got hurt, but we got put back in "The Hole."

We tried a lot of ways to escape. On one farm, we dug a hole right through the corner of a building, which was made of mud blocks. Sometimes we would be on a job, forty-two of us, and one or two guards couldn't watch us all. They'd have to trust us. I was a sort of head guy, and I learned to speak German better than most of them. Each morning, the farm boss would relate to me to tell those guys what they were supposed to do. It wasn't too hard to fool the one or two guards, and we would just take off. I don't know of anyone who ever really got away, to the Allied lines, or even back to the States.

"The Hole" was pretty bad. It was just a little place. You had to sleep in there and it got pretty cramped. They took you out twice a day, for an hour or two, to exercise. Then they put you back down in there. The first time I was in there, it was three days. The second time was nearly five days. It was pretty tough. If I had to go to the bathroom, I told the guard, and he'd open the door for me and I'd go.

To survive, we had to learn at least a little German, and the first word I learned was *essen* — "to eat." And *Arbeit* is "work," and *schlaffen* is " to sleep." Those were the first three words I learned. I got to speak pretty good German. We could barter with some of the guards. We made little stoves. Cranked them up to make tea. Then we would save all the tea, put it back in the bag. We'd trade that. We would get different things off of them. They liked chocolate, especially the D-bars in the Red Cross boxes. Then we'd get cigarettes and cigars. Sometimes we wouldn't get a Red Cross box for a long time. There would be two or three packs of Lucky Strikes in there, and the Germans liked them. Bad guards wouldn't wait to barter. They'd just open our packages and take what they wanted, cigarettes, canned meat. Generally, the guards would punch holes in the cans so that we had to eat the contents right away. Otherwise, if we escaped, we'd take the cans along with us, and have food along the way.

The last time I escaped, we were pretty close to a big lake called the Bodensee (Lake Constance), right across from Switzerland. The name was Stalag VII-B. We couldn't find a way across. There was supposed to be a guy there with a boat, but he wasn't there. We started walking, and we walked right into a youth camp. There were all these German kids wearing Swastikas. They were all eight, nine, ten years old. They surrounded us, and boy, they were happy when they got us. They put us on a truck and put us in jail. I remember there was a lady guard there. She was like a sheriff, or a cop, but she was a pretty nice lady. She asked us if we had any coffee or tea.

We had Nescafe. So she made us coffee, and she wanted to barter for some of those packets of Nescafe. She wouldn't steal, and she said she would give us something, but I don't remember exactly what she gave us. But we were there for three days in this jail.

Then we got sent to another camp. What the Germans called the *Unteroffizier* "Under Officer", would come every week or so. He was a great ping-pong player. He asked me, "How come you guys don't have a ping-pong table?"

He talked to me in German. The guys kept asking me what he was saying.

Then he said, "I'll have one made for you."

And, by God, he did. The next day, there was a big ping-pong table. One of our guys was pretty good at the game, and he played the officer. If the kid beat him, he wouldn't do as many favors for us.

We worked on the Bismarck Farm, in East Prussia, up in what would become the Russian Zone. There were all kinds of tunnels there. When the Russians got close, the Germans moved us out. We just walked and walked. It seemed like we walked in circles. It felt like we walked a thousand miles. When we left, it was pretty close to the end of February, and we walked pretty much the whole month of March 1945.

Then I was liberated the month Franklin Roosevelt died, April 1945, by English troops, after twenty-seven months as a POW. The day I got liberated, the guys broke into a warehouse and took brand-new motor bikes. They rode all over the place on them. I was in the hospital at the time. The Germans couldn't get any medicine; they couldn't even give us an aspirin. They gave me a clean bed to lie in, and that was it, regardless of what was the matter with me. I was down to about 90 pounds. When I went into the service, I weighed about 125, 130. Later on, Americans came in, and they flew me to an English hospital.

I stayed in England for about a month, then I got on a hospital ship and went home. I landed in South Carolina. I stayed in a hospital there for about two or three days, then they sent me to DeSchonn General Hospital. I had some bad times. It was no picnic.

When I was captured, my family had no idea whether I was dead or alive. After six or seven months, my sister found out that I was a POW through Vatican Radio. My sister was very active. She belonged to some kind of a club. Parents of POWs would listen to radios, and they'd tell names. When this priest came back from our camp, he took all our names and went to the Vatican. After a few months, the Germans allowed us to write to our parents. Everything was censored. I still have some of the letters, and some of the stuff is blacked out.

I got a Purple Heart and a POW medal. I was discharged in November, 1945. While I was in the hospital, I got tired of being pushed around. I had enough points to qualify for discharge, and I wanted to get out so I could get married. As soon as I got home I got my old job back, got married and had two children.

Allies dropped propaganda and safe conduct leaflets over German troops at the front to encourage their surrender.
Reprinted from CNAS/Buchanan Men of the 704.

The Waffen-SS identity papers and hospital tag of SS officer, Fritz Hofmann, who was captured by troops of the 4th Armored Division. Fritz left the papers at the 704 Tank Destroyer Battalion's field hospital after he had been treated and evacuated. *Courtesy of Mrs. Thomas J. Evans.*

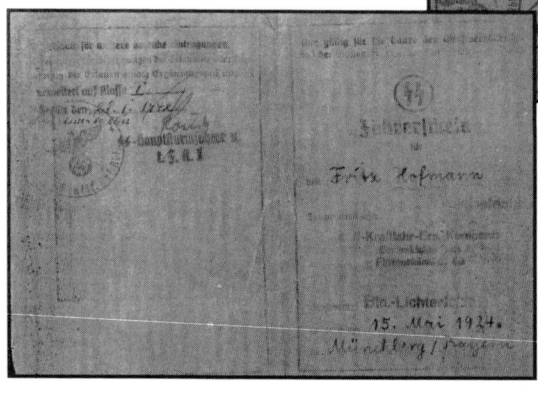

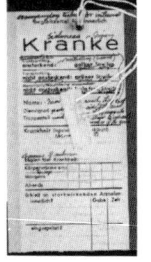
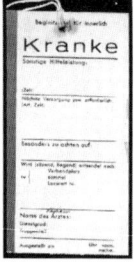

"The River Ran Like a Snake."

David Locke, M.D.
63rd Infantry Division, 263rd Combat Company Battalion, Headquarters and Service; Munhall, Pennsylvania

"Three days later we started to cross the river and begin our introduction to what we trained for. I didn't realize what was happening until I met a dead body."

I WAS IN THREE CAMPAIGNS during the war: Ardennes/Alsace, Central Europe and Rhineland. After the fighting, I was transferred to the 84th Division, then to the 37th, to the 100th and finally to SHAEF, Supreme Headquarters Allied Expeditionary Forces. In 1936, I started working at J&L Steel as a chemist. I was the only college-educated employee in the department at that time. Although I could have been deferred from the war because of that job, I was single and they were beginning to draft married men into the war. That did not seem fair to me.

I tried to get into the Navy, but I couldn't pass the physical because of my eyesight. Later, in August 1943, I was drafted into the Army. Our group left the Pittsburgh Pennsylvania and Lake Erie station, and went to Fort Meade. We all took the M.O.S. test to determine what jobs we would have. After three days, I went south by train to Camp Blanding, were we picked up some non-commissioned officers. After that, we headed further south to Centerville, Mississippi, to Camp Van Dorn. After debarking, I stood with a huge mass of men. They called out our names and we were placed in different groups. My group assembled under the sign "Engineer." All the trainees were loaded into trucks that took us to the various companies. I went to the Engineer Battalion. A sergeant met us by the duty room, an unpainted wooden structure, called us to attention, and marched us to another long, wooden, unpainted shed where they issued us two uniforms, underwear, shirts, shoes, socks, two handkerchiefs, a cap, and a barracks bag. In an hour we had changed into Army clothes, put our civilian clothes into a bag, marched back to the supply room, got our rifles, a gas mask, bayonets, knives, and helmets. The next day we sent our clothes and personal items back home.

Camp Van Dorn was in the process of being built. The land the camp was built on was a cotton field. All of the structures were made of mostly fresh, southern pinewood. The buildings were covered with tarpaper. Wooden sidewalks went from building to building. It was considered a two-division camp, which meant that two divisions were training at the same time. There were 69,000 men there.

One of the Army's tricks was to hold inspections on Saturday after marching the company for an hour around a dusty courtyard. Every one of us rookies had dust on our equipment after the march, and, because of that, we got demerits. Demerits meant that we had duty, got no passes, and did not leave camp for five or six weeks. Every Sunday the rookies who had received demerits were sent to work groups to work in the cotton fields. For the first six Sundays, I retrieved old barbed wire from the cotton fields. We had to tear up the fences and rewind the wire, which the Army re-set in coils for protection, or in areas of potential infiltration. That was my introduction to Army life. We really appreciated passes when we got them.

The nearest town was Centerville, a population of about 3,000. Most of the men in camp were Northerners, and the Southerners were bitter toward us. They saw fit to raise their prices, but we learned to go to towns further away, towns like McComb, Natchez, Baton Rouge and Hattiesburg, rather than pay what they wanted.

I became a Private First Class in the 63rd Division, 263rd Combat Battalion, Headquarters and Service Co. My M.O.S. number classified me as a chemist in the water purification section (S–4). This was changed to bridge carpenter assigned to S–3 section. As an S–3, I helped build camps, construct ramps, and repair bridges. I also helped build simulated Nazi villages for training, artillery ranges, roads, concrete bunkers, railroad tracks, and I learned to use demolitions. I was also trained in the basics of soldiering, map reading, use of the bayonet, night patrol, house to house fighting, use of camouflage, first aid, knot-tying, and crane work, among many other skills. I did this for the first six weeks of training. The men in H & S Company were part of the Battalion along with A, B and C companies. One combat company was to be assigned to one infantry regiment, but could also be interchanged if the need arose. During the second six weeks, I took advanced operational training with my unit. We were trained in keeping combat maps, and we went to Hattiesburg for three weeks for training in bridge building.

In June, I was sent to Rocky Mountain Arsenal, Denver, for chemical-warfare training. At Rocky Mountain, I learned to assemble and repair flame-throwers and fog machines. I also learned to make various explosive devices using plastics, TNT, dynamite, and black powder. After that I got my T4 stripes, equivalent to a sergeant, and I became a CWO, chemical-warfare noncom. Denver, Colorado was a good GI town, the folks were terrific.

In December 1944, before I was sent overseas, I got one free night at Camp Shanks, New York. The Army still made us wear our summer uniforms so that any spies would assume that we were headed for the Pacific. We didn't even get winter uniforms until we were ready to sail.

We left on the *President Harding*, a liner revamped for troop transport, and landed at Marseille, France. Our "bunks" were hammocks, six-men high. We spent all of our waking hours on top deck. When it got dark, we weren't allowed to smoke outside. We passed the time by playing cards, using decks that a group of Puerto Ricans had made from cardboard, or we searched the ocean, looking for the periscopes of German submarines Taking a shower was an unusual event. The showers on board used saltwater, and the only lights at night were red lights. In the red light, plankton in the water looked like tiny sparks coming out of the showerheads. A fun game was trying to keep our meals down in the rough seas, but since the ship was Navy, the food was also Navy. Breakfast was steak and potatoes, lunch was soup with Nabisco cookies, and dinner was a sandwich.

We knew nothing about our course across the Atlantic. It took us seven days to get to France, because we zigzagged in order to avoid enemy submarines. The second day out, the weather got warm, and then it got cold again. We found out later that we first sailed south to Florida, then zigzagged to the coast of West Africa, and then went up the Mediterranean Sea. When we reached port, the ship could not get in because the harbor had been bombed. So, they loaded us into barges and took us in. Ashore, we pitched tents and brought our equipment in. Then they put us on trucks and took us northward through France.

On the trip through France, whenever the column stopped, the French would trade black bread and red wine for our K-Rations. In Dijon, a little girl stood outside a fenced park where we camped for the night. She bargained with us for soap, in exchange for which her mother would wash our clothes, clothes we had been wearing for weeks. The girl lived in a two-room flat with her mother and *grandpere*. Her father had been fighting in the French Army, and they didn't know whether he was a prisoner of the Germans, or dead. We gave *grandpere* cigarettes. Using my poor French and some sign language, I was able to communicate with them.

After a three-day trip, we arrived at Sarreguemines in the Colmar Pocket and Alsace. Our division was assigned to the Seventh Army under General Patch. We were the flank company so that we could be transferred between the Third and Seventh Army, wherever we were needed. We went into action at Sarreguemines, and spent a lot of our combat in the Neckar River valley. The river ran like a snake, so we had to build many bridges before we reached the German Siegfried line.

One night, three of us were on guard duty. A Jeep came up the road. I hailed the occupants, asking them for the password. My two companions were hidden off to the side of the road. When they hesitated, and did not seem to know it, I challenged them. They claimed to be with General Patton, but we forced the issue, leveled our rifles, and prepared to fire. One of them gave the correct password, and we let them go on. Two days later we were called to Lieutenant Colonel Coan's office. Shaking in our boots, he asked why we had threatened General Patton while we were on guard duty. As we prepared to get demoted or worse, the Colonel smiled, something he rarely did. He told us General Patton ordered him to commend us for sticking to our Army orders. That was a time when the brass showed their cool.

At Sarreguemines, the Engineers took over a castle and prepared for battle. Among our supplies were confiscated explosives. Because they were German explosives, we had to test their fuse timers and powder. Three days later we started to cross the river and begin our introduction to what we trained for. I didn't realize what was happening until I met a dead body. At times, we hid in foxholes, shell holes, homes, barns, cellars, and haystacks.

A common trick of the Germans was to string out small anti-personnel mines. They were made of wood, and were the size of a pound-box of sugar. Inside, they put

TNT and ball bearings, or anything they had, like nails, nuts, and bolts. These mines weren't made to kill, just maim. When they exploded they tore up ankles, legs, and genitals. The Germans liked to put them down just before a snowfall. That way they would get hidden. I saw many of our men writhing in pain. The Engineers found that by welding chains onto the steamrollers or bulldozers, they could clear out a path for four to six men. Another German trick was to attach a large mine to several other mines so that when one went off, it would trigger the others to blow also. They would leave pistols, swords and cameras booby-trapped in a home. When these items were pilfered by U.S. troops, the house would blow up. Building bridges was also dangerous because the enemy would lay hidden in the riverbed. As you worked, you were like a sitting duck in an amusement park rifle range.

Piercing fortifications like the Siegfried line with its concrete projections, dragon's teeth, and concrete pillboxes was extremely dangerous. In a usual night project we had to creep along with various explosive devices to try to disrupt the pillbox guards and explode the dragon's teeth so that our tanks would have room to maneuver. Unlike the French Maginot line, which only faced toward Germany, the Siegfried line had guns pointed in all directions. The Germans were really set aback when we pierced their supposedly impenetrable fortification.

Not all of our soldiers were heroes. Drunkenness, rape and looting were common, even though the Army had rules against soldiers doing so.

I was fortunate after the fighting stopped to be sent to various schools. I was at the Sorbonne in Paris for three weeks and Epernay, where I had six weeks of welding experience. Then I stayed six months longer in the military government. For the first three months I was a guard at a Nazi prison. I was the only GI there to have seen action, so I was made 1st sergeant to the replacements sent in. Later I was put in charge of the Post Exchange at Stuttgart. That PX did $50,000 in business every two weeks, because it supplied all of SHAEF. Beside myself, there were nine German girls, a German secretary, and a corporal working there. The PX ran on the Army's one percent profit or loss system. The job put me in the position of having to stand up to Generals and other officers. Fortunately, I had a Major who trusted my judgment, and who had ties to General Omar Bradley. So, my backup was the best.

By 1946, I had more than enough points to be discharged. Points were obtained for length of time in, time in battle, and going overseas. I was offered a higher rank to stay another year but I wanted to see my family again. I was also worried about losing my job at J & L, which, by law, was only supposed to be held for one year.

After I returned home aboard the *Zanesville*, and with encouragement from my uncle, I applied to medical school. While I was in school, I continued at J & L in the summers. I became a doctor.

"Little Crow, Little Crow!"

John Martino
81st Chemical Mortar Battalion; Greensburg, PA, 20 August 1924

"All I heard was guns shooting. I was numb, scared. Praying to God I wouldn't get hit. I had my face buried in the sand. Everybody was a hero that day on Omaha Beach in Normandy. Everyone was my brother. We all helped each other. It was a feeling that nobody will ever understand except the ones who went through it."

I WENT INTO THE SERVICE when I was nineteen years old. My reception center was Fort Meade, Maryland. From there they shipped me to Camp Sibert, Alabama. I took my training in Camp Sibert for thirteen weeks then I went to truck driving school. From there we were going to go into jungle assault. They changed that in a hurry, and put me in 4.2 mortars. Everybody said we were going to a chemical school. Here, I thought I was going to have a white outfit to wear. I didn't know anything about chemicals. It happened to be chemical warfare with the 81st Chemical Mortar Battalion.

The 4.2 were called "chemical mortars," but we fired High Explosive (HE) rounds in a twenty-eight pound shell. When it exploded, you knew it hit. We had to wear earplugs. A lot of guys went deaf because they didn't always have a chance to think about wearing earplugs. They had to fire those shells quick, too. Every time you fired a shell, the 150-pound base plate would sink deeper into the ground. If you fired 100 rounds without first putting sandbags underneath the plate, you had to get a Jeep to pull it out of the ground.

Each squad had eight men and one mortar. Each guy took turns firing. A mortar shell had what they called powder rings on it. They would call from the OP, the outpost, how many rings to put on your shell. Everything would get set up on the barrel, the azimuth and deflection, which way and how high the shell was going to go. The more powder rings you put on the further the shell would go. To hit the target, we had to know what target to hit, or where the infantry was so that we could set up smoke screens for them. That's when we would fire so many rounds of White Phosphorus. You didn't want to get that stuff on you, because there was no way to get it off. It just burned a hole right through you. It was wicked. Dead duds in the barrel were scary. We had shells that blew up in the barrel; guys got killed. In an attack, the barrel got very hot because we were firing one WP, then an HE, then another WP, then three HE.

We learned how to use gas, phosgene, mustard, and other. We never had to use it. We got the term "chemical" because we used White Phosphorus. You could hear the Germans hollering when we used that stuff, but we used it to make smoke screens for advancing infantry, most of the time. The Germans were scared of that stuff.

In our unit there wee six or seven guys who couldn't speak English. There was a little Mexican from Texass named Martino. He didn't know what two and two was. He couldn't add, talked broken, but in training he got to be the best soldier in the outfit. We had a lot that went AWOL, Absent Without Leave, "over the hill." I had a buddy, Ralph from New Kensington, Pennsylvania, who went in the service with me. We got down to Alabama and took training together. He always wanted to go AWOL and hide in his uncle's mine.

I said, "Are you crazy, Ralph?"

"No. I'm not taking all this hiking and stuff."

He would talk Italian to me and I would talk Italian to him, and the officer didn't know what we were talking about.

The officer would say, "What did ou say, Soldier?"

We'd say, "Oh, nice day," or something like that.

I spent another six months in Alabama, at different schools, Fort McClelland, Aniston. They were nice people, especially the people in Birmingham. On weekend passes, we'd go to different homes for dinner and an overnight stay. Of course, a lot of them had nice-looking daughters, and this made things interesting. After church on Sunday, they'd give us dinner, and we'd get back to camp in the evening. In Gadsden, about sixty miles from Camp Sibert, we could buy moonshine for fourteen dollars a pint. They called it "White Lightning."

When we had to go to our POE (Point of Embarkation) to Camp Shenango, on the other side of Pittsburgh, Ralph got pneumonia, and he cried like a baby because he had to stay in the hospital and he wouldn't be leaving with us. I left him down in Alabama. I didn't see Ralph until I got back home. He got over to Europe with the 83rd Chemical Battalion, after the war was over

At Camp Shenango I knew I was going overseas. They shipped me straight to New York, Camp Shanks, for about three months, where we took some more training. Then, we got on a boat for Southampton, England, where we trained for six weeks before they loaded us into boats for the big day, D-Day. Everybody was shaking, scared. I had a buddy named Tony Pittari. I'll never forget him. He was from New York. Before we left Camp Shanks, we all went over his house. His mom and dad had spaghetti and all that for us.

Tony told me, "Johnny I'm never going to come back home."

He knew somehow. When we landed on D-Day, Tony got killed right beside me.

We landed on Omaha Beach, during the first hour of the invasion. While we approached the beach, bullets from the heights were hitting the side of the landing craft. We had the mortars on the carts, and we were supposed to wheel them off the landing craft. Each cart had life preservers wrapped around it so they would float. The mortar, alone, weighed about 275 pounds. At the right time, they dropped down the landing craft door. They said, "You had your fun in England, now go to Paris and have fun."

I didn't know how to swim. I had a life preserver on, plus my full field pack. The life preserver was like an inner tube that you wrapped around your stomach. It had a capsule. When you pinched the capsule, the tube would inflate. It was supposed to hold you up in the water while you swam to shore. You hoped it would, at least.

I expected white water. Instead it was all the color of blood. Bodies were floating all over the place. My mom had given me a set of rosaries and a prayer book. I prayed and prayed going onto that beach. I just lay in the sand, hoping to God I wouldn't get hit. My buddies were screaming for help, getting hit, getting killed.

The Germans were ready for us. Their beach defenses had been there for a long time. They were dug in pillboxes, trenches, and bunkers. Their guns were above, and they were firing at everything that moved. The Lord saved my life. The Rosaries helped me out. I still have them. The beads were black when my mother gave them to me. Today, they shine like brass.

All I heard was guns shooting. I was numb, scared. Praying to God I wouldn't get hit. I had my face buried in the sand. "Hero," everybody calls me. Everybody was a hero that day on Omaha Beach in Normandy. Everyone was my brother. We all helped each other. It was a feeling that nobody will ever understand except the ones who went through it.

When we got on top of the escarpment, to the town of Colleville Sur-Mer, we saw that the Germans had killed civilians, men, women, and babies. The French people tried to escape in covered wagons. The Germans just killed them, killed the horses, and turned the wagons over. They didn't have any mercy on anybody. There were dead horses, dead cattle. What a smell there was! I saw a dead German. He had his rifle bayonet stuck in the ground, and he was leaning on his rifle. I kicked at him and he just fell over. At first, I thought he was alive, but he wasn't.

The fight for Hill 192, around St. Lô, in the hedgerow country, was the worst battle we ever went through. We fought there for a good month (July 1944) until we got over that hill. We fought and fought day and night firing WP and HE. The infantry had the little 88 mortars, and we were right behind with the 4.2s. In the rear, supporting us, were the 105 and 155 howitzers, after that the 240s, and after that, in the English Channel, were the big cannons of our Navy ships.

At night, we dug in, two guys to a foxhole. One guy tried to get some sleep, another guy stayed up. We just lay in there. We didn't move around much or make much noise. The Germans would sneak up on you, and then just bayonet you. We didn't sleep very much, if we slept at all. Aside from worrying about the Germans, the holes sometimes got water in them, and there were bugs and night crawlers. We lived in those foxholes. We never dug one under a tree because of tree bursts. The Germans tried to hit the tops of trees with their artillery shells. When they exploded not only shrapnel rained down, but also pieces of wood and other parts of the tree. Two of my buddies were no more than fifty feet from me, dug in under a small tree. The Germans started with their .88s. I couldn't help them. They were hollering, "Help me! God! Help me God!"

They were both killed. Two years ago I went back to Normandy and visited their graves.

    We had a hard fight getting through St. Lô. Our bombers leveled the place. After that we broke out, and had the Germans on the run. Some days we'd go 500 feet, other days maybe four miles, other days maybe a mile. It all depended on the Germans. Once we had them on the run, though, we didn't stop. Night and day we went. We didn't sleep much. I don't care what they say about Patton, that guy got the war over. He made you move, night and day.

    We got to Paris. That was a happy day, but we went right on through. We weren't allowed to stop. The French people were breaking cognac bottles on the side of the Jeep. It was a ball! There was a lady in a hayfield who took off all her clothes. She kept singing "Praise the Lord, and Pass the Ammunition." An old lady on a hay wagon was singing "It's A Long Way to Tipperary." It was a great day, going through Paris, and seeing all the happy people!

    We got into a little town in Belgium where my captain, the platoon sergeant, and a couple other guys got captured. I got lucky and didn't get caught. Four of us were in a barn, and when we saw the Germans coming, we got way under the hay. Our Jeep was in the barn, with the motor still running. The Germans, figuring we were in the barn, stuck bayonets into the hay. One almost hit me in the forehead. The captain left his hiding place with the sergeant and the other guys and ran across the road. That's when the Germans caught them. I guess the Germans figured that was all of us. After the Germans left, we got out, and the Belgian people fed us for couple days until our outfit came up.

    The Battle of the Bulge was fierce. Men got frozen feet and trench foot from the cold and wet. The ground was so frozen we had trouble digging foxholes. Again, we had to be quiet because the Germans were always close around. We had those big army coats, and tried to keep warm. Most of us had blowtorches, and everybody cooked with it, if and when we had food. We ate what we could get. We didn't even have K-Rations because our guys couldn't get supplies to us. We'd raid chicken coops for chickens and eggs. We'd just pluck the feathers out of a chicken and cook it with a blowtorch. I don't know why we didn't poison ourselves. The Belgian people helped us when they could, but they didn't have much either.

    One morning in a small town in Germany, we lost twenty-six men. The Germans used jet planes on us. We were eating our first hot meal in three months. We were waving our aluminum mess kits around as we watched the mess truck come up the road. The German pilots must have seen the flashes from the kits. They came down so quick we didn't realize what had happened. I ran into this house for cover. They plastered the house, and it came down on top of the table I was under. I was lucky. The other guys weren't. I heard our guys hollering, "Little Crow. Little Crow." That was my nickname. My dad's nickname was Big Crow. Also, I named my Jeep, Little Crow. Anyway, I couldn't talk, I was so scared. They dug me out from under the table, and I got back to my outfit. I'll never forget that day. Most of the Jeeps had flat tires. But worse, about thirty guys were wounded, and twenty-six of my buddies died. Needless to say, we never did get our hot breakfast, but the morning was one big mess.

In Germany, we had to be wary of everybody, soldier or not. Even women called in our whereabouts to German artillery. Even kids! Toward the end, the Germans had twelve and fourteen-year-olds in their army. Once we had to shoot a woman out of a church tower because she was a sniper.

One day, in Germany, we were bedded down in a slaughterhouse with our mortar position outside. A German Messerschmidt dove down on us, but our ack-ack shot him down. He belly-landed right near our mortar position. He got out on the wing and started to fire at us with a burp gun. So, we killed him. I got his jacket, I got his cap, and some other guys got his rings and wristwatch. One of the guys couldn't get one of the rings off the German's finger, so he cut the finger off.

Between our drive from Hill 192 and the slaughterhouse it had turned winter. We kept our Jeeps white-washed so the German pilots would have trouble seeing them from the air. We even whitewashed our helmets. Everything was whitewashed. We had to put wire cutters on the front of our Jeeps. We had to have them, because they were lifesavers. The Germans would string steel wire across the road, and we had quite a few decapitations. You couldn't see those wires at night, and they were so thin, you could hardly see them in the daytime. The wire cutters on the Jeep cut right through them. There were land mines all over the place, as well. Our engineers usually went ahead to clear mines and mark safe paths. They would do this first, before anybody else made a move.

During the night, we traveled on the Autobahn, no lights, no anything, except one small reflector on the Jeep. We followed a little phosphorus paint on the Jeep ahead of us. The Germans, of course, knew we were on the road. Bed-Check Charlie would come over and lay flares all over the road to light everything up. We just hit the ditches because the Germans would open up on us from wherever they were.

A concentration camp we liberated had thousands and thousands of murdered Jews in it. I'll never forget that morning. The smell was unbearable. We loaded the bodies on trucks, dug ditches with bulldozers, and just dumped the bodies in the ditches. It was hard to take.

We had a corporal in our unit, named Cooper, a little Jewish guy, who was an immigrant to America. He had been born in the area we were in. After we liberated the camp we captured a bunch of Germans in a town. Cooper lined them all up. The Germans were shaking in the cold air. Cooper had a Thompson sub-machinegun.

Cooper kept saying, in German, "Who did this? Who killed my parents?"

How Cooper recognized the bodies of his parents in that pile of corpses, I'll never know. Anyway, Cooper took one of the Germans out of the line, made him take all his clothes off, then shot him. Nobody said or did anything to Cooper about it.

When the war ended I was in Salzburg, Austria, near Berchtesgaden, Hitler's hideout. Up in Salzburg they had the bunkers and a hospital. Everything was underground, generators, supplies, everything. I swear I walked down 150 steps to get there.

Salzburg is where I got an accordion. Through my wartime career, I was the only one in my battalion who played the accordion. Of course, we had guys who played the saxophone, clarinet, guitar, whatever, but whenever someone found an accordion they brought it to me. I had about twenty-one accordions over there. A lot of them got shot up, and this is the only one that made it home with me. This thing is history. It has to be eighty-five, ninety years old. Coming home on the ship, we had an orchestra, we had a ball.

After Germany surrendered, they were getting ready to send us to the Pacific after a thirty-day furlough out of Camp Lucky Strike in France. They already had our Jeeps packed in Cosmoline. The war in the Pacific ended while we were at Camp Lucky Strike. Boy! We tore that camp down, tore the latrines apart. A lot of guys stayed over there and did occupation work. I left Europe on the *SS Jonathan Edwards*. It was the ship's tenth voyage. In September 1945, I was back home.

When we got back to Fort Miles Standish, my buddy Tiberio says, "You're not carrying this accordion off, I am. I don't want you to drop it off in the ocean. You got it this far."

And Tiberio carried it off the ship. I play it at every unit reunion we have. I'm going to give it to the museum at Fort Leonard Wood in Missouri. That's were our monument is.

During the war I was a Sergeant. Then I got broke to Corporal. Then I got broke to PFC Then I got back to being a Corporal again, and I ended up as a Corporal coming home. Stripes didn't mean anything. All I wanted to do was get home alive, and see my mom and dad. Before you went to the army you didn't think much about your parents, but when you came home believe me you were a different guy. It wasn't easy, but we made the best of it. Thank God I got home safe and am able to talk about it, but it makes me feel bad that my buddies didn't make it home. Once in awhile, I sit down and think about it.

I can see it all in my mind. I can track everything. In 1993, I went back to Europe. The Mayor of Colleville Sur-Mer made our veterans honorary citizens of the town. Two years ago, we were over again. We visited the place where we hid in the haystack. Matter of fact, the barn is still there, and you can see the shell marks still, and the marks from the machinegun bullets. My wife couldn't get over that. The Germans didn't blow that barn up. I don't know why. They had to know we were in there. That morning was just as bad as D-Day. We were as scared, and nobody moved. Actually, we were scared every minute of every day. We never knew.

Joe Horant, John Martino, and Chet Skoraszewski of the 81st Chemical Battalion relax in a behind the lines rest area. *Courtesy of John Martino.*

John Martino plays his "captured" Hohner accordian at Berchtesgarten, Hitler's retreat. It will be placed in the 81st Chemical Battalion Museum at Fort Leonard Wood, Missouri

Privates Coscarilli (New Kensington, Pennsylvania), Cardella (Greensburg, Pennsylvania), and John Martino pose for a photo in Gadsden, Alabama (25 December 1942) while the 81st Chemical Battalion trained at Camp Sibert.

Art Carrier and John Martino, 81st Chemical Battalion, in front of the slaughterhouse, Saarlautern, Germany, 29 January, 1944.

Francis Satler, George Cardella, John Martino pose on the wreckage of a Bf-109 Messerschmidt, shot down by American ground fire.

John "Little Crow" Martino's Jeep, "Little Crow."

John Martino plays an accordion as buddies from the 81st Chemical Battalion show off souveniers taken from the enemy. Charlie Tarr, is dressed in a German uniform, La Mar Coleman and Andy Anderson hold the Swastika flag, Cooper displays a Luger 9mm pistol. Metz, Germany.

John Martino, driver, in a German motorcycle-halftrack, with buddies from the 81st Chemical Battalion. Left to right: Ed Poore, Arnold Tuttle, Alex Odom.

Going Home at last. John Martino aboard the *SS Jonathan Edwards*.

The 81st Chemical Battalion arrives in Boston at the end of the war.

"We Got Used to the Night."

Nicholas P. Matro

Twentieth Air Force, 6th Bomb Group, 313th Wing, 39th Squadron
Boeing B29 *Lucky Strike*, Crabtree, Pennsylvania, 23 June 1921

"We lived in tents for a long time and each crew had their own tent. Our tent was at the end of a line of tents. Prior to our getting there, the Army or Marines, I don't know which, had hung, from a tree near the tent, about twenty Japanese skulls painted different colors like Christmas tree ornaments. They swung back and forth in the breeze. We saw them everyday, and never thought a thing about it."

I fought the war in a B–29. Whenever a crew was shot down another crew would take the responsibility of watching over their tent. We would take turns doing this, and it was very emotional. There would be a shoe tossed over in the corner, or an open book lying on a cot where a guy had laid it down, maybe a half-written letter, things like that. It made an indelible impression on me. I still think back with sadness about those young guys who didn't make it.

I came out of the war with a Distinguished Flying Cross with one Oak Leaf luster. That meant it was the equivalent of two Distinguished Flying Crosses. I got the Air Medal with five Oak Leave clusters, making it six Air Medals. I got the Pacific Campaign Ribbon with five Combat Stars, and a Presidential Unit Citation with one Oak Leaf cluster, the equivalent of two Presidential Unit Citations. I also got a Good Conduct Ribbon! The funny thing is, I don't know where all those medals are. Just the other day, someone asked me about them, and I didn't know. I'm sure they're in the house somewhere. I'm sure of that. They're probably tucked away in the back of a drawer I haven't opened in years

It was a Sunday. I was walking home after visiting my grandparents. Someone stopped me and said, "Did you hear the news? Pearl Harbor has just been bombed!"

After that attack, going into the service for us was a natural thing to do, draft or not. It was as natural as starting a new school year. I hated to leave, but I didn't think about the downside too much. I looked upon it as a great adventure.

I went into active service in November 1942, and went to Nashville, Tennessee, before being assigned to a pre-flight school in San Antonio, Texas. I became an Air Cadet. We did the usual basic training, but it was more like going to school, or being in an ROTC unit. We learned the techniques of flying, even if we didn't do any. We also learned Morse Code and navigation techniques. We were busy from morning until night, so we didn't have much time to think about home.

I took primary flight training at El Reno, Oklahoma. I soloed, and went to advanced flight training, but I washed out because of what they called, "Mechanical Flying." That meant that I knew how to fly, but I lacked, at least in their assessment, the "feel" for flying. They gave me the choice to be trained as a bombardier or radio operator. I chose radio operator. They transferred me to Scott Field, Illinois, and then I went to advanced B–29 training in Sioux Falls, South Dakota. After that, I was assigned to an aircrew at Grand Island, Nebraska. From Grand Island we went down for a week or so to Cuba and Puerto Rico to learn how to fly over large bodies of water.

In late January 1945, we staged from Mather Field in California. There we were outfitted with new flying clothes, uniforms, and we were issued a brand-new airplane. We left Mather Field on 28 January. Our destination was Tinian Island in the Marianas. We were assigned the bombardment of Japan.

Our route was to take us from Mather to Honolulu, and from there to Kwajalein Island in the Marshalls. Enroute to Kwajalein, one of our engines caught fire. We managed to extinguish the fire and turn back to Hawaii. About halfway there, we remembered that there was a small atoll called Johnston Island, a Navy refueling station, actually made into an island by Seabees, who had dredged up coral to extend a runway into the sea. The place was a little over one-mile long and about a quarter-mile wide. We managed to land there, and ours was the largest plane at the time to do so. We spent ten days on that place! Not a blade of grass, not a tree in sight, nothing but coral, and a lot of Navy people. Ships would come and leave oil and gas to be stored for refueling ships. We installed a new engine ourselves. Fortunately we had our crew chief with us. He headed up our ground crew, and he knew what to do. If we hadn't taken him along, we would have really been in trouble. While we were there, another troubled B–29 came in. We got to know the other crew pretty well. We played a little softball or basketball to pass the days. That crew was later lost over the Pacific.

Eventually, we got to Kwajalein. We took off from there and landed on Tinian on 10 February. Tinian had the most ideal weather I had ever experienced. The temperature year round was in the range of eighty or eighty-five. Rarely was it much higher than that, and I never knew it to be much cooler than that. There were rainy seasons, but it was a very pleasant climate. It was a great island to be on. There was no malaria there either. It had been used by the Japanese to grow sugar cane. The Japanese had used Korean forced labor, and, after we took the island, we continued to maintain the camp that the Japanese had built for them, and in which they had to remain. I visited them on occasion. Their little houses were immaculately kept. They passed their time growing vegetables and raising a few animals for food. We used to trade them for the trinkets they made. They were a docile bunch, maybe because the Japanese had treated them so badly.

On 18 February 1945, I flew my first mission to a Japanese base on Truk Island. We dropped some bombs, but it was nothing spectacular. There was a little gunfire but nothing much more than that. From then on we flew missions on a fairly regular basis, usually, once a week.

Our next mission was on 25 February, over Tokyo. We had waited a long time for this one! We averaged about fifteen hundred miles, each way, and took about sixteen hours to complete. We came in at 26,000 feet, and I think we caught them by surprise. Our bomb bays got stuck open, and the rest of the planes pulled away from us. We were a little apprehensive. Mayo, our tail gunner, got in a burst at an enemy fighter, and he left us alone.

Later, we flew night missions, and came in very low, five or six thousand feet, an unheard of level, especially at night. That was Curtis LeMay's idea. On those later missions, we went in one plane at a time, dropping incendiary bombs on residential areas, just burning the daylights out of them. On those nights, after we had dropped our bombs, it looked like a dozen Chicago fires had been lit.

The B–29 was never intended to fly low-level missions but, for saturation bombing like we were doing, low-level, night attacks were undoubtedly far more efficient, and darkness gave us a sort of cloak of protection. The first time we went in, we were apprehensive. LeMay ordered that we strip the planes of all armament except the tail gun. There were two reasons for this; first, we lightened the load and could carry more bombs, and, second, because of the darkness, LeMay didn't want use shooting each other down. We got used to the night.

We were always in awe of the immensity of the conflagration. We didn't actually see flames, just a huge, orange glow. It was impressive! We didn't think much about what was happening on the ground, to all those people trying to escape the flames and the high winds they created. We were just doing our jobs.

The first few planes that went through would be in pretty good shape, but after that there would be anti-aircraft and whatever night-fighters that might be flying. The Jap fighters at times would be very daring. They'd dive right through our formation firing their guns and barrel rolling so that they presented a really scattered pattern of machinegun fire. Other times they'd fly out and stay out of range and just fly around us, almost as if they were observing. There was no way to tell. We sometimes thought the way some of them reacted that they might have been on dope or something because they were so reckless.

The Japanese fighters used some weird weapons. Phosphorous bombs were one. They exploded in mid-air, and the phosphorous spread all over the sky, like a firework. They used what we called the Baka Bomb, the "Stupid" or "Foolish" bomb. The Japanese called it the *Oka,* 'Cherry Blossom.' It was a flying bomb, and it meant a one-way trip for the pilot. They were rocket powered, and the pilots were supposed to ram our bombers with them. They had the maneuverability of a rock, and we could avoid them with just a little evasive action. The first time we saw one, was on a trip back from our target. We saw a ball of fire following a bomber, but we didn't know what the hell it was at the time. If they didn't hit anything, they soon ran out of fuel, and down they went.

The searchlights were the worst things. The Air Corps issued us dark sunglasses to take on our night flights! We thought that weird, until we realized why. If a plane got caught in a searchlight, the whole interior would light up like a sunny day. Every aperture, every window, every bubble, every reflective surface, would light up. Very often, when searchlights did zero in on a particular plane, all the anti-aircraft guns and night fighters went after it. We did everything we could to avoid the searchlights.

The effect of the heat and the smoke that arose from the ground was unbelievable. Not only did the fires create tornado-like winds on the ground, but also the heat from them created dangerous turbulence in the air. Big B–29s would be tossed around like corks, or thrown up or down several hundred feet. Some were even turned upside down.

Fighting a war from a bomber is vastly different from the kind of war an infantryman fights. We didn't have personal contact with the enemy. We were several thousand feet above them, remote from them. Years later, I got an appreciation of what our incendiaries were doing to people on the ground. One of our guys got his hands on a book written by a Japanese fellow. The title is *Tokyo Dai Kusuh* 'The Great Tokyo Raid.' He had the book translated, and he gave a copy to all of us at one of our reunions. The book described the horrors of those fire bombings. People headed for rivers to escape the heat and flames, only to find that the water was boiling. The devastation was terrific, and actually greater than what we achieved with the Atomic Bomb.

In any case, war has a tendency to dehumanize. We lived in tents for a long time and each crew had their own tent. Our tent was at the end of a line of tents. Prior to our getting there the Army or Marines, I don't know which, had hung, from a tree near the tent, about twenty Japanese skulls painted different colors like Christmas tree ornaments. The skulls swung back and forth in the breeze. We saw those skulls every day, and never thought a thing about it.

We had other missions like dropping anti-shipping mines in the Tsushima Straits. Those were rather hazardous missions because we had to fly in very low and expose ourselves to Japanese shore batteries, and Japanese naval anti-aircraft was much more accurate that their land-based guns.

Our briefings for those missions gave us an indication of what headings we would follow, and, on special maps, markings as to where we were to drop the mines. The actual dropping was done by radar, because radar gave us a precise outline of the coast, and enabled us to more easily locate positions for the mines. The mines we laid were insidious devices, tremendous in size, and set to explode by pressure or sound. Some would explode when the first ship passed over them, others on the third pass, and others on the twentieth pass, as so forth. That made them difficult to sweep. We dropped them by parachute, so that they would have a "lighter" impact on the water, reducing the chance of premature explosion.

One of our more interesting mine-laying missions on the coast of Korea, in the Shimonoseki Strait. General John H. Davies of the 313th Wing came along with us. The general had several ammunition cases brought on board, and we didn't know what the heck they were for. As we got into the twenty-hour mission, the general opened the boxes. They were filled with celery and Hershey bars. We hadn't seen fresh celery for ages! Had we gotten killed on that mission, we would have died happy. We had celery and Hershey bars! It was our first mining mission to Korea. It was supposed to be a relatively easy mission, a surprise attack, but it turned out to be very difficult. Our plane was hit twenty-seven times, but none of us was harmed.

The Pacific Ocean is vast, and we spent a great deal of our airtime over it. We were to react in certain ways if we took damage. If we absolutely had to bail out, try to get into the hands of the Japanese military. At least they would be interested in information, and we might have a better chance of survival. Civilians would likely beat us to death. If we were damaged, and if we could, we should nurse the plane back to Tinian or Saipan. We also had submarines we called "Dumbos" stationed a certain distance apart. Near the end of the war, they would be in Tokyo Bay, close to the Japanese mainland. We were told to fly a damaged ship out as far as possible into the bay, break radio silence, and then ditch. Hopefully, one of the Dumbos would pick us up. My hat went off to those Dumbo skippers. They really stuck their necks out for us, because there would also be Japanese destroyers and patrol boats in the bay.

When the Marines took Iwo Jima, it shortened our trips, and being able to land there saved many lives. The first bomber to land on Iwo was piloted by Raymond Malo. After him, twenty four hundred others made emergency landings. We had to land there five times with a shot-up plane or lost engines. One of those times was 14 May 1945 on our fifteenth mission over Nagoya when we took several hits. It was a 500-plane daylight raid, and the largest ever to hit the Japanese Empire. Our only thought was to get back to Iwo safely. Gasoline poured out of our plane, and when we finally made Iwo, a typhoon was just in its infancy. Ground control radioed that anyone coming in to land would have to bail out because conditions were so bad. We were down to one engine, at a very low altitude, and our commander decided to not follow instructions. We did make it in, but we were the last plane to do so. All the crews coming in after us, and even a couple before, bailed out.

We stayed on Iwo and weathered the storm. They put us in tents, and during the night the tents blew away. As we lay there in the wind and rain, we decided that the best and safest place to be was inside our plane, so we went back to it, turned it into the wind for greater resistance, went inside, and spent the night, soaking wet as we were.

After the storm, we took a tour of the part of the island under our control. Japanese corpses and body parts were all over the place, having been exhumed by the storm. Mayo kicked a Jap helmet, and a skull dropped out. The guy had been buried the way he died.

The Marines were still fighting for the island, and a squad of them came by and offered to sell us some rum. We were so cold and so wet that we decided why not? So they sold us a bottle of rum for fifty dollars. They left and we opened the bottle. God only knows what was in that bottle because we couldn't drink it. It was something they had just made. The following day the typhoon passed through. The Air Corps sent in planes to pick up us and other downed crews and take us back to Tinian.

The B–29 was excellent! It was the Cadillac or the Rolls Royce of the bombers because it was pressurized. Consequently, we could fly in light flight suits. We carried heavy suits in the event we lost pressurization through gunfire or shrapnel, but other than that the atmosphere inside the plane was pleasant. The B–29 was faster, it flew higher, and it was more comfortable than any other bomber. The guns were far more accurate because they were remotely controlled by radar. The gunners didn't have to have hands on a gun, so there were no vibrations to throw off their aim. The radar factored all the information for leading a target. It was the last word in the aerial fighting machines of 1945. Still, the plane wasn't perfect. Early on, the engines were prone to fire. The plane was heavy to begin with, and when we loaded it up with tremendous amounts of fuel and ordnance, takeoffs were hazardous. Our airfield at Tinian was only about ten-feet above sea level. Once we were off the runway, we were awfully close to the water, and we had to generate enough speed to start a climb. We would be so close to the water that it wasn't uncommon for sea spray to enter slits in the bomb bay doors and soak people inside the plane. There were quite a few planes that crashed on take-off, simply because they never developed enough speed to get up off sea level. Once you did, unless you developed engine trouble, you had a relatively comfortable flight all the way up to the Japanese coast.

I saw planes that didn't make it on take off. There were even times when we weren't flying and we'd see or hear a great big explosion in the distance. And, I mean explosion. Ten thousand gallons of high-octane fuel and several thousand pounds of incendiary bombs make one terrific blast.

We had two commanders on our B–29, the *Lucky Strike*. The first was Captain Robert Rodenhouse. After our fifteenth mission, headquarters made Captain Rodenhouse a staff officer, and that was the end of his flying career. Then we were assigned Captain William Lemme, and we finished out our missions with him. Our copilot was Dick Bumgartner. Our bombardier was 2nd Lieutenant George Kemp. Our navigator was Second Lieutenant Bill Sullivan. Our flight engineer was Staff Sergeant George Bayha. I was the radio operator. I was a staff sergeant at the time, and my position was in the front compartment.

The B–29 was in two compartments. There was a big tunnel, about thirty feet long, big enough to crawl through, that connected the two. In between these two compartments was the bomb bay. Our radar operator, Lou Volmen, who later became Warren Bush the film producer, occupied the rear compartment. Our central fire-control gunner, Charles Fitch, was another staff sergeant. Our two side gunners were Bill Moritz and Sidney Youngner.

Our tail gunner was David Mayo. We called him "Yo-Yo." He was the youngest guy on the crew. Most of us were around twenty or twenty-one, and Mayo was eighteen when he came aboard. He had already seen combat in B–25s, and had earned a Purple Heart! I don't know how, but Mayo enlisted when he was fourteen. He wasn't mentally light, but he didn't use a great deal of common sense. He loved combat, and he loved the war. He was consumed with it. After his wound, he could have sat out the war in some cushy stateside job, but he didn't. Mayo carried two pistols, a compass, and a huge Bowie knife.

Once, our pilot complained about our tail being heavy. On take-off, he was a little concerned about it because he had a hard time adjusting the stabilizers. They were a little sluggish. They checked all the mechanical aspects, and they couldn't find anything wrong. They just went over it with a fine-toothed comb. Nobody ever thought to check Mayo's gun compartment, which was an isolated position. Once we were pressurized, there was no way for Mayo to get in or out, and no way for us to check him.

Eventually, when they couldn't find anything mechanically wrong with the plane, they went into the rear and found the problem. Mayo felt that he hadn't enough ammunition with the normal allocation he was given, so he kept sneaking bands of .50 caliber back into his position. He had about twice as much ammo than he was supposed to have. In addition to the ammunition, Mayo was taking hand grenades aboard. We couldn't figure out what he was going to do with them because he sure couldn't drop them from the plane, especially after we got pressurized. It that wasn't enough, Mayo managed to get his hands on several flak suits (we all wore one over target), and lined the interior of his tail compartment with them.

Mayo didn't get court-martialed, but he got his ass chewed out good and proper because he could have killed us by putting all that considerable extra weight in the plane. From then on, our ground crew always checked the plane to make sure Mayo brought no more ordnance aboard than he was allowed to.

I went on one mission without my crew only once, and so did Mayo. He was with me. A radio operator on one of the lead crews was unable to go on a mission, so they assigned me to the plane. Mayo wanted to go with me, so he talked a gunner on the plane to fake some sickness or other.

Mayo and I were in the lead plane into the target, and as soon as we hit the coast, we took several hits. We lost a couple engines, and were forced to leave formation. The other crews reported that we had crashed, but we managed to limp back to Iwo. Along the way, we jettisoned our bombs into the sea.

Back on Iwo, and waiting for a plane to take us back to Tinian, Mayo and another kid went out to look for souvenirs. The Marines were still fighting on the island, and I had tried to talk them out of going. Mayo, however, was determined to get some souvenirs.

"I won't go too far. I'll watch myself," he said.

Another thing about this kid that plays into this story is that the rest of us wore flying clothes, but Mayo always wore a dress uniform, and he adorned it with all of his previous campaign ribbons. He looked much different from the Marines, who were always grimy. Anyway, Mayo and this other kid get to poking around in a cave when six Japanese soldiers came out and surrendered. They thought Mayo was some kind of high-ranking Air Force Army officer. Not too many Japanese were surrendering on Iwo, and not too many Marines were taking prisoners. These guys must have wanted to live instead, and decided to surrender to someone they recognized as non-Marine.

"I was scared," Mayo told me. "But I didn't let them know that. I fired over their heads to scare *them*."

Mayo and the kid were taking the prisoners down the road, when they met a group of Marines who took them off their hands. The Marines brought them back to their headquarters, and ended up giving Mayo and the kid everything that was in the cave.

Before Mayo and his buddy got back, a plane had come in for us and we left for Tinian. Back on Tinian, we started to hear stories of an Air Force guy capturing a bunch of "Japs." We laughed and said that it was probably Mayo. And damned if it wasn't!

Mayo got back just in time for our next mission. He took his cave loot — Japanese money, Saki, blankets, radio equipment — and he shared it with all of us. He gave me an opium pipe, and some money! We didn't know that he also brought back some Japanese hand grenades. He stuck them in a basket, and put the basket under some blankets. Then he put the whole lot under his cot. Japanese hand grenades were notoriously unsafe. You didn't pull a pin to activate them, like you had to do with an American grenade. There was a little knob on the end of their grenades that you hit down on a hard surface to arm them. Mayo had about fifteen of them in that basket, and it was conceivable that, if any one had accidentally kicked that basket, the whole Quonset hut would have gone up, with all of us in it. That was Mayo. He walked to a different drumbeat. We ran him and his hand grenades out of the tent. He hid them somewhere else. We never found out where, but at least they were out of our quarters.

Mayo stayed in service after the war. I still see him occasionally. He has a hundred-thousand-dollar gun collection. I asked him why he had all those guns. He replied that he wanted to be ready to defend the country again if he had to. Sometime after he came home, he went to a surplus auction and bought what he thought was one drum of brown camouflage paint. It turned out that he had purchased several. He painted his house with it.

As crew, we lived together, except for the officers. Still, we spent most of our waking hours together, fishing, beach combing, and things like that. One of our guys was a botanist. He'd go out and find unique plants. We spent a lot of time writing letters, and we had mail call every day. We got six-week-old letters, but they were like gold. We also got packages. Our head gunner, Charlie Fitch, a nice guy, but a little annoying at times, and a little on the beefy side. Well we used to delight in doing things to annoy Charlie. About once a month Charlie would get a box of Tampa Nugget cigars. We knew the size and shape of that box. We wouldn't touch his mail, of course, but the minute he opened it we all dove on Charlie and took the cigars. We would leave him a few, and we all went around smoking his cigars! Poor Charlie, he'd be mad, but there was nothing much he could do about it. When we got cookies, they were always stale. Charley Fitch's cigars were what we really waited for!

Gambling was a common pastime. So was booze-making. Some guys had homemade stills, and they would make some kind of booze out of sugar cane or whatever they could get their hands on. They were always trying to get raisins off the cook.

They were crude stills, and the booze came out one slow drop at a time. Nobody really got drunk on that stuff. It was mostly the fun of making it.

We ate what we got, and it wasn't always that good. We made jelly sandwiches to take on missions, but they were always stale. We got lots of goat meat from New Zealand. We liked to make friends with the Seabees. They liked to take rides in the planes, and we accommodated them, not always for unselfish reasons. They worked hard, and were entitled to the Navy food they had access to. In gratitude for the flights, they stole gallons of boned, cooked chicken and gave them to us. That was stuff we couldn't even dream of. We took that chicken on missions, whenever we had it. When we got back, we gave the jelly sandwiches to the Marines. They were happy to get them.

We had an open-air theater, like a drive-in. We sat on benches and watched really old movies three or four times a week. We built a kind of service club out of a tent. It was a crude place, but good enough to get together in and drink Coca-Cola and beer, when we could get beer. We did a lot of reading as well. They had a loud speaker that played music when it wasn't broadcasting orders or announcements. Trouble is, we had only one record, "Sentimental Journey, and they played that over, and over and over again. If it hadn't been for Tokyo Rose, we wouldn't have heard anything from the Hit Parade. She was the Japanese equivalent of Axis Sally, and she said pretty much the same stuff, like, "39th Squadron when you come to Tokyo tomorrow you'll all be shot down! You'll never get to see your loved ones again!"

We were always mystified by the fact that Tokyo Rose knew more about our bomber groups and squadrons that some of us did.

Dress was very casual. There were only rare occasions where we actually put on our Army dress clothes (except for Mayo), and that would be for maybe a visiting general or some very special occasion like granting of awards and medals. But, for the most part, we went around in shorts and shoes, that's it!

We were still thinking in terms of an invasion when the war ended. We felt we had softened up the Japanese mainland to the point where it would be a little easier for our people to invade, but there was always that concern that a lot of our troops were going to be killed because of the fanaticism of the Japanese people. Then we dropped the Atomic Bomb.

We had no indication of the missions to Hiroshima and Nagasaki even though we were on the same island when they brought the 539th Squadron in. The crews were absolutely segregated, and you couldn't get anywhere near them. The security was unbelievable!

It was hard to even comprehend the devastation those bombs created, but that didn't matter to me. They shortened the war, as far as I was concerned. It was the right thing to do, and no one will ever convince me otherwise.

After the bombs were dropped, they transferred us to Saipan, and we got on a ship for home. There we were, out in the middle of the Pacific Ocean on a hot, overcrowded ship. All we had for breakfast was beans, then sandwiches for lunch and sandwiches for dinner. We couldn't take showers, and the lines to the heads were endless. Most of us slept on deck, it was so hot on that ship. The sailors sold us jugs of ice water for five dollars, and sandwiches of thin baloney for two. They were stealing it all from the mess hall and making a fortune. If we had a poker game going, the Shore Police would come by and take a cut on every game. Japan surrendered while we were en route, and it didn't make it any better listening to broadcasts of the wild celebrations coming from the States, and wishing we were home.

I first heard about Pearl Harbor as I was coming home from my grandparents' house. It came full circle. When I got home, my old Italian grandfather, Carmen Matro, tapped a keg of special wine he had made three years before. All of his grandsons, returning from the war, got a glass of that wine.

Sixth Bomb Group bathers on Tinian strike a modest pose. *Courtesy of Nicholas Matro.*

B-29 pilots and crews pose in front of their casino on Tinian. *Courtesy of Nicholas Matro.*

Nick Matro takes a brief rest on some bombs on Tinian.
Courtesy of Nick Matro.

A knocked-out Japanese locomotive on Tinian.
Courtesy of Nicholas Matro.

Nick Matro in front of an early helicopter on Tinian.
Courtesy of Nicholas Matrol

Defunct Japanese "Meatball" tanks on Tinian. *Courtesy of Nicholas Matro.*

"The Rest of the Story."

Hal Mayforth
United States Third Army, 4th Armored Division
25th Cavalry Reconnaissance Squadron
Boston, Massachusetts, 25 February 1921

[Sergeant Mayforth through John DiBattista, who served with him in the 4th Armored Division's drive across France, passed on the following comments to the editors. Sergeant Mayforth prominently appears in Mr. DiBattista's narrative "Cowboys and Germans" included in the Center publication The Long Road: From Oran to Pilsen, 1999.*]*

We arrived in Normandy on D+38, and went into combat on the second day. The three line platoons left their vehicles under camouflage nets and proceeded to the hedgerows to fight as infantry. Ordnance had worked feverishly to transform ou Peeps from casual to combat dress. They abandoned the glass windshields in the hedgerows, and replaced them with armor plate. Vertically, on the front bumper of each Peep they welded heavy-duty, four-foot lengths of angle iron. They did this to save our necks — literally. The Germans, deliberately targeting Peep personnel, had a nasty habit of stretching neck-high piano wire across roads.

Our planes had completely annihilated a horse-drawn German supply train. The horses were still in their traces and boated by the hot, July sun, but the wagons were still intact. In the spirit of red-blooded GIs, we stopped for a look-see at what might be taken for loot. At first, nothing interested us until we chanced upon a wagon-load of brand-new, blue-gray, knitted sweaters, four of which we looted — one for each crewman. Knowing that the sweater would give us extra warmth when winter arrived, we stored them in our M–8 armored car. But more about the sweaters, later.

In early August, my unit was augmented by a French paratrooper named Tony. How he happened to join us remains a mystery. We just adopted him. Tony had been raised in England, and his unit had jumped into France about a month before D-Day to do as much damage as possible to bridges and communications. Tony was absolutely fearless. He parents had suffered from the German occupation, and his sister had been raped. Thus, Tony fought under a Vendetta, and he took no prisoners. Tony spoke impeccable English with a slight British accent. Since it was our job to discover from the French the route, location, and strength of *Wehrmacht* units, Tony was a valuable asset.

One time, the females in one French community, ecstatic over being liberated, showered us with affection. They asked Tony, "How do you say in English, 'Kiss me." To which Tony replied, "Kiss me quick, you sonofabitch!"

Thereafter, every GI passing through was greeted by the young women with outstretched arms, imploring, "Kiss me quick, you sonofabitch!"

In mid-August, we had just returned from a westward jaunt into the Brittany

Peninsula, near Lorient, and were heading east. Third Platoon, for reasons unknown to us, had been temporarily assigned as the reconnaissance element for the 8th Motorize Infantry Division. Because the Germans were in full flight they had outrun our contact with them. Our job was to seek out the enemy. Once we engaged them, we would radio back their position and estimated strength. Then the combat teams would go through us, while we scurried to protect their flanks. Late one evening, just before dusk, I felt the full weight of my gunner, Frank Sanginario of Needham, Massachusetts, on my back. At first, I thought he had lost his balance. Then he shouted, "Krauts!"

We were on a small rise with hedge-rows on either side of the road. From his elevated position at the .50 caliber, Frank had spotted several German helmets to our left. It was a machinegun nest. When my driver, Henry Therrien, of Brookfield, Vermont, brought the Peep to a halt, we dove for the ditches. Once we got prone, the Germans greeted us with a "potato masher" (hand grenade). We stared at it for an agonizing second, but nothing happened. It was a dud! We retaliated with several of our own grenades and got satisfying results. Both sides had resorted to hand grenades, because the hedgerows obstructed any field of fire. The second peep had stopped right behind us, and the armored car, commanded by Leo Trepanier of Worchester, Massachusetts, our platoon sergeant, backed up, and directed fire at the enemy. Abandoning our Peep, we retreated along the ditches, accompanied by the boys from the second Peep. In the meantime, Trepanier alerted the infantry, and they moved through us to pursue the attack. The platoon then moved to protect our southern flank. A G-2 officer (Intelligence) called me back to Infantry Command Post for debriefing.

I gave him a full account of the encounter. With a great deal of emphasis, I added that the shoulders of the road had been lined with anti-tank Teller mines, extending to the area where we had been ambushed. The following morning, our platoon regrouped on the same road and got ready to move out. Six of us from had to double up with other crews, because the Germans had absconded with the Peeps we had abandoned the day before.

The column sat in the middle of the road for an eternity. Suddenly, I heard the distinct sound of a Peep approaching at high speed. It appeared over the small rise where we had been ambushed. The driver saw us and swerved onto the right shoulder of the road. There was a tremendous explosion. The ground shook, and a coal-black column of smoke rose in the air. I knew immediately that the Peep had hit one of the Teller mines the Germans had set there. Either G-2 had been negligent about relaying my information, or the engineers had been engaged elsewhere and couldn't remove them.

Not only had the speeding Peep and its occupant (an infantry messenger) been obliterated, but also two of our platoon, Henry Therrien and Alfonse Alfano of Brooklyn, sitting in a Peep nearest the explosion suffered severe wounds and had to be evacuated. I saw them both after the war. They were fully recovered from their wounds, but their hearing had been permanently impaired.

The mine explosion further delayed us. Sometime after we finally got on the move, I found my Peep smack in the middle of the road. The Germans had burned out the clutch. They left the machineguns, but ransacked our musette bags, and relieved us of all the rations. They must not have known about the glove compartment, because my wallet was still in there, full of ninety dollars of invasion money. We reported the Peep to Ordnance. They repaired the vehicle overnight, and returned it to us. The other Peep remained forever lost.

Toward the end of August, Henry Therrien, was evacuated with severe shrapnel wounds from a German Teller mine. Since he was a French-Canadian, and thus bilingual, I was on my own with my smattering of secondary school French. We had lost contact with the enemy. Not only was it 3rd Platoon's order of rotation to lead B Troop's column, but also the entire Combat Command to which we were assigned. As scout sergeant, I rode in the lead Peep.

Previously, we passed through a small French farming community where I quizzed the locals about the location of the enemy. *Dupuis quand avez vous les Allemands*? "When did you last see the Germans?"

Il y a une heure. "An hour ago."

Avec les fusils, les tanks, les canons, les mutrioyettes? "With rifles, tanks, artillery, machineguns?" *Combien des soldats?* "How many soldiers?"

From their answers, I gathered we might eventually encounter a force of about 100. With this information the column moved out, and set a pace normal for advancing into hostile territory. About half-an-hour later the road straightened out for about three-quarters of a mile, then disappeared up a hill where the higher elevation on both sides converged. It was an ideal location for the Kraut to set up a line of defense, or so I thought. I slackened speed so that we could investigate further. Suddenly, my radio blared out a command in the raspy voice of Captain Fred Sklar from Louisiana, our fearless troop leader riding in the rear echelon. "Sergeant, step up the pace. Move out!"

I grabbed the mike and replied, "Sir, I'll move out as fast as the safety of the column will permit."

Then Sklar said, "Mayforth, come to the rear of the column."

My driver turned the Peep around and started toward the rear of the column. On the way back the troop greeted me with enthusiastic encouragement. "Atta boy, Hal." "You tell 'em, Hal."

Though I appreciated the troop's encouragement, I was more worried about what lay in store for me. I was afraid that I had disobeyed the direct order of a superior officer, and that I had done so in an impertinent manner.

My Peep fell in behind Sklar's half-track. I was prepared for the kind of savage dressing-down of which Sklar was capable. He ignored me, and nothing ever came of the incident. I didn't even get the chance to explain my moment of extreme caution. It was just as well, because what I thought might have been an ideal situation for a German ambush didn't materialize.

We moved fairly rapidly across Europe, but came to a grinding halt in September at Arracourt, France. We were out of gas. Eisenhower had diverted our fuel needs to Bernard Law Montgomery and his ill-fated Operation Market-Garden. As the result, the Germans were given a chance to regroup. Soon, we would be engaged in Europe's biggest tank engagement, the "Lorraine Tank Battles." "A" Company of the 10th Armored Infantry had met heavy resistance. When we last heard from them, they were dug in about two kilometers from us. Toward dusk, I was standing with some of our men at a road junction, and I witnessed an exchange between an officer of our Combat Command and the commander of an M–18 tank destroyer from the 704th Tank Destroyer Battalion. The commander of the tank destroyer had been ordered to establish contact with the 10th Armored Infantry. He said, "In no way am I going to sacrifice my crew and vehicle by going up there!"

Then Captain Fred Sklar of "A" Troop said, "Sergeant Mayforth, take your armored car up there and find out what the hell's going on."

I got map coordinates, and started west. Eventually, we left the road and headed south, down into a defilade. We could see the silhouettes of half-tracks to our left flank. We stopped and I dismounted, and then walked toward the vehicles. Someone yelled, "For Christ's sake, take cover!"

A squad leader from the 10th told me that his unit had been pinned down the whole day, and had suffered many casualties. He pointed to dead bodies covered with tent halves. I heard the clatter of German tanks maneuvering somewhere in the distance. I dashed back to my armored car, and radioed the situation back to Sklar. "Okay, mission accomplished. Get the hell out of there as best you can. Forget your vehicle!"

It was almost total darkness by now, and there was only slight visibility. We knew that 37mm anti-tank shells were as effective as ping-pong balls against German armor, but we fired a few rounds at the tank sounds just to let the Germans know that we had some fire power. After we fired, I yelled to my crew, "Take off! Every man for himself!"

I took off in a zigzag pattern toward the path we took when we left the road. I had been a halfback in college, and had never performed a piece of broken-field running like I did that night, probably because I was running for my life and not a touchdown. Machinegun bullets seemed to nip at my heels. The firing stopped only when I dove into a ditch. Almost everyone made it back except one guy, our radio operator. Chester Leherman, or "Chestnuts." Chestnuts was a good radio operator, but he would have been far happier elsewhere. During mail call, Chestnuts sometimes got letters from Navy buddy whose part in the war effort consisted of roller-skating messages around the Great Lakes Naval Training Station. Chestnuts really felt that his calling should have been more like his buddy's, and not dodging bullets and shrapnel in the ETO. Chestnuts lived in mortal fear of combat. The only time he ever emerged from his buttoned up compartment in the armored car was to answer a call of nature. I constantly admonished him with, "For God's sake, Chestnuts, get out of that vehicle and dig in where you'll be a helluvah lot safer." It was to no avail. Anyway, next morning we got a radio transmission from an infantry unit to our north. "We've captured a Kraut over here. He claims he's one of yours. Can you come over and identify him/"

Someone went to see, and, sure enough, the "Kraut" turned out to be none other than Chestnuts. Having been forced to leave the safety of his "cocoon" in the armored car, they found him without his sidearm, helmet, or jacket. His blonde hair was disheveled, and his eyes were wide with fear. The only piece of clothing he was wearing on his upper body when they found him was a blue-gray, knitted German sweater!

After Arracourt, we got R&R. Third Platoon got assigned a billet in a small hamlet, a cluster of about fifteen farmhouses. The owners had long since fled, but they had left everything intact. I discovered a feather-mattress in the "master bedroom." If there every was a place to get a good night's sleep this was it, or so I thought. Instead, after tossing and turning for what seemed an eternity, I moved to the hard floor, something I had grown accustomed to, an promptly fell into a deep sleep. The next morning, we made a hamlet-wide search of empty houses, in search of anything that would enhance our comfort. Overstuffed chairs, sofas, rugs, tables, and whatever else we found became part of our household's decor. What prompted our behavior was partly our own tendency to barbarity, but more so our adherence to the ancient phrase, "To the victors, belong the spoils."

When we were in combat our mess kits were given a rest. We did have a kitchen truck named "Belly Robber (each vehicle in the 4th Armored had a name the first letter of which designated the company or troop to which it was attached), but since our arrival on the continent it had served us only one meal, on "Franksgiving" (Roosevelt had changed the date of Thanksgiving Day), and our mess kits overflowed. In combat we had a high-energy, chocolate bar, the "D Bar" that tasted like Baker's unsweetened cooking chocolate. We also had a fruit bar. It was like a fruitcake that had been subjected to high heat and pressure. We could much on those while on the move, and they satisfied the pangs of hunger. In the evening, we had K-rations, packaged in what looked like an over-sized Cracker Jack box. The K-ration box also contained toilet paper, a brand of cigarette called "Chelseas" that I never thought were intended for civilian use.

When we moved into our R&R hamlet, we initially subsisted on Ten-in-One rations, cans of various vegetables and SPAM. These needed no cooking, but the hamlet's wood-burning cook stoves made a lark out of heating them. Once we had our food ready, we created a new dining experience. Not only did me make use of our "hosts'" China and dinnerware, but also their table linens and napkins. We took the term R&R seriously. We became lazy and slovenly. We never washed the dishes, and after several meals we had exhausted the supply. That didn't bother us because the had the rest of the houses in the hamlet from which to "liberate" new tableware. The chickens and geese running around the neighborhood helped us vary our meals. Thomas J. Stankevitch, one of our platoon also known as "Stoneface" because of his expressionless nature, revealed himself as having been a butcher in civilian life. He slaughtered the local poultry with a smile, and its population dropped off dramatically.

Our R&R lasted a week. The increase in our *avor-du-pois* gave evidence that we have been well nourished, and well rested. Aside from a serious decline in the population of the hamlet's chickens and geese, the only thing we really pilfered, their homes and possessions remained intact, and for that I assume they were grateful.

Around the same time, in the village of Holzen, near Luxembourg, six of us were billeted in the Mayor's house. He and his wife had graciously extended their hospitality to their twenty-six-year-old niece to keep her safe from combat to the east where she and her husband had their home. We reciprocated their hospitality by being very generous with our rations, especially our good American cigarettes. In the evenings after supper we played games and cards at the dinner table. Then everyone turned in for the night. After about three weeks, the Mayor approached me, and asked if I could get a vehicle. He explained that his niece was restless and wanted to return home, a round trip of about forty miles. To use Army vehicles for other than official business carried serious consequences, but the Mayor had been such a congenial host, I couldn't refuse him. Besides, it was night and the trip would have the element of stealth. I got a Peep, and set off with the Mayor and his niece. The trip to the niece's town and back was uneventful. We had no trouble finding it, especially with artillery booming in the distance. The louder it became, the closer we knew we were coming to our destination. It was only on our return to Holzen that we had a tense moment. We encountered an MP at a roadblock. At that time, it was over a month since von Runstedt's offensive through the Ardennes. It had been repulsed, but one phase of it still had the Army on edge, and that was Otto Skorzeny's special force of English-speaking Germans masquerading as American soldiers and driving captured American vehicles. It had been a clever ruse, and it had caused much havoc.

There I was, driving an illegal Peep, and in the company of a civilian. I know the MP thought he had a "live one." He asked me what I was doing on the road. I gave them my serial number, 11055758. When they asked me when and where I had been drafted, I told them I wasn't drafted, that I had enlisted in Barre, Vermont. The answers appeased them, and they let us proceed. The first digit of my serial number indicated that I had enlisted. The second number indicated Army Zone #1, which comprised all of the New England states. It was hardly information to which an English-speaking German would have been privy. We got back to the Holzen, and I took the Peep back to where I had gotten it. No one was the wiser.

Later, while we were billeted in a school house near the city of Luxembourg, I learned the real reason for the niece's "restlessness." Before we hunkered down for the night, Ignatz, regaled us with his sexual exploits at the Mayor's house. What began as "footsies" under the dining table, had turned into a full-blown affair. When everyone had retired for the night, Ignatz waited for the everyone to fall asleep, and then he tiptoed down the hall to the niece's room. For him to get there, Ignatz had to pass the bedroom of the Mayor and his wife. By our standards, they seemed quite elderly, but they had 20/20 hearing. They soon found out what was going on. It was the Mayor's decision to send his niece home to her husband, no matter how embattled their homeland.

In the words of Paul Harvey, that was "the rest of the story."

We'll Put You in the Medics."

Harry McCracken
99th Infantry Division, 395th Regiment Medical Detachment,
Headquarters Aid Station
Westmoreland City, Pennsylvania, 16 May 1922

"As a medic, I usually had people around me all the time, but if I was in a foxhole, most of the time maybe I had one guy to talk to. A lot of times, I was alone, wondering what was going to happen in the next five minutes, but, really, I just lived from day to day, because I never knew what was going to happen. I never thought of being adventurous. I was trained to do a certain job, and I figured, 'Hey, I'm here to do it the best I know how.'"

MY PARENTS, Frank E. McCracken and Cora Mattie Dullinger-McCracken, had sixteen children. I am number fifteen. Some of my brothers and sisters were married and had children before I came along, so I was an uncle before I was even born.

As a young man, my father was a professional loader of coke ovens. He was very familiar with all the coke ovens around our Mt. Pleasant area. He knew more than Henry Clay Frick himself. Frick, himself, would come to our house and talk my dad into staying, telling him to stay away from liquor, because he had a bright future with the Frick company. But you know how alcoholics are. It was a sad situation. Today they have medication and help for people like that, but in those days, there was nothing. As he got older, my dad never really had a job. That's how it was.

So, I was really raised by my mother. In today's world, probably the courts would've taken us away from my father, and put us in a foster home some place. That wasn't the case then, but my mother kept track of us. She was a good Christian mother. She raised us the way we were supposed to be raised, and we all ended up half-decent.

My mother took in washing and ironing, and she did sewing and mending for people around the neighborhood. Fortunately, with Westmoreland City being a small town, everybody knew our situation and, I guess, felt sorry for us. When our neighbors got new clothes for their kids, I would get the old ones to wear. I started working in a grocery story about fourth or fifth grade, passing out hand bills and selling newspapers, trying to make a few cents with things like that. In the Depression, no one was fortunate.

My sisters and brothers, they worked, and they would support us. When one brother would get married, it became the responsibility of the younger brother to help out. I helped the janitors at Norwin High School. I got ten-dollars a month for that, and I gave that to my mother. My first real job was with the WPA (Work Progress Administration). I helped build a football field at a high school. I got paid fifty-two-dollars a month. Of course, that check went to my mother. So that's how I grew up.

After a while, when I was nineteen, I had saved enough money to buy a 1937 Chrysler. It had radio in it. I had just picked up the car on a Saturday; on the next day I took my family for a ride. A news flash came over the radio that Pearl Harbor had been attacked. I will never forget that announcement.

Not long after, I went into Pittsburgh to join the Marines. There were a lot of movies at the time about the Marines, and how fancy their uniforms were. I guess they were trying to attract young men. It worked with me, and I fell for it.

Because of our situation during the Depression, I didn't get much dental care, so I had a lot of bad teeth. Twenty-one of them needed fillings, and until that was done, the Marines wouldn't even talk to me. I was working for Westinghouse at the time, so I had some money, and had all that dental work done. I went back to the Marines, and they gave me a date when I could go in, but in the meantime my draft notice came. The draft board wouldn't let me wait the two months the Marines had given me because they had a quota to fill. That's why I went into the Army.

Most of my friends enlisted. One went to the Air Corps, and the rest went to the Navy. They all wanted to stay away from the Army. So did I. I thought that everyone in the Army was an infantryman, but when I got in I found out that there were all kinds of branches. Still, I was kind of disappointed, but by hindsight, had I gone into the Marines, I never would have been able to liberate my brother from a German prison of war camp. Everything worked out.

I didn't know anything about the military. I was confused. I'd never been away from home before, and, when the time finally came, I didn't want to leave my family. In 1942, a group of us went into Greensburg for our physicals, and they told us that we were going to leave on 4 December. On that day, we all met at the Irwin draft board, and marched down to the railroad station on Main Street. There were people lined up on both sides of the street. We got on the train, and there were a lot of older guys on it. I was just a kid, and they must have been twenty-five or so.

The train ride to New Cumberland was a disaster. They had sack lunches for us, like a couple sandwiches and soft drinks, but a lot of those guys had alcohol. They were half drunk. They were urinating in bottles and passing them on to other guys.

At New Cumberland, they stripped us and gave us Army summer clothes. I didn't know it at the time, but we were all going down to Mississippi. We got our shots. They treated us like animals, just lined us up. One guy put a shot in one arm, and another guy put a shot in the other arm. Mass production! I got a weak feeling from that, but I survived.

We ended up in Camp Van Dorn, in Centerville Mississippi, a real mudhole. The place was just a temporary-type army camp; the barracks had black tar paper all over the outside of them. Nobody had been in there before; we were the original guys. Of course, I still had no idea where I was going, what I was going to be, or anything like that.

Once we got into that camp, they started to interview us, and, of course, they asked me if I knew anything about First Aid. I said, "Not much."

They said, "Okay. We'll put you in the Medics."

Van Dorn was where we got our basic training. Then we went to the Louisiana Maneuvers, which was three months of living in woods and swamps. Then we transferred to Camp Maxey, in Paris, Texas. At that time, it was a permanent camp. It had a real nice two-story barracks. We thought we had gone to heaven.

We received our medical training whenever the infantry soldiers were out training with their rifles. We had six doctors with us, so we went through classes and practical training, like managing splints. Of course, our training didn't really start until we got into combat. Once we got our basic medical training, we had to take infantry training. The only thing we didn't do was actually handle weapons, but we had to do everything else, and qualify as Infantry Expert. We had to go through the infiltration courses. They were firing live ammunition like eighteen inches over our heads, and we had to crawl through barbed wire. One of our guys raised his foot too high, and he got hit in the foot with a bullet from one of the machineguns. That's the only casualty I know of from our endurance training.

Basically, we were taught how to treat wounds. We had all the splints. We were trained to treat back injuries. We had all the different pain drugs, like morphine. We had blood plasma. While we were in the camps, we administered the semiannual malaria and tetanus shots to the troops. I had dental training, surgical training, and medical training.

When we were on maneuvers, they would bring guys in for regular dental care. They had a foot pedal drill assembly. As long as I pedaled, the drill kept going around. I helped mix mercury fillings. If it was a front tooth, we tried to match the color of the teeth. There were three of us guys who were all about the same age, and we more or less all competed to be first. No matter what we did, one of us three guys would end up there, one, two, three. Officially, I ended up as a medical technician, meaning I could assist in surgery, which, in fact I did, just before we crossed the Rhine River when one of our men was wounded in the foot. The doctor decided to amputate. He said, "If we don't take his foot off, he's not going to survive. The blood isn't coming back up his leg."

We cut the guy's foot off right there. I held his foot and did whatever the doctor asked me to do. Once we got it off, I dug a hole in the ground, buried his foot, and they sent him back to the hospital. I did whatever I had to do.

In training, once in a while we'd get weekend passes and go into Vicksburg and visit the Civil War battlegrounds and cemeteries. On Sundays, we'd always go to church. We knew that if we did some family would invite us home for Sunday dinner. Sorry to say, that was one of the main reasons we went to church.

I trained from December 1942 until the end of September 1944. We were combat ready, and I knew we were going to Europe, because I was in charge our supply preparation. At first, there was no room in England for more troops, so they kept us home until after the invasion of Normandy in June 1944, after which we started loading to go. We went back to Camp Maxey, then to Miles Standish in Boston. We got on board ship at Boston Harbor, and made rendezvous with ships from other ports until we had enough for a convoy. There was an aircraft carrier with us. Headed for the North Atlantic, we first went through the Gulf Stream, where it was warmer and fish were diving in and out of the water. Then it started to get colder. For fifteen days we zigzagged, avoiding submarines.

Harry McCracken somewhere in Germany, 1945.
Courtesy of Harry McCracken.

I was assigned to a six-inch gun in case there was an alert. We had several of those. Each time, I took my medic equipment, and went to that gun, prepared to help if any of the gunners got wounded. Once, there might have been a submarine in the area, but that was never validated.

We were supposed to go straight to Le Havre, France, but when we got nearer to England, we were told that those already in France had used our Jeeps, trucks, and equipment in the initial invasion. So they rerouted us. We went to England and stayed there for three weeks until we got refitted.

When we were getting ready to go to the Continent, we were short of blankets, so they sent a truckload of blankets. They were all different-colored civilian blankets. I was supply sergeant. I said, "We're not taking these with us!"

We got an English guy, gave them to him to sell throughout England, and then gave him a commission for selling them. We all made some money.

We loaded in Southampton. I ended up on a German ship that had been captured by the British. After we left the port, they announced that if the ship we were on got torpedoed, we had sixty seconds to abandon it. The ship was open-hulled, meaning that it had no compartments that could be sealed, so it would go down fast. That was nice to know! Anyway, we made it into Le Havre, went in on landing craft. Everything we owned was in our barracks bags, and they went down with us, over the side, on rope ladders. Trucks met us on the beach and took us to a bivouac area where we stayed until morning.

There were 127 of us medics ready to man four aid stations, Headquarters, and First, Second, and Third Battalion. I was with the Headquarters Aid Station. There were two doctors attached to each station. There were two dentists with Headquarters, and none with the battalion aid stations. Litter bearers worked out of each aid station. Each battalion had four rifle companies. Two medics were attached to each of those, and so on, down through the regiment. That's how we were organized.

They told us we wouldn't be doing any fighting in France, so we headed right into Belgium, to a town called Aubel, where we staged. Then the combat troops went from there to get the Germans out of Belgium. There wasn't very much happening on the line, but everyone was edgy. One of the first casualties was one of our own men who was shot by another one of our own guys. One of them was out one night walking around, and the other guy heard him coming and shot him. He didn't try and find out who it was, or anything. He just shot and killed him.

We no sooner got into Belgium when it started raining, then snowing. It was muddy. Really ugly weather. German buzz bombs flew low over us, headed for Antwerp. We could actually see them coming over. In fact, they were within rifle range, and some of the guys fired at them. Some even managed to hit them. They'd hit a wing, and the thing would just go in circles until it hit the ground and exploded. Word came around, "No more shooting at them! Let them go on to their destination."

I suppose the higher-ups didn't want those things dropping among our troops.

We had constant, harassing artillery fire. It wasn't really heavy, but the Germans knew we were there, and they would try and keep us on our toes. We'd fire back. Until we actually started to go into an attack, the artillery was spasmodic. Under General Hodges' First Army theory, like when we were assigned to capture a certain town, our artillery would present a solid, consolidated type of fire for maybe two or three hours prior to us starting to advance.

When we were in combat, we were on the line all the time, and we were always in combat. In spite of that, Hodges wanted clean-shaven, neat-looking soldiers, like we were in the States, but we didn't have the facilities; we couldn't shower, take a bath, or shave. Most of the time there was very little or no water. The food wasn't always there. On one occasion our evening meal was after midnight, and we were to pull out and attack at four o'clock in the morning. So at three o'clock we were eating breakfast. Within three hours, we were eating two meals! We never knew when we were going to eat.

As a medic, I usually had people around me all the time, but if I was in a foxhole, most of the time maybe I had one guy to talk to. A lot of times, I was alone, wondering what was going to happen in the next five minutes, but, really, I just lived from day to day, because I never knew what was going to happen. I never thought of being adventurous. I was trained to do a certain job, and I figured, "Hey, I'm here to do it the best I know how."

Most of our attacks started after midnight, maybe two, three, or four o'clock in the morning. The medical personnel were in direct contact with our infantry soldiers. Our commanding officer had maps, so he knew where our attacks were going to be. He would pick us out a town on the line, and we would go there and set up an aid station. We would make it clearly visible, so the wounded or people bringing in the wounded could easily find us. So that we could get the wounded in a sheltered structure rather than a tent, we always tried to find a house, but that was hard to do, because the artillery rarely left one that had four walls.

Prior to the Battle of the Bulge, I was assigned to 3rd Battalion, in an area called Hofen. I was assigned to an engineering outfit, whose job it was to blow up pillboxes on the Siegfried line. I would go with these guys just before daylight. Most of the time, the Germans had pulled back to their units for the night, and come back in the morning. The engineers first checked for mines, then headed for a pillbox and check for Germans. They laid a white tape behind them, showing where mines had been cleared, and the medics would follow. An engineer would drop a grenade into an air vent. Then they'd go in, check for live Germans. If there were any, they would eliminate them. Then the engineers would set up TNT charges. We'd fall back, and the engineers would detonate the charges. For a long time, little pieces of concrete would fall, like a hailstorm. Once we were finished, we'd go back to our area. Next night, we'd be assigned another pillbox. As far as I know, they never said that there was anybody in the pillboxes. I did that for a couple weeks, and then went back to my own unit at Rocherath. I was there two weeks or so, and then the Battle of the Bulge started.

At around five or five-thirty in the morning on the first day, the first shells started to fall. Our artillery was firing as well, and you could see shell bursts "walking" across a field. I told my commanding officer that we had better watch out. He just dismissed the whole thing. He said I didn't know the difference between a shell coming in and one going out. But I did! When it was daylight, the German shelling stopped.

The second morning, it started up again, and again I told the commanding officer, "Those shells are coming in pretty heavy."

He ridiculed me. Then the shelling stopped, again. On the third day, I was in charge of the aid station, and we were moving all of our equipment to the basement of this house. Of course, the commanding officer sort of made fun of me a little bit. The guys moved into the basement, but the commanding officer and a couple other officers went to sleep on the first floor. A German shell exploded near the house, a piece of shrapnel tore through somewhere, and landed on his bunk. He and two other officers got into a Jeep and took off. Next time I saw him was in 1985, in a Pennsylvania hospital. He never came back to the line. I assumed he was afraid of being hit.

By that third day, the basement of our house was filled with wounded soldiers. We were treating and evacuating them back from the front for further treatment. We had two ambulances on the ready to do that. On the third night, Rocherath really got hit with artillery. The ambulance drivers said they couldn't evacuate any wounded because the roads were blocked off. We just loaded the wounded up with morphine so they wouldn't be hurting.

A lieutenant from the 2nd Infantry Division came in and asked, "How come you're not sending these soldiers back for treatment?"

I said, "The ambulance driver said the road is blocked. He can't get through."

He said, "You load them all up onto the ambulances and vehicles, and we'll try to get them through."

He had a squad with him. Whether they ever made it or not, I never knew.

We had approximately fifteen people working in that aid station. In that basement, that night, there were at least thirty wounded soldiers. Most of them had shrapnel wounds. Many people think that bullets hit most soldiers during the war, but it was mostly shrapnel that did the damage. There were about six dead. That day, an officer said to me, "Why don't you load up these dead soldiers and try to take them back to Graves Registration?"

We put them all on litter racks, and I drove all over that area, but I couldn't find where I should take them. Really, it wasn't our job to do that anyway. I couldn't find any Graves Registration, so I brought them back, and we just laid them right along the outside of that house. When we left that house, they were still there, along with a lot of other guys that had been killed. We loaded up our equipment and went. We had to go down the road about a mile. There was a crossroads, and we were under constant German shelling. I told our guys, "Nobody rides the trucks down that road. It's under fire."

Except for the drivers, we went by foot off to the side of the road. If we heard incoming, we'd have a chance to hit the dirt and survive. Had we ridden, we'd lose not just a driver, equipment and truck, but fifteen guys riding in the back. We got to a crossroads, and, by that time, there were a lot of vehicles in the convoy. We jumped on some trucks, then. It was the middle of the night, and the ground was very muddy. The truck I was in got bogged down. Everyone got out and started to walk again. We came to a crater, about twelve by twelve and four feet deep. It was covered with tin sheets. We crawled in there for the night.

When morning came, we didn't know where we were, or whether the Germans were around, and if we would become prisoners. One guy stuck his head out, but didn't see anything. We got out of the hole. An Army truck came past. We stopped it and asked for food. The driver gave us each a can of C-Rations. They were frozen solid. We ended up chewing ice and vegetable soup at the same time. That was our breakfast.

We started walking in the direction we were supposed to go. Not far away, I spotted one of our trucks. I waved to the driver. He had been looking for us. We climbed onto the truck, and came to the town of Elsenborn.

We set up an aid station at a crossroads, where we would be easy to find. After a couple days, orders came down that there was a German tank coming up the road. We just had treated a guy who had a bazooka. My buddy and I took the bazooka, and went down into the basement of a house that had a little window facing the road. We had no training on how to use the weapon, but, if we saw a tank, we were going to shoot at it. A lieutenant came down, and asked, "What are you guys doing?"

I said, "We're waiting for this tank to come down. We're going to shoot at it with this bazooka."

He said, "You guys are nuts! If you would fire that in this little cellar, the concussion would kill both of you!"

Anyway, the tank had already been knocked out.

We were under constant fire and shelling there, so I said to our major that we were in a bad spot, that we were right in an intersection where German artillery was bound to zero in. I got that feeling sometimes. It must have been instinct. The major went out then came back. He found a good-sized, stone schoolhouse, so we moved our station there. The place was built like a fort. A day later, the house at the crossroads took a direct hit from a shell and got leveled. We were glad we moved.

On Christmas Eve, a German fighter plane strafed me. That was my Christmas present. I was a passenger in a Jeep loaded with medical supplies. We were going through an intersection when the pilot opened up. I didn't see the plane at all. All I heard was a sound like popcorn popping. The driver lost control and crashed against a tree in a nearby wooded section. We ended up under the Jeep somehow. My buddy grabbed a five-gallon water can and held it over his head. I was laying across a ditch, with the back wheel of the Jeep against my leg. We looked back toward the intersection. The MP who had been directing traffic was on the ground. We went over to him. He had been shot through the shoulder, so we patched him up. Then I noticed that it felt kind of gushy inside my shoe. I looked, and the shoe was filling with blood. I had been hit, but I didn't realize it, until just then. A bullet that ricocheted off the road and came up through the floor of the Jeep must have hit me. My buddy's jacket was torn; he had one of the old type fountain pens in his pocket and it was broken, ink all over his jacket. I still think of that today, how close those bullets came to us.

The bullet was imbedded in my leg. I bandaged it up. We were about a mile and a half from our aid station, so we walked to it. Of course, the doctor wanted to send me back to the hospital. I said "Hey. You're a doctor. Do the same as you would to anyone else."

He bandaged me up and said I would have to go back if it got infected, and, a week later, it did just that. A piece of the bullet was still in the leg. The doctor looked at the wound, and dug out a piece of metal that had been working its way out. I didn't want to go to the rear, to a hospital, because I was afraid that when I healed they would send me to another outfit. I didn't want that to happen. I wanted to stay with my own guys. After a month or so, I was all healed.

Once the Bulge ended, we moved forward again. In every field we crossed, there were dead soldiers everywhere, the enemy's and ours. Fortunately, it was so cold that there was no smell of decaying flesh. One guy was frozen in a kneeling position, as if he was firing a rifle. If that's the way you froze, that's the way you stayed. The Army brought in trucks, picked up the dead, and stacked the bodies in piles at an intersection. From there, other trucks brought the bodies to the rear. Whenever they would load these guys up, there'd be arms and legs hanging out over the edge of the trucks. I watched guys cutting off fingers of the dead to get rings. I thought that was kind of cruel. I don't think they should've done that. I never did that. I didn't think that was right. We came across burned out tanks, got up on them, looked inside, and saw whole crews, just burned up. It was sickening, but I got hardened to it. I was trained to do a job, and that's what I did. That was war.

After the Battle of the Bulge was over, we headed toward the Cologne Plain to the Rhine River. It still bothers me, and it bothers all of the guys in the 99th who survived. We were the troops who were initially hit, and we held our ground. When anybody today talks about the Bulge, all you hear about is Bastogne. To me, Bastogne was secondary. If the 99th hadn't held, there never would have been a Bastogne. There were American troops who fought that battle for a week before the Germans tried to get through at Bastogne. Fortunately, the true history is starting to come out, from the German and the American side. I'm not saying that the boys in Bastogne had it easy, but our 3rd Battalion, 395th Regiment, never moved an inch in the Battle of the Bulge, and they got the Presidential Unit Citation for that. When I went back to Bastogne, years later, the 99th Infantry's name is right on top of the monument there.

Our last big battle before we reached the Cologne Plain was at Bergheim. The Germans had it heavily defended, and we took a lot of casualties. After that, we moved right across the plain with few problems, right up to the Rhine River. Actually, we were the first infantry division to reach the Rhine, and the first full division to cross it. We figured to get a good rest, but we got word that the bridge at Remagen had been taken, and we got orders to load up. We got no rest at all. We drove all night, through Cologne, to Remagen. By the time we got there, only foot soldiers could cross. The bridge was so shot up it couldn't take vehicles. Troops were crossing, under heavy fire. We had to wait until the engineers could set up pontoon bridges. As soon as they did, they routed us and our vehicles across, then tanks and other heavy equipment. There were many casualties.

One of our boys captured a German doctor, and he worked with casualties in our aid station for a day or so. He was a young guy, and he could talk pretty good English. He said he had some training in some college in Chicago. I asked him how old he was; he said he was twenty-four. I asked him what he would do if I let him go.

He said, "My job is to take care of my troops. I'd go back over the line and take care of my troops."

I said I couldn't let him do that, because if I gave him off to somebody else he'd probably get shot. So we sent him back to the POW camp.

After we crossed the Rhine River, there was the German Autobahn. Once we reached that, we had free range over that part of Germany. Then, there was word that came out, that in the Ruhr area, just across the Rhine, to the north, there was supposed to be 100,000 or more German soldiers, trapped. As we headed there, the 395th was ordered to turn south, toward the Danube River and the POW camp at Moosburg. This was in April 1945.

My brother was in the Fifteenth Air Force, out of Foggia, Italy. I knew he had been shot down over Yugoslavia. I was still in Texas when my family got word that he was MIA. When I came home on leave, a telegram had come, saying that he as a prisoner of war. While I was in Europe, my sister got information through the Red Cross, telling her where all the German POW camps were located. There was one in Nuremberg, and when I got there, the camp was empty. A buddy of mine from Philadelphia could speak some German, and, after talking with some civilians, he was informed that the prisoners had been marched south. As we moved further south, the German civilians had little notes the Air Force guys had given them. The notes said things like, "Take good care of these people. They gave us water; they gave us bread."

We knew we were on the trail. We got to Moosburg, and set up our aid station. It was kind of quiet, so I just sort of roamed around.

There was a tank and two Jeeps with guns mounted on them, and I just happened to hear one soldier say, "I think there's a prison camp around here, what do you say we try to find it?"

So I said to them, "Do you want a medic to go with you?"

He said, "If you want to come along, come along."

I went back to our aid station, and a buddy from Minnesota and our commanding officer got in our Jeep. The tank went first, and we followed in the Jeep. We went across this field, and we could see the camp with all the barbed wire. The tank went straight through the barbed wire. The German guards ran the other way.

Once we got into the camp, all the prisoners of war mobbed us. One guy said, "Can we take a ride in your Jeep?"

I said, "If you want to take a ride, go ahead."

It looked like twenty guys were hanging all over that Jeep as we rode around the camp. They stripped it of everything that was loose, for souvenirs.

I asked, "Is there an American officer in charge of this camp?"

They told me where the officer was. I went up to him, and asked, "Is there anybody in this camp by the name of McCracken?"

"I think there's a couple guys in here by that name," he said. "But you have this whole camp so confused by the way you came in, you'll never find anybody. If your brother's here, I'll have him come into this office. Come back tomorrow morning, and if he's in this camp, he'll be here."

I saluted him and went back out the door. When I walked out the door, my brother was standing there. He had watched us coming across the field. He sort of looked at me, like, "It couldn't be. It's impossible!"

We had a big reunion. They started putting MP's at the gates so guys wouldn't start roaming around, because the war was still going on. They weren't going to let anyone out. I took my combat jacket and my steel helmet, and I said to my brother, "You put this on."

So he went out in my uniform! I took him to our aid station, and he stayed all night. Then the next morning, he wanted to go back with his crew. He wasn't so bad off, though he had lost a lot of weight. He had been a prisoner for a year. He said that German draftees, not SS, had guarded him so he had been treated fairly well. I once said to our doctor, "If I find him, and he's in poor health, we'll send him back through the medical channel."

My brother explained that when they got Red Cross packages, they would trade the cigarettes for bread and other food. He did develop stomach problems in that camp, though, and he had that problem from then on, until the day he died. His camp might have been bad, but maybe not as bad as some of the other camps. My brother stayed with his crew for two weeks, then the Army started flying the prisoners out.

All through the war, I wrote home pretty frequently, but the censors wouldn't let us say anything about where we were, or what we were doing. Sometimes we used a code. Sometimes it worked, sometimes it didn't. When I wrote to say I had found my brother, the censors wouldn't let me mail it. I said to the company commander, "Here's the biggest event of my life. I'm not allowed to tell my family?"

He said, "You give me that letter, and I'll say I went over it and everything is clear."

He signed his name to it and I sent it home.

The Germans wouldn't surrender, even when they knew they were beaten. We ran into one group, several hundred, of older German troops. We knew they couldn't win, and they knew they couldn't win. We had a couple boys who could speak German, and so they asked this one guy, "How come you didn't surrender?"

There were several hundred of them. He said the SS troopers were behind them, and that if they didn't fight, they were going to shoot them in their backs. They figured they were going to get killed one way or another, so they might as well keep fighting.

Of course, I was happy when the war finally ended. I figured we were done with everything. Then the Army started telling us that we needed so many points in order to be allowed to go home. I was something like five points short, so I had to stay there with the occupation for a while. The 99th was scheduled to go through the Suez Canal to the Pacific. The Army assigned General Hodges to that theater of operations, and the first division he asked for was the 99th. He was supposed to capture Tokyo. I don't think I would have made it the next time around. Luckily, we dropped the Atomic Bombs, and the Japanese surrendered. Then the Army told us to unpack, because we weren't going anywhere.

I came home on 9 January 1946, on a Victory Ship, one size up from the Liberty Ship. We left from Marseilles, France. There were three thousand troops on board. Halfway across, we ran into a bad storm. I thought, "Oh, man! I've gotten this far, and now I'm going to drown at sea!"

The storm was so

Harry McCracken (right), his brother Milton (left) and Walter Pawloski at Moosburg, Germany, the day Harry found his brother in the POW camp there. *Courtesy of Harry McCracken.*

bad, we were getting SOS calls from other ships. One had lost its rudder. Our ship was closed up as tight as a drum. We had the hatches closed for three days. No one could go outside. They would have been swept overboard. That ship bounced all over the Atlantic Ocean.

We came past the Statue of Liberty in the middle of the night. We were all up on deck. What a sight that was! We got off the ship, and they took us to a camp, where they gave us all a steak dinner. Our waiters were German prisoners of war. After a day or so, I went to Indiantown Gap. They asked me if I had seen any atrocities, if there was anything wrong with me, if I needed medical help. I said no to everything, and got out of there as fast as I could. Waiting to get home was the worst time of my life in the United States Army. I was ready to go back to Westinghouse, but they were having a strike. I got into the 52/20 Club until July, when the strike ended. I went back to Westinghouse, and stayed there forty-two years, without a layoff. I retired in 1982. My wife also worked there, and we were married on 8 May 1946.

I came home with a Purple Heart that didn't have my name engraved on it. When they engraved a name, that meant that the owner had been killed. I also got two Bronze Stars, but, after all, all combat medics got one. I got a Certificate of Merit for treating the MP at the intersection after the German plane strafed us. I never read it. It was supposed to be sent home, but they changed it to the second Bronze Star I got. I got three medals for being in three major battles. I got the Good Combat Medal, and the Combat Medic Badge. They gave me an Expert Infantry Badge, but I wasn't allowed to have a Combat Infantry Badge, because we weren't supposed to get or handle weapons (though I was going to use a bazooka, once). The Combat Medic Badge paid me ten dollars a month more over my regular pay. I'm proud of all of my awards, especially the Combat Medic Badge.

I still think about a lot of things we did. We had plasma for anybody that needed blood. At that time it was just a bottle with powdered blood in it, just the white corpuscles, then we had another bottle of saline solution. We had to mix the two together and then give it intravenously. We didn't want to waste it, so we had to make sure a soldier was really losing blood, or had lost a lot of blood, before we would do that. Once, I gave a soldier six pints. We thought he died, so we put him off to the side, covered him with a blanket. Then we noticed the blanket moving a little bit, so we started another IV, and put him in the ambulance. Whether he made it or not, we never knew. After the wounded left us, we never knew how they made out.

Hundreds of soldiers in the foxholes got frostbitten feet, especially at Elsenborn Ridge. Feet also got rotten with trench foot. Really, we had no way to care for our feet, or general hygiene. We had few clothes to change, and we wore the clothes we had for six weeks at a time. Still, they told us that we should wash our feet every night and put on dry socks. We'd bathe frozen feet in lukewarm water, and then bandage them. Some guys couldn't even put on their four-buckle Arctics. As long as they could sit or stand and hold a rifle, we weren't allowed to evacuate them, because there was no one else to take their place. It was a sad thing. Some of the feet had turned black, and, eventually, maybe years later, those guys would lose their feet. Then the Army came out with a ruling that anybody with trench foot would be treated the same as someone with a self-inflicted wound. So our army doctor told us, when we evacuated anybody, we were not to use the words "trench foot." We were instructed to use the words "frozen feet" instead. We treated a lot of German soldiers and civilians, just the same as we treated our own guys. Displaced German civilians roamed. That was one of our problems. During combat, they roamed from one town to another, hauling their stuff in horse-drawn carts and wagons. They blocked the roads, and really held things up. Many of them would see our Red Cross flag, and come in for medical care. Most of them were sick with one thing or another; some of them had infections. We used Sulfa on them, and, later, when we had it, Penicillin. They weren't bad people.

We were going into this one town, and the women and their kids were standing on the streets. We asked them what was the problem. The Germans had told them the Americans' job is to kill all the women and children, and they were really scared to death. Then we started giving them chocolate bars and all that kind of stuff; they found out that wasn't our goal. One woman came in with a little boy; I'll never forget him. His hand was all infected. So I treated him, put the sulfur powder on it, bandaged it all up. He was a real nice looking little boy about three, with blond hair and blue eyes. When our doctor came back, he wasn't there at the time, I said, "We've got to make a house call."

"What are you talking about?"

"Well, there's a little boy there up the street. He's in pretty bad shape; I wanted you to look at his hand."

We did, and the doctor told me I had done a good job.

The Hitler Youth created a lot of problems. They were really belligerent. They brought one with a broken arm into our aid station one day. He spoke English. He started giving me a lot of lip, and I was thinking of sending him back through the medical channels. He said we were no good, and that they were the master race, and all that. Then I said, "You're not the master race today. You're going back to POW camp. You're not even going back through the medical channel."

I sent him back to a POW camp. That was the way I treated him. On the other hand, the regular German army troops were like us. They knew that they weren't going to win the war, but it was still their job to be soldiers, and they did it the best they could. We didn't have any problem with treating those guys. There was a lot of flu and diarrhea, and we had medication for those. Most of the diarrhea was caused by contaminated water. Guys were supposed to put Halazone tablets in their canteens to counteract it, but most of them didn't. We had a lot of nervous conditions from lack of sleep and stress. That gave the guys upset stomachs. We'd use Phenobarbital for the nervous conditions and stomach upsets. The medics didn't sleep much. We were always too busy treating casualties. There were only twenty-four hours in a day! That made us a little edgy.

One time there was an MP who had lost his arm; all we did was use the forceps to close off the blood vessels. Another guy, the whole front of his forehead was taken off. I mean, it was just brains and everything down in there. He talked to me. He said, "Did I get hit very bad?"

"Oh, not too bad, I said."

Really, there wasn't much we could do for him. We gave him morphine, covered his wound, and gave him blood plasma. I asked the doctor, "Do you think he'll survive?"

The doctor answered, "He has a good chance for survival, but he'll probably be blind."

Just a year or so ago, I ran into a guy who was with him when he got hit. He told me that the soldier didn't survive. The main thing that sticks out when the Battle of the Bulge was going on was combat exhaustion, people who went mental. At Elsenborn one day, I was called to a house. There was a big, strapping guy in there down on his hands and knees, digging into the floor with his hands, trying to get protection from the artillery. I knew right away that he was gone. I knew he was mentally gone. He was a big, strapping guy; you'd think nothing would ever bother him. After we crossed the Rhine, we had an aid station in a castle. I found one ofs our medics curled up in a corner like a trapped rat. He was gone. I think we'd have all eventually been that way if the war had lasted longer. If a guy got hit with shrapnel or something, you could patch him up. Mental, I often wonder if any of those guys ever got OK.

They brought one guy in who had gotten hit with shrapnel. His leg looked like four pounds of ground meat. All I could do was apply Sulfa for infection. We just loaded that leg up with Sulfa and bandaged it. I never knew if they saved his leg.

In addition to being a medical technician, I was a supply sergeant, so I had to make daily visits to our aid stations with our commanding officer. We'd check on the various needs, then go back to the depot and pick up supplies, especially C-Rations and K-Rations. In Elsenborn, when we had a lack of food, we'd butcher a pig or cow. The civilians had all gone, leaving the animals to wander around. We figured we might as well eat them, even though to do so was a violation of Army regulations.

I treated one SS guy, and that was right after we crossed the Rhine River. We were up at our aid station in the castle when they brought him in. They shouldn't have done it, but they interrogated him right in our aid station. Those guys, they didn't talk. One soldier took his wallet. He had some pictures and stamps with Hitler's picture on it. He made the SS trooper eat those stamps. He still didn't talk. They took him out of there to a POW camp. The SS were tough. We were fortunate that there were no more of them than there were.

Today, I think anyone who is going into combat, or who has been in combat for a while get psychological counseling. In my war, the Army didn't tell us a thing. They asked us a few quick questions when we got back, but they usually just gave us our discharges and sent us home. That was it. Every once in a while, I still dream German soldiers are coming over a hill after me, but it's not as bad as it used to be.

"May I Volunteer for the Airborne?"

Peter Messer
Assistant Military Attaché, U.S. Embassy, London, England;
17th Airborne Division, 155th Glider Anti-Tank Battalion
Yokohoma, Japan, 3 September 1913
Rector, Pennsylvania
31 January, 2002

"I had to take a leak. I didn't want to go under fire with a full bladder, so I opened a little canvas door that the gliders had, got down on my knees, and then peed out over the French countryside. As we got over Germany, I saw a bunch of German soldiers in the distance running away. Most of them wanted to surrender, but nobody told their flak gunners that. Headquarters had seven gliders, and lost two. Everybody in them was killed. My glider got hit in the tail, and started to go down. We came in level enough, and headed straight for a tree. We hit the tree and took six feet off a wing. We climbed out, and as we did I saw some Germans standing around in a meadow. I simply said, "Come on," and they followed me as prisoners of war. I put them in a trailer next to some houses where our guys had gathered. We must have looked like some mean chaps. I didn't think I could have shot anyone, but those Germans didn't know that."

I WAS BORN IN YOKOHAMA, Japan, the son of American parents. I lived there until 1923, the year of the Great Earthquake. We lost everything and had to leave. We took an Australian ship to Shanghai, China. We stayed there six months, and then went to England on a Peninsular and Oriental Line ship.

In England, we lived just north of London. I went to English Prep Schools, which are elementary boarding schools. I was very much an outsider, being an American who had lived in the Far East. But English schools are very rigid, but pretty soon I became pretty much Anglicized. I went to Cambridge University and read English for only one year, because that's all my father could afford. After I left Cambridge, I worked for a publishing company that eventually started Penguin Books.

Since I was an American citizen, my father sent me back to New York, alone, to find my way. I traipsed around, and I got a job at the Oxford Press in New York. I was there a few months, but I didn't know what the hell I was doing, so they fired me. I loved New York, which in the 1930s was a fascinating city. Eventually, I got a job selling antique furniture, which I hated. Happily, my father was able to raise enough money to send me back to Cambridge for a degree.

While I was at Cambridge, I spent my summers in Germany, in the area of the Rhine River. We were so blind to reality that we couldn't see that Germany was preparing for war. Hitler had already taken over Austria, and *Kristallnacht* had already happened. I saw signs saying JUDEN *VERBOTEN!* ('Jews Forbidden'), but the evil of that didn't register. Before my family left England for America, they visited me in Dresden, and they, too, were fooled. We saw men in brown shirts and *Swastika* armbands running about on weekends feeding the poor and so on. Hitler Youth marched around with shovels on their backs, going out to work in the countryside. The country just seemed to rise out of the ashes. It all looked happy. All Germans seemed to be working together, and everything ran on time. Germany was very prosperous, so tourists rarely got the feeling that anything bad was going on. I never saw people pulled out of their houses and beaten or anything. I graduated in 1939, right before the war began. I left for America in May 1939. Three months later, on 1 September, Hitler's army invaded Poland. It was the beginning of World War II.

I had no interest in business, so I got a job in New York at a brand new Episcopalian boys' boarding school. The job paid peanuts. While I was there, I got my peacetime draft notice. It was New Year's Eve 1940. I wasn't making much money at the school, so I volunteered to go into the Army just before the school year ended. I went into the Army on 1 April 1941, for a tour of duty that was supposed to last only six months. Now I was just a number. No one knew who the hell I was, and no one really cared. They took my civilian clothes and gave me a uniform. When they said, "Fall in," I fell in. After awhile I couldn't stand it. It was awful! There was a real nutcase who trained with me. He kept saying, "I'll shoot their balls off." I realized that nutcases get drafted, too.

I went to an induction center somewhere on Long Island. A few days later, I was in Williamsburg, Virginia. When the train pulled into the station, we had to sit in the cars for hours. Finally, an officer came in and said, "You are all going to Coast Artillery. It's an elite branch of the Army!"

Coastal Artillery! For God's sake! After three months of training, everyone got shipped out except me. Because I had been a teacher, they held me back to teach the next class. That sort of thing happened to me all my life, and it was not very heroic. By July, I was teaching the next group of draftees. One day, the captain came up to me after class and offered me a chance to go to Officer Candidate School for Coast Artillery in Fort Monroe, not far from Williamsburg. When I got there, the Army decided that Coast Artillery was an outmoded name, and they changed it to Anti-Aircraft.

I didn't know much about the Army, but I had a good sense of what it meant to be unprepared to fight a war. My unit had World War I Springfield rifles that we never took out of the god-awful Cosmoline they were packed in. Fort Monroe was even fully developed. We had no radar, just searchlights. We didn't even have artillery.

When I became a second lieutenant, I went down to a National Guard regiment outside of Savannah, to a place called Camp Steward. The Table of Organization there called for more first lieutenants, so they made me one. I had been a second lieutenant for less than a month! Everyone got shipped out again, some to Guadalcanal, everyone, that is, except me. The Army sent me down to Wilmington, North Carolina. My job? Teaching incoming officer candidates. That was the extent of my combat training. I was lucky, but not happy. I needed to get the hell out of teaching officer candidates. I didn't really understand why the Army thought I was qualified to run an Officer Candidate School, anyway. Then someone told me that our embassies needed military attachés. They needed people who had had some foreign experience. I made a contact in the Pentagon, got interviewed, and became Assistant to the Military Attaché in London. I thought I had gone to Heaven! I took four weeks instruction in embassy protocol at the Pentagon. After that they gave me a diplomatic passport. Jesus! I had gone from PFC, to lieutenant, to diplomat in the time it took to take a breath!

England was a little island at war for almost four years, and short of everything. Now there were a million American military there with money in their pockets and screwing all the girls. There was a lot of hostility. The British often said, "Those Yanks! Overpaid, oversexed, and over here!" As for myself, I had my own apartment in London, which the Army paid for. I could get any kind of liquor, diplomatic liquor, by the case. The ordinary citizen couldn't find a bottle of whiskey in the whole city. It was tough duty. My job was to go out to British bases and observe their anti-aircraft defenses. I spoke the same sort of language as the British, and I got along very well with them. When I wasn't doing observation, I took generals on tours of the country.

One day, my boss, a general, decided that there was no need to write reports on anti-aircraft facilities any more. After all, the German *Luftwaffe*, by that time, was virtually powerless. I went to him and asked, "I've got to get out of this. I can't end the war in this job. May I volunteer for the Airborne?"

Even though I wasn't combat trained, the general assigned me to the XVIII Airborne under General Matthew Ridgway. Ridgway then appointed me to serve under General Miley, commander of the 17th Airborne. The 17th had not seen combat, but it was considered an elite division, and my understanding was that they were there to do the Rhine Jump.

Miley assigned me to the 155th Glider Battalion, which had been antiaircraft, but now was anti-tank. The 155th had six batteries, and three of them had antitank guns, British six-pounders. We also had three machinegun companies. The plan was that when the crossing of the Rhine was to happen, the American 17th and the British 6th Airborne would both take off from England and drop across the Rhine.

Gone now was the London apartment and all the other perks I had been enjoying. Suddenly, I was sleeping on the floor in a sleeping bag with a bunch of Airborne guys, getting up at six thirty every morning, and running two miles. I got to be good friends with all of the guys. I signed up for Jump School that was to start by Christmas 1944, but I never got there. We got shipped out to France and the Battle of the Bulge.

Most of the division flew over, but Headquarters went over in an LST. I had six men and a couple vehicles. We got to a French *caserne*, a military installation near Rheims where the 101st Airborne was before they got sent to Bastogne. A few days after Christmas, we were ordered to the Bulge. I traveled in a Jeep with the colonel. Shit! It was cold! It wasn't snowing when we left, so we drove into the night. One night after we got settled, we were sleeping in a factory when the goddamned phone rang. The officer at the other end ordered me and my driver, Sergeant Nat

Youngblood, to move to a town called Neufchateau. So, Nat and I got on the road at two in the morning. We couldn't see much, because our headlights were just cat's eyes, slits. Nat hit a pile of dirt and turned the Jeep over. I hit my head and got bloodied up pretty much. Nat broke is leg in several places.

Luckily, a bunch of black soldiers from another unit came along and took us to an aid station. Somebody gave me a shot of whisky, and then bandaged me up. After that, I passed out. I woke up in an evacuation station in Verdun, site of a great battle in World War I. There they gave me morphine, and put thirty-two stitches in my head. I was there about a day. Then I went to a little hospital somewhere, where I slept in a comfortable bed. Everyone else was out there getting killed, and there I was, the victim of a Jeep crash. Eventually, I got back with my outfit, and I was glad to be with them.

By the time I got out of the hospital, the Battle of the Bulge over, but we still had to cross the Rhine. In March the 17th was in a huge tent camp outside Rheims getting organized for the crossing that would occur on the twenty-fourth. We all got into 40&8 boxcars and left for an airfield outside Paris where C–47's were waiting for us. The Army called the operation "Varsity," and it was the biggest Airborne operation in history. We met up with the British over Brussels. I looked out and saw mile after mile of gliders.

I had to take a leak. I didn't want to go under fire with a full bladder, so I opened a little canvas door that the gliders had, got down on my knees, and then peed out over the French countryside. As we got over Germany, I saw a bunch of German soldiers in the distance running away. Most of them wanted to surrender, but nobody told their flak gunners that. Headquarters had seven gliders, and lost two. Everybody in them was killed. My glider got hit in the tail, and started to go down. We came in level enough, and headed straight for a tree. We hit the tree and took six feet off a wing. We climbed out, and as we did I saw some Germans standing around in a meadow. I simply said, "Come on," and they followed me as prisoners of war. I put them in a trailer next to some houses where our guys had gathered. We must have looked like some mean chaps. I didn't think I could have shot anyone, but t h o s e Germans didn't know that.

On the second night, we dug in. There wasn't any fighting that I could hear, but the flak display across the Rhine was spectacular. Then we just drove further into Germany. There was no one to fight. We stopped at Munster, and then we were pulled back to occupy Essen, where the bomb devastation was unbelievable. We didn't even see a mouse. We humans build, we destroy, and we build again. War is stupid!

When we occupied a town, it was my job to deal with the mayor. One thing that made me feel good is that were weren't any death camps in our area. There were, however, forced labor camps. We cleaned the people out of those camps and took them to a German officers' rest camp on the end of a lake. There were thousands of displaced persons like these, most of them Russians. I wondered how they would ever get back home.

Near Essen, I had some unique experiences. The Krupp family, the steel and weapons barons of Germany, had a huge estate outside the city called the Villa Hugel. The XXII Corps knew about this wonderful estate because it hadn't been bombed, and they wanted to turn it into a hotel for visiting dignitaries. I got to be the hotel manager, and I used the Krupp staff, all Germans. A lieutenant colonel, who had been a hotel desk clerk in civilian life, knew exactly how to assign rooms. I stayed there for almost a month, running the hotel and drinking the best wine in the land. Jesus, what wines they had in that wine cellar. The German cooks were incredible. They made American rations into gourmet meals.

One day a colonel from XXII Corps came in and told me, we've got a lot of reporters coming in. Give them a good dinner and sell them lots of wine."

There was no whiskey, but lots of brandy in the wine cellars. The colonel said, "Before dinner, instead of whiskey, give them brandy and Coca-Cola."

I went the German major-domo and gave him the colonel's instructions. He said, "Brandy and Coca-Cola! Those Americans are barbarians."

At the Krupp villa I met the great photojournalist Margaret Bourke-White. I told her about Nat Youngblood and the wonderful drawings he was doing of the war. I had Nat come up, and I introduced him to Bourke-White. She looked at some of this stuff, and then gave him some contacts to follow up on after he left the service. It must have worked, because he got a job with the *Pittsburgh Press* and stayed with them until he retired. I ran into Nat often over the years.

When the war ended, the division in was a resort town near Metz called Contrexeville. We lived in a huge hotel where we waited for discharge or reassignment. I had collected a lot of points while I was working at the embassy, points that I hardly deserved, so I was in a better position to come home than most. The rest of the 17th went down to Bavaria.

The thing I admired most about American soldiers during the war was their enormous flexibility. The American soldier was very much of an individual. I've often wondered about the "Greatest Generation," and all this interest about the war now, and how wonderful people think my generation was. Well, I don't know that we were all that wonderful. We did what any generation of Americans would do in a similar situation.

After I came home, Mrs. Richard King Mellon asked me to establish the Valley School in Ligonier. I did, and administered it for thirty-one years until I retired in 1978.

The United States Air Force's "Little Friends" that escorted the B-24s and B-17s on their missions and helped protect them from enemy fighter planes. The Lockheed P-38 "Lightning," the Republic P-47 "Thunderbolt," and the North American P-51 "Mustang." *United States Air Force photos.*

General George S. Patton arrives at Stalag VIIA, Moosburg, Germany, 29 April 1945. *Courtesy of Robert Nelson.*

"The Flag is Passing By"

Alexander Robert Nelson
Fifteenth Air Force, 449th Bomb Group,
716th Squadron; Irving, Illinois, 26 December 1921

"An American captain told us just to stay put because the battle was continuing in Moosburg. As the captain spoke, one of our guys goes: 'Hey there goes the American flag!' And we could see the tower over in Moosburg, kind of the county seat. Our flag was going up. The German flag was going down. Well, you can imagine! I mean all at once it was Fourth of July, Christmas, New Years Eve, everything all at once! We were free men again!"

AFTER PEARL HARBOR, I sort of got the feeling that I needed to be more involved. The whole world was exploding. The Nazis were doing their thing, Mussolini was doing his thing, and the Japanese were doing their thing. I still remember the feeling I had: "If I don't get in there now, I'm really going to regret it!" I wanted to fly, so I went down to the local post office and enlisted in the Air Cadets. I had flown a little bit out at the Latrobe Airport (Arnold Palmer Regional Airport) in a Piper Cub, but someone else was always the pilot. On 26 August 1942, the Cadets called me in. Instead of sending me directly to the Air Cadets, they sent me to an Air Force training location in St. Petersburg, Florida. What a great place to be from August through December! I learned all the neat things that went with being a soldier before I got into the Air Cadets.

Hour after hour, train after train, men arrived in St. Petersburg for training. Our superiors pulled some of us out of our duties to meet one of the trains and help the Military Police process inductees coming from New York City. It was a wild thing! The train pulled in and there were about thirty military police there with shoulder arms and side arms and there were six of us. We got these guys out of the passengers' cars and some of them were just pie-eyed drunk. Others were just out of it, for whatever reason. We lined them up and shook them down. Out of 130 inductees we managed to find some eighty pistols and about 200 knives, and we took those away from them. Then we lined them up and marched them off to the barracks. They were a tough bunch. I was very glad they did not assign me to them because there were fights every night in that place. They got them out on the drill field where there was a second lieutenant that was spit and polish down the line. He got those guys going in a couple of weeks. It was just amazing!

This lieutenant worked on a series of demerits. As someone accumulated demerits, all of a sudden he would be doing 100 pushups, or get put on KP for a week, or whatever. Very soon a person got the idea that if he did what the lieutenant wanted he would be in very good shape, but if he didn't there would be lots of extra duty, like carrying a fifty-pound pack and a rifle for an hour-and-a-half. We called that "walking the distance." Those New York guys turned out to be a crack organization, a real example of the kind of change that can take place when someone has a focus.

I was a KP "pusher" in St. Petersburg, making sure people did their jobs. Our kitchens were sparkling clean, and the food was a good as anywhere. Despite the fact we that ran ourselves ragged every day, we all managed to put on weight. Three full meals a day, and they were full! It was all cafeteria style, and we could load our plates with anything we wanted. But we had to eat it all, otherwise we would get KP. A master sergeant stood at the end of the line, and if someone didn't get that last bit of food in his mouth before he dropped off his tray, the sergeant took his name and that was it!

By 1 January, my orders came through to report to Louisville, Kentucky, where I was finally inducted into the Air Cadets. From Louisville, I went to Maxwell Field for pre-flight training. Then they sent me over to Ellington Field for basic training. I'm not sure whether it was a good thing or a bad thing, but I washed out because of poor depth perception. They put me into navigator training. I thought, "Well if I can't be a pilot, I'll be a navigator. At least I'll still be flying."

It was a big disappointment washing out, but they were absolutely right. I was pleased with being a navigator. I always had a tendency toward logic, mathematics, and why things are the way they are. To me, celestial navigation was fascinating. I was very proud when I got my wings and commission. When I took my oath I really understood what "Duty, Honor and Country" meant. We got it instilled into us. I felt good about myself.

Navigation School took place in San Marcos, Texas, a backcountry town, to be sure, but it had a university, San Marcos University. I settled in there for about six weeks, by which time I was flying training missions in twin engine trainers with two other navigator trainees.

I saw my first B–24 in Alamogordo, New Mexico, the area where they would test the first Atomic Bomb. The place wasn't much at the time. It was just sand, sun and tumbleweeds. They assigned me to the 716th Squadron ["The Toppers"] in the 449th Bomb Group ["The Flying Horsemen"], which they were just then forming. We were destined to go over to Italy.

At Alamogordo, I met my crew. There were ten of us. The pilot was George W. Foote. Quentin Madigan was the copilot, I was the navigator, Jack Murphy, from Boston, was the bombardier, Jim Gorrel was the top gunner, Harry Lain was the ball-turret gunner, Walter Gates was one of the waist gunners, and Al Yano was the other. Ellwood Farmer was the tail gunner, and Skidmore was the nose gunner.

We flew to Bruning, Nebraska, in the coldest and snowiest weather that I had ever experienced. The B–24 bombers were eighteen feet high. The snow was so high on each side of the runways that the B–24s had to be in the air before you saw them, if you were off the flight line. The ground crews plowed and threw the snow up in twenty-five foot drifts.

Until Bruning, most of us officers had not had any training in .50-caliber machineguns. Some bright person came along and said, "OK, you guys have to learn how to shoot. So, we're going to issue you all shotguns and we want you to go through the fields up north of the camp and shoot at pheasants."

That was our training in how to lead a target, and how to shoot. But most of us had guns at home, you know, so we thought that was ridiculous, but that was one of the ways they trained us to shoot machineguns.

The training missions were probably pretty typical. We bombed "targets" in North and South Dakota. They took a couple thousand acres out in the wilderness, and made them a bomb target, just big circles on the ground. They put a photographer in the plane whose photos showed how accurate our bomb strike was. We got up around five o'clock in the morning, had breakfast, and got to the briefing room around six. They would have a big map of the area on a wall. They would say, "OK, here's where you are and we want you to fly up here and drop your bombs here. We want you to fly back here. This will be your Initial Point (IP), this will be your target, and then come back here."

We'd take off and I'd tell the pilot what heading to take to the target, about a two-hour flight. We'd get to the IP make our turn into the target, the bombardier would take over at the IP, he would come in and drop his bombs. Then we did a "three-sixty" to see how the bombs would hit, and then we would head back to Bruning, take a shower, have a couple of beers and go to bed. That was day after day after day. Then we started to fly formation where the whole squadron would take off and bomb the target.

In Bruning, we took what they called the POM (Preliminary Operations Missions) inspection, something every bomb group had to pass. A group of senior officers would come in and the whole bomb group would fly a simulated mission, and they would grade you. If you flunked, you had to go back for more training, if you passed you went overseas. The first POM we flunked. They said we just weren't efficient enough to get in the air and to get into formation. The whole group flunked! *Four squadrons*! Two weeks later they showed up again, we take off and they say, "OK, you've passed the inspection. You can bomb, fly formations, your ground crew seems to know what they're doing."

In late October, we flew to Topeka, Kansas, where the planes were shaped up for overseas duty, and where the Army issued us overseas equipment. We got a .45 and a knife, first-aid equipment, a gas mask. We had duffel bags that we filled as full as we could. And then we were briefed about what we were going to do and how we were going to do it.

From Topeka we went to Morrison Field, in Florida. I had been to Florida before, to Miami, but a couple of the guys hadn't, so they asked me to show them around. We went "over the fence" (they didn't allow us to leave the base). We weren't really AWOL; we just wanted to go into Miami. We spent the night there, and got back before reveille the next morning. At reveille they said that we had to report at noon for our briefing and orders to go overseas. They told us that eventually we would end up in Grottaglie, Italy. We flew from Morrison Field to Trinidad. Imagine a twenty-two-year-old who has never been more than fifty miles from home, and then, suddenly, he's in Trinidad.

Trinidad was a beautiful island. As we were coming into the air base, they told us that there were some brief showers between where we were and the field. And there were, but these brief showers were like what we would call storms, because the rain would be so heavy we couldn't see, so we had to go on instruments to find the field and land. At one end of the field the sun was shining and at the other end it was just pouring down rain. We refueled, stayed overnight, and from there we flew to Belém. In Belém, they outfitted us to cross the Atlantic to Dakar, Senegal.

There were a lot of wild parts to the world then. Places are a lot different today. Belém, for instance was just a field that they hacked out of the jungle, and no matter where you walked you were in the jungle. As soon as we were on the ground, they briefed us and said, "Look, these are not the streets of New York City. There are panthers out there, there are alligators, there are you name it and they're out there. So we want you to understand that we don't want you to get off the base other than by accepted pass."

They lined us up and gave us a number and when that number came up it meant that we would be ready to go across the Atlantic. We picked up another crew and so there were actually two crews in one airplane, so we were packed in there like sardines. We took off at three or four o'clock in the morning.

In celestial navigation, when you're in the Northern Hemisphere your navigation stars start with the North Star, but in the Southern Hemisphere it starts with the Southern Cross. And so I had to use my sky charts to make sure what I was shooting when we got off the ground. So we got off and we headed out across the Atlantic, twenty men in a big, lumbering, airplane. We could hardly make 150 miles an hour, we were so heavy. We were from 500 to one thousand feet off the water, because the prevailing winds were best for us closer to the water.

It was just fabulous to be in the dark. I and the other navigator made a couple of star shots and made sure of our plots and our directions. We were checking our wind drift, and so on. Then we settled in. Just absolutely settled in as we started across the water. Fortunately, we had very decent weather. Scattered clouds that were not any problem, and every hour then we would take a sun check to make sure what longitude line we were on, and we would check each other out. We could chart ourselves pretty good as we started across the Atlantic.

When we got to the Equator, they told us, "Everybody! OK! We're crossing the Equator back into the northern hemisphere again."

Everybody wanted to look down and see where the line was. There is a "point of no return" when you're flying over the Atlantic. That meant you had enough fuel to get to the other side, but you didn't have enough fuel to get back, so if something happened to the airplane you couldn't turn around, you had to keep on going straight.

We were doing well. The gas consumption and the engines were holding up pretty well. We didn't think we were going to have any problem.

The other navigator, Jack Henry, and I, had a little competition. I had to get something going, you know. We decided we would plot out what we thought our arrival time would be, and whether we would be on target or not. So we kept separate records, and took separate shots. As we got closer and closer, I laid out my plot and he laid out his plot and we compared. We were within about five minutes and about fifty miles. We ended up five-minutes late, but we were just delighted! Fourteen hours in a B–24 is a long time.

We got off the plane in Dakar, Senegal, a French colony. I went into culture shock. I was one of the first who got off underneath the bomb bay. I stood up and here was a Senegalese soldier dressed in a French Foreign Legion uniform. He was in bare feet and saluting me. I saluted him back. He had a gun on his shoulder, and you always respected somebody like that. He said that there was a command car waiting for us, and that the ground crew would take care of our plane.

We went over to the BOQ (Bachelor Officers' Quarters), and had some dinner. They immediately corralled us while we were at dinner and said, "We want you to understand that you are not to go outside your barracks, or outside any building without having your clothes tied at the wrist and at the ankles, and something over your head, and bug spray on, because here if the mosquitoes bite you you'll get malaria."

They said they had to tie down the airplanes every night because if they didn't the big mosquitoes would come out of the jungle and grab the airplanes thinking they were big mosquitoes and take them back in the jungle!

After three days, our ship was serviced and ready to go, and we took off for Marrakech, French Morocco, where Winston Churchill went to paint his pictures. He found the atmosphere there to be the clearest and cleanest. We came in from the south, and flew over the Atlas Mountains. It was high noon, and the sun was shining on Marrakech. It was the most beautiful thing I had ever seen. Everything was pure white. Gold shone from the mosque minarets. It was right out of the movie *Beau Geste*.

In Marrakech they put us into twelve-man tents, just off the base. At noon the temperature ran to 105 degrees. At midnight the water froze in the buckets we kept outside. They tried to heat the air by building big bonfires along the streets, but it didn't do much good. In fact, we went back to our ships and got our fur-lined flying boots, pants, jackets and hats to wear to bed.

We went into town to one of the bars. I was having a Cognac. They had no beer. All they had was Cognac and wine. I had to go to the men's room. I said to the bartender, "Mr. Bartender I would like to go to the men's room, where is it?"

He said, "Go down the hall, turn left, and it's the first door on your right."

I went down the hall, turned left, and saw the first door on the right. I opened the door and walked in, and there were two women standing at a basin combing their hair! I excused myself and got out! That was the first time I ever heard of a coed bathroom. It took a little while to get used to that, but of all the places I ever wanted to go back to, Marrakech was it!

We got off the ground again, and went to Constantine in Algiers. Finally the day came. It was December 1943, and they told us we were bound for Grottaglie. Sunny Italy? Grottaglie was all mud, cold, snow, rain, no facilities, and our ground crews had not shown up yet. They were coming in by ship. We had to gas our own planes, we had to bring our own bombs in, we had to steal people from other places, and our ships sank down into the mud. We were quartered in a cold building because they didn't have our tents and Quonset huts set up yet. We had no shower facilities. It was just as primitive as you can imagine. I remember that by Christmas time we were still not operational because we just didn't have the means to be.

We had metal mess kits. Christmas dawned and we were told we were going to get a turkey dinner. We were delighted about that, because we had been living on GI rations and all that other kind of messy stuff. At about eleven o'clock that morning we're lined up for dinner, and it starts to rain. Bless Colonel Alkire! He was our CO at the time, and he was dishing out the turkey and all the trimmings. We even got coffee. Then it started to pour rain, all over us, and into our mess kits. Everything became a watery mess. It was a bad day!

In early January, things started to clear and we dried out a little bit, and a couple of the ground crews showed up. Then things started to happen rather quickly. We got decent places to live in, we set up a mess tent. We flew our first mission in early January, to an airfield near Zagreb, Yugoslavia. We missed the target by a mile. We saw flak for the first time, but no fighters. We were "blooded" and ready to go.

Our mission briefings included instruction as to what to do if we were captured. They gave us maps that had escape routes marked on them. We got special instructions if we got shot down over Yugoslavia, where there were two opposing groups, the Partniks and the Chetniks. We were told to seek help from the Chetniks, because they would help us get out of Yugoslavia. The Partniks were likely to turn us over to the Germans.

On each mission, the main thing that concerned us was getting the ship off the ground. The plane, itself, was one, huge bomb. It was loaded with gasoline and ten five-hundred-pound bombs, plus ammunition for all the machineguns. We were always overloaded, and we used every bit of runway we could. Some crashed on take-off. Others couldn't manage to get high enough and hit trees and went in.

When we took off the navigator, bombardier and nose gunner and top gunner all sat on the flight deck, right behind the pilot and copilot, and it was only after we got into the air that we went to our stations. We couldn't see anything, but we could feel the damn ship shaking like it was coming apart. The noise was ear splitting. Once off the ground we breathed a sigh of relief. We were all well trained, but our reactions were different. Some were white-knuckle people, and others were just enjoying it thoroughly. I'll say this for myself, most missions that I flew, with one or two exceptions, did not bother me at all. To begin with, I was too busy constantly checking the course. I had to deal with information about where the flak barrages were going to come in, where the fighters were going to come in, what time we were supposed to hit the IP, what time our bombs were supposed to drop, what direction we had to take once away from the target, and which neutral countries we could get to if we needed to, or getting back to the Adriatic Sea, or getting to Yugoslavia, or whatever. Then I had to constantly maintain my log — speed, direction, coordinates, and flight history.

The worst part of any mission for me was when we got to the Initial Point. Then the bombardier took over, and I didn't have a damn thing to do but stand there. And I had to keep my hand on the salvo lever. The bombardier had control of bomb trigger. When he hit the trigger a bank of lights on the left-hand side of the compartment would start to go out. If any of the lights didn't go out, that meant that a bomb was hung up in the bomb bay. Then I had to hit the salvo lever, a mechanical thing that kicks a hung up bomb out of the bomb bay.

Most of the time the intelligence we had was good. Sometimes they would screw up because it was something they couldn't know. For instance, German fighter units that were supposed to be in one place might have been called back into the interior for rest and recreation. As luck would have it, they would be near one of our targets, and come up to meet us. That was never fun.

There was radio silence after we got into the air. The gunners would then test their guns. The bombardier would go check his bombs to make sure they were all right. By that time we would be at 10,000 feet, and we would all have to put our oxygen masks on, because at 10,000 feet and above you can get into oxygen deprivation very quickly.

As navigator, I had laid the line we were supposed to fly on a map of the area even before take-off. I worked out what would be typical fifteen-minute periods along that flight line, and every fifteen minutes I would check where I was supposed to be against where we actually were, if I could see the ground, that is. If not, then I adjusted to the speed and the altitude and direction that we had gone in for the past fifteen minutes, and then noted in my log what had happened in that fifteen-minute period.

I would do this if I were what they called a "following navigator." There was a "lead navigator" and all the rest of us were basically "following navigators." The lead navigator was the one who was taking the group into position. We did all this because if we lost an engine or if the ship came under attack the navigator would know where the ship was so he could plot a course back over the Adriatic or wherever, to safety. As we got to the Initial Point, usually this would be at a right angle to the target. In other words the formation would fly up to the Initial Point (about fifty miles from the target), make a ninety-degree turn, and by the time we would get straightened out and level, we would be coming into the target. Well, the bombardier by this time would be in the nose of the plane and I would give him our approximate position, time remaining to the target, so that he could get set up. He would open the bomb bay doors, he would set the electrical systems up for dropping the bombs in sequence, which is basically the way you would do it. You didn't drop all the bombs at once.

At about two or three minutes from the target he would call into the pilot and say, "I've picked up the target. Give me control of the ship."

He would then take control of the ship. He had two knobs, one that moved the ship to the right or to the left, and another that brought the target into focus. Of course, all the data would be in the bombsight about the trajectory of the bomb. So, whenever the bombsight mechanism would tell the bombardier to drop the bombs, he would hit the trigger.

Immediately after we dropped the bombs, the bombardier would say, "Bombs away!"

The pilot would then take control of the ship, and close the bomb bay doors. Usually there was an evasive action set up and the formation would go either to the right or to the left or go up or down or whatever the evasive action was for that particular target on that particular day. We would then head back for the Adriatic. As soon as we landed in our regular echelon form, we would pull into our revetment where we parked, if we could do that, and when we got out of the ship there would be officers there to debrief us immediately. For this, my log was very helpful. They wanted to know what we saw, where the bombs dropped, what the flak was like, did we identify any fighters, and what happened to the ship and to the formation.

We went through the debriefing, and after the debriefing we would get our gear together and they would haul us back to the BOQ. Then, whatever time of day it was, we would usually go directly to the mess hall and get something to eat. Then we went out or went to bed, depending on how much energy we had left. When you're on oxygen for a long period of time, you're burning up an awful lot of the natural forces you have in your body, so it took a little while to get them back. We knew they would call us the next morning between four and five o'clock to be briefed for the next day's mission.

In January of that first year, we had wonderful flying weather, and the whole Group flew twelve missions in a row, twelve days in a row. Usually, we flew three successive days, be off two days and then three days and two days. So there was a rotation depending on what happened. In my case I flew more missions because we were very short on navigators, most of whom had to fill in for units that were short handed.

They credited me with forty-five missions by the time I was shot down. I actually flew thirty-one. Every mission was enough to scare me, but a couple stand out in my mind. Our Bucharest mission was a fascinating one. Our group got a Presidential Citation for that. We wiped out a railroad-marshaling yard. We went in with forty-nine bombers each loaded with ten, 500-pound bombs. All of the bombs hit the target. We blasted that marshaling yard out of commission for about four months. It was just great! When we came back across we hardly made it over the Yugoslav mountains. Our oxygen was shot out, and we had to drop out of formation and come down below ten thousand feet. We came streaking across Hungary and Yugoslavia and got to the mountains before the Adriatic Sea. We just pushed the engines up over, and burned one of them out. We made it back.

The Bucharest mission was horrendous, despite our success. From about the time we hit the Rumanian border until we got back to the Adriatic Sea it was one constant fight, but the heavy fighting was right around Bucharest before and after the bomb run. We lost ships, and the Rumanian pilots shot the hell out of the guys who were parachuting down. After that, if anyone bailed out, he didn't pull the ripcord until the last minute.

The beachhead at Anzio after we invaded Italy was something to see. We came in at ten to twelve thousand feet, and we were being shot at with everything they could throw up at us. We had anti-personnel bombs that we dropped on German troops. Then there was one mission where they wanted us to bomb a hillside so that it would block a major road that the Germans were using for transport into that area. That was a funny one, how do you bomb the side of a mountain, what do you do? We did though, and it did block the road.

One of our most exciting missions was a double strike on a Regensburg marshaling yard in the south part of Germany, and this was probably the major target for destroying the infrastructure of Germany. They set up a scheme where the Eighth Air Force [England] and the Fifteenth Air Force [Italy] was to put every ship in the air and rendezvous them over Regensburg, then turn around and go back, or bring some of the Eighth Air Force down to Italy because it was closer. So, they called a one thousand-ship mission, and every bomber they could get into the air they got in the air. They perfectly timed how we were coming in. What happened was, of course, Murphy's Law; if something can be screwed up it will be. So, when we turned at the IP, B–17s from England were above us. We're coming in from the northeast, and they're coming in from the north. We're both heading for the target. We dropped our bombs. Just as we got off the target, the planes above released their bombs. We put on a lot of heat getting the hell out of there. Anyway, we knocked that target right off the map!

We made the third Ploesti raid, to the Rumanian oil fields. I went into the briefing room before the mission. The map on the wall had arrows on it, all pointing to Ploesti, and pointing away from Ploesti. The arrows coming back meant that we could get back, but none of us was very happy. Ploesti was heavily protected. An old Tennyson poem kept going around in my head; "Theirs' not to reason why, theirs' but to do and die."

We got off that morning and started across the Adriatic. We were a little concerned because there was cloud cover, and of course you just can't throw fifty bombers up in the air and have them fly through clouds because they'll bump into each other. We had to have eye contact. We got over the Yugoslav coast and headed toward Ploesti. It was a long mission, six hours, and we hit a little bit of flak over the coast. We really didn't get any enemy fire until we got about 100 miles from the IP, then both the German and Rumanian fighters hit us. At that particular time, we did not have fighter cover. We had P–38s, but they could only fly in so far, and then they had to turn around and go back. We were huddled together like dogs that were trying to keep warm, except it wasn't the cold we were worried about.

We were flying "Tail-End Charlie," the low squadron on the left. And the 454th

Bomb Group was off to our right. The fighters hit the 454th first, and then they peeled off and came at us. Our gunners got a lot of action, and we shot down one fighter. The fighters hung on for about twenty minutes, and by that time we were at the IP and turning. Then the flak started to come and the fighters left. We were briefed that the Germans had built a camouflage model of the Ploesti oil fields just short of the actual Ploesti, and we had to be aware of this. The cloud cover had gone and we could see both the decoy and the target, so we headed on into the target. The flak got so heavy we could not see the ground, and that's hot lead that's all over the sky. We started to lose planes. Off to our right one B–24 took a direct hit. Its wing came up and the plane just fell out of the sky. We saw about a half-a-dozen guys bail out of that one. The lead plane of the 718th, above us, got hit and had to drop out of formation. I was looking right at him when he got hit. We got through the flak, got our bombs away, and started our evasive action.

By then, the formation had loosened up, but the fighters came back, so we tightened it up. Again, we were still "Tail-End Charlie," and we were not happy about that because that was usually the place the fighters went for. Fighters hit another ship in the high flight, and it fell out of formation, burning. We saw parachutes open, and we saw the fighters go down after them. We were furious.

We were in good shape. One of our other ships dropped out. We moved up in the formation, and we headed back. Occasionally, someone would call out "Fighters!!" But they would be going after the high groups, especially the 450th.

We usually encountered two types of aircraft; the Bf (ME)–109 and the FW–190. Focke-Wulf–190. They were very tenacious. Once we were the high squadron, and this German fighter brought his ME–109 right up, and just sat right in the middle of our formation. He just sat there because he knew none of our gunners would shoot because they were afraid of hitting our own planes. Finally, he winged over and dropped out. They were good. They knew their business! Their tactics were perfect. Whenever we saw them, we knew we were in big trouble. The worst time I think I saw the fighters hit was at one of the first raids over Wiener-Neustadt. Twelve or fifteen fighters hit the 98th Bomb Group. And they just racked them through. I think they lost half their bombers that day. Watching it was wild. Then, as the air war continued, more and more of those experienced German pilots got killed. They brought up the younger, inexperienced people. Then we could get at them more easily.

We had twelve German fighters to our credit when we were shot down. Almost every time we went to Ploesti or Wiener-Neustadt or Regensburg, one of our guys would get credit for or would get partial credit for a kill. I think probably the one that I remember was when our nose gunner, Skidmore got one, and it was rather funny because I remember him yelling out: "My God, there's one coming right at me!"

I was right behind Skidmore, looking out through the nose. The plane was coming head-on, and the pilot was firing the guns. Skidmore pulled down on the triggers, and literally blew the German plane's nose off. The plane had gotten so close that Skidmore couldn't miss. We got hit with the debris, but we didn't take much damage.

It was pretty exciting while it was happening!

The fourth time we went to Wiener-Neustadt, Austria, we got shot down. Our mission was to bomb a factory making airframes for Messerschmidt. They were also building the FW–109. The fourth mission was just as bad as the first three, except we didn't come back. Jack Murphy, the bombardier, was on his fiftieth mission, and his last. He was slated for rotation back to the States. Skidmore had become what we called "flak happy," and had been grounded. So, we had a new nose gunner, a guy by the name of Audrey Salyer, a nice young man. When we took off, we were the lead plane of the 716th squadron. It was also the low squadron. We went through the usual route, across the Adriatic, up along the Yugoslav border, and into Austria. It was an absolutely beautiful day in May 1944. The sky was blue and sunny. We couldn't have asked for better flying weather. It was another one-thousand-bomber mission. The 449th, 450th, 97th, and 376th Bomb Groups went into Wiener-Neustadt; the other wings went north, to Nuremberg, Germany.

We made the turn and, as usual, they knew we were coming. The Abbeville Kids, the *Jagdeschwader* 26, a crack German fighter outfit, were there at the time, doing R&R. We recognized them by their yellow nose spinners, and we knew their reputation from crews who had to cross France to bomb Germany. They were based right in our flight path. They had some fun with us, but for some reason they quickly broke off.

As we turned on the IP, the flak was devastating. We went in straight and level. We were sitting ducks. We opened the bomb bay doors, dropped our bombs, and started a ninety-degree turn to the right when BOOM! They hit us in the number four engine with a shell, they hit us in the bomb bay with a shell (thank God our bombs were away!), and they hit us on the flight deck with a shell. Those four shells killed the copilot and the top gunner. The ball-turret gunner got out of his turret, but his clothes were on fire. We put out the fire, put his chute on him, and dropped him out of the plane. His chute didn't open. Jack Murphy and I got Audrey out of the nose turret. We opened the nose-wheel door, which was our escape hatch. I was facing the cockpit, looking at the flames. Foote, the pilot, was fighting the flames with a fire extinguisher. Murphy sat with his feet outside the plane. He was wearing his chest chute. He turned and looked at me, I waved him off, and he left. Audrey was standing behind me. I sat and jumped out. By this time, the ship was falling off on one wing. When I got out, I tucked my hat underneath one of the harness straps. Why I did that, I have no idea.

We had learned our lesson about not opening our chute too soon. So, it was freefall. There was a cloud cover below us at about four thousand feet. As I got to it, I pulled the chute ring, and the chute—zip!—came out. You're falling at 200 miles-an-hour and all at once you're falling at twenty feet-per-second, you come up short, and I remember looking up and I said, "My God it worked!" It was the first time I ever used a parachute. None of us ever practiced jumping. We just remembered being told that if anyone's chute didn't work, he could take it back and the manufacturer would give him a new one!

I came down through the clouds over the Vienna Woods! It was beautiful forest from one end of the horizon to the other. I knew I was going to come down in a tree, not a pleasant expectation since you could get pretty well cut up depending on how you hit the tree and at what angle you hit it, and how fast you were going when you hit. Fortunately I came in feet first with hardly any sway. I ended up twenty-feet off the ground, swinging back and forth. My back hit a limb. It knocked the breath out of me. I just hung there, half-out and half-in consciousness. I have no idea how long I hung there, but eventually I came back to full consciousness. There I was, hanging there on a big white chute draped in a tree. I had to get out of the harness and onto the ground without breaking any bones.

About thirty-feet away on my right, a patrol of German soldiers came up the path, talking, laughing, having a great time. I thought I'd had it, because we knew that one of the things they did was hold target practice for people who were hanging in chutes from trees. I closed my eyes and said a prayer. The patrol went by, never pausing, never seeing me. The old heart is just Boom! Boom! Boom! You talk about excitement? That was enough for me. I crawled back up on the shroud lines to take the pressure off the clips that held the chute. Once I got them out, I was hanging by the shroud lines. There was only one thing left to do, and that was drop. So I dropped twenty feet and hit the ground—Boom! Knocked myself out again.

We were shot down at 12:21. By this time, by my watch, it was about two o'clock when I finally woke up. I took my .45 off and buried it. I buried everything else that could identify me as a combatant. I took my officer's pins off and put them into my pocket. The adrenaline was pouring through me. I even buried my hat! I struggled to the path, and decided I'm pretty much three-quarters the way up a mountain. I started to walk fairly well, although it was very painful, and started to walk down. I must have walked a mile or a mile-and-a-half when all at once I heard, "Hey, Lieutenant!"

And out of the wood came Walter Gates, the waist-gunner, and he was the best-looking thing I ever saw in my life. We compared notes. He jumped after I did. He told me that Foote got control of the plane again, and kept it level so that the rest of us could get out. Foote went down with the plane, and Walter always thought our pilot should have gotten the Medal of Honor. We discussed plans, and decided to continue down the mountain through the woods. We stopped at a house, and asked for some water. A young woman gave us some, and didn't seem concerned about us, or the fact that we couldn't speak German.

Late in the afternoon we looked for shelter. We found a cottage, broke into it, and found some cold gruel. We ate that, and fell asleep. The next morning we got our heads together. I was in very bad shape. My back was hurting about as badly as it could, but over a period of about an hour it limbered up to the point where I could at least get up. Walter and I held a little conference, checked our escape maps, and decided that our best bet would be to head south and west and get to the Yugoslav mountains and see if we could get with someone who could give us a hand as far as getting back to Italy.

I said, "Walter, you can move a lot faster than I can. You should take off and head for the hills. At least you might get through."

He answered, "Well, I guess I could, but I'm going to stay with you. We'll tough this out together."

By this time it was around nine o'clock in the morning. We kept going across fields, through forests. We knew the direction we wanted to go, we knew we wanted to stay off the roads, and we knew we wanted to avoid people. We stopped at streams for water, but we didn't have anything to eat. Still, we were doing very well. If we kept at it we would get to Yugoslavia in two days.

Toward sundown, we started looking for a place to sleep. We came to a farmhouse. The place looked lived-in and there were animals in the barn, but there were no people. We got into the kitchen, got a loaf of bread, a couple hunks of meat, and then we took off for the barn. We crawled up into the hayloft and ate. By that time it was night; the animals had settled down. It was very comfortable. Nobody showed up, but that was our real concern. What would happen when someone would come in to feed the animals?

About ten o'clock that night, people came in. We stayed quiet in the loft. Early the next morning, before the sun came up, we took off. My back was very stiff, very sore. It took about two or three hours before I could really start to move again. Around noon, we saw the mountains. We were just delighted! We went across a road, and a young lad came by on a bicycle. He was a good distance away, so we didn't think he took much notice of us. We kept going on in the same direction. We got into some thick woods. We figured we were about twelve miles from the Yugoslav border. We came out of this very thick forest into a meadow. Instead of skirting it, we just cut straight across. We were pretty confident, and this was our undoing.

When we were halfway across the meadow, out came a car from the other side, going like hell. It pulled up to us. Two guys brandishing pistols jumped out. They were the local police. The kid on the bike must have alerted them. They put us in the car, took us to a small town somewhere, put us in jail, took us before a magistrate somewhere, gave us something to eat, and put us back in jail. The locals had a very uncomfortable jail. All they had were plain, wooden boards for us to sleep on. Anyway, I had to stretch out on the bed, and that did my back some good, even though I had trouble with it for six weeks or so. We didn't understand German, and there was no one there who understood English. We were lucky it was the local police. When they found out we were airmen, they turned us over to the *Luftwaffe*. Had the SS captured us, we might have been shot on the spot.

The Luftwaffe put us in a command car and took us to Wiener-Neustadt. They put us in a holding room with about twenty-five other captured fliers. Some of them were pretty badly banged up, heads bandaged, splints on their arms and legs. There was nobody from our crew. Late that afternoon by the way, the Fifteenth Air Force came over and bombed again at Wiener-Neustadt. We loved it! We stayed there that night.

The following day they took us by truck to a train station somewhere in the area, and put us on a train to Regensburg where they had an *Oflag*, a place where they screened and interrogated POWs. Then the RAF bombed with their Mosquitoes that night. The next morning, the Eighth Air Force came in and bombed. Nobody had thoughts of escaping. On the contrary, we kept as close to the guards as we could because the civilians were not very happy about us being there, especially after the bombings.

A bunch of guys were taken to the hospital, so there were about fifteen of us who went for interrogation. It was a very simple process. They stripped us, gave us a shower and some prison clothes. The clothing was really Army Air Force issue that they had taken from other airmen. In other words, every time a bunch went through, somebody else was coming back, and they got our stuff, and we got the guys' stuff that went ahead of us. They put us into solitary confinement, a room about eight-feet long and about six-feet wide with a straw mattress bed, a chair, and a light bulb that was always on. The door was just a standard wooden door with an eight-by-eight inch, barred window.

They didn't allow us to associate with anybody. They took away our watches. We didn't know whether it was day or night because there were no outside windows in the room. I was exhausted. My back was in really bad shape, and I remember stretching out on the bunk and just zip! — going out. It was probably a good thing for me to be in solitary where I could let go of the tension. I didn't know whether I was going to get shot, hanged, tortured, or whatever. Every once in a while, they opened the door to give us something to eat, and that was it. I just lost track of time completely.

The sanitary facilities were rudimentary. They had a slit trench outside, and if I had to go I banged on the door until the guard came, and then I told the guard what I wanted to do. He would take me out and then bring me right back in. I never saw anyone. I never talked to anyone.

Our people had warned us several times that if they ever captured us to be very aware that there were going to be Germans posing as Americans who would try to get information from us. One time I was stretched out on the bunk and there was a knock on the wall. Then someone said, "Hey, are you new here?"

I was immediately suspicious. I answered, but I didn't say much, except to tell him that I wasn't feeling very well. At some point, a guard came for me and took me to the interrogation room. The place was very bright. Inside was a noncommissioned officer sitting at a desk.

"Would you like a cup of coffee, Lieutenant?" he asked.

He was trying to make me feel comfortable. He spoke excellent English. He told me that he had spent some time in Kansas City, Kansas, and had gone to school at one of the universities in the United States. He asked what group I was with, and I answered, "My name is Bob Nelson, 0–690697, and I'm a first lieutenant."

He kept at me. "Well, you were with the 449th Bomb Group."

"My name is Bob Nelson, 0–690697, and I'm a first lieutenant in the Army Air Force."

When I wouldn't answer his questions, he did it for me! He knew a great deal about what was going on. Later we found out that the Germans maintained a clipping service of American newspapers. Every time we graduated from any of the service schools they had our pictures with our names underneath in our local newspapers. Interrogation went on for about two hours. At the end of two hours he said, "Since you aren't going to talk, we'll have to keep you here for a while."

So, back into solitary confinement! They came for me a second time. Now there was an officer — a captain or major — who pounded the table, and who really got stormed up about what I knew and what I didn't know.

Finally I told him, "You're wasting your time. I said I'm a first lieutenant. My name is Bob Nelson, 0–690697. That's all I'm permitted to tell you, according to the rules of war."

He stopped pounding the table, and we talked for a little bit. Then they took me back to solitary confinement. Less than an hour later they got me again. This time they photographed me and gave me a "Kriegie" (*Kriegesfegangener* 'Prisoner of War') number. It was 9507. You don't forget those things. Then they took me to a holding pen where we waited to go to a camp. While we were there, the American Red Cross had packets for us that contained things like toothbrushes, soap, towels, and other toiletry things. We also got food parcels.

They took us by train back to Regensburg and then from Regensburg they took us to *Stalag Luft* III, near Sagan, half way between Berlin and Breslau. It took us about a day-and-a-half to get there. There were probably twenty of us in one car. We had a gun pointed at us all the time. Most of us were still in a state of shock. At one point we were flying bombers, dropping bombs, and the next thing you know we're prisoners with guns pointed at us. We had no freedom at all. They told us what to do, when to do it, where to do it, and how to do it. And if you didn't do it you got a rifle butt in your head. And that happened often enough.

At Sagan we were processed by the German administration. Stalag Luft III had an administrative section, a north camp, a south camp, a center camp, an east camp, and a west camp. They assigned me to the west camp. We got to the camp entrance, and they opened the gates to let us in. I was astonished! Colonel Alkire, my CO from the 449th Bomb Group who had been shot down earlier, was standing there. I saluted him and came to attention. He said, "Relax! Smoke 'em if you got 'em. Rest. It's great to see you! We've been expecting you for some time!"

This time our interrogators were Americans. They wanted to know whether we were somebody who we weren't, like German spies. Because I was from Colonel Alkire's group, he could vouch for me. It was a very simple thing. I told them exactly what had happened to me, and how it happened. Afterwards they assigned me a room and a bunk. From that time on I really understood what it was like to be a prisoner.

We ate whatever we could. The Germans gave us a kind of thin pea soup and black bread. We called it "Goon Soup." The Germans called it "Fart Soup." If we had Red Cross parcels, we would use some of the food, and try to ration the rest. In the afternoons, we did clean-up details in around the camp and in the barracks. When we had free time, we did exercises like "walking the perimeter," an hour walk around the perimeter of the camp. Despite the fact that we were malnourished, we never missed the chance to exercise.

After exercising, those of us who had been assigned to escape committees would go to our assignments — drawing maps, making bogus money, re-tailoring uniforms to look like German uniforms or civilian suits, putting together whatever was necessary for the next approved escape. That didn't say that there weren't people who tried to get out on their own. Some of them made it through the gate, and some of them didn't. But, generally, nobody escaped just by saying, "I'm going to escape today."

The YMCA provided books and playing cards. We formed a bridge competition. We played an awful lot of bridge. The YMCA gave us musical instruments. Those who were interested in music would go over to the central meeting barracks and practice or write tunes. They did a good job, too. We also had our own choir and a choir director, so there was always practice going on. The YMCA also provided baseball equipment, and we formed teams.

Sometimes, in the afternoons, we dug up tree stumps to use as firewood. There were plenty of stumps, because when they leveled the field they didn't have bulldozers, so they just cut the trees down and took the lumber away.

We had roll call in the mornings, and at four o'clock in the afternoon, we had a second roll call. We went through the whole miserable process again. At one time we used to confuse them a little bit, but we found that wasn't much fun after all, because the thing about the German mind is that it had a definite routine. For them it was $1+1=2+2=4$, right down the line. We substituted people, eliminated people or moved people around, just to confuse the hell out of them. The only trouble was we had to stand there as they did it all again. So we stopped playing games with them. The second *Appel* was over in about an hour or an hour-and-a-half, because they wanted to get us in before dark. We could light lights in our barracks, but we had to close the shutters, which were sealed so that no light would get out for our Air Force to see.

Nighttime was when we were sure there was no one around to hear us, and that was when we made most of our plans for the escapes, and passed on information. What was difficult was moving from barracks to barracks. Nobody did it unless they were ordered to, because the Germans would let attack dogs loose in the camp after dark, and we had to be very careful about that. We were very careful about what we did and how we did it. Then "lights out" was at ten o'clock. Zip! All the lights would go out, I mean all the power went off. Anyway, by that time, we were weary.

There were many abnormal days, when there would be trigger-happy guards who would all at once start shooting up the camp. If they found a tunnel, or if they would find something out of line, all hell broke loose. They would lock us all in the barracks and wouldn't let us out, or they would take us out on the parade ground and make us stand there until they got everything organized again.

Sometimes guys "hit the wire." That was always a tremendously upsetting experience. The guys who did that had really lost their minds. There was a fence line, and you were not permitted to cross that line, unless you wanted to be shot without warning. Seeing somebody shot like that was difficult, because they would be climbing the wire and BANG! BANG! BANG! — a dead man!

Around January 1945, the Russians were coming in from the east, and the Germans decided they were going to use us as hostages and take us into Austria. On Christmas Eve, when we were at church in the west camp, they announced to us that within the next week we would be leaving, and that we should prepare ourselves to go. It was the coldest winter in Germany in about thirty years. The temperature dropped below zero, it was snowing, and one night around midnight they pulled us out of the barracks and started us down the road under heavy guard.

Snow, below zero, cold, it was probably the worst three days of my life. I got as close to dying as one could possibly get. Guys fell by the wayside and froze to death. The Germans picked them up and threw them in horse-drawn wagons. Some of the Germans died, too. They got us into a pottery factory that was still operating. It was warm in there, and they came in and they gave us some soup. I have no idea what the soup was, but it certainly was helpful. We were rejuvenated, a little. Two days later, they put us in boxcars, and locked us in. Things were pretty bad. Half of us could stand while the other half were lying down, so we took four-hour turns doing that. Sometimes the train moved, sometimes the train didn't move. We were in that boxcar a couple days.

We got to Nuremberg (Nürnberg). They took us off the train put us in a camp that Italian POWs had used. It was the dirtiest, filthiest, lousiest place I had ever been in my life. In addition, none of us had taken a bath or shower for about two weeks. We didn't bathe for another three weeks, and by that time we were about as bad as the camp was. I refused to sleep in the bunks. They were filthy and full of bugs. I wouldn't even go close to them. I stretched out on a couple of benches, instead. I think that saved my life.

When I was shot down I weighed 202 pounds. At this point, I weighed 160 pounds. When I was liberated, I was down to 140. We were all pretty skinny and weak. You could count ribs. That first night we were there one of my buddies died. His resistance was so low bug bites had infected him. Bugs just covered him. We took everything out the next day and burned it to try to clean it up.

We were there from 1 February to just after Easter. Easter came early that year. They marched us toward the southern part of Austria, still hostages. The Russians were overrunning everything, and on the other side the Americans were coming in. So, they decided to head us south. We were making some twenty kilometers a day. There were 1600 of us. When we started we numbered about 2,000. Four hundred of us had died. We were on the road about four weeks. They took us to the Moosburg Stalag VII/A, and it wasn't much better than the one at Nuremberg. We knew things were winding down, and the Germans were nervous and trigger-happy.

A couple of prisoners that had escaped coming down from Nuremberg to Moosburg had been picked up again. They told us that Patton was coming in from the west and they felt any day something could happen. But nothing did. And it wasn't until 23 April that we heard this battle going on. Suddenly we could hear the whistling of the shells and crackle of small-arms fire. We really didn't know what to do because the Germans were on the one side, the Americans on the other, and we were in the middle. So we did the best we could. There were a couple of brick buildings handy. We clustered as close as we could for protection. I was sitting with my back to the one wall facing the fence, and about eleven o'clock in the morning, suddenly, all the firing stopped! Suddenly, out of the woods rumbled this mammoth American tank! The muzzle of the tank's cannon traversed back and forth. It headed right for the fence. The tank hit the fence, and it came down. All hell broke loose. I mean it was a time! Oh, we ran for that tank, jumped on it, pounded on it! It was fabulous! [*Editor's note: The American tank was accompanied by a Jeep in which rode Harry McCracken, who would liberate his own brother. Mr. McCracken's story appears in this volume*].

The Germans were encircled. A group of infantry had gone up around to the entrance and had blocked off any escape from there. We rode the tank up to the entrance of the camp. We were yelling at the Germans and calling them names, trying to scare them a little bit. Our troops finally marched all the Germans off. We were just delighted! An American captain told us just to stay put because the battle was continuing in Moosburg. As the captain spoke, one of our guys yelled, "Hey, there goes the American flag!"

And we could see the tower over in Moosburg, kind of the county seat. Our flag was going up. The German flag was going down. Well, you can imagine! I mean all at once it was Fourth of July, Christmas, New Years Eve, everything all at once! We were free men again! Next day was just great. They told us to stay put, not to move, then they said, "We'll have food into you tomorrow."

The next day, along about eleven o'clock in the morning, a Red Cross truck comes in and two women get out and start serving coffee and donuts. They were that close behind the troops! The Army kitchens got there around noon, and we had our first cooked meal in a year. The following day Patton himself came in on his command car and talked to us. He was just as much a commander as you could imagine — pearl-handled revolvers, shiny boots and shiny hat! I mean he was all there! We had to stay there about two weeks because they couldn't get transport for us. Once they did they took us to an airfield and put us in DC–3s and flew us up to a processing camp up near Bordeaux, France. It was called Lucky Strike. There was Lucky Strike, Chesterfield, Camel, you know, all those good cigarette places. The first thing they did was burn our clothes and de-louse us. Here we were stark naked. We had the option of getting our heads shaved, because of the lice and all the other stuff. Most of us said, "Shave it off! Shave it off! Get rid of it!"

We knew we weren't going any place for a while. I went through delousing, shaved my hair off. I was pallid. We were the most disgusting looking bunch. I could count every rib in my body. My hipbone stuck out. We got new uniforms, then they said, "Time to go eat!"

That's all they wanted us to do. After a while the back got to be okay. We got our physicals and got our records all straightened away and then we went to the mess hall. I couldn't believe the food — fresh bread, eggs, chicken, steak, veal, you name it, and they had it! And every one of us got sick. Our systems couldn't take it. Even the smell of that food revolted us. I ate, anyway. I ate continuously.

We had no duties. All we had to do was report every morning at eight o'clock for reveille, and the rest of the day we had off. We could go to the PX, we could go to the movie, we could take a walk, and we could do whatever we wanted to do, especially eat. We wrote letters, of course, and tried to get a little bit back in touch with what was going on.

I and a couple buddies went down to the motor pool and waited around until we could commandeer a Jeep. We got one, and went to Paris where we stayed for twelve days. We were absolutely AWOL, but we didn't care. We had back pay and everything we needed or wanted. We got a small room, and did very well for ourselves.

Twelve days later, at four in the morning, there was a knock at the door. I opened it, and there stood a couple of tough-looking MP's.

"You're Bob Nelson?"

"Yes, sir."

"You're so and so?"

"Yes, sir."

"Well," they said, "Come on!"

So, we gathered our stuff up and went down to their command car, and they drove us from Paris to Bordeaux and stood around while we got checked into the ship that was going to bring us back to the States. They didn't punish us. In fact, they knew we were in Paris the day we got there. The concierge that we got the room from made her money by telling the MP's if there were any American troops around. I got on board the ship and here again is Colonel Alkire, my CO, on the ship. I kept bumping into this guy!

He said, "Okay, Bob, you're appointed Officer of the Day on the ship."

Well, that was okay with me. I didn't mind that at all. That was supposed to be my punishment, and it was great because I got a stateroom with another lieutenant who was Officer of the Guard. We didn't have to go down in the hold where all the other guys had to go.

On the way back we stopped at Trinidad. Then I went to New York, to Fort Dix, got processed, got some money, got a ninety-day delay, then got on a train to Pittsburgh, stayed overnight in a hotel. Next morning, I got on a train to Greensburg, threw my duffel bag up over my shoulder, got off the train walked up the street to my house, knocked on the door. My mother opened it, looked at me and said, "My God! It's Bob!"

And I said: "Yep, it's me."

I gave my mother a big hug. She was crying. She called my dad, and my dad came over. She made me something to eat. I was starved, if you can believe that, because I had been eating like a pig and had gained fifteen pounds. Around noon Dad was going to go back to work, and I told mother that I wanted to go to bed. She said, "Go ahead, the bed is all made up."

I woke up at one o'clock the next day. I slept twenty-four hours. My mother later told me that she checked on me every couple of hours. She said, "I was going to call the doctor, because I thought you were in some kind of coma!"

My dad calmed her down a little by saying, "Well, at least he's still breathing!"

I woke up ravenously hungry. I proceeded to eat everything in the house. Dad had saved up all his gas stamps, and Mother had saved up all her food stamps. So Dad had all these gas stamps for me; there was still rationing at the time. Dad had bought a two-door Mercury, so I could get in the car and go any time I wanted to.

Physically it probably didn't take more than six or seven months before I was back to a fairly decent weight, fairly decent physical condition. When I was separated, I got a clean bill of health, so in six to eight months I was in pretty good shape. Mentally? Probably it took a year for me to get out of the military thought processes. I started undergraduate school at the University of Pittsburgh. I went from the military into academe, and that was like going from Antarctica up to the Equator. Here I am, twenty-three-years old, having helped bomb half of Europe, and I'm sitting in a class with seventeen-year olds. It took about a year to adjust to being a civilian.

Emotionally? It was about five or six years before the nightmares stopped. My wife was great about this. I would get up at two or three o'clock in the morning, get in the car, and I would drive for two or three hours. It wasn't until fifty-years later that I found out I wasn't unusual, for there were a lot of people going through the same things. We didn't pay much attention to it. It was just a normal way to readjust to society. We did our job, and didn't make excuses.

I don't know why, but it was fifty years before I thought about looking everyone up. I was reunited with Walter Gates with whom I shared the mountain in Austria. I was reunited with my bombardier when I went to his retirement party. I went to the fiftieth reunion of Stalag Luft III in Cincinnati, and I went to the fiftieth reunion of the 449th Bomb Group.

Of all the things I came out of the service with, two things stand out: one was a great appreciation of discipline, and a great appreciation of what the words "duty, honor and country" mean. "Duty, honor, country?" When you're in war, when you're in combat, you recognize that you will kill or be killed. There isn't any other way of surviving combat. But when you're in combat and you get up in the morning and you go to briefing and you get in the plane, you go, and you fight your way through fighters, you get through the flak, you drop your bombs, you come back, and the next day you do the same damn thing. Duty! *It's your duty to do this*! When the fighters are coming in at you and you're holding down the trigger, and despite the fact that they're shooting at you, you're shooting right back at them. You just get in that frame of mind that you're going to kill, kill, kill! It isn't another airplane over there, it's another human being, and you're going to do it.

Honor? This is probably the thing you remember the best. You and nine other people are in that bomber and you're all depending on each other and you are not going to let them down. People say to me, "Bob why did it take fifty years before you saw Walter and before you saw Murphy, and Al Yano, and Audrey Salyer?"

And I answer, "It's very simple. You never forget!"

Country? I spoke to a group of nine-year-olds up in Akron in one of my granddaughter's classes, and they didn't understand country, because I asked them. I said, "When I say duty, honor, country what does country mean to you?"

They looked at each other and finally one of them piped up and said, "Well, that means that you love where you live."

I thought that was pretty good. That goes together, but they had never thought on these terms.

If I could describe what country meant to me—it was one of the last flights we made to Wiener-Neustadt, and we had a maximum effort, and we put one thousand bombers up in the air. We were in the far left-hand side of the echelon, and as far as you could see were bombers. Then you realized that there were a thousand bombers up there, and those ten men were all doing the same thing. Ten thousand men! All intent on one purpose: defending their country. To a lot of people today especially, defending your country is a very loose phrase, but there is a poem called, "The Flag is Passing By."

And the first phrase goes, "Hats off. The flag is passing by." And that's your country!

Alexander Robert Nelson (first row, right) with his crewmates at Bruning, Nebraska.
Courtesy of Alexander Robert Nelson.

Two pages from Alexander Robert Nelson's Stalag diary. He wrote the diary on scraps of paper taken from cigarette packages. *Courtesy of Alexander Robert Nelson.*

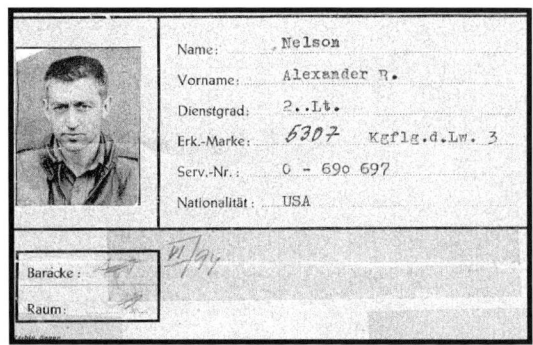

Robert Nelson's "Kriegie" (Kriegesgefangener) Prisoner of War ID card. *Courtesy of the Nelson family.*

Wally Gates, who was captured with Robert Nelson in Austria after they were shot down over Wiener-Neustadt. *Courtesy of the Nelson family.*

"Thumbs Up, Yank! We All Can't Go!"

Fielder N. Newton
Eighth Air Force; 389th Bomb Group;
Farrell, Pennsylvania, 23 September 1923

"A typical mission would start the night before. They alerted us that we would be flying in the morning. So we got to bed as early as we could and fell asleep as quickly as we could with the things that were on our minds. It wasn't always easy."

WIN THE WAR! That was the feeling of the time. All the industrial companies in Pennsylvania were busy with war work, and proud to get the Army and Navy "E" for Excellence in war production. People put aside their differences and worked together for the common good. The unions were willing to cooperate, and were not looking for more money and other perks. The folks at home made sacrifices, too. There was rationing and people accepted it. I grew up in Sharon, Pennsylvania. In 1941, I went off to study Petroleum Engineering at Texas A&M, but Pearl Harbor changed everything.

From the time I was a boy, I'd been interested in flying. I took the Air Corps exam and enlisted in the Army Air Corps in 1942. They allowed me to stay in college until the spring 1943, when I would finish my sophomore year.

After basic training, I went to Slippery Rock, Pennsylvania, to the College Training Detachment, a waiting place for Air Force cadets waiting to get into the regular cadet program. While I was there, I got ten hours of training in the Piper Cub. From Slippery Rock, I went to Nashville, Tennessee for classification. It was there that I went through a battery of tests that ultimately decided what part of the Air Force I was suited for.

I was sent to pre-flight school at Maxwell Field, Alabama, and the Air Force Academy at that time. In pre-flight school we learned a lot of things that we needed to know for flying, but we never put our hands on a control stick. We did only classroom work.

After I completed pre-flight, I went to primary-flight training at Lakeland, Florida, where I washed out. I always felt it was not entirely my fault. By that point in the war, December 1943, they were trying to reduce the number of cadets they had. So it was a given that a lot of us were not going to make it as pilots. In primary flight school, we flew the PT–17, which were open-cockpit biplanes. We had the same instructor for the entire time we were there. We went up with the instructor until such time as we had enough skill and hours to solo. I never reached that point, though. Incidentally, the primary schools were all civilian-operated. If you flunked the check ride with the civilians, the Army gave you a courtesy ride, which was done to put the final stamp on your washing out.

Fortunately, I scored well enough in the examinations that they sent me to navigation school. Before going there, I completed six weeks of aerial gunnery training at Fort Meyers, Florida, and was classified as a gunner. Gunnery school was more fun than anything else, because we got to shoot off a lot of rounds, starting with .22 rifles on a range similar to something you'd see at a carnival shooting gallery, except we shot at little airplanes that were farther away and went faster than carnival ducks. We were being trained to lead a target. From the "shooting gallery" we shot skeet with shotguns mounted on turrets. They would release the skeet from a high tower. We tracked them with the turret and shot at them. Then we trained on a skeet range from the back of a pickup truck that had a shotgun mounted on an O-ring. There were skeet houses stationed here and there around a mile track. They would release the skeet at random, and you had two things to think about, the motion of the truck, and the motion of the skeet. There were many variations on the same theme. Finally, we got to fly in B–17's, and fire at towed targets.

There was a lot of other instruction with the .50 caliber machinegun, taking it apart and putting it together, blindfolded and wearing silk gloves. Training with the gloves was important because, at altitude, hands would freeze to metal if they weren't protected.

After I finished gunnery training, I went to Selman Field, Monroe, Louisiana, to study navigation, including celestial, pilotage and dead reckoning. We flew the twin-engine Hudson. Usually there were four navigators in training, with a pilot flying them. One of the navigator-trainee cadets would fly in the copilot's seat and do pilotage navigation. The other three would be doing dead reckoning at three desks with compasses. Then, at night, we'd practice celestial navigation.

Pilotage navigation was basically just looking at the ground and comparing what you see visually with what's on the map. You could do that in the daytime or at night, though, at night, it was more difficult because distances could be deceptive.

Dead reckoning used information based on weather. From the weather people we'd get the wind velocity and direction. Using the heading from the compass, and adding to that the velocity and direction of the wind, whichever direction it might be forcing the plane, I could get position relative to the ground.

Celestial navigation used stars to determine a line of position. By taking three shots on three different stars, you could get three different lines of position. Those, hopefully, would cross and form a triangle, and at the center of the triangle would be where the plane would have been twenty minutes before, because that much time passed by the time I did my calculations. Then I took an average course between those fixes and eventually got to where I was going.

I also used a radio compass. I could tune into a radio station, and the arrow of the compass would point to wherever the antenna was. It was a very risky method to use for those people flying over the ocean during the war. They were sometimes lulled off course by German submarines that surfaced and sent out signals. I could also use a radio beam and cross it in the daytime with a line of position of the sun and determine where I might be.

When we started flying missions out of England, we had additional methods of navigation. One was a special compass developed by the Navy. If I knew my longitude and latitude, I would set that into the compass, and the compass would follow the direction of the plane. I would add the wind velocity and direction, and get my position. The Navy compasses weren't that suitable for us, however, since they were designed for pilots flying off carriers. They didn't fly as far as we did. They became less accurate over longer distances. The Navy compass was a good aid, but I couldn't rely on it to a great extent.

I graduated from navigation school on 7 August 1944. After that, I married Marjorie, a second-grade teacher in Lewiston, Pennsylvania. It wasn't as smooth as it was supposed to have been. It was a short honeymoon. My promised two-week leave became a seven-day delay-en-route. Marjorie went back to finish at Penn State, and I went to California to train with my crew to go overseas.

They sent me to the San Joaquin Valley of California to staging area. I was there for a week or so, got my shots, and had my physical records updated. While I was there, some of us went to a bar in town. The bartender asked one of the pilots for his ID. He was only twenty, and the bartender refused to serve him. It seemed strange to us that a guy could pilot a complicated aircraft, go out and defend his country, possibly get killed, but was too young to drink.

After San Joaquin, they sent us to March Field, in California, a permanent base for B–24s. I trained there with my crew for six weeks. Our pilot was J.C. Dodman, from Michigan. Our co-pilot was Paul Rochette, an orphan who was raised by an uncle, a career Army man. Paul became a good friend of mine. He enlisted in the Army after getting out of high school, and was assigned as a radio operator to the first B–17 squadron created by the Army. When the war started he applied for and got into OCS, and then was commissioned into the Signal Corps. He spent some time in Greenland, but didn't much like that duty. So, he applied to the Cadets and went through pilot training as an officer.

Our bombardier was L. E. Dowell, from Kansas City, Kansas. L. E. was the youngest officer on the crew and a bit immature, but he was a good guy and a good bombardier. Our first flight engineer was a fellow from Brooklyn. When we were in the staging area to go overseas, from Camp Kilmer, New Jersey, we had a twenty-four-hour pass and he went AWOL, and never did come back. I don't know what happened to him.

Clifford Brace was our second flight engineer, but we didn't get him until we got to England. I think we were fortunate, because he was a better flight engineer than the guy who went AWOL. Gene Richardson, from Michigan, was our radio operator. I got to know Gene's parents because they visited him in California when we were out there. He was a lanky Texan, probably eighteen or nineteen at the time we went overseas. Dick Bidlack, from Ohio, was our waist gunner. Jim Ward was our nose gunner. He got to be the closest to me, because he was right in front of me in the nose turret.

At March Field we familiarized ourselves with the plane. None of us, except the pilot, had ever flown in a B–24. We did a lot of cross-country runs for navigational purposes and so the radio operator and flight engineer could become familiar with what they had to do. The flight engineer was responsible for checking the fuel and switching tanks when one would empty. His job became very important on a couple of the missions we flew.

At Hamilton Field, San Francisco, the Army issued new B–24Ns. Hamilton was a staging area for the Pacific Theater, and that's where we were supposed to go. To me, it was a lot nicer plane, because I had a desk on the flight deck where I could sit down. On the older version, I had no desk, and had to stand for all of our flights. We were slated to leave Hamilton Field and go to a point of debarkation at another air base. We were flying our final fuel consumption run south out of San Francisco when, as we neared Bakersfield Tower, they radioed us to return to Hamilton Field. The Army had changed our orders. When we got back they took our B–24's away from us and said, "You guys are going to Europe."

The hardest-hit were our enlisted men whose nice-fitting olive drabs were taken from them. The Army gave them new khakis that they had to get re-fitted. We got on a train, ten crews in all, and we went from San Francisco to Camp Kilmer, where we got a twenty-four-hour pass. When we returned we were quarantined. We had no contact whatsoever with the outside world. We didn't know where we were going until just before we left in November 1944.

We left for England on the *Il de France*, a ship that traveled fast enough to avoid enemy submarines. It didn't need the protection of a convoy or escort. Our course was to the south, toward Bermuda. It was November, but we were on deck in our shirt-sleeves. We had quite a conglomeration of troops on board. I got acquainted with a signal officer from the Canadian Army, and helped him get his boys, the first Canadian draftees, on board. He had several of them go AWOL from the train they boarded in Montreal. They didn't want to go to war. There were Army troops on board, glider pilots, Army nurses and OSS girls, civilian secretaries. It took us seven days to get across.

We anchored in the Firth of Clyde, and they transported us in small boats to land. From there they put us on a train and our ten crews went to Stowe, England, the classification center for the Air Force in England. Our barracks were built of concrete block, and they were cold. From there we were transferred to East Anglia, England, to the 389th Bomb Group. By the time we got there, the Army had increased the number of missions a crew had to fly to complete their tour of duty. At the beginning of the war it was twenty-five. Now it was thirty.

Our first mission was 2 January 1945. Koblenz was the target. We bombed the rail yards and a bridge crossing the Moselle River. Needless to say, everybody was scared. It was a trip to the unknown, our first time in combat, but once we got airborne and into formation, we were ready to go. Flak was meager, which was a good way to start. We hit additional flak coming back and our resident comedian, Bill Denton, had a piece of shrapnel hit him on the bridge of his nose just above his oxygen mask. He

Right: Lieutenant Fielder Newton, navigator of the "Sky Wolves," with Lieutenant Paul Rochelle, copilot. Courtesy of Fielder Newton.

got scratched, but never got the Purple Heart. His friend, Ring, was to hold onto the piece of flak as proof of the wound, but he lost it, and it was a point of contention with them for years. Bill's was the only blood ever drawn on our missions.

Flak was our greatest fear. The Germans had many anti-aircraft guns, and they concentrated them. We used to say, "The flak was so heavy you could walk on it." It was a bad omen when the Germans fired colored flak. That was a signal to their fighter planes that the flak barrage was over and that they could attack. Toward the end of the war, The Germans must have been low on ammunition because they fired everything they had at us, including the colored flak. We got flak on the way in and on the way out.

A typical mission started the night before when they alerted us that we would be flying in the morning. We got to bed as early as we could, and tried to fall asleep as quickly as possible, and that wasn't easy. There would be a lot on our minds.

They woke us up very early, three or four o'clock, depending on the length of the mission. We dressed quickly, got on our bicycles, and rode to the mess hall. We always got a good breakfast before a mission — eggs (to our liking), bacon, coffee, and toast, whatever we wanted. After breakfast, officers and enlisted men went their own way. The navigators met with the squadron navigator who, in conjunction with the group navigator, outlined our course to the target. The bombardiers met with their group to go over pictures of the target, decide on the IP (Initial Point, where the whole bomber stream got into close formation to proceed to the target). Then, we all got together for the final briefing, got into our flying clothes, and headed out to Army trucks that took us to the area where our planes were parked.

Our flying suits added a lot of pounds to our bodies. We all wore flak vests, which were like catchers' vests, only they went down the back as well as the front. We had the option of wearing a back parachute or a chest pack. The chest pack could be put on when we needed it; the back parachute was worn all the time. I chose the back parachute because I wanted to have a parachute on me all the time. We wore a silk, heated suit and a flying suit, which was an alpaca-lined jacket and pants, and flying boots, which were sheepskin-lined leather boots. There was no heat in the plane, and the temperatures at altitude could go to fifty below.

Once we were in the planes, we waited for the green flare that told us to start engines. Then, we proceeded in our turn to the runway and off we'd go with a full bomb and gas load, more than 10,000 pounds worth. Most of our missions were long, because most of the good targets were beyond the American lines, and it was my job to get the plane there.

Once we got airborne we went to point where all the squadrons rallied on the lead crew. Once they were formed, each bomb group formed on the division leader and then we'd go off in a stream of maybe 500 aircraft. We headed over the English Channel, usually over Holland and into Germany. Once or twice, we went down through France.

We flew to the initial point, and started our bomb run. The run lasted long enough for the bombardier to fix his Norden bombsight on the target and set the speed of the bombsight so that it would synchronize with the speed of the airplane. The sight was connected to the automatic pilot, and the bombardier, at this point, was actually flying the aircraft. When the bombardier released the bombs, it was my job to pull the "salvo lever" to make sure none of the bombs got hung up in the bomb bay.

For the most part, we hit our targets quite well. Of course, we were doing saturation bombing, too, that's why we were in formation. Every bomb wasn't going to go on the exact point of the target. But it was saturated around the target enough that the target would be destroyed. The main thing was, if we could fly visual all the time, it would've been great, because we'd know what we were hitting. But, when we were in overcast and using radar-directed bombing, all we knew was that our bombs had hit the ground. We couldn't see where they hit.

We bombed bridges and railroad yards. We went all the way to Czechoslovakia to bomb an airstrip that was a jet base that the Air Force wanted put out of commission. We got hit a couple of times by the jets. They weren't that accurate, because they were coming through the formations so fast. Typically we would get hit by ME–109s and Focke-Wulf–190s. We never saw any other kinds of German aircraft at all. Strangely enough, we had a pilot on our airbase whose name was Johnny Messerschmidt. He was a cousin of the Messerschmidt who developed the aircraft. I don't know why they ever sent him to Europe to fight, but they did!

We couldn't eat on these long missions because we wore oxygen masks from the time we got to ten thousand feet. What we did have were little packets in wax boxes that contained hard tack and Chicklet Chewing Gum. That was all we had for a long, nine-hour mission. Sometimes I'd chew gum for so long my jaws got sore.

When we came back, the medics met us. Our medics were very good to us. To pep us up a bit, we got a good shot of American whiskey. After that, we made our way over to the Red Cross girls who had sandwiches and coffee. That was the first food we had, and we needed it after that shot!

Then we went into debriefing. Usually, our bomb group commander, the colonel in charge of the 20th Combat Wing bomb group commander, and his adjutant, the actor Jimmy Stewart, would debrief us. We went over the whole mission — what happened, what didn't happen. We also checked out photos taken during the raid. The photos had been developed immediately after the planes got back.

Many planes never came back. But we were lucky. Once we were coming back from a mission over Berlin. We had lost an engine over the target from flak. The pilot was forced to feather the prop, and we started back behind the bomber stream. A B–24 used more fuel with three engines than with four, because you had to rev the other three up pretty fast. The B–24 flew with a lot of thrust from the engines and less lift from the wings. We were coming back across Germany and over Holland to get back to our base in East Anglia, England. The pilot and I, talking on the intercom, decided that we'd better find an alternate route in case our fuel got too low. I plotted a course to an emergency field in France. We got near that and we felt that we had enough fuel to keep going to the next emergency field, right on the English Channel.

We headed for that point and about halfway across the Channel, the pilot said, "Let's go home."

I gave him a heading for home. We landed.

Just for fun, I asked Brace when we got out, "How much fuel did we have left, Cliff?"

He checked the gauges. We had fifty gallons left. We came in pretty light. We were very fortunate. I suppose we might have gone around the airstrip a couple of more times and that would've been it.

The weather affected a great many of our missions. Once, we were on board our plane waiting for the green flare to go off. We waited and waited and waited and ultimately, a red flare went up. This meant the mission was scrubbed. It had been scrubbed because the cloud cover at the rally point was too high. There was no way we could rally in the clouds and go together as a group. The ceiling at which we could successfully fly was about 25,000 feet. We could go maybe to 30,000. So, if the cloud cover went all the way up to 24,000, they just couldn't afford to send us out.

We did go on a mission that we didn't get credit for. We formed up and started out over the channel and they recalled the mission. The ground weather had deteriorated to the point that the airbases were becoming fogged in. By the time we got turned around and back to our airbase, we couldn't find it. We headed north, where the weather was supposed to be a little better, and searched for some place to land. We found a hole in the clouds, and saw an airbase under it. We went down through the hole and radioed in. It was a Canadian RAF base and they gave us the green light to come in. We landed there and stayed overnight. We lost five aircraft that day just trying to land.

After about two or three missions, we were elected to be a lead crew. Our pilot had polled the crew about whether we wanted to become a lead crew or not. The majority of us said, "No, let's get our missions in and get them over, and get out of here."

That was probably a mistake, because they wanted us badly enough as a lead crew that they didn't fly us for a week or two. That meant that we weren't clocking missions. Finally, we decided that we weren't going to be getting out any sooner, so we might as well go ahead and become a lead crew. As a lead crew, we fell in line to become squadron officers. As missions tallied to the maximum, the pilot would become a squadron commander, the bombardier a squadron bombardier, and the navigator the squadron navigator. That carried another rank upward. We would have all been captains instead of first lieutenants, but that never occurred, because the war ended before we finished our tour of duty.

Between missions we would get periodic passes. The nearest large town was Norwich, England, twenty-five or thirty miles away. They'd load us into a truck and take us there. There were USO or Red Cross quarters there where we could get a clean bed and a hot bath for fifty cents. We always visited the local pubs for some beer or Scotch, and then go to a movie. When we went to London, the passes lasted a little longer. Again, we would stay at USO Clubs. On base, the Army held dances at the officer's club. The girls from town would come to the base.

We really didn't take the opportunity to make friends with the British. There are people that I know through the Eighth Air Force Historical Society that made friends over there, and still correspond with them. I admire that they were able to do that. We just didn't seem to meet anybody that wanted to be friends. In fact, you had the feeling at the time that some of the British were getting upset with so many Americans being around. One of their favorite sayings over there was, "They're overpaid, they're oversexed and they're over here."

There were British civilians working on the air base, and when we loaded onto a truck to get out to the aircraft, some of them would give us another favorite saying, "Thumbs up, Yank!" We all can't go!"

We were well paid compared with the British soldiers. The pay was pretty good for a first lieutenant in the United States Air Force. I made about $368.00 a month, which was quite good for 1945. In fact, when I got out of college, I started at Youngstown Sheet and Tube for $300.00 a month. You can see that the Air Force was pretty good money!

When the war ended, everybody celebrated. We had trolley missions that involved taking ground crews on sightseeing tours of the damage that was done to Germany. Those ground crews were real supermen. They kept us flying and these sight-seeing tours was one way we could pay them back for staying up all night to have our planes in top condition for the morning mission.

We finished up the war with seventeen missions. We got the Air Medal with two oak leaf clusters and the European Theater of Operations Medal with four or five battle stars. We got a battle star for each battle that went on when we were in the theater, whether we participated or not. We got a Presidential Unit Citation and a Victory Medal.

Our group had flown over 300 missions and was approaching 325, when the war ended. Being an older bomb group that also flew on the famous Ploesti raid, it was broken up and the young crews were sent home immediately because it was thought that they might still go to the Pacific Theater. Those of us who had been there some time longer were assigned to another bomb group, the 364th. We took an aircraft fitted with wooden racks in the bomb bays so that we could carry mechanics, tools and all kinds of aircraft parts, along with ten ground crew personnel. We got on board with our ten passengers and flew to an airbase in Wales, spent the night there and the next morning headed for the Azores Islands. On the way there, we went on an air-sea search, because the day before an aircraft had been lost and we were sent looking for survivors.

We arrived at the Azores, and the weather grounded us for three days. The wind velocity and direction was wrong for us to have enough fuel to fly to Gander Lake, Newfoundland, our next stopover point. We flew from the Azores to Gander, left there the next morning and flew to Bradley Field, Connecticut. It was there that we left our airplane, said goodbye to our friends in the crew and went home for our thirty-day leave.

I was then assigned to a base in Sioux Falls, South Dakota. While I was at Sioux Falls, V-J Day occurred. Then it was just a matter of waiting until it was my turn to get out. Of course, the separation centers were flooded with people. A lot of the combat veterans had a lot of points. The point system determined when you could get out. They sent me to Love Field in Dallas, Texas, an air transportation base. I was there for two or three months, waiting to be discharged. Finally, my number came up and I was discharged from Sheppard Field in Wichita Falls, Texas, came home and had my terminal leave. The date of my discharge was 8 December 1945. I did stay in the reserves until 1953. I went back to college and finished my degree. I graduated from Penn State in 1948 with a degree in Mechanical Engineering.

The war taught me a lot about this country. I think duty was the important thing, and so was patriotism. We were all ready to fight for our country.

British Air Marshall Portal and United States Air Force General Ira Eaker play in concert. A cartoon that demonstrates the unity between the United States and Great Britain concerning the "Round the Clock" bombing of Nazi Germany. *London Illustrated News.*

"Are There Any Mines There?"

Orlando Pietropaoli
629th Engineer Light Equipment Company
Greensburg, PA, 31 January 1924

"When I was over there, it never ever entered my mind that I would get shot. It was like I just had to do a job over there, and I did it. One time when our planes were bombing, this one fellow, who was under the tractor with us, was shaking and crying so hard we could hear the matches in his matchbox rattle. My buddy and I didn't think anything about the bombs. It was just another day."

JAPAN HAD ALWAYS been a good neighbor, and we were always sending our extra steel over there. They bought it up like crazy. After Pearl Harbor, I saw a cartoon in the paper of a Japanese soldier putting a knife in Uncle Sam's back. It was only a matter of time. I was inducted into the Army and ended up at Fort Meade, Maryland. I wondered what I was getting into. When I was through with my interview the sergeant said, "I'm going to send you to a good outfit."

So, he put me in the Combat Engineers. Two hundred and fifty of us went into training. Only 125 made it through. They took only the best, and made most of us sergeants. They made the rest officers. We had one corporal, and he worked in the kitchen.

We had our maneuvers down in Tennessee. We did a lot of damage to the roadways and had to fix them, especially the farm roads. Sometimes we made a deal with a farmer. A farmer might say, "I won't worry about my road if you dig me a pond over there."

Then one of us would say, "We'll give you a pond if you have a chicken dinner for us."

We had a lot of chicken dinners, and corn whiskey.

When we went overseas, we went to Scotland first, and then took a train down to England, to a place called King's Park. While they were unloading the trucks, one guy hollered my name. I turned around to see who it was, and there two guys who grew up with me. I met them a couple more times in Europe, once when they were putting up pontoon bridges across the Rhine at Remagen. They were engineers, like me. Small world. I never expected that.

An English guy came over to me and said, "We really build some good machinery over here."

I said, "That's not your machine. This dozer was made in the United States."

He said, "Right! We built that over here. We do that all the time."

I said, "Well come over here and look. What's that say? It says 'Made in the United States.'"

When we tried to land on Omaha Beach on D-Day, we couldn't get in because all the landing craft were backed up. We were like sitting ducks in the water. On the second day we got in, and it was like the Fourth of July. All night long shells burst all over the place.

After we broke out of the beach I saw dead, bloated animals all over the place, cows, horses, whatever. I spent a couple days just bulldozing the dead animals. The stench was terrible. Strafing aircraft constantly interrupted us. Every time a plane went over, the three of us (I had a truck driver and an assistant) would dive under the dozer, and in the middle of all that stench. We would say, "Aw, I hope we don't have to go under there today!"

But we always had to. Dan Price, the driver, was a big guy about six foot and 230 pounds. I don't know how we all fit under there, but we did.

At St. Lô, we were sitting on top of a hill waiting for the big carpet-bombing of the German Lines. Operation COBRA it was called. We set out smudge pots all along our lines so the pilots would see the smoke and know where we were and where the Germans were. When they started bombing, the wind shifted and blew the smoke in the wrong direction. That must have confused the pilots because bombs dropped into our own lines and killed a lot of guys.

The Germans were still able to put up fighter planes, and they would come around and strafe. One time, during a strafing run, we got under a trailer because there was a little more room there than under the dozer. We had steel skids, and we put them along the side of the trailer to make us safer. Dan Price got tired of the strafing, so he jumped up, got up on top of the truck where we had mounted a .50 caliber machinegun, and he started shooting away. He actually shot one plane down.

Around this time we came across a knocked-out German tank. We found a blowtorch clamped on the tank. The Germans used them to heat their manifolds in cold weather, but we used them to make hot water to shave with. We'd take the liners out of our steel helmets, put the water in, and use the blowtorch to heat it. That blowtorch was great.

One time we came upon one of our tanks stuck in a crater. There was nothing the matter with it; the tanker just couldn't get back out. They had a tank retriever, a big truck, and even it couldn't pull him out. The lieutenant from the tank came over and said, "I'll hook you right next to the tank, and I'll put the tank truck above you."

Well, that didn't work, either. I said, "Let's just switch it around. I'll get up front and we'll get more traction."

It worked.

I said to my buddy, "Let's eat!"

We sat there eating our K-Rations, just looking around at all kinds of blown-up machinery. I got up and walked over to this burned-out half-track to have a look. Here and there was a leg, a finger or two, and a head. I got the heck out of there.

The Engineers were a little different from anyone else. We never saluted anyone.

Our own officers wanted it that way because the Germans might see the salute and pick the officer off. One time when we were checking on new equipment, we walked right past a general, a colonel, and a captain.

I heard the captain say, "Those guys didn't salute us."

Then one of them said, "Those sonsofbitches never salute anybody."

Once we had an ammunition dump on fire, and we were supposed to go and put it out. At the time my own dozer was out of commission, so I went up as an assistant, just in case someone got hit and I had to take over. A master sergeant from Texas and his driver took me there. When we got to the bottom of a hill, the sergeant said, "I'm not going any further. There's shellfire and bullets all over the place, plus there's that burning ammo dump."

I argued with him, "You're supposed to go up there and see that this work is done."

Then I said to his driver, "Okay. Let him stay. You and I are going up."

The driver looked around and said, "Okay. Okay. I'll go with you."

The sergeant changed his mind and came along. We got up there and there were four dozers working in different directions.

I said, "This is never going to work. You're never going to cover the place up."

I called the guys together and said, "Get all your dozers together, blade against blade. Everybody push the at same time."

We got the dump covered in about an hour. The other guys all ended up getting a medal. I got nothing, because I don't think the master sergeant liked me for dragging him up there.

Near Paris the guys got into a big stash of liquor. I didn't know where they got it, but they wanted to see me get drunk. And they did. The lieutenant laughed and said, "You'd better get in good shape to travel tomorrow!" He told me later that I kept calling him by his first name, Larry. He was such a nice guy; I named my first son after him. He even came to see me once, after I got home.

We got into Paris and stayed just long enough to see Notre Dame and the Eiffel Tower. The cathedral had sandbags all around it. I went to the top of the Eiffel Tower. It was a great view, about as much as I would ever see of the city. After that, we took off again. We did have drivers who would go to Paris for supplies, but I never got to go with them. After Paris, we got up around Malmedy, in Belgium, at the time of the Battle of the Bulge. We heard that the Germans had broken through somewhere, but we didn't know exactly when or where. I pulled guard duty, the only one I ever pulled during the war. Then they assigned me to another outfit. I had to drive there myself because my driver took sick and had to go to the hospital. I drove down to a place called Trois Pontes, and parked the truck, the dozer, and the trailer. Then I went headquarters and reported in. Trois Pontes was just a madhouse. They were loading all the trucks and moving out because the Germans were on the advance.

The lieutenant in charge said, "You have to go back and get your machine. Where is it?"

"It's over on the other side of Trois Pontes."

"You got to go back and get it."

"No way. There's Germans all over the place, I'm not going back there."

"What are you going to do?"

"I'm going to go with you."

"Well," he said, "'we're moving out."

"Okay," I said.

"What can you drive?"

"That big truck back there."

"Okay. You get in the back of the line because you're going to be holding us back."

"Where are you going to be?" I asked.

"I'm going to be in the Jeep," he answered.

"I'm going to be right behind you," I said.

Nobody knew where to go. The lieutenant kept reading the map.

I said, "Lieutenant I don't where you're going, but you better move from there."

"Why?"

"Look. There's four tanks over there, their guns are starting to turn this way, we better move."

We moved.

Around Christmas time, we were reorganizing and trying to push the Germans back. We had a lot of snow, and it was really cold. I had the machine running, and we were all sitting around. The infantrymen had white coveralls on to camouflage them in the snow. I was sitting on the seat, me and my buddy, and I kind of dozed off. When I woke up, I saw all the infantry guys standing around my machine. I wondered what was happening, and then I realized that they were trying get warm by the heat of the motor. Actually, I think they were keeping the machine warm.

I had been clearing snow off the roads. There came a little thaw and the snow was starting to melt. The trees on the side of the road had been wired to blow and block the road. The Germans who must have done it were there too, and all of them were dead, maybe eighteen of them. They were all in the middle of the road. One was in a Volkswagen staff car.

I said, "Now what?"

Our trucks were going to come through soon, and I had to clear the road. So I said, "There's only one thing to do with them."

There was a big hole, probably a shell or bomb crater. I put my blade down, took my time, and pushed them all into the hole. I never hurt one of them, never pulled off an arm or leg. I just pushed enough to get them off the road.

A lieutenant wanted me to clear the road into Bastogne.

I asked, "Are there any mines there?"

He said, "I got a whole group of men up there cleaning the mines up."

So I went down there. I'm pushing snow when, all of a sudden, I see these black things going flip, flip, flip. They were mines flipping off the edge of my dozer. I stopped. The lieutenant came up with a one-star general. He jumped all over me.

I said, "You told me this road was cleared of mines. Just look at those mines up there. You didn't do your job."

The general said to the lieutenant, "I want you to put a BAR guy on his dozer, two guys up above sweeping for the mines, two guys in front for guards, and two men behind. If anything happens to that dozer or that man, you're dead."

Another time we were really pushing. My buddy and I had worked all night in the cold. We saw this big house, about four-stories high. There were a lot of our guys in the place. One of them said, "Any place you find to lay your head down, go ahead."

I said to my buddy, "We'll stay here over night, then we'll go tomorrow."

We were sleeping maybe an hour when this guy comes in and yelled, "Who's running that dozer out there?"

I said to my buddy, "Don't even answer that guy. I'm not going back out. I'm frozen now."

Finally, the guy said, "All I want is for someone to move it. One of our guys is wounded and needs help. The dozer's blocking the road."

I went out and moved the dozer, and pushed another dozer off the road while I was at it. Somebody had a tank dozer out there, and they kept complaining that the clutch was slipping. They wanted me to go out and fix it. I told them I wasn't going back out. They asked if they could borrow my dozer. I let them. I didn't see it again for three days. That was fine by me. I hadn't had any rest for three days.

When I went into the Army, I weighed 155 pounds. After the Bulge, I was down to 119. I had to fight for my food. They had ten rations in one box, what they called Ten-in-Ones. Convoys would go up a hill pretty slow. One time, I jumped on one of the convoy trucks and threw some ration boxes down to my assistant. He picked them up and put them on our truck. When I got back to the outfit, the sergeant came around and asked, "Do you have any rations? We don't have anything to eat around here."

I said, "Yeah. I got two boxes."

"Well, you got to turn them in. Captain's orders."

"The hell with you buddy. Nobody fed me when I was out on the road. I'm going to keep them. I got to go back out on the road. I don't get anything to eat out there."

"Well, I'm gonna go talk to the captain."

"Hey, talk to the captain. Do what you got to do."

The sergeant went and talked to the captain. Pretty soon the captain came around and said, "I understand you disobeyed direct orders. You have rations on there?"

"Yes, I have two boxes on there."

"You were ordered to turn them in."

"I know but nobody fed me on the road. I'm going back out on the road. That's my food."

"You know I can take all your stripes off you."

"Take my stripes. Put me in the stockade. I don't care."

"You smart sonofabitch. Go ahead and go. Keep your rations."

The captain was a good man.

I was always kind of spicy. I knew what I had to do, I did it, and nobody questioned me about it. When I was out on the road, whatever my decision was for me and my two men it went. I didn't care if a guy was a lieutenant or whatever because I was in charge of that truck and that machine. Whatever Headquarters needed, they got. Most of the time I was away from my outfit, doing what Headquarters wanted me to do, and I was on the front line all the time.

We kept going, right into Germany. The first time I ever saw a jet was in Cologne. There was this big smoke stack there. We saw two of our planes, then all of a sudden, we saw this German jet. Our guys took after him, and they got pretty close. Then we saw a big burst of flame come from out of the rear of the German plane, and he was gone. Our guys couldn't catch him.

At the Rhine River's Remagen Bridge, I had to build a ramp off the main road, down to a pontoon bridge, so we could get our vehicles across. After we got across, I we went up the Autobahn, Hitler's superhighway. One day I was clearing up, and the Germans had put a lot of railroad ties across the road. I had to knock them off, so our guys could drive through. When I finished what I had to do, I went to meet my driver down by a bridge and tunnel where we parked. I saw a guy, a Military Policeman from the Black Hawk Division.

I said, "You with the Black Hawk?"

"Yeah. Why? You know someone?"

"My brother's in that outfit."

"What's his name?"

"Vince Pietropaoli."

"Oh, just keep your eye on that tunnel. He'll be on the first Jeep that comes through."

I said, "Oh yeah?"

I didn't even have my helmet on, but I did have my souvenir, my German P–38 pistol tucked in my belt. Sure enough, there was Vince, just like the MP said. I waved him down. He couldn't believe it was me. I jumped into the Jeep and said, "I'll run up the road with you, but not too far, because I have to walk back."

Vince was a messenger. He said he would come back later, but I told him, "No. I won't see you. Don't even try to come back because I'm on the move."

He told me later on he tried to come back, but his lieutenant wouldn't let him go. They sent another guy, instead. On the way back, the other guy ran over a mine with his Jeep and got killed.

I had another brother, Joe, who was a tanker in Italy. His tank took a direct hit. The blast laid open his toes and burned his face. He jumped up through his turret, and rolled off the tank. He couldn't see. He started running. All at once he stopped and turned around and started running in the other direction, right into his sergeant's arms. At first, he was headed right toward the Germans, but something made him turn around. When he came home, they had to graft skin on his face. His face wasn't too bad, they did a pretty good job, but his hands, you know how it is when you get burnt, they're a light color. He came home with a Purple Heart. He was the only one to get out of the tank alive.

My mother was always sending packages overseas. I kept telling my mother, "Send all this stuff over to Joe."

Joe would say, "Send all this stuff over to Orlando."

We took care of each other, my brothers and I.

I got Bell's palsy in my face from driving the open cab truck. That was it. I went to the hospital. They told me I was done. They sent me home on a hospital ship, a converted French luxury liner. When I got to the States, I went down to Tennessee.

On the way back on the ship, a guy came around and said, "Anyone have any guns or ammunition. You have to turn it in."

I thought, "That's just bullshit. That guy is just taking that stuff and selling it."

I said, "I have a German P–38."

"Well, you got to turn it in."

"No. I'm not going to turn it in. I don't care what you say."

"How about turning the ammunition in."

"You can have the ammunition. I'll just keep one round so I can get more when I get home."

I still have that pistol.

I was glad to get home. They wanted me to rejoin, but I had had enough. I was discharged on 25 November 1945. The only thing that scared me over there was airplanes. After I came back, I had nightmares about those planes. I'd run in my sleep like crazy, trying to get away from them. My wife would have to wake me up.

When I was over there, it never ever entered my mind that I would get shot. It was like I just had to do a job over there, and I did it. One time when our planes were bombing, this one fellow, who was under the tractor with us, was shaking and crying so hard we could hear the matches in his matchbox rattle. My buddy and I didn't think anything about the bombs. It was just another day.

Artist Jes Wilhelm Schlaikjer painted this recruitment poster in 1942 for the U.S. War Department's Bureau of Public Relations.
National Archives.

"I'd Better Get the Hell Outta Here!"

Antonio ("Tony") Martin Priolette
24th Infantry Division, 21st Infantry Regiment,
3rd Battalion, Company I; Greensburg, Pennsylvania
11 November 1917

"The next day, our Jeep boy, the one who drove the captain around, was going down to the field hospital on an errand. I asked him to find out about Sergeant Sliven. He came back and told me, 'The sergeant can't talk too well. I had to put my ear right up near his mouth, but he said he was, okay.' Then he told me that Sliven had the whole side of his jaw blown off below the ear by shrapnel, that all he could see were Sliven's eyes, nose, and mouth. The rest of his head was bandaged. He also told me that the docs were going to take a jaw off a dead man and try to use it to replace the one Sliven lost. He said that Sliven kept saying, 'It's okay. It's okay.'"

IN BASIC TRAINING, my buddy Johnson marched behind me. He always stepped off on the wrong foot. He was always stepping on me. It was fun! Johnson was raised on a ranch in Colorado. He eventually got wounded on Leyte. I got through basic with flying colors. I tried to be a good soldier. I did everything that they wanted me to. I became a sharpshooter. I went in at 175 pounds. When I came out, I weighed 136. I was as solid as a rock. I could run with a bayoneted rifle, hit the ground with my shoulders, flip back up and be ready for parrying. I would never have survived without the kind of training we got!

After Pearl Harbor, my dad said, "No, Tony, don't sign up. You might have to go overseas! Wait, and you may never be called."

To the day he died, he regretted ever telling me that. I guess he just didn't want to see me leave. As it turned out, I was one of the first to be drafted, so I figured this was it. I'm gone! This was in January/February 1942. I was twenty-four-years old at the time.

We got to the Court House at seven o'clock in the morning, and got on a train to Pittsburgh, where they checked us over and sent us on another train to New Cumberland, Pennsylvania where we were sworn in. From there we went to Camp Wheeler, Georgia. I was there for twelve weeks basic training.

The only leave we got while we were in basic training was a twelve-hour pass. We'd go down to Macon, Georgia, but had to be back by midnight. It really wasn't much of a pass. Andy Cholock, a guy from Scranton named Kusik, and I, walked into a bar and said, "We want a shot and a beer."

The bartender said, "I can serve you beer at the bar, but if you want whiskey you have to sit at a table."

We got to a table, and then decided to drink rum and Coca-Cola, instead. So, we bought a fifth of rum. We finished that bottle, and never got up to go to the restroom. The guys wanted to order another fifth. I looked at my watch, and said, "We don't have time to drink another fifth, let's just get a pint."

We finished the pint. Andy was really sloshed. I knew what I was doing, but my legs just didn't want to go. I'd take these two-foot high steps trying to get out of the place. We made it back to Camp Wheeler just in time. When we got back, we decided to take a shower and sober up. Andy came into the shower room dressed in a tee shirt and shorts. We were buck-naked. I said, "Andy, are you going to take off your shorts and tee-shirt?"

He said, "I'm not wearing any clothes."

He got into one of the showers, singing, and soaping himself all over his shorts and tee shirt. The shower didn't help. We couldn't get back upstairs unless we went up on our hands and knees. Andy just jumped into bed, wet tee shirt and shorts. He slept in them all night.

One day, my name was called over the PA system. I said, "I'll see you guys later, I'm going over to Command Post."

There was about twenty or thirty guys lined up at the Command Post. The captain came out and said, "Fellas, all I can tell you is that this is a break for you. Where you're going, I can't tell you, but I can tell you that it's a good break."

I turned to this guy and said, "What'd you do in civilian life?"

He said that he was a baker. I turned to another guy and asked the same question. He answered that he was a mechanic. It turned out that half the people there were either mechanics or bakers!

We ended up in Pearl Harbor, the first troops to arrive there after the attack. They really worked us there putting up defenses on Oahu because they were getting ready for a Jap attack. It never came. We had to straighten barbed wire out in the ocean in water up to our waists. When the tide went out, we'd drive these steel pegs into coral reefs with sledgehammers. Then after we got all that secured, we had to dig pillboxes. They had old pillboxes that were made out of railroad logs and we had to put new ones there beside them. We had to dig with pick and shovel in that coral rock. I'll tell you, you throw a pick down at that corral rock and it will bounce back at you! That's how tough it was.

We were housed at Schofield Barracks. I got put in command of a police dog. They'd send up K-Rations for me, and thick, round steaks for the dog. I fed the dog the K-Rations, and fried up the steaks for myself. Actually, I think it was horsemeat, but it was good, and better than the rations.

Every day an officer of some kind would come up and say, "The names I call, step out!"

So he'd call maybe four or five names and each of them would step out and they'd be gone. In late December 1942, I was one of the six guys left. An officer called our names out and said, "Follow me!"

He put us in the 24th Division, and that's how I lost all my friends. Everyone else went into the 25thDivision, and they went to Guadalcanal. We left for Rockhampton, Australia, in different units, from May-September 1943. When we got off the ship, they loaded us on trucks and took us to this old racetrack where there were tents. We stayed there two or three weeks and then made our first invasion. I think it was more or less a dry run, really, because we hit Goodenough Island and there was nobody there. Then we got back on the landing barges, turned around and came back.

Our first real landing was Tanahmerah Bay in Dutch New Guinea around April 1944. Before we hit that area, they briefed us on it. We were warned that there were natives that shot poison darts. We were also advised not to ever hike up in the mountains unless there were six or more of us because they had big monkeys that would attack a single hiker. When we landed, it was about 100 yards of beach and then it was jungle. Once in the jungle it was more or less swamp. They didn't tell us much about the Japanese defenses. They only told us about the poisonous darts, and the natives. I guess the Dutch who colonized the place couldn't reach the natives up in the mountain areas because they were too savage. We set up a perimeter because they said the Japs in the mountains would get hungry and come down to get food. That's when we were supposed to capture them. I never saw a live Jap there. I saw a few dead ones there, but that was it.

In the Pacific, the way that we fought was to get into single file, and wherever we took fire, that's where the battle was. As we went through the jungle the head scouts and the second scouts cut paths for the rest of us. The ground got soggier and soggier. Our supply sergeant came over, picked me out and said, "Priolette, here I want you to carry these."

I already had my canteen, first aid kit, and two bandoleers of ammunition across each shoulder, and he wanted me to carry mortar shells! Besides, I wasn't in a mortar company. I was a rifleman! He slipped the shells over my head on top of my bandoleers, three shells in front and three in back. They were heavy. Pretty soon I'm up to my waist in the swamp, and the only thing holding me up was my right knee, which was resting on a root or something. I could have drowned. I held out my rifle, and two guys pulled me out. There was a lot of suction. I took the mortar shells off and threw them into the weeds. I said to the Sergeant, "If you want to court martial me, then you go ahead, but I'm not carrying them!"

We got into a clearing and set up camp. It smelled like goats, and it was all rock. I was so tired that I just lay down on the ground. I couldn't dig a foxhole through the rock, anyway. We set up a perimeter with machineguns on each corner. I didn't really sleep. I was in a sort of stupor. Then, all hell broke loose at the north end of the perimeter. There was a lot of gunfire. I took my shovel and started to dig. Suddenly, everything quieted down. I kept digging, but all that was coming out was stone. All night long I tried to dig a foxhole.

After that night, they had us put up a company street just to keep us occupied. They picked the thickest jungle that there was and told us to clean it out. We had it looking pretty good by the time we finally left Dutch New Guinea.

We set up bivouac at the Hollandia airstrip. Company H was down on the lower side of the perimeter. They opened fire on some Japs that were coming from one mountain to another. They didn't know we were there. I went down later to see what all the shooting was about. I saw one Jap machinegunner whose head was missing.

In Dutch New Guinea we used native scouts. We had an old guy there. One time he stopped and held up his hand. Everybody stopped, and dispersed on both sides of the path. Then put his ear to the ground, got back up, went back to the lieutenant and said, "Six coming this way."

I wondered if this guy was full of shit, or what. How would he know that? The next thing I knew, here comes six natives carrying sticks on their shoulders. They were friendly, and kept going. That scout was a good man, I'll tell you.

One day, I went out to look for some coconuts. Usually, some native kid would be around, take your belt, put it around his ankles and a tree, and then climb up and get coconuts. This time I was alone. I took out my .45 and fired at the stems. I hit a couple, and the coconuts came down. all of a sudden, I see this old, gray-haired native standing there. He got down on his haunches, smoothed out the dirt, took twigs and broke them, then pushed them into the ground. Then he pointed at the tree. He was trying to tell me that he had planted the trees, and that I should stop shooting at them. I gave him a salute to show him I understood. Those natives weren't dumb!

We had a first aid station with one doctor. C–47s would drop us off food, but they couldn't drop it off half the time because we were up so high that we were covered with clouds. So, we didn't eat. Then we got orders that we could go out and hunt. There was a native named Tena, who would hang around the camp. I said to Tena, "Where's the birds? So we can shoot them and eat?"

He said "Okay. You come with me."

He could speak English because the Dutch taught him. He took us out to this thick jungle. When he put his hand up to his mouth and whistled, the parrots came around. I got two or three of them with my M–1. We went back to camp and Tena said he'd cook them. He skinned them, cleaned the insides of them, washed them out, and put them on a stick around the fire we built. I got dengue fever, and I blamed it on eating the parrots. I felt lousy, and would sweat, get chills, sweat, get chills. All the doc could do for me was give me some aspirin, and put me to bed. I lay in bed for two days until the fever broke. That sickness never got into my military records.

The kid who led me to the parrots was a nice boy, but he followed me around like a little puppy dog. I'd give him rations. They loved chocolate bars. He'd go for water, or do anything you wanted him to do. All those native boys were good boys. They suffered along with everyone else. One time I went into a hospital tent where a medic was working on a native boy who must have been seven or eight years old. His intestine was sticking out of his rectum about eight inches! Red as a beet! His mother was there. The doctor used Vaseline and rubber gloves to push it back in. The kid was hollering and screaming to beat hell. After he got it all in he packed it with gauze. I don't know how the doctor communicated with the mother because she didn't speak

English. The kid had eaten too many bananas. It bound him up so bad that when he went, it just took his intestines with it.

After we were secured and put the company street in, they had a course for a volunteer jungle squad. I hated guard duty, so I volunteered for the squad. Fifteen of us volunteered, and we went out with a lieutenant and first sergeant, making maps and looking for good places to set up machineguns. That's the first time I saw a camouflage uniform. They also gave us boots that came up to our knees. They looked like long tennis shoes. I wore the bottoms out of them, and the rest just rotted away. We went eighty-one days without stopping. At that time, we broke all the records for the infantry as the longest to ever fight without taking a break. We would radio back for supplies, but the planes couldn't make the drop because they could never locate us. Even when they did, by the time we got to the drop, the natives had been there first and stole everything.

Up in those hills we had two-man foxholes. Everybody had to buddy up with someone. My buddy Johnson from Colorado and I were in a foxhole on the outside perimeter, when it started getting dark. I went out and set tin-can booby traps with wire and cans from the kitchen. I'd put a stake here and a stake here, and string up the cans. Anyone who hit that string would cause the cans to rattle. Then about five or ten feet closer to us, I'd string another stake here, stake here, and a wire, but there I'd put grenades. I fixed the wire and the pins so that anyone coming through would detonate the grenades and have a hell of a time!

Later, we were in the foxhole talking and he said, "Did you hear that?"

I heard it, but I didn't want to shake him up, so I said, "No I didn't hear anything Johnson."

He said, "There's something out there."

I said, "Johnny if something was out there, they'd rattle the cans and I didn't hear no cans"

And first thing you know, I heard it again. It sounded like breaking twigs or branches. He said, "Did you hear that?"

"No, I didn't hear anything Johnny You're getting goofy in your old age."

I was kidding around, trying to keep him cool and yet at the same time I'm getting scared. First thing you know, the cans start rattling.

"Now," he said "do you hear that."

"I heard that."

He said, "I'll be the machinegunner, you be the feeder."

I agreed. Now, we were supposed to fire in short bursts. I pulled the lever and set a round in the chamber.

"Johnny, let her go."

We had orders that if we fired we'd better have results or we'd be court-martialed, which was a crock of shit, now that I think about it. He opened up and I'm feeding. He just held onto that trigger and I'm hollering, "Johnny, release it, release it, release it!"

We got two belts off, then lay down and listened. There was no more noise, all of a sudden, a lieutenant, said "Priolette, Johnson, don't shoot I'm coming down!"

He's crawled up on his belly, and got in the hole with us. We explained to him what happened.

The lieutenant said, "Oh, there'd better be something out there tomorrow morning."

I said, "Well I'll tell you, I have a feeling that there is going to be something out there because the noise stopped."

Next morning we woke up, and started down. There we saw a bunch of natives carving up a water buffalo we had riddled. They already had two-thirds of it carted away. We never heard anything more about it.

My first sergeant's last name was Sliven. One time we dug a two-man hole together. We got set up in there, and somebody yelled, "Hey, they're bringing up the water truck!"

I said to Sliven, "I'm going to get my canteen filled."

I asked Sliven if he needed his filled. He said that he had a full canteen. I went up a dirt road to the water truck. While I was filling my canteen, a shell came in. Everybody scattered. I ran for a tree and hit the ground. Maybe that wasn't smart of me, because of tree bursts, but I squeezed up against a big root, figuring that a shell wouldn't hit the same place twice. A few more rounds came over, but I didn't find out what was going on until later.

The Japs had a five-inch howitzer on tracks inside a cave. They'd pull it out, fire a few rounds, then pull it back. Our planes couldn't locate it. I was lucky that I went for water, because a shell got Sliven. When I got back, he was covered in blood. Another guy and I carried him back to the water truck, and laid him down on the road. There were fifteen other guys, dead or wounded, lying there, too. The medic took one look at Sliven, then left him to bandage some other guys.

The next day, our Jeep boy, the one who drove the captain around, was going down to the field hospital on an errand. I asked him to find out about Sergeant Sliven. He came back and told me, "The sergeant can't talk too well. I had to put my ear right up near his mouth, but he said he was, okay."

Then he told me that Sliven had the whole side of his jaw blown off below the ear by shrapnel, that all he could see were Sliven's eyes, nose, and mouth. The rest of his head was bandaged. He also told me that the docs were going to take a jaw off a dead man and try to use it to replace the one Sliven lost. He said that Sliven kept saying, "It's okay. It's okay."

That same night we sent out a patrol. They took fire on the way back, and they left Mickelich, another guy from Michigan, like Sliven. Mickelich was wounded, and unable to retreat with them. I would never have left him. I wanted to go up after him, but the officer wouldn't let me. The next day, we pushed through and found him dead.

The officer who wouldn't let me go was Lieutenant Dino, a heck of a nice guy. He became company commander when the one we had got killed. Dino and I both had heavy beards. We decided when we left, we weren't going to shave. Mine grew straight out and I looked like a werewolf. When we got back, the guy that outranked him wanted him to shave the beard off and gave him direct orders to get all men shaved.

Lieutenant Dino came over to me and said, "Priolette, you got to shave your beard."

"I'm not shaving it. We made a bargain that we weren't going to shave it off."

"Yeah, but we're off of the mountain now. You'll get me in trouble if you don't shave."

"Okay, I'll shave."

I went over, got my helmet, took the lining out of it, scooped up the water in my helmet, carried it over, built a fire, heated the water up, and then I tried to soak my beard as best I could. All I had was an old pair of scissors, so I used one of the blades and cut a little at a time. It took me over an hour to shave.

Jesus! It was scary up on that mountain. Guys got so scared they cracked up. I could tell three days before a guy would fall apart. His eyes would get glassy. One guy put his M–1 right against his leg and pulled the trigger just so he could get out of that place. They took him out and I never saw him again. We had a lieutenant just in from the States. He carried two pearl-handled .38s that he had gotten from his father. He must have thought he was King Kong or General Patton. He was a real chickenshit officer, "stand at attention," and all that bullshit. When we got into a jam, he started running up the road yelling, "Fire! Fire! Fire!"

He went totally out of his head. They took him back, too. One guy who cracked up got put on graves registration. One day, while we were making an advance, I saw him near a medical detachment truck loading dead bodies. I thought, "Of all the things to put him on! The guy is half nuts now, and they have him digging up bodies!"

When they pulled us back from the mountain, I said to everybody, "What do you say we all kneel down and say a prayer. Any religion you are, and if you don't have a religion just thank the good Lord."

We all knelt down and I was surprised to see this guy named Cooke kneel because he was Jewish. We knelt down for what seemed like ten minutes although it was probably only two or three minutes, and we all said a prayer. That's when they took us back and gave us replacements and whatever clothing we needed.

They said they were going to give us a rest so they had us guard sixteen-inch guns that were firing at enemy ships. The Japs were sending out harassing parties that threw grenades at our artillerymen. They had three batteries of four guns each. They would fire by battery, and by the time the last four would fire, the first and second would already be reloaded. The Japs thought that the guns were automatic. The guns fired all night long. We guarded those guns for two or three nights and then they pulled us out, put us on trucks and took us to the ocean and put us on an LST. We were to land on Mindinao, south of Leyte.

I was on deck when they announced over the PA that ninety Jap planes were headed our way. They were 100 miles out. I got behind a Jeep that was strapped down

Our first real landing was Tanahmerah Bay

"Oh, there'd better be something out there tomorrow morning."

in front of the officers' con. To my right was a machinegun position. Pretty soon, all hell broke loose! Our planes from Leyte went up to intercept them, but out of ninety Jap planes, twelve or so got through. One of them picked out our ship. He came right at us, and I watched as that machinegun opened up. I hollered at the gunner, "Atta boy! Keep it right there! You're right there!"

His tracer shells showed that he was making hits on the plane's engine, setting it on fire, but the plane didn't stop coming. When the plane got too close for comfort, I ducked behind the Jeep. The plane crashed and exploded right above me, in the officer's con. It must have been carrying a phosphorus bomb, because stuff landed all over my head and back. My hair was on fire. My back was on fire. I looked at my hands, and saw that the skin was just hanging there from the wrists down. I couldn't stop the burning. I turned to run, and there were two men lying on the deck in an "L" shape. I managed to get my Mae West on. I jumped over the bodies, slipped on an oil slick, across the deck and under a tarpaulin. The tarp was in flames. I looked up, and the officer's con was in flames. I could have jumped off the ship right there, and I still don't know why I didn't. Instead, I ran toward the elevator. There was a sailor with a hose there. He hollered, "Turn on the water!"

I looked at him and thought, "Buddy, I don't know where to turn on the water."

I knew the ship was loaded with gasoline and ammo, and that it could blow any second. I ran right across the elevator, up to the bow, and I looked over the railing between two pipes and there was nobody, no heads, nothing in the water. Then I looked way out, and I could see heads bobbing in the water, and I thought, "Boy, how long have I been on this ship!?"

I crawled between the two pipes, and over I went. From the bow down to the water was a long way. When I hit that water, I went straight down. I kicked as hard as I could. But I kept going down. Then I started to come up. Once on the surface I tried to swim away from the ship, but the current kept carrying me back. I struggled around the fantail. There was a four-inch pipe that went from one side to the other. One of my buddies was sitting on the pipe. I told him the ship was going to blow up, but he was afraid of the water, and refused to jump in. So, I said, "So long, then."

I kept swimming. The sky was all covered with flak. I spotted a raft and started toward it. I reached the raft and tried to grab it, but a wave brought me down, and brought the raft up. It was like I was in the bottom of a big cup. Then I was at the top of a wave. I could see the whole convoy, and the raft was a good distance away from me. Then I noticed another raft to my right, much closer. I started swimming toward it, but I was exhausted. There were six guys on that raft. They joined hands and came over to me, got me to the raft, and threw me in. As long as I lay in the raft with my hands in the water, I didn't feel any pain. I looked up into the sky. A Jap Betty bomber came in, looking like it was going to go for the raft. I thought, "Oh, Jesus, here we go again!"

But the bomber passed by. I moved around a little and watched. He zigzagged through the convoy, and headed for a cruiser. The bomb bay doors were open, and a bomb came out. It seemed funny to me, because the bomb went ahead of the plane.

The bomb hit the water, but when the Betty pulled up, it must have got hit with a five-inch shell. It got blown to hell!

Twenty and 40mm shells from our ships were splashing all over the place. I thought, "Jesus, if the Japs don't get this raft, our guys will!"

A landing barge came up to us near dusk. Some guy hollered, "Is anyone wounded?"

They said, "Yeah, we got one!"

I heard a voice say, "Priolette, is that you!?"

I said, "Yeah!"

It was a guy from our company. How he got on that barge I don't know, and I never saw him after that. He said, "Don't panic, Tony! Stay there. I'll get you off!"

Some of the guys on the raft panicked and tried to get on the barge. One guy reached for the barge, but the waves lifted the raft and he fell out right into the barge's propeller. That was it for him! Then the guy from my company jumped onto the raft and helped me get on the barge. By that time, it was dark. We got to another LST. They lowered a bull rope. It must have been an inch-and-a-half in diameter. They tied it around my waist. I couldn't hold on to it. My hands were burned so bad. They were pulling me up when the rope slipped up my back. God! The pain! I kept swinging and hitting the side of the ship. Finally, I got to the top and they helped me over the rail. Two navy medics cut my off my shirt. One of them hit me in the arm with a needle. I went out. I woke up three days later on a hospital ship. Then I thought, "My God! How long have I been out?"

There were some other wounded guys in the compartment with me. I didn't know I was on a hospital ship until they told me. One morning I woke up, and there was no one there. I got out of bed and walked out on deck. I got talking to the guys, and I said, "What are you doing out here? You left me all by myself?"

"Hell, you stunk so bad! We had to come out here!"

They had me all wrapped up in Vaseline gauze, and the flesh started to rot, and it stunk like hell! I couldn't smell it, but they could. I guess I had gotten immune to it after three days. The only thing that wasn't wrapped on me was my eyes, nose and mouth. A sailor would take me for lunch and for dinner. He would sit with me and feed me. It was embarrassing as hell. Finally I got off the hospital ship and they took us to Manis Islands, and I recuperated in a field hospital there. After that they said, "Priolette! You're in charge of these six men. Here are their papers. When you get there, you give it to so and so."

We got on a ship. The officer in charge said to our group, "Who's in charge here?"

I said, "I am, sir."

"Okay follow me!"

We followed him down a couple of decks.

He said, "These are your quarters. In the morning when you get up the best thing to do is to make up your hammock, mop the floor, and get the hell out of here for the rest of the day. When they inspect it, they'll find everything nice and neat."

I said, "Well, fellas you hear that? You two take it the first day, you two take it second day and you two take it the third day."

I got to look around the kitchen. I asked the sailors if I could help. They said I could. So I went in there and I helped them cook, and serve the sailors. They all seemed to like me, and one day the head cook said to me, "Priolette, do you know how to cook spaghetti?"

"Yeah. If you've got the stuff."

"We'll get you anything you want."

They took me to their walk-in cooler. They had some beef hanging there, and I told them I wanted a big piece. They cut off a big hunk. I got all the canned tomatoes, sauce, onions and spices I needed. Whatever I wanted they got for me. I prepared the sauce, and the whole kitchen smelled good! The officer in charge came in and said, "Boy, what is that smell?"

"That's Priolette. He's gonna cook us spaghetti."

The officer said, "Hey, if you're cooking spaghetti don't forget me and the captain!"

They said, "Oh, no, no! We won't forget you!"

They got a little leery because they thought they were going to catch hell, but he didn't seem to mind. So I put water in another vat and boiled it and threw the spaghetti in. Just then he came in and we were fixing the spaghetti and sauce on plates for the captain and he said, "Where's your plate?"

I said, "I'll get it."

He said, "No, no. Get Priolette a plate first."

Then he said, "Come with me."

He grabbed two plates and I grabbed mine and we went into the captain's quarters. Right in the center of the room they had a galvanized tub filled with ice and beer! I ate with them and had beer! That's when I asked the captain, "Why don't you keep me on the ship as a cook?"

He said, "Boy, I'd like too, but then you'd be AWOL."

I said, "Yeah, but when they found out where I was, you can tell them I lost my memory."

He said, "Naw, we can't do that!"

I had it made there! At night I'd go up and help the bakers for a couple of hours. The sailors would sneak by and say, "Hey, Priolette! Make us some sandwiches."

I guess I wasn't allowed, but I'd sneak back there and I'd take a loaf of bread and slice it up and make sandwiches. They had ham and bologna and any goddamn thing you wanted!

One night I was down watching them playing cards. One of the officers was playing and he got called away. He said to me, "Go ahead, Priolette. Play my hand while I'm gone."

When he came back, I had a nice pile for him. He said to me, "Well, you did good! Maybe I should stay away longer!"

He got called the second time, and I built up his pile more. The third time he was called out he grabbed all his money and left a handful for me.

He said, "Go ahead you play. This is yours. I'm out."

I couldn't even get a pair after that.

Finally, we got to our destination, Leyte, October 1944. The guys who piloted the landing craft didn't want to hit the sand too hard or come in too close and get stuck. They wanted to get out of there as soon as they could. I couldn't blame them. When they dropped the doors of the barges down, we exited. The water must have been eight feet deep. I sank some, but I know I would come up and be okay. There was a little Mexican guy next to me who couldn't swim too well. I grabbed him by the back of his shirt and dragged him in. There was no resistance when we got onto the beach. Otherwise, we would have been wiped out because we had 200 hundred yards to cross before we the hit jungle. I was first scout. After I got this Mexican on land, I took off straight as I could to those woods. I hit the ground a couple of times before I got there. When I did, I looked back and waved everyone to move out.

Once we hit the trees, we regrouped and got into a single file. The regular scout was out first, then the second scout, then the first sergeant, then the lieutenant, and then the rest of the squad. There wasn't anybody near us, and I didn't see a soul, except our men. Eventually we hit a road, and hiked up it until we ran into a mountain and the Japanese. That was what got to be called the "Battle of Breakneck Ridge."

We got to the top of a hill. A buddy and I were in a Jap foxhole, and we could see Japs down in the valley going back and forth past an opening in some kind of wall or fence. I said, "Watch me get one of them"

I put the sight of my M–1 on that opening. Sure enough, one came by, and I fired. He went down. They didn't drag him away. They just let him lay. Another one passed. I fired. He went down. He fell on behind the wall. I got about four or five of them.

The Japs were good fighters. They weren't afraid to die. They had spider holes, which were as big as a man's body and maybe six feet deep. They'd climb up and fire from those, then drop back in. There were snipers, too. Ralph Johnson from Colorado, the one who fired the machinegun with me the night we killed the buffalo, got hit in the shoulder with one of those Jap .25 calibers. Then a sniper put a couple more rounds into him. There was a big hole in him that kept gushing blood. I took an empty machinegun belt and stuffed it in the wound, then put his first aid kit on top of that and pushed as hard as I could, but I couldn't stop the bleeding. The sniper was still firing. Johnson was a big guy, about 200 pounds. I got my arm around his neck and said, "Okay, Johnny, let's go." I'd run ten feet or so, then hit the ground. The dirt kicked up around us from the sniper's bullets. I finally got him down to the aid station, where they took care of him. Along the way, I had to get rid of my rifle, and his. I found a .45, and went back up.

We were going up a trail at one point, and we saw a place where our bombardments must have got a whole Jap regiment on the move. Before we got to that spot, our bulldozers had widened the trail. They just dug a big trench and pushed all these dead Japs into it, then covered it up. I could see arms and legs sticking out everywhere. There was even a mule's head sticking out. I guessed they used the mule to pull a cart or something.

At one point in the battle we were moving along with tanks, the first I had seen in battle. They drew enemy fire like nothing else. They would get us, the infantry, to guard the tanks because the Japs would strap mines to their bodies and run into the tanks. When we came upon bunkers, the bulldozers that were with the tanks would go up, drop their blades, and bury the Japs alive. We guarded the tanks for about three or four miles, then we got to the edge of a valley where the Japs were well dug in. We called for air support and navy bombers with Marine pilots came in. They flew over the valley, took off to the left and flew out of sight. Before I knew it, they were coming right back in again. I was down on one knee with my new rifle in my hands, watching those planes. The pilot would machinegun until he'd got down so far, then he'd turn up and he'd drop a napalm bomb. Then the tail gunner would strafe. I'll tell you it was beautiful to see them! When napalm hit there was a big cloud of smoke and flames. You'd swear nobody could ever live through that, but, by God, when the Navy planes were gone and we were waiting to advance, the Japs started to fire mortar rounds at us. I was still down on one knee and I swear I could have reached up and grabbed the rounds! Before I could hit the ground, one landed behind me. It knocked me ten feet onto my face. We had been taught that when one got fired, there would be two more to follow. I thought, "I'd better get the hell out of here!"

I made a right turn, and started off. There was grass there about two feet tall, and an old building there that was half blown apart. There were logs lying there, and I crawled in between them and then I thought, "Hell, they might think this is our CP and start bombing this old, broken-down building. I better get the hell out of here!"

So I took off into a field, and crawled through the high weeds and finally found a little depression in the ground and I lay there and I thought, "They'd have to get a direct shot to get me here."

I lay there it seemed like ten or fifteen minutes, though it could have been only two or three. I saw guys getting up, so I got up. One of the guys was a medic. He ran over to me. "Are you hit, Priolette?"

I said, "No, but look at my hands."

They were bleeding. He didn't say anything. He walked around behind me and he said, "The hell you're not hit, you've got three holes in your shirt and all three of them have blood coming through them!"

I thought it was just the concussion from the mortar round that knocked me for a loop. Another buddy named Johnson, Bernie Johnson from Fargo, North Dakota, got one in the shoulder and he was hollering to beat hell! I calmed him down.

I said, "What the hell's wrong with you!? You only have one and I have three!"

They sent us to the rear where the medics were set up. They gave us a fast check over. One fella had got it in the throat. He was gurgling and hollering in pain.

They said to him, "Grit your teeth!"

He said, "I don't have any teeth!"

They flew him out, but he died on the plane. The rest of us they put on two-and-half-ton trucks and took us to a field hospital. The doctor came in each morning to fix my dressing. They had a big jar, with a big wide lid on it and there was Vaseline gauze in there. They'd take tweezers and pull this Vaseline gauze out and shove it into my back. The shrapnel was about as big as my little nail, but it made a hole about as big as a thumb. God! That was painful! I'd lift the cot and him and everything else up! He said, "I know it's painful but I got to do it because we want it to heal from the inside out because if it heals on the outside then you've got a pocket in there, then you're in trouble."

They took two pieces of shrapnel out, but the third one was too close to my spine. He said, "It's better to leave it in because they're red hot when they go in so they're sterile. It's better to leave it in than going after it and causing more damage."

Believe it or not, despite being wounded, some of us had to stand guard after we got fairly well healed up. Stupid! They had a wooden box set up in a field about fifty yards away from the last tent. The guard was supposed to sit on this box for two hours until he got relieved. Anyway, some of us were sitting around in a tent bullshitting. We heard this explosion. I thought it was a bomb, but I found out later that it was some Jap out there harassing us with a grenade. I jumped out of the tent into a two-foot deep, two-foot-wide trench. At first, the guys started laughing at me, then they got their asses out of there as well. I'm crawling up this goddamn trench, but I was in pain, and could only go so far before I had to take a break. I ran into a nest of big, black ants, and they started to sting the shit out of me. I thought, I'd better get the hell outta here!"

I finally got to headquarters. It was really dark when I got there. I managed to get the ants off of me. I thought, "Now, where am I going to stay tonight?"

I sneaked into a tent where the rear echelon had some cots stacked up. I stole a blanket. I crawled in the aisles between the cots, found a place, laid the blanket down, rolled myself up in it, and went to sleep. I went back to my own tent in the morning. The guys were still there. The lieutenant and first sergeant were getting ready to go back to the front line, but before the lieutenant left, he handed me my Purple Heart.

The guys on guard the night before were recruits, fresh from the states, and they were always scared to death. The night before, after the explosion, this kid goes down to relieve the guard, and the guard panicked and shot him. I went down to see. He was still laying there, all covered up. I pulled back part of the blanket, and, hell, it was a kid I was talking to the night before.

I had a buddy in there with me who was also wounded and he got out and was sent back to the rear. He came one day and said, "Tony, they just called your name on rotation."

I said, "I guess I'll be out of here tomorrow."

The next morning the major came, and I said to the major, "Major, when am I getting out of here?"

He said, "Well, what outfit you from?"

"Company I, 21st Infantry."

"Oh, they're hitting it tough up in the mountains. You don't want to get out. You're better off staying here in the hospital."

"No, I don't want to go back up there, but I'm on rotation. I could go back to the States."

"Oh, why didn't you tell me that in the first place. You'll get out in the morning."

He filled out the papers and the next morning I got out. I still had bandages on. No matter how I turned, or where I leaned, it ached steady all the time. But I figured I was going home, so I got the hell out of there and went to the rear. Back in the rear they gave me a dress outfit and a work outfit. I put it in my bag with everything else I owned.

By the time I got to headquarters, where I was supposed to go, I had a hole in my new barracks bag and I was losing half my stuff because I was dragging it along the dirt, I couldn't lift it because of my back. I lost two matchboxes full of gold that I had panned on Dutch New Guinea. I said to one of the soldiers there, "Hey, buddy. Do me a favor. Throw this on the truck for me."

He threw it onto the truck, then helped me up. When we got to Leyte, they processed us out. They asked us different questions then said, "Every morning you get up, all we ask of you is to make roll call. If the fella calls your name, you're going home. If he doesn't you're free for the rest of the day. You can go back and sleep in your bunk if you want."

I was there two or three days, and they finally called my name. Then we got on a Liberty ship for home. We got to San Pedro, California in thirty-three days. There was a band playing for us when we got off. We went through a building where the Salvation Army had coffee, hot tea, or cocoa, and donuts. As we came single file through there we just got what we wanted and kept moving. From that building, we got onto a train. From there they took us to the desert. I don't know where it was located, but we got there about two o'clock in the morning. That's the first time that I saw WACS. They were driving two-and-a-half-ton trucks. They loaded us on those, and took us to the camp.

They assembled us in a big, floodlit field. A general got up on a platform and told us we would be going home as soon as possible. We got hot showers and anything we wanted to eat. I had never seen so much food! We fell out the next morning, and got on a train. I got to Indiantown Gap, Pennsylvania. One night while I was there, I went to the PX for a beer. I hadn't seen one for a long time. All the time I had been gone I never met anyone in the service from Greensburg. As I was walking up the steps to the PX, Vincent Collaruso was coming down. Not only was he from Greensburg, he was my neighbor! We all called him "Pivot." We hugged each other and went into the PX for a few.

The next day they told me I could leave. The quickest way out of there was by bus. I asked the driver, "Would you let me off in Irwin."

At Irwin, I got off, grabbed my barracks bag, and walked over to Route 30. I stuck out my thumb, and got a ride immediately from a nice couple. The man got out of the car, opened the trunk, and threw in my bag. We rode the six miles to Greensburg, and when we stopped at a red light on Hamilton Street, I said, "This is fine."

I thanked the man and his wife, got my bag out of the trunk of the car, threw it over my shoulder, and walked the rest of the way home.

"What Did I Need a Gun For?"

John Paul Priolette
United States Navy, Task Forces 37, 38, 50 and 58, Northern Carrier Group;
U.S.S Monterey
Greensburg, PA, 24 January 1921

"One day I developed a tooth ache, and went to the dentist for it. It was a wisdom tooth. He just got through pulling it out when the battle station bell went off. He stuffed some cotton in my mouth, and I got up to the deck. The sky was black and red with flak and tracers. A plane was headed right for the ship. I got so excited I swallowed the cotton! The pilot let his bomb loose too soon and it exploded in the water. Then the plane got hit and got blown all to hell."

WHEN THE WAR BROKE OUT my brother, Antonio, was the first to be drafted. He wrote back to me when he was in training and said, "Whatever you do stay the heck out of the army!"

So, I went and joined the navy. I took it for granted that they needed *me*. My brother had it worse than me. He carried a gun, and fought in the jungle. What did I need a gun for? My job was to fix shot-up airplanes.

On the train to our basic training area, I was shaving with a straightedge razor. That train was rocking from side to side, and a bunch of guys were taking bets on whether or not I would cut my throat. When I got to the Great Lakes Training Center in Michigan, they made me get rid of the straight razor, and they gave me a safety razor. I cut myself more with that safety razor than I ever did with the straight edge.

The first night we were there the chief said, "Lights out!"

The guys on the top floor ignored him. They went on talking and laughing like they were having a party. The chief came back in, turned on the lights and said, "Everybody up!"

Even though the guys upstairs were to blame, the chief took us all out to the marching track and marched us around. It seemed like forever. Then he told us to stand facing each other. The guys from the top floor had to run between us while we whacked them on the asses with our belts. That was my initiation into the United States Navy.

The next thing I did was take a test so that I could qualify for something. It was easy for me, because I was just out of high school. One kid from Pittsburgh beside me was a little slow, so I wrote my answers down and then showed them to him. He couldn't get them fast enough, though, and he got a low grade. When we were all done, they told me I was in the top ten of the class, and that I could choose whatev-

John Priolette in Hawaii with two friends.
Courtesy of John Priolette.

er job I wanted. I said that I wanted to be a gunner. They said, "Boy, you can't be a gunner. You fixed wrecked cars back home. You're gonna be an aviation metalsmith."

They sent me to school in Chicago at the Navy Pier that sticks out into Lake Michigan about three quarters of a mile. I was supposed to train to be a metalsmith, but for the first month I helped prepare food for the mess hall. I cut up lettuce and other vegetables. I did that until the previous class finished and a new class came in.

After I was trained, the Navy assigned me to the *U.S.S Monterey,* a cruiser that they had converted into an aircraft carrier. It was a small carrier, and we carried only about fifty-five planes as opposed to eighty-five for a regular carrier. We carried Hellcats and Avengers. There were five of us from Greensburg on that ship. The commander, Gazze, was from Greensburg. Ninety-nine percent of us had never been on a ship before. I didn't know there were colored guys on the ship until I saw this little guy they brought up to man the water hose. He was scared as hell. He didn't know what to do with that hose. On the hose there were two levers; one gave a spray, and the other gave a steady stream. The chief warrant officer yelled, "Turn on the water!"

That poor little guy got scared and he pulled the lever all the way back, and a jet of water shot out and hit the chief warrant officer, knocking him down into a three-foot pit near the plane elevator.

We went to Trinidad for shakedown, and then to San Diego. After that, we headed for Hawaii. We had one thousand extra troops on board.

When we got to Pearl, one of the fellas from Greensburg said, "I'm going home."

"You can't go home!"

"I'm going home."

He pulled out and left. I saw him after the war in town. I asked him, "What happened to you?"

"They caught me up around Idaho. They put me on another boat."

Hawaii was our home base. We'd make ready for sea, go out for three or four days and then we'd come back. We did that three or four times. The last time the captain said, "Well, this is it. This isn't practice now. We're going to the Gilbert Islands. We aren't going to try and take them. We *are* going to take them!"

And we did, eventually. The battle for Tarawa was the first battle we were in, and, during it, we crossed the Equator four times in one night, because Tarawa was smack dab on the Equator. We stayed there for a month, softening the place up. When we got done with the bombing, there wasn't a blade of grass left on that island. During the battle the Japs looked for the wake of our ships at night. The wakes showed up white, and they would use them as reference points for their torpedoes. One missed us by twenty feet. We could see it go by from the flight deck.

If one of our pilots bailed out of his plane, we would radio a destroyer to go and rescue him. Then we would shoot a line over to the destroyer. The line had a little metal chair on it, and the rescued pilot would ride back over to us on that. One time a pilot called down to us and said that he couldn't get his right landing wheel down. So he brought it in and I thought, "Oh, boy this one's gonna smash up that whole damn flight deck!" So we watched him coming in. He circled around and he came down and landed real good and the tail hook grabbed hold and pulled him back and the plane tilted on to its side. It just dented the end of the wing. I thought there would be more damage than that. Sometimes a plane that crashed on deck would catch on fire. We had crew men assigned to deal with any fires that broke out.

Paul Danks was one of the people on the ship from Greensburg. I said to him, "Paul, you got to get into something, otherwise you'll be a seaman all the time, and get all the dirty work." Myself, I was only on the ship six months, and I was a petty officer. After that, Paul got a job working the arrester hooks, which were thick cables that went across the flight deck and stopped the planes that were landing. One day, after the last plane had landed, an arrester cable knocked Paul overboard. Some guys threw their life jackets down to him, hoping he would be okay. We didn't stop for anything. We went about two miles, and threw a smoke bomb into the water, and then we radioed destroyers to pick him up. By they time the destroyers got to where Paul had been, it was too late. I listened on the earphones until it got dark, getting information from the destroyers, but I knew that we had lost Paul, forever.

During a fight there were battle stations all over. Some were on the flight deck, some down below. My station was on the hanger deck, and I always had the earphones on so I'd hear whenever the bogies were coming in. I'd yell to all the guys things like, "Eighty bogies at eighty miles!" Then everyone would get to the battle stations and wait. Then I would hear through the earphones that they were getting closer fifty miles, forty miles, thirty miles. I'd tell the guys, "Hey! They're getting close. They're only twenty miles away!"

There was nothing we could do about it. We'd just stay at our battle stations. They wouldn't pay much attention to me until the last minute. Then the guns would start to go off and they'd yell at me, "Why didn't you tell us they were right on top of us!"

I yelled back, "What do you think I've been telling you!"

I remember one day we had to push six planes overboard to make room for those coming in! They'd land and hit the barrier and flip over and get damaged beyond repair. Before we pushed them overboard the guys stole the clocks from the planes and the instruments. They'd be on a plane ripping that stuff out even as it was being pushed overboard!

This illustration and the one on the following page are from the *U.S.S. Monterey's Newsletter* edited by Gerald Ford who would become President of the United States. *Courtesy of John Priolette.*

SALTY JOE THE BOOT
U.S.N. Anywhere
SHADRACK
L. Lusk
DON'T BE A PIG
SPLATTER
SPLASH
USN
LIBERTY CALL
FOO FOO
LIBERTY BOAT AT THE GANGWAY
OH BOY!
TOWN
BRING YOUR MONEY CHUB
WOOPIE
EAST MAIN
CLICK
DOG WRENCH
AFTER HOURS DIVE INN
PLAIN MAIN
HEY LOUIZEE
SPEED
ALL WELL THAT ENDS WELL!
FREE SMOKES
LOVE
U.S.O.
WELL COME!

I still think of Ensign Smith. He was hit pretty bad, both he and the plane, and was circling the ship, getting ready to land. He kept coming down, but before he got to the tail of the ship he hit the water. The plane sank, and I kept saying, "Come on! Get the hell outta there!"

But he never came up.

One day I developed a toothache, and went to the dentist for it. It was a wisdom tooth. He just got through pulling it out when the battle station bell went off. He stuffed some cotton in my mouth, and I got up to the deck. The sky was black and red with flak and tracers. A plane was headed right for the ship. I got so excited I swallowed the cotton! The pilot let his bomb loose too soon and it exploded in the water. Then the plane got hit and got blown all to hell.

We got news and entertainment in a little ship's newspaper our assistant navigator helped produce. His name was Lieutenant Junior Grade Gerald Ford. He became President of the United States.

Toward the end of my time on the *Monterey*, one replacement came on board that was fifty years old! I said to him, "What are you doing here!"

He said something about a wife and two kids. I think it was his wife's idea! He was a regular sailor. I thought he was great. He was a scrawny, little guy named Joe Colombo from New Jersey. Joe was my replacement, so he was responsible for getting me off the ship. Another guy took my battle station. His name was John, like mine. He was the first sailor to get killed when the *Monterey* went back out to sea. A Kamikaze hit the ship, right on top of my old battle station.

After I got back to Hawaii, they put us on a ship for the mainland. It was an old ship, and on the way back to the States the engines broke down, and we were dead in the water. Usually, transports like that had a destroyer escort, but this one didn't. That was the only time during the war that I was really scared. I got off at Bremerton, up near Seattle. I got assigned to a beautiful base that had bowling alleys and a theater. I lived in a nice, brick barracks. What was more important is that the base also had WAVES on it! One morning they told me that I had enough points to go home. So, I went and waited for transportation. We waited for ten days. Halfway through that time, I said, "Release me! I'll hitchhike if I have too!"

But they wouldn't do that. Finally, I got up to Vancouver on a bus, where I boarded a Canadian train. I traveled in a first-class Pullman car. I got anything I wanted. I even got my bed made for me. When we got into New York, we passed the hat around for the train's porter. The guy had been so good to us that we threw in fives and tens. He got a pot of money! I got back home to Greensburg with eight dollars and fifty cents in my pocket. I was glad the whole damn thing was over with.

"Patriotism Was Typical"

Paul Danks
United States Navy, *U.S.S Monterey*
Greensburg, Pennsylvania July 9, 1924; Killed in Action July 11, 1944

[John Paul Priolette speaks of Paul Danks in the preceding story. Center staff compiled the following from the recollections of Paul's brother and sister, Tom and Anne. Paul was washed overboard and drowned while serving on the carrier U.S.S. Monterey].

Anne: On Sunday 7 December 1941, all the bells in town rang. We went to church and prayed. Even though our brother, Frank, was married, he was drafted anyway on 29 April 1941, into the Air Force. Paul was just seventeen, but he went in 1943. They jiggled the numbers a little. Everybody was going in. Everybody *wanted* to go in. Mother tried to talk him out of it for a long time. She wanted Paul to wait. She didn't want him to go unless he was drafted, but he wanted to go. Patriotism was typical of kids then. I know when anyone around here went into the service, everybody that possibly could, went to the train station to see him off. They had bands playing, and always gave them a big send-off.

Tom: We helped out with the war effort at home. I had a paper route and I had to buy stamps all the time. The old man made me buy stamps and then I got a bond. I wanted to do more than that. I was only fourteen. If I had been old enough, I would have gone, too

Anne: It seemed like everything was rationed. Mother bought SPAM. I still laugh when I see it in the store. My father got outrageous with it. He'd do everything possible with that SPAM. He'd put some pineapple on it to dress it up! He hated it! We had Victory gardens where we grew our own vegetables. That way we saved on food stamps. Everybody had a little patch of ground for a garden, and we helped each other out.

We followed very closely what was going on in the world through newspapers and the radio. We had blackouts for air raid drills every six weeks or two months. We waited for the mail to come to see if there would be a note from Paul. He wasn't a big writer, but he did write from time to time. After he did his shakedown cruise, he came home only once, and then he went overseas.

We got a telegram from California one day. Paul's sister, who was four years older than Paul, went to the Western Union office to get it. It was coming from California. No family wanted to get a telegram in those days. The telegram told us that Paul had been killed. We asked ourselves, "How could that have happened?" But that's what war is.

Tom: I was pretty broken up when I found out Paul had been killed. After the war, two Navy men came to see Mother and Dad. They had been on the *Monterey* with Paul. One of the men, Johnny Priolette, was from South Greensburg.

Anne: I was pretty young at the time but I always admired my mother and father for the way they handled their bereavement. If they could have brought Paul home it would have been so much better, but that never happened. Paul was gone in the sea. Mother kept her emotions pretty much to herself. She did her crying alone. A few times she asked one of us girls if we could take a little walk with her. We'd just walk the streets and maybe we wouldn't even talk with each other, but it just seemed she had the desire to get out of the house, especially in the early months. We'd take a walk for a few blocks and then she'd say she was ready to go back home. Our mother joined the Golden Star Mothers after Paul got killed. She faithfully met with the group at the American Legion. She was even president of the group at one time.

Tom: You know, when we heard the war was over it was kind of a hollow feeling because Paul wasn't coming back. The whole town went goofy, though. They marched and celebrated, but we didn't feel like doing that. When the war was over I realized how fast I had grown up. And five years later I would be in the Army fighting in Korea. I just guess it was my turn to go.

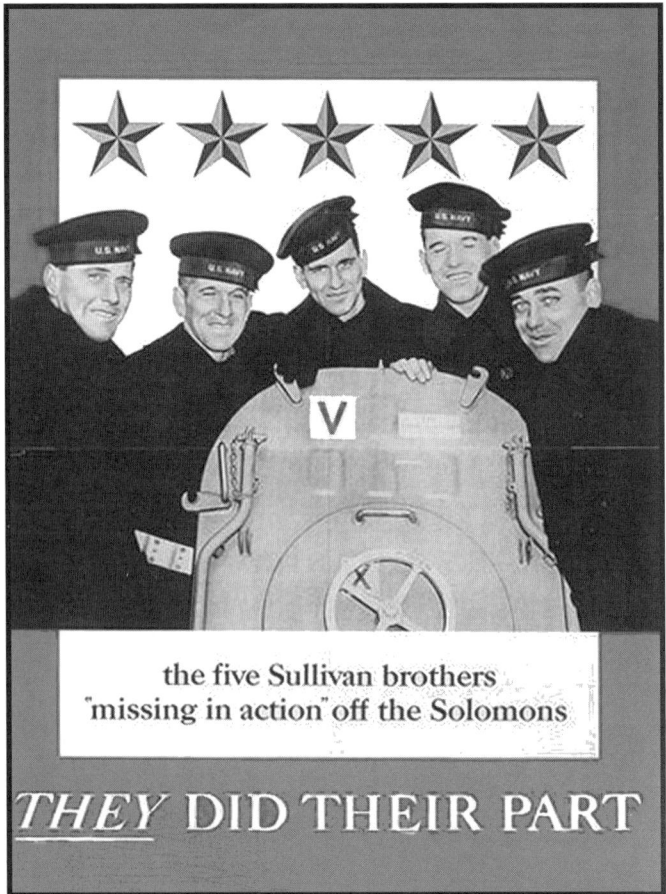

Albert, Francis, George, Joseph and Madison Sullivan were born in Waterloo, Iowa, between 1914 and 1920. George and Francis enlisted in the Navy in 1937, and their three younger brothers followed suit in early 1942. All five were assigned to the *USS Juneau* in February 1942. All were lost with her on 13 November 1942, a tragedy that received wide publicity in the United States and resulted in a new Navy policy discouraging family members from serving together in the same ship.
National Archives.

"Clyde Ain't Coming Back"

Michael Rudy

83rd Infantry Division, 200th Field Artillery Battalion (Replacement Unit),
Ligonier, Pennsylvania, 1924

"After basic, we went back to Fort Meade. This was 11 May 1944. We still weren't part of any unit. We were going overseas as replacements. After a couple days, we boarded the USS Whitfield. There was a lot of hollering going on. I couldn't figure it out. Then I saw them bringing guys on board who were tied down on stretchers. They didn't want to go! I was eighteen-years old. What the hell did I care?"

IT WAS JUST ANOTHER WAR. Nobody knew much about Communism and Fascism and everything else that was going on. I got my draft notice when I was eighteen, and I left for the service on 9 October 1943. They sent me to Fort Meade, Maryland. We stayed there just long enough for them to holler at us. We stood there in our civilian clothes, and they were trying to tell us all these things about "attention," and "about face," and "left face," but we still looked like we just walked off the street. There was this one kid with us from Export. He wore size fourteen shoes! He was a big guy. He couldn't turn, march or do anything. Boy, that sergeant hollered at him! We were all pretty bad at it. We got scared. After a couple days they gave us a little duffel bag full of clothes, and then put us on the train.

The train took off toward the south. The corporals wouldn't tell us where we were going. We pulled into Raleigh, North Carolina. At some point they split the train into two. One part headed one way and the other went someplace else. The scuttlebutt was the other half went to Florida. I'm glad we didn't go to Florida. Those guys ended up in the infantry. We went to Fort Bragg to be trained on 155mm howitzers. It was winter, and it was the coldest one in years. A lot of guys got sick. Our firing range was on a hill. After a while, we gave the hill a name. We called it "Pneumonia Hill."

We went on overnight hikes. A couple friends would sneak into the bushes, hide out there, and then catch the march on the return. I was too scared to do that. I did learn to always follow close behind the lieutenant. When he stopped for a five-minute break, I stopped. A lot of guys would straggle, so, by the time they caught up, the break would be over.

Guys in our battalion came from all over the place. One of them, Dussendorf, had been born in Germany. He became an American citizen, and got drafted out of Walla Walla, Washington. He was a lot older than us, or he seemed to be. When you are eighteen, someone in his thirties looks like a fifty-year old. When we were in combat crossing the Cologne Plain, he would tell me what was up ahead. He knew the area because he had been born in Cologne. I noticed that when we had to shell a place, he would go real slow bringing a shell over, like he really didn't want to do it.

After basic, we went back to Fort Meade. This was 11 May 1944. We still weren't part of any unit. We were going overseas as replacements. After a couple days, we boarded the *USS Wakefield*. There was a lot of hollering going on. I couldn't figure it out. Then I saw them bringing guys on board who were tied down on stretchers. They didn't want to go! I was eighteen-years old. What the hell did I care?

We docked at Liverpool, England on 20 May, and got off the ship next day. They sent us down to Southampton. We got ready to go over the Channel. It seemed that they told us a couple times on 6 June to get ready to go over. Then they said, "Not today, boys."

Then everyday it was the same. Get on the trucks. Get off the trucks. Finally, on 13 June, they loaded us up for France. We were all scared, but we joked around to ease the tension. This kid from Sharon, Pa. said, "Just remember, when the bullets start flying, they're your ticket home."

We were replacements, the whole boatload of us. We didn't know where we'd end up. We just knew that we would finally be going into combat.

We got onto the beach on 16 June, D+10. Planes flew back and forth. There was a lot of smoke. Barrage balloons hung over the ships. It was incredible. We had to go down a rope ladder from our transport into the landing craft. We got in only so far, then had to wade the rest of the way in water up to our knees. After ten days, the invasion force had pushed about thirteen miles inland. We moved off the beach and headed for the front line. We got to the top of this hill. There was a house there where a French lady lived. From what we understood, she had married a German. She had shot one of our guys, and another of our guys shot her. There were dead bodies everywhere. I came across a group of dead Americans with an Indian patch on their shoulders. I knew they were from the 2nd Division. There was a dead German, but I was too scared to go near him. His throat was all swollen, and it looked like it was going to burst. A guy came up to me and said, "Don't worry about him, he ain't gonna hurt you!"

Around that time they started sending the replacement to different outfits. I was put into the 200th Field Artillery. The first night we were up in this orchard a couple miles off the beach. I just dug a little foxhole. This sergeant came over and said, "Hey, buddy! Hey, soldier! You're not going to dig that hole like that. You better get that thing down there. You don't know what's gonna happen tonight."

Then I dug pretty deep. I learned other things pretty quick, like when you get shelled, they tell you if you hear a shell, when it whistles, don't worry about it. The one you can't hear, that's the one that's coming your way. That's what they always told me, but whenever one hit, I'd jump in the hole it made. They never hit in the same place twice. I wasn't taking chances.

One night this German plane flew over dropping flares. Then he dropped a five-hundred-pound bomb. He must have seen something. A few holes over from mine the guys were playing cards by candlelight. They had a tarp over their hole, but it's possible that some of the light showed through an opening. I was down in my hole with a canvas cover over top. That bomb hit and all hell broke loose. The blast sent all this dirt up in the air and it came showering down on top of my tarp, just like hail. I thought it would never stop. I looked out of my hole after the dirt stopped falling and saw a five-hundred pounder stuck in the ground about three feet from my hole! He had dropped two. One went off, the other was a dud. It was a miracle. I'll tell you what. I had a Catholic missal with me. I wore that thing out by the end of the war!

The next day I saw this fella Burns from Massachusetts in the chow line. He was one of the guys playing cards. The bomb that exploded was closest to his hole.

I said, "Hey, Burns, I bet you shit your pants!"

"Naw," he said, "We just reshuffled the deck."

After chow we saw that they had marked off the area around the dud.

Not long after that, we were in a field. I didn't dig a foxhole, but my buddy next to me did. I got in my sleeping bag and zipped it up. We heard the command passed around that there was going to be a tank and infantry attack at five in the morning. It was starting to get daylight. It was foggy. I heard this noise. I looked up and our tanks were fifty feet away from me. This goddamned tank just came roaring up toward me. I tried to get out of my sleeping bag, but I couldn't. I just kept rolling in that bag until I got out of the way. The tanks went by. My buddy, a kid from Idaho, had dug himself a pretty deep hole, and one of the tanks rolled right over it. Afterwards he said, "I felt the treads of that tank tickle my chest!"

Our job in the 200th Field Artillery was to shell the enemy's front line positions. At St. Lô, we were doing this in preparation for the big breakout, which happened at the end of July. After the breakout, we went to Paris. After that we moved fast through France into Luxembourg and the Ardennes Forest. Autumn came, and along with it, the first snow of the year. You know what I remember about being in that Ardennes? The snow. Deep snow! Two or more feet of it! One morning, the sergeant sent me around to wake up the men. I couldn't find them at first, because the snow had covered them up while they slept in their foxholes under their tarps.

Then all hell broke loose. The Germans broke through the Ardennes Forest, and the Bulge started. So much happened in so little a space of time that sometimes I can't remember it all. The 106th, the 28th and 99th Divisions were the ones that took the first German attacks. They sent us up there from the south to help relieve the troops being attacked. They put us in trucks, and we rode all night. The moon was shining. It was so cold. The guys were smoking cigarettes, cupping their hands around the lit cigarette to keep them warm. Some guys were taking their gloves off to do this. I kept mine on, I wouldn't take my gloves off in that zero weather! At some point in the night we got shelled. A lot of trucks were blown up, but none of our guys got hurt.

Our job was, again, to shell the enemy front lines and break up their attacks. We used forward observers. If we were in a town, we'd send guys up into the highest point, which was usually the church steeple. One time we had two guys up in this steeple and Germans sent over some 88s trying to hit it. The guys in there slid down the rope attached to the bell and got out of there. The next round hit the steeple.

Being in the artillery we didn't have to worry too much about German tanks, but one time we did. The Germans had broken through with some Mark V tanks. Our sergeant came to me and said, "There's a Mark V tank coming up the road. Get the bazooka."

He told me and another guy where to go and wait for the tank. We weren't going to be out there alone, but it felt like it. There was supposed to be another bazooka team, but I never saw them. The sergeant said, "Go out there and get in front of him. Get behind something."

Imagine facing something like that! You've got to figure, if you miss him, you're going to get it. I turned and said to the guy next to me, "We miss that sonofabitch, we're dead."

There was a gully there on the side of the road, and that's where we waited. We heard him coming. He's coming slow. Then we saw him. I didn't see any infantry with it. They might have been behind it. The next thing I know, I hear airplanes. They're ours. These P–47 fighter-bombers came flying up the road. I looked up, just as they were right over us. I saw this thing drop from one of them; it looked like it was coming right at me. It hit the ground, skipped up the road and exploded right underneath that tank! That saved a lot of infantry guys. It was the most beautiful sight I ever saw.

Around this time, I watched a lot of dogfights. One day I looked up and saw this German plane on fire. The pilot jumped out, and his parachute opened. He was coming down close to us. I was up on a half-track behind the machinegun. I turned to the sergeant, "What should we do?"

"Shoot him when he lands," he said.

The wind blew him away from us. I was glad. I didn't want to kill him. I don't think I would have.

Another time a German twin-engine fighter crashed in a field near us. It was burning when we got to it. There was a guy in back, and when we pulled him out, his legs fell off just above the knees. His thighs were on fire. We put him on the ground, and I threw dirt on what was left of his legs to put the fire out. It made his skin smolder. The pilot gushed blood from his forehead. Our ambulance came and took them away. I don't know what happened to them.

I stayed with the 200th Field Artillery all the way through to the Moselle River in Germany. Because the Army had taken so many casualties during the Bulge, they took some of us and put us into the infantry. That's how I became a part of the 83rd Division.

There was supposed to be non-fraternization with the German civilians, but that order was not always followed. Two of our guys raped some girls at gunpoint. Some of us were ordered to go into this orchard. We stood there at attention, while a captain marched the girls past us. One of them looked at the guy next to me and pointed. I got scared. I thought for a minute that she was pointing at me. I turned sideways, and saw that guy's face turn red. She moved on, and pointed to another guy, and then they took her away. An American translator came with the next girl, and she did the same thing. After that, they took the guys away. They put one of them in a farmhouse. The sergeant came up to me and said, "Rudy, you guard this guy. Don't let him out of there until the MP's come."

They left and I locked the door to the farmhouse. Soon I hear this knock come from the cellar door. "What do you want?" I asked

"I want to get a drink of water."

"I can't let you out of there."

"I won't do nothing."

"You better not."

"I'll just get a drink of water and go back in."

I let him out and followed him over to an old sink that had a hand pump. He got some water and went back down. I locked the door. Boy, was I relieved, because if he had gotten away, I might have had to serve his time. That's what they told me, anyway. The MP's came and took him away, and we never saw Willie again. Somebody said they sent him to Leavenworth Penitentiary. The other guy was back in a month. They put him on hard labor in the rear. Hell, he had it made!

When we met the Russians, we found out that they had no problems raping the German women. I could speak a little Russian. When we were in Bavaria, right on the border of Germany and Austria, a young Russian lieutenant said to me, "Come over."

I said, "I'm not supposed to."

"Come on. There's women over here."

Eventually, I did sneak over. I saw some big Siberians there. I mean they were big, and they had wristwatches the whole way up their arms. The lieutenant told me about them.

"They really can't tell time, you know," he said. "They only put them on because they got them off dead Germans. The watches are trophies for them."

It got dark. He led me into this town. These Siberians were raising hell. They were going into houses and dragging out screaming women." The women started screaming.

I said, "I'm leaving."

The lieutenant said, "No, stay. Have a drink. We're going to have these women here."

I left. Those Russians raped those women, and nothing ever happened to them, as far as I know. I guess that was all part of their revenge for what the Nazis did in Russia.

Myself, I got to be friendly with a Bavarian girl. She wanted me to stay in Germany with her; she didn't want me to go back to the States. She was seventeen, and I had just turned twenty. Her mother wanted me to stay too, because she wanted her to marry an American soldier. Her mother was wary of me at first, but then she saw I was different than a lot of the other guys, and she relaxed. Her husband was killed on the Russian front. The mother did my laundry. Eventually, it came time for me to go home. I asked the mother for my laundry, but she had hidden it someplace and wouldn't give it to me.

She said, "Are you going to come back over?"

"I don't know. I've got my mother and dad at home. So maybe I'll come over."

It took me over fifty years, but I did go back, in 1996. My cousin went with me, and he could speak really good German.

I said, "Let's take a trip up to Bavaria, to this town. Let's see if that girl's house is still there."

I showed him the building we used as a barracks. It had become a restaurant. Then we went past this little farmhouse up above a little Catholic church. I told him to just go slow past it. We couldn't see anybody.

He said, "We'll stop and go in."

I said, "Don't you dare."

We didn't stop.

The war ended, and they were sending everybody home. We had been occupation troops for several months, and there were a lot of guys that got to know German families. We were down at the train station getting ready to leave, the scene reminded me of the train station in Latrobe when I first left home. There were girls screaming and crying. They wanted to get married with these GIs. They had to pull one of the girls from the train.

One girl said to me, "Clyde will be back. He told me he's coming back over to get me."

I knew the guy she was talking about was married already. I didn't tell her anything, but I thought: "Clyde ain't coming back."

I've been to a lot of reunions in the last couple of years. The 200th Field Artillery guys are starting to die off, and there aren't too many of us left. I belong to Veterans of the Battle of the Bulge. Last year we had some German soldiers attend our reunion. One of them had been a paratrooper. He told us he was glad he surrendered to the Americans because the Russians would have shot him. "Well we wouldn't want to waste the bullet on you."

I guess there's a certain friendship with these Germans now, years after the war.

"I Figured I had Bought the Farm."

Ross Saunders
66th Infantry Division, 262nd Regiment, 3rd Battalion, K Company
Bovard, Pennsylvania, 30 November 1924

"The HMS Brilliant came alongside our ship again and with a bullhorn the captain told Colonel Martindale that the ship was sinking and he should have his men abandon ship. The ship was listing badly, and I went into the water by sliding down the side. I told my friend, Fred Walstrom, to stay close to me because I couldn't swim. Then something, a steel net or something on the side of the ship, caught my leg and rolled me under water. I was under water and figured I had bought the farm. Next thing I knew I was going up, up, up, it was like I was going to heaven. I thought, you know, is this the way I'm going to die – after all the training I'd had."

DURING THE DEPRESSION if one of us had an apple, we'd share it. If my dad was out in the yard digging a hole or something, a few neighbors would come over and give him a hand. You don't see much of that sort of thing today. For us, in a way, the Depression was a good thing.

I grew up in Bovard, Pennsylvania, a coal-mining town. Poles, Slavs, Italians, were all pretty well meshed together, and we played together. We were so poor; but we didn't know we were poor, because everybody else was poor. I spent a lot of time in the woods, and playing ball. We'd hang around shacks and shanties, or we'd play street games at night. A guy named Jim Murphy, a Marine veteran, lived next door to us with his mother, and they had a big shack in their yard. We loafed in there, and made model airplanes. On Monday nights in the early to mid-thirties, the United Mine Workers showed movies for ten cents. Most of the time we didn't have ten cents, and we'd sneak in. Sometimes they'd catch us, and throw us back out.

My Dad was born and raised in the area before Bovard even existed, when our family worked the farms. My Dad's dad had a house and barn. When the Keystone Coal and Coke mine was opened, the company used horses. So, my grandfather became the stable boss, and my uncle became the wagoneer. They hauled coal back and forth. My dad was an electrician in the days when, if you could connect two wires together, you were an electrician. My grandfather, actually, was a tenant farmer; he didn't own the property, he just worked it.

My mother's maiden name was Helen Ruth Buttermore. They were from Greensburg, and her dad was a boss with the West Penn Power Company. At that time they had electric streetcars, and he was the boss over the crews that maintained the system. He retired when I was a kid. My grandmother, in fact, all my grandparents were born in the 1860s or early 1870s. My grandmother on my dad's side had two brothers in the Civil War, and my great-grandfather who was on that side of the family was in the Civil War. His name was Adam F. Sanner and he had a nephew by the same name. They served in the 11th Pennsylvania, so he changed his name to Sanders because all the mail and the pay and everything was getting mixed up. Our last name eventually ended up being Saunders. Dad was in the 79th Division in World War I. He fought in the Argonne, Verdun, and St. Miehel, terrible battles. He was gassed a little, but he never went into much detail about it.

I went to grade school in the Hempfield system till 8th Grade, and then to Greensburg High School, where I played a little football and basketball. I quit sports after the second year of high school because we didn't have any transportation, and you couldn't very well play sports unless you wanted to walk home all the way to Bovard every night. We had bus service for the first two years, but for the next two we had to get there the best way we knew how, which was mostly by hitchhiking. Most of the kids just quit school and went to work in a coal mine or some other job, but Dad was adamant that I finish school. I was in the Army at the time of my graduation in 1943, and I had enough credits to graduate. My mother got my diploma for me.

I entered the army on 27 March 1943, and wound up with the 66th Infantry Division at Camp Blanding, Florida. I became a rifle-squad leader. I stayed with the 66th until the war was over. After that, I knocked around Europe for several months, and I came home early in 1946. A lot happened to me from March 1943 to the end of the war in 1945. I was only seventeen when the Japanese attacked Pearl Harbor. I don't remember how I heard it, but I know I went to school the next day, and we had a meeting in the assembly room. They turned on Roosevelt's speech about "a day that will live in infamy" That's when I first really realized what had happened. My reaction at first was, let's go kick somebody's butt! They can't do that to us! I think we all felt a little like that in those days. "We're not gonna take this!"

After we heard Roosevelt's speech, everyone was all Gung-Ho. Another fellow and I went to Pittsburgh to join the Marines, but they would not take seventeen-year olds without parental permission. I got all the papers I needed in Pittsburgh, came home, went to the police station where they signed a statement that I was not a criminal. Then I put the papers on my father's dinner plate. When he came home from the coal mine, he sat down to eat, saw the papers, picked them up, read them, then slowly got up, lifted the lid on the coal stove, and threw the papers in the fire. He turned around and said, "When you're old enough to go into the service without my signature, you can go."

That was the end of that. You didn't argue with my father. He had been in World War I, and he knew about combat. I didn't. My friends and I were all young, and we figured that we would live forever, and everyone else was going to get killed. My dad did me a favor that day, no doubt about it.

When we were old enough, five of us from our community went to the Draft Board and got our numbers pushed up. Two were rejected for medical reasons. Three of us went to New Cumberland, Pennsylvania, where the Army had a staging area. After that, we got separated. One guy went to Louisiana, to an armored outfit. George Koluder, who lived across from me in Bovard, got sent to Camp Blanding with me. George got into the 66th, in Artillery. I wound up in Company K, 262nd Infantry Regiment, 3rd Battalion, Company K.

When we arrived in Camp Blanding, our train backed in and started unloading. I saw all these officers with crossed rifles on their collars. I told my friend George, "You know, this is the Infantry. This is not the Air Corps."

They took us into a big field and started calling out names. Henry Stairs and I were the first two privates to go into Company K, 262nd Infantry. The first thing I learned was not to volunteer too much. They had us picking up cigarette butts. As soon as I got done doing that, and I did it as fast as possible, I'd tell the sergeant, figuring that I could go back and loaf around or take a nap. But he always gave me something else to do. After a couple times, I realized that they were just keeping us busy, that we would never get done. So, we just took our time doing any job we were given.

Training was not only tough, it was dangerous. In one particular week, our division had twenty killed during a maneuver. We were making a night river crossing, and everybody had his full field pack. One of the boats tipped, and about twelve guys drowned. Ten or so more got killed in explosions. Then an artillery caisson ran over two artillerymen and killed them. One time, I had three of my men get slightly wounded with rifle-grenade fragments. One guy fired a rifle grenade and it hit a strand of barbed wire about fifteen feet away and exploded. The Army figured that if you lost a couple guys in training, so be it.

Part of our training was learning personal hygiene. Some guys never took baths, especially those from the "backwoods," who might not have been very bright. Those guys would get a bath, whether they liked it or not, with help from a few people and a GI scrub brush. I remember one guy who got that treatment. This same guy never changed his socks, either. After that GI shower, though, he started to keep himself a little cleaner.

Some guys were just nuts. We called them "Section-Eights." One guy pulled his own teeth out. The guy was from Eastern Pennsylvania somewhere. It all happened one day when we went on a hike. It was a pretty good long hike, I don't know how far, but this guy wouldn't do anything. Sergeant Paskowski and I, we were the two biggest sergeants in the outfit, tried to make him hike. So we had him, one under each arm, and we had to drag him for I don't know how many miles. And Paskowski would say, "Why don't you run?"

He said, "No. You'll shoot me."

Paskowski said, "Damn right I'll shoot you."

This nut then pulled his teeth out, laid in a ditch and wouldn't move. I didn't see it, but he got under some kind of vehicle, and he pulled some teeth out. I don't know how many. He was crazy. I think maybe he deserved to get out if he wanted out that damn bad. He said he was going home to buy Bonds. He got a Section Eight discharge.

After Camp Blanding, we moved to Camp Joseph Robinson in Little Rock, Arkansas, where we did maneuvers. We lived outdoors, and slept on the ground, just like we would do in combat. One day we marched thirty-six miles, trying to outflank somebody or something. We started out at one o' clock in the morning and walked till dark the next day, with a ten-minute break every hour. Of course, we were all nineteen-years old, and in pretty good shape. I became a staff sergeant fairly fast, and that kept me in the States longer than most others. When they started needing more bodies for combat, they came and took all of our buck privates, PFCs, corporals and second lieutenants and shipped them overseas. That's when Henry Stairs left our outfit. Until late 1944, I was basically a Training NCO, because after I trained one group, they shipped out. I trained another group and they used them for replacements. The third group I trained was the one I went overseas with, in November 1944, about six months before the war ended. The Battle of the Bulge started while we were in England, and was ongoing when we crossed the English Channel for the Continent.

Before leaving for Europe from Camp Shanks, New York, we got some leave. After that, we put five thousand troops on the *SS George Washington*, joined a convoy, and had a pretty uneventful trip across the Atlantic. We landed in Southampton, England, and organized in Dorchester. On 23 December, we boarded a train to the coast. Since the Battle of the Bulge had started on the sixteenth, the Army decided to get us across the Channel earlier than planned.

At Southampton, they loaded us on to a Belgian ship, the *Leopoldville*. The ship was loaded with ammunition and rations. We were kind of young and stupid, and we were itching to get into action. Some of the older guys might have been a little worried. As I was going up the gangplank, I said to the guys behind me, "Anybody want a quit slip now?"

We started across early in the morning. Each squad leader had to get lunch for his people. It was slop. They gave it to us in a tin can the size of a coffee can. My men wouldn't eat it; they threw it over the side. We weren't allowed to eat the D-bars because we didn't know when we would have another meal. Some guys had candy bars and other things squirreled away, and they ate those.

Shortly after we sailed, we ran through a boat drill. I was second in command of our boat station. After the drill, we just lounged around on anything that was handy, tables, chairs, whatever. All of a sudden there was one hell of a BOOM! I smelled cordite. I knew we were hit by something. Right away I said to my men, "Get your preservers and get on deck."

I went on deck and we started organizing our people, trying to figure out where to stand. When an officer arrived to take over, another sergeant and I went back below deck to pick up more life preservers. A lot of guys had come on deck without them. The other sergeant went lower to see where the ship had been hit. He found a sad sight. Men were trapped and they were dying. Medics were crawling in there trying to shoot them with morphine to knock them out. We went through crews' quarters gathering up life preservers. We both had our arms full of them. I said, "We better get back up on deck with these preservers."

"No," he said. "I'm going back to help those boys."

"No," I said. "You can't help. The medics are doing everything they can. Come on with me. Lets get these preservers up."

He refused. He gave me the preservers he was carrying, and I took them up with me. He went back down, and he stayed there, permanently. I passed the preservers around to anyone who needed one, and we all just stood around. Rumors started to fly that we were only six miles out. We were going to get towed to shore, the rumors said. And that's what they started to do. It was getting dark and cold. The ship kept listing, so our company commander marched us around to the other side of the ship. When that started to list, we went around to the other side. They figured shifting weight would help the ship right itself a little bit, but it didn't work that well.

Another troop ship was right in front of us, and when we got hit they headed for the port real quick. As we were being towed, a British destroyer, the *HMS Brilliant*, came alongside and a number of our people jumped onto it. Some guys just jumped into the water. We were on the port side by that time, and the ship kept listing. Finally the destroyer backed off. It couldn't take on any more people, and because of the way the *Leopoldville* was listing, the *Brilliant* had to pull back and away. The captain of our ship never came out of his quarters, and our crew of Africans, Congolese, got into the lifeboats and left. That left just the troops onboard, and Lieutenant-Colonel Martindale, from California, took command.

The *Brilliant* came alongside again, and using a bullhorn, the captain told Colonel Martindale that the *Leopoldville* was sinking and he should have his men abandon ship. I went into the water by sliding down the hull. I asked my friend, Fred Walstrom, to stay close because I couldn't swim. Then something, a steel net or something on the side of the ship, caught my leg and rolled me. I was under water and figured I had bought the farm. Next thing I knew, I was going up, up, up, like I was going to heaven. I thought, you know, is this the way I'm going to die, and after all the training I'd had! But still, I wasn't overly frightened. It didn't seem like I was panicking or anything. I popped to the surface, at least 500 yards from the *Leopoldville*. My leg was hurt, but it wasn't broken. The undertow must've pushed me out. If I had been on top of the water, it might've pushed me in. That's what put me that far away from the ship.

The water was so cold I couldn't feel anything. We were paddling around when some smaller ships came to pick up the living and the drowned. I saw a soldier drop his head down in the water. I picked his head up, and he was still breathing, so I put his arm under mine, and my other arm around a piece of wreckage. Five or six people panicked. They wanted to grab that piece of wreckage, and they pushed me under, and I lost that kid. Some were yelling, "Save me, save me."

I hit one kid. He came over and he wanted me to save him. I was having problems saving myself, and he jumped on me, pulled me underwater, and when I came up I jumped up as high as I could and belted him one and got away from there. "You save yourself, I'll save myself," I thought.

That's really the only bad bit of panic I saw. Most the guys were pretty calm, but

I decided that I was going to get the hell away from everybody, so I paddled off by myself, to an empty spot. A small harbor craft came up and rescued me. I saw its bow coming right for me, so I slid alongside it, and someone threw me a rope. My hands were too cold to grab it. Someone told me to wrap the rope around my arm. I did, and that's how they pulled me up.

I was in the water at least a couple hours. Someone told me later that my long underwear acted like a wetsuit and kept me from freezing. Guys who weren't wearing long johns froze to death. Many of them were wearing nothing but T-shirts and shorts. When I wound up on that little ship, I just fell on my face. My leg was hurt worse than I thought. They helped me down into a little engine room, and there was a sailor there, a mechanic. He gave me a cigarette, the best I ever had in my life. Martindale was the only one on board that I knew. They took us into Cherbourg, France, put us on an ambulance, and took us to the 280th General Hospital. I had swallowed a lot of salt water. I got in the ambulance with Lieutenant Solomon from I Company. I said to him, "I guess we owe those sonsofbitches something for this, don't we, Lieutenant."

He must've been hurt worse than me. He didn't say anything. He just sort of moaned. Then, when they got me to the hospital, they had German POWs carry me in. I'd never seen a live German before, and I thought, "Holy hell, am I safe with these guys?"

They put me in a ward, which, of course, was crowded with casualties from the Bulge and from our boat. I was put in the Venereal Disease ward! They had it divided with a screen, with the VD patients on one side, and the battle casualties on the other. Nobody thought to look for me in the VD ward, so, for a couple days, my outfit thought I was dead. There were about fourteen of us in the beds. After a couple days, one of my lieutenants walked by and saw me, and he came in acting like he had found his long lost brother. He and I didn't even get along that well, but at least my outfit then knew I was alive.

I was in the hospital with some pretty crazy people. There was a tanker in the bed next to me. He had the whole top of his head laid open. Tankers had leather helmets. A German tank had fired an 88 and the shell just grazed the top of the leather helmet and took part of his head with it. They had put his head back together, but the pieces of his skull didn't meet very well. He was goofy. They would give him pills and he would put them under his pillow. He said he was in Patton's Third Army. I said, "Did you get hit with a piece of shrapnel or what?"

He said, "Shit! I got hit with a whole 88!"

I said, "I can't believe that."

There were a couple Combat Fatigue guys in there with us. They were really nuts. Every time the radio would go, "Roo-oo, roo-oo," or something, they'd holler about buzz bombs and dive under their beds. They were getting them ready to ship out of there. The place was a menagerie.

One of the worst things during the time I spent in the hospital was in not knowing how many of our men had been lost when the *Leopoldville* had been hit. My division had a battalion on that ship, about 600 men. In total, about 800 soldiers and sailors were lost, and many of their bodies were never recovered. Twelve hundred were rescued. I lost four men of the twelve in my squad. We got pretty well torn up.

Well, my leg wasn't broken. It was smashed. A "Subversial Contusion" they called it. That didn't mean a thing to me. I just knew I couldn't walk. I was in the hospital about eight days. I started walking a bit. In the meantime, a colonel came in and pinned a Purple Heart on me. I was supposed to stay in the hospital, but I begged to get out. Once the guys found out where I was, they came around and told me the outfit was moving out. I didn't want to lose my outfit; I had been with those guys for two years. I begged the doctors to let me out, even though I was still hobbling pretty good. They let me out, and I went with my outfit to a combat area.

We were sent down to the St. Nazaire-Lorient area to relieve the 99th Division. The 99th was sent east to the Western Front, and we stayed on to close off the German pockets in St. Nazaire, Lorient and Bordeaux. What happened was that the 4th, which had taken Brest, suffered such heavy casualties there the brass decided to ring off the those fortress cities, and just keep the Germans bottled up. The 99th had been taking care of that, and when we got decimated from the sinking, they moved us down there to take over from them. We held the Germans in there, more or less, until the war ended. There was patrol action and artillery duels, but it wasn't fierce combat compared to what was happening in east, in France, Belgium, and Germany. Thank God! I didn't have to see that! Still, it wasn't a picnic.

I got back with K Company at St. Nazaire, back to my old job. I had to be the oldest squad leader in the army, having had the job for three years and eight months. I never did get promoted, and I was kind of mad about that. I felt I should have been a platoon sergeant, but, even though I had all that background, they wanted an older fellow, somebody about twenty-eight. Anyway, we went up, the three squad leaders and the platoon sergeant, to where the 99th had been. They already dug foxholes. I got my assignment, which was to cover an area of about 500 yards. Then I went back and got my men.

Mostly our patrols were small ones, but sometimes we'd take out a combat patrol, about forty men, a platoon. My first experience under fire was scary. It was artillery fire. The Germans had been there a long time. They knew where every damn point was, every crossroad. So when they started shooting, you'd better get in a hole. The Germans always used creeping fire. They would shoot once here, then they would move up one, then move up another, whereas the Americans would bracket fire: one short and one long, and back short, and this and that. Then, when they would get on target, they would shoot ten or fifteen in succession. So, one day we're back at the hedgerows eating, me and Pat, my assistant squad leader. We heard the artillery in front of us, so we ran into our hole. We were laughing at the Germans, saying things like, "Hey! Raise them up, Fritz. You're too damn short!"

Then the shells started creeping up, to right in front of our hole. It threw dirt in on us, and the concussion was pretty bad. I looked at Pat, and he looked at me, and if I was as white as he was, we were both pretty white.

"Jesus! I hope they don't fire for effect now!"

They didn't. They raised their fire up one more time, and hit an empty field. They must have fired fifteen rounds into it. We were lucky, but it was funny at first.

Once in a while, the Germans launched an attack. One time, on the line, M Company, a heavy weapons unit, put up a heavy machinegun in the corner of the basement of an empty house. All we had were light machineguns, manned by a crew of five or six. My lieutenant told me to take some men up and see what was going on. There had been a lot of shooting, then it had gotten quiet. I took half of my squad and we went up there, sneaking around. We went into the house. Nobody around. I had my rifle ready. I heard a door creak. I pulled it open, and there stood a guy as black as the Ace of Spades. If he had had a weapon, I would have shot him. My heart was going, "Boom, Boom, Boom!" What I didn't know was that the Germans had been there and gone, taking the machinegun with them. This guy had crawled up the chimney and spread-eagled himself so he wouldn't fall back down. He was covered in soot. The Germans didn't find him. He was so scared, he couldn't talk. We took him back, and it was hours before he could explain what had happened. The Germans had come upon them very fast, captured them, except for him, and took the gun. He was lucky that I didn't shoot him.

The Germans didn't use any tanks in our area, but we did. One of our attacks came through my position. A sergeant from I company led it. He took out a platoon of infantry and five tanks. I knew he was coming through, and I had to make sure there were passages through the hedgerows for the tanks. The reason for the attack was that some big shot back at some safe spot wanted some prisoners. Well, we lost two tanks and seven men. One of the medics went out to get the wounded. His name was Chung Fat. He was Hawaiian, and he was as ugly as sin. When he came back down that hedgerow, he was carrying a sub-machinegun, kicking those prisoners in the ass. He machinegunned some of them!

On combat patrols, we spread out and advanced. There were these little, abandoned, French villages. If there were Germans there, they would start shooting, and we would shoot back. We couldn't see them most of the time. We just shot into an area. We only went in so far, figuring that we'd run them out. Then we'd go back to our own lines. One time, on one of these patrols, a kid in my squad ran across a road, and a bullet hit his rifle sling and glanced off. He was lucky. Everybody had close calls. Once, when we were on a four-man patrol and Sergeant Rawlis shot a German, and they chased *us* home. We heard bullets that sounded like they were going through a piece of paper, and we knew they were pretty close. Of course, we had to move back, but we didn't just get up and run. Three guys stood fast while one guy moved back, and so on. When we got to hedgerows, I called mortar fire down on a spot over a 536 radio, which had a range of a mile or so. Before I did that, Sergeant Rawlis, who started the whole thing, came near and fell down. I thought he was hit. I asked, "You hit, Jack!"

"Naw! I'm just tired."

"You better get your ass through the hedgerow, because you're not safe lying out there."

I put cover fire down for him, about sixteen rounds, two clips from my M–1. Hopefully, I could keep the German heads down while Rawlis got through. Once he did, we started running, one of us on each side of the hedgerow. Damned if our mortar guys didn't drop rounds right on top of us, and we couldn't stop, because the Germans were right behind us. Neither of us got hit, but it was like running through raindrops. When I got back to the line, I dragged that mortar sergeant out of his hole like I was going to kill him. But, short rounds happened, and so was death by "friendly fire."

In World War II, an infantry division had a Cannon Company in each regiment. Once, after our tanks got back from an attack, there were still two of our tanks sitting out there disabled, right in front of me. We didn't want the Germans to have those tanks, so our Cannon Company was moved in behind us to destroy them. They even fired phosphorous on those tanks to ruin them. They didn't hit a damn thing!! That night, after things quieted down, we could hear noises out there; Germans talking. The Germans got so sick of hearing all that artillery going off, they helped us by blowing up the tanks themselves! The next morning our artillery moved out, and things quieted down.

There were FFI troops on our right. They were a different breed! They had a 20mm sitting on the road, and they fired it all the time, at nothing, or whatever. And then they would come over and would want to trade wine for soap and other things. They had some women up there with them. When we went on patrol we would take four men, spread out and sneak. The French would sling arms, about ten of them would march down toward the Germans, whistling and making noise. Soon as a German shot at them they'd all fall down, shoot all their ammunition, and come home. They weren't very well trained.

One day the French were on a hill across from us and we were watching them. They were piling up ammunition. Well, the Germans were on a higher hill, and they could see the French, too. The Germans never fired a shot until it got to be about five o' clock, when they figured the French must've had most of the ammunition placed. Then they blew that place wide open. We all sat there joking with each other, "Jerry's waiting! He's waiting till you get it all in there, and Jerry will blow it all up!"

Which Jerry did.

Compared to those FFI, the Germans were good troops, even though we weren't up against the elite. We didn't see any SS. When the war ended, we went over and disarmed them. They were just *Volksturm*, Peoples' Troops, but they were trained. They were okay. We didn't mess with them, or figure we were smarter than they were.

Sometimes, the Germans were so close, we could hear them talking. We couldn't understand what they were saying, and we didn't much care. We just held our own, and watched that none of them broke out of the ring. They had some Screaming Meemies that they fired at us, and we didn't like them. They were called *Nebelwerfers*, and were supposed to fire rockets that laid down smoke screens, but the Germans used them to fire regular rockets. They screamed when they came in. They also had a big railroad cannon hidden in a tunnel somewhere. That's what they used to do with those big guns. They'd bring that out and fire it every once in a while, then take it back in a tunnel. It was harassing fire, mostly. The shell from that thing left a hole nine-feet wide, and five-feet deep. We had an artillery observer, a lieutenant, who had a radioman with him. They kept trying to get a line on the gun, so that we could open up with a counter-battery. The lieutenant said the shell sounded like a "flying shithouse with both doors open" when it went over. We counter-fired, but the Germans had the gun back in the tunnel. The closest one of those shells landed to me was about 600 yards to my left. They didn't fire it too often. I don't think they had much ammunition for it, except what they could bring in from the sea, if they could.

We got a new guy in the squad, a replacement. There was an older guy in the squad named Donny Van Hoozer, who could steady young soldiers. Donny was in his thirties, and he was destined to be a private all his life, but he was a good private. I put the new guy with Donny. One night, this kid kept hearing Germans all the time, even though there weren't any Germans out there. He panicked, grabbed a grenade and threw it out of the dugout. When he threw the grenade out, a big clump of mud fell down inside the dugout. Of course it was dark, and Donny thought the hand grenade had fallen back inside. Donny was on his hands and knees, trying to grab what he thought was a hand grenade before it exploded. Poor Donny, he was steady, but not steady enough to be around that kid.

Once, Donny was on a little patrol down in this abandoned village. He went off to one side while we were checking these houses. He came around the corner of a little house and he ran smack-dab into a German. They both dropped their rifles and ran. We used to kid him: "How many Germans you see down there, Donny?"

He would answer, "I seen beaucoup of them!"

We took a thirty-man patrol back down there to get his rifle. When we got Donny's rifle, we found the German rifle right around the other corner. We picked that up ,too.

I got a Purple Heart for the leg wound suffered in the sinking, and I turned another one down later. This happened after we were in action in southwestern France, when I got hit with a piece of shrapnel right between the thumb and forefinger. A medic, whose name was Ralph Gadoo, picked the little piece out of there and put some iodine on it, and he said "Do you want the Purple Heart?"

I said, "Hell, no. I've already got one."

As it turned out, after the war, they counted five points toward discharge for each medal. Hell, I could've had another five points!

It was tough letting people back home know what was happening. It's like when I sent my Purple Heart home. I put a note in with it, together with the citation that described the date and the circumstances of the medal. The note told my parent that I was all right. The censors took the note and other stuff out. All Mom and Dad got was the Purple Heart, and Mom thought I was dead. The censors especially didn't want anyone to know about the *Leopoldville*, which the Army kept quiet for almost fifty years after the war. The only ones that knew about it were the people that were there, and a couple of writers.

Although we weren't involved in the main push into Germany, I felt what we were doing in the St. Nazaire-Lorient-Bordeaux area was very important. We were keeping fifty thousand Germans bottled up so they couldn't be used elsewhere. We bombed the hell out of St. Nazaire, Lorient, Brest, and Bordeaux. One day I saw the whole Eighth and Ninth Air Force coming back from a raid on Bordeaux, right over top of us. All morning long, the sky was black with B–17s and B–24s. I was glad they were on our side. This was about ten o'clock in the morning, and a German 88 on a hill in front of us opened up on those planes. One plane dropped out of formation, went over the top of the hill, and dropped a stick of bombs where the 88 was. I figured they must have radioed around to see if anyone had any bombs left, or didn't drop any bombs for some reason. When we got into St. Nazaire, after the war ended, we found out that all of the planes could have saved their bombs. The submarine pens they bombed had nine feet of concrete over top of them. Hardly a scratch on the sub pens.

We made all the Germans in St. Nazaire pile up their weapons. There was a beautiful, chrome Mauser with a white stock, and a pistol some German submarine commander turned in. Years later, I gave the pistol to my boy, Greg, who still has it. Shortly after we disarmed the Germans, we got sent up into Germany for the Occupation. I got tired of carrying the rifle, so I gave it away. I wish I'd have kept it. Beautiful rifle! But I'm not much of a gun man. I'd had enough of that. I had slept with a rifle for a long time.

I survived combat, and the *Leopoldville*. I've been asked if I ever worried about losing an arm or a leg, and I guess I can honestly say that I never did really think about it. I didn't even think about getting killed. I was taught that a good soldier makes sure that the enemy dies for his country; you don't die for your country. When I was young, I had no concerns. I didn't have anything. I didn't have a girl friend. I just had my parents. That's why the military likes twenty-year-old soldiers. Forty-year-old soldiers are smart enough to be scared.

We weren't up there very long in Germany, when we got orders to go near Marseilles, France, to a place called Arles. We built a great big tent city, and staged to go to the war in the Pacific. I wound up being a mess sergeant in charge of a 500-man mess, and a dozen or so German POWs, who did all the work. I also had guards who watched the POWS. All I had to do was make sure everyone got fed. I had one German interpreter, a sixteen-year-old kid. My head cook was a seventy-year-old German. I also had a couple American cooks. They knew what they were doing. I didn't. They had a menu, supplies, and everything they needed. The Pacific war ended while I was in Arles.

If we hadn't dropped the Atomic Bombs on Japan, I have no doubt that the 66th Division would've been sent to the Pacific. A lot of people say we never should've dropped that bomb on Hiroshima. I tell you one thing, they figured we would take a million casualties, and maybe I'd have been one of them, probably would've been one of them. So I'm damn glad they dropped that bomb.

We didn't know what an atomic bomb was. The headline in *Stars and Stripes*, said one of Japan's cities is missing. We started reading about the first one we dropped. Then, in the next couple days, we dropped another one. Then it was announced that the Japs surrendered. Of course we had a big party. Anywhere we could find some booze, we drank it. We had a good time, and shortly after that they broke up the division and sent it home, and they sent the guys that had fewer points. We were in combat for four months, but we only got one battle star, because we stayed in the same place. I know of guys who went through replacement depots, never even got into combat, and got four or five battle stars, because every time they moved into a different area, they got a battle star. They counted five points apiece for them. Same as that Purple Heart I could've gotten, for an additional five points. Anyhow, I didn't care. I had a good time while I was there.

I wound up back in Germany, then I went into Austria. I was put into a ten-ton quartermaster truck company. I was an infantry sergeant, and I had no duties whatsoever except to tell those trucks where they were going the next day. And then I went on a couple of furloughs to Italy and out to Nice, and they sent me into St. Wolfgang in Austria. I had no duties there. I was sergeant, and all I had to do was every seventeen days was be in charge of quarters. I'd just go run around, go to town, do whatever I wanted to do. Then they shipped me to a place up in the mountains of Austria, where there was nine feet of snow. I went up there and I got in with the 83rd Division. They were coming home. So they processed our equipment and everything, put us onto 40&8 boxcars and took us up to Bremerhaven. We stayed there in camp for two days, and then got on a small ship, the *Sea Porpoise*. And that's when I got seasick, coming home on that thing. I said, "Is that the ship that's gonna take us to the ship that we're gonna go home on, or is that the ship we're gonna go home on?"

It wasn't very big; maybe even a little less than a Liberty Ship. Anyhow, my buddy Tooey from Pittsburgh, he was on another ship the same size. They went on a northern route, and they got hit with a small iceberg. Of course, they had watertight doors. One of their cargo compartments was flooded, and they just shut it off. He was on the Leopoldville too, when it got torpedoed. Tooey said, "You think I wasn't nervous?"

When we pulled into New York, we passed the Statue of Liberty. We got off, and boarded trains that took us to Fort Dix. We got a leave into New York City for one or two nights. Then they processed us for discharge. They gave us our final pay, and took us to Philadelphia to get a train home. Tooey and I came home together on the same train. When we got to Greensburg, I got off and he went on to Pittsburgh. I didn't see him after that for a long time. He eventually became a captain in the prison in Pittsburgh. The warden was from Greensburg, and when his mother died, Tooey came up to Bacha's funeral home to see the warden's mother and found out that I lived in Bovard. He came here and knocked on one door at a time until he found me. This had been about twenty-five or thirty-years since I'd seen him. Tooey died last year.

In Greensburg, I got a cab home. I was a big shot, and I could afford a cab. When the cab came around by the Honor Roll in Bovard, I saw that coal had been stripped out of our baseball field, and it was nothing but a big hole. That made me sick, because I had played baseball there as a kid. I popped in on Mom and Dad. I had sent them a telegram or something to tell them I was coming home from Fort Dix. That was it. Home. I didn't have a job, so I just loafed around for awhile. Joined the 52/20 club, which gave me twenty dollars a week for fifty-two weeks. I thought of going to school, but I never got around to it.

I worked a little in the steel mills, and I worked a little on the railroad for awhile. Then I joined the National Guard, where I got a commission as a second lieutenant. When the Korean War broke out, I was called to duty. I went to Europe, where we were worried about the Russians, instead of Korea. The kids that ended up in Korea, got no recognition for what they did, not like us who served in World War II. I commanded a company in Germany. I might have stayed in the Army, because I would have made Captain, but I wanted to get married, and I didn't think my wife would have liked life in the military. I came home and married in 1952. We had eight children, six boys and two girls. I worked for the telephone company for thirty-four years and retired in 1987. I've enjoyed the good life ever since.

Wooden spoon made from a a wooden beam in BAD ORB Prisoner of War camp, Germany, by William E. Simpson, Co. "B" 110th Infantry, 28th Div. Simpson was captured on the second day of the Battle of the Bulge. The spoon was carved with broken stone and glass.

MM 88.1.1

May 1993. A boxcar typical of the kind used by the German military to transport prisoners of war. *Courtesy of Leroy Schaller.*

In prisoner of war camps, cooking facilities (if and when there was something to eat) were primitive and makeshift. These served as stoves in Stalag Luft 1 in Barth, Germany. *Courtesy of Pat Seanor.*

Home of Pierre Eicher, Marnach, Belgium, destroyed on 16 December, the first day of the Battle of the Bulge. *Courtesy of Leroy Schaller.*

"Today Is Our Day, Tomorrow May Be Yours."

Leroy "Whitey" Schaller
28th Infantry Division, Pennsylvania National Guard, The "Keystone" Division, 110th Infantry; Fountain Hill, Pennsylvania
19 November 1922.

"Most of the rooms were empty. The Germans came upstairs twice, but on both occasions they did not look into the room we were in. We were not as lucky the third time, when they came up again. We heard them head back downstairs, or so we thought, but not all of them did. Our door was like a shallow closet door. It opened, and I knew it was up! We couldn't do anything. It would have been foolish to shoot. His first words were, 'Good morning, Gentlemen. For you the war is over!' As they marched us away, he turned to me and said, 'Today is our day, but tomorrow may be yours.' He must have known that this offensive of theirs was their last attempt at winning the war. War is strange, indeed. We later discovered that he had been educated at the University of Pennsylvania."

MY FATHER, ROY E. SCHALLER, rigged up the first airplane ever to fly upside-down. During World War I, he was a mechanic. He never got overseas, but he trained mechanics and flyers in Plainfield, Texas. There was a French general who came over to the airfield to observe American troops. The general said he couldn't teach Americans a damn thing, and that they were a bunch of damn fools. The general's pilot wanted his plane rigged to fly upside-down for the military review. My dad took a one-gallon gas can, rigged it so that when the pilot flipped the plane over it would feed the carburetor. Supposedly this French general saw this plane fly past upside-down and was very surprised to learn that an American had fixed it up like that.

My father was a paperhanger. For a time, I was a fourth-generation paperhanger. I learned the trade when I was in tenth grade. The Schaller family goes back to the time of the Reformation, and most of them came from Switzerland to the United States in the mid-1800s. My mother was Grace Fenstermacher, and her family came here in the early 1700s. One of her ancestors, Lisel Boekel, helped nurse Lafayette back to health during the American Revolution.

I was born in Fountain Hill, a little borough in the Lehigh Valley, between Allentown and Bethlehem. The area had been on the southern edge of an ancient glacier. When I was a kid I found hatchets there that men from the Stone Age had used. It wasn't long before I realized that there were left-handers in the Stone Age, because some of the hatchets were made to fit one or the other hand. There were a lot of arrowheads in the area, plus a huge grindstone that must have weighed several tons. The place got built up while I was overseas, and all that stuff disappeared.

Unfortunately, during the worst of the Depression, my dad broke his leg picking cherries for some extra money, and he was laid up for three years. They reset his leg two times, and finally the Veterans' Hospital in Philadelphia had to chisel bone off. So my mother went to work in the silk mills. My sister and I were too young to work, so we did the housework. But, we always were well fed despite the hardships.

I got my first job when I was in high school. A neighbor was trying to start a potato chip factory, so I used to peddle potato chips on Saturdays. They were fifteen cents a bag. I think people bought them more because I was just a kid. I was quite shy, so much so, that if I got a new shirt or a new pair of trousers, I didn't want to wear them because I felt everybody was looking at me.

I went to Penn State to study Forestry. I was fair-skinned with blonde hair. My roommate called me "Whitey," and it's been Whitey ever since. On Sundays, five others and I helped in the kitchen of a private dormitory. We were peeling potatoes, when over the radio came the announcement that Pearl Harbor had been attacked. We all stood up. A fellow named Kowalski went to the sink, rinsed off the potato peeler, set it down, dried his hands, and left. Two weeks later, his mother requested that we pack his clothing and send it home. We found out why. The same day the announcement came over the radio, Kowalski went to Pittsburgh and enlisted. We didn't hear from him again until after the war. The pressure was on me to stay in college, but I was in an accelerated program and sort of tired of it. Even before Pearl Harbor there was a feeling in the country that we would be at war at some point. We had a small high school graduating class, and I remembered our commencement speaker telling us to look around, that it would be the last time many of us would see each other. He was right. Soon, many of my friends were in the service, and I had lost a couple, and others had been badly wounded.

Finally, I just said, "I'm going into the army." I decided this partly because I knew of the GI Bill that was going to come, and I could finish college after the war. I enlisted in November 1942. I was twenty-years old. But I didn't go on active duty until May 1943. I was still in college during that time. They told me, "When we want you, we'll call."

Eventually, they did call. I was inducted at Fort Meade, Maryland. Then they sent me by train clear up to Chicago and then down to New Orleans. It was a two-week trip on coach. The dirt and dust were awful! My orders said TC Corps. I thought, "Tank Corps! That's good!"

I felt that if I was going to be in the war, then I was going to fight. When I got down to New Orleans, one of our commanders set the record straight. TC turned out to be not the Tank Corps but the Transportation Corps, the highest priority service organization at the time. I was assigned to the 17th Mobile Port. Two of us got stuck there because of our forestry and surveying background. We were good at it. We could step off a mile within fifteen feet. The idea was that Mobile Port would follow the front lines through the Pacific, set up a port and turn it over to somebody else.

I had been in ROTC, and immediately got the rank of Private First Class. Most of us were College Enlistment Reserve Corps. A little sergeant there hated college kids! He'd sit in the shade while we drilled. We'd do fine until some officers came along. Then he would get up and show how well he had trained us. But we would deliberately screw up something awful. That poor sergeant! During rifle training, I was one point shy of "Expert." I felt that if I had had a second chance at it, I could have made "Expert." As it turned out, I became "Expert" enough.

They put us to checking cargo at the Port of New Orleans. It was a real eye-opener. One day I checked in thirty-two ambulances that arrived from the North African campaign. It was obvious that aircraft had strafed them all. After that, I came to know that the rules of the Geneva Convention didn't really mean much.

I didn't like the Transportation Corps. The idea of business as usual when somebody's shooting at me? I wanted be able to shoot back. They told us, "If you're unloading a ship, you got to unload it, never mind the bombs."

I wanted to get out of the Transportation Corps, and there was a classification officer that tried his damndest to help me. He got me into the ASTP, Army Specialized Training Program. They sent me to a Star Unit at Louisiana State, and then to Johns Hopkins. I figured that I would screw that up, and eventually make my way into the infantry. But by that time they had dumped everybody out of the program and put them in replacement pools. That's how I finally made it into the infantry, and to the European Theater of Operations.

I crossed the Atlantic on the *U.S.S. Sea Porpoise*, in a convoy. The food was terrible! I learned that they were given so much money to provision the ship, and they made some short changes. All we were getting were potatoes! We had a riot. It was getting pretty nasty. MP's settled it by coming around and passing out food. I swore that if I ever met the captain of that ship I'd beat the hell out of him! It's the only grudge I've ever carried. I still get steamed thinking about it!

We arrived in Liverpool, England, 2 June 1944, just as an air raid was going on. We weren't yet in port when two German fighter-bombers picked us out as an alternate target. They made a quick pass, dropping their bombs and strafing us, but they missed. My guess is they were just unloading what was left of their bombs and just wanted to get the hell out of there. The MP's chased us all down into the holds. When it was all over and they let us back topside, we saw holes in the ship's funnels. After some inquiry, we learned that those holes came from our own green gun crew who fired at the attacking planes. We had a good laugh about that.

After we landed in Liverpool they whisked us away like we were some big secret, but how do you hide thousands of men? We went up to central England, where we waterproofed vehicles. We'd test them by driving through a pond. Sometimes we'd get stuck and have to swim back to shore. It was cold! I still think that summer in England was the coldest "winter" I ever experienced. Other than what we did, they didn't know what else to do with us, so they'd send us on hikes, lots of hikes! We did get passes to go into a nearby town, but we didn't fraternize much with the locals. There was a sign in town that I didn't appreciate. It said, "Dogs and U.S. Soldiers Keep Off the Grass."

On 6 June airplanes filled the sky from one horizon to the other. It was D-Day. Wounded men arrived during the following days. We got to talk with some, asking them what it was like. When we shipped out to France, there was a guy with us who had been wounded at Omaha Beach. They declared him fit for duty. He was being sent back with us as a replacement. We landed at Omaha and when he saw the beach, he passed out on the spot.

We crossed the Channel from Southhampton on 20 June 1944. We got ashore and there were piles and piles of C-Rations and supplies just sitting on the beach. There was this crazy guy yelling that these were the worst living conditions he'd ever seen in his life, and he was going to write his congressman. Considering what had happened there, all the men who died taking that beach, what this guy was saying was pretty ridiculous and inappropriate. I was still in a replacement pool. It was frustrating because D-Day had already happened and here we were still sitting around as replacements even though we were in France where all the fighting was going on. They sent us down into the Cherbourg Peninsula. We went past St. Lô. There was one tower standing there, the rest of the town was leveled. We saw a lot of guys with the diamond shoulder patch of the 9th Infantry. We thought we were going to end up with them, but we didn't. They turned us around and we went past St. Lô again. That last tower was down this time. Apparently there was a German sniper using it, so they shelled the hell out of it.

We went through Paris in a boxcar. They passed the word that we were going to be sidetracked for hours. They didn't know for how long, but they said we could take off, and that they would sound the train whistle when we had to get back. Well, some of the guys imbibed some local Calvados. The French use only a few drops of that stuff to make Coffee Royale. One of our guys had two cups half-and-half. Three days later, his eyes still didn't focus. In September, when we got into Mons, Belgium, the first thing they did was caution us about the local Calvados! They already had three guys in the hospital with their livers shot.

They put me in the 28th Division on 10 November 1944, the Keystone Division from Pennsylvania, the Keystone State. I still have gaps in my memory of my first days with the 28th. You see, we went in as replacements right in the thick of the battle in the Hürtgen Forest. If you lasted the night in Hürtgen you were a veteran. That was one of the division's worst battles, as it was for a lot of others. In my particular company, B Company, when we came out of Hürtgen, there were no originals left, just the replacements. Events of 10–16 November, when we came out of the Hürtgen, are pretty much missing from my memory. I pondered the benefit of going back through it all, possibly under hypnosis, and to reclaim that information. I've asked Army psychologists, and two of them have said, "Leave it alone."

I know I was part of a forty-four-man team sent to knock out pillboxes. Two of the guys carried flame-throwers, and a number of the guys carried forty-pound satchel charges with three-second fuses. I had one of those charges. I had to prop the charge up against the aperture of a pillbox, light the fuse, and then hit the ground. The explosion was supposed to pass over me, but kill those inside the pillbox. I don't remember if I ever used that charge, and I don't remember any of the men on my team.

I went back in 1986. I was with Charles MacDonald, who wrote *A Time for Trumpets: A History of the Battle of the Bulge*. During the trip I had a sense that I had been in certain places before. They were driving us around in a tour bus, visiting the battlefields. For forty years I had been wondering where Vamose was. The bus stopped at a place, and I looked out the window. Suddenly, I knew that I had been here before. It was once a vista that had a sign that said, "Vamose." For all those years, I remembered only the sign, not the place. As I looked out the window, I remembered the MP who stood there, waving our truck through. We stopped and one of the guys jumped out to take a piss. The MP told us we had to go another way because a buzz bomb had hit just up the road. If we had not stopped there for a time that bomb might have hit us. Then, the vista was cut out of the woods. Now it was denuded, and there were cattle grazing there. I saw another place on the map, Simonskull. They drove the bus up there. The bus stopped and was turning and then I saw the sign for Simonskull. Things started to come back to me. We went to a German cemetery. There was a nurse with us and she followed me around, knowing that I was becoming upset. I started to hear the moaning and cries of the wounded. A cemetery, pockmarked from artillery, the graves spilled open, flashed in my mind. I saw a church steeple on fire.

I lost track of time in the Hürtgen. It seemed like two days, but we were in there for almost a week. I do remember hearing mortar rounds. I yelled and dove to the ground, smashing my nose on my own rifle. For that, I got a Purple Heart. I couldn't breathe for months.

After we left the forest, we moved into an observation post. It was an open area, and we could look down across the Our River. It was a beautiful mountain scene. To the rear was a wooded area and an abandoned town. It was a rainy night when we moved in. I was in a BAR position under a tin-roof. They told us that a minefield surrounded us. While we were there, things got hotter and hotter. Ordnance would come up, set up machineguns and mortars for trial, fire off a belt and some mortar rounds toward the German lines, and then head off down the road. Then the Germans would open up, and we would catch hell.

At night we heard patrols out in front of our position. We didn't think too much of it until we heard a German swear. I thought maybe he had fallen into a slit trench. Apparently, the minefield wasn't all that big. Shortly after that, HQ brought up a heavy-weapons section. They moved into two houses below, and, in spite of our warning, they each proceeded to build a fire. Smoke started to come out of the chimney. Two artillery rounds came in, knocking off the chimney.

On another rainy night, something jumped up on the parapet of our observation post. I realized it was a cat. The next day we started shooting all the stray cats there, because they were tripping mines and booby traps, and it had us unnerved. When we pulled out of there the Germans gave us a farewell by sending some artillery over on top of our replacement squad. Fortunately, no one was killed. The Germans must have noticed all the activity as we moved out. We pulled back into the town. We were standing outside a church waiting for a truck to pick us up when a round came over and hit the church bell. We got covered in plaster. We were all still jumpy as hell from the Hürtgen Forest. We were glad to get out of there.

On Thanksgiving Day we enjoyed a meal with the citizens of a Belgian town. I was to have dinner with a minister. I knew they liked hog's head. I wondered if that's what they were going to have for dinner, and whether I'd be able to eat it, but luckily they had roast duck.

We'd had a shower, the first one in three months. I slept in a bed, and the only duty we pulled was night guard duty. I was sitting on the bed, talking to some of the guys. I kind of pulled my feet up and I had my arms around my shins, and they were ice cold. I massaged them for hours. I couldn't get the warmth back in them. They had gotten frozen.

On 15 December, they moved us into Luxembourg. Five of us went out on patrol, trying to establish contact with the enemy. At two-o'clock in the morning, we came back in. Just before that we ran into a German patrol. We could hear them coming downwind, and we knew from the sound that it was a heavy, combat patrol. It was uncommon to hear a patrol of that size in that sector of the line. I heard them before anybody else, and I stopped the patrol. We stood in our tracks. They passed within thirty feet of us, and never knew we were there. After they passed us by we came to a church. We stopped there to warm up, but the one guy had a bad cough and his coughs were echoing through the church. We decided to get back to our own lines as quickly as possible. Ultimately, the Germans passed right through our lines, which would not have been difficult since they were so thinly defended at the time. They got into the town we were occupying and attacked us from behind. Most of them didn't make it out.

I don't think we were any more suspicious of an attack after that encounter, but maybe we should have been. Two weeks before, two civilians were going around the town setting up electricity in the houses. What bothered me was that one of them was a big, healthy, blonde-haired fellow. If he wasn't a German or a German sympathizer, then why hadn't he been conscripted by the Germans into their army? I asked my sergeant, "Have these guys been checked out?"

He answered, "Oh, I'm sure of it."

So, the matter was dismissed. But when German shells started coming in at five-o'clock in the morning of 16 December, the morning of the start of the Battle of the Bulge, every building that housed a weapon, a vehicle or troops was hit with uncanny precision. They were sending over incendiary shells to set fires. I was near a staircase on the third floor of a building, looking out a window. For a split second, I saw one of those shells coming right at me. It looked like a ball of Mercurochrome, with different colors swirling around in it. I stepped back toward the head of the stairs, ready to throw myself down them or out the window. Luckily, the damn thing landed outside and burned harmlessly in the snow.

Marty Larson was with me on the third floor, and we had other troops downstairs and throughout the house, in the village of Marnach. Marty took up position at another window. We stayed in that building through the artillery barrage. When the sun came up, the Germans started moving toward the town. We set the sights on our M-1s at 400 yards. It was obvious that they were trying to outflank the town and surround it. Then I spotted a German general officer in the square below. It was Field Marshall Model, commander of the entire Ardennes offensive. I had him in my sights, but chose not to pull the trigger. If I had, I'm sure that every GI in the building and in positions nearby would have died on the spot. I thought it was better, instead, to lay low and hope to break out after the Germans passed us by. The officers moved out. Later, a bunch of other Germans in a field in front of our position were trying to set up mortars. They were using haystacks as cover. Marty and I fired some tracer rounds, trying to set the haystacks on fire. A couple rounds hit at the bottom of the stacks and came out through the top. Germans kept popping out from behind the stacks, and we sniped at them, saying things like, "I'll bet you a nickel I got him."

It got quiet later in the day. The German tanks were still bottled up across the Our River and their infantry had pretty much gone around us. That night they started firing their 88s. Five of us moved to a farmhouse. Between us we had thirteen rounds of M–1 ammunition, an empty bazooka, and two hand grenades. We figured we'd just hide out. By seven o'clock the Germans were pretty much in the town. We laid low. At eleven o'clock I heard a scream, and an exchange of shots. The scream sounded like a woman's, but it was probably a young boy, one of those the Germans had in their army at that point in the war. Then it got quiet.

Half an hour later, German tanks came through. At first we thought that we were being relieved, and then we realized that they weren't our tanks. They went through doing a reconnaissance by fire. They shot the whole town up until they decided the place was empty of live American troops. I found out much later that the tanks were part of an armored infantry that eventually penetrated all the way to Bastogne.

Sometime in the night a column of German infantry passed by the farmhouse. We could hear the clank of their mess gear. This time, I was on the second floor. I thought for a moment about throwing my two hand grenades at them, but I had second thoughts. The next day they backed a tank into a garage beneath the house. Between us and the Germans below, there were just some loose floorboards. They also parked two half-tracks in front of the house. Cautiously, I looked out and down the road. I counted thirty-three Panther tanks. We just sat still.

We were above that tank all night. We thought about stuffing the muzzle of the tank with our grenades, but with the loose floor we were afraid to move. Sometime in the night I must have dozed off. I awoke to someone saying what sounded like, "Whitey."

After the second call, I was ready to answer, but it was someone downstairs who answered! We thought of ways to get out of there, but the farmhouse had no back door, and we couldn't get past the Germans downstairs, anyway. There was a stepladder propped up against the second floor window. We could have climbed down the ladder, but we would have ended up on the tin roof of a small shed, and we would have made one hell of a racket.

Most of the rooms were empty. The Germans came upstairs twice, but on both occasions they did not look into the room we were in. We were not as lucky the third time, when they came up again. We heard them head back downstairs, or so we thought, but not all of them did. Our door was like a shallow closet door. It opened, and I knew it was up! We couldn't do anything. It would have been foolish to shoot.

His first words were, "Good morning, Gentlemen. For you the war is over!"

As they marched us away, he turned to me and said, "Today is our day, but tomorrow may be yours."

He must have known that this offensive of theirs was their last attempt at winning the war. War is strange, indeed. We later discovered that he had been educated at the University of Pennsylvania."

They marched us down the road and past the field where the haystacks were. I passed the body of a dead German, one I had shot. I had hit him in the stomach, and he lay there with a look of agony on his face. War was a hell of a way to settle an argument, I thought. We passed a bunch of tanks. They were bumper to bumper. There was only one road for them to use. I thought that surely our commanders should've known that and attacked them.

An airplane came over, one of ours, a Thunderbolt. The ground haze wasn't that bad. I had a gold watch and tried to flash it in what sunlight there was. He side slipped and flew over us. I expected he took some pictures. The Germans saw me flashing the watch, and they took it from me, together with my wallet. I was glad that's all they took!

As they marched us away, I turned and saw a church steeple. I wondered what lay ahead for me. Today, I am glad that I couldn't have known. When I returned to Europe years later, I took a picture of that same steeple from approximately the same spot I first saw it.

They put us in a cave. It looked like the entrance to an old coal mine. I think we were there for two nights, though I'm not sure. Some of the guys thought the Germans were going to blow the entrance of the cave and bury us alive. We had no food. The only thing we had eaten since being captured were some half-rotted apples we had taken from the farmhouse. None of us really had an appetite, though.

They interviewed every one of us while we were in the mine. We gave them name, rank, and serial number. For the most part, *they* told *us* where we'd been in the last several weeks and months. They even named some of our casualties. They knew more about us than we did.

The German officer who interrogated me wanted to know about our frontline road signs.

I said, "I don't know anything about it."

Then he asked, "What do you people mean by unconditional surrender?"

I was very happy to tell him.

He told me his last name was Schaller.. He said, "Perhaps we're related."

He might have been right, but I wouldn't admit it. It was possible, but he was from northern Germany, while some of my ancestors had come from Bavaria, in the south. He offered me cigarettes and coffee and tea and a candy bar. I didn't particularly care for cigarettes, although I could've taken them and given them to some guys who were smokers. But I wasn't about to take any of it. I refused all of it, and he just got a smile on his face. He knew I was just being stubborn, and he knew damn well I wanted some of that stuff. A candy bar would've really been nice.

They started marching us again. Their first words were, "For every one of you that tries to escape, we will shoot three."

That did it for us. There was no real thought of escaping after that. We were prisoners. They could shoot us at any time, especially since there was no registration of us with the Red Cross, although that didn't always mean anything either. They could always say we tried to escape. They gave us half a loaf of bread and some marmalade. They didn't tell us this was to last us for the next six or seven days. That's when we lost our physical strength. We went long periods without water. Some of the guys drank water out of mud puddles. The shots we got in the States protected us from some water-borne diseases, but the cold took its toll on us. We started marching on 18–19 December, and were not fed again until we got to Geralstine, Germany, on Christmas night.

During the march, one of the German officers threw a blanket on the ground, and everybody that went by took their cash and threw it onto the blanket. Somebody estimated they took over $10,000 from us. One night we slept out in the snow, which was as high as a man's knee. Some of the guys were barefoot. A few of us had overcoats. Fewer still had gloves. Our German captors took anything they could use. Some of them took our guys' shoes and exchanged them for their own, which were worn to the point that toes stuck out of them. We huddled together in groups like coveys of quail. Those who had overcoats occupied the outside perimeter and those without coats went to the center. We really didn't sleep, but several times during the night those with overcoats shifted around a bit so that one of them was not on the outside all the time.

They marched us through a German town. The people were lined up like they were going to watch a parade. Our capture was a great morale builder for them. There was a lot of shouting and spitting. One little kid came running our and kicked the guy in front of me in the shins, as hard as he could. The little shit wasn't more than ten years old. When they saw him do that, the crowd cheered. The guards with us were worn out, old-aged men. They couldn't control that kind of stuff.

One day, on the march, we saw an American fighter plane get hit. The pilot bailed out. When we saw him, his face and a quarter of his body were severely burned. They marched him with us for two days until they were able to hospitalize him.

They marched us over 100 kilometers. In Geralstine, they put us up in a Catholic church for the night. They didn't feed us until after midnight, after Christmas was over. I still feel they had denied us the food on purpose. The church was on a hill above the houses, and there were a thousand of us jammed into it. A woman from the town came to the church with a pitcher of water. A guard barred her passage, but she just pushed past him. Then four or five women came up the church steps carrying buckets of water. It was an act of kindness I have never forgotten. In 1993, I made contact with a chaplain in Pittsburgh, who contacted his son-in-law in Iowa. From there it went to a young man in Belgium. The young man knew an English/German speaking priest who contacted a priest in Geralstine. I sent a letter and flowers to that church in Geralstine, and I got a letter back from some of those women who were still alive and who remembered the incident.

On 26 December they loaded us into 40&8 boxcars. Trouble was, there were

"She came up there with a pitcher of water."

sixty of us in each car. The only way we could get rid of excrement was with our steel helmets, that is, the helmets of those who still had them. One end of the car had a small opening, and we were able to empty the helmets there. While on that train our own planes bombed and strafed us. The cars ahead of us were the recipients of the bombs. The Germans stopped the train, and we struggled to get out of the car. A fella from the 100th Infantry and I shook the door, trying to open it, but the latch would not break. We both got down to where we could look through the keyhole of the latch to try and figure out how to open it. Our heads were tight against each other, and the guards shot through the car. A bullet caught him under his right ear and exited out his elbow. It took the rest of us ten minutes to get him stretched out, we were so crowded together. He died within that time. They didn't open the car until we got to our destination. The guards kept their rifle butts handy, and they used them. They removed the dead body.

They took us to a prison camp, Stalag IXB, in Bad Orb, Germany, near Frankfurt. One fella from the 106th Division had a twin brother. They both had been captured separately. When he arrived, somebody said, "My God, we just buried you yesterday!"

That's how he knew his brother was dead.

Stalag IXB was one of the foulest POW camps in Europe, and it was crowded, 290 to 500 men per barracks. There were a few British and a lot of Russians and some Serbians there. The Russians gradually, mysteriously, disappeared. The Germans separated the noncoms from the officers. The privates were nothing, and we were pretty much treated that way.

We all had to make a lot of adjustments. A lot of smokers suddenly had to quit smoking. There was no food of any appreciable amount, just poor German food that couldn't begin to sustain us. We got very few Red Cross packages. I shared one fourth of one Red Cross pack with four or five other guys. That was it. We got some packages from the Serbians in the camp who'd been long-term prisoners. They would build a supply of packages up. Every once in a while we'd get something from the Russians. They'd throw a loaf of bread over the wire to us.

Our regular diet consisted mainly of a kind of watery soup and *ersatz* tea in the morning. Really, it was just warm water. In the beginning, we could see a few barley grains in the soup. We could count them. Finally, there were none. I ate out of my helmet liner. Some guys ate out of tin cans. We didn't have spoons. Try eating soup with a helmet liner. You can't tip it up. What I did was dip my fingers in the soup and lick them. Then I scooped the last of it out. A buddy made a wooden spoon for me with a stone and a piece of broken glass. That spoon is now in the Military Museum in Boalsburg, Pennsylvania. One of the fellas found a horse's hoof somewhere. We made soup out of that. They used the frozen tops of beets, too but that didn't help us, it probably hurt us. All of us had diarrhea. One of the hardest things I witnessed were guys that had been protecting each other just days before beating each other over the head with rocks over spoiled, half-frozen potato peelings that the Germans had thrown out and covered with ash to make them unpalatable. Some of those rocks required the use of two hands.

There were no medications except what a few of the fellas carried in on them. We had nothing to wash with, which didn't help in trying to stay healthy. I did not have a shower for more than three-and-a-half months. We had problems with lice, fleas and bed bugs. I didn't have nearly as much trouble as some of the other guys because my skin temperature ran lower than normal. The bugs really didn't go after me. A lot of the men were all bitten up, especially the ones who had pneumonia and high temperatures. It was cold! Old "Pop" Simpson and I looked out for each other. He had an overcoat that he'd open up, and we could both fit in there. That was our blanket. There were no other blankets. There were very few bunks, as well. We slept on floors covered with straw. Even the straw quickly disappeared because we used it as toilet paper.

As time went on, we got weaker and weaker, and more and more communicable diseases developed. Dysentery was a problem. One of the guys from my squad, Carl Reinhardt, from Minneapolis or St. Paul, died of spinal meningitis. There were other communicable diseases toward the end. My honest feeling is that if we had not been liberated in early April, if we'd have been there when the weather got warm, very few of us would've come through. Even with the spinal meningitis, they came through with some hot lime and spread it on the floor — that was it. They had nothing else, or at least they weren't about to share it. Anyone who died was taken out and buried in a mass grave.

The camp was unmarked. One day we got strafed by our own forces. An American fighter plane was pursuing a German jet. The jet came down low over the camp to avoid the American plane and as he made a pass over the camp the American fighter shot at the jet. Seven of our guys were killed. The camp was unmarked. After that incident the Germans marked it as a POW camp.

One night two of our guys got into the camp kitchen and were scrounging for food. A German guard came in to investigate the noise and got clobbered with a meat cleaver. The next day they turned us out of our barracks and made us stand in the cold for hours in front of this ditch. Guys were passing out from the cold. I thought they were going to machinegun us all. Here they were trying to find out who attacked this guard. They eventually got the two guys, and I'm sure worked them over and shipped them out to another camp. I recently found out that the guard survived. One of the fellas who attacked him ended up dying of natural causes a few years ago. The other is still alive. We all thought that the two were so weak that they really didn't have the strength to actually kill the guard.

Escape was always on everyone's mind, but there were no organized attempts to do so. The camp had gun towers, electric-wire enclosures, and we stayed away from them. Even if we would have had the opportunity to escape, we were too weak to really try. Still, one time I did get the chance to escape. I figured I was in better shape than most of the guys, so I volunteered to cut wood for our own use. They took the woodcutting crew outside of the camp. On the way back, we had a ten-minute break. I stepped off of the trail into the woods to take care of myself. As I was getting ready to come back, they were forming up the prisoners for the march back to camp. I figured I'd just stay there. I had a pretty good idea which way Switzerland was! Unfortunately, my buddies kept saying, "Where's Whitey?"

They were so loud about it, I just stepped back in line. I probably wouldn't have made it, anyway.

It was important to be active. I walked the perimeter every day. The guys that just lay down and gave up? They died. We did have a guy "hit the wire." He was a black man, one of two we had in the camp. One day he had had enough. He ran into the forbidden zone and jumped on the wire fence. A guard shot him dead, and he hung there for several days.

I was kind of a "chaplain" to this guy from Pittsburgh. Every other day he'd ask me, "Whitey, are we gonna get out of this?"

I'd tell him, "Oh, sure."

That seemed to satisfy him. Recently, I got a book concerning ex-POWs, and he's listed as deceased, but I know he made it back home. I was determined, at any rate, that I was going to get out of there. I was determined that they weren't going to kill me off. That was my attitude, and I think it helped.

The British in our camp had a radio that they made out of tin foil wrapping from a Red Cross package and other things they scrounged up. They were getting information about the outside world. Also one of the guards was somewhat friendly with one our men. He told him of the progress the American troops were making, so we knew they were coming, and we knew the Germans were taking a beating. We could see Frankfurt from our camp. In a three-day period we watched American bombers level a good bit of the city. One of our guards lost his wife and two daughters after one of those raids. He got pretty rough with us after that.

There was a guard who was a nice guy. His name was Schmidt, but we called him "Schmitty." He was regular army, the *Wehrmacht*. He was on that woodcutting detail, the time I thought about escaping. I had a container of soup with me for lunch. Three other prisoners and I had just sat down to eat. Schmidt came and sat down with us to eat his meal. He hung his rifle on a tree branch, and he took a knife out to cut his bread. He shared his bread with the four of us. Then he took that knife and ran the dull edge along the back of his wrist and then my wrist. He drew blood. He said, "The blood is the same."

Schmidt tried to pick up on American slang. He stayed in the camp when we were finally liberated, and we interceded on his behalf. The Americans who liberated us were roaming around the camp freely, and one of them was reaching for his pistol to shoot Schmidt. Fortunately, we stepped in and prevented him from getting shot. I think Schmidt returned home eventually.

We were liberated on 2 April 1945. I was in camp for 115 days. I weighed 185 when I was captured. When I was liberated, I got into one of the buildings and there was a scale. Even with three and a half months of dirt, my boots, field jacket, long johns, everything but the helmet, I weighed 110. And that was pretty much normal, I think. I had lost about forty-five percent of my weight. And I was an easy keeper. Some of these guys were in a bad state. When we were liberated, there were medics that came through there with tears in their eyes. We didn't realize how bad we were, because we were all losing this weight together. We didn't realize how bad we smelled, how bad we looked, until we saw them in tears. These guys looked like football players compared to us. Now that more than fifty years have passed ,the evidence is obvious that this camp director really wanted to kill us all. Some of our noncoms got the word that if we were close to being liberated they were going to march us down the road and shoot us all and say we tried to escape. But many of the German guards would not go through with it.

The unit that liberated us was the 106th Reconnaissance Group from the 44th Infantry Division. They heard that there were Americans in the camp and they went ahead of their lines by forty miles. They came through the front gates waving empty machineguns. They hardly had any ammunition left. Years later, the commander of the outfit spoke at one of our reunions. He told us that one of the worst days he ever had in the army was the day he liberated us and found out that the houses and buildings in town were full of Red-Cross packages that had been meant for us. He said it was a good thing they were low on ammunition. He and his men would have used it up, then and there.

I just sat down somewhere and thought about things. I had no energy left. The Russians who survived danced all over the place. Some of the Russians got out of the camp and went into town to beat up the women. They were enraged at the Germans. Some of our guys went into the town, but most of us had no strength for any of that. We stayed in the camp. I and five buddies were the only ones left out of our original squad of twelve. One of them found a five-pound bag of sugar somewhere. When I came into the barracks, they were sitting there with big smiles on their faces. They said, "Whitey, put out your hands and close your eyes."

I did, and they poured something into my hands. When I opened my eyes, it was sugar. With that first dab of sugar on my tongue, I could feel the heat go right down to my toes.

They couldn't get a kitchen up to us, so they brought in some C-Rations instead. Two guys died from eating a can of those rations. Their stomachs had shrunk so much that they ruptured. A few more guys died the same way later, at Camp Lucky Strike in Le Havre. They had gorged themselves on donuts.

The guys with jaundice were immediately transported to a hospital. They trucked the rest of us out of there. We went through delousing, and then they gave us brand new clothes.

Shortly after that, I was on my way home to New York Harbor on a hospital ship. Oh, some of these poor guys on that ship! Some didn't have chins or lower jaws. Some were blind. Some were vegetables. They were celebrating VE day in New York as we came into port. We saw the Statue of Liberty. Nurses brought these blind men up on deck to see the Lady of the Harbor. It was an emotional time.

Photographers and news people were all over the place. They had German prisoners in the cafeteria, and I guess one of the Germans said something to somebody, and one of our guys went after him with a table knife. Just that quick the German prisoners were out of there. After that the MP's served on the KP line.

I called home when I got a chance to let my folks know I was back in the States. Months before, my family received word that I was missing in action. They did not receive any further word about me until Easter 1945, when they learned I was a prisoner. A few days later they learned that I had been liberated from the father of one of my college friends who owned a newspaper. He recognized my name when it came across his Teletype. He phoned my parents and told them. A couple days later the Red Cross told them the same thing.

I told my folks I'd be home in a day or so. I dragged my feet and so did some of the others. I didn't know how to face them at home because of what I had been through. When I got to the railroad station at home, I saw something in my mother's face. Later she told me, "You didn't look at us, you looked through us."

And I was aware of it. I had the "Thousand-Yard Stare."

A fellow named Marty Talpus, from Nazareth, Pennsylvania, came home with me on the train. Marty got up to Nazareth, and he stood on the corner, trying to remember. He didn't know where his home was, anymore. Fortunately, the local police chief came along and said, "Hop in, I'll take you home, Marty."

They had blown us up quite a bit back on the hospital ship. At Lucky Strike, also, they just loaded us up with milk, ice cream, and vitamin pills by the fistful. It just made us puffy. We looked pretty good, but I was so weak even when I got home, if I squatted down I couldn't stand up unless I could also pull myself up. Also, I couldn't write my name anymore. I could print it one letter at a time, but I didn't have the coordination to write. I didn't get it back for at least a month, and, even now, I sometimes don't have it.

I worked with my dad once I got home. I really didn't like the business, but I wanted to help. I did go back and finish my forestry degree. I met my wife around that time. And then I stayed on and took a degree in horticulture and genetics. I was really one of the first forestry geneticists in the state, and I was employed as such.

About five or six years after the war I got restless, but I didn't know why. I may have been in denial, but once we came to our farm in Ligonier, Pennsylvania, during hunting season. I had sleepless nights because I heard gunfire in the distance. I really didn't put it all together until forty years after I got out of the service. My feet were hurting so bad that I went to the VA. There, they gave me a POW protocol exam and really made me aware that I had what has become known as Post-Traumatic Stress Syndrome.

Forty years ago, I couldn't talk about this. Sometimes I can't talk even today. I'm choked up a little now. But I don't have any sleepless nights anymore. I was glad to serve. I was glad to be associated with some truly heroic people.

"We Could Have Been Good Friends."

Joseph ("Sam") Seanor

106th Infantry Division, Field Artillery; New Alexandria, Pennsylvania,
15 February 1925

"The 106th was caught in the middle of the Kraut attack. Little groups of the division would hold out in a firefight for a little while, and then down they would go. Some lasted two or three days, but they had little ammunition, no heavy guns, no supply, no nothing. The 99th was on our left, and the 9th armored was dug in all around us, and they damn near all got wiped out too. Those jerks had their goddamned tanks dug in and they froze in the ground and couldn't get out."

I DIDN'T TURN SEVENTEEN until the February after the Pearl Harbor attack, so I wasn't old enough to go into the service. I got a job at the coal mine, and bummed around for a month. I didn't much like it, but I wanted to make a buck or two, and all the employers were begging for workers because many of the guys had enlisted. I was pretty lonesome myself because all my older buddies were in, and I was anxious to join them.

I got drafted on 18 February 1943. I didn't care which branch of the service I went into. My father would've liked me to stay home and help him work a farm, and my brothers were still in school, but Dad had a military background, and he understood. My mother didn't want me to go. I don't think any mother wants her son to go off to war.

On 2 March 1943, I went into Field Artillery at Fort Bragg. I ended up with a group of ROTC boys from Harvard, all of whom were drafted as a group. They were well above the intelligence of the average soldier, but they were nice guys all the same.

The Army had a program called ASTP (Army Specialized Training Program). Anyone who passed the entrance test, and who had an IQ above a certain level was automatically sent to school. Why? I have still not figured it out. I think they wanted to protect the geniuses so they wouldn't get killed! My IQ was quite beyond the minimum, and they sent me to Ball State Teacher's College in Muncie, Indiana, to a crash program there. I guess they wanted to see how much pressure we could take. I was slowly going down the chute, washing out, so I and a couple others in the same situation kept watching the bulletin board for other service possibilities.

One day the Air Corps came looking for people. We all signed up. A couple days later we were in the Air Corps. They took us down to Florida, and we went back to basic training in the Air Corps. Basic training was ridiculous, because I knew more than some of the instructors did. The drill sergeant usually sat under a palm tree while we bummed around. After basic training, I went to Basic Flight School in Walnut

Ridge, Arkansas. I was there for about seven weeks. A bulletin came through that all personnel previously trained in the ground forces would be returned to the ground forces. So I wound up with an infantry division on maneuvers in Kentucky. That was it. Tough! I thought I was going to die. I had been living a pretty easy life until then.

The Army put me in the 106th Infantry Division at Camp Atterbury, Indiana. The Army had sent all the privates and corporals in the division to Europe as replacements. All that was left were sergeants and ranks above that. We were filling in the gaps. The camp was near Ball State, where I was in school, so I knew the area. I became a pretty popular guy, a social promoter. I'd take the guys up to the college for fun and recreation.

Since I was trained on artillery, they put me in a cannon company. I worked with a low-silhouette 105mm howitzer. It was easy for me, and I knew more than the officers. They immediately made me a corporal, in charge of two howitzers and six guys. In late August 1943, we shipped out to Camp Miles Standish. We passed through Greensburg, and I saw some people I knew walking on the bridge above the train station. I wanted to call out and wave, but I couldn't because troop movements were supposed to be secret.

We went over to Europe on the *Queen Elizabeth*. After staying in England for a while, we boarded a small fishing boat that only held about thirty-five guys and crossed the Channel to LeHavre. The Krauts had the harbor blocked with sunken ships, and we had to wait for high tide. Our big stuff had to go back to England. The whole division went in bits and pieces. Whoever landed first just started to walk inland. And we walked the whole way across Europe into Belgium and the Ardennes Forest area where we set up a staging area. After the rest of our people and gear caught up with us, we went to St. Vith in Luxembourg. They assigned me to outpost duty for a tank and cannon company, and I was in charge of communications.

At dusk, we'd go out on patrol and return at daylight. We holed up in a little cement block creamery. From there we looked into a valley at the bunkers and tank traps of the Siegfried Line. We could see the Krauts coming around for chow. They were about a thousand yards away, and too far for any of us to take a shot at them. A lot of guys from the front needed a rest area, a quiet zone. The 2nd Division had taken a lot, so they pulled them back for rest and put the 106th up front on the second line. Everyone figured the Krauts didn't have much fight left in them, anyway. Ours was a green bunch, and never suspected otherwise. We didn't know what was in store for us.

It was December 1944, the coldest winter in Europe in decades. The fog, when it came in, was thick and damp. It got colder, and it started to snow. Then the sun would come out and the fog would lift. Then the fog would come back in, and it would snow again. When the fog was in you couldn't see, but you could hear for miles. It got colder and colder each day,

Around 13 December, we heard heavy motors start up in the valleys. It seemed odd. Then we heard the sound of tank treads, and all kinds of rattling noises. I called in every night for three or four nights. I'd tell them, "There's something going on up here."

A couple times I shot up some flares, hoping to see something. Nobody paid any attention to my messages. An officer said to me over the radio that the Krauts were just trying to scare us by playing those sounds over loudspeakers. Nobody paid any attention, at all.

And then it came. A big artillery bombardment. We got out of that creamery, and started down over the edge of the ridge. The barrage went over our heads, but we knew as soon as it stopped the Krauts would be coming for us. And we were right. We heard them yelling. They came to the creamery and blew the back out of the place. We set up a little machinegun. We kept them pinned down for a little while. This went on for quite some time. Finally, the end came.

The 106th was caught in the middle of the Kraut attack. Little groups of the division would hold out in a firefight for a little while, and then down they would go. Some lasted two or three days, but they had little ammunition, no heavy guns, no supply, no nothing. The 28th was on our right, and the 99th was on our left, and the 9th Armored was dug in all around us. They damn near got wiped out. Those jerks had their goddamned tanks dug in and they froze in the ground and couldn't get out.

We kept trying to find some shelter back in town, but we were cut off from everything. We got into a little house that had thick walls. The Krauts didn't seem to want to bother with us, like we were just some unimportant satellite or something. I don't know why, because we were doing some damage to them. We were in that building two days, and we put a lot of hurt on those Kraut troops.

My company captain and a whole squad of guys got killed trying to get to us. They'd come up to try, but we saw them all get killed trying to cross a field. It was strange. To me there didn't seem to be a lot of noise. It was all kind of muted, all the rifle and machinegun fire. Maybe it was the thick snow that muffled everything. I wasn't scared. I was too busy to be scared. I got scared later. I still get scared today when I talk about it.

Finally we ran out of ammo. They got in downstairs, and started shooting up through the floor. Then someone yelled what sounded like "Comrade." He was. In German. *Kamerad.* Then "Surrender" in English. Things got quiet. Somebody was on the steps outside the room.

We had two or three rounds left. I said, "Okay, if he comes in the door, we'll talk to him. Maybe he knows a little English. If he shoots one of us, the other two shoot him."

He came in the door, and he was holding a sub-machinegun. I never looked so hard at anybody in my life. He was just a kid, like me. He was a blond, blue-eyed, nice-looking kid. He could speak a little English. "Do what I say, and you will be alright," he said.

What could we do? We surrendered. We were worried. We had killed a bunch of them, and I know we wounded a lot more than we killed. They might have shot us right there, but they didn't. They took us back to the creamery, or what was left of it. They had their wounded in there, and some of our guys, too. When they found out that I had some medical training, they put me to work taking care of theirs and ours. I did that for seven days. At the end of that time, I was so exhausted I could hardly walk. I think playing medic sort of saved my butt. They were troops, just like us, and after we got acquainted with each other, we both realized that none of us really wanted to be there. Had it not been for the war, we could have been good friends. I learned sometime later that we were lucky the unit we confronted wasn't SS.

The kid who captured me came around four or five hours after he took us prisoner. He was shot through the knee. I dressed and bandaged his wound. He got his knapsack out, cut a big slice of bread and a hunk of some kind of salami, and gave it to me to eat.

A little while after we got captured, one of our trucks came down the road. What the hell they were doing coming down that road, I'll never know. Two guys were in front, and one guy was in back, the canvas cover was down. The Krauts just riddled that thing from side to side. The guy in back started screaming. His intestines were laying out in his hands and he was trying to push them back in. He lived maybe for a minute. A minute was long enough! One guy in front rolled down into the ditch on the other side of the road. He got captured. The other guy got shot through the head, right between the eyes. He ran twenty yards before he fell, but it was all just reflex. I know he never knew what hit him. He was a big, strong guy. He just kept going with that wound in his head, like a fullback going through the line. At the end he just took this dive, nose first, into the ground.

We left that dressing station. Four SS took us up to a big bunker in a collection area on top of a hill where they interrogated us. There were all kinds of Kraut brass in there. The little guy who questioned me could speak better English than I could. He had spent many years in our mid-West. He'd ask all kinds of questions, and every once in a while he'd throw in a sneaker. He knew more about me than I knew about myself. "Ah, yes. You are from Pennsylvania? You are about nineteen? You are from the secret 106th Division, finally come over from England?"

He gave all that kind of crap. He looked to be in his thirties. We were at that headquarters for one day. Then they loaded us into boxcars. We traveled all night. The wooden slats on the boxcars had big gaps in them, and we knew when we crossed the Rhine River. Finally, they put us in a prison camp, Stalag XIIA. At night, the Krauts launched V–2 rockets from down in a valley.

There was a sergeant with me, a Syrian from Alabama. There was Wilcox from Cleveland, and O'Brien from Watertown, New York. We got to be close friends. Right around Christmas time, the English decided they were going to bomb the shit out of the area. When the RAF bombed at night they would send three big Lancasters out, and they would drop flares in a triangle. Then they would come in and they would blanket bomb everything inside the triangle. Well, this night they miscalculated, and the triangle picked up about half the prison camp. The bombs killed a bunch of people, including two of my officers, Lieutenants Devlin and Newman. They were both in the same building. Nothing was left of it but a hole in the ground. Wilcox had a good voice, so he conducted the service. After we left that camp, I never saw

Wilcox or O'Brien again. We got split up.

For days after the bombing, all we did was clean up the rubble. Then they put us on boxcars again. We rode the whole way across Germany, through Berlin. We lay over in the Berlin rail yards and were scared to death. We figured the way those rail yards looked, all bombed up and all, that we were going to get caught in another British or American air raid.

We weren't treated too well. When we left the first prison camp, it was colder than hell. They told us not to take blankets, but a couple guys did. They wrapped them in strips around their legs. The Krauts found the blankets, and they beat the shit out of those guys, just hammered them to hell with rifle butts.

We got to Pomerania, a part of Poland. We could see smoke on the horizon. The Russians and the Krauts had a tank battle the night before. We were real close to that, or so it seemed. It was very flat country, and the smoke was much farther away than it looked. On my first day in the new camp, they put me in the hospital. I was in bad shape. My feet were frostbitten; I couldn't eat. I also had hepatitis; I was all yellow. I was down to about 120 pounds, which, for me, was pretty damned thin. I started out at 185 pounds. For a time, the doctor in the camp was a British captain who had been captured early in the war, sometime in 1941 or 1942. I always credited him with the fact that I made it home. The doctor had to use bandages that looked like crepe paper. He had no sedatives, nothing. The flu I had broke up, the frostbite cleared up, but left scars. I watched the doctor scrape one guy's feet clear up to his ankles. Some of the guys didn't keep their feet. They had to be amputated.

Eventually, they took all the walking prisoners out of that camp, and they left twenty of us back there with the doctor and the American medic, a young kid from Iowa. We stayed there several days, until the Krauts came back. There were three or four SS officers on a flatbed truck. They loaded us all on, except for one guy. The doctor convinced them that if they moved him then he would immediately die. The Krauts didn't press the issue. We climbed onto the truck, got to a railhead, and boarded another train. It was an anti-aircraft car, with two anti-aircraft guns on each end. We laid down flat, between them. We went north, then west. Somehow, I could sense that.

Suddenly, I smelled the ocean. We had traveled up near the Baltic Sea, where we were sent to an officers' camp. There were thirty thousand British and American prisoners there. They couldn't believe what we looked like. We were half-frozen and filthy. They made us post our names and our hometowns. Soon, four or five guys from Pittsburgh and Western Pennsylvania were taking care of me. I had a couple-inch beard, and I was crawling with lice. By March, I could get outdoors for short walks.

Our boys had a big bulletin board (they had it hidden so the Krauts wouldn't find it) all stuck with pins showing where the Russians were, where the Americans and British were. They had a terrific communications system. They knew more about the war, I think, than most of the generals on both sides knew. When a Kraut would come around, that bulletin board would disappear so fast you could hardly see how. It was in little sections, and all they did was take it apart, piece by piece, but in a hell of a hurry.

I had a little tin pail, oval-shaped with a wire handle, and a wooden spoon. Those two tools were our lifeline. The only way I could clean the spoon and pail was to scrape them with a stone. We called our rations "grass soup." I think it was made of vegetable tops and horsemeat. We got that once a day with a slice of heavy black bread. We were all poorly nourished, everybody. I don't think the civilians around the area had that much to eat at that point, either. It was pretty bad.

Some of the prison camps got Red Cross parcels out of Switzerland or out of Sweden, but at that first camp there were no parcels, there was nothing. When I first got over to Pomerania there were some Red Cross parcels. We all got milk, raisins, and a bit of chocolate. The second camp was the one the Krauts allowed the Swedish Red Cross to visit, so they kept high standards. The Swedes would come in, take a look, and go back saying, "Oh, my, look these people are doing good; they're taking good care of them."

The compound next to us was full of Polish prisoners. The Krauts used them as forced labor. They would march them out every morning and bring them back every night. The guys were disease-ridden, especially with diphtheria, and we were told not to go near the fence with any of them. Every morning a one-horse cart left their compound carrying a couple dozen frozen bodies. I never found out what those Polish guys did, but I suspected that they were repairing rails after bombing raids. They led a horrible life, but they were tough. Believe me, they had to be.

Eventually, the Russians overran the place. When they first came through, they looked like something out of Buffalo Bill's Wild West Show. The first wave stormed in on American Jeeps. They looked like Mongolians. They all had sub-machineguns, and there would be seven or eight of them hanging, crazy-like, all over those Jeeps. I'm sure that when they got back to their homes in Russia, they never again rode on anything that had a motor. Those Mongols shot anything that moved, and they thought we were gods. If you wanted something shot, all you did was point to it. BRRRRRRT! It got done. All their stuff was made in America. Here they came, driving a herd of cattle, Jeeps all spread out, and those loud bastards firing into the air. Crazy! Oh, my God! When they got into camp, they put up some cooking tripods, built fires, and started to slaughter the cattle for us to eat. Big mistake for me! I ate some, and then threw up all over the place.

I couldn't get out of that camp for weeks after my liberation. Our brass had to arrange transportation, negotiate with the Russians, and so on. When the "real" Russian army got there, they looked almost like a real army. They were all real sharp guys.

The Russians established a Corps Headquarters right outside the camp. The Krauts had mined it, so the Russians had to spend time de-mining it. Then the B–17s started to come in, a steady stream of them, and I flew out on one of them, back to France. The depot there had a constant chow line, but I passed out every time I got near the food. I weighed 118 pounds, and I was very ill. They took me to a General Field Hospital in Paris where I took a month recuperating. I got out a little bit, and

I got to see some of Paris. There was a subway stop right near the hospital, and I'd go out with a map of the city, and everyday I get off at a different stop. In the meantime, they kept telling us we were going to go home.

They came in one day in July 1945 asking for volunteers to help on a Liberty Ship that they had converted into a hospital ship. It was like a stampede with everyone trying to sign up. I managed to get on the list, and I came home. We were supposed to land in Boston, then New York, but we finally ended up landing in Virginia.

It was a fun ride, in a way. I never wrote to my parents. I don't know why. I was missing in action, as far as they were concerned. While I was in the hospital I had a nurse write to my mother to tell her I was okay, and that I was coming home. So, my mother knew I was all right. They didn't know when, but they knew I would be coming.

I had a sixty-day leave coming, after which I went to Fort Oak, Georgia, to a military correspondence unit. All I did all day was process papers discharging guys for medical reasons. I went to the doctor. He said, "OK, Seanor, you can have a medical discharge!"

Back home, through the Veterans' Administration in Pittsburgh, they gave me a fifty percent disability pension. I couldn't walk very well because my frozen feet weren't completely healed. The pension lasted for three years until the Army stopped it.

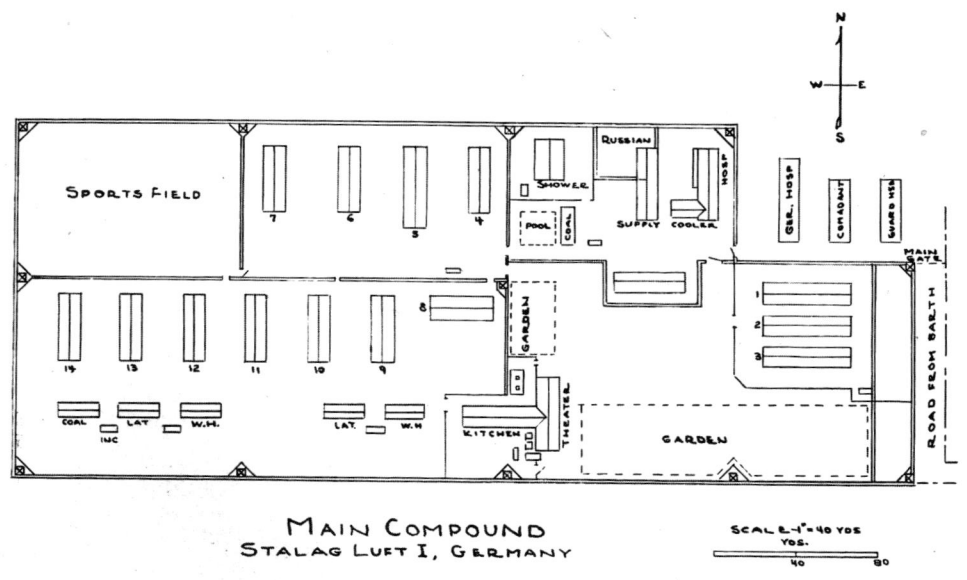

Diagram of the main compound, Stalag Luft I, Germany. *Courtesy of Pat Seanor.*

Pages from a Red Cross booklet given to John Seanor and his fellow POWs after their liberation.
Courtesy of Pat Seanor.

"NIX BARLEY!"

"That's Jones — Just returned from a P.O.W. camp!"

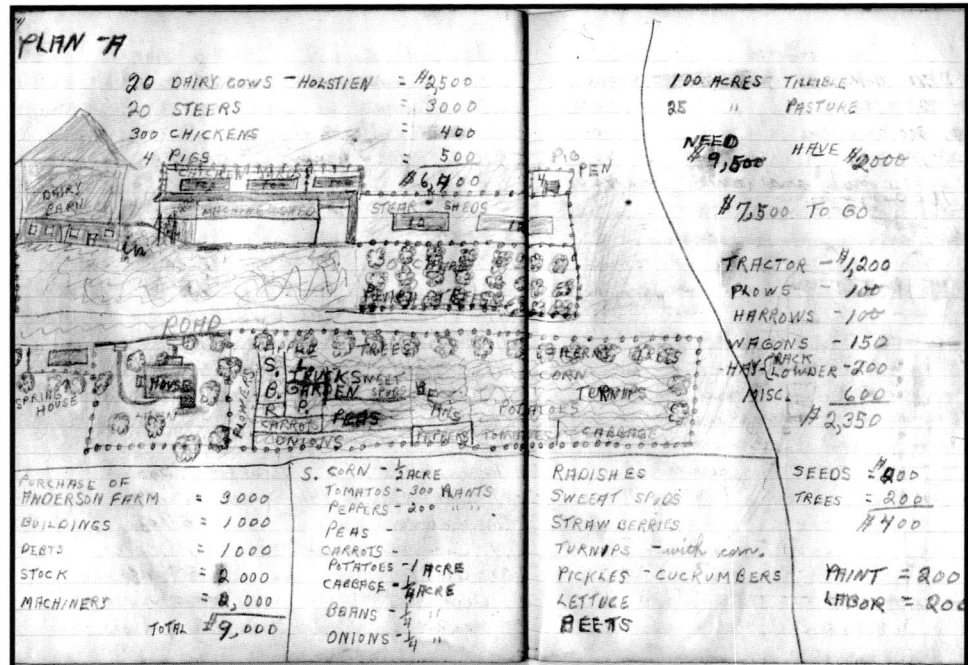

Pages from Joseph Seanor's POW diary. The men occupied themselves by planning their future after the war. Here, Mr. Seanor has drawn up a cost analysis for the purchase of a farm.
Courtesy of Pat Seanor.

"My Dear Boy! Are You All Right?"

John S. Slaney
Royal Air Force; Birmingham, England; Greensburg, Pennsylvania
1 March 1922

"We went past this place that I'd just shot up, and it was a shambles—body parts and bodies all over the place. I concentrated on not looking too satisfied with my work. I could feel this corporal press the Luger harder into me. He was obviously under some emotional stress, passing his dead buddies the way we did."

I WAS CALLED SAM during the war. The senior sergeant pilot on the first squadron I got to gave that name to me. I'd told them my name was John when I got there. And he was looking over my shoulder as I was writing up the next-of-kin and all that, full name and all that sort of stuff, and I wrote down "John Samuel Slaney" and he said, "Hey, this chap's not John, he's Sam!" So everybody started calling me Sam. He was killed two weeks later. That was in 1941. The name stuck all the way through the Air Force.

I went to Mosely Secondary School. I liked Latin and Math, but they threw me out of the Latin course after the first year because I was no good at it. I left school when I was fourteen. So my education was somewhat truncated. Eventually, I realized that I'd better do something about not having matriculation, which was the entrance to university, or a school certificate. In the early part of 1940, I got a first class certificate in the City & Guilds of London examinations in metallurgy.

I became an apprentice in a foundry and stayed in that job until I was nineteen, when I joined up. I made two dollars a week, for a forty-hour week, from eight in the morning to five-thirty in the evening, Monday through Friday, and then eight until one-thirty on Saturday. Low pay. Besides, I had to take deductions for insurance and unemployment. Working conditions were quite reasonable, actually, but they didn't heat the place.

In 1938, Neville Chamberlain, our Prime Minister, had called for one thousand pilots, but I was too young at the time. In the early part of 1939, he called for another thousand. By that time I was old enough. I went to the Volunteer Reserve, which is to say, "Weekend People." Once I got there I found a roomful of people all wanting to be pilots. A guy taking down names asked me, "What do you want to be?"

I said, "Pilot."

He said, "We're full up."

"Okay, I'll be an observer."

"We're full up there, too."

"Okay, I'll be an air gunner."

"Okay, we need some of those."

I filled in the forms and went home. In September 1939, Hitler attacked Poland and we were at war. My sister called me at work to say that there was an OHMS letter, "On His Majesty's Service." We worked not far away from each other so we met for lunch. I thought the letter was for my call up, but it said, "Owing to the present emergency, we've suspended recruiting in the Royal Air Force Volunteer Reserve." I thought it funny that they would turn down people who wanted to go in. Then the letter went on to say that if I still wanted to serve, I could join the RAF as a regular. I tried to do just that, three times. One time the office was closed, the next time they weren't doing any recruiting, and the third time it was something else. I thought, "Well, to hell with this; they don't know what they're doing."

So I stopped trying to join up.

Then in the early part of 1940, they issued another call up for pilots. Then I went to what they called a Combined Recruiting Center, which was in the YMCA. There were four tables, Army, Navy, Air Force and Ministry of Labor. I went to the Air Force guy and he asked me what I wanted to be.

"Pilot," I answered.

He told me to go over to the Ministry of Labor guy and he'd sign the form and they'd be calling for me. So I went to the Ministry of Labor guy and he said, "You can't join up."

"Why not?"

"You're in a reserved occupation. You can't join up."

I went back to work and saw the manager of my department. As luck would have it, he was an old Royal Flying Corps pilot from the First World War. I told him I didn't feel essential to the war effort. He said, "I can understand how you feel, my lad. I'll tell you what I'll do. I'll write a letter to the Ministry of Labor and tell them that you're absolutely useless to me, and that I want them to classify you as no good at all. Then I'll write another letter to the Air Force and tell them that this is merely a subterfuge, to take no notice of the classification, that this guy's all right. If you don't get in as aircrew, no joining the Army or the Navy. This is just to get you into aircrew. If you don't get into aircrew, you'll come back to work." So we had a gentleman's agreement on that.

I went along and I gave this letter to the Ministry of Labor people and the guy looked at me as though I crawled from under a stone. He gave me a form and threw it back at me. Then I went to the Air Force. I gave them the form from the ministry of Labor, and then I gave them the letter from my boss. They thought it was rather funny. They smiled about it. That's how I got in. That was 5 May 1940, shortly before the Germans broke through at Abbeville. *[Editors' note: Abbeville is a small French town in the Department of the Somme, about seventy-five miles northeast of Paris. The German breakthrough on 14 May completed the encirclement of Allied forces on the Channel, and hastened the fall of France in June 1940].*

For "swearing in" as we called it, I went to Cardington. I spent two days there, getting medical exams and all that sort of stuff. I remember going back and telling the guys about all these tests they gave me. One chap asked why they did all that testing. Another chap said, "Well, they can't have unfit men lying around dead, you know."

It was kind of a gallows humor.

At what was called "Receiving Wing," I got fitted up with uniforms and stuff. We did our six weeks of "square bashing" (basic training) at Aberystwyth, on the west coast of Wales, at an Initial Training Wing. We got lectures on such things as *esprit de corps*, general nonsense like that, and things like when to salute, and how one didn't stand around with hands in pockets, particularly with officers around. And then we did a lot of marching back and forth, and some training in ordering squads around, and doing guard duty at the hotels where we were billeted. The young girls would come around and giggle at us. I spent the first two weeks wishing I hadn't gone to all that trouble to get into it. I didn't like the restrictions and all that stuff. But, I soon got over that, and I got to like the Air Force.

I joined up as an AC/2, which was Aircraftman, Second Class. Then when I started flying training I became an LAC, a Leading Aircraftman. Then when we got our wings, one third of the course were commissioned and two thirds were made Sergeant Pilots. I was made Sergeant Pilot. Then I went to OTU, Operational Training Unit, and then to squadrons. After I'd been in a squadron about six months, I was commissioned as a Pilot Officer, or 2nd Lieutenant. After another six months or a year, I became a Flying Officer, or 1st Lieutenant. Then, after I'd been in different squadrons for about two-and-a-bit years, I took over a flight, which is half of a squadron, and became a Flight Lieutenant as it was called, which is like an Army Captain. Then I got shot down about six months after that, so that's where I stayed. They didn't give me any more promotions.

Elementary training was at an Elementary Flying Training School [EFTS] at Woodley from 12 October to 4 December 1940. I soloed in Miles Magisters, 100-horsepower with fixed undercarriage. If we didn't solo in ten hours, we were thrown off the course.

From 15 January to 15 May 1941, I attended Service Flying Training School at Tern Hill in the Midlands, and then I went to Number 56 OTU, an Operational Training Unit at Sutton Bridge. Sutton Bridge is on the east coast, where they were flying Hurricanes. That was from the 3 June to 14 July 1941. Then I joined Number 257 (Burma) Squadron at Coltishall, which is in the north of East Anglia just south of Sutton Bridge. That was from the 15 July to 8 November, and that's were I made my first victory, shooting down a Dornier 217 bomber that was attacking a convoy. Then we were posted to a place called Honiley for night defense of the Midlands. We were there from the 8 November 1941 to 6 June 1942. From there we went to High Ercall on the same job until 11 September 1942.

At that time we had been training with the Boston (Douglas A–20 Havoc). They had fixed lights on the front of these planes to assist us in night fighting. They had to put so many batteries on the Boston to power this light that they couldn't put any guns on it. In those days the airborne radar couldn't see closer than about one thou-

"Then there was readiness. We had to be in the air in five minutes."

sand yards, which wasn't too bad on a moonlit night, because the pilot could then edge forward and pick up the target. But, on a really black night you couldn't do that. So someone had the bright idea of putting this light on to illuminate the target. Since they couldn't put guns on the plane, they had a Hurricane fly with it.

Just after Pearl Harbor was attacked in December 1941, an American squadron was brought over from the States. I was talking with the Yanks in the mess about deflection shooting. They'd never had any instruction about front-gun fighting, and they didn't know what I was talking about. And they were an operational squadron! So they said, "Our CO ought to hear this."

They went and got their CO. He said, "I think the whole squadron ought to hear this. You just say when and I'll have all the squadron in the middle of the runway to listen."

I said, "Fine, I'll talk at your dispersal tomorrow morning."

So we spent the whole morning there talking about how to estimate deflection and that sort of stuff. After that, he said, "Well, what can I do for you?"

I said, "I don't want anything. We're all on the same side."

He said, "Would you like to fly one of our aircraft?"

I said, "Oh, yeah!"

A British squadron commander would never have offered that. Americans were much freer about it. He took me out to his own aircraft and showed me the switches, and off I went. When I came back, everybody on the station had heard that Sam Slaney was going to fly one of the American aircraft, a P–39 Bell Airacobra. In that plane the undercarriage retraction was just an electric switch, where on the British aircraft you had to pull the hydraulic lever up. It became quite a trick to keep the aircraft steady while you were doing that. With the Airacobra, all you did was click the switch and the undercarriage popped up. So everybody was very impressed with this straight takeoff I did. The Americans said, "Didn't you find that there was little space for your head and that the controls were far away from you?"

I said, "No, I thought it was very nice."

They said, "You didn't find that your head was hitting the top?"

The guy turned to the man next to him and said, "Hey, this guy's built like a monkey."

The Airacobra had a very low roof because the air intake for the engine was right behind the cockpit canopy. I had a short body and long arms. I was a perfect fit for the Airacobra.

Then we got re-equipped with Typhoons and these things cruised at 300 knots, while the Boston cruised at about 180. So you can imagine trying to formate at night, when you're really supposed to be flying at 300 and you're flying at 180, damn near your stalling speed. They decided to form squadrons called Turbinlites, and they'd have Hurricanes formatting with them. They formed No. 535 Squadron, and our CO was told to post six pilots from his squadron to make up the Hurricane pilots for No. 535 Squadron. So he posted the six newest and worst pilots he had. The order came back from Group, "This was no good. It's obvious you're sending your worst pilots. You've got to send experienced pilots."

It turned out I was one of those pilots. We figured if he couldn't send his worst pilots, he'd send the ones he liked the least!

Shortly after that 257 Squadron flew off down south to do some day defense. At that time the Focke-Wulf–190s were coming in with bombs under the wings and they were just dropping them on the seaside towns and going back again, so they stationed Typhoon squadrons there to fend off the 190s. We six were left at High Ercall with No. 535 Squadron from the 12 September 1942 to the 22 January 1943. There were six of these Turbinlite Squadrons and the only thing that ever got shot down was a Short Stirling, which is a very slow-flying British bomber. So they disbanded these squadrons on 22 January 1943.

On 23 January 1943, I was transferred to the No. 247 Squadron, which was called "British." Shortly after, they seconded me to Central Gunner School where I learned advanced tactics. We'd have discussions and some of the top marksmen would talk about aiming and fighter tactics and all that. Then we'd go off and do it, in Spitfires. The funny thing there was, they had WAAF's, Women's Auxiliary Air Force doing maintenance. You had to be a bit careful with them. I remember once I went up in this Spitfire and it was left-wing low, so you put a bit of tape on the aileron on the other side to bring it up level, those were the very rudimentary kind of methods we used.

I said to this girl, "It's left-wing low, let's get something on the aileron."

So the next time I went up in the same aircraft, it was still left-wing low. So I came down and started to bawl her out and she started to cry. We weren't used to aircraft mechanics crying.

At the tactics school, I learned some things, but it didn't add much to my basic knowledge. I learned a little about deflection shooting. Once I was on patrol over the north end of a convoy and I heard over the radio, "Fighters! Fighters!"

I looked around, and down at the south end of the convoy was this Dornier 217. I went tearing down after it, but I didn't get to him before he'd already bombed one ship, and he went around to have a crack at another one. As I was closing in, I was working out the deflection. I thought, well, he's doing about 200 miles an hour. I'll close at about thirty degrees. As I was closing in on him, I remembered what they'd said: "Whatever you think the deflection should be, double it."

So I doubled it, and POW! I hit him in the left engine. When I closed on him, I expected his gunner to fire at me with 7.62 machineguns, and I wasn't too bothered by that caliber. His rounds seemed to come at me slower than they should have. I learned later that the gunner was using a 20mm cannon!

At gunnery school we also learned how bombers worked. At one stage of the training we flew in a bomber's tail turret to operate the guns and watch what a fighter looked like coming in. Then we learned that after attacking a bomber to throw on hard right or left rudder and throw the stick in the same direction. That was a violent maneuver, very uncomfortable, because you get thrown around in the cockpit. But it throws the enemy gunner's aim off. I never got to do that maneuver in actual operations. I either couldn't catch the bomber or I wasn't involved in that kind of operation.

My first night combat mission was an unfortunate one. We were running convoys up the east coast and the Germans would come in and attack them. I'd gone out with my flight commander (we used to go out in pairs), and the idea was to patrol around the convoy until you lost contact with your Number One in the darkness, and then you carried on until you figured you couldn't see anything anyway. Then you went back home.

I lost him in the dark, but I could still see the ships, so I thought I'd stay around for a bit. I got low on fuel, steered west, but couldn't recognize the coast. I saw what we used to call a "scarecrow," which were lots of searchlights all around an airfield. The idea of that was if an enemy aircraft came in to attack at low level, all these searchlights would blind him. But, I was naive enough to think that ours was the only airfield in the area with searchlights around it. So I flew to this airfield, I could see by the buildings that this wasn't my field. I was lost. So I called for a homing, and they gave me one.

On a night approach, you have the engine on to control your descent. I was about a mile or so from the airfield and the engine conked out. I'd run out of fuel! I'd gotten my wheels down by this time, but not my flaps. I knew I had to get the flaps down. So I selected flaps and pumped them down with the hydraulic hand pump. I got my speed down as low as I could. I saw out of the corner of my eye this huge black shape glide past and then, BAM! I thought I was going to be killed. Then there was this was this BANG, BANG, BANG! I was being knocked around the cockpit. Suddenly there was this damned great PLUNK! I got thrust forward and caught the bridge of my nose on the reflector side. I thought, "Well, I suppose I'm dead now!"

I wasn't an agnostic then, and I wondered if I was going to meet old Saint Peter. Then I saw the phosphorescent instruments and realized I was still alive, so I got out of the plane as fast as I could. I ran away from it in case it blew up. All the crashing about, I discovered, was my having run through an iron fence in front of a rather well-built farmhouse. The plane had gotten tangled up in that, a good thing because it stopped me from going straight into the house. The big, black thing that I'd seen go

"Sometimes we had rockets. Sometimes we loaded thousand-pound bombs."

by turned out later to be a very solidly built church tower. I'd landed across from the best field in the neighborhood.

A little old lady came out carrying a light. She didn't know whether I was German or English.

"My dear boy! Are you all right?" she asked.

"Oh, yeah, I'm okay."

"Well, you've got blood all over your face! You'd better come into the house. My sister is making tea. Would you like a cup?"

I thought about all the racket the crash made, and imagined what the scene in the farmhouse was like and the conversation:

"What was that awful noise?"

"I haven't the slightest!"

"Oh, you go out and find out, while I make a pot of tea."

Those two were remarkable. Totally unflappable.

I had a cup of tea with the ladies, and then asked them if they had a phone. They didn't. They directed me to the village police station. In the meantime, an Army guy had shown up. I asked him to guard the plane while I went to call the airfield. I went down to the police station and got hold of my flight commander, who was pretty teed off about being disturbed at that time of the night.

He asked, "Where are you?"

I said, "I'm in the police station in the village."

"Who's looking after the airplane?"

"There's an Army guy watching it."

"Well, you're all right, aren't you?"

"Yes."

"Well, you'd better get back and guard the airplane!"

The next day I was called before the station commander, a Group Captain. I told him that I'd run out of fuel, that I'd run out on main tanks and then switched over to gravity. But, it turned out I still had about three gallons of fuel left in the main tanks.

He said, "You've got fuel in your main tanks."

"Ah, yes."

"You asked for a homing."

"Yes, Sir."

"You should have asked for an emergency homing, shouldn't you have?"

"I didn't think it was an emergency, Sir."

"Well, it was an emergency because you were lost! You were careless, weren't you? That's what it amounts to." You were careless, weren't you, Slaney?"

"Yes, Sir!"

The long and short of it was I was admonished, got seven days extra duty pilot, and a notation of carelessness in my logbook. If there was any night flying to do, extra duty pilots had to go down to the end of the runway and marshall the planes, an early version of flying control.

I flew combat for two years and eleven months. There was a period when I was in a fairly quiet sector and so that's probably why I lasted so long. In January 1943, Squadron 247 had twenty-five pilots. There was a guy in my tent who had a list of the pilots. Every time someone would get killed, he'd put a cross against the airman's name. I thought this was a pretty bizarre kind of activity. Anyway, one day he got killed. And I looked at that list and put a cross against his name. And I kept putting crosses up there, so I had a rough idea what was going on with this squadron. There were only six of that squadron left alive at the end of the war. And one of those got killed just after the war. But this was a fairly busy time, operationally.

If our mission was a defensive one, there were several states of readiness. One was release, of course. Another was thirty minutes, the time we had to get into the air. Next was readiness when we had to be in the air in two minutes or less. Then there was standby, and there we had to be in the air in less than a minute. Readiness meant having our Mae West life jackets on, parachutes either on or in the aircraft, and the engines warmed up and ready to go, so I could just start it and go. Of course, the ground crew would be out at the aircraft, ready to help. For standby, we had to be at the end of the runway, strapped in, helmet on, and ready to go. That was when we were defensive against the 190s that were coming in during the latter part of 1943. They were coming in low down, with very little warning, and we had to get off quickly. The other state of readiness was on patrol. We would fly on a patrol line for an hour, low down so we could get a chance to see them coming. What we would do at that time was, we'd do a patrol, go back and then immediately come up to thirty minutes. Then the next hour we'd be up to readiness, the next hour on standby and the next hour we'd be back on patrol. We were spread pretty thin. We didn't have too many squadrons available for this kind of work. The Typhoon was the fastest aircraft we had at the time. We were getting rather tired doing that.

Here is a story that points out something about the nature of war. One night, between July and November 1941 (we were really a day squadron), the Germans were bombing at night, so they used to send us up to see if we could see anything. I went up over East Anglia near the east coast. I intercepted a twin-engine, single-fin aircraft. And that far north you get a faint glow in the northern sky. Against the glow I could have sworn he was a Junkers Ju–88. So I slid behind him, got him in my sights and was just about to open fire and I took another look. Now he looked like a Bristol Blenheim, one of our aircraft types. I moved back beside him, and got him against the light again, and he looked like a Ju–88. I went back behind him and he looked like a Blenheim. I couldn't make up my mind. So I called control and asked him what was in the air, Ju–88s or Blenheims?

He said, "We've got both up there. You'll have to make up your own mind."

So I checked the plane a bit more. I decided to let him go. I thought it better to let some German escape, than kill some of our own.

Later on, when we were defending against Focke-Wulf–190s, I was getting a bit teed off. We were on patrol constantly, and I was getting tired, especially because of the longer, summer days. I called the operational controller one day and I said, "Look, this is stupid. We're chattering away on the patrol line, they know we're here, it's a total waste of time, this. They'll never come. But if we keep radio silence, then they'll think we're not here and they'll come and we'll get them."

And the controller said, "Hey, Slaney, have you forgotten what we're doing this for? We're doing this so they won't kill our civilians. And you want to use our civilians as bait so you can go chasing them?"

By 1944, just after the invasion, I was a flight commander. The CO would lead one operation then I'd lead one, then the other flight commander would lead one, to spread out the load. I had the squadron and we were in front of the bomb line, which the army was not supposed to cross. Once we crossed the bomb line, we could attack any military stuff we saw. So I was way down, maybe thirty or forty miles past the bomb line with the squadron, looking for stuff to attack. And drawn up in one of the side roads was all sorts of British equipment and tanks. I carried on and did an orderly turn about, which didn't give them any indication I'd seen them. I knew I was way south of the bomb line. I thought it was either our people who had ignored the bomb line, or those were tanks that had been captured and the Germans were keeping them there, waiting to launch a confusing attack. So I thought, the hell with it. I went down on them with rockets and knocked a lot of them out.

It turned out later that they *were* British who, in fact, had ignored the bomb line. After Dunkirk, when the British Army was driven out of France, the Army hadn't thought much of the Air Force's effectiveness. Well, they hadn't seen any of our planes because the pilots were behind the lines, fighting the Luftwaffe. So the Army didn't really think the Air Force was all that effective. And these guys had just ignored the bomb line and gone on. So the next day, our Air Officer Commanding (Broadhurst) was at our dispersal.

He asked, "Who was it that attacked those British tanks yesterday?"

I answered, "I did, sir."

I thought I was going to get "torn off a strip," as we used to call it.

He said, "It's just as well. The Army ignored the bomb line and thought that we were ineffective. Not very many of them got back, but they know now that when they call for us, that they'll get results. Good show, my lad."

So you see, I'd slowly changed from a guy who'd rather let some Germans go than possibly killing our own people, to actually killing some of my own people. Of course, it wasn't cold blooded. There was every reason to attack, really, but it lives with me all the time.

Our time before we contacted the enemy varied. If we were going over to France, and of course, during 1943 and the early part of 1944, we were always going across the Channel, we'd be about fifteen minutes before we were over their territory. Then we might get shot at by flak or tangle with fighters. Sometimes we had bombs under our wings and sometimes we had rockets. It depended on how far we were going. If we were going beyond Paris, it would take about three-quarters of an hour to get there. Most of my fighting was in a ground attack role, but I did get into a few scrapes in the air. I feel sure I got a 190 off Le Havre.

I was flying with another chap; Atcheson was his name. He was a Scotsman, and was later killed. We were on a long-range trip to stir up some trouble deep into France. We had long-range tanks on. The idea was you'd use up all the fuel in the extra tanks, then switch over to main tanks and drop off the long-range tanks. You couldn't cross that coast unless you were above 8,000 feet or in cloud. All along the coast the Germans had light anti-aircraft batteries, which could reach up to 8,000 feet. So it was more than your life was worth just to go over in daylight, let alone in clear skies. So if the weather was too bad for big operations with lots of aircraft, you'd take another aircraft, sometimes four, but usually two. You had to be able to use the clouds for cover. Once you got over the coast, you were safe.

When we got there, it was clear. No clouds at all. So I thought we'd take a sweep down the coast and not cross the coastline, to see if we could find any German aircraft to shoot at or something to attack. But I kept the long-range tanks on, because I didn't want to waste them or the fuel that was in them. We saw a couple of aircraft inland from us, and then we saw a couple of 190s further out to sea. They must have seen us at just about the same time, because they turned to attack. I told my wingman to drop tanks, but one of my tanks came off and the other wouldn't. So we battled below 500 feet with these two guys, and I kept going into a spin, you know, because the tank was still on.

Then I found myself coming at him head-on. And my thoughts went back to the comic books I used to read when I was a kid. In them, the World War I German pilots always turned away from head-on attacks. So I thought, that's what I'd do. I kept straight on and I opened fire and he didn't. He turned away. My Number Two was dealing with the other one. He was getting onto the other guys' tail, but we'd been around there long enough for them to have alerted their field. I thought we'd better get home. So we flew back. I did actually damage him; I saw the strikes on him, and he was going down. It was very likely that he did go in because we were so low, but I didn't actually see him hit the ground. The rules were you didn't claim it unless you actually saw it go in or saw parachutes from a single-seater.

Since we were familiar with German airfields around Caen and Amiens-Glicy from which the Germans took off on night raids and were seen by our radar, we'd go down to radar control in Manston and sit around wearing dark glasses in a low-lit hut, getting used to the dark. They'd get word that the Germans were coming up from Amiens, for instance, and the guy in charge would say, "Who knows Amiens?"

Someone would raise a hand and say, "I do."

Then we would fly over to Amiens and hope to catch them on their return flight. The idea was that I could catch them making approaches with their navigation lights on. But I never did have any success with that. Actually that was about the loneliest kind of job I ever had. I was out there in the dark on my own, the whole time wondering if there was someone out there doing the same to me, trying to catch me from behind.

When we would be bomber escort, we would be fairly low, about ten thousand feet. The Germans would come down at a hell of a lick, and as they came down, we'd wait until they were just about in firing range, then we'd break formation. Number Twos would try to hang onto their Number Ones. That was important to survival. If you were lucky enough to get a German in your sights, you'd give him a squirt. Many times when you broke you'd find yourself all alone. It's incredible how quickly the sky emptied. And also how quickly one could get clobbered.

I finally got shot down. That day we'd gotten up at about four o'clock in the morning for a predawn attack on a defended locality. Then we were to land on a strip on the Normandy beachhead. We went over with rockets and attacked a place that was holding up some of our troops. By that time the Army was really getting used to the idea that they had the protection of Typhoons carrying six-inch rockets, equivalent in power to a round from a six-inch gun on a cruiser. We were the only mobile thing that could knock out a Tiger Tank.

We took off in the dark and got over there by dawn and hit this place. Then we landed on airfield B–3. We just hung around there waiting for another job. While we were there, I saw one of these big graders, with the blade on it for building airfields. Then, in came this Flying Fortress, a B–17. And who should pop out but Ike Eisenhower. He got into a Jeep and went off to visit somebody or other.

Right about lunchtime, I said to the guys, "It's about time we see if we can get something to eat around here."

So we got a Jeep from somewhere. Eight of us were hanging onto this Jeep, and when we passed this mobile command post a guy yelled, "Are you 245?"

I said, "Yeah."

He said, "We've got a job for you."

They wanted us to do an armed reconnaissance of the Caen-Falaise Road, which meant to go up and down the Caen-Falaise Road and knock out anything we saw. We waited for some DC–3s to take off with wounded going back to England, and then we took off in a great cloud of dust.

I went up and down this Caen-Falaise Road and there was nothing there. The Germans weren't moving in the daytime then. So I moved west to see what I could find there. And I found some halftracks deployed around a wood. I thought, "Ah, antitank guns!"

So I left one section upstairs and took the other section down to rocket these halftracks. We used to fly in eight, two sections of four. They weren't antitank guns! They were four-barreled anti-aircraft guns. I gave them a squirt of cannon fire to throw off their aim, but it was useless. I found out later that it wasn't the usual bunch of inexperienced conscripts manning the guns; they were veterans from the Eastern Front, and no amount of cannon fire was going to intimidate them.

I saw my aileron tear away, and the tail plane must have been hit because the control column wouldn't move. The bottom of the cockpit was on fire. I was going in at about 450 knots, and I knew I had better get out. I decided to let them have the rockets, so I ripped off four pairs. I jettisoned the hood (canopy) and started to get out. Of course, the air at that speed was like a brick wall. It tore my helmet off and blew my face around. I got stuck with my parachute on the combing of the cockpit and I couldn't move. So I bent back down and wiggled my way back in and squatted on the seat. I pounded the control column, which had a little bit of movement, and that shot me out of the plane. Of course, I was gamboling and I saw ground, sky, ground. When I saw ground the second time, I pulled the ripcord so hard that the cable came out. I let it go, and, as it fell away I thought, "Damn! The Royal Air Force is going to take that out of my pay!"

Then the parachute opened, Bang! I swung three times and hit the deck. I was so low, in fact, that nobody saw the parachute. Everybody thought I had been killed. I actually saw my burning aircraft hit the ground. On the third swing, I looked back, I was swinging backward, and I saw this bloody big barn coming. I thought, I'm going to get mashed against a barn and killed, anyway. But, fortunately I hit the ground and gamboled. I stuffed the parachute under a hedge. I was in the backyard garden of a French cottage in this little hamlet. I ran down through the garden and there was a young woman there with a little boy and an old lady. Years later I met the woman. It turned out that she was eighteen when we first met, and I was twenty-three.

The old lady was looking at me wide-eyed and I said, "I'm English."

The young woman said, "Yes, I know. Go upstairs."

I don't know how she knew I was English. So I went upstairs and looked out the window. I saw Germans going into all the houses in the hamlet.

I went back down again and said, "Look, I can't stay here. If they find me here, they'll kill you for sure."

The young woman said, "No, go back up!"

I went up again and had a look around. I couldn't see anywhere to hide at all. I went back down.

"No, I can't stay. Where are the *Boche*?"

The woman kept telling me to go back upstairs. She was a tremendously brave woman. So I asked the little boy where the Germans were and he pointed in three directions. So I ran in the direction he didn't point, and I ran into half a dozen of them. They were SS, and they had *Leibstandarte Adolf Hitler* bands around their cuffs. I figured I was in for it! They put me on the back of a truck, sort of like a Jeep, and this corporal put his Luger down my neck. They took my Smith and Wesson .38 from me. I used to keep an empty chamber under the hammer for safety. When the Germans saw that, they couldn't figure that out why anyone would keep an empty chamber in a revolver. We went past this place that I'd just shot up, and it was a shambles—body parts and bodies all over the place. I concentrated on not looking too satisfied with my work. I could feel this corporal press the Luger harder into me. He was obviously under some emotional stress, passing his dead buddies the way we did. Fortunately, they took me to their CO. They held me there for a time, and then sent me down the line to a large house that was their headquarters. A couple guys were standing around with submachineguns.

Soon, their CO came up, a *Hauptmann* (captain). He wasn't a bad chap, actually. He, too, was wearing the Adolf Hitler cuff band. The captain and I chatted for a while, and he asked me what I was flying.

I said, "Sorry, can't tell you that."

"Ah, orders?"

"Yes."

Then he said, "I'm sorry, but we've had our midday meal. I'll have some food sent up to you when we have our evening meal, then I'll send you back down the line. You understand, if you try to escape, we shoot to kill."

Then he asked me if I was wounded.

I said, "Yes." I had this scratch where my cufflink had been torn out. He thought that was a good joke. We laughed over that. I still have the other cufflink.

Then he gave me a Nazi salute, saying *"Heil, Hitler!"* So I gave him a proper British salute. He left me with this young fellow who had a machinegun. I was looking out the window trying to appraise my situation when this young chap pointed to his gun and said, "Hmm. Many bullets in here for one man."

The captain sent me back in his staff car, which was rather nice. There was a driver and a sergeant, a *Feldwebel*, in the front. They gave me cushions and blankets so I could sleep if I wanted to. They were pretty nice, actually. I would soon run into a couple of bastards, however. The driver was drinking Schnapps, and he offered me the bottle!

The other one wasn't about to give me any. *"Nein!"* he said. The other one said, "*Nein*!"

He wasn't about to let him give me schnapps.

The roads were absolutely jammed with equipment. I thought, "Boy, if only I could get back and tell them to drop some flares over here, they could really do some damage to them."

They got me and a bunch of prisoners in a school in Chartres, in one of the dormitories. They'd got machineguns at either end. There were a whole bunch of British troops, people who I'd been supporting early on. They had been quite far forward and they had been surrounded and captured.

A sergeant said, "I'm going to tell them I'm a cook."

I said, "No, you don't do that. You just tell them your name, rank and number and nothing else. Don't tell them any lies. You tell them that and nothing else."

These guys didn't have a clue about interrogation methods. They hadn't been taught about that sort of stuff. I told him to gather the men around. I jumped up on a nearby table and said, "Now look, you guys don't seem to know about German interrogation methods. You don't tell them any lies. You just tell them your name, rank and number. Don't trust anybody you didn't know before you were captured. Don't trust me, don't trust the padre if you didn't know him before."

Then I heard a couple Germans cock their machineguns, so I thought I had done enough instructing. Shortly after I'd given this talk, the padre, who'd been dropped in an ecclesiastical stick of paratroopers with his portable altar and such said, "What do you mean by telling the men not to trust me. They've got to trust me. I'm a padre."

I said, "It's okay if they knew you before, but you could be anybody. The Germans could have planted you here."

I kind of calmed his clerical feathers down. He was really ruffled. He thought I was being sacrilegious or something. Shortly after that they pulled me out and took me in town to the civilian jail. There I ran into a real bastard, another interrogator.

"Oh," he said, "Where were you born?"

"Sorry, can't tell you."

"So," he said. He sneered and showed his gold filling, and from that time on, I kind of disliked gold fillings.

"You are not born?"

"Well, you could say I was born."

"Who is your commanding officer?"

"I can't tell you that!"

So he opened a kind of a curtain on the wall and he said, "We've got all of your order of battle, and we know every commanding officer, every flight commander. We don't find your name on it."

When I saw it, he'd had an old battle order. It was 16 Wing, which was now called 121 Air Field. I said, "Well, I can't help that."

He said, "Well, the only conclusion we can draw is that you're a *franctireur* (terrorist). We're going to send you to the Gestapo. You know about the Gestapo?"

"Yeah, I know about your Gestapo."

"Well, I've finished with you. You can go to the Gestapo."

They marched me off to solitary confinement in a French civilian jail where I spent a few days. My cell was full of bed bugs. After a while they sent me back to the others and we were off to Paris. While we were waiting in a rail coach at the Gare de l'Est, the French were very good to us. They cheered us and laughed. A very good-looking young woman about my age came over to us holding a tray filled with bottles of *vin ordinaire* (common wine). She passed the wine to us, and we drank it up. She went back to a crowd that was being kept back by the Germans. As senior officer of the group, I said to the guys, "Anybody got any escape money?"

Before we left on flights, they always gave us escape money. Funny that they hadn't taken it all away from us up to then. We had a look around and got some money, and I called this woman back and I said, "Go and get us some more wine." Which she did. The German guards didn't seem to know how to deal with that. Anyway, we were soon on our way to Germany.

American P–47s would make tactical strikes while we were on the road. Each time the Germans would stop the train and pile out into a ditch, but they'd keep us in the train. I spoke to the officer of the guard. I said, "This is a bit silly. There's no point in having us as targets here. How about if I give you a parole, and when an attack's on you let us get into the ditch? Then when the attack's over, we'll get back in the train and the parole will be over."

He wasn't really a military man. He'd been a lecturer at Heidelberg University. He said, "Okay."

So, one time when an attack came, he'd let us get out of the train and we were all over the place. Now, I'd told our guys, "Now, for God's sake, none of you escape while this is on, because I've given a parole for all of us."

So our guys were all over the place in ditches and around this French farm that was just by the railway line. I was talking with this French farmer.

He said, "Come on, I can hide you. I can take you around the back here."

I told him, "Sorry, I can't do that because I've given a parole during this attack."

And the Frenchman said, "Oh, piss on that!"

But I honored the parole.

Just out of Paris the train started up an incline, and it was going very slowly. We were in an ordinary French third-class carriage with wooden seats. And it had a corridor. I drew the guards away in conversation about the V–1s. One of the guards had lived in Chicago and he said, in an American accent, "What do you think about our V–1s?"

I said, "They're not very good, really, because they only carry one-thousand pounds of explosives. They go over and they're finished. They don't come back. Our Lancasters take 20,000 pounds of explosives and come back again, most of them."

While I had his attention, five of the guys jumped off the other end of the coach. After this, the officer with whom I arranged the parole, said "When did you last see them? I can't be nice to you! Why did you do this to me?"

I said, "Well, I'm sorry, we've got to escape. It's our duty. But, I saw them just was we were leaving Paris."

We went on and we got to Frankfurt. Oh, there was terrific damage. Every building was gutted. There were no roofs, just some walls standing. In late afternoon, they took us by light railway to a *Dulag Luft* (a main interrogation center for airman) at a place called Oberusel, near Wetzlar. They gave us two pieces of bread, and then I was put in solitary from 1 to 15 July 1944. Usually people stayed in solitary only one day, but they kept me there for two weeks. Afterwards I realized why that was. It was most likely because they'd got me tagged as a troublemaker, you know. I was the senior officer of this group and five guys had gotten away. They interrogated me quite a bit there.

These interrogators were Intelligence people. They had a red patch on their shoulder. And I think they had the zigzag, so that was something to do with the SS. They said, "It is evident that you're a *franctireur*. You've told us that you're a flight commander."

I hadn't told them I was a flight commander, but I had two bars on my shoulders that meant I was like a captain.

He said, "You're a flight commander, and we've got no record of you in our British battle order. So we're just going to ship you off to the Gestapo."

And, by golly, they took me back to my cell. I heard a great clattering. They came down the corridor and slammed open the door of the cell next to me and started yelling at this guy in there. They put chains on him and led him off and let him know that they were taking him to the Gestapo.

I thought, "Christ! They're going to do that to me!"

But then they didn't do anything, and I thought, "Well, they were giving me a show to try and get me to believe they were going to do that."

And they always called me "Mister Slaney." They wouldn't call me "Flight Lieutenant."

Then after a while this guy came into the cell and he said, "Flight Lieutenant Slaney?"

I thought, "Ah, they're going to let me out"

"We're moving you to a POW camp today."

Then it was over.

In the *Dulag*, the guards were old enough to be my father or grandfather. For breakfast, we got some *ersatz* (fake) coffee with no cream or sugar in it and two bits of bread with some *ersatz* margarine on it. For lunch we got a bowl of thin soup. Then for dinner, we got two more bits of bread and some more of this coffee stuff. So, I would save a bit of the bread so I could mop up the soup to get every last bit of it. I also saved a bit of bread for afternoon tea, because they'd let you have a bottle of water in your cell. I mean, I had bread and water, kidding myself that the water was tea!

One lunchtime I was scraping away around this bowl to get the last bit of soup. I was bloody hungry, you know! And this old guard came in. He was a gentle kind of an old soul. He said, "*Haben sie Hunger*? 'Are you hungry?'"

"*Ja, Ich habe Hunger.*" I knew enough German to tell him that.

So he held his hand out for the bowl, and I gave him it and he went out. He came back with another bowl of soup for me.

Eventually I got out of that *Dulag*. They took us back to Frankfurt on a light railway, where we got into a first or second-class coach, very comfortable, but it had bars on the windows, specially made for POWs. Just before we got to Berlin, we were stopped next to another train and I got to talking to one of the guards, who was from Alsace. We conversed in French as well as we could. There was a German man in the other train and he looked at me and his eyes were flaming. He turned to the guard and asked "*Terrorflieger* 'terror flyer'?"

The guard said, "Ja."

I figured if that guy could have gotten his hands on me he would have murdered me, because they were suffering tremendously from Allied bombing raids.

As we approached Berlin, the officer of the guard said, "You will be kept overnight in one of the stations in the center of Berlin. I ask you to tell your men to keep all the blinds drawn, because I can't answer for the consequences if the civilians find you."

I appreciated the good sense of that.

An air raid developed that night. That was something. I'd been in some air raids in England, but that one in Berlin was terrible. We weren't very far from a flak tower. They had these big flak guns, big ones. Those things were thundering away, and the bombs were coming down. Fortunately, the railway station didn't get hit at all. But, that was some attack.

After that we were moved north to Barth, which is between Rostok and Stralsund near the island of Rugen on the Baltic coast. In our compound there were about 300 RAF and about 800 Americans. Then there were three other compounds, and they were all Americans. There were about one thousand in each compound.

We were in huts with rooms on either side, with about sixteen people in each room. There was a corridor down the middle of the hut. Everyone gave their place a name. I remember one was called "Quit Your Bitch-Inn." Our room was called "Australia House," because that's the name of the Australian legation in London. There were a bunch of Australians who didn't have a flight lieutenant and the Germans insisted that at least a flight lieutenant be in charge of each room. So these guys asked me if I'd be their flight lieutenant. So I was living with a bunch of Australians. I stayed there until the end of the war.

We had set routines in the camp. In the morning, there would be an *apel*, which was a count, and in the evening there would be another. We'd have to get out and parade and they'd count us. And whenever anybody got away, that was a big time, because people would move between the ranks to screw up the count. The Germans couldn't work out what the hell had happened. They weren't sure if they'd lost someone or not.

A few people got out, very few. It was difficult because the water table was only about four feet below the surface there. So you couldn't go down deep with a tunnel, or you'd be in the water. The escape committee had taken our bed boards to shore up the shallow tunnels. The Germans used to drive a heavy oxcart around the outside of the fence every so often to collapse any tunnels that might be around. They did find one. The Germans also had microphones buried in the ground to catch the sounds of any tunneling that was going on. I never got onto an escape group, because you had to be in the POW camp for some time and work your way up.

First of all, you started as a "Penguin." The Penguins had long bags down their sleeves and tied around their necks, which were filled with the soil from the tunnel. The Penguins would walk around the compound slowly dribbling the soil out of their sleeves, so it would get scattered around and wouldn't be noticed. Then you could become a member of the XYZ Organization. They did all kinds of things—planning escapes, making committee assignments, forging papers, and so on. Then you got into the tunneling. Then you got onto the escape crew, the ones who were going out. It took a long time to work your way up. I was POW for only eleven months, so I didn't have time to work my way up in the hierarchy of the tunneling business.

Shortly after I got there, there was this American chap standing near our tent. We were living in tents at this time, because they didn't have enough space. There were these guide ropes, and suddenly this American nipped up the side of our tent and cut one of our guide ropes off. I said, what the hell are you up to? He said, "XYZ."

So off he went.

I yelled after him, "XYZ. What's that?"

He answered, "Go see the captain."

So I found this captain. He told me they needed the rope for the escape organization. So XYZ could do anything. The idea was that you supported XYZ. I don't know what they were using the rope for.

You weren't supposed to escape unless you had some sort of permission or were part of a plan. One American did go out on his own, though. He didn't get very far, before they picked him up again and brought him back. When they did, von Mueller, the camp commandant asked him, "How'd you get out?"

The chap said, "I jumped over the wire."

Now the wire was about ten-feet-tall barbed wire and there were two lots of barbed wire. They were about six feet apart and in between them was barbed wire entanglement. Some ten feet from the fence was what was called the warning wire. And you weren't allowed to go past that wire. You weren't allowed to approach the fence. Otherwise, you got shot!

Von Mueller looked at him and said, "I don't believe you."

The guy said, "Yeah, I did. I just jumped over. I waited until the guards in the posterns weren't looking and I jumped over."

Von Mueller said, "If you show me how you got out, I won't put you in the cooler."

So the guy showed him. He ran at the warning wire and kind of leapt over the wire, grabbed the top, went over and down into the entanglement, then jumped up again and over the top and did it again. He was a real athlete. Von Mueller was as good as his word. He didn't put him in the cooler.

We had long periods of boredom. Once they let us out to go swimming in the inlet to the Baltic. This was in the summer of 1944. We all had to sign a parole that we wouldn't try to escape. So we figured it was worth it just to get outside the wire for a bit. Most of us did that. They took us in groups. It was all very controlled and nobody tried to escape during that period. It was quite pleasant.

Occasionally they'd let us take baths. In eleven months, I guess I had about three or four hot shower baths. Apart from that we bathed and washed clothes in cold water with Ivory soap. We couldn't get anything very clean, so we'd make up a batch of *ersatz* coffee and put the underwear in that to give it a coffee color. That way we couldn't tell if it was dirty or not. Of course, having baths was rather difficult in cold water.

Occasionally we'd get some new people in, people who'd just been shot down and captured. I remember when our Group Captain came in. Group captains weren't supposed to fly, but he'd got a bit antsy and he'd gone on a show and got shot down. He saw me when he got to the camp and said, "Hello, Sam. Thought you were dead."

We were hungry most of the time, though, of course, we got Red Cross parcels, British and American. We got those in proportion to the number of people we had in the camp. We had a table, a stove, a food locker, and benches to sit on. There were eighteen people in my quarters. In the Christmas parcel from British Red Cross was bully (corned) beef, a tin of salmon, some jam, sugar (four ounces), margarine (eight ounces), cheese, egg powder, bacon, biscuits, condensed milk, dried fruit, mixed vegetables and meat, rolled oats, cocoa, tea, soap, cigarettes or tobacco, and some chocolate. There tended to be more variety in the British parcel, somehow. The Americans, though, seemed to have more stuff. There was a tin of American Spam, a tin of salmon, a tin of bully beef, you'd either get Spam or bully beef. Then there was jam, sugar, margarine, cheese, meat pate, like the Underwood Deviled Ham, biscuits, powdered milk, that was whole milk, and we'd beat it up. The Christmas package contained a twelve-ounce tin of turkey, a twelve-ounce tin of plum pudding, a packet of dates, and tins of butter, cheese, deviled ham, cherries, honey, jam, a box of bouillon cubes, mixed nuts, two fruit bars, assorted sweets, packets of tea, a pipe, tobacco, and cigarettes, a face cloth, a pack of cards, an indoor game, chewing gum and a photograph. I don't remember what the photo was.

We had special tools we'd make from tin cans and bits of wood from the fence and things like that. We made a mixer for mixing the powdered milk into liquid milk. In the wintertime, we'd allow this stuff to settle and get cream on the top. And we'd take the cream off and mix some sugar in and put it outside. It would freeze, and we'd have ice cream.

We used to use these milk tins, open them up and flatten them out and we had a special way of joining them by cutting a piece of tin to connect them into a sheet. We'd make a baking tin out of them. The packages also had prunes, raisins, coffee, soap, chocolate, pepper and salt, vitamin tablets and cigarettes. I didn't smoke, so I saved my cigarettes until the parcels ran out, and then gave the smokers two each a day. I got to be very popular as a source of cigarettes. We got one of those packages once a week until they gave out. When they gave out, the German food gave out, too.

We had a "food acco" as it was called. It was a sort of marketplace in a room that the American guys ran. Everything you got from the Red Cross was given a point value equal to one cigarette. So, bully beef was worth eighty points. You could take a bully beef can in and get a credit of eighty points to buy something else. You couldn't buy food with cigarettes. You could buy other cigarettes if you wanted to, but you couldn't use cigarettes to buy food. The "food acco" commission was four percent. English jam was quite popular.

Toward the last few months of the war, the Americans were coming over in the day time in their Fortresses. And we'd cheer like mad and act like dervishes. So the Germans said, "Whenever there's an air raid warning, everybody's got to go inside the huts. No more of this stuff."

Anyway one American evidently hadn't heard the warning, or something, and he was walking in the middle of this open area. He must have realized that there was nobody around. So he turned and ran back to his hut, to get where he was supposed to be. There was one guard who drew a bead on him and followed him with his rifle. When the American got to the doorway, he kind of stopped and said, "Whew!" That's when the German fired and killed him. That wasn't very long before the war was over. They immediately sent this guard away somewhere, because a search was put on for him. The prisoners were going to get him and hang him.

The SS and Gestapo had executed fifty or so escapees from Stalag Luft III, the camp that was in the movie *The Great Escape*. There were also rumors about that Hitler had the same fate in store for all POWS, so we formed a fighting force in our camp. We'd had all the prisoners from the Arnhem airborne attack and we formed companies of 200 people. Each one had an Army man in charge. My group was comprised of officers of all ranks, and our commander was a sergeant. The idea was that we'd form up into threes, under the cover of the huts, if they started to shoot, you know, with machineguns, we were just going to rush the postern boxes [guard towers]. A lot of us might get killed, but we would overpower them with numbers. There was no point in just waiting to be killed.

Anyway, that didn't have to happen. What did happen was the British were about forty kilometers away on the Elbe and they stopped, because they'd agreed to meet the Russians there. So the senior German officer, Mueller, spoke to the senior British and American officers. He told us he was going to march us west, the whole bloody lot of us. He said we had two hours to get ready.

Our people figured that Russians and British were strafing columns of marching men all over the place. Our senior officers went back a few hours later and said,

"We're not going, because it's bloody stupid."

The Germans said, "Well, *we* are."

And off they went, leaving us to wait for the Russians.

By this time, I'd gone down to eighty pounds. You know how your belly-button goes in? Well, mine was sticking out because everything around it had shrunk away. A few weeks before the end of the war, some Canadians had driven some trucks up through Germany with Red Cross food. So the food came and one of our guys who'd been a POW for many years had made himself a great big "kriegie cake," which was crushed up hard tack biscuits, moistened, then heated in the camp oven. He ate so much of it that he choked and died.

When the war ended they couldn't get an agreement with the Russians to have the B–17 Flying Fortresses to come into this airfield to pick us up. During the hiatus between the time the Germans left and our getting out, we saw the people in the forced labor compound at the nearby Luftwaffe airfield. They were in terrible shape. They were just skeletons. They were brought in to work on the new German jet aircraft, the Heinkel 162 that had the jet engine on the top of the fuselage. A lot of them were dying. That was terrible.

A Russian chap would come in and visit; sometimes he'd come with a private and other times he'd come with an officer. They seemed to be quite democratic in the Russian Army. And he'd got a German belt on, it said *Gott Mit Uns* 'God with us'' and a Swastika on it. And he wore it upside down and he'd filed off the swastika, or at least he'd tried to. Evidently, he had been taken prisoner by the Germans, then the Russians had overtaken the camp where he was being held and he'd just joined up again and carried on. He didn't feel like going home. A tough bunch, those Russians.

Anyway, this Russian had a very nice watch, and one of these paper serviette things with gold spots on it. We couldn't speak a word of each other's language; we did it all by sign language. He was talking with me and another guy and he evidently put equal value on these two things, the serviette, which was worth a hundredth-of-a-cent, perhaps, and this watch, which was quite a good one. So as a gesture of good will, he gave the watch to this guy I was standing with, and the serviette to me. It was funny, that, because he thought they were both pretty, and he was trying to be nice.

When the Germans left, we had a big parade and the band got out and we sang the American national anthem and the British national anthem. It was quite a moving experience. While we were there, we got a message from Eisenhower. It said, "Message to Stalag-Luft 1: Stand By." They didn't want us straggling across Europe in groups, because it was interfering with the war. So we stayed there. But a lot of guys didn't. They just walked west and picked up with the British.

When the final evacuation came, we of the fighting force went out last, in groups of twenty. The Fortresses would come in and land and go around the perimeter track. The door would open, twenty people hopped in, the door closed, and off they went. We landed very close to the place I'd taken off from when I went over to the beachhead. Of course, we hadn't any money, so we walked over to a pub that was nearby.

We made some reverse-charges telephone calls home, to tell people we were back. We just hung around the bar and looked around and people were buying us beer. We were a pretty motley bunch. I'd got khaki trousers on and no hat, all kinds of clothes. We just looked like a mess.

They took us up to someplace in the Midlands where they gave us something respectable to wear, and then we went home. When we got home, of course, our uniforms were there. They'd sent them home for us to dress properly. When I got home, I found out that I had been awarded the Distinguished Flying Cross, but the family had not written to tell me because they thought the Germans would not be "nice" to me!

The RAF kept telling me to stay on leave. The war was still on, but it was coming to an end very soon because they'd dropped the atomic bomb on Japan. I said, "Well, if you're going to keep sending me on leave, why don't you discharge me, because I'm doing nothing right now."

They did that, and I went.

So, I had my war, and I think about it often, about the people, and the planes. The British had good planes, as good as anybody's, and I flew quite a number of them. The Hurricane was very maneuverable, but wasn't very fast. That was okay on defensive work, because you could keep on turning and if you didn't get inside of the other guy, he'd eventually have to go home because he'd be running out of fuel. When we were going over to the other side in Hurricanes, we couldn't get away from the German fighters. This was funny, because we used to read the newspaper reports that the Germans had, "turned and fled," or something like that, whereas if we were over there, we had "disengaged." You see, we were both doing exactly the same thing, just trying to survive.

The highest I ever went in an airplane was 32,000 feet, and that was in a Hurricane. They could get up there, but they were very sluggish. If you made a mistake in a turn you'd lose one-thousand feet just like that. The Spitfires, particularly the later marks of Spitfires, which were designed with slightly longer wings and more boost in the engine, could operate up there very well, much better than the Hurricane could.

The Typhoon was a big aircraft. Hurricanes and Spitfires had Rolls-Royce Merlin engines, about twelve hundred horsepower. The Typhoon had a Napier Saber engine, which was a twenty-four-cylinder "flat-H" and it was about twenty-four hundred horsepower. It was a much faster airplane. These things cruised at 300 knots, which is a bit more than 300 miles-per-hour. We really could go like the clappers.

A big problem we had with the Typhoon was the engine would stop. They had sleeve-valve engines instead of poppet valves. The sleeve-valve would wear out. The Bristol engine company had been using sleeve-valves for some time, but Napier hadn't, and I don't know whether Napier just wouldn't ask Bristol or if Bristol wouldn't tell Napier how to make them. But eventually the government told Bristol, "You'd better tell them."

This guy in our squadron, Brayshaw, was just off the coast and his engine packed up. He landed on the sea and went down to the bottom. When he hit the bottom, he waited for the water to come in, then he jettisoned the hood and undid his harness, opened his Mae West and popped to the surface. There were a couple of guys in a fishing boat nearby and they came over and picked him up. In early 1944, he was hit near Le Havre, so he turned around and headed out to sea, thinking to do the same thing again, I suppose. It didn't work out the same way. He drowned.

Another thing that would happen to the Typhoon in the early days was that the tail would come off. That was particularly disturbing, because nobody ever got out of that, because the aircraft would start going down like a bomb. When we were at a place just east of London, the Germans were coming in over East Anglia at about 30,000 feet, screaming down to 20,000 feet leveling out, dropping bombs then nose diving again to scream out at a hell of a lick. It was very difficult to catch them at that. So anti-aircraft gunners tried to get them. And they had to be very accurate.

We used to have to do a stooge at about 20,000 feet for the anti-aircraft people. That is we would fly at exactly 20,000 feet so they could check the accuracy of their rangefinders. This was on the west side of London and the day was particularly clear. I looked down to the east and I could see my airfield on the east side of London. So I stuck my nose down and screamed down. By the time I reached the airfield I was doing a hell of a lick. So, to wind the speed off, I just went round and round the airfield, slowly getting my speed down enough so I could put my wheels down.

I told the guys about this. And to do this stooge was a terribly boring thing to have to do, to fly back and forth at that height. I said one thing you can do is to shove your nose down and come screaming down to the field. I went on leave then, and the next day another guy was flying, and I think he was flying my airplane, I'm pretty sure he was, and he did the same thing. He was going around and around the airfield at a hell of a lick and, pop, his tail came off. Of course, he was killed. Eventually, they got over those problems and we stopped losing tails.

Before they corrected the Typhoon's engine-stopping problems, I was flying to France and was over the Channel at about 200 feet. At that altitude, we could get under the German radar. As soon as we got to where we could be seen anyway on radar, we'd climb like mad to eight thousand feet to get above the effective range of the coastal flak. We had what we called "flying spares" with us, replacement planes in case somebody's plane acted up on the way over.

At 200 feet, my engine stopped. I closed the throttle, and then opened it up again. The engine caught! I carried on towards France. The engine stopped again. I closed the throttle and opened it. The engine stayed dead. So I closed it again, opened it up, and it picked up, so I carried on. A bit later on the engine stopped again, so I closed the throttle and opened it up and it didn't start. I closed the throttle and opened it up, it didn't start. I closed it and opened it up, but it didn't start. I closed it again and opened it, and it picked up, but I thought, that was enough, so I waggled my wings and went back home. The flying spare went in my place. When the guys came back from that operation, they said that when my engine picked up, it blew spray up from the sea, that's how low down I was.

I remember some of the people. When I got back onto mostly day fighters, the squadron I was posted to had all been on night fighting. I was the only one in the squadron who had any previous experience at day fighting. So the CO would go off to a briefing to find out where we were going, say escorting bombers or escorting some American squadrons. He'd come out and buttonhole me, put his arm around my shoulder and say, "Sam, we're going to be escorting some Marauders to so-and-so, and we're going to be mid-cover. What kind of formation do you think we ought to fly?"

I thought, "If something happens you won't know what to do."

And sure enough, I was right. We were bounced by 190s. I spotted these buggars coming down and I looked to the CO and I gave the squadron call sign, "Garbo squadron, bandits six o'clock."

And there was no reply. I didn't seem to get any response from the CO at all.

So I said, "Bandits are coming closer!"

Then I said, "Okay, Garbo Blue, be prepared to break!"

What was supposed to happen is that we would watch them come in right close, do a quick turn to throw off their aim, then engage them. And nothing had happened still. They were coming and they were just about in firing range and I said, "Garbo Blue, break!"

And as I pulled away, I looked back and saw the CO flying along, enjoying our protection. He was going home with the bombers. We were mixing it up with these 190s. There were just four of us and I don't know how many 190s there were. I don't think we hit any of them, because at that point we were more interested in surviving.

Anyway, we got away from them and we got back to the airfield. Of course, we were later than the others. We kind of dragged into the dispersal carrying our parachutes. What was going on there I don't know, but the CO was telling the intelligence officer that there was no reaction, that he hadn't seen anything. And he hadn't. It wasn't that he was a coward; he just didn't see anything. He was a hell of a nice chap, personally, but, as a CO, he was just plain awful. He used to worry me to death when I was going off with him, because I knew I couldn't rely on his doing the right thing.

Wing Commander Erik Haabjoern took over for him and it was like night and day. This guy was a bloody good shot and he knew how to lead. He could see aircraft long before I could see them. He had fantastic eyesight. There was another guy who had fantastic eyesight. His name was Stapleton. He could see things long before I could.

Haabjoern was a Norwegian national. He'd escaped from Norway on a British destroyer when the Germans invaded Norway. We'd made an abortive attempt to stop them, the British did, and we sent some destroyers and aircraft. He was in the Norwegian Air Force when the Germans were closing in and he was evacuated from Narvik.

Then there was Coxswain Bloggs. We used to do a lot of patrolling along the North Sea. Of course, a lot of ships were bombed or torpedoed and were sunk. It wasn't very deep water there, and very often you could see their masts sticking up.

Coxswain Bloggs was the coxswain of the Great Yarmouth lifeboat. A ship had been hit and was sinking. It was low in the water and the bridge and the forecastle were above water, while the decks of the ship were below water. I was patrolling this thing, because we had to make sure the Germans didn't come over and bomb it again. There were a lot of guys on the bridge, you see. And Coxswain Bloggs steered his lifeboat between the forecastle and the bridge and held it there while these guys jumped off. It was incredible, because the sea was running like hell through there. I guess the tide was going out. Then when they all got off, he just drove away like he was driving a car out of the park.

After the war, I joined the University Air Squadron as a Flying Officer. It was a volunteer reserve, and we flew on weekends. Around the same time, a chap from the Ministry of Labor came around and asked ex-service people what they wanted to do. I said I was going to pick up studying metallurgy again. And he said, "Well, you're a bit long in the tooth for doing it the way you were in the evenings."

We had something like the GI Bill, and he said since the war had interfered with my education, and if I'd like to apply for a full-time grant, he'd support me. So I got to go to London University. I finished up at the Royal School of Mines, which was part of the Imperial College, which was part of London University. I ended up with an honors degree in metallurgy, in 1950.

After I graduated, my wife Elizabeth and I went to South Africa to do gold and uranium extraction metallurgy in the mines. There, it became increasingly evident that the government policies just didn't agree with our ideas, and the job was pretty boring. So we decided to leave. We saved up for a long time until we'd got enough money to leave, then went to Canada. I'd gone six months ahead, mostly because we hadn't enough money to get us both out and a baby, too. So I went and saved and sent some money back to Betty to come out. I had been offered a job in the Gaspe' Peninsula. I'd written to this friend there and said that I'm thinking of coming to Canada to find a job in extractive metallurgy. He wrote back and said that he'd spoken to the chief metallurgist with a big Canadian company. He offered me a job at a place called Murdochville, which is on the right bank of the St. Lawrence. I arrived there just before Christmas, and was it cold there. Forty below! I'd scarcely taken more than a glance at the place and realized I wasn't going to bring my family there. So I called long distance across the Atlantic and told Betty I wasn't going to stay.

In the meantime, my boss there had said, "Call Operator 23 in Toronto."

I said, "What's that, what do you mean?"

He said, "Well, call Operator 23 in Toronto. There's somebody there who wants to get in touch with you. Call there and they'll see that the message gets passed on. They'll put you in touch with the person who wants you."

I called and it was an old boss of mine from South Africa. He'd gone to Canada and wanted me to go and work for him, to do some development work. He was offering good pay, so I said, "Okay."

I worked for him for a while and he paid me well. It lasted about six or eight months, but it was in extractive metallurgy, and I didn't want to stay in that. Then I got a job in materials engineering with Orenda Engines. Then I became chief metallurgist at De Havilland of Canada. I worked for them for a while, then went to Canadian Pratt and Whitney, where they were developing an engine. I was in charge of the materials for that. Then I was offered a job in Utica, New York, and this was in super-alloy development at a place called Special Metals. There I solved the problem of sigma phase embrittlement in superalloys. The gas turbine blades, which live in the hot blast of the jet engines, were developing sigma phase that made them brittle. If you'd dropped them on the floor, they'd snap. The whole industry just didn't know what to do. And I solved it. So I became rather well known in the industry for that!

In 1968, we came to Greensburg, Pennsylvania, and I took a job with Latrobe Steel about eight miles to the east of Greensburg. They wanted someone to develop a new multi-phase alloy that was useful at higher temperatures. It was also too dependent on cold work. So I made an improvement on that. That alloy is now holding on the nose wheel undercarriage of the Boeing 747.

Eventually, we became American citizens. We've felt very much at home in America, so this is where we stayed. Of course, I escorted quite a few American bombers during the war, so I felt a kind of fellowship for Americans anyway. It was all a long time ago.

John Slaney"s 247 Squadron, 1943.
Front row, left to right: Ken Gear (survived the war); Gonfra Burton (killed when his plane's tail came off); John Slaney; Ian Burns (Intelligence officer); Bill Shimmons (OC 'A' Flight);
Jim Mellville (Squadron OC); Gerry Gray (OC 'B' Flight); Taylor (Adjutant); Brayshaw (sank to sea bottom twice, drowned second time).
Second row, 6th from left: Van ,Van Zuilecom (KIA); 9th from left: Aitchison (KIA); 13th from left: Alex Robertson (Killed in mid-air collision).

John Slaney boards a Tiger Moth trainer. *Courtesy of John Slaney.*

John Slaney in 1941, standing on the wing of his Hawker Hurricane after shooting down a German Dornier 217 Bomber over the North Sea. At the time, Mr. Slaney was with 257 Burma Squadron. The squadron's logo appears in the photo just below the cockpit rail. *Courtesy of John Slaney.*

RAF Typhoon pilots and ground crew prepare a personal 500-pound greeting for Adolf Hitler. *Courtesy of John Slaney.*

Bombing up a Typhoon for a cross-Channel "Rhubarb." *Courtesy of John Slaney.*

| Abschuß am: | 14./16.6.44 ? | bei: | Caen, Frankr. | | Flugzeugtyp: | / |
| Gefangennahme am: | wie oben | bei: | | | | |

Nähere Personalbeschreibung

Figur:	schlank		Augen:	blaugrau
Größe:	1.72		Nase:	gerade
Schädelform:	längl.		Bart:	-
Haare:	braun		Gebiß:	gesund
Gewicht:	63 kg			
Gesichtsform:	oval		Besondere Kennzeichen:	
Gesichtsfarbe:	gesund			

John Slaney's POW ID. Mr. Slaney "liberated" the card from the Stalag Luft office after the Germans had left and before the arrival of the Russians. *Courtesy of John Slaney.*

John Slaney points to the name A.E. Miron on the Noyers Bocage Memorial. Miron was Mr. Slaney's Deputy Flight Commander. *Courtesy of John Slaney.*

"Sometimes We Didn't Need the Dog Tags."

William R. Smith
28th Infantry Division ("The Bloody Bucket"), 110th Infantry Regiment
2nd Battalion, Headquarters Company, (63rd Infantry Division)
Woodale, Pennsylvania, August 21, 1920
(Wilpen, Pennsylvania)

"When people ask me, 'How many Germans did you kill?' I answer, 'I didn't kill any!' I didn't draw up on a man and shoot at him. I fired the rifle a lot of times, but I don't think I hit anybody. I didn't always see what I was shooting at. 'You see guys shooting and getting shot in the movies though,' they say. And then I say, 'I know, but I wasn't in the movies!'"

I NEVER WENT VERY FAR IN SCHOOL. I joined the National Guard in 1940, and in 1941 I went on active duty. I put thirty years in the service. Before I came out I went to the first sergeant and asked about promotion to one rank up so I could get a better pension.

He said, "Well, I'll see what I can do."

I went round a couple of days later.

"I can't do anything for you. I can't get you that promotion."

"Why? You've been doing it for other people."

"Well, you never went to high school."

I said, "Well, if that isn't something!"

I didn't say it to him that way. I had different words to use at that time. All that many years, from private, clear up through the ranks to master sergeant, and then they told me I wasn't qualified.

Why did I go and sign up all those years ago? Lately, I've thought about that. I guess it was because the buddies I was running around with at the time, they signed up. I went over to the Scottdale recruiting station, and they told me they were full up. The major said, "If you really want to get in, I'll take you over to Connellsville, sign you up there. When we get to camp, as soon as we get an opening, I'll transfer you back to the company in Scottdale."

Scottdale was a service company. Connellsville was a tank company. I had more fun in Connellsville. When we got to camp we trained on "artillery" pieces." We went to junkyards and got old axles from cars, put a piece of pipe on them for a barrel.

Eventually, I went down to the Carolinas for maneuvers. I had a nice job there. I never stayed out in the field. I stayed in hotels and ate in restaurants. I just drove the Claims and Damage officer around to the different homes and farms. Some of them got damaged during our maneuvers, so he would make out claims for damage and the

Army would pay for it. I got back to Pennsylvania five days before everyone else. The officer and I just drove straight through to the "Gap" (Indiantown Gap).

I got a week's leave, and I hitchhiked home. I was with my girl friend at her house, listening to the radio. The news about Pearl Harbor came over. Just like that I was back in camp, all leaves canceled. Soon, we got orders to ship out for Louisiana. We continued to train on our "artillery." There were five of us to a "gun." We'd go through the drill of loading and firing. If a guy got "hit," someone would take his place. It was all preparation for the real thing.

Meanwhile we continued to train on our fake artillery. It was all routine and preparation for the real thing. In the fall of 1942, we went to Florida for six months of amphibious training. I learned to swim. We jumped off ships, swam around a little, and then climbed back up the sides of the ships.

We didn't know where we would end up. They never told us. We went to Camp Pickett for more training and then to Camp Miles Standish for embarkation in 1943. I was on a ship called the *Cristobal*. Most of the ships our Army went over on were converted liners. We were overloaded, twice what we were supposed to have. It was a rough crossing.

As many of us as there was, there was a continuous, twenty-four-hour chow line. We'd get our trays and food, and then ate standing up at a high table connected to the wall. The ship leaned over one way, and the trays and the jam cans slid down the other way. They the ship leaned the other way, and the jam cans came back. I'd try to grab a can as it came by. Trouble was, guys would get sick and barf all over the table and the jam cans. It was the worst thing I ever saw. After a couple days of that, with no one bathing, the stink would just hit you. I don't know. Maybe that got us used to the smell of death. We were still on the ship on Thanksgiving Day. Some of us got the sick guys chow cards and went down to the mess hall to get second helpings.

When we landed, the 110th went to Pembrook Docks, down in South Wales. The Welsh people were nice, and we had a lot of fun. They had a dance for us every Saturday at their community building. I was with a service company, 2nd Battalion, 110th Infantry, gathering up garbage, hauling rations, loading supplies. When I got into combat, I stayed with Headquarters Company. We weren't back very far from the lines. I got a little brave.

We knew the invasion was coming. We left Wales and went fifteen miles outside of London. At three o'clock in the morning, everybody got out of bed, went down to the docks and started loading up equipment. For two or three weeks, these turned out to be dry runs. When the actual invasion came on 6 June, I was at a London PX getting supplies, candy and cigarettes and such, when some C–47s flew over. I didn't know what was going on, but I had an idea. A little less than a month later, we were on Omaha beach.

I took the ammunition right up to the troops in a two-and-a-half-ton truck. When the Germans sent over some shells of their own, all the guys would run away from that truck. When we had a truck full of ammo, it was a pretty good pile of BOOM! We carried so much small arms ammunition, so many mortar rounds, and so many hand grenades. We generally had quite a number of grenades because our troops used them up pretty fast. As a matter of fact, the troops on the line used up ammunition faster than we could get it to them.

The Germans had us held up in the hedgerows. After we broke out, the Germans took off with us after them. It was just a big rat race all over France. We stopped in Paris, let the French army go in first, then we paraded through the streets, the whole division. It rained, pouring down. We got in there at night; nobody knew a thing. We just drove the trucks around, and then decided to park them. When daylight came, we all got organized for the parade. We dressed in Class A uniforms. The streets were crowded. We marched around two sides of the Arc de Triomphe. We enjoyed it, because we got lots of kisses from the women! They crawled up onto the trucks, and we had to push them off of us so we could keep going. We were going right through, and we didn't know what was waiting for us on the other side of the city. That was the worst part. A lot of times you can talk about the fun part, but when it comes down to the other thing, your mind goes blank. I don't remember crossing the Channel, and I have vague memories of climbing up from Omaha Beach. I don't remember much about the Hürtgen Forest, except that I delivered mortar shells in there. I guess we all have a tendency to forget the horror, and remember stuff that seemed funny at the time.

When we were attached to the 1st Division, the Big Red One, we were in Aachen, and I looted a bank. We weren't supposed to do that. I stuffed millions of German marks into suitcases. I thought I was going to be rich, but the money turned out to be useless. Another time, before the Bulge, we got up to the Dragon's Teeth of the Siegfried Line. We were sitting around, bullshitting and smoking cigarettes, when the German artillery started giving us holy hell. We all dove under the truck for protection. It was pure instinct. But the truck was full of ammunition!

We always dug double foxholes, and then parked the trucks away from us. We parked close to a creek one night, and then climbed this hill. It seemed a nice place, so we dug in for the night. When you heard an artillery round, you didn't much worry about it because it was going over. You worried about the ones you didn't hear. My buddy and I thought we'd have a smoke, so we sat down on a pile of dirt and lit up. This thing came in and hit the ground. It just stuck in there. It didn't go off. It must have had a defective fuse, or the fella upstairs must have been riding it. We picked up our shovels, and back down the hill we went, laughing like hell.

The 28th was in the Hürtgen Forest for twenty-one days, and it never moved a foot forward. For twenty-one days I hauled ammunition in, and hauled the dead out. And there were as many dead Germans in there as there were Americans. We'd pick up our dead, wrap them in a blanket, throw them up on the truck, and then take them back to Graves Registration. We knew who they were from their dog tags, but sometimes we didn't need the dog tags. That's the part you block out, A direct hit killed a buddy of mine. He was in his foxhole, and an artillery shell came in. All I saw in the air was blood and bones. I don't know why I'm telling you this. I never even told my wife, and I've know her almost sixty years.

The Battle of the Bulge started on 16 December 1944. It was dark, just before daylight. We heard the Germans down by the river, revving up their tanks. Then the tanks came up. They had searchlights on them, and they just lit up the whole place. We just took off! My assistant driver started the truck, and guys jumped on. He drove off, and I didn't see the truck again until we got to Bastogne. There weren't too many that made it through.

I got with a bunch of guys and we wandered around. We didn't know where we were. We'd start up one way, and then go another, picking up guys along the way. We didn't have any ammunition, so we avoided places were there was shooting. We had no rations. Soon, there were a dozen of us. At some point, six of them took off on their own. They were afraid that a large group had more risk of getting shot. We crawled around on our bellies part of the time. In the day, we hid out and watched. Anytime you could get five winks, you took it. I ended up getting frozen feet. Our overcoats got wet, and they weighed a ton. We were trying to get back to the rear where the division was, because we knew they had been pushed back. There was a part of division headquarters that was shot up pretty bad. The 112th and 109th had been on our flanks. They didn't take the full brunt that we did, but they lost a lot of people, too. We ended up coming out in Bastogne. We left Bastogne and we headed back for another town, where they told us the division was assembled.

I went down to the medics and they poured alcohol on my feet.

They said, "You could get a Purple Heart."

I could have got one, easy. I know a lot of guys who just scratched their hand on a barbed-wire fence, and they went down to the medics and got a Purple Heart. That bothered me. I mean there was guys laying there that couldn't even move. They deserved it more.

One day the war ended. When it did, we were down in southern Germany. I didn't have to haul ammunition anymore. I was transferred from the 28th to the 63rd. We went into occupation duty. I didn't come home until October 1945. I came home on a Liberty ship with five hundred other guys. I didn't get sick going over, but I sure did coming back. We came into Boston. They put us on a train, and sent us to the "Gap." We marched into this big building and they said, "Throw your bags in here, and go home."

They didn't give us papers or anything. They just told us to come back in fifteen days. I stayed with the Pennsylvania National Guard for thirty-three years.

When people ask me, "How many Germans did you kill?"

I answer, "I didn't kill any!"

I didn't draw up on a man and shoot at him. I fired the rifle a lot of times, but I don't think I hit anybody. I didn't always see what I was shooting at.

"You see guys shooting and getting shot in the movies, though," they say.

And then I say, "I know, but I wasn't in the movies!"

A 94th Division infantryman checks his carbine during a lull in the fighting in the Bannholtz, Sinz, Germany (Saar-Moselle Triangle). The fighting at Sinz was fierce. (See Martin Burke's account in this volume). *All photos on this page are Courtesy of Richard "Doc" Buchanan, M.D.*

Mail call in the Bannholtz, Sinz, Germany. Rollins in his M-18 gets the mail from Mail Clerk Masirovits.

Eisenach, Germany. 4th Armored troops and members of the 704 Tank Destroyer Battalion's medical detachment watch a dogfight between a Bf-109 and a P-47. The Bf-109 was shot down.

"I Was Gone a Year."

Antonio Spanish
Merchant Marine

"One night, Joe, another guy named Al Bakeoff, and I were in a restaurant spiking our coffee from a bottle of booze. There were three or four girls there, and we got to talking with them. Then a couple sailors came in and broke into our conversation. We were quickly at war. We turned tables upside down, and just about tore that restaurant apart. The police and the Shore Patrol came in. We were in civvies, so the cops took us away, and the Shore Patrol took the guys in uniform. One of the cops got me down on the ground and hit me over the head with a billy club. They threw the three of us in jail. We slept on the concrete floor. The next morning we had a hearing."

I grew up in Detroit, Michigan. After my father died I went into a children's home, and stayed there until I was fourteen. I worked in a bakery for a few years, and when I turned eighteen I went to work at the Cadillac plant. I was there when Pearl Harbor was bombed. Like many people my age, I wanted to join the Navy. I went with my buddy who had already planned on joining up, and on the way we saw a sign advertising the Maritime Service, what they called the Merchant Marine at the time. I said to my buddy, Joe, "Lets go in there and inquire about this Maritime Service. You're planning on going in the Navy, and I am going to get drafted anyhow, so let's see what they have offer."

We went in and talked to a guy in an office. We asked him how long would it take before they took us in. The guy said "We'll take you in one month."

I said, "I'm signing up."

Joe really wasn't old enough for the Navy, so he gave that idea up and went into the Merchant Marine with me. Within a month we went to Sheepshead Bay, New York for training, which was similar to the way the Coast Guard and Navy trained. We learned specific jobs like swabbing decks and working in the boiler room. We also did marching, and emergency drills, like dropping and manning lifeboats. We learned how to swim, and how to row a boat. It was twenty-below-zero at Sheepshead while we were there, and it really got us ready to go into the North Atlantic.

After our first six or eight weeks of boot camp, we were allowed to go into New York City. In those days, Times Square was packed with guys from all branches of the service, and there were sailors there from other parts of the world. Because of the air raid blackouts, New York was dim, compared to the bright lights of today. We spent our pay, about thirty dollars, in one night. Flat broke, we went to the Pepsi Cola Canteen, right off Times Square, where we could get free pop and sandwiches. They also gave out tickets to see shows. We always stayed at the Mansfield Hotel 47th and 9th Avenue. Right across from there was a place called the Algonquin, where the Broadway stars hung out. One night, some big movie star got falling down drunk, and Joe picked him up off the floor. I saw a lot of stars there—Frank Sinatra, Jack Benny, to name a couple.

One night, Joe, another guy named Al Bakeoff, and I were in a restaurant spiking our coffee from a bottle of booze. There were three or four girls there, and we got to talking with them. Then a couple sailors came in and broke into our conversation. We were quickly at war. We turned tables upside down, and just about tore that restaurant apart. The police and the Shore Patrol came in. We were in civvies, so the cops took us away, and the Shore Patrol took the guys in uniform. One of the cops got me down on the ground and hit me over the head with a billy club. They threw the three of us in jail. We slept on the concrete floor. The next morning we had a hearing.

That magistrate said to me, "What do you have to say for yourself?"

"Well I am not saying anything," I said, "There's our spokesman Al Bakeoff. He's going to do all the talking."

So, Al stepped in and told the magistrate what had happened; "Our ship's laying in the harbor down there. It's ready to sail tomorrow. We want to get back on it."

The magistrate said, "I'm going to let that man go, but I am going to fine you two."

Sixty bucks was the fine. The problem was, we didn't have a dime. So, Al went back to the ship, borrowed sixty bucks, and brought it back. We gave it to the court, and they let us go.

Our training at Sheepshead bay ended in April, and we shipped out soon after, on a Liberty Ship, and headed out into the Atlantic. We were bound for the Mediterranean and Oran, North Africa. Even our ships bound for the Pacific left from New York, but on return trips, we docked somewhere else, like Norfolk, Virginia, or Mobile, Alabama. The Liberty ship was designed specifically to carry supplies. It had three big holds that were loaded inside with everything from tanks to ammunition. We used to carry stuff on top even, anywhere we could, and as much as we could. Down below were the engine room and crews quarters, the galley and the holds. Up top were the officer's quarters and the guns. We had a five-inch gun we practiced on but didn't use in combat. We also had a three-inch gun, and on each side of the ship were four 40mms, for a total of eight.

The crew quarters were tight. Our bunks were three high, and we slept in shifts according to our watch. Each duty station had specific quarters, so if a guy worked in the engine room, everyone in his quarters also worked in the engine room. In the Atlantic, the seas got so rough our heads would bounce in our bunks when we tried to sleep. On the sea, it was always "lights out," no smoking, no nothing. The enemy submarines could see any kind of light.

We had about forty-five Merchant Marines on board, and about twenty-five Navy guys. The Navy served as gun crews, had separate quarters and mess hall, and was called the Naval Armed Guard. We didn't have a brig, but we never had any problems, so we never needed one. We had no hospital facilities on board. Our purser, the guy who handled the payroll, doubled as a medic.

The United States already controlled Africa when our ship got there. Oran served as our homeport for the delivery of supplies to Sicily, after we invaded the island. Unloading a ship always took a couple of days. It was heavy, dangerous work, and it had to be done slowly. I hate to say this, but when we were in North Africa unloading, they used to make colored troops come and unload our ships. I think that's all they let those guys do, even though they were all Army personnel, like everyone else.

I became a seaman after that first trip, and stayed in that capacity throughout the war. My job was to stand watch and steer the ship. I worked four hours on and eight hours off. I worked that way for thirty to sixty days until we got to a port. I picked whatever watch we wanted. There was a little bit more freedom in the Merchant Marine as compared to the other services in respect to choosing duties and such. When a ship was at sea, there was one ordinary seaman and two able-bodied seaman on watch. Down in the engine room there were a fireman, an oiler and a wiper. As soon as the ship docked, I went on straight eight-hour watches. There were no rotations. When we docked, I also did maintenance work, like painting and scraping.

When we weren't on duty we played cards, or, if we could get ashore we did. We did a lot of gambling. We bet on baseball games a lot, and I had a clever way of keeping track of baseball. There was a phone in the crow's nest. When I went on watch, I took the phone wires and connected them to the wires coming from the radio shack upstairs. After that, I could hear all the ball scores. I could get the scores, but no one else could. Then I would bet on what I already knew. I also took part in the Black Market; we all did. We used cigarettes in place of currency. Once we got far out to sea, we opened what was called the "slop chest." We could buy as many cigarettes as we wanted for fifty cents a carton. Since I wasn't a heavy smoker, a pack usually lasted me a week. So, I would get to a port like Australia, and I would have ten or fifteen cartons, stacked up. A couple packs bought me a bottle of Scotch, which I could easily turn around and sell for twenty bucks. It was quite an enterprise. We rarely sold the liquor we bought, though; we drank it. We would sneak things into our stateside homeports, because everything in America was rationed. In Norfolk, Virginia, I once sneaked in twenty-five pairs of socks filled with cigarettes.

The food aboard ship was the best part. For breakfast I could have anything I wanted–scrambled eggs, fried eggs, sunny-side up, pancakes, bacon, whatever. At noon, I had mostly boiled foods, like meat and potatoes. Suppers were mainly fried food–steak, chicken, rabbit, roast, pork chops. There was one kid who could eat a dozen chops all by himself. The first time I shipped out some guy walked by me on the ship and I looked at him, he seemed familiar. We had 300 soldiers on the ship and he was part of that group. They got basic Army food.

I said to the guy, "Hey I know you."

"Yeah. Me and you used to live together in Detroit on Woodrow Wilson Street, at the children's home."

It was really something to see him, such a small world.

He asked me, "Tony, how can I get something better to eat?"

"Don't worry I'll take care of you."

Well he ate what we ate. I sneaked him our food, which he appreciated.

As a seaman, I was paid a base of seventy-two dollars a month. In a combat zone, we got more. We got a bombing bonus, and if we were bombed in port, we got a hundred dollars. When we got in enemy waters, they gave us five extra dollars a day. The regular soldier didn't get what we got.

On my first trip I went through my indoctrination, the same one sailors go through when they cross the Equator.

I told them, "You're not going to catch me."

Well, they came up into the crow's nest and got me. "We'll relieve you," they said. They took me down, and true to their word, they "relieved" me. They cut all my hair off. Then they made me strip, and covered me in something like tar. They had two or three other things they used to do as well. Then I was the same as them. Then I could do the same to those who came into the service after me.

In a typical supply convoy we had a hundred ships that were protected on the outskirts by Navy destroyers and escorts. They were supposed to sink any German submarines with depth charges before the subs could get to us. I never saw a submarine in all the time I was with the Merchant Marines, but I saw plenty of enemy airplanes when we were in the invasion of Sicily. That's where I was wounded. It was dawn when we arrived there. There were all kinds of ships around us and there were a couple big battleships bombarding the beaches, trying to soften it up. All our ships had big wires going up with great big balloons at the end of them. In case any enemy planes dove low the wires would take their wings right off.

There were fifty Liberty ships like ours. There were landing craft everywhere with soldiers on them, heading into the beach. We could see all the enemy bombs dropping down near us churning up mud and sand. A couple of our sister ships during the invasion got hit and sunk. My ship was there three days and aside from that first day when it was hit and I was wounded, it remained untouched. When I was wounded, we were getting bombed by thirty or thirty-five German aircraft. One of them dropped a bomb on my three-inch gun position. Shrapnel hit my legs and broke both of them. I was taken off of my ship to a Coast Guard ship, the *U.S.S. Samuel Chase,* and they operated on my legs there. Then they transferred me to a hospital ship that had a big, white cross on it. The hospital ship took us back to Oran, where I stayed in a regular hospital for eight weeks. Then I went to a convalescent hospital.

When I was in the hospital, in Oran, we were right next to a prison camp. Most of the prisoners were Italians. They'd march them up and down every day. They went out to do work and we could hear them singing at the top of their lungs. I don't think I ever saw any German prisoners, and I never saw any Japanese when I got to the Pacific, although there were still many left in the jungles when we landed.

When I was almost recovered, I went into a little nearby town, where I saw the guys from my ship, which had returned to Oran. They said, "We came back to load again."

I told them, "I'm going to try and get back on with you."

They released me from the hospital and I was lucky enough to get back on my ship. After that we came back to the United States. That was in November 1943. The Merchant Marines gave us a thirty-day leave, something they did each time we returned home. Anyone who didn't return after leave, would have his name sent to the Draft Board. When they caught up with him, they placed him in the Army or another branch of the service. Of course, I always returned. I tried to stay away from getting on a ship that was going into the North Atlantic. There were U-boats everywhere there, and we lost a lot of ships up in that part of the ocean. When I signed on I would go to a big hall where they had a bulletin board showing which ships were going where. We were allowed to turn down two ships, but we had to take the third, no matter where it was going. Some guys went on those ships across the Atlantic to Russia because they wanted to, I never understood that. Some of the guys didn't take the thirty-day leave when they finished a duty either. They went back and signed up on the same ship as soon as the first trip was done. That was their home, I guess. Not me. I got leave and I took it.

I signed on with a ship going to the Pacific. At the time, the battle for the islands was pretty much over. We went to Australia and New Zealand to pick up supplies, and drop them where they were needed. The trip took about seven months. When I came home, I met the girl who would be my wife.

My buddy Joe lived in Pittsburgh, so I came home with him one time between voyages. That's when I met her, downtown at the dance hall. Most of the guys were gone to the service, so there were a lot of girls around. Well I met her and then I shipped out again, came back, and we decided to get married. That happened a lot during the war.

After I got married, I shipped out again.

I said to my wife, "I'll be gone three or months."

I was gone a year.

I went to the Pacific again, through the Panama Canal. In the Pacific we didn't travel in a convoy. We went across by ourselves and we had the ship up to ten or twelve knots, as fast as we could go, because we wanted to outrun any Jap subs that might be around. They said it was safe, but we never knew. In a convoy, in the Atlantic, we only went six to eight knots. That was a big difference, and the ocean was altogether different. The Pacific was like a sheet of glass all the time. The Atlantic was rough and stormy. There weren't any normal ports in New Guinea or Guadalcanal, like we had in North Africa or Europe. We could tell there had been one heck of a fight on some of those islands, though. We could see where the trees were all blown down from bombs and shells.

We were in New Guinea, in a club, when somebody came in and said we dropped something on the Japanese, and that they might surrender. We couldn't imagine what the heck they had dropped on them to make them surrender. We later found out it was the Atomic Bomb. We thought we were going to come right home after that, but we didn't. They took us and they loaded us with all kind of shells, empty shells, because brass was scarce. We took all that brass back to the United States. That was January 1946.

When I came home, I went back into the Maritime Hospital, because my legs swelled up from an infection. Then they took me to a hospital in Lawrenceville, Pennsylvania, where they took the shrapnel out. I lay there for about two months, until July.

I think if I had not gotten married I would have stayed in and served twenty years and retired. I always liked ships, and going on trips. I saw the world, as they say. The way I look at it, if it wasn't for the Merchant Marine carrying supplies over, we might not have won the war. We go largely unrecognized for what we did. We had to do it, that was our job, no matter what happened, no matter if we were scared. They didn't even include the Merchant Marines as part of the branches of service until fifteen years ago. Even though I was listed as being in the Naval Reserve, we didn't get recognition or benefits like the other services did. We were paramilitary, you might say, when we were in an invasion. Other than that, we were just ordinary workmen, like we would have been in peacetime. Per capita, we lost more seamen than any other service. It was even more dangerous for us, because the enemy knew we were carrying vital supplies.

My discharge papers say "Naval Reserve," so, to me, anyway, I was in the service. The Merchant Marine had its own decorations. I got one for being wounded, one for being in a war zone, and one for being in the Pacific. Once we were recognized as a branch of the service, I got back pay in the amount of twenty-five thousand dollars. I didn't get a real Purple Heart, and so I think we are finally getting a bit of well-deserved credit.

National Archives

"You're Not Going to Make It."

Marvin R. Spencer
80th Division, 317th Regiment, 3rd Battalion, Headquarters Company
Okalla, Texas, 5 December 1921

"When I jumped over trees, you know, I saw the biggest German that I had ever seen waiting for me. He was on his knees, just waiting for somebody to come over. He caught me in the stomach with a bayonet and it slit me about five inches up. Well I caught him and got rid of him. The battle lasted a long, long time and when it was over you couldn't take three steps in any direction without stepping on a dead German or a dead American."

I WENT INTO THE ARMY in July of 1942. I was inducted at Lubbock, Texas. I went from there to Fort Sill, Oklahoma. I stayed there five days, and went from there to Camp Forrest, Tennessee. That's where I joined the 80th Division.

The 80th took part in the Tennessee maneuvers and then we went to Camp Phillips, Kansas. From there we went to Arizona for desert maneuvers. From there, we were supposed to go to the South Pacific, they told us. We got new clothes and everything to go where it was hot and they came back the next morning and told us we were going Europe. That was the way it went. We had to turn in all our new hot weather clothes. We went to Fort Dix, New Jersey and we trained there and then we went over to embarkation.

We went to Camp Kilmer to get aboard the ship. We were there about a week and we practiced getting on the boat and off the boat and all that stuff. Then we got on the *Queen Mary* and went to England. The *Queen Mary* took us over in five and a half days. Then it took me twenty-one days to get back home on a hospital ship after I got wounded.

After some time in England we crossed the Channel to Omaha beach. It was in August so the beach was secured and cleared by the time we stepped onto it. Right after we got off the beach, a plane came down and almost hit the truck I was on. My platoon leader, Lieutenant Belloc, jumped off the truck and was killed when he hit the pavement. That shook everybody up.

Then we didn't have any more big trouble for a while. It was all light fighting for about a month. We went to the Moselle River and made that crossing. I went over on a riverboat and the end was shot off so we all had to swim back and cross again. I had to cross twice.

One big fight was in Argentan, France. It was hedgerow fighting and I remember it was all mixed up. The 317th, 318th and 319th Regiments were all assembled in the area there. I don't know why they chose us, but we went over the hedgerow first. They set our schedule up by eight minutes to try and throw the Germans off. The Germans thought it was going to hit at five o'clock. When I jumped over the bushes I saw the biggest German that I had ever seen waiting for me. He was on his knees, just waiting for somebody to come over. He caught me in the stomach with a bayonet and it slit me about five inches up. Well I caught him and got rid of him. The battle lasted a long, long time and when it was over you couldn't take three steps in any direction without stepping on a dead German or a dead American.

I don't remember the next battle. It's kind of complicated, you know, because they didn't tell us exactly what we were going to do. They just told us to go forward. That's the way the Army is. We'd go from one hill to the other and cross a river and so on.

One of the biggest fights was Hill 109. It was my job to get the ammo to the guys. We took grenades up the hill, and it was so steep that we had to push them up ahead of us, take our trench knife and stab it in the ground and pull ourselves up. When we finally got up there we found out they were really low on ammunition. So they sent two more guys and me back to get a re-supply. We didn't know exactly where the ammunition dump was and we got lost in the brush. It was just before dark and we ran into about thirty Germans. Our old company commander, Robert Smith, came up and he had about thirty men with him. He saved our lives. After that we ran into Sergeant Jones and he told us where a Jeep was he had hidden. We got the Jeep and went to where the ammunition dump was.

On the way we ran into a chaplain. I mean, he was just out there in the brush, in the middle of nowhere. After we picked him up, we went on for several miles and we ran into about 100 Germans. They could have torn us up if they had known the situation, but they were tired of fighting and wanted to give up. We had a .30 caliber on there so we fired a few rounds and they all just gave up. I was lucky I had that chaplain with me because he could speak German as well as they could.

I told him, "Tell them to stack their arms up and wait till we send someone after them." We stacked as many as we could on the Jeep and carried them back. Lieutenant Turner was at the dump, and I told him about it. He took some men and went back there and got the rest.

The next morning we pulled out and we came to a crossroads, where we started to take fire. We could tell it was coming from below ground and not the trees. Then we spotted a pillbox. I told another guy to fire over my head while I crawled over and dropped in a grenade. A couple seconds after I tossed in the grenade and it exploded, someone stuck a white flag out of an opening in the pillbox. We thought whoever was left was going to come out and surrender, but they changed their minds. So, I threw another grenade in. This time they surrendered. Twenty-two of them came out. I don't know how many were still in there that my grenades killed. We put them out on the road and made them lay down and we searched them. We cleaned them out and got them up to march them out to our trucks.

I was standing beside them in about the center of their line. All of a sudden some went one way and some went the other way, and I knew something was about to happen behind me so I whirled around and got caught a bullet in the right arm. About that time an old boy from Beaumont, Texas, the same one that patched me up when I was cut with the bayonet, arrived. He doctored me up, gave me shots and so forth. He tried to put a tourniquet on but it just wouldn't work. So he put a K-ration wire on the wound and got it chocked down pretty good. I didn't want to give my rifle up. I didn't have but one arm, but I could still shoot it you know? When that guy shot me, he knocked me down to my knees, and my rifle hit the ground and I just picked it up and I shot that guy twice. I didn't kill him, and he tried to surrender again, but my buddy emptied his rifle into him.

After the medic worked on me they took me back and the next thing I knew it was about two or three o'clock in the evening. The chaplain talked to me when I woke up and he said he'd write my wife a letter. I don't know what I told him to tell her, but she did get the letter. Then they sent the ambulance in later and they took me back to a field hospital. There was an old sergeant driving the ambulance. I told him, "I still got feeling, and I understand what's going on. I would like to be put on top."

So he put me in last. It was full and when they were going across the shell holes it was pretty rough. They got me back to the field hospital and there was a ward boy there.

He said, "If you don't get that blood stopped pretty soon, you're not going to make it."

I told him, "I know that."

Two doctors came in and he talked to them. They said they were going to try and get me out of there because I couldn't live over an hour and a half without stopping that blood.

They had to set my arm first. It took five of them to do it. The one took this hand and squished the bones back into place, and I passed out again. After that they moved pretty quickly and a C–47 transport, took me to England. I was in the hospital for about two years there.

When I got back to England, they put me in a private room, the only private room that I ever had while I was in the Army. They operated on me and put me back in the corner.

Captain Myer was the doctor. He said, "We had to put you in that room because you whipped me and all the ward boys and everybody you could get hold of."

I didn't know anything about that, but I had tried to fight them off. They finally got me subdued and put me in that private room.

I couldn't eat anything, just chicken broth. They gave me broth twice a day. I asked the doctor one day if I could have more.

He said, "Well I'm going to let you eat today but I'm going to send two guys with you to watch you and just eat a little bit. Promise me you won't eat too much?"

I said, "All right."

I didn't eat too much but it was pretty good, you know, to eat again. Then about three weeks later they put me on a hospital ship and I came to South Carolina. And then I stayed there three days and they sent me to Texas, Longview, Texas. After that I got out of the army. That is my story.

Ralph Sperber with his mule, AOO5, during a break in the action. *Courtesy of Ralph Sperber.*

13 May 1945, Arco Area, Italy. Brigadier General David L. Ruffner, Artillery Commander, 10th Mountain Division, pins the Bronze Star on Ralph Sperber. *Courtesy of Ralph Sperber.*

"The Days Didn't Matter Any More"

Ralph Sperber

Fifth Army, 10th Mountain Division, 616th Pack Field Artillery,
Headquarters Battery; Greensburg, Pennsylvania,
10 September 1925.

"The days didn't matter anymore because guys were getting their arms and legs blown off right in front of me. We fixed up Jeeps to carry the wounded. If they were badly wounded, chaplains would ride with them. Some guys died in those Jeeps."

My first job was selling ice cream at a local drug store. I worked there for a couple of years before going into the Army. I was only seventeen when I joined. I spent three months at Fort Bragg, where I was attached for a short while to the 82nd Airborne Division. The Airborne guys got drunk and fought each other all the time. Then I heard that the Army was forming a new division of ski troops. To get in, I had to get three letters of recommendation, which I got. Then I was shipped out to Camp Hale, Colorado and the 10th Mountain Division. The British had sent more than 5,000 German prisoners from North Africa there who had fought with Rommel. When we arrived at Camp Hale, there were Germans all over the place. We thought we had been invaded! They were happy to be prisoners because they were receiving plenty of food and clothing. Since there were not that many guards with them, some of the German POWs escaped all the way into Texas or Mexico. Some of them went into hiding in the US. I never found out if they managed to get messages back to Germany or not.

There were 19,000 of us at the camp. They had guys coming in from Harvard and Yale who were professional skiers, and experienced mountain climbers. I was taught the rudiments of skiing, but I didn't have to worry about getting very good at it because they assigned me to an artillery outfit within the division, the 616th Battalion. We used 75mm pack-howitzers, and gave close support to tank infantry. I ended up being a forward observer, directing fire. To get guns up into the mountains, we had to dismantle them and put them on the backs of mules; big, strong mules from Missouri. They would do anything for the lumps of sugar we all carried, and they could go where some vehicles couldn't. We had about 5,000 of them. It took ten ships to get them all to Italy. Going up the passes in the Italian mountains with eighty pounds of GI equipment on my back, I would hold onto a mule's tail to help balance myself. My mule's Army ID number was A005.

We shipped out from Newport News in Hampton, Virginia. The scuttlebutt was that the Germans knew when we were going to ship out, and had positioned submarines all along our intended route. We stayed on deck, afraid. Fortunately, we never saw a German sub.

We landed at Livorno, Italy in December 1944. They put us on an LCI [Landing Craft Infantry], the same kinds of boats they used on D-Day in Normandy. We ran into a really bad storm off the coast of Africa, going into Italy. These landing craft didn't do well in rough seas and we took on a lot of water and we all got soaked. The waves would really rock the ship so everyone was seasick, but we finally made it to shore. We made camp at Mt. Vesuvius, in Naples. The last couple of days the volcano was getting active, so we had to get out of there. Then they shipped us up the boot with the 1st Armored Division to Pisa. We stayed there for a couple of weeks going through final preparations for combat. Before our division went into combat the Italian partisans took some of us who were forward observers up into the mountains to scout out the German positions. The one mountain that was particularly important in the German line was called Mt. Belvedere, and our division would fight its first battle there. I was really scared because we went up there at night and the Germans sent heavy patrols all through our area. We dug holes and camouflaged them with rocks. We'd get back to our outfit and report what we saw. Soon after we marched into the Apennine Mountains to relieve the 92nd, an all black division. Once we got into combat we took heavy casualties in the Northern Apennines because the Germans were dug in well. They had holes so deep that our bombs and artillery were useless. We had to use ladders to get down to them.

The Germans laid mine fields, and sometimes the infantry had to go along and use bayonets to dig them out of the ground. Other times we would machinegun whole areas to detonate the mines. The ones that were the worst were "Bouncing Betty's." They'd pop out of the ground and explode, spraying ball bearings all over the place. "What did I ever do to get over here?" I thought. The days didn't matter any more because guys were getting their arms and legs blown off right in front of me. We fixed up Jeeps to carry the wounded. It they were badly wounded, chaplains would ride with them. Some guys died in those Jeeps.

One time I told our chaplain, Father Moran, "I think that I am going to get killed."

He responded, "What ever made you think that? You can't get killed. You're needed here."

Then he gave me this certificate that said I would never be killed in action. Once the other guys heard that I received it, everyone wanted one, and Father Moran had to print more. We all thought that since we had that piece of paper we wouldn't get killed. I know it was a white lie, that it wasn't going to guarantee anything, but it was good to know I had that in my pocket. I helped Father Moran with the wounded for about a month, and served as an altar boy whenever he said Mass. I felt a great deal of respect for him because he helped me get my mind in shape and make me realize I had a job to do.

I found out if you didn't stay in your foxhole at night you were almost certain of getting hit with shrapnel. The Germans would send over these little nuisance planes,

"Bed-Check Charlies," that would drop a couple of bombs and sometimes machine-gun our positions. The Germans also shelled us with their 88s. One time shrapnel was coming through the air from one of those guns. A piece hit me in the leg, cutting it open just above the knee. They said I'd get a Purple Heart for that but my records were lost somewhere along the line. The Germans could drop a shell anywhere and their gun positions were always well concealed. We were pretty good at that too.

The infantry had to take this place called Riva Ridge, and we supported their attacks with howitzer fire. We got the German positions, what kinds of weapons they had, if there were any tanks, information on the units, and then we'd fire support. We used a technique to measure or estimate how far the Germans were from our guns. Based on these measurements, we were able to kill a lot of Germans. We also had 220mm guns back of the line. We'd radio back the coordinates on the German positions and pretty soon those big shells would be lobbed over our heads. Those guns were so loud, it sounded like the world was coming to an end when they went off.

At times we worked behind enemy lines trying to capture prisoners for our intelligence officers. We got pretty good at capturing their officers, who were responsible for making the battle arrangements. In Italy, most of the German prisoners I saw and talked with were fed up with fighting and wanted out of it. When we brought them back and gave them cigarettes, they were the nicest guys. We made sure that they ate well and were taken care of. We had a prisoner who fought on the Russian front. I got to talk with him and I used to give him cigarettes. He showed me pictures of his four daughters back in Berlin. I could have been court-martialed if the Army had found out about that because there were strict rules about fraternizing. It didn't matter that the war was coming to an end. There was still shooting going on, and the Army wanted us to stay hard-nosed.

After taking Mt. Belvedere and Riva Ridge, we were joined by the 1st Armored Division in our push across the Po River Valley. We rode on their tanks right up to the river. After we secured the Po, we were to go into the Brenner Pass and get information on the German defenses from the Italian Partisans in that area. One of the guys in our outfit, Miles Sevetti, was given money by the United States government to pay the Italian partisans.

We got to the Po River and crossed it in DUKWs. They were heavily loaded and we lost four or five of them in the water. Some guys drowned. While we were there I got to work the battalion switchboard quite a few times, That's how I found out a detachment of 10th Mountain infantry was going to try and capture Mussolini. It came through intelligence that he was in the area, and heavily protected by the Germans. We wanted to take him alive, but, as it turned out, the Partisans got to him first. They shot him and people mutilated his body. They hung him in Milan from a gas station sign, first by his hands, then by his feet, along with his girl friend and a couple other guys. The Partisans posted a heavy guard around the dead dictator, because they didn't want anybody to touch his body, especially us. We nearly got into a fight with them over it. They let the local Italians walk past so that they could throw stuff or spit on the bodies. They hung there a couple days. I saw them, and it was a horrible sight!

In the meantime, they took a lot of our tanks from us and sent them to Belgium where they were needed because they lost a lot of armor during the Battle of the Bulge. Ours was a front of secondary importance, I guess. I learned about Bastogne while I worked the switchboard. I also heard about the Tuskeegee Airmen, the black pilots who flew support for our bombers and us. One day, before we were to launch an attack, about eight of their pilots came up to the front to check out the positions we were going to try and take. We were pretty close to the German lines, and these fellas wanted to be sure that they wouldn't bomb or strafe us. I showed them the positions on a map. By that time in the war, they were using napalm. The next day, they attacked the German positions. One of their planes crashed into a mountain. I couldn't tell if it malfunctioned, or if it was hit by ground fire.

When the war ended, we all thought we were going to go home, but we didn't. In Yugoslavia, Tito had been fighting a guerrilla war against the Germans, and when the war in Europe ended, he got into it with the Italians over Trieste. We went up there to try and resolve the conflict, and we ended up losing a couple of our guys even though the war was supposed to be over. They pulled us out because they didn't want us to get any more involved, and then we started to get outfitted for the Pacific Theater. We didn't need our mules any more so the Russians got all our mules, heavy equipment, and tires. I wish we could have kept our mules. They suffered with us.

We got word that they were flying us home. We loaded up in North Africa and Southern Italy, and then the big transport planes took our equipment and us all the way to California with many stops in between. We were supposed to take amphibious training in California for a month, after which we were to go to Okinawa. In the meantime, they dropped the Atomic Bomb, saving us from having to go into combat again. I was young and full of pride, but, still, I was really glad the war was over. I just came home and went to work.

When I got home, I got a job at Thomas' Drug Store, in Greensburg, Pennsylvania. Mr. Thomas was going to pay for me to go to pharmacy school, but that fell through. Then I worked at a rubber plant in Jeannette, Pennsylvania, where I made tires.

Just before we left Europe, I had seen some kids in Trieste, kids about twelve-years old, running around wearing helmets and carrying toy guns, playing war. That's what we were, too, just kids.

"We Were Still Kids"

Henry M. ("Hank") Stairs, Jr.

66th Infantry Division, 30th Infantry Division, 28th Infantry Division (Korea); South Greensburg, Pennsylvania, 1924

"While we were still in Repo-Depo, we were on a bivouac on a hilltop, and another group was to our rear. They had arrived just after sunset after a long hike and were too tired to dig in. Almost every night a German recon plane flew overhead. We called him "Bed Check Charlie," and we had a very firm rule not to fire on him. Somebody did. Charlie made a big circle, came back over, and dropped a load of anti-personnel bombs on the newcomers. I was about five feet from my hole when I heard him coming. I dove headfirst for cover. My rifle flew in another direction. The bombs plastered those guys, killing and wounding scores. Among the dead, we later learned, was a chaplain. Several of my buddies visited the hilltop the next morning. I wasn't that curious. I figured I would see enough later, and I was right."

My father was in World War I, with E Company, 110th Infantry, 28th Division. He served with the 28th in France until September 1918, and then was sent to Officer Candidate School. The new "Shavetail," Henry Stairs, was assigned to Company M, 364th Infantry, 91st Division. He told me he was leader of the last white man's platoon in the Army. Divisions above the 91st were made up of African-Americans.

I was standing outside a little theater in Youngwood, Pennsylvania, called "The Pearl" (ironic?) with some other guys when the usher, a big tall skinny kid named Jerry, came out and said, "The Japanese bombed Pearl Harbor!"

Somebody said, "Oh my God! They bombed Pearl Harbor!"

Well, first of all, we didn't realize that Pearl Harbor was the naval base of the Pacific, and, secondly, we didn't realize that there was so much devastation from the attack. So I have to be honest; I wasn't terribly impressed. I was too ignorant to know what the hell was going on.

By early 1943, I was eager to join the military, especially since many of my friends had already gone in. We knew we were going to be drafted sooner or later, so three of us decided to volunteer for service. We were told that, as volunteers, we would have our choice of service branch. I wanted the Navy, another kid wanted the Marines, and the third had no preference. Anyway, we were all "accepted" by the Army. In March, two hundred of us headed for the induction center and boarded a train for New Cumberland, Pennsylvania. It was no big deal, because there were so many of us leaving at once. My girlfriend (now my wife), some friends and I, had a beer party, but I don't remember any great sorrow or hilarity. There were a lot of "Good Lucks." It was fun on the train. One guy was intently reading a newspaper. His buddy took a match, sneaked over, and set the paper on fire. Our feeling was, "Hey, goddammit, we're going! There's no reason for us to get out of it. Let's get going!"

We were still kids. What did we know?

New Cumberland was not a very happy place. It was our first exposure to military rank. A skinny, little corporal, a barracks leader, gave us such a bad mouth. I was shocked to realize that a lowly two-striper had the authority to sound off like a big shot. But we "rolled with the punches." Soon came the crew cuts, long lines to get our uniforms, long lines to get chow, and long lines for shots (yes, a few guys passed out!).

Back at the barracks, the corporal said, "Everybody out at five thirty for Police Call!"

What the hell did that mean? What are we going to do, direct traffic? Little did we know that "policing" meant picking up cigarette butts, or any other trash in the area. That was the first time I heard the phrase (there were many more to follow) "All I want to see are asses and elbows!"

It was the first time I experienced "KP," short for "Kitchen Police." I hated KP. It was elbows deep in soapy water, scrubbing pots as big as fifty-gallon drums, operating a dishwashing machine with blinding steam billowing back into your face, washing five hundred plates with someone in the background yelling for you to hurry up. I still won't do dishes. What a mess the kitchens were, scrubbing and slopping, heat and vomit.

After New Cumberland, we got on a train for a long ride to Camp Blanding, Florida. It was April. I stepped off the train and my foot sank up to the ankle in sand. "Why the hell would anyone spread all this sand at a railroad siding?" I thought. What did I know about Florida!

We assembled in a nearby field, and were told to sit down and relax. An officer was standing on a platform with a bullhorn under his arm, giving us unit assignments. He proceeded to go through the roster, "Ross Saunders, K Company, 262nd Infantry; Henry M. Stairs, Jr., K Company, 262nd Infantry."

I suppose every service unit had its misfits, but we had some who were outstanding. One was from Pennsylvania, and he was absolutely uncooperative. He wanted a Section Eight Discharge for being mentally or physically unfit for military service. During one of our long hikes, he refused to march. He sat down, and would not get up. My buddy, Ross Saunders, was ordered to march behind him with a fixed bayonet up this guy's ass. The guy was under guard all day. Finally, we stopped for a break. The guy crawled under a Jeep trailer and proceeded to pull out his teeth with a pair of pliers. That clinched it for him. He got his Section Eight.

Our division was transferred out of Blanding to Camp Joseph T. Robinson, not far from Little Rock, Arkansas. Our training included overnight, simulated combat exercises, no lights, no matches, and no cigarettes. After a long march, we arrived back at our training area and hit the sack right away, because there was an early morning call. After breakfast, we were supposed to get a brown-bag lunch. I was the last man to go through the line. No lunch! Someone ahead of me had taken two. I didn't have the guts to raise hell about it.

All day long we ran problems, which means running and hitting the ground, getting up, advancing, doing that over and over again. Damn strenuous! Later in the afternoon, the exercise over, we started the hike back to the barracks. By that time, I was low on energy. We were taking a break when some friends of mine came by in a Jeep and tossed me a pack of Camels. I really enjoyed that smoke! The break over, we continued our march. After a few minutes, I got light-headed. Smoking on an empty stomach made me sick. We were hiking on a dirt road that had just been scraped, and there was a mound of dirt running along the side. I was determined not to just drop out of line and sit down. I thought, "If I fall, I'm going to fall into that soft dirt." The world dimmed and, whoop, I passed out face first into the mound of dirt. I came around, rested, got up, finished the hike, and staggered into the barracks.

In time, I was selected to go to Radio School. For four weeks, I was excused from the long hikes, and that met with no objection from me. Each morning I reported to the school and practiced Morse code and "Voice." There was no school in the afternoon, which meant that I was supposed to report back to the company. Instead, I spent the afternoons at the Service Club. The Army called that "f—-ing off."

After completing Radio School, I was transferred to Battalion Headquarters. I hated leaving Saunders and the other guys who had suffered basic training with me, but I had a new MOS, and a new title, Rifleman/Radio Operator.

There were GI's shipping out of the division every week. Finally, it was my turn. "Pack your gear and prepare to ship out." Yeah, I was pissed, but it turned out to be a blessing coupled with a little Irish luck. Had I stayed with the 262nd Infantry, I would have been on the *Leopoldville* on Christmas Eve 1944 and possibly lost at sea. A German U-Boat sank the ship and a lot of guys got killed. Ross Saunders, my good friend, was one of the survivors. Radio School was another of my four-leaf clovers, because it got me out of being a rifleman, though I had been trained as one. Being attached to Battalion Headquarters would keep me fifty to 500 yards behind the front lines — most of the time.

I went overseas, via Camp Shanks, New York, to Port Rush, a temporary camp on the northern tip of Ireland. The trip over convinced me that I would have made a terrific sailor. I loved the fourteen days it took to cross. I got sick, but not seasick; I got candy sick. I bought a box of Hershey bars, and ate too many. I had one meal a day and a snack. I did a lot of calisthenics, played cards, shot craps. It was a great time, except for one thing. I pulled KP.

One of the most impressively ugly things at Port Rush was the condition of our latrines. They were little two-hole buildings with a board across and a big bucket underneath. Once a week, this Irish guy would pull his pony cart up. The cart was as big as a table and close to six-feet off the ground. The Irish guy wore a big, leather apron. He'd throw the contents of the buckets over the top edge of the cart, splashing everywhere. I heard they used that stuff to fertilize their fields.

As a lowly PFC, I sensed a different attitude from many of the officers and senior non-coms while I was at Port Rush. There was less "spit and polish," and the atmosphere was much more relaxed. It seemed to me they were aware that, in the near future, we would be placed in a position where we would have to rely on each other. Still, there was no breakdown in discipline. Our respect for rank remained unchanged. Training continued, but much of it was boring. We did a lot of close order drill, marching in unison, and immediately responding to commands. This was an important part of our training as infantrymen, because it became practical in combat. It was important not to hesitate if given an order.

We left Port Rush in April 1944, went to Bristol, England, and then trucked to Warminster, near Bath. Though there was some more very boring "dry run" practice with our rifles, we got some new training in how to accompany and protect tanks. In early June, we transferred to a camp near Southampton. Thousands of troops, miles of trucks and supplies filled the landscape. We were getting ready for the invasion of Normandy. 6 June came and went. We were still in isolation at an assembly area. Then, on D+18, we boarded a ship and headed for France. Some prayed. Some played. I was no good at cards or dice, so I just wrote letters home or lay in my bunk, alone with my thoughts. Was I scared? No, at least not on the way over. I knew I was going to come home. I just KNEW it! I suppose there were guys that didn't have that same attitude. A guy could be scared as hell that he wasn't going to make it, but I didn't think he could survive with that attitude.

A few days prior to our landing at Omaha Beach, there had been a terrific storm that destroyed the breakwater along the shore. Large boats had been scuttled there to provide a sheltered landing area. We had to unload farther out than we had planned, but it wasn't a serious problem. On 26 June, we went over the side, and climbed down landing nets into the landing craft.

We climbed the hill at Omaha, following a path that was lined with white, cloth tape. The area outside the tape had not as yet been cleared of land mines. There was no need to dig foxholes. We just got into those that were dug by the troops ahead of us. I didn't have much to do, except write letters, or bullshit with my buddies. I got lucky and was sent back to the beach on a work detail. KP again! But, this time it was a pleasure. I was assigned to the chow serving line, and passed out food to the personnel clearing the beach. I had all the pancakes I could eat!

I was a replacement, of course, in the Replacement Pool, nicknamed the "Repo-Depo." It was there that I witnessed my first casualty. One of the GI's in my group was demonstrating to a friend that our sidearm, the .45, would not fire if you pushed hard on the muzzle. Unfortunately, the demonstration failed, and the gun went off. The slug went through his hand and hit his buddy in the chest, killing him.

While we were still in Repo-Depo, we were on a bivouac on a hilltop, and another group was to our rear. They arrived just after sunset after a long hike, and were too tired to dig in. Almost every night a German recon plane flew overhead. We called him "Bed Check Charlie," and we had a very firm rule not to fire on him. Somebody did. Charlie made a big circle, came back over, and dropped a load of anti-personnel bombs on the newcomers. I was about five feet from my hole when I heard him coming. I dove headfirst for cover. My rifle flew in another direction. The bombs plastered those guys, killing and wounding scores. Among the dead, we later learned, was a chaplain. Several of my buddies visited the hilltop the next morning. I wasn't that curious. I figured I would see enough later, and I was right.

After the breakout at St. Lô, several of us were assigned to the 30th Division. We were near a small town called Percy. During our time in Repo-Depo, we had heard of the reputations of the 29th, the 1st, and the 30th Divisions. Since combat was inevitable, to be assigned to any of those divisions was okay.

Thirty of us were sent to an assembly area for an indoctrination speech by the regimental commander, Colonel Walter Johnson, from Montana. He was a little, short guy with a handlebar moustache, and he wore his .45 slung low on his hip like a western gunfighter. "Look to your right, now look to your left. One of you is going to be a casualty; two of you are going to be damn good soldiers and serve the 30th Division. We're gonna do our job and kill one hell of a lot of Germans!"

I became part of 1st Battalion Headquarters Company. I arrived there with five or six others, and we immediately began digging our foxholes. The battalion sergeant major approached and asked if any of us could type. I said I could.

He said, "Come over here and type."

I started to type, "Now is the time for all good men . . . ." Before I could finish he said, "Okay, you're our battalion clerk."

That was on 4 August 1944. Later that evening, we had a visit from Edward G. Robinson, the classic movie star gangster. Three days later they loaded us on trucks driven by the black troops of the "Red Ball Express." It was a short ride to the front, close to a small French village, St. Barthelmy. Our mission was to relieve the 1st Division, and maintain a strong defensive position. As we were jumping from the trucks, one of the drivers said, "Man, look at them four P–47s circling up there."

In an instant, the planes peeled off, dove down, and strafed us. P–47s? Like hell they were. A few strafing runs, and they were gone. One of the guys from the "Big Red One" said, "Hey, you guys are lucky. There's nothing happening up front with the Jerries. You can take over our foxholes and communication wire we laid, then you can relax!"

The next day the Germans launched a major counteroffensive, and the Battle of Mortain began. Hitler himself conceived the offensive. He called it "Operation *Luttich*" (Liege). The Germans wanted to drive a *Panzer*/infantry attack through the American lines to the French coastal town of Avranches, split the First Army from Patton's Third, and cut off Patton's supply routes as he pushed toward the south. The thick fog concealed the German movements from Allied aircraft. In their first thrust, they overran our roadblocks, and other forward positions. A and C Companies suffered severe losses, as did B and D. Plus, we lost several strategic defensive positions.

A guy named Leon Zilakowski and I shared a hedgerow foxhole we inherited from the 1st Division. It was about three-feet deep, long enough to lie down in, and, except for the entrance, covered with logs and dirt. We were well protected, except for our lower legs. In the predawn hours before the German advance, their artillery shelled the hell out of us with fragmentation shells and "Screaming Meemies." There was a tree burst right over us. After the barrage, we crawled out to discover the ground around us peppered with shrapnel. How we survived without so much as a scratch, I will never know. Irish luck, again!

One of the sergeants came running to our hole and said, "Okay, boys, the Germans are coming this way. We are now on the front line. You two go up to that hedgerow, and find a defensive position."

"Welcome to combat, Hank," I thought. "This is your baptism of fire!"

We had only our rifles. I heard the clank of approaching tanks, and that sound is forever imbedded in my memory. I knew I could shoot any German coming at me, but if a tank came through, I didn't know what the hell I would do. I crawled through the hedgerow into a five-foot deep ditch, trying to get a better view, and looking for an escape route. Nothing came, for the moment. A few minutes later, the enemy artillery resumed, and I heard the "freight train" sound of our own artillery overhead, and the chatter of small arms. This all contributed to a damned exciting morning. I asked myself, "If this is combat, how the hell does anyone survive?"

Then, in the early afternoon, the English appeared overhead in the form of RAF Typhoons. They came in so low we could see the pilots clearly. They strafed and fired antitank rockets. We cheered them on. More than fifty years later, I met one of those pilots. His name was John Slaney.

Our battalion commander, Lieutenant Colonel Robert Franklin, from Jackson, Tennessee, was manning a forward command post when a German tank moved up and stopped beside the building. Franklin was with his operations officer, a radioman,

and a couple enlisted men. As he turned toward his rear, he saw two GI's walking by with their hands raised. He promptly shot and killed the German captors. He ran out of the post, shot the tank commander, climbed the tank, and fired into the open hatch, killing the tankers inside. He never got recognition for that.

There was occasional incoming artillery after the heat of the first two days of the Mortain battle. Several of us were enjoying a brief respite, sitting in a hedgerow, when several shells came in. After being in an artillery barrage several times, we learned to tell by the sound whether they were going to land in our immediate area. We knew that these shells were not heading for us. They didn't land far away, but they were not close enough for us to panic. We weren't concerned about shrapnel tearing through the trees above us, until one of the guys sprang to his feet, and started into a weird dance that included a vigorous rubbing of his thigh. We thought he had been hit, but, as it turned out, a hot, quarter-sized piece of shrapnel had dropped from a tree and landed on his thigh. It was not enough to make it into a movie script, but it did invoke some smiles.

The Battle of Mortain lasted almost a week. It was there that I saw my first combat wounded GI, my first German prisoner, and my first dead German. Our battalion received the Presidential Unit Citation for the defensive stand that disrupted Hitler's plans. Another Unit Citation was given to a group of our guys who were surrounded for four days on the area's highest hill. Their accurate adjustments of heavy artillery fire caused Jerry to lose large numbers of tanks, support vehicles, and personnel.

A few days later, we, as part of the First Army, swung to the south, then turned north with Patton's Third Army in an attempt to surround German forces retreating east after their defeat at Mortain. We expected Field Marshall Montgomery to drive south and close what was supposed to be a pincer movement to trap the Germans in the Falaise Gap. He failed to do so, and thousands of crack German troops escaped through the opening. In this action, I listened to radio transmissions from our little Piper Cub observation planes describing the effects of our artillery laying waste to Germans retreating toward Paris. "Unbelievable! Beautiful! Direct hit on that lead tank! There goes an ammo truck!" were the excited comments of the pilots. The reports went on for hours.

The Falaise action cleared the combat in Normandy. Goodbye and good riddance, hedgerows! We advanced across the plains of France toward the Seine River, north of Paris, sometimes in vehicles, much of the time on foot, and I mean MUCH of the time. We walked, and we walked, and we leapfrogged with trucks, for 125 miles. Even though I was in excellent condition, the physical demand was so intense, my ball and socket joints felt like they were lined with sandpaper. In their retreat, the Germans had destroyed the bridges over the Seine, but, in our area, at least, there was enough left of some of the structures for infantry to walk across. The German rear guard resisted, but it had more nuisance value than anything else.

We advanced another 120 miles, in trucks and on foot. We stopped for a rest at the French town of Evreux, near the Belgian border. We were treated to a USO show featuring Dinah Shore, who was from Tennessee. It was only natural that she should entertain the 30th Division, the Tennessee National Guard.

In early September, we were attacking again, this time across southern Belgium, to Tournai. Our battalion was the first troops to enter Belgium. Our purpose was to liberate Holland. There was more stubborn rear guard action. During one of these confrontations, I chased a Jerry, but he was too far ahead for a good shot. I hoped I had scared hell out of him, at least. I was always an avid hunter, and I was a damn good shot, but not that time. Was I prepared to kill? No question about it. I would not have hesitated. I did not think of the Germans as human beings, as sons, husbands, fathers, or brothers. They were the enemy, simply put. Their job was to kill or wound me. My job was to do the same to them.

When we got into Holland in mid-September, we were walking single file up a small hill near Heerlen, when our column got an order to halt. There was a mine directly in our path. The platoon leader of the Ammunition and Pioneer Platoon was called forward to disarm the mine. There was an explosion, followed by a rising cloud of black smoke. There was nothing left of the soldier, and since there was no body for positive identification, he was declared MIA (missing in action). I thought that was wrong. We all knew he had been killed disarming the mine, and his family would just go on hoping that he was still alive unless they were informed of the truth.

I tried to write home every day, but sometimes we advanced so fast that I couldn't write. Even when we did write home, the Army censors would cut out any references to our actions and positions. That was a shame, because if those letters had remained intact, they would be invaluable primary sources for historians. What difference did censorship make, anyway? The Germans knew exactly who we were, where we came from, and where we were. In Alsdorf, Germany, for instance, we had a radio and listened to a female disc jockey that broadcast for the German propaganda machine. She played all the popular American tunes of the day, especially those of Glenn Miller and other big bands. We knew her as "Axis Sally." After a song, she would say things like, "By the way, you boys from the 30th Division, in case you haven't heard, your password for tonight is (then she'd give the password)." She always got it right.

If the German propagandists ever thought that Sally was in some way instrumental in destroying our morale, they were absolutely wrong. She'd say, "Listen, boys, is your wife back home sleeping with that good-looking draft dodger neighbor? Don't you wish you were there to put a stop to it?"

And we'd say, "Cut the bullshit, Sally, and get on with the tunes!"

When we got to the Siegfried Line (West Wall), our battalion was in reserve. The rifle companies were practicing unique river-crossing techniques. The Wurm River crossed our front about 300 yards short of the line of pillboxes that were the border defense of the "Fatherland." The Wurm was called a "river," but to me it was only the size of a small trout stream, about eight feet wide and waist deep. Our plan was to have the leading assault teams carry sections of a prefabricated footbridge, two-feet wide, ten-feet long. They dropped one section onto the near side of the stream from shore to midstream, the second across to the opposite shore, in line with the first. This made a V shape in the water. The final section spanned the V to make a small footbridge. Some of our riflemen were trained to use flame throwers, and two types of explosives. One was the "pole charge," consisting of a piece of lumber, ten-feet long and three-inches wide. At the end was a canvas bag, two-inches thick and one-foot square, filled with TNT. The idea was to crawl up to a pillbox, place the charge against the wall, and BOOM! The other used the same kind of explosive, but it had a canvas loop sewn on it so the GI could fling it. This was what we called a "satchel charge."

The pillboxes were made of reinforced concrete about the size of a two-car garage. The walls were thick enough to be safe from most artillery, bazooka rounds, and most bombs. There were thousands of these in the Siegfried Line, and they were arranged so that they would catch an approaching enemy in a crossfire. Most pillboxes were in the fields or in the line itself, but some of them were in the various towns. They were camouflaged to resemble regular houses. By the time we got there, Germans had lost so many seasoned troops, that the pillboxes were manned by the less experienced, some of them very young boys and old men. Anyway, they could still pull a trigger and kill you.

On 2 October 1944, we were ready for the attack on Hitler's West Wall. We watched the bombs from our medium bombers fall and explode. P–38s dive-bombed and dropped Napalm. That was the first and last time I saw Napalm used. The pillboxes were so effectively protected that most of our bombardment, especially from artillery, was useless. I had no doubt, however, that the Germans inside them were plenty scared. At eleven o'clock in the morning, the rifle companies crossed the Line of Departure, and were followed by my company and the reserves. There were no Dragon's Teeth or other tank and infantry obstacles in our sector. By the time the forward elements reached the Wurm River and crossed the railroad immediately in front of the pillboxes, they were damned tired, but within two hours, all the pillboxes in their sector had been captured, and our boys formed a line of defense. Our rifle companies suffered many casualties, especially C Company.

When I reached the small town of Palenburg, I met troops from the 2nd Armored Division, the boys who attacked on our left. A GI from the 2nd Armored, standing in a doorway, looked awfully familiar to me. It was Earl Leonard, one of my bunkmates during basic training. After we chatted for a few minutes, I went on my way. Today, I still wonder if he made it through the war.

That night, Headquarters Company personnel were ordered to go forward and dig in. We had to fill a gap in the front line. Early the next morning, volunteers, including me, went back to pick up the dead from Company C. Since the area was still under enemy observation, we were ordered to leave our rifles and sidearms, and put on Red Cross armbands. Six of us went back to the open fields with stretchers, picked up our dead comrades, and brought them to the area where Graves Registration would collect them. In the C Company zone, there was a barbed-wire trap. In an area twenty by twenty feet, there were wooden pegs driven into the ground

BATTLE OF THE BULGE   STAVELOT, BELGIUM, DEC. 19, 1944 "FIVE AMERICAN JEEPS FILLED WITH GERMANS IN GI UNIFORMS MADE A WILD DASH TO CROSS THE BRIDGE."

HANK STAIRS 1ST BN 117TH 30TH D

30th Division commanders prepare for the assault on the Siegfried Line using a SANDTABLE.
Courtesy: Hank Stairs

about two-feet apart, and a twelve-inch-high mass of barbed wire was woven between the pegs. I had never seen that kind of obstacle before. It seemed awesome to me.

In a day or so, we were off toward Ubach. During our advance we came under fire from a dug-in tank. The Jerries had dug a sloping trench wide enough for their tank. Only the gun turret was exposed. I ran like hell to a nearby school building. Enroute, I passed a couple fallen Americans. One was a second lieutenant. A gold bar on his collar flashed momentarily in the bright sunlight. For some reason, seeing him hit me pretty hard.

Someone took care of the tank, and we moved out. After a mile or two, we reached Alsdorf, a mining village. We waited for several days, while the division helped in the encirclement of Aachen. When that was completed, we got a "Big Day" in Alsdorf; we all got to take a shower. We didn't get clean uniforms, but that was the least of our worries. That was the night Axis Sally gave us our password.

Showers were rare, and everyone smelled the same say, bad. Hygiene, in general, was a problem. Our helmets had a plastic liner, inside of which were a few strips of webbing about an inch wide, crisscrossing the interior. We would slide a small roll of toilet paper from the K-Ration box between the liner and the webbing, together with our extra socks. This kept the socks and the paper dry. If nature called, you jumped from the foxhole, took your entrenching tool, went a few paces, and dug a small hole. If you were under fire, you simply used your helmet, without the plastic liner, and cleaned it later. Of course, first you removed the toilet paper and the socks. You did what you had to do, then covered the hole. A common problem was where to go when we were on trucks. If you had to defecate, you were in big trouble. Again, you had to use your helmet, unless you could hold it for a stop, but, with what we ate half the time, that wasn't always possible. Many times, I urinated from a moving truck. It wasn't easy.

Body lice were a common parasite, but they really didn't cause any great discomfort. We got them from sleeping on straw in our foxholes or in barns, or on damp mattresses. I recall removing my wool sweater and it was crawling with bugs. "Seam squirrels," "crotch crickets," "mechanized dandruff," we called them. In spite of lack of bathing, we still had to be clean-shaven, and we had only cold water and no shaving cream. I estimate that between the time we left for the Continent until the war ended (eleven months), we didn't have more than ten baths.

The 30th Division was preparing for a 16 November offensive in the Wuerselen/Mariadorf area, which was later called "The Perfect Infantry Attack." While that preparation went on, several of us in the battalion were sent back to a monastery in Kerkrade, Holland for rest and relaxation (R&R). It was great! We slept in bunks, between sheets and in our underwear, sat at a table, ate off real china. No enemy activity! Absolutely nothing to do but write letters home and relax. Someone took a picture from the second storey of us playing touch football. It made it into my *Battalion History*, but it is of very poor quality. When I visited the monastery in 1999, I went up to that same second-storey window, and took another picture. During that rest period, I did get a chance to visit Heerlen again and get a proper portrait taken.

Around 14 December, the division was ready to cross the Roer River. The battalion was near the town of Warden, Germany, were we had a one-man Mickey Rooney show. I was impressed. He carried all the sound equipment by himself, set everything up, and gave us a real show. It was there that I saw my only German jet plane. It looked like a stubby cigar zooming through at a very low level. It had short wings, and single jet at the rear of the fuselage. I don't know what happened to it. I don't think it was shot down, it went through so fast. We watched a movie, *The Song of Bernadette*, starring Jennifer Jones. I fell in love. Then came the order, "Pack up and move out."

It was 17 December 1944, and the Battle of the Bulge was on. We were told that the Germans had broken through in Belgium, and that we were going down to help stop them. Axis Sally reported that the German attack through the Ardennes could not be stopped, despite the impending arrival of the 30th Division, President Roosevelt's "SS Troops!" All night long we ran bumper-to-bumper, with blackout lights on. Someone had to jog in front of our truck so that we wouldn't rear-end the one in front. German planes were overhead, dropping flares, but they didn't bomb us, although some of the 30th guys reported otherwise. From time to time, we were ordered out of the trucks to take cover. On one of those leaps, my steel helmet crashed down on my glasses and gashed my nose. We never used chinstraps. I could have gotten a Purple Heart, but I refused. To accept one would have been blasphemous.

We arrived at Malmedy, Belgium, tired, sleepy, and cold. The battalion was ordered ten miles east to Stavelot, along the Ambleve River. We had no intelligence on the enemy, and no one knew where they were. We made a U turn and circled to the rear for several miles, finally stopping within a few miles of Stavelot. As we detrucked, there were some American troops sitting by the side of the road eating K-Rations.

"The Germans ran us out," they reported.

Colonel Franklin ordered the battalion into tactical formation, one company to the left of the road, one to the right. The reserves, D and Headquarters companies, followed. A mile down the road we came upon a burned-out gasoline dump that had been set ablaze by Belgians. Thousands and thousands of cans, some still smoldering, lined the road. The dump had been a prime objective of Joachim Peiper's *Panzer* troops. The gasoline was denied them. When they saw the ruined dump, they had turned east. The first inkling we had that many of Peiper's SS troops were disguised in American uniforms was when an "American" halftrack sped across the Stavelot Bridge and started firing on us. The halftrack was quickly dispatched. In another incident, an "American" approached a two-man foxhole and asked, "You guys want a cup of coffee?"

The GI's accepted the offer. The "American" shot and killed them both. From then on, the general order was to shoot anything on the other side of the river that moved. The next day, 19 December, five Jeeps, loaded with "Americans," came speeding across the Stavelot Bridge. Four of them came under a hail of rifle and machine-gun bullets. The fifth turned and escaped.

19 December was a day of artillery fire and counter fire. Our Headquarters command post was set up in a small house to the rear. A barrage of German artillery came in. A few of us were outdoors, and made a mad dash for the building to get some cover. All but one of us made it. He came in, hopping and cussing about a shrapnel wound in his foot. "Damn!" he kept yelling.

"Quit your bitching," we said. "You have a million-dollar wound there, and it's enough to send you back home!"

Around 20 December, a company of SS infantry, either boozed up or jazzed up by a pep talk, started *wading* across the river in a fanatical charge. They never made it to midstream. It was a slaughter.

While we were bunked in the basement of the Headquarters building, a few of us were standing outside the basement door, looking toward the German side of the river, and watching our artillery pound the place. Suddenly, roaring up the river to our right, came a German fighter, a Bf–109 (Messerschmidt). He was very, very low, about tree top level. As he came even with our line of sight, the pilot made an abrupt climb, turned upside down, and FELL OUT OF THE PLANE! One of my buddies turned to me and said, "The guys in A Company will have his flight suit before he hits the ground!"

His comment was so funny, it has remained with me for over fifty years, assuring me that I did not dream the incident.

One day a German prisoner was brought back to battalion for transport to the rear. Someone asked, "Who wants to take this Nazi back to Regiment?"

I immediately volunteered. The sonofabitch was dressed in GI clothes. He was even wearing GI dog tags. He should have been shot. He was the perfect image of the Nazi SS, arrogant, firm-lipped, steely eyes. He was probably one of those who massacred innocent Belgians and our own POWs. I kept thinking about the two guys who were shot in their foxholes in cold blood. I thought about shooting him myself on the way to Regiment. I was filled with hate, and wanted so much to do it. I was almost ready to become like he was. I was ashamed to admit it to myself.

In early January 1945, the division was relived and sent to Sart, Belgium, for rest, refitting and replacements. We were housed with the locals, and they were great people. Then we attacked in the direction of St. Vith. During the attack, we passed the site of the Malmedy massacre, where nearly 100 of our troops, prisoners of war, had been slaughtered by Peiper's SS. Later, we were delayed for nearly an hour on our approach to St. Vith. A general came over (he wasn't from our division) and asked, "Why are you stopped?"

We said, "There's a tank up there, General, and it has all this terrain covered. We're waiting for an artillery hit."

He said, "Oh, gimme your rifle."

So, the general took a rifle from a guy, went to the front of the column, and fired. Looking back, I guess he wanted to include in his memoirs that he was the only one brave enough to fire at, "that damned tank." As any idiot knew (perhaps not), you couldn't hurt a tank with a rifle, and don't be surprised if it fires back. Which it did.

But the general got his Combat Infantry Badge, and we got one of our guys killed.

The Battle of the Bulge was over for us by 25 January 1945. On or about 1 February, the 30th Division was about to disappear. We removed all division identification from our uniforms and vehicles. The plan was for us to return north, and cross the Roer River without the German generals knowing it. We got ready to make a hush-hush move around midnight. On our way north, Axis Sally announced that the 30th Division was in convoy moving north. Some secret! On 6 February, the battalion was happy as hell to return to the monastery in Holland for some rest.

On 23 February, facing the Roer, we awoke to the sound of artillery. It was the biggest barrage fired by our artillery during war in that part of Europe. After the barrage, the Roer crossing got underway. The battalion was in division reserve and did not play an active role, but for the remainder of the month, we were involved in several heated actions, including one night attack. I hated night attacks with a passion. First Battalion captured a huge, self-propelled, 380mm howitzer.

In mid-March, we prepared for the Rhine River crossing. For the third and last time, Headquarters Company planned the strategy over the SANDTABLE. The first time we did it was when we attacked the Siegfried Line; the second time was when we attacked in the Wuerselen/Mariadorf area. The SANDTABLE was about a six-foot square, a three-dimensional model of the battlefield. We built boxlike tables, put in a large mirror, then put sand on top of that. From contour maps and aerial photographs, we formed hills, valleys, and plains out of the sand. Then we put in small painted blocks that were buildings, obstacles, pillboxes, and other structures. We used wire for railroads, small sticks and weeds were wooded areas. Then we removed sand to expose what were rivers and streams. The SANDTABLES were terrific training aids, and using them saved lives. Every unit down to squad leaders was given an orientation on the SANDTABLE by Headquarters staff and senior NCOs. Squad leaders especially were encouraged to bring their team of eight or ten soldiers to view the model terrain.

H-Hour was 23 March, at night. We marched to the vicinity of the Rhine in column. As we neared the water, I saw an Army sedan parked along the trail. It belonged to Generals Eisenhower and Simpson, the Ninth Army commander, and ex-commander of the 30th Division. Behind the river dike, was a line of small boats. It was dark when we reached them, and a GI directed us to stand by "our" boat. The assault teams were off ahead of us. We were the third wave. There were eight of us to a boat, plus one to operate it. GO! We went four on each side, grabbed the boat, pulled it up and over the dike, and down into the water. The engine roared to life, and we were off. The guy operating the boat was in the Navy! I said to him, "You have a hell of a job, taking men across the river."

He said, "Yeah, but I get to come back!"

While we were crossing, two machineguns were firing tracers high overhead to mark the landing zone, one to the left, one to the right. Aside from that and the noise of the boat motor, there was nothing. I expected to be shelled, but that didn't happen. Thanks! The flat-bottomed boat scooted onto shore, and we promptly jumped out, ran up the dike, and down the other side. I got separated from the rest of the guys, and realized I was alone. Off to my right came a faint call for help. We weren't under fire, so who was calling for help? I heard the call again, and this time, I saw a wounded German soldier who was ready to give up, to *anyone*. I told him I couldn't help, and that he should just sit there and wait. Sooner or later a medic would show up. He was wearing a watch, and I asked him if I could have it. He gladly gave it to me.

Having some idea of where our command post was supposed to be from the SANDTABLE, I continued toward a tiny village called Ork. When I got there, I saw no one. I had fallen behind, talking to that wounded Jerry. I went into a cellar where I found a frightened old man and girl. I took off my steel helmet, and started to relax a bit. I saw a baby carriage nearby. I was going to throw my helmet into it, but I thought, "I wonder if there's a baby in there." I hesitated, then looked inside the carriage. Yep, there was a baby. I was glad I didn't toss the helmet.

All German civilians, now mostly old men and women, feared us. There were damn few young men, I mean, damn few teen-age boys. Even at that age, they were in the German army. Once in a while we would come across a non-German person who was a maid or a farmhand. A couple of them weren't too happy about being liberated. I think the life that they were living as a servant was probably better than the one that they left behind.

The battalion continued its forward movement for the next two weeks. I lost a good friend, Patsy Liscio, a replacement from the 66th Division who was in basic with me. In early April, we captured Hamelin, of Pied Piper fame. I found eggs preserved in a clear liquid (*wasserglas*), and I ate a dozen. Lowell Thomas visited our battalion while we were there.

From Hamelin, we were off again, driving south of Hanover, toward Brunswick, where there was some resistance, but, by this time, German troops knew that their defeat was a certainty. We captured them in large and small groups. Toward the end of the first week in April, a small group of German soldiers carrying a white flag approached company A. Among them was the commanding general of the Brunswick troops. He asked to meet with General Leland Hobbs, our division commander, to discuss surrender terms. The German proposed permitting the evacuation of his troops, and leaving the town to us. Hobbs replied, "Hell, I don't want your town. I want your soldiers!"

After Brunswick, we continued on to Magdeburg, on the Elbe River, which we took in mid-April. As the battalion approached the city, a Nazi flag was still flying in an upstairs window of a building along our route. I took off, ran into the building, and tore the flag off the pole. I still have it among my souvenirs.

We weren't supposed to do any looting.. I suppose taking the flag was okay, but I'm talking about looting. When we would enter a German town (after the civilians had departed) our platoon leader would say, "Communications will take those buildings."

My "foxhole" buddy and I worked as a team on those occasions. One of us would grab a mattress from an upstairs room and drag it to the basement, where we would be protected from artillery fire. The other would look for booze or food. We always found lots of booze, wine, Cognac, Schnapps, sometimes Champagne. I found an unusual meal, a whole chicken stuffed into a sealed, glass canning jar. Many times we found good bread, which, when we sliced it, we could see full grains of wheat. We'd force open drawers, cabinets, or anything else to look for "war trophies," like cameras, guns, ceremonial daggers. I made a great find in Magdeburg. It was a machine pistol, with an ammunition clip attached, stored in a hollow, wood container carved into the form of a gunstock. The pistol could be connected to the gunstock and used as a shoulder weapon. I traded it for a camera. The box also contained the German equivalent of our Expert Infantry Badge, and paper money. Once, somewhere in Germany, I ducked under a viaduct for protection, and discovered on the ground hundreds of silver one-Mark coins. I stuck as many as I could in my pockets, and when it was all clear, I went on my way.

We were ordered to stop at the Elbe and await the Russians. Berlin was only ninety miles away. Thank God, no more casualties, no more war! On 4 or 5 May, our battalion staff welcomed the Russian commander to our command post. We joined hands, and drank a toast to victory, but behind the smiles and joviality, I sensed an uncomfortable aura. A few of us walked to the river to meet our Russian counterparts. It was a friendly gathering. I had medical alcohol mixed with lemon powder in my canteen, and I offered the Russians a drink. Then they offered me some Vodka. WOW! It was the hottest liquid ever to go down my gullet! We shared a healthy laugh, tried to talk, but we really couldn't communicate. I did understand their requests for cigarettes, and I obliged.

The war in Europe was over. On the way home, I was processed out at Camp Lucky Strike. The processing camps were named after cigarette brands. We celebrated. One guy had Cognac, another had wine, another had Orange Liqueur, and one guy had Buzz Bomb Fluid, some sort of alcohol concoction. Did we get drunk? You bet we did. The next morning was unpleasant.

We left from Le Havre for Southampton and came home on the *Queen Mary*. We left the day Japan surrendered. When we hit New York Harbor, the Statue of Liberty came into view. As we sailed up the Hudson River, a big blimp came overhead to greet us. So did tug boats and fireboats firing water cannons. The 30th had been listed in shipping notices all over the country, so there were many relatives at the pier. We anchored on my mother's birthday, 26 August. I got home. I don't remember a flood of tears, but, for sure, there were wet cheeks. Dad didn't show a great deal of emotion, but I could feel his love in a warm, firm handshake. We now had a common history — war. At breakfast, we were seated in a small, breakfast nook. Suddenly there was a loud, whistling noise, PSSSSSSSS! I froze for a millisecond. It sounded like an artillery shell on the way in, but it was just the safety valve on the radiator. Dad and I had a good laugh!

I enrolled at Seton Hill College in Greensburg for a year, prior to attending Carnegie Tech in Pittsburgh. In the meantime, I joined the 28th Division, the Pennsylvania National Guard, the Keystone Division. It was called that because

Pennsylvania is known as the "Keystone State." Then came the Korean War. The 28th became federalized, and, after my junior year at Carnegie Tech, I was back in the United States Army. I was pissed. I had no one to blame but myself for attending all those Guard drills as Master Sergeant gave me a few extra bucks that came in handy for a married-father-student.

We got sent to Camp Atterbury, Indiana, a training nucleus for a great number of soldiers that were sent to Korea. It didn't feel great to know that they would be sent into combat, but I did my best to give them what Dad, ten years earlier, said I should have, a damned good, hard, basic training.

In November 1951, the 28th was on its way to Ulm, in Bavaria, as the Army of Occupation, and a "Cold War Force." It was only five years since the defeat of Germany, but I was not aware of any hostility toward us. We were there for Christmas, and since my car had been shipped over, some of us drove into the surrounding villages to get away from camp. On one of those trips, we stopped in a *Bierstube* for a beer and snack. There was a Christmas party going on in an adjoining room. A young German, about our age, came out and asked us to join the party. We did, sang some carols, and drank some beer.

Another time, during *Oktoberfest*, we joined a big party under a large tent. There was a German band on a raised platform playing Bavarian music. They were dressed in the local attire, *Lederhosen*, Tyrolean hats, the whole bit. After several beers, the bandleader called one of our guys, Chuck van Pelt, a sergeant, to come up and lead the band. Chuck got up on stage, rolled his GI trousers up as far as he could, borrowed a Tyrolean hat, and started leading the band. The crowd was delighted. Suddenly, from out of nowhere, appeared an MP. He yelled to Chuck to get his attention. No response. He yelled again. Still no response. Finally, the MP cracked Chuck on the toes with his Billy club. Chuck responded. The MP yelled, "Get down off there, soldier, you're out of uniform."

The crowed booed. We headed for the rear exit, trying to decide whether to leave or stay. While we debated, a young German came out and asked, "Sergeant, do you want us to take care of the MP?"

"No, thanks," I answered. "We don't want to cause you people any trouble."

Great American image you displayed, MP!

Our occupation time in Germany lasted only six months. I came back in 1953, and finished up my education as an Industrial Designer. I worked for Talon Zipper Research in Meadville, Pennsylvania. They closed in a year, and I joined a design consultant firm. Five years later, I went to American Standard. Thirty years after that, I retired as Manager of Industrial Design for American Standard Plumbing Products.

During World War II, with the exception of Mortain and the Siegfried Line, I operated to the rear of the rifle companies. I did not always face their danger, but I am qualified to give them praise, because I was trained as a member of an infantry rifle squad. I thank God for his blessings, and Irish ancestry for passing on good fortune my way. This is my story, these are my words, but no words can be spoken or written without remembering the sacrifices of those of my comrades who gave their full measure.

"It Was All Luck"

Lewis Jacob Steck

2nd Marine Division, 2nd Marine Regiment, 3rd Battalion, L Company
Yukon, Pennsylvania April 2, 1922

"I saw a lot of people get killed. I saw a lot of people get wounded. It bothered me more when the person was wounded real bad than if the person was killed out right. You don't forget about them. I'd see a Marine who was wounded real bad I'd wonder, "Is he gonna make it? Is he even gonna make it back to the ship before he dies?" A lot of times the fellas who I thought were wounded real bad were taken off the island. Later on they came back to the outfit! It was like a reunion! Then there were the times when I'd never see them again. A lot of the stuff has come back. I never talked very much about it, and a lot of the things that happened I just let go by, and I didn't even want to think about them. In the war, some of the best people were the ones that didn't come back. And I often wonder how the world would be if they were all here."

I WAS THE FIRST THING my parents raised on the Steck Farm! They moved here in March 1922 and I was born on 2 April. We were a big family. Eleven kids. Four died in childhood. I went to a one-room schoolhouse just down the road. There was twenty-three of us in that school. Then I went to South Huntingdon High School, and graduated in 1940. My father came from the old country, from Slovenia, but then it was in the Austro-Hungarian Empire. My father married my mother over there, where she was a cook for a well-to-do family. Dad worked in a mine for a while in Germany. In Austria, he was a carpenter, and he also worked in a brickyard. He was in his twenties when he came over, and worked in the mines for a time. Then he was able to get a forty-nine-acre farm in Arona, Pennsylvania. My father was a wonderful farmer. He lived to be ninety-four years old. We delivered milk into Yukon and Wyano. A lot of kids grew up on our milk. Of course many families couldn't afford to pay for it since it was the Depression, but Pap, he would just give them the milk. He'd say, "If you can pay a little bit, fine."

My friend, Mike Babich, and I wanted to go into the Marines together, but they wouldn't take him. I don't know why, he was a big guy! He went into the Navy instead. On 3 November 1942, I went into the Corps. I was going to be drafted anyway, so in September I signed up. They told me they would call me when they were ready for me. So I got all the farm work done in the fall. I was the only one from my family who went into the service. I was nineteen years old.

I left from Pittsburgh and went by train to Parris Island. The rifle they gave us to train on was the old Springfield '03. The one they gave me had a pitted barrel and I couldn't get it clean. When the DI inspected the bore, it looked dirty, so he made me "ride the range" where I had to clean the top of the mess hall stove with a rag and salt. If I had sores on my hands, it would sting like from the salt and the heat of the stove.

In boot camp we did everything at attention. When we went up to the main station from our barracks, we had to march at attention. When we went through the chow line, we had to stand at attention. We weren't allowed to talk, laugh, or do anything. Our drill instructors walked up and down the line watching. One day, two guys were in chow line talking. The DIs caught them talking and pulled them out of line. They put one kid on one coal pile and the other on another pile. One had to yell, "I'm a shit head!" The guy on the other side had to answer, "Me, too!"

And they had to keep doing that all through chow.

Boot camp lasted eight weeks. After that there was no more training. One day they had us all lined up ready to get on the train. I was standing next to this kid from Canton, Ohio, whose name was Bacon. They were calling guys' names to get on the train and Bacon, myself and this other kid weren't called. They didn't have our record books, so we couldn't leave with our buddies. We weren't about to be left behind, so we went back to the barracks and found our record books. We hurried back and showed them to the CO. He said, "Get your gear down here."

We put our gear in where the officers had theirs. The officers had their own cabinets for their stuff, and they had their own rooms with three compartments, a bathroom, a seating area with a table, and a sleeping compartment with an upper and lower bunk. Because they screwed up our records, we ended up staying in this luxury compartment! We were like officers! We went all the way across the States that way. We even had our bunks made up for us. But the good times stopped when we got to the West Coast.

We boarded a big ocean liner that had been converted into a troop ship. We got to American Samoa, and then transferred to an old lumber schooner that took us to British Samoa. On board they fed us C-Rations dated 1916! They had those rations stored in some big old warehouse all that time. We could still eat them, but they weren't good. When we got to British Samoa they lined us all up and said, "You men are going to mortars. You men are going to machineguns. The rest of you are riflemen!"

I was in a replacement battalion, and was put into the machineguns. On Samoa we made a lot of fire lanes. We'd clear a place out with axes and saws, and then set up a machinegun. I had this buddy, Tinch, who had worked for a tree-surgeon company before the war. I got along well with him because we could both wield an ax or saw. I learned all that from my Pap. I'll tell you, Pap could cut a tree down that was leaning down hill and he could make it fall uphill!

It was hot and damp on that island. Miserable! I went into the PX on Samoa to get some cigarettes, and they were moldy, but we'd smoke them moldy cigarettes. Chocolate would get a whitish mold on it, but it was good once you scraped the mold away. It would pour rain like crazy, and then stop all of a sudden. We'd go outside, and there would be just one cloud passing over.

Soon I was shipped to New Caledonia. But we never even got off the ship there.

We went straight to New Zealand, a beautiful country. We got there in the Spring of 1943, which was actually their winter. Fellas were coming back from Guadalcanal to Wellington, New Zealand, where they were reforming the 2nd Marine Division. There were the 2nd Marine Regiment, the 8th Marines, the 6th Marines, and the 10th Artillery. I ended up in the 2nd Marine Regiment, 3rd Battalion, M Company, a light weapons company of machineguns and mortars.

The guys that come back from the Canal had a lot of liberty so they could get rid of their tensions, but they all had malaria. They would go on liberty, and sometimes wouldn't show up for days. That was because they would be in the hospital in Wellington with high fevers. We had a little charcoal-burning stoves in our tent, and sometimes I could hardly stand the heat from that thing. When these fellas came back from the hospital, they'd get the chills and fire that thing up!

We got all kinds of training in New Zealand. The guys from the Canal taught us how the Japanese fought. They fired our weapons and Japanese weapons so that we could distinguish the difference. We made simulated landings, and we made actual landings along the coast of New Zealand. We had an LST blow up on one of these landings and there were some casualties. Guys would get their feet cut between the Higgins Boats and the LSTs. What would happen is the toilets, or "heads" as we called them in the Navy and the Marines had these long tubes running down the sides of the ship almost to the water. They had openings at the bottom, and this is where all the crap would come out. The Higgins boats would draw right up beside the LST's and our guys had to climb down the landing nets into the Higgins boats. The rough sea would make the Higgins boats go up and down. If a Marine wasn't careful, and had his foot on the gunwale of a Higgins boat when the sea swell drove the boat upward, he'd get his foot caught against this "chute!" We were always warned about that. They told us not to step on the gunwale of the boat when it's coming up at you. They told us to jump into the boat off the net.

By the time we were ready to go into combat, there was nothing but the Marine Corps! Naturally, we were serving our country, but the business of doing it for the Corps was to make us Gung-Ho. Really, we looked out for our buddies and ourselves. We did anything to save our buddies. We were family.

They told us we were going to hit Betio Island in the invasion of Tarawa. My battalion was to hit Red Beach One. We got up at midnight on the morning we were to land. We took a shower and everybody had to shave, because, if anyone got wounded in the face, a beard would make the wound get infected easier. For our breakfast we had steak and eggs, the same thing we got to eat before every landing. We got into the Higgins boats around four o'clock in the morning, as part of the third wave.

Since I was part of a machinegun squad, I carried in part of a .30 caliber. A machinegun platoon was made up of four sections. The sections were made up of squads and there were eight men in a squad. The number-one man carried the tripod. The number-two man carried the gun, plus the spare parts kit. The third man, who is what I was during the battle, carried the water can or a box of ammunition, which has a belt of 250 rounds in it. The rest of the guys carried two boxes of ammunition.

We had carbines as our personal weapons, and the number one and two men had .45 pistols.

I'll tell you, the Navy bombed that island like you couldn't believe. The Japanese thought it would take a million men to take that place. And we were figuring on taking it in ten hours! So something was wrong somewhere!

We were in the water going around in circles for hours. The Navy had to move the big warships back because our Higgins boats were in the line of fire. The first wave of Amtracs was supposed to land around eight o'clock. They didn't start to land until ten after nine. The Navy was supposed to make a last bombing run with dive-bombers. It didn't materialize so we just waited in the water. Meanwhile they were worried about the tide. If we waited much longer our Higgins boats might not be able to get over the reef, like the Amtracs could. The water depth was real shallow on one side and on the other it dropped thousands of feet! Those guys in that first wave got the hell shot out of them. The Japanese had these big naval guns, one of them a British gun they had captured on Singapore. They had concrete pillboxes built up with sand and coconut logs. Bombs did little damage to them.

Guys in the Higgins boats got seasick, and everybody was scared. When we started in, we couldn't get over the reef. The Higgins boats were supposed to hit the beach, and then the front doors were supposed to drop, letting us out. We couldn't do that, so we went over the sides of the boats and into the water. The water was anywhere from over our heads or up to our knees, and we were 800 yards away from the beach! We had to wade in all that way, and it was slow moving. I lost a lot of buddies. Most of the fire we were getting was small arms fire, but it was as thick as you could imagine. I could see the bullets hit the water, and the ones that didn't hit the water I could hear them snap as they went by, and there was a continuous snapping! I kept thinking, "Which one's gonna hit me?"

My buddies fell all around me. A couple guys weren't hit too bad, and could make it the rest of the way. I had to drag a few guys in. Some thought they were hit worse than they were, and after dragging them a few yards, they realized they could make it on their own.

One of the worst things was not knowing where all the fire was coming from. We didn't know where to shoot. There was a sand bar about two feet high and close to the beach. On the seaward side we could get down in the water behind that thing, but the guys who went to the landward side found out that the Japanese had a heavy machinegun zeroed in there. I could see a couple of our dead on that sandbar. We knew that the Jap gun had a clip of thirty rounds. What we did was stay down until the gunner fired his thirty rounds. Then we'd take off while he crammed another clip in his gun. That's how I made it to the beach, but to this day I don't know how.

As scared as I was I kept moving forward. I was resigned to the fact that I *had* to do what I was doing. Some guys carried lucky charms with them, but still got hit. A lot of them had their girl friends' pictures for good luck, and there was plenty of that. One fella got hit in the front of his helmet; the bullet spun around inside, and then came out the back. Didn't even singe his hair! It was really *all* luck, I guess.

I finally got up against the sea wall and saw the guys from the first wave still there; a lot of them killed right in their Amtracs. The Japs had anti-boat guns placed, and when the Amtracs went over the sea wall, they'd fire at the soft undersides. There was so much fire going on at that seawall, I didn't have time to think. Corpsmen ran back and forth along the sea wall taking care of the wounded. Somehow they managed to get these guys onto rubber boats out to the reef and from there they'd take them on to the ships. By the time it was all over, we lost seventeen out of forty-three in the original platoon.

Everything was disorganized because we didn't have our company commander. He was still out there somewhere in a Higgins boat. The batteries in our SCR–300s backpack radios went dead, and we had no way of getting replacements.

It was noon before anyone even went beyond the sea wall. I picked up the ammo to our machinegun and followed the rest of the guys. Finally we got our machinegun set up in a temporary position, because we really couldn't see anything to shoot at. L Company was actually a rifle company that day. As machinegunners, it was our job to protect their right and left flanks. I was on the left flank. We did keep up a continuous fire towards the Japanese lines to keep their heads down while our riflemen moved forward and knocked out the next foxhole or shell hole. We did have some trouble with Jap spider holes, steel drums with lids buried in the sand. In each was a Jap rifleman. They would lift up the lids and snipe at us from the rear. They'd do it so fast sometimes we couldn't tell where the shots came from. They also had zigzagging trenches. If a shell dropped in one section, it wouldn't affect those in another section. One of our guys jumped in one of these trenches, and there was a Jap in behind one of the zigzags. He threw a grenade over and killed the Marine.

About the only way we could get into those bunkers was by using flamethrowers, and if we hadn't had those we would have been in real trouble. The openings to those bunkers weren't straight in. They were offset. We'd throw demolition charges in them, but they wouldn't go in far enough to do any good. Then we'd use a flamethrower. It wasn't so much the fire itself, but what the fire did. It sucked all the oxygen out of the bunkers, and the Japs would suffocate. A lot of times we'd cover the flamethrower guys with our machineguns while they got on top of the bunkers and drop quarter-pound TNT charges in through the air vents. The Japs would stick it out in those bunkers, but they must have known they'd had it, once they saw the flamethrower guys. A lot of them just committed suicide by throwing themselves on their own grenades. Some of the pillboxes were actually Jap tanks dug into the ground. Our tanks took those out easily with their 75mm guns.

We moved forward again on the same day, and I hadn't seen a live Jap, just dead ones. As we were moving forward, we came across a lumber pile. We went to the left side of the pile, and a Jap came out from the other side. He was just walking, and with all the shooting that was going on! He said, "Uh-oh!" And took off!

Nobody shot at him! Everybody was stunned! He probably got it later on. He was the first one I saw alive.

We set up our machinegun for the second time that day, and started firing across the island into this Japanese held area. We were told that there was a lot of activity over there. Our fire was having a pretty good effect they said. We lost our water can for the machinegun along the way, but the gun would still fire as long as there was steam in the water jacket. We ran out of ammunition soon after that.

That evening we had to move all the way back to the beach. What we gained during the day we had to give back because we didn't have enough men to hold onto what we had. That wasn't too good for morale. Water was a bad situation by evening. We had two canteens of water and rations for three days. We hadn't eaten much at all that day, but we drank a lot. It was hot! But, I was pretty good about conserving my water. I still had some left at the end of the day.

It was nighttime and nobody was firing. Things got quiet. The Japs were testing us. They'd holler for help, pretending to be one of our wounded. I didn't get any sleep that night! That night a Jap Betty bomber came over real slow. We called it "Sewing Machine Charlie." You could tell whenever he would bomb. With each bomb he released came a "click." He never seemed to hit anything. I think he actually dropped his bombs in the area that was still being held by the Japanese! We didn't even shoot at him because it didn't seem like he could hit the island, no matter how hard he tried.

In the morning the 8th Marines came in to reinforce us, and they got slaughtered. Their battalions had more casualties than any other battalion the day before, and we couldn't help them in any way. After that we started inland again. We had to put colored panels in front of us so that the Navy fighter planes would know where to strafe. Sometimes it didn't help because we were so close to the targets that they killed some of our men. We called for the offshore destroyers to send in shellfire. They opened up but had to stop almost immediately. The highest point on Betio was about ten feet, and the destroyers ran the risk of hitting us, instead of the enemy.

We had the machinegun set up in another flanking position that day. I was on the gun and I saw out in front of me what amounted to a squad of Japs moving to a new location. I pulled the trigger and caught them all as they were going across. We didn't think too much of the Jap soldiers. It was either you or them. I'll tell you what hurt, though. Your own people getting killed. Some of them got hit so bad you knew they weren't going to make it. Then the corpsmen would take them away, and you set your mind on other things that were happening. I saw a dead Marine who had thrown himself on a grenade to save his buddies. When we were in training, they said that that was one of the things we might have to do. Guys that did that kind of thing probably didn't think too much about it; they just did it.

Before we got relieved we took two prisoners over to the command post. They were naked except for a loincloth. No shoes, no nothing. They didn't talk or anything. I don't know what happened to them. We found Jap photo albums with letters in them. It was a Japanese guy who had been over in the States going to school. His picture was in there, and he was posing with some Americans. I guess he got stuck in Japan when the war started and had to go into the army there. I buried the album on Tarawa, but never got a chance to get it again and bring it home.

After some time, the 1st Battalion, 6th Marines came up to relieve us. As soon as we got relieved we took our clothes off and dove into the water. We didn't know if it was mined or not, and we didn't care! The whole island had a terrible odor to it, what with all that heat and decomposing bodies. Everything we tasted had the taste of that smell. The swim was welcome.

The day after we were relieved, we were back on the line, working down through the island cleaning out the remaining Japs. That's when we really ran into the spider holes. While we were mopping up, I was surprised how much American stuff they had. In one of their motor pools I found a bunch of Champion spark plugs. Their trucks were 1937 Chevys, just like Pap had on the farm at home. I looked under the hood and the engine and everything else was exactly the same. The trucks were made in Japan, but the Japs were great copiers. They'd get foreign equipment, tear the stuff down, study it, and then build something identical to it.

After seventy-two hours, sixty-two more than planned, the island was declared secure. I came out of it all with just a minor shrapnel scratch on my arm. I didn't report it to the medic because it was nothing compared to what happened to other guys. That was the only combat wound I would ever receive. We sailed back to Hawaii where we built a camp that we named "Tarawa." By then we were pretty hardened to combat and we tried to teach the new guys just like the old fellas from the Canal taught us. In Hawaii I got transferred from M Company to Headquarters Company and became a Jeep driver, a radio Jeep equipped with a TCS receiver and sending unit. We stayed at Camp Tarawa until June 1944, the month we got sent to Saipan.

The 2nd Marines made the Saipan landing during the day, and, toward evening, brought the radio Jeep in. The radio kept up communication with tanks supporting the troops in the forward line. I joined the company that night. I dug a foxhole right by the Jeep, and put a poncho over the hole to keep out the heavy rain. After the rain stopped, a bright moon came out. I'm facing the back of the hole when all of a sudden I saw a shadow. Immediately, I thought it was a Jap trying to infiltrate. I got my carbine ready. I came around real quick, but I didn't shoot. Here it was a white goat! We kept it as a mascot. We named him Zero, after the Jap fighter plane.

The fighting I experienced on Saipan was altogether different from Tarawa. It wasn't as intense for me as it was for some of the other guys. My outfit's job was to take Mt. Tapotchau. That was the highest point on the island, and we also had to take the town of Garapan. Saipan was the first island we hit that had any kind of a town on it. They had a small railroad where they hauled sugar cane. We had guys with us trained to run the railroad so that we could use it later on.

One evening I was with a buddy of mine and we had the radio Jeep set up on the road to Garapan. The Japanese were up higher on the ridge, and they could look down on us, so we moved the Jeep to another spot after dark. Japanese binoculars were much better than ours. They were actually German made, and the binoculars set on a big tripod. You could see a man's cartridge belt from seven miles away with that thing. I knew they had spotted us, and I also knew that their artillery and mortar fire could be very accurate because they had the advantage observing from high ground.

I told my buddy, "I have a funny feeling tonight. I think we ought to dig a foxhole."

A lot of times before on Saipan we didn't dig a foxhole. We just sort of took a chance, which wasn't a very good idea! This time, though, we dug our foxhole right in front of our Jeep, and put logs around it for extra protection. We settled down for the night. I took my boots off for the first time in a month. My feet were filthy. I got a bucket of water and washed them. I had just put the bucket down in front of the Jeep and got in the hole when the Jap mortar rounds started falling. They walked those shells right down that road. We got down as deep as we could in that hole. One of the mortar rounds hit right outside of our hole, but the logs took the blast. Another round landed right in the bucket I had been using to wash my feet in. It was still full of water. The blast wrapped the bucket handle and the top rim of the bucket around the drive shaft of the Jeep. The Jeep and the radio were completely wrecked. We got out of that scrape okay, and went back to get another Jeep. If we hadn't had that foxhole, that would have been it for us.

One afternoon soon after that night, our machinegun squad spotted the Japs setting up a mountain gun on a ridge to our front. We watched them maneuvering this gun into position, camouflaging it and everything else. We knew that night they were going to use the gun to fire on us, so we set our machinegun up to fire on the emplacement. We pretty well knew what elevation we needed to have to get rounds up there. Soon, as night began to fall, we saw them going into their positions. There was still a little daylight when we opened fire. They left there in a hurry, and I'm sure we killed some of them. They sure worked hard getting that gun set up, but all that work was for nothing!

We drove through Garapan one day after the street fighting was over. There was a Jap bank there and someone blew it open. There were Yen notes everywhere. We stuffed bunches into our pockets and bags. I carried that money with me for the rest of the war, and used it when I got to Japan.

There was a Headquarters Company guy, Mark Snyder, who also was a radio operator. I was driving the Jeep along this road past these L Company guys who were moving up on the line. They stopped me and asked to put their packs on my Jeep. I told them to go ahead, so they piled their stuff up and even hung packs on the spare tire and every place they could put them. I told them I would meet them up the road a ways. I was going along and I drove into a shell hole. Snyder's pack fell off, and I wasn't about to stop and pick it up because we were in a forward area, and I didn't want to make myself a target for another mortar attack. When I got to my destination, I parked the Jeep in a sheltered area behind this ridge. Eventually, L Company came up the road. Snyder came over to get his pack. When he found out what happened he raised hell with me. We almost got into a fight over it! It's funny, but we got to be the best of friends after that, and he's the only one from the war that I'm in touch with today.

We had trouble taking Mount Tapotchau because the Army's 27th Division between the 4th Marine Division and us wasn't moving as fast as we were. Our feeling was if you keep them disorganized and don't give them a chance to set up, they can't shoot back at you. Here the 27th worked differently. They were more concerned about taking casualties in the assault. But we had to hold back, and were losing men just sitting there! Our battalion commander got the commander of the 27th removed. After that, we all moved forward together to finally take the objective.

By the time we got to the other side of the island, the battle was nearly over. We made a push down to the sea, and got to the part of the island we came to call "Suicide Cliff." The cliff was where the Chamorros, the natives of Saipan, threw themselves and their kids over in order to escape us. The Jap officers told them that we would torture and kill them, and the people believed them. In actual fact, and as they found out, we took care of them. We would give the civilians our chow, and give the kids our candy and water. That was rough watching those families kill themselves, but we were pretty well hardened by combat. It didn't seem to bother me much then, but it bothered the hell out of me later on. Sometimes the Japanese soldiers shot the civilians who wouldn't jump, and then they would kill themselves. Still, you had to be wary of some of the civilians who had been armed by the Japs. One time an old woman threw a hand-grenade at a buddy of mine, and it went off. He got wounded. He lay on a stretcher, all shook up about that old woman. I talked with him, and tried to calm him, but he was really disturbed. He was evacuated, and I don't know what happened to him after that.

There were some Japanese soldiers mixed in with the Chamorros. We had an interpreter with us. He had lived with a Japanese family on the West Coast before the war and could speak Japanese real good. He called a bunch of them to come away from the cliffs. He tried to get the Jap soldiers to surrender as well. Williamson was a guy from Seattle, Washington. His dad owned a trucking company there that had employed Japanese. Anyway, here comes this Jap up to surrender and Williamson recognized him. The guy had worked for his dad's company before the war! We took those who surrendered to a compound where they were well treated.

Toward the end, the Japs sent in a Banzai attack, and broke through our lines. They got all the way to the positions of the 10th Marine Artillery Battalion, and got stopped cold. The Marines had set their shell to explode at one-fifth of a second, about 100 yards in front of the guns. They got into trouble. Some army officer said, "You can't do that! You can't set your shells like that for safety reasons!"

Hey, there were no safety reasons during a Banzai attack!

After Saipan, we got ready for the invasion of Tinian. That was on 25 July 1944. It was an altogether different island with big fields of sugar cane, and we used tanks armed with flamethrowers. The Japs would run into these sugar cane fields and we'd set the tanks up on either side and just burn the whole field with the flamethrowers. A lot committed suicide in those sugar cane fields rather than burn to death. The smell was awful!

Tinian was so close to Saipan that we got a lot of our supporting artillery fire from Saipan. I was still in Headquarters Company, and when we went into Tinian I was on the radio Jeep again. We sealed off the spark plugs, the breather on the rear-end housing and the air-intake which went up along the windshield in case we had to drive the Jeep through the water on to the beach. Sure enough, they dropped me off in the water from the LST. The water was all around me in my lap! The waterproofing worked, and the Jeep didn't stall. Once we got inland we had to take all that stuff off because it would overheat the Jeep.

During the fighting on Tinian, our B24s came over to bomb the Jap caves on one end of the island. They came in high. It looked like they were going to bomb us, and we scrambled to get out of the way. The bombs landed on the cliffs, just like they were supposed to, though.

I had the same duties I had on Saipan, communicating with the front line. We used to change frequencies on the radio and pick up Tokyo Rose, who came on at seven in the evening. She was the Japanese propagandist, but she played all the latest hit tunes. I'd park that Jeep, and the boys enjoyed those songs! Tokyo Rose tried to make us homesick with her announcing, but it didn't work with us. We were just interested in the music. I don't think she should have been tried at the end of the war for what she did because she provided the only entertainment we had!

Another thing that kept up morale was mail. I got the local paper, the Greensburg *Morning Review*. It was old news, but for me it was good news, and it was better than nothing. I read those papers over and over and over. I was never a good letter writer, though. But there was this one fella that I would write letters for. Actually they were love letters! It wasn't his wife then, but his girl friend. I guess it must have worked out all right. I heard from him after the war that they got married!

After Tinian, we went back to Saipan, where they built a camp for us halfway up Tapotchau. We had a good view of the Asilito Airfield, and we watched the B–29s land after raiding Japan. We also watched them take off, always around three in the morning, in three-minute intervals, loaded with bombs and fuel. Some of them came back shot up, some crashed into the sea. One came in with a wing half shot away. There was a roar, then a big explosion. The plane couldn't make it over Tapotchau. The plane parts scattered over a three-mile area.

Snyder and I went over to the air base to get their really good chow! We found out that they were going to "slow time" one of the planes, that is, they changed the engines and were going to take it up to see if everything functioned okay. We asked for a ride, and the crew told us to go get parachutes.

We came back out and said, "They won't give us one unless you sign for it."

The pilot said, "Get a Mae West then."

They wouldn't give us that either. So we went up with nothing. We wanted a ride! I was in the tail, in the gunner's compartment. The pilot had a relative of his up in the cockpit with him, and he was trying to make an impression on him. He put the 29 almost on its tail, straight up. When he stalled it, that old tail was just swinging back and forth from the vibration. I thought the whole tail was going to come off! They had a fighter base there, as well, and I got a ride in a P–47 Thunderbolt because a friend of my sister was the pilot. He flew that plane sitting on my lap. He dove at the ground and pulled out real low.

He looked over his shoulder and said, "Are you all right?"

"Yeah! Yeah! I'm all right!"

Actually, I think I passed out during the dive.

Okinawa was next. We weren't told where we were going yet, like always, but we knew it was going to be a big operation. We got on the ships and ended up in a group of islands called the Kerama Retto Islands that were right off Okinawa. The 3rd Battalion was to make a diversionary landing on one sid of Okinawa, while the took place on the other side. It was Easter morning, about five o'clock. We were standing in the chow line on the *U.S.S. Hinsdale* heading into the mess haul for our traditional steak and eggs. We were walking through these watertight doors, really like holes in a steel wall about two feet off the deck. We had to step up and over. A buddy of mine was walking in front of me. He had just stepped through the door when a Kamikaze hit our ship. There was an explosion, and the blast drove my buddy back through the doorway, and he smacked his legs right on that two-foot-high piece of steel threshold.

He said, "I think my legs are broken!"

Everything happened at once. The bombs going off, my buddy flying through that door, and everybody yelling and running every which way! I bent down and picked him up off the floor. I started to run with him, holding him up and carrying him as best I could, right up a ladder that led topside. He wasn't a heavy fella to begin with, but here I'm having all this help from below. All these guys are charging up that ladder below me, pushing and shoving to get up on deck. We practically got shot up that ladder; those guys were in such a hurry! Topside, my buddy started to walk! Turned out his legs were just badly bruised. Then we saw this huge hole in the side of our ship where the Jap plane hit, killing sixty-five Navy personnel.

It was a bad day for our battalion. Headquarters Company and all its equipment was on this troop ship, the *Hinsdale*. L Company, I Company and K Company were on LSTs and Kamikazes hit all three of them. We were picking our men up out of the water, when the ship started to list. We had to be towed down to the Kerama Retto Islands, where we transferred to another ship. We transferred stuff all night and into the next day.

The Kamikazes weren't finished with us. Five o'clock that evening more of them came in. They knocked out a good many of our ships. One plane came in right off the water, right through a wall of tracers. I wondered how those planes could get through all that fire. The five-inch gun on the back of our ship tracked him in. They could set their shells to go off at a certain height. When they thought he was in the right place they opened up and blew him to bits.

I lost track of my battalion. They were all on different ships heading back to Saipan because most of our gear was gone. I and about thirty-eight other guys from Headquarters stayed on this ship up in the Kerama group. We had quite a life there eating ice cream and not worrying about having to make another landing for a while. I grew a beard because it was over a month before we got back to Saipan. When we came back to Saipan, I was walking into the company area and whom do I run into but our battalion commander!

He didn't say, "Hi-ya!"

He didn't say anything like that.

The first thing he said to me was, "Get that damn beard the hell off!"

They wouldn't let us grow beards. I never even gave it a thought that I had it.

We started more training back on Saipan. It was getting time for the invasion of Japan, what would be Operation Olympic. I think we would have been the first wave in, at Kyushu, and we were worried about that, because it was all cliffs.

While on Saipan we were put on guard duty, guarding something, but we didn't know what. Later, we found out that it was part of the Atomic Bomb that we dropped in August on Hiroshima. When it happened, we couldn't imagine one bomb could do what that one did. Two days later they dropped one on Nagasaki. The Japs surrendered after that. Those big bombs saved countless American lives. They had it figured the first waves on Kyushu would be wiped out. I'm certainly glad Truman made the decision to drop those bombs, especially for my own sake.

Five weeks after they dropped the Bomb on Nagasaki, our ship pulled into Nagasaki Bay to begin the occupation of Japan. I guess they weren't too worried about radiation, but there's a lot they didn't know then. One of the first things I saw that was a result of the Bomb were boats from Nagasaki Bay thrown inland about 200 feet. The blast must have emptied that bay and thrown the boats towards the land.

We built a camp in a rickety Japanese naval barracks. That was to be our home. We found out that they were rickety on purpose. They had been built that way to withstand earthquakes.

Once we were settled, we moved out into the town. We went up into the area where the Bomb hit the hardest. It was completely flat. Even most of the stone structures were destroyed. Anything wooden burned up. It must have been such an intense heat. I noticed one thing in the blast area. The backs of the buildings that had been facing the blast were blown out, but the rest of the building was still standing! There were areas where there had been trees and it looked like a bull-dozer took them and pushed them over. Anything that was round, like telephone poles and electrical poles, were still standing. I guessed that's because the blast curved around things that were round in shape.

The streets in that town were real narrow. They had transoms above the doors to their houses. We would pull the Jeep up close and look in and there'd be Japanese civilians sleeping on the floors. They looked like they didn't have much. We had a lot of blankets with us, so we threw them in through the transoms. These people looked like they had escaped the blast. We did see others with terrible burns, but we didn't go to any of the hospitals. The thing that struck us was the people themselves were very pleasant. They weren't against us in anyway. The population didn't want that war. That's politics, I guess.

One of the assignments we had was removing the breeches from these big naval gun emplacements they had along the coast. One place we went to was way up in the mountains. A goat would have had trouble walking up there! We took a Jeep up this road and through this tiny village that had maybe seven houses to it. I don't believe those people ever saw a white man before in their lives! We saw smoke coming out of a chimney, but nobody was around. We had an interpreter with us, and he called out. The first thing we saw were the little kids they sent out first. They figured we wouldn't hurt them. Then the older kids came out, then the adults, and then the old. We took our rations out and gave the kids the hard candy that came with them. We always saved that for kids. One time we stopped by a school. School had just let out and I started passing candy out. They just swarmed me! I didn't have enough for all of them, and I felt real bad when some of the kids went away empty-handed.

We stayed in Japan several months and then came back to the States. We hit some bad storms on the way. I'd be pouring coffee, and it would come in one side of the cup and out the other! Sometimes the ship would list and everything on one end of the table would go, zoom! The fronts of our dungarees were greasy from food. We came into San Diego, but there was no band playing. They took us to an old raider camp, Camp Delouse, for a week. Then we got liberty. We went to San Diego for the weekend.

We were walking down town when this fella said to me, "Did you check the bulletin board?"

"No."

"When you get back, go check it."

I checked the bulletin board and my name was on it. I thought I was on my way out of the service, but we had to go to Camp Pendelton for some reason. After our weekend liberty we reported to Camp Pendleton. Some of the Marines there said, "Our replacements have come in. We can go home now."

I asked one of them, "How many points do you have?"

"I've got fifty-one points."

He was never out of the States yet. I was three years out of the States. I had sixty-five points. I got to thinking, "What the devil's going on?"

We started calling home telling our folks we had to stay longer. Some of the guys called their Congressmen to complain. After spending all that time overseas and then go back into duty again! I called home and found out Pap had pneumonia. My mother told me she had sent a telegram through the Red Cross, but I never got it. I went to the Red Cross offices at Camp Pendleton. They told me to state my claim and then they would direct me where to go. I told them there was a telegram that came through the Red Cross and I didn't receive it.

They said, "It might be with your outfit."

I said, "I checked with my outfit."

I was told to go to another desk. I went to that desk and I was pushed to another desk and another desk! Four different desks until I was back where I started from! Then I got a little curious that maybe the telegram was on that first desk! They never sent it out. I went back to our barracks and I told the guys what happened. We started raising a lot of hell with our Congressmen, and they finally discharged us in San

Nagasaki, Japan. After the dropping of the atomic bomb.
Courtesy of Lewis Steck.

Diego. We were given our mustering-out pay and train fare for home. I came into Pittsburgh, and from there took another train to Greensburg. I got off the train and was going up the street when the guy running the streetcar recognized me. He gave me a ride down to Hunker. A fella in Hunker stopped me when he saw my uniform and gave me a ride all the way home to the barn.

It was five o'clock in the morning and mom was there making breakfast. There was bacon and eggs on and Dad was in the barn milking the cows. I wasn't even in the house yet and I smelled bacon and eggs! It was very touching.

I worked on the farm until 1949, and then I married my love, Kay. We will be married fifty-five years come July 2005. I retired from Westinghouse Research in 1986

I saw a lot of people get killed. I saw a lot of people get wounded. It bothered me more when the person was wounded real bad than if the person was killed outright. I don't forget about them. I'd see a Marine who was wounded real bad I'd wonder, "Is he gonna make it? Is he even gonna make it back to the ship before he dies?" A lot of times the fellas who I thought were wounded real bad were taken off the island. Later on they came back to the outfit! It was like a reunion! Then there were the times when I'd never see them again.

A lot of the stuff has come back. I never talked very much about it, and a lot of the things that happened you just let go by, and you don't even want to think about them. In the war, some of the best people were the ones that didn't come back. And I often wonder how the world would be if they were all here.

Lou Steck and comrades at Nagasaki, 1945

"Hellfire and Damnation All the Way"

Earl Vincent Stratton
63rd Infantry Division ("Blood and Fire"), 254th Infantry Regiment, 2nd Battalion, Company H
Stillwater, Oklahoma, 25 January 1924

"I could tell that he cold-blooded killed this German even though he meant to fire over his head, or so he told me. I could tell that it had shaken him up a little. The other German prisoners just stood as still as they could. I waited with that kid for what seemed like hours. There was never any word about that dead German. It was war which meant hellfire and damnation all the way."

WE LIVED IN THE DUST BOWL. The sky was always red with the dust and filth, and there were locusts everywhere. Maybe walking alone through the dust and locusts prepared me for the things to come. I shot on the rifle teams in high school and I shot on the ROTC and Pershing rifle team in college. I did everything to prepare myself academically and emotionally to be able to take my place in that war. I was a freshman in college when Pearl Harbor got attacked. I didn't rush into anything. I continued with my education until 8 December 1942, when I enlisted, one year and one day after Pearl Harbor

I had an older brother, Robert. During the Depression he and I worked together. He rented bicycles and I set up a soda-pop stand next to him. He was great with anything mechanical. He'd make skateboards for my friends and me and fix our bikes. I learned a lot of this stuff from him. One time he got this old Model T that didn't have a top. A homemade convertible, I guess you could say. He fixed that thing up and we went cruising. He'd kid around and take the steering wheel off while he was driving, and hand it to me. Then he'd pull out a pair of pliers and steer the car that way. My brother was killed trying to land his PBY in a heavy fog. He crashed into the sea. That happened two weeks before he was supposed to get his gold wings in the Navy Air Corps. He was only twenty-two. The Navy gave him a big military funeral. I touched his body while he lay in his casket. It felt like clay.

When I went overseas, I made certain that I had no attachments. I didn't want any of that. I stayed single, while others got married. One of my buddies got married. They had a baby before he went over. He was blown to smithereens. I believed my calling was for infantry combat first. Then, when I finished with that, I would be in the front lines as a minister in the pulpit. I knew that I didn't really have to go into combat because I was a last surviving son, but I felt that's where I was destined to go.

In spring 1944, the Army sent me to Fort Sills for induction. We were preparing for the Pacific, ready to bake in 100–degree heat on some island, but they needed us in Europe. So, we froze instead, in the ice and snow.

At Fort Benning, I took my OCS training. I became a Ninety Day Wonder. They made us run and throw ourselves on barbed wire so that our buddies had a path to run through. They told us not to move. I didn't think it would hurt, but it did. We had the volunteer spirit. We looked out for each other as best we could. None of us wanted to fail. On twenty-five-mile hikes, we'd go out with full field packs. Sanchez was a squad leader in my company. He tired out one time on the march. Mike Wolfe was my assistant squad leader, and he took Sanchez's pack off of him to help him out. He gave me half his pack in addition to my full pack. We didn't let anybody else see what we were doing. We got him through those miles, and put his pack back on him. When we got back to camp, the band struck up a march, and those packs seemed to get as light as feathers. I still think about those marches, about coming up those last, long hills, when we were young and the future was still uncertain, and I still think about Sanchez. Sanchez got killed on an island in the Pacific.

I was a second lieutenant when we went overseas, making $40.00 a month. I sent my pay home, because I didn't need it where I was. In January 1945, they made me a first lieutenant. After that, instead of having a yellow bar on my helmet, I had a white one. That bar was a great target for the Germans.

My division formed up at Camp Van Dorn, Mississippi, where I started training in the heavy-weapons company. 81m mortars were what I went overseas with. They packed a hefty punch.

We staged to go overseas at Fort Hampton, and we were told to keep our mouths shut. Our regiment got on board this huge Italian liner, under blackout conditions. They gave us lectures on the way over on what to expect from the civilian population of France, and how we were supposed to behave towards them. They told us to stay away from the women. During the trip, I often talked about my career plans with our chaplain, Reverend Monroe. He always philosophized about our mutual calling. He still held services when we got into combat. The night before our first big battle, we had a service in a barn. He asked me to say a prayer, and I did.

The next day we went into battle. Colonel Warren had gotten our regiment over first and committed it with the 3rd Infantry Division in the Colmar Pocket. The 3rd Division had veterans from Africa, Sicily and Italy. No matter how trained we thought we were, once we saw those veterans we knew what true training is. They were haggard, weary, and tough.

In my baptism of fire, the Germans fired into the trees with mortars and artillery. Before this barrage came in we made sure our mortars were well dug in. We came across some lumber, and we made roofs for our mortar pits out of four-by-fours. Then we piled earth on top of those, leaving room for our tubes. When the first barrage came in, I was out of the hole and too far away from it to get back in. I knew I had made a stupid mistake because we learned about tree bursts in training. I hunkered down by the base of a tree and hoped I wouldn't get sprayed with shrapnel. I thought I had made a fatal mistake, but, luckily, I came through.

Hill 216 in the Colmar Pocket stands out in my mind. It was a bloody encounter but we were able to drive the Germans off. We attacked just before dawn with the 3rd

Division and the 254th artillery plastering the northern flank of the German positions. I had gotten up into a shot-up church steeple as a forward observer. I watched in awe as big shells burst against the snow-capped hill. Along a one thousand yard front our infantry went "over the top." There was only silence as they advanced. Then came countless, dull explosions. Our troops started to fall. There were cries of "Medic, help me!" There were no shell screams, no mortar whistles, just mysterious bursts. Then I realized that the battalions had entered a field full of German *Schu* mines, deadly things made of plastic or wood that would blow your feet off. The heavy snow coupled with the brisk winds perfectly hid the mines, as well as the footprints of the Germans who laid them.

The men immediately removed the bayonets that they had fixed to their rifles, and began to probe for mines before moving on. Then came the German mortar and 88mm rounds. I learned later that rounds from this barrage that fell into our rear killed Reverend Monroe. Mortar and 88s started to come in.

As daylight improved, the Germans started with their machineguns. My battalion hadn't gone into the attack yet, but we were bringing down as much mortar and machinegun fire as we could on the Germans. Casualties increased at an alarming rate in the 1st Battalion, but through sheer courage they moved forward toward the top of Hill 216. Going down the other side of the hill was nearly as bad – more mine fields, more artillery and small arms fire.

It was then that I first witnessed the death of a German soldier. There was a house that was within the German lines. I was about to set it on fire with some phosphorous rounds, when a colonel, because it was a French village, ordered us to ceasefire. A short time later, the Germans sent a patrol into our lines, and a fellow officer was shot just outside of a barn in a skirmish with the patrol. I was with my squad and we spotted the Germans moving back to their own lines. I was afraid they were going to call in a fire mission on us, so I ordered my men to open up on them. One German got hit, and fell to the ground, rolling and groaning. I thought about going up to him and shooting him, but I thought better of it. I didn't want to give our position away, and he was pretty well finished, anyway.

We moved into this town the next day. That night a German came out of a barn about twenty-feet away from me. I didn't shoot at him because I would have been firing in the direction of my own men.

I yelled to one of my men who was in a better position, "Shoot him!"

He did.

I was put in charge of twelve German prisoners that had been rounded up from the town. I was guarding them with an enlisted man who was armed with a BAR. I was still concerned even though the Germans had been disarmed. It was still night, and I wondered what would happen if one of them pulled a pistol, would I be able to see it in the dark?

I thought I saw one of the Germans with a burp gun. As I looked over at him, I heard a shot. The German stiffened, and he slid down a wall, deader than a doornail. The guy with the BAR was the one who shot him.

"What happened? What did you see?" I asked.

"I thought I'd give them a warning shot over their heads." he answered.

He might have meant to aim the gun over their heads, but he never fired there. He just shot directly at them. I talked with him very steadily and calmly so that he wouldn't get more nervous. I could tell that he cold-bloodedly killed this German. I could tell that the incident had shaken him up a little. The other German prisoners just stood as still as they could. I waited with that kid for what seemed like hours. There was never any word about that dead German. It was war, and that meant hellfire and damnation all the way.

We drove the Germans off Hill 216 and east toward the Rhine River. We closed off the Colmar Pocket and the Vosges Mountains. Then we moved north to Sarreguemines where the rest of the 63rd was conducting patrols for our push against the Siegfried Line. Now, for the first time, we would fight as a full division. It was in February when we started our push. I was out as an observer when I got hit in the side and fell down thrashing. I had never been hit so hard. There was another lieutenant with me and he grabbed me and said, "You're going to get a Purple Heart."

I reached back to feel the wound and there was a metal fragment embedded in my webbed belt. It never pierced my body. I said, "Purple Heart? Thunder!"

I threw the fragment as far as I could.

The 63rd saw a lot of combat in front of the Siegfried Line. A company commander, a captain, was killed. A first lieutenant took over and pulled the whole company off the line like rats leaving a sinking ship. We got the call to lay down a barrage in an S pattern to cover their retreat. I was concerned because they were calling in coordinates that were within twenty-five yards of our own men. An 81mm throws a lot of shrapnel out. We laid down a continuous barrage blocking that whole area from counter-attack. It was very deadly. I fired my mortars so much the base plates embedded into the ground and froze there over night. We couldn't get them out when we had to move so we removed the tubes and got replacement base plates from the next supply truck.

We emptied two regimental ammunition dumps on the Siegfried Line. There was a wall of fire laid down on that thing for days so that no German reserves could move up in support. I was glad that I didn't have to endure anything like we let go on the enemy. The whole earth shook from the firepower of our artillery. Everything was illuminated both behind us and in front from the muzzle blasts and the explosions. It was a terrifying sight, even to those who did the firing. There were blinding flashes and deafening noises. We had to deal with that at night all the time. Never had I experienced anything like it.

When it was over, and as I was walking up through the upper trenches on the Siegfried Line, I came across a whole bunch of dead German troops. They all looked whole, almost alive. I couldn't figure out how they died. I had the eerie feeling that they were all going to rise up. But they didn't. They all had been killed by concussion. To this day, I have visions of that scene.

Combat contains the smoke and smell of death and destruction. The bodies have a grayness that sets in on them, and then they turn like clay when they are dead. I often thought about my brother in his casket when I saw all the dead on the battlefield. They piled them up and crossed them over like cordwood. Once I came upon a German in a ravine whose legs had been blown off. He was still alive. I sent for a medic. That was all I could do, because I had to move on. I think it was my mortar fire that blew off his legs. Our artillery hadn't been firing toward the ravine. Yes, it was probably my mortars that got him. I remember him, too.

One night, when we were in reserve, a corporal told me that some of the noncoms were "inebriated," and that they were threatening to kill some officers. Then he told me about the liquor that the men had "liberated" somewhere, and suggested that we get rid of it.

I responded, "If you can get that stuff in a Jeep, then we'll do it."

He got it boxed up and into the Jeep. I don't know how he got it past them, but he did. Then the two of us went out at night risking land mines and everything. When we got out a certain distance, we broke all the bottles.

There was another time when I took a knife away from a drunken and probably a slightly shell-shocked corporal. I kept hearing a loud commotion coming from a barn. It kept getting louder and louder. I found out later that a lieutenant had gone down there twice, but hadn't done anything. I went out to handle the situation myself. I put on my leather palm gloves. I moved through some soldiers and here was this corporal with a knife about to kill a hog. His knife was bloody and around him were the carcasses of dead hogs he had killed. I went straight at him and grabbed the blade, and tried to trip him to the ground, but he got behind me. Finally, I tripped him. The guys with him thought I was going to kill him, because I really ground him into the dirt. I got the blade from him, and then I told his buddies, "Now, you take care of him!"

It was frustrating to have to face things like that when you had just come off the line. Human beings just can't take constant combat and violence. It wears them down. One time during the Siegfried Line battles I got this man transferred into my squad because they felt that he was a coward. I took him up on a hill where I could see the Siegfried Line, and they could see me. They started firing, and I kept him with me. He showed no cowardice. I used him as a radioman after that. He was broken in again.

Once I was assigned to go out on night patrol. Just when I was about to leave they said I didn't have to go. My superiors realized that I was weary from being out front as forward observer all that time and that I wasn't in peak condition. They sent fresh officers out there and it was a good thing because they ran into a large German patrol that would have required quick decisions, and I don't believe I would have been up to it.

We had another guy, our interpreter, who went over the edge. We were all down in a ditch waiting to fire our mortars. Suddenly, the interpreter walked out into the open. We yelled at him to get back but he said he was going to talk to them.

The troops were yelling to me, "This guy is nuts!"

I called him by name, I gave him an order to return, but he just kept going. Then the Germans opened up, killing him. I still believe even if we had run out after him he would have run away from us. I still believe that he thought he was invincible, that he could walk to where the Germans were and convince them to surrender.

I captured a German toward the end of the war. Prisoners were coming in by the thousands. We were still in battle, but the war was winding down.

He said, "Now we go fight the Russians!"

He was probably one of those die-hards who thought that the Communists were the next battleground. He turned out to be right in a sense, since we did go through fifty-years of Cold War.

When the war ended, I was happy to find myself still alive. We stayed in Germany as occupation troops until early 1946. Then they put us on a ship for New York. After eighteen months away, we became very emotional when we saw the Statue of Liberty. I had a great family reunion, except that my brother wasn't there.

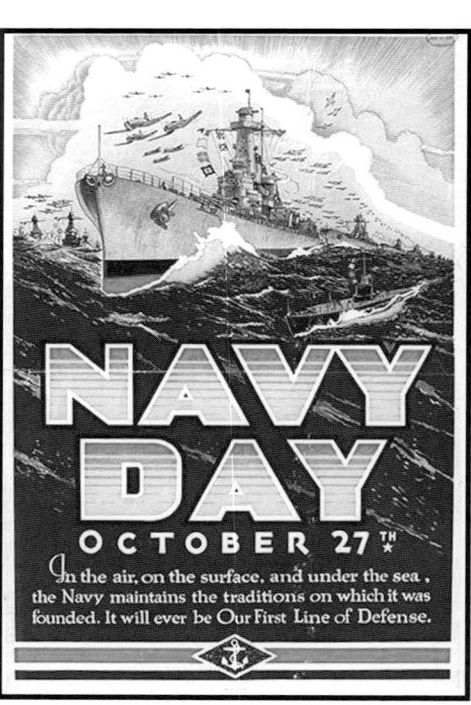

National Archives

"Who Knew All This Stuff About War?"

Jim Takitch
United States Navy, Destroyer USS *Kidd*
Hecla, Pennsylvania, 28 June 1926

"I went back to watching the dogfight. Another Japanese aircraft was close to the ocean deck, looking like it was going to crash into the Black, but the pilot gained altitude, dropped his wing tanks (the after battle report suggested that he did that, hoping to set the Black on fire), and headed for us. The pilot dropped down close to the water. We couldn't use our five-inch guns because the Black was in the line of fire. The Black gun crews weren't as considerate as we were. They opened up on the rear of the plane. Then we opened up with our smaller guns. The plane came on, and I had the feeling that it was targeting me! My first reaction was to throw my arm up over my eyes. I peeked out and saw the pilot firing his machineguns. A bullet tore through my lower left jaw, took out part of my jaw bone, knocked out two teeth, and because my arm was over my eyes, the round lodged in my upper left bicep. I lost consciousness very soon after I was hit."

MY FATHER'S NAME WAS JOSEPH TAKITCH. He came here from Czechoslovakia when he was about two years old. My mother, Julia, was a naturalized citizen. They had thirteen kids, including me. Two of my siblings died right after being born, and another died at the age of two. We had a large family, to be sure, and we all took care of each other. My older brother, Ed, who spent thirty years in the Navy, died six years ago.

My father was a yard boss, and he oversaw operations at the coke ovens in Hecla. When the Depression hit, and the mines closed down, he went to work with the Works Progress Administration (WPA). His paycheck was $52.60 a month. Because my father was a foreman, he had the first opportunity of buying the company house that we lived in, a two-story, single dwelling. There were three or four houses for supervisors like that in Hecla. We had running water, a furnace, an inside bathroom, and electric lights. Around 1939, my father was forced to buy the house. He got the place for $1100.00, paying $25.00 monthly until the debt was paid.

I heard about Pearl Harbor on a Sunday afternoon. There was a place behind the schoolhouse, called "The Green." We were playing football, and someone came over and told us that the Japanese had bombed Pearl Harbor. I didn't know where Pearl Harbor was, and I didn't know much about the Japanese either. I was only fourteen. I never thought that I would become involved in the war effort. It seemed so far away, and I never really gave it too much thought because I was just getting ready to go to Hurst High School. Out of 276 freshmen, only 136 graduated. That was because many went into the service or into war production.

In March of my senior year, I got a job at Robertshaw Thermostat Company in Youngwood, Pennsylvania. I worked the midnight shift, and after work I went home on the streetcar. I'd get home around seven thirty in the morning, run up the hill to the house, wash, change clothes, have breakfast, then run back down the hill to catch the street car up to Hurst High School. School started at eight thirty and went until two thirty in the afternoon. I didn't get much sleep, and I kept that schedule through the summer. In August, I quit working because I received my draft notice. I didn't want to go, but since everybody else was, I felt I might as well go, too

They put me in the Navy, where I always longed to be anyway. My older brother was already in the Navy, and maybe that's why I got in. Thirteen fellows ahead of me asked for the Navy, but they put them in the Army. I stayed in Pittsburgh the rest of that day, taking my physical. They looked at my mouth, teeth, ears, eyes, and listened to my heart. They made me bend over and checked me for hemorrhoids. There were other guys who got rejected. One of the fellows I went to school with was rejected. He got a little nervous during his physical so they rejected him because of emotional instability. A fellow from Scottdale, who worked with me at Robertshaw, and I wandered around Pittsburgh for a while, and then we went back to the induction center at a specified hour. Soon after, we boarded a train for Great Lakes, Illinois. I had no idea that I would be sent directly into the service, so my family had no time to give me a sendoff.

The train ride to Great Lakes was miserable. There was no heat on the train. When we got there, no one knew where he was supposed to sleep or eat. They gathered us all up, took us into a big room where I got my papers. Between filling out the different forms, they gave us all a hunk of steel wool and told us to put it under our shoes, pick a board on the floor and scrub it. I shuffled it back and forth, and then somebody behind me followed with a broom and a dustbin to clean up the dirt. All the other sailors were doing the same thing. That is how we were supposed to clean the floor and keep the woodwork shiny. I was up there from 28 September until 11 December 1944.

At the beginning of our training, they took us out on the lake in a boat and told us what to do in order to survive if our ship should sink. It was ice-cold in the Great Lakes region, so we never had to jump into the water, though the waves were pretty high, and we would get wet. We also had to identify different things about different ships. I received a *Blue Jacket Manual* that contained everything I was required to know about the Navy. Of course, we had a drill instructor. He had been over in the Pacific on a ship that had sunk, and he was pretty tough. He didn't let anything go by the wayside. We had to do it his way or else. The Navy tried to keep boys from the same town separated, so there wasn't anyone from Hecla. There had been some friends of mine from Windber, a town near Johnstown, but that was earlier on, and they had since gone. I looked at the roster one day, and saw the name Kostelnick.

"Hey, who is Kostnelnik?" I asked.

The fellow came up and said, "How do you know my name? Nobody pronounces it that way. They always say 'Kostelnock' or something."

"Well, there are people living right where I live with that same last name."

I got to be close to him. He turned out to be from a small town named Smock, and he lived about three doors down from my uncle, a good friend of his. He was killed later on in the war.

On Saturdays we had competitions and entertainment, so it wasn't always hard work. The Navy was pretty strict about cleanliness. The company that had the best weekly record for cleanliness, shoe-shining and bed-making won a flag with a rooster on it. My company won it for ten weeks. There was this guy in my company that had a bad habit of not bathing. A couple guys took him out of bed one night, threw him into a shower, and scrubbed him with a brush. That was a common punishment for guys who wouldn't keep themselves clean. We also competed in cross-country running. We also had basketball teams. On Sunday nights, inside a large Quonset hut, we saw movies. Great Lakes had a football team, and we got leave to go to the games. Most of the guys smoked, but I didn't. I didn't start smoking cigarettes until I got out of the service. On a Saturday afternoon, it looked like a big coke oven was in operation as 30,000 sailors smoked away at the football games.

We had about 120 men in our company. Every man got a kitchen detail for one week, and my kitchen detail started at three-thirty in the morning, and sometimes I wouldn't finish until eleven at night. Furthermore, Saturday was inspection time, and they had some officer come through to make sure that we cleaned every speck of dust. If he said, "Not good enough to pass," we'd have to clean some more, clean some more, and clean some more. One Saturday, the officers came through, and a coffee cup had a stain in it. Well, not only did they force my company to clean the cup, but they also forced us to clean all the cups and dishes. As a result, it taught me good discipline when I returned home. Today, I still think twice before throwing my clothes around or leaving things out of order.

Training lasted until 11 December 1944, when I came home for a ten-day leave. After the leave, I returned to Great Lakes. On Christmas day, they sent me to Shoemaker, California, a distribution point. I was assigned scullery duty on the same day. I put on boots, rubber trousers, a hat, coat and gloves, and steam-cleaned all the cooking pots. I did that for the whole of Christmas Day 1944. On New Years Day, thirty-nine men and I were assigned to a ship called the *USS Kidd*. We were sent to Mare Island, California, which is right next to Vallejo.

The *Kidd* needed some refitting and repairs. After they got through with her, we went on a "shakedown cruise" around Alcatraz prison, Treasure Island, and under the San Francisco Bridge. This was the time that I first got seasick. I was sitting in a chair getting a hair cut. I ran out onto the ship's superstructure and threw up. I'm glad there wasn't anybody down below me; otherwise they would have been splattered. The second time I got seasick was when a couple of guys played a prank on me. I was walking beside a ladder and these guys hung some greasy pork chops on a string, and swung them at me as they were going down the ladder. When the chops hit me, I threw up.

On one of the "shakedown cruises," the mechanics made repairs on the boilers, valves, gauges, and other components after they had been purposely damaged. One night, we were traveling at about thirty-eight knots. Suddenly, the boiler room workers were told to reverse the propellers. The ship continued forward as the propellers spun feverishly in the opposite direction. The entire back-end of the ship hovered up and down above the water. What a racket! I felt as if the ship was going to go down. The experience was a real "shakedown."

During the daylight hours, we simulated how to tow the ship after it had broken down. To do the simulation, we tied steel cables or ropes in front of the ship and hooked them onto another ship. As the tow ship began to move, it exerted a lot of pressure on the line. At that time, there were thousands of seagulls following the ships, looking for garbage that the cooks would throw overboard. The cable snapped, and it coiled like a spring. The cable killed about a thousand seagulls, and they went crashing down into the ocean.

I was just an ordinary seaman on the shakedown cruises. Once I got to know the ship and the different areas, I earned the privilege of requesting other duties. If an officer became aware that I was capable of doing a job on the ship, he would ask me to transfer from the deck gang to doing something else. One time, I was asked to leave the deck gang and go down into the belly of the ship as a fireman. I didn't want to go down there because I wanted to see where I was at all times. I preferred the deck. My brother, Ed, on the other hand, spent all of his time aboard ship below decks. He loved it. Under no circumstances would he work above the decks.

The Navy required us to train on all the various guns on board, from the 20mm to the larger guns. I practiced every day. Every morning we had to get up for "general quarters." Everyone had to get up even if some of us only had two or three hours of sleep. They rang a bell and sounded a horn. Then we went to our battle stations. My battle station the entire time I was aboard the ship was lookout. Using binoculars, I'd stand up, look around, and report whatever was going on. I had no weapons at my disposal while I was on lookout.

At first, I didn't like living in the destroyer. There were over 350 people on board, and everything was cramped. To me, the destroyer was nothing more than a floating arsenal. We had ten torpedo mounts with five nine-hundred-pound torpedoes on each. These were either rolled or shot off to the side. We had one thousand rounds of five-inch powder and five-inch shells. We also had 60,000 rounds of 20mm and 40,000 rounds of 40mm. Finally, we had to top off our 300,000-gallon oil tanks every third day from another ship. All of that ammunition, storage and oil space took a lot of room, not to mention the fact that it wouldn't have taken much to make the ship blow up. I never wanted to go below decks with all that stuff on board.

One of the most annoying jobs on the ship was painting. No one wanted to paint. Luckily, the ship that I was on had a brand-new coat of paint. However, when we went to Pearl Harbor we had to paint the decks from gray to green because the colors of the decks of the ships in Pearl Harbor were green, at least the pilots overhead said it was. Personally, I thought it was a very odd regulation, and just something instituted to keep sailors busy.

The food was good, anyway. We even had an ice cream machine. The bathing facilities, on the other hand, were terrible. Since not enough ocean water could be purified for everyone, I had to bathe in salt-water showers. Once I was on oiling detail. The tanker came alongside the ship, got into position, and sent over a large fueling hose. I noticed that the hose seemed to be stretched more than it should have been. I didn't want to say anything because I was just a green sailor. I turned to walk away, and the hose parted, hit me, knocked me down on the deck, and made me look like a glob of tar. I went aft, took my clothes off, and threw them overboard. Then I went down to the engine room, washed myself with diesel fuel, and then took a salt-water shower. Because of the salt-water, I felt like I had glue on me for the rest of the time that I was onboard.

"A tanker came along side..."

"My battle station the whole time I was aboard ship was lookout."

Accidents were common. Another fueling hose incident ended tragically. This time coiled ropes going through pulleys supported it. Again, the hose parted. A fellow we called "Boy Blue" got his foot entangled in a rope as it was being siphoned through the pulley. Boy Blue got swept off the deck, into the pulley, and his leg got mangled. Someone cut the rope, and Boy Blue crashed onto the deck. He was transferred onto the battleship *South Dakota*. After I got wounded and ended up in the National Navy Medical Center in Bethesda, Maryland, I ran into "Boy Blue." His leg was still in bad shape. After I was discharged, I lost track of him. Later, I found out that he passed away.

Finally, we sailed to Pearl Harbor, and from there to Ulithi in the Carolina Islands. It took us thirteen days. The weather was quite good, and the waters were calm. We met up with three carriers. There were nine destroyers in all, running escort. On 18 March, we were preparing for the April 1 landing on Okinawa when the carrier *Franklin* got hit with two bombs. She was dead in the water, and destroyers were running a circle around it. I was assigned to go up on submarine lookout. The cruiser *Santa Fe* sailed in and picked up as many survivors as possible. I thought to myself, "Why do I have to be here?"

From Ulithi we went to Okinawa. We were called to "Sunrise General Quarters," because there were Japanese aircraft in the area. I was on lookout, and I spotted a twin-engine Japanese bomber, flying level with the ship. We didn't fire at it because it surprised us, coming out of nowhere as it did. That perplexed us, because we had advanced radar, but didn't pick up any signals, then, or later. Every now and then we would come across a floating mine. The ship operators would slow down the ship to allow the crew to take Tommy guns and rifles to shoot at the mines. Our ship's doctor got to be quite good at it.

It was the "Day of the Kamikaze's," Thursday, 11 April 1945. At first, it seemed a typical day. Everything was quiet. At two o'clock in the afternoon, I took steering duty. Over the loud speaker I heard, "Many bogeys, fifty miles!"

They alerted us to battle stations. My assignment was the lookout deck, the highest deck one could walk upon on board the ship. When my relief came to take the wheel, I went up the bulkhead ladder to the lookout deck. While I climbed, I heard that our fighter cover had downed four of seven planes heading toward our ship. Cleverly, to divert our attention, two of the Japanese aircraft off the starboard side were faking a dogfight. At the same time, off to port, one plane looked like it was going to crash into either the destroyers *Walker* or *Chauncy*. Both ships turned vigorously. The diving enemy missed them and crashed into the ocean.

I went back to watching the dogfight. Another Japanese aircraft was close to the ocean deck, looking like it was going to crash into the *Black*, but the pilot gained altitude, dropped his wing tanks (the after battle report suggested that he did that, hoping to set the *Black* on fire), and headed for us. The pilot dropped down close to the water. We couldn't use our five-inch guns because the *Black* was in the line of fire. The *Black* gun crews weren't as considerate as we were. They opened up on the rear of the plane. Then we opened up with our smaller guns.

The plane came on, and I had the feeling that it was targeting me! My first reaction was to throw my arm up over my eyes. I peeked out and saw the pilot firing his machineguns. A bullet tore through my lower left jaw, took out part of my jaw bone, knocked out two teeth, and, because my arm was over my eyes, the round lodged in my upper left bicep. I lost consciousness very soon after I was hit.

The plane had hit the ship less than fifteen minutes after I took the wheel. The hull was only five-eighths of an inch thick, so that was not much armor protection. The 500-pound bomb the plane was carrying passed through the ship four or five feet above the water line on an upward trajectory, and it came out where the hull and main deck intersected. As it came out, it exploded, pushing the superstructure inward. The explosion detonated many of our oxygen and acetylene tanks that were lined up on the main deck.

When I regained consciousness, I heard steam whistles, fire whistles, and bullhorns. The steam whistles were going off because the airplane had ruptured a majority of the steam lines. The ship was burning in the storage locker and the forward fire room. The steam escaping from the steam lines helped keep the fires from spreading, but many men were scalded to death. I lay on the deck, supporting my left arm with my right. Blood ran out of the cuffs of my shirt. I saw the ship's doctor, who was taking a film of the plane as it was coming in. One of his eyes was gone. His stomach was wide open, and he was holding his intestines in his hands.

Someone came to help me. He cut my foul-weather jacket down along the zipper with a knife, cut off the sleeve, and took off my belt to use as a tourniquet. Then he left me to help others. I was one of two survivors on the lookout deck. The rest were dead. To get me off the deck above, someone set me on his shoulders and took me down the ladder step by step. Once we got on the deck below, he put me down and I was escorted to the first aid station in the middle of the ship near the washroom. I caught sight of myself in a mirror. In the first aid station, they placed me on a mattress in a sitting position with my knees pulled up. Afterwards, I began to straighten my feet out and my left knee began to hurt. I found out I had a hunk of shrapnel lodged in my left knee. Thereafter, the first aid workers applied sulfa powder to my face and drugged me with morphine.

I was in considerable pain. My arm hurt very badly, and the pain was worse than in my face. To keep the bone in my upper arm separated so it would not be rubbing against adjacent bones, the doctors put a wire-basket in the shape of a cone over my arm. The large end went up to my shoulder and the small end went down to my hand. Around six in the evening, I heard gunfire. More Japanese airplanes had come to finish us off, but we drove them away.

The next day, I, along with four other injured men was transferred from the *USS Kidd* to an oil tanker called the *USS Sarenac*. We were moved on a cable-stretcher that connected the two ships. Whatever I drank ran out the corner of my mouth. My beard grew in because I couldn't shave. I spent most of the time lying down. Side by side, the *Sarenac* and the *Kidd* sailed down to Ulithi. From Ulithi, we were only four days and four nights in sailing distance from Okinawa. They took me from the tanker and put me on the hospital ship *USS Bountiful*.

On the *Bountiful*, I was taken into the operating room where they straightened my arm out as best they could. Next, they put a cumbersome body cast on me to support my left arm. I had no feeling in my thumb and two other fingers. In fact, I used to take cigarettes and touch my fingers with the lit end, and not feel any pain. I also would take a pin and put it under the skin and not feel it. The doctors wanted to do a nerve operation on me, and showed me the different procedures they do for nerves. They had pictures of bodies, and where they would cut. I refused. Afterwards, my fingers swelled up like sausages, but they eventually healed to a certain extent. Today, I can feel myself rubbing my fingers together.

I was afraid of disfigurement, but everything turned out all right. Today, my jaw is in good condition, and no one can notice any distortion, at least at first glance. I still have three pieces of shrapnel inside me! My arm is still slightly crooked.

Eventually I was transported to Hawaii. Because I was going to be flying at a high altitude, the medics covered the roots where my two teeth had been with something to prevent bleeding. Despite my torn jaw, I could still talk fairly well. I really enjoyed the flight in the airplane, a C–54, four-engine passenger plane, equipped with stretchers on the fuselage, and in the center isle. However, the heaters did not work and the cumbersome body cast on me transferred the cold air to my body like a magnet. I had to be covered adequately throughout the entire ride to avoid hypothermia. I stayed in Pearl Harbor for two weeks until they removed the body cast and replaced it with a simple arm cast. Next, they flew me to the Oakland Naval Hospital in Oakland, California.

My arm still remained very painful, and even a small tap hurt. Despite that, I was able to walk. Sometime later before I was scheduled to leave Oakland, I was asked what hospital I would like to go to. I had a choice of a hospital in Corvallis, Oregon or a Naval Hospital in New York or Maryland. Before choosing, I called my parents. My parents didn't have a telephone, so I had to call a nearby neighbor. They got my mother, and as soon as she picked up the telephone, she began to cry. I told her I was probably going up to a hospital in Corvallis, Oregon. Deeply concerned, she wanted to know if I still had my legs and eyesight. I tried to convince her that I just had a broken arm, but she was too concerned about my well being and feared the worst. In the end, I chose the National Navy Medical Center in Bethesda, Maryland. One of the nurses had recommended it, and it was closer to home. When I arrived, they put me on the ninth floor with sixty other men.

I was given a thirty-day leave not too long after I arrived in Maryland. By then, I was just wearing a sling. When I returned to the hospital, the doctors started work on my face. The gum had grown over the roots of my two broken teeth. They took the roots out and decided that plastic surgery was the best option to restore my face. I had three different operations on my face to cut away the scar tissue. I was sutured with 112 stitches after the three operations. When they started to remove the sutures, the wound hemorrhaged. I told the doctors, "Leave it the way it is. Don't bother with it any more."

Next, they wanted to take a piece of bone out of my leg to put under my jaw. I told them, "Nothing doing. I'm going home. I've had enough of this place."

I witnessed others in pain, and I could sympathize. When I was in the hospital on Guam, I had an experience with a young black man in the bed next to me who had a cast on his right leg. He used to tell me, "Takitch, there's something crawling in my cast."

He told me they had put maggots in his cast to eat the dead flesh! He was part of some kind of construction team, and they had been teaching him how to run the bulldozer as he stood up on the fender of the bulldozer. He anticipated the driver to go one way, but the driver went the other way and knocked him off. Before the driver could stop, the track ran over part of his leg and took all meat off his calf and the back of his leg. Also in Guam, a man had one of his legs cut off, and he'd scream all night long saying his toes were hurting, but there was nothing there.

The worst I saw were sailors from the carrier *Franklin* who had been badly burned. The stench from their burned flesh was terrible, and that odor and many others filled the wards of all the hospitals I was in during the war. At that time, certain medications and treatments were not available. For example, when I had the cast on my body, the wound would drain a liquid that seeped down to my wrist with such a rancid odor! The odor was constantly present, and my worst experiences with it were when I would roll over while trying to sleep at night and be awakened by the stench of the draining liquid! That was enough to kill me!

Most of the time at night it was so hot that I didn't want to sleep, especially wearing the body cast. The heat combined with the healing wounds would start itching and there was virtually nothing I could do about it. I was given sticks with cotton swabs attached to the end so I could scratch myself, but the itch was still unbearable. The odor and the itch: it is an experience that no one would ever want to go through.

A piece of shrapnel under my cheekbone wasn't removed until thirty-five years after the end of the war. Originally, I had no idea that a little scar on my cheek was a result of the shrapnel that went under my cheekbone. The shrapnel must have been so hot going through that it cauterized itself. Years later I started to feel pain in my cheek. The doctor thought it was a cyst that had to be removed. It wasn't until the actual operation that he discovered the "cyst" to be a souvenir piece of shrapnel. I never really had the feeling that I was going to die after I was severely wounded. I was only eighteen years old. Who knew about all this stuff about war?

When I came home I had no difficulty adjusting to civilian life. I was still the same person I had been before registering in the Navy. I did not pity myself because I had a disability, but rather lived with it. Although my wife says I had a difficult time tying my shoes, I eventually learned to tie the laces with one hand, and light matches without any problems.

People who hear my story say, "Boy, you are a big hero!"

"What are you talking about?" is always my answer.

U.S.S. Kidd. Courtesy of United States Navy.

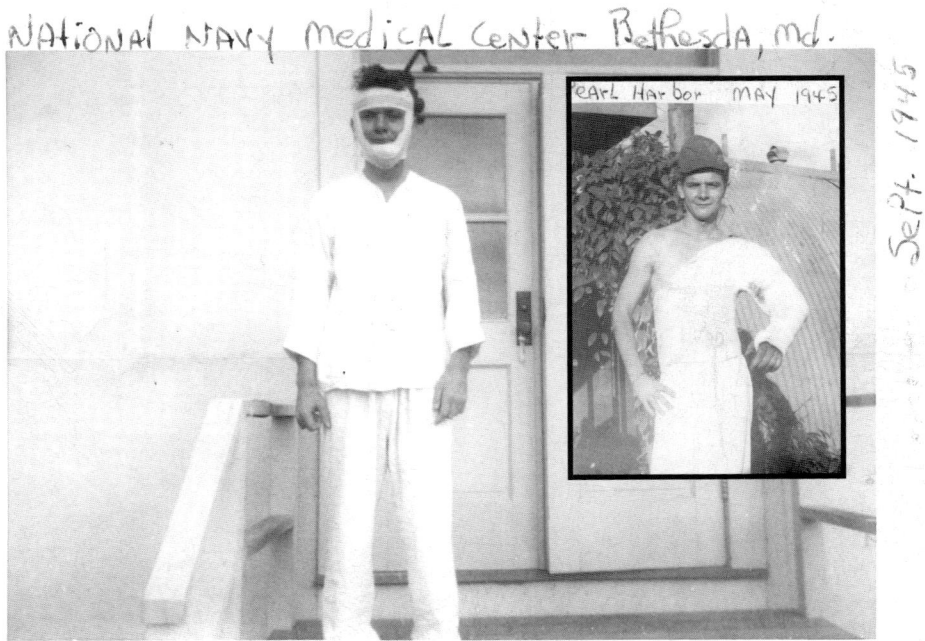

Jim Takitch recovering from wounds. *Courtesy of Jim Takitch*

Medics of the 704th Tank Destroyer make use of a captured German Volkswagen "Schwimmwagen."
Courtesy of Richard "Doc" Buchanan.

Bringing in the Wounded

Hank Stairs

"We Weren't There for Love."

Peter Talarovich
26th Infantry Division, 101st Infantry Regiment
Third Battalion, Headquarters Company
Bradenville, Pennsylvania, 26 February 1923

"We came upon these dead Germans in a barnyard. This one was a giant of a fellow. He had his whole rear-end shot off. Must've been a direct hit. One private looked at me and said, "You know, his sergeant must have really chewed his ass out." I mean that's the type of humor you found. I guess it's about the only thing you could find in a place like that."

WE HAD A BIG FAMILY. There were twelve of us. I'm the only surviving brother. The flu of 1917 killed three brothers. My youngest brother was in the 3rd Marine Division, and he was killed on Iwo Jima. Before that, he got wounded on Saipan. He was awarded the Silver Star. He and another fellow from Missouri killed twenty-six Japs in one attack.

My mother and father, Peter and Anne, came to the United States from Austria in 1894. My father was sixteen. They met and married in America. My mother died of hospital pneumonia when I was fourteen. It was a common way to die, back then. She had gone in the hospital for a gall bladder operation.

During the Depression we had nothing, but we had enough to eat. We lived off the land. We grew our own vegetables and canned for the winter months. We had a big garden and two cows. There were always potatoes and vegetables. We went barefoot in the summer, because we didn't want to wear out our shoes. We shaved our heads, to cut down on haircuts. We had no running water, just outside pumps that froze in the winter. We used coal for cooking and heat, and we heated only two rooms. It was cold when we got into bed, and then we covered ourselves with quilts mother made from the feathers of our geese. In the mornings, we'd brush the snow off of the quilts. That's how bad the house was. The snow would blow right through the cracks around the windows.

My dad was a coal miner, but he worked in a system that was like White Slavery! The company gave him nothing. If a miner didn't buy at the company store, where the prices were higher, they'd tell him to get his tools out of the mine and leave. I'd go to the store with a list. The store manager would call the company bookkeeper and ask, "How many wagons of coal does Peter Talarovich have loaded today?"

They'd tell him. The manager would look at the list and say, "You can't have this, and you can't have this."

The companies were unconcerned about the worker. One time a man was crushed in a mine accident. There weren't too many motor vehicles at the time, so they brought him home on a horse-drawn wagon. They put him on his living room floor and said, "Here's your man, missus."

But, it wasn't all bad when we were growing up. One neighbor had a radio. On summer evenings, we'd all sit on his front porch, he'd bring the radio out, and we'd listen to the Joe Louis fights, and all the other heavyweight fights. We played a lot of baseball during the day.

When I was eleven, I got a job working for a farmer, first for fifty cents a day, then for seventy-five. That was the only money we had coming in, because all Dad's wages went to the company store. I'd work from six in the morning until dark. The farmer gave me two meals, breakfast and lunch, and they were good meals. Those farmers really had the food!

After high school, I worked for the Civilian Conservation Corps for six months. I cut pathways through trees for telephone lines. Living conditions with the CCC were good. We had comfortable barracks, good meals, work clothes, shoes, and whatever we needed. It was better than what I had before. I got thirty dollars each month, and sent twenty-two home. After that, I worked for a candy company in Johnstown, Pennsylvania, and then I went to work for Carnegie Steel in Pittsburgh. Japan attacked Pearl Harbor while I was working in Johnstown. One day, one of the guys came in and told me about the attack.

I said, "Hey, where's Pearl Harbor. I never heard of it."

I was ready to leave the candy company job and go to work in Pittsburgh. I kept waiting for my call-up. I waited and waited. Finally, in January 1942, I went to the Draft Board and told them I wanted to volunteer. My brothers were already in. My father wasn't too crazy about any of us going, but what could he do about it. Everyone was going. A month after I talked to the Draft Board, I was on my way.

We reported for service in Ligonier, Pennsylvania, and from there we traveled by train the twenty miles or so to Greensburg where we got our physicals. From there we got sent to Indiantown Gap, Pennsylvania. After a week passed, they put us on trains and sent us to Camp McCain, Mississippi, where they were organizing the 87th Infantry Division, a new division.

They kept us busy in basic training. Live-fire training was something! One time we were playing war, advancing toward the "enemy." They were using live artillery in what they called "rolling fire," when the troops would advance behind the shells. One round fell short and killed three guys. We'd crawl under barbed wire while they fired live machinegun rounds over our heads, and they'd set off explosions as you crawled under the wire. They did that so that we would get used to it. We didn't get used to it. We never got used to it.

After basic, I was promoted to PFC. A month later I made corporal, and a little while later I was a buck sergeant, drilling troops. Then, the whole outfit went to Fort Jackson, South Carolina. Down there I trained three different groups in eleven-week training periods. I trained them in close-order drill, the M–1 rifle, the mortar, the .30 caliber machinegun, the .50 caliber machinegun, the 37mm anti-tank gun, and the

57mm. Eventually, I got tired of the routine, so I volunteered for overseas duty.

It was thirty others and I who went up to Camp Miles Standish in Boston. We were there a week. They put us into a replacement pool. Then we shipped to England on the *Queen Mary*, a converted British luxury liner with British sailors on it. It was eleven o'clock at night by the time they finished loading the *Queen Mary* up. We steamed out in the morning. When I got up and looked out, there were ships as far as you could see — battleships and cargo ships, troopships and destroyers. They fed us British food. Boiled bacon and mutton for breakfast! I tell you that was hard to get used to! Otherwise, the trip over wasn't bad, even though we slept in hammocks.

We got to England and they put me in a cadre of twelve, plus a couple officers. The cadre made up the schedules for the replacements. We had to keep these guys moving. They'd come in, be with us for three or four weeks, then ship out, then a new batch would arrive. I did this for five or six months, and then I shipped for France. We crossed the channel on transports, and then climbed down cargo nets into the Higgins boats. This was D-Day plus forty-five. The first town we entered was St. Lô. There wasn't much left of it. I didn't know where I was going.

They said, "Get on this truck."

Other guys got on the truck with me. They took us up to the front line. A sergeant greeted me.

He said, "Do you know why you're here?"

"I guess I'm replacing somebody."

"No, you're an expert in the 57mm anti-tank gun. We had the 37mm before but they took those away and gave us the 57mm. We don't know anything about them. You're here to show us."

I was there to give them a quick lesson. They didn't even have the things zeroed in. I showed them how to zero them in and what to watch for. A truck pulled the 57mm. It was a big gun but it wasn't effective against Tiger tanks unless you got them from the back or you aimed for the tracks. But it was very effective on the half-tracks and any other vehicle.

Shortly after that was when I was assigned to the 26th Infantry Division, 101st Infantry Regiment, 3rd Battalion. I was in what they called a "Bastard Platoon." That is, when one bunch didn't need our guns, they'd send us to another bunch that did.

I learned pretty fast the things I should carry into combat and the things I didn't need. We all ditched the gas mask. What we did carry was a light pack with our mess gear and our sleeping bag and toilet articles. When I got into combat, I had a carbine. After my first combat experience, I threw that carbine away and I got an M–1 rifle. I was well trained on the M–1, and, in a pinch, I could use it like a club. Then I ran across a half-track and found an M–3 submachinegun. The thing resembled a grease gun, and that's what we called it, the "grease gun." I took it, and I had it strapped around me with the M–1 rifle. I also had a .45 pistol. For short range I had my submachinegun. I'm glad I did that, because that submachinegun came in handy quite a few times. It had a clip of twenty rounds. I strapped two of those together and whenever I used up the one I just flipped it around and snapped the other one in. I generally carried one bandoleer of ammunition for the M–1. It depended on where I was going and what the action was going to be.

It wasn't long before I got into a minor skirmish. We were moving through a town. The guys with me had been through this before, but this was completely new to me. We got a burst of machinegun fire over our heads.

I thought, "Hey, that isn't for me!"

We moved up. One guy would advance and we'd cover him, then we'd move up and somebody else would cover. It was called, "hedge-hopping." I moved up again and jumped into a crater. There were three Germans in it! They were as frightened as I was. They immediately put up their hands.

"Hey, come here! I got three Krauts!" I yelled.

They could've killed me, but I think they were ready to surrender. Lucky for me! I didn't have to fire a shot

My first real combat was when we had to take a town in the Saar Union. After we took it we set up an outpost to guard against any counterattacks. We camouflaged our guns and set them up so that we could watch all the access roads. We had armor-piercing rounds and anti-personnel rounds, but compared to our 105s or 155s our 57s were like firecrackers. Nobody told us that there was a counterattack coming. The Germans came right down one of the streets with five Tiger tanks and supporting infantry. We were supposed to have L Company riflemen with us, but their lieutenant pulled his men out when he saw the Germans coming, but we didn't know that at first. The Tigers came in firing their 88s and machineguns. They had infantry all around those tanks. We didn't even have a chance to take a shot at them with our gun. Rounds popped all around us.

The Germans knocked out three of our guns. I don't know how many of us got killed. There were six left in our platoon, and we ran into a building. A shell hit out in front of the building. I was standing next to an old steam radiator, and a piece of shrapnel missed my left foot, and took four ribs out of that radiator. We were cut off. Only one way out. We looked up. There was a window with bars. One guy got up on another guy's shoulders and they spread those bars apart. Out the window we went, and across a little field into a barn. We went into the hayloft, Germans all around us. So what do they do? They roll a Tiger tank into the barn. We're up in the loft, and they're downstairs. We looked at each other, and by sign language we decided we were going to fight. We waited. Things cooled down a bit. We could hear the Germans talking. One German started coming up the ladder into the hayloft. Then another German called him back. As soon as we saw him coming up the ladder, everyone had his rifle ready to go. I don't know what would've happened after that. They probably would've burned the barn down with us in it. Anyway, the Germans went back down. We were stuck there for the next thirty-six hours, staying very quiet.

We had some C-rations with us, and some chocolate bars, but no one ate. We weren't hungry. We had our canteens and we'd take a drink every now and then, but we tried to be as quiet as possible. The next morning, some more German armor and infantry came up. Then, during the night, they pulled out. We heard all of this confusion. We didn't know what was going on. We just stayed still. They pulled back, we got out, and that's when we found out that the rest of the guys were either captured or killed.

After the battle in Saar Union we went from town to town. We took part in the battle for Metz and the forts that surrounded it. That was a tough one. We got the hell beat out of us there. After that we were supposed to be on R&R in a rest area when the Battle of the Bulge started. It was December 1944, the coldest winter in forty years. The order came for us to move out. We didn't have a full platoon. We never really did have one. We started our march, and then they put us on trucks, together with our guns and ammo. Then, the next afternoon they told us to get off the trucks because they needed them to carry supplies. So we marched again, and our gear went with the trucks. All we had was our rifles, and from then on we were riflemen. Like I said, we were a Bastard Platoon. We went wherever we were wanted, and we did whatever they wanted us to do. We marched all afternoon, all night, and into the morning, through mud, slop, and snow! Then the order came down, "We don't know where the enemy is — march till you meet him."

The next day we met him, and from there on it was hell. When we met resistance, we fanned out, took cover, fired our weapons, and advanced. That's what it was like for days and days, and from town to town. We had some tank support from the 3rd Armored Division, and we fought alongside other infantry units. We were just a blip in the whole operation. We knew pretty much what our platoon was doing, and maybe we knew what some of the division regiments were doing, but we didn't really know what other divisions were doing. My old outfit from the States, the 87th Division was there with us, but I didn't know that until after the war.

On Christmas Day they brought up a kitchen truck and served us a hot meal of turkey, gravy, and potatoes. While we were eating, a German fighter plane came in low and strafed us. He didn't hit anything on his first pass, so he turned and came in for another one. Someone opened up with a .50 machinegun. The pilot must have seen those tracers coming up at him, and he turned and flew off. We went back to our dinner.

We had been getting information that English-speaking Germans were dressing in American uniforms and driving captured American equipment. We were told to watch out for things like a Jeep full of guys, with only one guy doing the talking. He'd be the one fluent in English.

"Hey, buddy. What part of the States you from?" we might ask.

"I'm from New York."

"Whereabouts in New York?"

Then we might keep the guy talking. We knew American slang, but he might not. Then we might tell him to keep quiet, while we questioned the other guys. They wouldn't be likely to know English. I told some of the new guys who came into our platoon, "You've been in the Army long enough to know how a GI talks. A cuss word here and there, that's what you watch for."

Another thing we found out is make them drop their pants. They might have had our uniforms and equipment, but they never had GI issue underwear!

Around Christmas time we set up our guns on a small hill to cover a crossroads. One of our companies laid a mine field there and we had our guns covering it. The Germans were about 400-yards away in this hollow. Another fellow and I sneaked down and we watched them. They were making a lot of noise. We must have been within fifty yards, and they're down there clanging their utensils and talking. We tried to figure out how many there were. When we got back I had the coordinates of their position, but no radio. I sent one guy back to headquarters to see if we could get artillery to fire on them. Our artillery didn't respond, and the next morning the Germans attacked us. We were cut off, but we didn't know we were cut off until later. There was no action to our front, but all on our right flank. We heard this fighting going on but couldn't see any of it. Then we heard this voice out of the woods in front of us.

"Good morning. Where are you? Good morning. Where are you?"

I told the fellows, "That's no GI. A GI doesn't talk like that. That's someone talking English, but he's not talking American."

We figured it must have been a German pretending to be an American soldier and trying to find out where we were. We never saw him. After a while we heard some Germans calling out in broken English, "*Kamerad, Kamerad. Wasser. Drink. Wasser!*"

We looked and here were two Germans coming toward us, holding up another German. They wanted a drink of water for this guy. He had his whole Adam's apple shot off. The air was coming out of the wound, and you could see the steam in the cold air.

The corporal there with me said, "Let's shoot them."

I said, "That's why I'm the sergeant and you're the corporal. Don't shoot them. We've got to have information. Take them back to headquarters."

They took them back. On the way, the wounded German died. They continued with just the two. They came running back.

The one said, "There's fighting on the ground below us and between us and our command post!"

"Okay," I said, "We're cut off. There's enemy between us and the CP."

"Sarge, what're you gonna do, what're you gonna do?"

The guys were starting to panic. Around this time a couple of GI's from M Company showed up. They said the same thing. The Germans had broken through. One of these guys was limping. He had shot himself in the foot to get out of it. Which is dumb, I think. Probably he got court martialed.

I said, "OK. We're gonna hook up the gun. One guy get on the .50-caliber machinegun. One guy take the .30 caliber to the left. We've got about a mile to go."

That's how far we were into No Man's Land.

I said, "We're pulling back. If we don't pull back now, we're dead ducks."

We went down this road back to the CP. We didn't meet any resistance at all. We met up with the platoon we had in reserve and set up a defense with them. Shortly after we left that hill the Germans brought up some tanks. They threw in shell after shell of 88s on our position. I was down in a foxhole with this other guy and a heavy shell comes in, plop! Right outside of the hole. We were waiting for it to go off. Nothing happened. Next morning, we look out, and it was just sitting there in the snow.

I said, "After a barrage like that, they're going to attack."

Everyone who had a gun set up a defense. Even the cooks and truck drivers got in on it. But the Germans never attacked. We had 600 men that went into that fight, and only 200 of us survived. Our platoon turned over three times during the war. I was in combat for seven months. I guess maybe that's why they called this guy and me from another platoon "the fugitives from the law of averages." I never got real friendly with anyone, because if I made a friend one day, tomorrow one of us would be dead. It was okay to have friends, but not close friends.

We stayed in the area for a couple of days, getting refitted and taking replacements. Sometimes the replacements were pitiful. A lot were from the Air Force, and didn't know how to use a rifle. Shortly after that, we were outside another town where I encountered one of the strangest things I ever saw in the war. We had our guns set so we could see about 600 yards down a hill into a valley. Suddenly, this German half-track emerges into the open and starts coming into our zone. He wasn't firing or anything. He was just driving along.

Our gunner says, "I'm gonna open fire, Sarge."

I said, "No. He might just be the point. Wait to see if there's anybody else coming."

That's how they did it. They'd send one guy in to see how much resistance he would meet. We waited about three or four minutes, and didn't see anything else coming.

"Okay," I said, "open fire!"

All hell broke loose. Everybody opened fire on that thing. It looked and felt like a thousand rounds went into that half-track. The Germans didn't get out. It was just strange the way they were out there all by themselves. I think they must have been lost.

On another occasion, we captured three German half-tracks. They were left out in a field after the Germans in them surrendered. Our Air Force saw them, and started strafing. We had to set up our color panels to let them know American troops were on the ground. They made two runs, but after we set up the panels they stopped. They came down and dipped their wings. They could've wiped us out. That was another instance where we could have been wiped out by friendly fire. Another time was during the Battle of the Bulge. We were in our foxholes. We had a hell of a time digging them. The ground was frozen stiff. But once you had the hole dug it was comfortable because you were out of the wind. You'd be surprised how fast you can dig a foxhole when you're in a situation like that. We usually had two-man foxholes. One guy would sleep, the other would watch. I was in this hole with a guy named Phillips. We were whispering and bullshitting back and forth. Then I heard something.

I said, "Phillips! Hey, keep quiet."

I looked out and saw these figures dressed in white coming right towards us. Phillips said, "They might be krauts."

I said, "Wait. Challenge them."

He challenged. They were a patrol of about six or seven guys from K Company. They had gone out on patrol, and were coming back in.

I said to their sergeant, "What the hell? You guys are crazy. We could've killed you. Why didn't you inform us that you were out there?"

"We got twisted around. We were supposed to come through another sector and we came in through your sector."

"That's damn dangerous."

That's how much information we were getting — in other words, *none*. We were on our own.

We tried to live off the land. Once in the Saar Valley we were set up in a house. We were on one side of the river and the Germans were on the other side. One of the guys came in and said, "There's a steer down in the stable."

I said, "Good. Go down there and butcher it."

"You're kidding."

"No. Get a couple guys and go down and butcher it."

We ate steaks for a week. We couldn't take it with us, because it started to spoil.

One thing that helped me find food while I was overseas was my parents' advice. They came from Austria and knew how most Austrians stored their food and smoked their meat. I figured that they did it the same way over most of Europe.

My father told me, "If you should ever get into that country, you'll find that the kitchen stoves are made out of brick and are wood burning. They're like an open fireplace and up in the chimney part is where they smoke their hams and their bacon."

The first one we ran into, I looked up in there, and said to the fellows, "Hey, we're having ham tonight!"

"What're you talking about?"

I reached up there and pulled out a ham. My dad also told me that people hid their bread in grain boxes. I went in there, dug around in the grain box, and I found two big loaves of brown bread. We got wise to where they kept the food. The same with their alcoholic drinks. There were certain places they would hide it, and we always managed to find it.

Some of these Germans' houses in the bigger towns were nice with modern kitchens and indoor plumbing. I don't know if any of these nicer houses belonged to Nazi officials or not. We didn't pay too much attention to that. But we'd get into one of these houses, use their dishes, and when we were done with them we'd throw them out the window.

Some of the guys started to crack under the strain of combat. We had one guy desert three different times. They always picked him up in Paris. I got word that they picked him up in Paris again, but this time they didn't send him back to the line. We also lost a squad leader to combat fatigue. I had to appoint somebody to take over the squad. I told this guy, "Hey. You're going to take over the squad."

"Me?"

"Yes, you."

"Okay."

The next morning he comes up to me crying.

"Oh, I don't want the squad anymore! There's three Germans in the basement of that house! They won't surrender. How am I going to get them out?"

I said, "I'll show you how to get them out."

We went down to that house. I threw a grenade through a window in the basement, and that took care of them right there. I guess they were just stubborn and didn't want to give up, but you can't fool around. You have to act; I guess that's why I survived.

I said to this fella, "You've got to take action! You can't just stand by!"

"I don't want the squad anymore! I don't want the squad anymore!"

That's all he could say. The guy was in tears. He was absolutely shook up over the whole thing.

By March 1945 it was a rat race! We were going about fifty kilometers a day and suffering very few casualties. Sometimes guys would get overly confident, and that was bad because the Germans were laying a lot of booby traps. They'd booby trap their own dead. There was one incident in a town while we were mopping up. We were going through building after building. Usually teams of three did this. We went into one building, and this guy was on the second floor balcony. It was cold out but the sun was shining.

He said, "Boy, what a beautiful day!"

He sat down in a chair.

I said, "Goddamnit, we're not finished mopping up yet. There's still snipers around. Get the hell in here!"

Just then, POP! Right in the forehead. Down he goes. I was about a minute too late telling him to get the hell out of there. We had to learn how to survive, and we had to be cautious. I was always cautious. One false move, and you're done. But I still got scared, regardless of how cautious I was. Once, inside a house, I heard something running in a room. I kicked the door open real quick, and a goat was in this living room. He jumped on top of a couch, looked at me, and went, "Baaa." I had a notion to shoot that son of a gun! He had me really scared for a minute because I didn't know what I was going to find behind that door.

Near the end of the war, the battalion commander offered me and another fellow a battlefield commission because we didn't have a lieutenant. Our lieutenant had shot himself with a *Panzerfaust*, a German anti-tank rocket. He unscrewed the head of it and had the propelling charge in his hand. He was showing a couple of recruits. We told him not to fool around with it.

"Oh, I'm just showing these guys what this *Panzerfaust* is like."

The charge went off and blinded him. They sent him back to the States. That's why the battalion commander offered us the commission. We refused, and he got so mad, it wasn't funny.

He said, "Just for that, you'll lead the platoon till the end of the war! You're not going to get an officer! You're going to do it!"

He kept his word, too. After the war, we got a lieutenant.

This new lieutenant comes up, and he said, "I'm your platoon leader."

I said, "You are?"

"Yeah. But there's one thing I want to ask you. Will you lead the platoon? These guys were in combat with you. They'll respect you, but they won't respect me."

"All right, no problem," I said. I never saw that many officers at the front, anyway.

Once we were setting up a defense, General Paul, the commander of the 26th Division, came around. I thought to myself, "If there's a general here, then we must be pretty safe." That's what I figured.

We got into Saldu, Czechoslovakia. We passed that place, and then we had to go five miles back, because we were in Russian territory. They said we couldn't take that, according to the Potsdam Treaty. So we came back to Saldu. There was no resistance but we had to outpost, anyway. One morning I had two guys out on the gun. They ran in, saying, "Hey, Sarge, come out!"

"What's the problem?"

"There's Germans all the way down the road!"

I looked out, and there was vehicle after vehicle with white flags. They claimed there were ten thousand that surrendered, running from the Russians. They could've overrun us but they'd rather surrender to us than the Russians, because the Russians probably would have killed them. We didn't know what to do with them. We put them out in a field. Then they loaded them in trucks and started hauling them back.

Some of these Germans said to us, "When are you going to fight the Russians? We heard that the United States and Russia are going to get into a war. When is it going to start?"

After what we had all been through I didn't want any part of this new war between Russia and the U.S. I hoped it would never come to pass.

I guess you couldn't blame the Russians for wanting to take revenge against the Germans. We had one Polish fellow join our outfit. He was a displaced person. A DP, as we called them. Sergeant Lucas spoke Polish and he found out this guy was a lieutenant in the Polish Army. When the Germans invaded his country they took his wife and put her in a camp, and they used her. He didn't know what happened to his two kids. He was a very intelligent fellow. He could read maps. He helped us locate a bridge on a map for us once. Took us right to the spot. The only trouble with him was, and I didn't blame him for this, every time we captured a prisoner he said, "I'll take him back."

The Command Post was a half hour behind us and he was always back in about fifteen minutes. This happened about three or four different times. The next time we caught a prisoner, I told Corporal Leads, "Hey, follow that guy. I don't think he's taking those prisoners back."

He didn't. He took those prisoners so far, made them kneel, and that was it. You couldn't blame him for what he did. From then on, depending on the importance of the prisoner, I was cautious with that guy.

Germans, old men and young boys were surrendering in droves. There was a lot of wreckage, and a lot of dead Germans and GI's laying around. The enemy was the enemy, but we had a different feeling for the GIs. You'd look at them to see if maybe you knew them and then bow your head and continue on. Once we came upon these dead Germans in a barnyard. This one was a giant of a fellow. He had his whole rear end shot off. Must've been a direct hit. One private looked at me and said, "You know, his sergeant must have really chewed his ass out."

I mean that's the type of humor there was.

There were always a lot of dead horses laying around. Civilians ate the meat from them. It seemed like they favored the hindquarters. We'd see chunks of meat out of the horse. The rest of the carcass was laying there.

We took town after town. They would usually be deserted. Most of the time, the civilians would all be crowded into a couple houses. One time we set up our gun to cover a crossroads, and it was near a house full of German civilians. I told a couple of the guys to go in that house and tell the Germans to leave and to check for booby traps. They came back a few minutes later and said, "There's thirty civilians in that house, and we can't get them to come out."

I went in there and said, *"Alles raus! Raus! Raus!"*

One girl said in perfect English, "You can't make us leave."

I said, "The hell I can't! Now you get out. I mean it. Out! We're occupying this place."

They got out all right. After all, we were at war. We weren't there for love.

We went through a small concentration camp. I only saw one survivor there. They told us to keep away from the place and the survivors, because of disease. That poor guy, he was looking through the fence. Take a skeleton, wrap skin around it, and put two eyeballs there; that's what he looked like. The Germans disposed of dead bodies in ovens. It reminded me of the old brickyards back home where they made bricks.

One day we learned the war was over. We were still in Saldu. Slowly, we started to settle down. Pilsen, Czechoslovakia, was to the east. The Company would send a truck up there to get a couple barrels of beer. Those couple of barrels didn't last long. It was just like kids eating candy!

They took us out to bivouac in a field where they planned on training us for the Pacific. We were going to get a thirty-day in-route furlough on our way to Japan. A guy in the pup tent next to ours was cleaning his .45. It went off. The guy next to me gets hit, but, luckily, the bullet hit his pistol that was hanging on his hip. The careless guy got disciplined. There was no call for what happened. Somebody could have gotten killed. To go through all that we went through, then get killed like that!

Then they dropped the Atomic Bomb, and the Pacific war ended. Instead of going there, they shipped us to Steyr, Austria, where we became occupation troops. I was given duty with the CIC that was investigating Nazis and anybody working in the Black Market. The GI's were selling to German civilians and Austrian civilians.

They'd take their goods down to Vienna, and they'd get a good price for them. They'd sell a pack of cigarettes for five dollars, and the guy they sold to could turn around and sell them for ten dollars. One day the CIC sent me down to investigate a prison full of Austrians. The place was a dump. The prisoners looked awful. I told the warden, "I want this place cleaned up. I want these prisoners to shave; they've got to bathe. They've got to wear clean clothes. I'll come back in a week."

A week later, I came back, and they're expecting me, and he's got them lined up like a bunch of soldiers. Everything was cleaned up. After I finished up with the CIC, my outfit was shipped to a camp in France. After a while, we went to Southern France and got on a Liberty Ship for home. We hit forty-foot waves in the Mediterranean. That ship would go up and the propeller would stick out of the water and the whole ship would vibrate from that. I thought it was going to fall apart. It took us two weeks to come back.

This one squad leader of my platoon Philip Ides, from Norfolk, Virginia, said, "I never get seasick. 'Old Salt.' That's what they call me."

That guy was sick from the day we left to the day we landed in Norfolk. I came off the boat and saw him, "Hey, Salty, how you doing?"

"To hell with ya!" he said

When we landed in the States, the first meal they gave us was steak. German prisoners were handing them out. I got in line, and this German picked up a little steak and put in on my plate. I said, "Give me that one there."

He gave me a bigger piece. He couldn't get away with that!

They put us on a train and shipped us out to Indiantown Gap. We were there for maybe a week for debriefing, to get prepared for civilian life. They interviewed me, and looked through my papers. "Well, let's see, what job are you suited for?" they asked. "Hey, you know any gangsters? It'd be a good idea for you to join them."

That was the way he put it to me. They brought us into a room where there was a captain trying to get us into the Reserves. Nobody spoke up. Nobody joined up. He looked at me and said, "Sergeant, why don't you set an example and join?"

"Sir, right now I wouldn't join the Christmas club."

That was it. I'll tell you what, except for the combat, I liked the Army. If it hadn't been for the Russians threatening, I probably would have stayed in the Army and made a career out of it. But I had had enough. After our debriefing they gave me my mustering-out pay and a ticket to Latrobe, Pennsylvania. From Latrobe I thumbed my way home. The second or third car that passed picked me up. He was on his way to Ligonier. On the way, I told him I was from Wilpen. He said, "I'll take you out there."

He brought me right out to my house, duffel bag and all. It was good to get back home with the war over. But I lost a brother in the war. I got word of that by mail around March while I was still overseas. My sister sent me the news in a letter. I was broken up over that. He was only nineteen-years-old. They brought him back, or so they say. He is buried in our church cemetery. The coffin is there, anyway.

I loafed for about three weeks, getting that twenty dollars a week from the 52/20

Club. I thought, "No, this isn't for me."

I had to find work. I went up to Ligonier and I got a job with John Hall Plumbing. Worked for him for a while. Then I went to the coal mines, because there was big money in the coal mines at that time. I worked there for five years. They slowed down, and I went to the mills. After I retired, I went into contracting. Then I figured no, I'm retired, so I quit contracting.

I didn't have any problems once I came home. I fit right in. To me it was like I never left. Maybe because I went to work right away. A lot of these guys loafed for a whole year, on that twenty-dollars a week. They got their check, went to the beer garden about every day and that was it. I figured there's better things in life than that.

I ended up with the European-African Ribbon with three Battle Stars, and I've got the Bronze Star, the Combat Infantry Badge, the Good Conduct Medal and the Presidential Unit Citation. The battle stars are for the Rhineland, Ardennes, and Central Europe. And they gave me the Victory Medal. I don't know what that means except we won, I think. They gave me the Bronze Star for a few things that happened in the Battle of the Bulge. Helped them set up that defensive line. We were under mortar fire, and one of the guys got hit in the hip, and he was out there exposed and fire was coming in. I dashed out there and grabbed him and pulled him in. Somebody saw it.

You only do what's natural, and some people think it's something great.

Outpost in Belgium

Hank Stairs

General Dwight D. Eisenhower gives the order of the Day. "Full victory - nothing else" to 101st Airborne paratroopers just before they board their airplanes to participate in the first assault in the invasion of the continent of Europe. Some of the men with Gen Eisenhower are presumed to be: Pfc William Boyle, _____, Cpl Hans Sannes, Pfc Ralph Pombano, Pfc SW Jackson, _____; Sgt Delbert Williams, Cpl William E Hayes, Pfc Henry Fuller, Pfc Michael Babich and Pfc W William Noll. All are members of Co E, 502d. The other men shown on the photo are not identified. 6 June 1944.
United States Army Signal Corps photo (Moore).

"I Was Just More Of What They Wanted"

Steven Richard Vella

101st Airborne Division, 506th Parachute Infantry Regiment,
Company D; Luxor, Pennsylvania, 22 July 1921

"I only weighed 112 pounds. I wasn't very heavy, but I could outrun just about anybody, and I was a good shot, too, because on the farm at home I shot a lot. I was just more of what they wanted."

I WAS ALWAYS A HUNTER, and I was always a meat cutter. When I was a kid, I cut meat for Kroger's market. I'd cut on Saturdays and after guys went into the Army I got more time. After the war, I butchered cattle for Saint Vincent College. My dad's name was Louie. He came from Sicily. My mother's name was Verona. She came from New Jersey. When he first came over, he worked for a coal company, and then he got a beer distributorship and store. My dad never wanted to talk about the old country. He didn't care for us to worry about Europe. He was more concerned about this country. He didn't want to go back. When he lived there, he had nothing, and people didn't treat him right. When he came here, he was free.

My brother Joe was a medic in the Army. Samuel was in the South Pacific. Angelo was in the Air Force. Carmine was in the Navy. Jimmy, the youngest, was in the infantry. Then there was me. I was a paratrooper. When the war came, I wasn't yet twenty-one, and I didn't think it was my business. I just kept on cutting meat. Then they started taking everybody. Then it became my business. I went to join up with a bunch of other guys. We went up to the Greensburg Armory.

The recruiter asked everybody, "Where do you want to go?"

I said, "I want the most money!"

"Will you jump out of an airplane?"

"If anybody can do it, I can do it."

And that's how I got in the Airborne, and I was there until the day I quit. They told the other guys, "Go home for a couple of days, and don't be running around and getting into trouble because within ten days you're leaving!"

The guy at the Armory said to me, "How soon can you leave?"

"Today."

"Be on the train at one o'clock."

They gave me a meal ticket, and away I went, straight to Fort Meade, Maryland, the same day I joined up. If they'd got a paratrooper, they figured, "We're gonna take him right away before he changes his mind!"

When I got to Fort Meade, I was disappointed. I didn't see any airplanes.

They said, "You don't do anything, just wait for your orders."

And I waited for a couple weeks.

One day I was watching some guys unloading a truck full of beef. I said to the lieutenant there, (you're not supposed to say anything when you're in the Army, but me, I was young and cocky) "Ya know, that's a one man job unloading that beef."

He said, "Well, you unload it!"

I knew how to do it from my butchering days. I picked it up, threw it on my shoulder and unloaded the whole thing. The lieutenant went to the CO and said, "Hey, I got a man here we ought to keep."

The commanding officer said, "Let me see his papers."

He saw that I was going to the paratroopers. "Don't you let him touch anything! He's going to the paratroopers. We'll all get court martialed!"

Then I didn't do anything, just ate and slept. If I had gotten hurt, they would have lost a volunteer who wanted to jump out of an airplane! I had a buddy in the camp that was also from Luxor. He always knew what was going on. His name was Chester Bartosh.

I said to him, "Hey, Chester. Find out what they're gonna do with me."

A little later he came back and said, "You're shipping out to another camp in Georgia. The name of it sounds like Camp Tobacco or something."

About a week later I was on a train. I don't know how long we traveled. I got off the train in Georgia and there's nothing, just a long road and a railroad track, and I was all by myself in the woods. About a half-hour later a truck came to pick me up.

The driver said, "You going to Camp Toccoa?"

"I don't know where I 'm going, buddy."

"Get in the back."

When we got to the camp, I was disappointed again because all it was all tents! I was looking for a place with airplanes. Then they told us where we were. It was a Boy Scout camp. Boy Scouts!

I took basic infantry training at Camp Toccoa, and then I went to Fort Benning for paratroop training. I jumped out of wooden airplanes, learned how to run with a pack, learned how to climb cliffs, and learned how to take orders. That was the main thing, learning how to take orders. The wooden airplanes were only about five feet off the ground. We moved forward in those things, grabbed the doorframes, made a step, and went out the door. Then we had a tower that we'd jump off of. There was a cable that ran past the tower. Our harness was connected to that cable by a rope. When we jumped, that cable would catch the rope, and then we'd slide all the way down into this big sawdust pile at the bottom. That was to get us used to the shock of landing. Then they took us up in this 250-foot tower. We jumped off that with parachutes, so we could get the feel of a chute opening up.

Very few had problems with heights on those towers. The thing that bothered guys the most was when they made their first jumps out of the C–47s. A lot of guys would vomit. We had a bucket for that. I never got sick, thank God, and I don't know why. The first time I jumped I was scared, and you had to make five jumps to qualify. Getting in the plane the first time, oh, Jesus Christ, it was rough! Once I got in, I cooled down.

On all the jumps we'd be flying along, and the jumpmaster would come back and yell, "Two minutes!"

Then, a red light came on, and we would hook our chute to a static line. The number one guy would go to the door. The guy behind you would check your equipment. Then everyone hollered that they were set.

I'd say, "One Okay!"

The guy behind me would say, "Two Okay!"

"Three Okay!" And so forth, down the whole stick. Then the number one man, he'd stay at the door looking out. The guy behind him was the jumpmaster and he said, "As soon as you get the green light you go!"

The jumpmaster stayed at the door to make sure everybody jumped out. Once my chute opened, I had no special feeling, except for the opening of the chute. It stopped us cold, every time. When we jumped, we didn't go straight down. We followed the plane, because our bodies were going just as fast. Then the blast from the engines threw our chutes back. We had to do that five times, to give us confidence that the chutes would open. I ended up in the 506th. I only weighed 112 pounds. I wasn't very heavy, but I could outrun just about anybody, and I was a good shot, too because on the farm at home I shot a lot. I was just more of what they wanted. You didn't get your boots till you went through your sixth jump. When we got the good jump boots it was all worthwhile, because we were paratroopers then! By the time I jumped into Normandy and Market Garden, I had twenty-six jumps.

The 506th made me a 300-radio operator. I had to jump with that thing, too. They kept our squad together. There were three squads of fifteen to each platoon. Fifteen men was a "stick" of jumpers. We ate together, slept together, trained together, and died together. We depended on each other, and that's the way the Army wanted it. Your buddy could save your life.

We left for England on 5 September 1943, from Camp Miles Standish. I couldn't write home. We weren't allowed to. We had to take off our divisional patches. We arrived in Liverpool, England, 15 September. They had us crammed in the ship like cattle. There were so many boats in the convoy, it looked like you could step from one to the other. We gambled as soon as we got on board, and we gambled all the way across the ocean. Gambling was the name of the game! When I came home on the *USS Wakefield*, it was the same story.

We got to Liverpool at night, in "secrecy." They gave us coffee and donuts, and we started unloading the ship. Somebody turned on a radio. We heard an English-speaking German guy say, "Congratulations to the 506th at Aldbourne-Wiltshire."

We hadn't been off the ship for a half hour, but we had no idea where we were headed. The Germans told us! Jesus, we all laughed about that! They knew more about us than we knew ourselves. Then the announcer said, "You'll soon have company when the 502nd comes in tomorrow."

They even know the name of the boat the 502nd was on. How did they know that, we wondered?

One thing we did know was that we were training for an invasion of Europe. We didn't know when it was coming, but we knew we would be in it. We started to make mass night jumps, because we knew we were going to do the same in the invasion. At night, we heard the German bombers and buzz bombs. We saw the British searchlights come together. When that happened, we knew they found a bomber. Then the ack-ack would open up, and we'd see a plane come down in flames. We were used to shooting and explosions from our training, but we were still scared, especially because we couldn't do anything to fight back. Our barracks weren't too far from town, and we'd go in and talk to British soldiers and the people. We'd have girlfriends, and sometimes they would come back to the barracks to see us.

One night, we got into our planes and didn't come back. They got us all together, and gave us an early meal. General Eisenhower came over and talked to us. He was trying to build up our confidence. He told us everything was going to be all right. Later, they explained to us our exact mission, the kind we had been trained for. And we were trained! They kept us worked up. We didn't do too much thinking. We all had the feeling, "The other guy is going to get killed, not me."

We went out to our plane. We had to be over France by midnight, six hours before the main invasion force. Just before we got on the plane, they gave us a little, black pill. I don't know what it was. Maybe a nerve pill, or a stomach pill. We took off from Exeter, and headed south over the Channel. We were getting some ack-ack from the Germans. Tracers were floating up at us like fireworks. A plane in front of us got hit. The green light came on in my plane, and I went toward the door. I jumped, and soon I was on the ground. We jumped into Ste. Mere-Eglise. They told us if we got lost or separated, to just watch the returning planes headed north, toward England. That would give us bearings.

After I hit the ground, I had to find everyone else. Guys missed landing zones, got separated, and didn't get with their units until days later. Some guys drowned in places that had been flooded by the Germans. That night was hell. I could see battle going on all around me. Everything was exploding, and, up in the air, it looked like fireworks. Oh, Jesus, all kinds of lights! Some of that was German anti-aircraft fire going up after our planes. A bunch of us was trying to get together, using the clickers they gave us. We were supposed to use them at night. One click was supposed to get two responses. It didn't matter which company anybody ended up with. We had to get together. Everybody was looking for somebody.

About daybreak, I found some D Company people. A day later, I found the company commander, who was dead along with three other fellows. We had a wide landing zone, and we had to search the whole area for the dead. It took a lot of effort. I was in the water for at least an hour looking for guys who drowned. Then we started to move forward, but along the way, we still looked for the dead. We made maybe a half-mile a day. We reached St. Bernard, and decided how to complete our mission. We were supposed to create confusion behind the German lines, and pave the way for our main invasion forces. Certain of us were assigned to blow up small bridges, rails, and take crossroads that the Germans might use. We moved forward, sometimes coming under fire. Somebody would holler, "Left flank, to the woods, fire for effect!"

A bunch of us would start shooting in the direction of enemy fire. We'd get up and move for cover, then fire again. When we'd get to the German position we'd find dead Germans. We never knew which of us killed them, because everyone was firing. We didn't stop to count the holes in their bodies. One, or ten, it didn't matter. They were dead. There was one guy in our outfit (I shouldn't talk about him because he's dead) who just *wanted* to kill Germans. He would go around to these dead Germans, take out his knife, and cut their ring fingers off, take the rings, then wear them on a chain around his neck. He took gold teeth, as well, right out of their mouths. He wouldn't take prisoners, either. He'd say, "I'm here to kill Germans!"

We were always looking for our planes. If we saw them, we knew we would have a lot of firepower behind us. One time, my buddy and I were on the side of a road near some woods, waiting to move out. We were just sitting there watching this dogfight between an ME–109 and a P–47. They were way up there, but they soon got down closer to the ground. We could hear that P–47's .50 calibers firing. The ME–109 came down low, and the P–47 was right behind it. Stray bullets came tearing up the road straight at us. My buddy said, "We're gonna get killed by our own planes!"

We started to run down the road by these woods and the next thing we knew this ME–109 comes crashing down in front of us about a 100-yards away! It tore up the trees in front of us when it blew up. We took cover in the woods and that P–47 practically shaved the tops of the trees off with its propeller as it flew over us! It's funny now, but when it happened, it scared the shit out of us!

I got wounded three times in the war. The only thing that I prayed for was that I didn't return home blind. That's what I dreaded more than anything else. Shrapnel hit me in my back, and in the eye, but that wasn't serious. The last time I was wounded, I broke a bone. We were on the other side of the Rhine. We got some machine-gun fire, and I hit the ground. I rolled down a hill and broke my hand. I thought that it was just bruised, so I wouldn't go to the hospital. They wrapped it up for me. When they X-rayed it, they found out that it was chipped. They wanted to operate, but I wouldn't let them. I wanted to get back to my outfit. Getting back to them was like going home. I knew I could trust those guys. Once I got back to the States, I always told my old buddies that if they were within a hundred miles I'd come and get them. Of course, we have our reunions, and we end up talking about what we went through. Some of them are drunks, but they're still my buddies. I'll never forget them.

1943. One of the first raids by the Eighth Air Force in Europe. The target was a Focke Wulf plant at Marienburg, Germany. German fighter planes destroyed eighty planes of the attacking force.
National Archives.

"It All Seems Like a Dream."

William Wachter
Eighth Air Force, 452nd Bomb Group
Wexford, PA

"Over there, we had a standing deal where there would be dances for the officers and non-coms. They alternated, the officers one week, the non-coms the next. The same girls would come to each dance. The only time I went to one of these dances was the time I witnessed an unfortunate circumstance. Our wing commander cut in on a lieutenant, took the lieutenant's girl, and went dancing around. The lieutenant went up to him, pulled him back, and knocked him out. Everybody just kept on dancing. Then the executive officer came up and the lieutenant knocked him out, too. There were the two of them laying side by side, a general and a colonel. Everybody ignored them, and kept dancing around. I thought that the lieutenant was going to be court martialed and shot the next morning, but nothing happened. In fact, they got those two guys off the floor. They got sent home, and never came back."

I ALWAYS FELT BAD about my grandfather. One of his relatives was a Colonel in the Irish Rifles who said that once the Irish got in the war, it would be over in six weeks. I made the wisecrack that I'd be over there winning the war for him. He never forgave me for that.

I started out as a member of the Army ROTC at the University of Pittsburgh in 1940. We spent our time attacking a hill in Schenley Park with wooden rifles and going through a lot of other drills that didn't mean much. There was nothing much in the way of equipment in those days. At the time, I had the impression that we were going to be in the war, and that was our main driving force. A year and a half later, we were called up from Pitt, and sent to basic training at Fort Eustace, Virginia. I got out of a lot of duty there working for a Major, the former head of the Mechanical Engineering Department at Georgia Tech. He was an old codger with the Regular Army commission of Major, which somehow outranked the commanding General at Fort Eustace. The Major didn't like the idea of having to walk or march everywhere, so he had us build what was probably the first "golf cart." We took old parts from a gun directory and hammered out this crazy thing. It used a gasoline engine that we stole off of one of the generators that supplied the power to these gun directories. By the time we got it built, we got orders for two more. I got out of a lot of other work by working with him.

At the end of that training period they announced that we were going back to Pitt, but I said I wasn't going. A buddy and I went to the Battery Clerk's office and asked for transfers to the paratroopers. It turned out that they didn't have any transfer forms for the paratroopers.

We asked, "What *do* you got?"

He said, "The only thing we got is Air Corps."

My dad had flown in World War I, and I always wanted to be in the Air Force. Plus, I had the notion that any war we fought was going to be dominated by air power. I knew at Pitt that someday we would be in the war, but I shied away from the Air Corps because my teeth were crooked. They turned you down if you didn't pass the so-called "64 Physical."

Without hesitation, I said, "I'll take it."

My buddy went back to Pitt. Four weeks later I had to explain to some psychiatrist why I wanted to fly.

We were a close bunch in the Air Corps. We were, you might say, free and easy compared to the other branches. When we were in pre-flight and flight school it was terrible. They had us doing everything, squaring our meals, and behaving like idiots. I guess all of that gave us a sense of order and discipline.

We had the usual training in Texas. Since I had studied astronomy, they automatically made me the navigator. We had quite a few losses in training, but our worst accident happened during tight formation flying. One of the planes hit another and it had a domino effect. We lost seven planes and seven crews.

After training, we boarded a British ship in New York harbor. The ship had been rammed and sunk, but they pumped it out and resurrected it, but it had a permanent curve in its hull. It took us thirteen days to go over because we were zigzagging to avoid German submarines.

Over there, we had a standing deal where there would be dances for the officers and non-coms. They alternated, the officers one week, the non-coms the next. The only time I went to one of these dances was the time I witnessed an unfortunate circumstance. Our wing commander cut in on a lieutenant, took the lieutenant's girl, and went dancing around. The lieutenant went up to him, pulled him back, and knocked him out. Everybody just kept on dancing. Then the executive officer came up and the lieutenant knocked him out, too. There were the two of them laying side by side, a general and a colonel. Everybody ignored them, and kept dancing around. I thought that the lieutenant was going to be court martialed and shot the next morning, but nothing happened. In fact, they got those two guys off the floor. They got sent home, and never came back.

We had a loose outfit. One day while we were inspecting our plane, we ran across a guy with a busted motorcycle. One of our gunners went up to him and said, "You having trouble, Bub?"

He said, "Yeah, yeah. I'm having a lot of trouble."

He was the commanding officer of our base!

We went to Stonehenge for classification. That was the coldest I've ever been in my life. It was the dead of winter, and it was awful. Then they put us on trains and we went to the various bases we were assigned to. We were made a lead crew from the beginning.

We were based out of Deopham Green, southwest of Norwich. It was a very unusual arrangement of Quonset Huts; they were spread out in different areas so one bomb couldn't get them all. We also kept the planes in separate revetments for the same reason. There was a bus service that took us to different places. The airbase was loaded with dogs that were either brought over by crewmen, or picked up there. The crewmen had either been shot down or been sent home, and the dogs would wait at these bus stops. The damned bus drivers would stop for these dogs, before they would stop for human beings. I guess the drivers figured the dogs were going to be there longer than we were. The dogs would ride the busses over to the mess hall, run out back, and get the scraps. I never found out what happened to those dogs after I left. I guess they turned wild.

When we were first there I slept in a mummy sleeping bag. I noticed that most everybody had sheets.

I went over to somebody and asked, "How do you get sheets?"

He said, "Well you got to wait until someone either gets killed or sent home, then swipe them off the bed."

And that's what we did. It was a very different world there.

For R&R, we went into London. Once I went to Albert Hall to hear the London Philharmonic. The Queen Mum came in with her daughters. She was beautiful, but her daughters looked like her husband – ugly. That was back when the German rockets were falling, but that didn't seem to bother the Queen Mum.

I managed to get tickets to a Sid Fields' performance in *Strike it Again* at the Prince of Wales Theater. Sid was known as "Britain's Bob Hope," but I thought he was pretty bad. It wasn't my kind of play, at all.

We went to eat at a posh restaurant, the Rogner House. The main floor was for regular officers only. The balconies were reserved for staff officers, and the top balcony was reserved for generals. You couldn't get away with that in our country, but in England, that was a different matter. One time a table of Britishers sat down next to us. They toasted us, and we turned back and toasted them, and I made the mistake of saying they were English. We almost had a knockdown fight because they happened to be Scots. They all seemed to hate each other over there.

We didn't get over there until the end of the war, so the missions weren't that difficult. We had a few experimental runs. We were the first group to fly napalm bombs. They first put the stuff in a P-47 fiberglass gas tank and hung them in our bomb bay like sausages. The fumes from the chemicals filled the plane. We always had to yell at the crew for smoking when we flew missions with ordinary bombs, but when we carried the napalm, we didn't have to tell them to stop smoking. Nobody touched anything that lit. After we dropped the napalm, the second group came over and dropped fragmentation bombs, and scattered the stuff all over the place. Our objective was 90,000 German infantrymen in the fields at the harbor of Bordeaux.

It was a little tricky flying over the enemy coast. We flew over German installations, and they would open up on us. They also had ingeniously come up with dummy radar signals, if we weren't on our toes, especially the navigator, those signals would take us off our course and over the flak guns.

The last people we would see when we boarded our planes were little old ladies from the Salvation Army. They were there in fair and foul weather, ready with coffee and a snack. They were always there when we came back, too. When we came back they gave everybody a bottle of liquor. Since there were several of us that didn't drink, the rest benefited by getting a double ration. Then they would take us into the debriefing room and you had to describe anything. Not only was I a navigator, I was also a weatherman. I had to record conditions to target and back, and then report my findings at the debriefing.

On 7 November 1944 the last big air battle over Europe took place. This was a month after our intelligence officer told us the *Luftwaffe* had been destroyed, so it came as sort of a surprise. Our group lost about half its members there including my best friend. He was the only one that had a legitimate job waiting for him back home. He was the first drummer in Sam Kenton's orchestra. In that battle the German Jets lured our fighter cover away, and conventional fighters hit our bombers. By that time, the German pilots were so bad, they had a lot of collisions with the bombers. My friend was killed in one of those collisions.

It was a heavy fighting day. Our group shot down nine Focke-Wolfe –190s and twelve Me–109s and two of our own P–51s. Our fighter pilots were told not to fly through the formations, but they did, on the tails of the enemy planes. They passed through a group of thirty-six bombers, each of which had twelve to fifteen guns, each firing 600 rounds per minute. They went down quickly.

As the war wound down we were notified of a bad situation in Holland. Thousands of people were starving to death. So they organized part of the Eighth Air Force and part of the RAF for a food drop. It was the first time that heavy bombers were used on a mercy mission. We flew over Rotterdam stadium where the Dutch had painted a huge bull's eye in the middle. We approached the stadium from one end, dropped our wheels to slow us down. We dropped the food, and then climbed back up. We flew there again, and this time a 500-pound sack of potatoes got hung up in the bomb bay. We held the radio operator head first out of the bomb bay while he freed the bag. Our bombardier kept screaming, "Don't, don't, don't!"

When we finally got the bag loose, it tore and potatoes flew all over the air like buckshot. We looked out and below were a long string of greenhouses. The potatoes were smashing out all of the windows. Years later, when my wife was president of the Brentwood Garden Club, they would invite the Dutch tulip people over. I always felt really embarrassed to meet them.

We flew another mission to Linz, Austria. We flew into the city and picked up a horrible collection of walking skeletons. They had come from the Nazi death and labor camps. We loaded them in like sacks of grain. I had ten of them in the nose of the plane. Today, when I see a B–17 at an air show, I look in the nose and still can't figure out how I got them all in there. All of them had been dusted with DDT powder. I kept the maps I used in the war, and years later, if I shook them, DDT still fell from them.

When we flew to Linz part of the way down the Danube River, it was the worst navigation chore I ever had. Everything looked alike. It was hard to pick up pilotage points and figure out when we were going to land. The bases over there were lined up with what they call the prevailing winds. Planes were landing at both ends at the same time. Two planes would come right at each other and, at the last minute, one would chicken out and pull up. It was more dangerous than our bombing missions. When I came back, kids were playing the game of chicken on the highway with their cars. That was nothing. They should have been trying that with four-engine bombers. After the mercy missions our job was done in Europe.

They brought the Eighth Air Force back. As a lead navigator, I had to check all the planes and their instruments. Then they sent us home on leave. After that, they got us collected at Sioux Falls Air Force Base. Their intention was to send us to the Pacific. But that didn't happen. The Japanese finally surrendered, thanks to two Atomic Bombs. Years later, at a dinner celebrating the first atomic reactor, I sat at a table with two Japanese scientists, and they didn't blame us. They blamed their own. They knew what was coming, and they desperately tried to get their rulers to surrender. They had been picking up fission fragments in the air, traces of our test explosion. The scientists resented us dropping the second bomb, however, but that second bomb saved a lot of American lives.

I am glad I did what I did. I am particularly glad I got a chance to fly those mercy missions. That is the most important thing we did, except for bombing the greenhouses with potatoes! I still wonder what happened to those poor people we picked up in Linz, whether they survived after we brought them to France.

When we came back we didn't talk about it, and we weren't cry babies. Actually, nobody really asked us to tell our stories back then. The Depression made us tough, and it had a solid effect on us. Of course, I think about my lost buddies. The war is so far away now that it all seems like a dream.

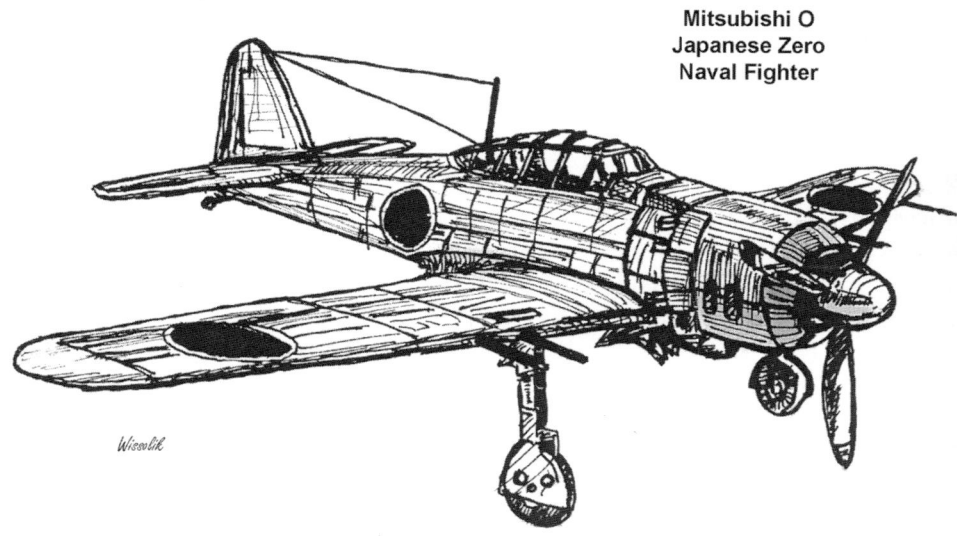

**Mitsubishi 0
Japanese Zero
Naval Fighter**

A Curtiss P-40 Tomahawk. Only four of these were able to get airborne at Pearl Harbor.
United States Airforce file photo, original source and date unknown.

"I'll Be Back in a Year…"

Robert Wasson
34th Combat Engineers, Headquarters Company
Indianhead, Pennsylvania, 1917

"Army pay was twenty-one dollars a month. When we got paid we said, 'The eagle landed and took a crap.' Pay came in a little brown envelope containing a ten-dollar bill, a five-dollar bill, five ones, and a quarter. They held back seventy-five cents for laundry. That was twenty-one dollars pay for getting shot at, and for taking orders. After getting paid, most guys headed to the Post Exchange or a gambling table."

THERE WAS A POPULAR SONG back then called, "I'll Be Back in a Year, Little Darling." I was a patriotic sort of guy, and in 1941 I told my wife I was going to put in my year in the service. What a farce that was, because once you held up your hand and took that oath, you didn't belong to yourself anymore; you were Government Issue, a GI, and you were expendable. Army decided what and when you ate, when you went to sleep, when you got up. I soon learned to despise the Army.

I was assigned to the 34th Combat Engineers. After training, they sent me to Los Angeles where I boarded a very, very old troopship, the *USS Grant*. We had no idea where we were going. Then, somebody spotted an officer's luggage. It was marked "Honolulu."

In September 1941, after ten days zigzagging in the Pacific, we arrived in Hawaii. Instead of hula dancers, a bunch of officers met us. They put us on a narrow-tracked train that was used to haul pineapples and sugar cane. We made a slow trip up a hill to Oahu. Halfway up, I caught a glimpse of Pearl Harbor in the distance. I couldn't believe my eyes! I hadn't been a military man for very long, but I wondered why, if war seemed to be so imminent, that we had lined our ships up like dominoes.

They sent us to Hawaii to build additional barracks for soldiers. After a few weeks, our battalion commander pulled me out of a work detail. "Are you married?" he asked.

I said, "Yes, sir."

"You didn't tell anybody you were married."

"That's right, sir. I'm here to put in my year."

"Well, in that case, I'll make you an offer. There's a vacancy in the officers' club kitchen. The pay's a dollar a day. This is in addition to Army pay."

Army pay was twenty-one dollars a month. When we got paid we said, "The eagle landed and took a crap." Pay came in a little brown envelope containing was a ten-dollar bill, a five-dollar bill, five ones, and a quarter. They held back seventy-five cents for laundry. That was twenty-one dollars pay for getting shot at, and for taking orders. After getting paid, most guys headed to the Post Exchange or a gambling table.

The extra pay looked good, so I took the job in the officers' club. I was on the job the morning of 7 December. Pearl Harbor was fifteen miles away. We heard explosions coming from the direction of the harbor, and, when we stepped outside to see what was going on, we saw big clouds of smoke. The telephone rang. The only officer in the club at that time answered it. He hung up the receiver, turned to us, and then told us what was happening. The Japanese were attacking Pearl Harbor!

As we ran out of the club, several Zeros went over us, machineguns and cannons rattling. I jumped behind a coconut tree. I looked at the tree and said to myself, "This is like hiding behind a corn stalk!"

I dove under a building that was built on stilts. A couple guys joined me. A Zero strafed the building but I didn't get hit. Another guy took a round in his heel. After shooting up our barracks, the Zeros headed for our airstrip, and then bombed and strafed the whole area. I had no rifle, no ammunition, no steel helmet, no nothing. And even the anti-aircraft batteries and numerous artillery battalions in the area had no ammo, nothing! We were caught with our pants down, unprepared! That's what I remember of Pearl Harbor. It was all over very quickly.

After that, everything was blackout, and blackout conditions went on for years after. We dug foxholes and bomb shelters. All of it too late! But if another attack came, we would at least be a little prepared. The raid seemed to me to have been very well planned. It was a Sunday morning. Most people would be asleep or getting ready for church. It was also the day after payday. The Japs must have figured that the GI's would be drunk or hung over or down with the prostitutes on Canal Street.

Something strange happened to me the day before the attack. I had been in Honolulu all day. I started back to the barracks late that night and I saw a copy of the *Honolulu Star Bulletin*. The headline read "War Declared." A few hours later Pearl Harbor was attacked. How could this be? What kind of generals and admirals did we have leading us?

There was no just pick up the phone and say, "Hey, mom. How are you?" Anything we wrote in a letter, if it implied at all where you were or what you were doing, would be all blacked out. The most you could say was, "I'm living."

Shortly after the attack, I was assigned to headquarters because I could read a map and determine coordinates and I knew some of the things necessary for troop location. So my days in the officers' club kitchen were over, so was the thought of getting home in a year. I stayed in headquarters a number of years until I became a tech sergeant in charge of G3, Operations. Operations identified and kept track of where all our units in the Pacific were. The section I worked had four or five men. We had maps on the officers' walls covered with a plastic film that we could write on with a grease pencil. We had various legends with symbols that denoted armies, divisions, regiments, and other information.

The first lesson I learned in the Army was self-preservation. They wanted me to come back to the States for Officer Training School. I refused.

I said, "I'm staying right here."

And I did, until near the end of the war, and then I was assigned to a task force to go to Okinawa. We spent thirty-three days zigzagging again across the Pacific to join in the attack on that island, the last stepping-stone to Japan. When we got there we came under Kamikaze attack. We spent four or five days under constant bombardment. I was grateful to get off the ship onto dry land because I didn't think we were going to make it out in the harbor. The Japanese philosophy of death made him a very dangerous opponent.

We landed on the little island of Ieshima, just off the coast of Okinawa. The Marines and the infantry had already infiltrated the island, and there were dead Japs and Americans every place you looked. We buried the Americans properly. The Japs we just scooped up with bulldozers and dropped in mass graves. The odor was horrible! It was the odor of death! The Japs were bloated like balloons, and their skin had turned black with decay. I took the wallet from a dead Jap. I pulled out a picture of his family, and, when I saw his wife, I became very sad. I thought of my own wife. There was a nearby schoolhouse. It had been devastated by bombardment. I picked up a textbook. Though I couldn't read the language, I could tell from the illustrations that the book told of the Jap hatred for the American flag. I still have the book. I kept it as a reminder.

I was still in headquarters. My duties were to map. It was only two miles one way and one mile in the other direction. Ieshima is the island where Ernie Pyle was killed. I was no more than a couple hundred yards away from him when he was shot. He was in a Jeep, and a sniper shot at the Jeep and missed. They got out of the Jeep and down into a ditch. Ernie Pyle made the mistake of raising his head to see where the shooting was coming from. He got shot immediately. Pyle was loved by the troops, because he wrote about them in human terms.

I had a Jap surrender to me. The area we were in was all rock, so it was near impossible to dig a foxhole, but we had slit trenches and shelters made out of logs. I was in one of these when I saw a Jap approaching me. He was waving a white shirt on a stick in sign of surrender. I grabbed my M–1. I bet I scared him to death, because I pointed it right at him. I escorted him right down to headquarters where he became an official prisoner of war. We found another Jap in our area, hiding out in the brush. A soldier stepped out of his hole to relieve himself and heard this movement. He left, came back with a hand grenade, and then threw it into the brush. That was the end of the Jap.

There were lots of caves, and the Japs hid in them. One of our sergeants went into one of the caves looking for a souvenir. A bobby trap wounded him. I thought, "Well, good for him. That was a stupid thing to do anyway."

The Japs bombed us every day and night, and that was tough to get used to. Sometimes, I would be so tired that I would sleep through the noise. One night, a squadron of Black Widows (P–61s) came in and landed on the airstrip we had laid out on the island. The planes were strange to us, and we wondered what they were for. We found out that night. The Jap bombers came over, their engines sounding as usual like old washing machines, a sound that distinguished them from our planes. The air raid alarm sounded, and the Black Widows took off. A few minutes later I heard a short burst of machinegun fire, and then I saw a light, just a spark at first, but then it grew brighter and brighter. It looked like it was coming straight for me. I woke up my buddy and we both watched this thing come down. We were right on the edge of the island. This fireball came down right past where we were, and down the other side of a cliff. A Black Widow had brought the bomber down. It could see in the night because it had been equipped with radar. The Black Widow changed everything, and it became suicide for the Japs to bomb at night. Day or night, they lost hundreds of planes to our fighters, the Widows, and radar-directed artillery.

After we dropped the first Atomic Bomb, they gave me orders to return home. I landed at the airport on Okinawa just at the time of the surrender. Every plane that had been going east to the United States was diverted to Japan and the other islands to liberate Allied prisoners of war. They got precedence, as they well should have. I couldn't get an air pass, but there was a colonel who decided we could go to Guam by boat. It took us four days to travel four hundred miles! We landed on a small island and decided to stay there, rather than go on to Guam. A mail plane landed there from Guam every day, and the pilot had permission to take one person with him when he left. Naturally, the colonel went first. I got to go next. It was a thrill to fly in that little plane. The island had such a short runway that I hoped it would get in the air before it hit the water.

On Guam, I got on a B–29. Gene Autry and his group had been doing a USO show on Guam and they also boarded the plane. There were not seats, so we all did the same thing. We laid out our luggage and sat on it. I got all the way to Hawaii on that bomber. The plane was not pressurized because it had some battle damage, and there were bullet holes here and there in the fuselage. The noise of the engines was terrible. It took months before my hearing got back to normal. I got to Honolulu, and from there took a flight to Seattle.

I took a train home from Seattle. When I got home, my wife presented me with a four-year-old girl. It was the first time I saw her, and, of course, she had never seen me. She wanted no part of a stranger, and it took her quite a while to get to know me. I had been gone more than four years. It was a hard time for me, and one that I would never want to repeat. I remembered that old song, "I'll Be Back in a Year, Little Darling."

"We Never Forgot Those People."

Harvey Waugaman
87th Infantry Division ("Golden Acorns"), 346th Regiment
Greensburg, Pennsylvania, 27 January 1924

"When it was time for bed, the family gave us their beds to sleep in. It was the first time in months we had seen a bed. We slept between clean sheets, under feather ticks. We were in Heaven! When we awoke in the morning, we found that the family had washed and dried our clothes. Before we left, even though their food was in short supply, they gave us breakfast. All they had was eggs. Off we went, again. We never forgot those people, and I'm sure they never forgot us."

WHILE IN HIGH SCHOOL I worked for my family's retail meat business that also served hotels, restaurants and institutions. I worked there until I got called into the service. I took flying lessons at the Greensburg-Pittsburgh Airport in Greensburg until it closed down and was made into the West Point housing plan. Then I went to Bettis Field near Pittsburgh for lessons. I soloed and got my license at the Latrobe Airport, now the Arnold Palmer Regional Airport. When they asked for volunteers for the Air Cadet program, I volunteered. I went to Pittsburgh and passed their physical, hoping that when I got called to the service I'd have a chance for the Air Corps. By the time I did get called, they had a surplus of people.

When I got drafted, I went to Fort Meade, Maryland. Since I had been in the meat business, they put me into a specialty camp in Camp Blanding, Florida, where they trained specialists like mechanics, radio technicians, communications people, bakers, cooks, and so on. I schooled there for about three weeks until they changed the camp over to a weapons camp. I trained there for another six weeks, then went to Boston, boarded a ship, and crossed the Atlantic Ocean to Great Britain. From there, the division headed for the Continent, and on 8 December was at Metz where we took Fort Driant. We were just moving into Germany when the Germans broke through the Ardennes Forest in the Battle of the Bulge. We were placed in reserve for a while, and then we joined the Bulge battle in Belgium on 29 December. On 15 January we moved into Luxembourg to relieve the 4th Division near Wasserbillig, a little rail and bridgehead between the Sauer and Moselle Rivers. Our orders were to clear the village so that our troops would have clear sailing to the bridgehead.

We assembled early in the afternoon, and were issued K-Rations and white snow-suits. At midnight, we left for Wasserbillig, following the railroad tracks. It was cold and snowy, but our snowsuits were warm and provided perfect camouflage against the snow. We entered the village in two columns. My squad went directly to a house on the left hand side of the street. We went to the second floor and set up machineguns. Another squad did the same thing on the other side of the street. One of the guys tried to suppress a cough. Without thinking, he lifted his hands to his mouth, and dropped two cans of ammunition he was carrying. That was enough to alert the Germans. We fought the rest of the night. A German tossed a hand grenade in through the window. One of our guys threw it back, killing the German. We held the town for three days. Usually the Germans counterattacked, but this time they didn't.

Our next big objective was Gold Brick Hill (Hill 649), and we fought our way there for two days through bitter cold. It was really Gold "B" Hill, but all the guys called it "Gold Brick Hill." At night we used each other's body heat for warmth. Gold Brick Hill was the beginning of and the highest point on the Siegfried Line, and from it the Germans could cover most of their front. We had to cover 700 yards without much cover to get to the top, where there were several pillboxes and a couple hundred crack mountain troops. We knew what was up there from a German officer some of our guys had captured. If we could take Gold Brick Hill, our officers told us, the German supply route into the Schnee Eifel (snow ridge) area of Germany would be taken away from them.

At one thirty in the morning on 8 March 1944, our regiment started across an open field for Gold Brick Hill. The Germans opened fire on us, and pinned us down. We lay in the field until dark, and then we moved back into the woods. There was a ditch running through the forest. We all got in there, head to foot, and got a little rest for the night. The next morning, as we prepared to move out, the Germans shelled us. We lost half our troops that morning, but Army wasn't concerned about our losses. Our orders remained the same. We lined up shoulder to shoulder and started up the hill, firing our weapons as we went. At the top of the hill, we came upon a camouflaged German pillbox. As we got closer, Germans came out waving white flags. What a relief that was to us! It didn't turn out to be the slaughter we thought it would be, but it was bad enough. By the time we were through, our division had destroyed seventy-nine of the 936 pillboxes in the Siegfried Line. The 346th lost 849 men killed or wounded.

After Gold Brick Hill, I went to Houffalize in Belgium. The people there were glad to see us, and they looked upon us as liberators. One family took two of us in for the night, out of the bitter cold. After we cleaned up a bit, we sat down with them and chatted. There was an older man, two older women, and a young girl who lived in the house. Hitler's soldiers had taken all the young males to work in labor camps. The young girl brought us out a medal that Hitler had ordered given to all the young girls who had borne children for his Master Race. They weren't proud of the medal, but they showed it to us anyway.

When it was time for bed, the family gave us their beds to sleep in. It was the first time months we had seen a bed. We slept between clean sheets, under feather ticks. We were in Heaven! When we awoke in the morning, we found that the family had washed and dried our clothes. Before we left, even though their food was in short supply, they gave us breakfast. All they had was eggs. Off we went, again. We never forgot those people, and I'm sure they never forgot us.

We fought our way through some woods, through the town, and through several villages. We got far ahead of our field kitchens. We ended up in a woods, and had very little food. Finally, our kitchens caught up with us. Some place along the way they "liberated" some hams, and made us ham sandwiches. We ate them as though there were no tomorrow. The bad thing was we had nothing to drink. All we were able to do was break ice on the frozen roads and drink the water underneath. We had to for survival, and we protected ourselves by using Halazone purification tablets. We huddled under the trees at night and tried to sleep.

We started out again the next morning. We didn't have any idea of where we were and where we were going, except that we knew we were heading toward the Rhine River. We moved day and night, for two or three days, finally coming to a high ridge where we stopped and regrouped. We just started to eat our K-rations when the Germans threw everything they had at us. It was a gruesome battle, and we took many casualties. After dark, on 25 March, we marched down a curving, windy road to a place called Boppard, at the edge of the Rhine River. The engineers had rubber rafts waiting for us. We got in the rafts and started rowing across the Rhine, a swift, wide river. Everything went well until we got half way across. Then the Germans threw up flares that lit up the whole river. It looked like Times Square. Immediately, we threw up a smoke screen. They couldn't see us, and we couldn't see where we were going. We finally made it across. On the other side was a steep bank covered with vineyards that we had to crawl through to reach the top. Our job was to establish a beachhead so our engineers could work through the night putting up a pontoon bridge. By morning they had the bridge up, and started to bring across tanks, trucks and other heavy equipment. We assembled at the top, put six men on each tank, three to a side, and started through Germany. German artillery fire had pretty well subsided by this time, but we had to contend with snipers.

We crossed Germany. For us, at least, the resistance was scattered. We ended up in Plauen on the Czechoslovakian border on 16 April 1945, where we awaited further orders. We were to be given a thirty-day furlough home. That was the good news; the bad news was we were heading for Japan. We had two choices of where to go first, one was Paris, and other was to the Riviera. We drew cards to see who would go where; the high card meant the Riviera, the low card meant Paris. I wanted the Riviera, but I drew the low card. The next day, three of us boarded a truck and headed for Paris.

It was a beautiful day when we got there. I felt good, the weather was good, and the war was over in Europe. One day, while I was walking down the street, sightseeing, I heard someone call out, "Hey, Harvey."

I knew nobody knew me there, so I kept on walking, looking around, sightseeing. A Jeep pulled up alongside. Lo and behold, driving the Jeep was a friend from Greensburg. I hadn't seen him in years. He had been stationed in an air control tower in Paris. He told me that he had made friends with a French family, and that they

Harvey Waugaman with a .30 caliber Browing machine-gun and a Nazi souvenier. Harvey sent this photo home with the notation "This is your Harvey in his fur jacket."
Courtesy of Harvey Waugaman.

Harvey Waugaman in Germany. April 1945.
Courtesy of Harvey Waugaman

Young Thierry poses with veterans in Belgium, December, 2004. *Courtesy of Harvey Waugaman*

> Velaine Sur Sambre 22.12.04
> POPPE Thierry
> 36/A2 rue Docteur Severin
> 5060 Velaine /S/Sambre
> Belgium
>
> Dear Mr Harvey Waugaman,
>
> I was in Bastogne the 18th December for a ceremony in your honour and your comrades in arms who give their life for me ... a child of Belgium.
> Thank you for all; you are a courageous, and brave young soldier in 1944... I life thanks to you!
> This is a real emotion for me and, you stay in my mind for every day of my life.
> This letter is a little testimony of my respect for you... my liberator!
> In this letter your find a double of your photo in Bastogne (Patton Ceremony)
> I hope a good news of you; (If you writte to me)
> Good protect you and your family
> Merry Christmas and happy new year 2005.
>
> ... Your devoted young Admirator from Belgium
> Thierry

Harvey and Gladys Waugaman at the ceremony honoring veterans of the Battle of the Bulge. December 2004. Gladys wears her Nurse Cadet hat. *Courtesy of Harvey Waugaman.*

were giving him a farewell dinner before he went back to the States. He invited me to go along. And so I went.

Of course, in those days, food was scarce, but the family had managed to get Belgian rabbits. They roasted them in wine. We ate those rabbits and drank wine all evening long. It was a French meal I shall never forget.

It wasn't long before we boarded ships for home. I had never seen the Statue of Liberty. When I left, I left from Boston. I figured that this time we would sail to New York and I would see the statue, but I was disappointed. We landed in Boston. My future wife, Gladys, was stationed at a hospital in Memphis, Tennessee. I called her from home and told her, "If you want to get married, you better get home now, because I'm on my way to Japan."

Gladys came home, and we set the date. We were to be married at seven thirty in the evening. Around twenty after seven I was listening to the news on the radio. An announcement came over that the Japanese had surrendered. The whole town went wild. We had a hard time getting to the church on time. I went back to visit the old battlefields some time after the war, but the most memorable visit for me was the one in December 2004, to commemorate the sixtieth anniversary of the Battle of the Bulge. The Belgian government arranged it all. Chester Lapa and I left Greensburg on 7 December for Washington D.C., and went to a reception at the home of the Belgian ambassador. After that, we took a plane from Andrews Air Force Base, and arrived in Brussels at noon, their time. They housed us at the military base until the next plane arrived. Then they moved us to our hotel in Houffalize. Next day, they gave us a bus tour of all the battlefields. We had a four-motor cycle police escort. They parked the buses and we got off in the Houffalize town square, where the honor Guard from Fort Campbell, Kentucky, presented the colors. They were followed by Navy bands from Spain, and the Belgian and Luxembourg military. After a short service, we marched through the town to a memorial where we placed a wreath. The streets were filled with applauding people shouting "Welcome! Welcome! We will never forget!" The stores were closed, and the schools were closed. We signed autograph after autograph. Kids from the schools waved American flags. It was a great feeling! It brought tears to my eyes, and theirs. The people were the greatest part of the trip. They were great to us during the war, and they were great on that day. The people of Luxembourg did not forget us, and we did not forget them.

"I Came from A Long Line of Soldiers."

Terance Arthur John Wickham, M.D.

Royal Army Medical Corps, 8th Indian Infantry Brigade, Field Ambulance Corps, B Company, Prisoner of War (India, Singapore, Malaysia, Thai-Burma Railroad)
Citation for Member of the British Empire (Military Division)
Central Chancery of the Orders of Knighthood St. James Palace, London, 25 September 1947
5 July 1914, Poona, India
Stroudsburg, Pennsylvania

"The end came. The Japanese came into the Civil Hospital. They were so confident that everything was going to go their own way they only sent one Jap. He couldn't have been much taller than five feet, and he had a very boyish face. He must have been about sixteen or seventeen. He was in full kit, and helmet. I went out of the operating theater and he was coming down the corridor and I waited until he got up to me and showed me quite proudly his bayonet with blood on the end of it. 'Chinese,' he said pointing to the blood. 'Chinese.' Then he kept on walking. I hate to think what happened in the Chinese quarter of the city."

I GREW UP IN POONA, INDIA, near Bombay, and spent my early childhood there. Later, I lived in a place called Chindwara, in the Central Province of India. We moved around because my father was an inspector with the police. India was a lovely place and the Indian people were very charming. We had several servants, which was the thing to have during the British Raj. My early education was in boarding school. There weren't many options for a boy in India. You either went into one of the services, like the Indian Civil Service, or you went into the military. I had an interest in medicine and I wanted to be a doctor, something I could become as a civilian by paying for my education, or by joining the military, and having the Army pay for everything. I always had a liking for the military because both of my grandfathers had been in the British Army, one of them in the Boer War, and the other in the Indian Mutiny. My father had joined up during World War I. So, I came from a long line of soldiers.

I studied in Calcutta, and it was a very happy time. We stayed in a barracks handy to the hospital across the road from us. All the buildings were part of a teaching hospital, and there were several hospitals that were part of this institution, the main hospital having been founded in 1835. Because we were military students, we were expected to wear our uniforms to the lectures, but we had no badges or rank at the time. We had to do a certain amount of work before we earned those. We manned all of the outpatients' departments, learned the local language, and helped the doctors. From the first day we went in, we had "hands-on" medical training. I did that for six years, and then went straight into the regular Army.

My first posting was to Quetta, in Baluchistan, on the Afghanistan border. I arrived there at night and it was snowing. We had to walk out to this place fifteen miles away, and the wind was blowing the snow sideways and piling it up on my left shoulder. When we got there, we set up camp, and lived under canvas. We were always quite glad to get moving every day to stay warm. We had two motorized ambulances with us just in case of any casualties from the cold, and we trained as a Cavalry Field Ambulance.

I had met my wife, Margaret Morrissey when I was in medical school, and after training at Quetta, I got a ten-day leave and, on 8 May 1940, we got married. We had a very happy life, but it only lasted a few months, and then I was mobilized. We had been getting news about the war in Europe over the radio. We knew about Dunkirk and things like that, and it was rumored that we were going to be sent to Eritrea in Africa to encounter the Italians. But they had sent a battalion of Gurkha before us, and the Italians didn't like the idea of these little men with the big *Kukri* knives and they surrendered. But since there were growing threats from the Empire of Japan, we knew sooner or later something would happen in our part of the world.

We went to Malaya in the autumn of 1940. We arrived in Singapore and stayed there for ten days, and then we got into a convoy, went over the Singapore causeway, and moved upcountry. My first posting was with a Field Ambulance, a unit consisting of a Headquarters Company, A Company, and B Company. I got B Company, with a rank of Assistant Surgeon, which was equivalent to Warrant Officer, Class I. I went with B Company to a place called Kuantan, halfway down the east coast of Malaya. We lived in tents on a disused rubber plantation for six months. The rains came in December, and we were still in tents. Water came up through the floors of the tents. Later we lived in huts raised off the ground. After six months, more reinforcements came, and then we were sent up to Kota Bahru, which is up in the northeast of Malaya. That's where the Japs made their first landing. We must have been in Kota Bahru for about six months before the war started.

I have to say this about Winston Churchill. He was a great chap. I think the world of him, but he had the tendency sometimes to blame people for things. He described the fall of Singapore as the most ignominious defeat in the history of British arms. I'll never forgive him for that, because we had no field artillery and no fighter aircraft. We literally had no air force, and what did arrive came a week before the Japanese attack. They sent us British Spitfires in crates, and they had to be assembled. One of the RAF chaps had been in the Battle of Britain. He went out and tried to fight the Japanese in biplanes that had been used in the northwest frontier bombing tribesman. There was a lot that went wrong. We had some planes with us near Kota Bahru. They were Brewster Buffaloes, which the States had given us, but they were no match for the Japanese Zero. It was sad to see these chaps going up and just getting shot out of the sky by these Zeroes. I knew some of those chaps. They came by on mess nights.

The Japanese landed on 8 December 1941. We had been told to move to our battle stations on 6 December. There were two World War I battleships that were sent from England, the *Prince of Wales* and the *Repulse*. There was an active Fifth Column, a spy ring, in Singapore, and the Japanese must have known the ships were coming. Japanese planes sank both ships with ease. That happened on the second day of the war, and it was quite shocking. Battleships at sea were supposed to be invincible against air attack. Later, we learned about Pearl Harbor and the Philippines, but we were too busy receiving casualties to worry about those places.

I had charge of an advance dressing station. B Company was with me. The casualties started coming in and we dealt with them as best we could. Some I could only give morphine to and send them on to a better facility for more complex surgery. I stitched up small wounds and stopped bleeding, and that's all I could do. We were there about two days. We could hear the fighting going on, only about a mile away. Some of the casualties were walking casualties and some were stretcher borne. We had very good ambulance drivers. There was a road that ran parallel to the beach. The army stretcher-bearers carried the casualties to the ambulances for transport to the dressing station.

My first two casualties were two rear gunners from bombers, and, funny enough, both had shrapnel wounds that had shattered their knees, one his right and the other his left. The Japs obviously had good antiaircraft fire. I gave them morphine, I splinted them, arrested what bleeding I could, then sent them on down the line. I expected each of them to have lost a leg, eventually.

We sent the wounded to a main dressing station. From there they were sent to a casualty clearing station. Those who recovered were sent back to their units. Those who lost limbs or had serious wounds were sent further down the line to the Base General Hospital in Singapore.

When the infantry retreated south from Kota Bahru, we went with them, our ambulances loaded with casualties. On the way, Jap reconnaissance planes flew over us. One dropped a small bomb. It made a big bang, but caused little damage. When we got to a railroad station, we loaded our casualties on an ambulance train and sent them further south. While we were there, a formation of three Jap planes came over the hills from the west. They dropped their bombs. The bombs reflected the sun like tinsel. We thought for a moment that they were going to fall on us, but they went over the train and hit the station where they were having a roll call. Two or three chaps were killed, and we got many more casualties to care for. I was doing sewing up and splinting and arresting bleeding and all the rest until we got orders to move. We were told to destroy all of our equipment, including our ambulances. They didn't want to leave anything behind that the enemy could use. We removed the distributor heads from the ambulance engines, threw them away into the bushes, and pushed the vehicles over into a ditch.

In the south, we got more ambulances, and we got back to receiving casualties. Our ambulances were clearly marked with the Red Cross, and the Japanese seemed to respect that. There was only one occasion when they fired at our ambulance. The troops fighting the Japs were exhausted and the brigade asked us to help in evacuating them. Since it would have been deemed an offense of the Geneva Convention to evacuate viable troops in ambulances, we smeared mud over the crosses on the sides and top of the ambulances. We evacuated the troops at night. After we finished this, we intended to wash the mud off, but being exhausted ourselves, we forgot to wash it off. I was traveling in one of these ambulances with some wounded when A Jap Zero came down at us.

I said, "Crikey, doesn't he see the Red Cross on top."

The pilot started firing. We could see the bullets hitting the road in front of us and ricocheting. Bullets went through the roof and the windshield between the ambulance driver and me, but fortunately none of the rounds hit us.

Around this time we took our one and only Jap prisoner. A Sikh Regiment attached to our brigade counterattacked. One of the Sikhs got a Jap, hit him in the head with the butt of his rifle and gave him a scalp wound. Someone brought the wounded man into my advance dressing station. A Japanese-speaking brigade intelligence officer came in. I sewed up the scalp wound while they talked. The Jap sang like a bird. He gave us a lot of information. The officer related to me that the prisoner was grateful for the treatment he received. We evacuated him down the line. I heard later that he was sent to India.

It was a very chaotic time. The Japanese had two lines of advance, one down the west coast and one down the east coast of Malaya. We moved south as they advanced. After a while we were not receiving any casualties, because we had gone through the Australian lines and they had their own field ambulances, so we were ordered on down to cross the Singapore causeway into the city. We had to pull to one side and let some of the British troops go over first. We took care of some of their casualties and then we went over about two o'clock in the morning. It was a beautiful tropical night, with full moon and stars. One felt like tiptoeing. The Norfolk Regiment and one of the Scottish Argyles Highlander regiments followed behind us. And here these chaps were playing their bagpipes! And here we were, trying to tiptoe across the causeway, trying not to make too much noise! After we got over the causeway, we blew it up and that was the end of the campaign on the Peninsula. It wasn't long before the Japanese were able to repair the breach. Then they came across with tanks.

After we crossed the causeway we were taken out of action, and told to rest. "Rest" was a good word! We were hounded from place to place because the Japs were firing field guns on the town all the time. They had an observation balloon up, and they were directing artillery fire from it. We could see it in the distance. We took refuge in one place behind Government House. There was a hill behind the house and on top of the hill was a water reservoir. The observation balloon must have seen us. I saw a youngster come up carrying a pile of white sheets and red blankets, and he walked around the top of this reservoir and then down the hill.

I thought, "That's very odd."

The youngster must have been doing this for the benefit of the balloon observer. Suddenly, they started firing at us. There had been an Australian battery in front of Government House firing back at the Japs. I took refuge in a storm drain behind

Government House. As I sat there, these Australians came in and one of them said, "I wouldn't stay there if I were you because they're going to put their sights up."

And off he went. I got up and got out of there, and right after there was a tremendous crash behind me, and a lot of muck and chips of cement came down on me. I waited till it was all finished, and I went back there and the place where I had been sitting was just a shambles. I missed that by a few seconds. If I ever saw that chap again, I would have thanked him profusely.

We had an orangutan with us. Evidently it had gotten away from the zoo, or they let it loose. We felt sorry for it. It didn't know what was going on and was terrified. It nestled up with us because it was frightened from all the noise. We adopted this orangutan. But not for very long. It all came to an end.

It wasn't possible to evacuate us. The Japs had total command of the skies. Any attempt at evacuation would have been fatal. As it was, one ship was to take the officer commanding the Indian Ambulance, Colonel Chopra, a Punjabi, and a very fine fellow and commander. He was ordered to go back with information on field ambulance functions. He came to us and said, "I've asked if I could take you all with me. But they said we can't take any more."

He shook us warmly by the hand. We heard later that his ship was sunk. It never got to India, and everyone on it was killed.

I assembled my field ambulance after the incident at Government House, and we thought we'd go and help out at the Indian Base General Hospital. One day, I had a little time off, sitting around, thinking of my wife, and Jap planes came over a big field behind me toward the hospital. They ignored the Red Cross on the roof and bombed it with incendiaries, setting it afire. Some of the patients who were bedridden died inside. Others got out, dragging splints and crawling alongside the field. The planes came back and machine-gunned them all. That was awful! Then, when they felt they'd done their bit, they flew off. Immediately, we went off, got stretchers, and prepared to take them to the Civil Hospital. One fellow was walking in his pajamas, and looked like he was about to fall. I tried to help him into the ambulance. I reached under his arm to lift him up and my hand went right into the side of his chest. His wound just caved in under the pressure of my hand.

We got them on our ambulances and took them to the Civil Hospital. We parked our ambulances in a Malayan schoolyard across from the hospital, and set up our field ambulance. Three of us went to the hospital and offered our services if they'd take our casualties. They agreed. Civilian casualties were coming in fast, and we dealt with them as best we could. We had eighteen-inch guns defending Singapore, and they were supposed to make the city impregnable. Unfortunately, no one thought that the city could be taken from the jungle side, so the guns were built to fire only out to sea, and they had no 360-degree traverse, except one that was situated on an island the Malayans called "Island of the Dead," where they buried their dead. It was firing directly into Jahore, across the Straits of Singapore. The shells sounded like an express train going over, but they were ineffective. There were no explosions! All of the big guns had been designed to sink approaching fleets, and all they had were armor-piercing shells. They just buried themselves in the moist Malayan soil. I don't know how many I counted, maybe a half dozen or so. They are probably still there as a potential hazard.

The final end came. The Japanese came into the Civil Hospital. They were so confident that everything was going to go their way they only sent one Jap. He couldn't have been much taller than five feet, and he had a very boyish face. He must have been about sixteen or seventeen. He was in full kit, and helmet. I went out of the operating theater, and he was coming down the corridor. He got up to me and quite proudly showed me his bloody bayonet. "Chinese," he said, "Chinese."

Then he kept on walking. I hated to think what had happened in the Chinese quarter of the city.

We later learned the Japanese went into the British Military Hospital in Singapore, herded all the walking wounded into a storage room, and tossed in grenades. Killed off the lot. There was a surgeon, Major Drummond, operating on a patient. The Japanese broke into the operating theater, rifle-butted him in the face, killed the patient, and just went berserk. These were the kinds of things that were happening in the days after the fall of Singapore.

There were no more casualties coming into our hospital so we went back to our ambulance unit in the schoolyard across the road. We thought we'd take our minds off the war by playing a little soccer. The Japs didn't disturb us at all.

I had one RAMC named Kumba. He wasn't afraid of anything. He went and stood out on the side of the road as the Japanese came by in their tanks. They came past the school, and he stood there waving at them. It's a wonder they didn't shoot him.

We got orders eventually to assemble at a certain place, and from there we were marched to Changi, a walk of about ten miles, the sad part of which was passing through Singapore itself. I saw an old Chinese woman as we walked by, and she gave us a "thumbs up." Tears rolled down her cheeks. Only God knows what happened to her.

Changi was an area in the eastern end of Singapore that held the garrison barracks just north of the military hospital and civilian jail. We got temporary accommodation in the hospital and the barracks, and then the Japs divided us into units. We came there with the 8th Indian Infantry Brigade. We were separated from the Indians, who were taken elsewhere. The Japs worked on them to get them to help in the invasion of India. Some of the Sikhs did join the Indian National Army, but were in trouble with their own kind after the war. Some of these chaps were given camp guard jobs just to humiliate the British further. One of them had been one of my ambulance drivers. When he saw me he stopped and stood at attention! I said to him in his language, "That's a very shameful thing you're doing."

He said, "They won't give us anything to eat unless we do this."

We settled into Changi fairly well. We occupied an area that had housed the people who manned one of these big eighteen-inch guns. The gun itself had been sabotaged by our troops. The explosion caused the barrel of the gun to point straight up.

This was dangerous for us later on because it became a lightning conductor. It was quite close to us, and lightning would strike this gun barrel with a hell of a crack.

We were there for a while, and we started to get organized. We were not doing well with food. Rice mainly. British troops were not very good at cooking rice. We always ate it all slushy. Only the Indian troops could really cook it. Occasionally we were able to buy vegetables. We didn't have meat, until they brought in a shipment of frozen sheep, but I think the Japs got most of that. Some of our chaps worked down on the docks for the Japs and saw them loading Red Cross parcels onto Japanese submarines. So we only got some of those. The ones we did get sat in a warehouse so long that the cigarettes got so mildewed you couldn't smoke them. We tried to wash our original uniforms, but eventually they just fell apart. The Japs found some other uniforms in a storehouse, and they issued them to us. Each of us got two shirts, two pairs of shorts, and one pair of boots or shoes.

Before the Japs took us to Thailand, we were leading a reasonably civilized life; we had concert parties and things like that. Every once in a while the Japs very "kindly" brought trucks containing fishing nets full of all the rubbish they had collected from the sea, prawns, the odd frog, and goodness knows what else. We boiled and boiled and boiled it until it was a kind of thick, fishy soup.

We remained in Changi just over a year, until the spring of 1943. And in that time all of us had lost a lot of weight. I lost about three stone, about forty-two pounds. It was at this point that we began to show signs of vitamin deficiency. Some people were getting a bit of foot drop, something that occurs when the muscle on the front of the shin that holds the foot up gets weak from vitamin deficiency. The soles of the feet get very hypersensitive. But it was surprising that, after awhile, the body adjusted to that sort of thing. The Japs started to give us unpolished rice, which was good. It smelled like cow dung when it was being boiled, but because the germ was still in it, it did away with the foot drop, and various other problems.

We had boiled tea, morning, midday, and at night, a pint of it. The food we were getting was boiled watery rice in the morning, like porridge, and boiled dry rice in the afternoon, and boiled dry rice in the evening, a cup of it each meal. When we got into Thailand, we got a bit more meat.

At the camp hospital in Changi, we had a couple of RAMC medical orderlies. When I went to the hospital to check on the chaps, I had to wear a brass hat that said in Japanese who I was and what I was. There was a big joke concerning those brass hats. A British officer wore one, and he had to salute the Jap guards. When he did, they roared with laughter.

"What the hell does this sign say?" asked the British officer.

Another British officer who was a translator interpreted the sign for him. He said, "It says, 'I am a prostitute.'"

We had to salute the Japanese no matter what rank they were. I nearly got walloped once because I didn't notice the chap. I was walking to the hospital and I saw a car coming toward me. There were Japs in it. I ignored them and kept walking. There was a screech of brakes and I heard a shout in Japanese. They never did anything in a gentlemanly way. They shouted at each other, let alone us! I heard this command and I turned around and walked back. There was a chap sitting in front looking down, and there was a big sort of Kempetai policeman sitting behind him saying, "*Shoko, Shoko.*" (Officer, officer!).

I went round and looked at this fellow and said: "Are you an officer?"

This fellow in the back was about to get out and give me a real beating. So I saluted and went off.

There was no idea of escape. Every morning the Japs counted us to make sure we were all there. When Singapore fell, or it was obviously about to fall, two Australians got a boat down in the dock and were trying to row themselves to Java or Sumatra, then work their way to Australia. The Japs caught them and held them in a jail. The Japs, when they knew they were going to send us up to Thailand, felt it might be easier for some of us to escape there, so they made us sign a pledge that we wouldn't try. A Japanese officer stood on a table to address us all about this in broken English. We had already refused to sign it twice, if we didn't sign it the third time, he was going to punish us all by stopping our food. To drive the point home, the Japs executed these two Australians by firing squad. Our colonel, who was made to witness the execution, came back and told us that if we signed the document, it would be under duress, and it didn't mean a damn thing anyway, and that we should try to escape if we ever got the opportunity to do so. So we all signed it.

In the spring of 1943, I was mobilized with H-Force. Why the Japs called it that, I didn't know, but each group of prisoners had a letter designation. We were sent in railroad goods cars to Thailand to work on the railroad. Since the cars were steel and hot inside, once we got moving the Japs opened the doors. We took turns sitting in the open door with our legs hanging out. They stopped every thirty miles so we could get out and relieve ourselves. We were cold at night because we were so malnourished.

We traveled from Singapore all the way to Thailand, to a place called Bang don Pong. There we got out of the train and we marched by night, and rested in the shade during the day. We marched about ten miles a day, and must have done 120 miles. On one stretch, we traveled by train, on flatcars that also carried rails. There were some awful bends in that rail road. We went through a swarm of bees once and a lot of us got stung. We stopped at a place called Kabin Buri, 8 May 1943, my wedding anniversary. It was raining buckets! We spent a little time there while recuperating, and then we got back onto the train to parts of the rail line that had been finished.

When we traveled on these flat cars, the Japs didn't stop much. When a chap had to relieve himself he had to go right over the side of the train. There was a method one had to go through in order to do this. His friends would hold his hands while he squatted with his bottom over the edge of the flat car. Once, while we were going through a town, an Australian felt the urge, and his buddies held his hands while he squatted. He let loose just as we were passing a station. A Jap officer stood on the platform. Plop! Right at his feet! He drew his sword, cursing, but it was too late; the train kept going. We all laughed.

We stayed in a transit camp for about a week, recovering from our four-day journey on that ghastly train. The Japs had built latrines right along a road that the locals used on their way to market. The open ends of the latrines faced the road, and when we squatted to use them, the locals couldn't help but see us. The Thais who did pass, however, tried to be respectful and looked the other way. But that's the sort of thing the Japs did to demean us. Some of them were real bastards! Of course, they're nice enough when they meet you under other circumstances. After the war, a group of about a dozen of them came around to the hospital where I worked. My chief technician knew what I thought of them. He stuck his head round my door and said, "That group of Japanese doctors is here. Do you want to speak with them?"

I said, "No thanks, very much."

He said, "I thought you'd say that."

We got to our work camp. I was the only doctor. There were sixty British, and a group of Australians around the same number. They had no doctor, but they did have an orderly. They were a fit lot, the Australians. They didn't often have anything wrong with them.

As the only doctor, I decided who went out to work on what we called "The Cutting." The Australians called it "Hellfire Pass." We were blasting away the side of a hill to make it flat so the rails could follow the river. That was backbreaking work! You could only do so much and then you'd have to blast some more off.

The Japs yelled "Speedo" incessantly. They had a strict timetable, and they needed as many men to come out for work as possible. The chap in our camp was a bit of a slave driver. He was not a Jap, but a Korean. If he didn't send up as many people as he could, then the Japs took it out on him, and he passed his anger on to us! And since I was the chap who decided who could go and who couldn't, the Korean would slap my face if I held too many men back. He started a slap from way back, but since I boxed in school, I knew how to ride it out. If I didn't, he could have broken my neck. "Get them out!" he would yell.

These were good fellows, these patients of mine. They'd tell me, "Doc, don't get slapped around. You're the only chap that can do us any good!"

And, for that, they'd crawl out of bed and stand up, and this Korean would go up to each one and make them open their mouths and put their tongues out. He made the diagnosis whether or not they could work. If I argued with him, he gave me a wallop. One thing we learned was never to fall if we got hit. Otherwise, the Japs would come at us with boot heels.

Well, in time, I had my revenge. Shortly before we were due to go back to Singapore, the Korean was sitting on the steps of his raised hut with his head between his hands. He saw me and beckoned me to come over. He was holding his stomach.

I said, "Come upstairs and lie down."

He went up and I examined his belly. He didn't have any tender points or acute appendicitis. I palpated his stomach, and I could feel that his spleen was about two inches below his liver. He had malaria, with a high temperature and all the rest of it. The ache he was getting was in his spleen. He insisted that he had something in his stomach.

I said, "It's malaria."

"Malaria? No! No!" he said.

The got punished if they got malaria, because it was preventable. They were supposed to take the quinine they were issued. Well, the customer is always right. He wanted something to move his bowels. I thought, "Well, I'll give you something!"

In the Army we had what was called a "Number Nine," a most effective physic. I gave him two Number Nines. I thought, "That'll move you."

The next day we were getting ready to leave and I saw him sitting there.

I said, "Very much?"

"Yes! Yes! Yes!" he said and he put his head in his hands.

What I had given him certainly made him go. He probably thought it wasn't even worth going back into his hut. But it hadn't cured his malaria.

I thought, "Good, you swine! Carry on with your malaria!"

It went against the grain a bit, but he had knocked me around several times too many.

There were Indians in Malaya whose families had been there for generations working the rubber plantations. Toward the end of the war, the Japs were bringing these Indians up to work on the railroad. They were clever about it. Indians were suckers for the cinema. The Japs would advertise a free movie at the local movie house. The Indians would go, taking their families as well. After the movie, as they exited, the Japs, who were waiting outside with trucks, would load them up, drive them to the train station, and send them off to Thailand. Kids, too! One lot that they had brought up lived just on the other side of our compound fence. They were thrilled to bets when I talked to them in Hindustani.

The Japs made all these people work, even the pregnant women! It was inhuman. They were exhausted, and many of them were dying of malnutrition. They were not particular about where they buried their dead. One day, during the rainy season, I was coming back from working at the cutting. The path we were on was muddy, and I saw a hand sticking up out of the mud. The Indians had buried someone there who had died of Cholera. I knew that because Cholera contracts the muscles. The hand had gradually come up through the mud. All I did was stamp the hand back down. It's things like that that come back to haunt you.

I think the most horrible thing I ever saw was this Indian woman get beaten. She was squatting on the ground and this Jap went up to her, shouted at her and kicked her right between the legs. She lay there in agony afterwards.

We knew this would all end some time. We knew we were going to win, because we got word from the outside world. We had an Australian chap who was in the Signal Corps. He built a wireless set into the bottom part of a water bottle while he was in Changi, and he tuned in to the news from New Delhi. He fixed inside the bottle a false chamber in which he kept water, so if there was any question about it he could take the top off and pour the water out. That was enough to dispel any suspicion. He only used the wireless once every two or three weeks to minimize the chances of getting caught. The wireless required a lot of pre and postoperative work.

The bottom of the bottle had a sewn-on felt covering. In order to get the radio out of the bottle, he had to carefully remove the thread from the felt, remove the felt covering, and then remove the radio from its chamber. Then he had to do all of this in reverse in order to get it back together. He had thread always tied to the needle, and he hid the needle in the felt so he could get at it quickly, and sew it back up quickly. He worked the radio off of a car battery. We had a truck to take the food up to a point before we had to carry it the rest of the way to where we worked. He was the driver of the truck. He'd listen to the news, and write it down in shorthand.

Besides getting news over the Australian's radio, I received three letters from home, two from my wife, and one from my parents, but I couldn't respond. The Japs gave us nothing to write with. One I received in Changi, and the others while I was in Thailand. They had been a month getting to me. I also received a radio message from my parents. For that I was summoned by the Japanese to their headquarters in Changi, after we got back from Thailand. The Japs got the message out of New Delhi. They always listened to radio signals from there in order to find out information.

I thought, "Good heavens! What have I done now?"

I went there and a Jap officer who spoke English said, "I have a message for you from your father in India."

And he read it out to me.

It said, "We are thinking of you and praying for you and hope you are well."

I was very grateful for that. I thanked the officer.

He said, "I hope this all ends soon and we all go back home."

He was as much against the war as anyone. I did meet some compassionate Japanese in these camps. One was a lieutenant named, Fukoda. He could speak English. He was also a medical student. He was about to qualify as a doctor, but he got conscripted. There was a base hospital at Kabin Buri. We stayed in a camp there after we finished with the railway line. We went there with our sick and dying, and he was in charge of this camp. We had a place at the end of one hut for skin diseases where he came to look at slides on malaria and stool specimens for dysentery.

It was a joke to us, but he'd say: "Tojo number one, Churchill number two!" He would say it and laugh.

We replied: "Churchill number one, Tojo number two!"

He was a good fellow. He was a human. We told him what we needed, and he'd get it for us from a supply depot, pretending to be getting it for his people. He gave me whatever drugs he had gotten. The bottles had labels printed in Japanese. I emptied the drugs into vials that had British labels, and then I destroyed the Japanese bottles. I did this because he said to me, "If find that you've got that, they will torture you until you tell them who gave it to you, and then I'll be in trouble."

He once asked me if I would take him on my rounds.

I said, "Of course you can come."

I took him round and did demonstrations for cases to him, and he was really grateful for that. He came from a better class of Japanese. When the line was finished, and just before we were to go back to Singapore, he came by with a bottle of Japanese wine. He poured it into little glasses and he shared it with us.

In the Thailand camps, we had to deal with a lot of injuries. In Hell Fire Pass, after they blasted, debris and pieces of rock fell down and some chaps got hurt. Other times, some chaps carelessly swung hammers, missed their mark and hit a foot. Many worked in bare feet, so the damage they did could be serious. We had been wearing the same boots for years, and they just fell apart. And walking around on crushed rock in the cutting played hell with the feet. Once the Japs sent up a pile of boots that were left by Australians and British who had died in the camps lower down the line. They were as bad as the boots we had thrown away! The Japs threw them into a pile and we helped ourselves. I was lucky because I had a small foot and the boots I found, no one else wanted. One was brown and the other was black, but I used those. They had a hole in the side that a chap cut out because he must have had a bunion. Some chaps made boots from motorcar tires. They cut the rubber out in the shape of a foot and got strings to tie across the top, and they'd walk around on those. Men wore hats when they worked in cuttings open to the sun. Many of the Australians still had their broad billed hats, while the British troops improvised with almost anything that could be had. A piece of tent flap worked well. They'd tie that around their heads.

We had to deal with tropical ulcers. I put it down to basically malnutrition, but I learned later that bacteria caused the ulcers, though I still think that malnutrition made them worse. There was a lot of Beri-Beri, caused by a lack of Vitamin C. If you worked all day, fluid collected in your legs, and your legs would swell. After you went to bed at night, and you woke up in the morning, your face and your eyes would be swollen because the fluid had shifted position in the night. Once you stood up, the fluid returned to the lower extremities, where it interfered with the body's normal defenses. Tropical ulcers would then take hold faster, and the flesh decomposed. I made the chaps with ulcers sit out and let the flies land on the sores. The flies ate the dead flesh, as did their maggots. Some men got sicker with ulcers than others, and the ulcers ate down to the bone.

We had an Australian surgeon, who, with his team, moved up and down the line to the various camps, (the Japs let him do this) where he performed operations. He had an ordinary dinner spoon that he had sharpened around the edges. It was razor-sharp. He gave patients a quick aesthetic, and then scraped out the dead flesh with that spoon. If the ulcer had gotten down to the bone, there was no point in using the scoop. We had to amputate.

The chances of surviving had a lot to do with having a rugged constitution, I think. But an awful lot died. The Australians were fairly rugged. The British troops from the 18th Division that had left from England and had gone all the way around the Cape of Good Hope in Africa, destined for Eritrea, were not so rugged. The Italians had already surrendered there, and the 18th was sent to Singapore, arriving only a short time before it fell. They had been at sea for three months, on limited rations, and were in poor physical condition when they became prisoners of war. Going on a diet of rice didn't do them much good. Then they were sent up to Thailand and they didn't last long at all. It was sad. As I drifted off to sleep each night,

I could hear those youngsters calling, "Mum! Mum!"

In the jungle we couldn't give the dead proper burials, because the jungle floor was all roots, and we couldn't dig very deep. In one camp, we found a crevasse at the edge of a river bank. That's where we buried our dead. We'd bring them on a stretcher, tip them over, and let the bodies slide into the crevasse. We'd hear them go right down. Lord knows how deep it was. It must have gone down pretty far because no flies bred there.

Often I worked at night by candle light. Even at night the tropical sky was bright, and my eyes got accustomed to the semi-darkness. The only reading material I had was a book of medicine that I read not only for its usefulness, but also for relaxation. I kept it through my captivity even though it weighed three pounds and I could have done without carrying it.

The railroad was being built from two different points, and eventually they were supposed to meet. After one section was finished, they moved us up to another camp that the Japs had surveyed ahead of time. We built a bridge we called "The Bridge of Cards." The Australians sabotaged it from their end. They had loosened the fittings. It fell over, and they had us all out there at night to get the damn thing up again. We used elephants to help us pull the bridge together again. We didn't have heavy equipment, so the Japs brought in the elephants. The elephants had a skid behind them, like a bobsled, on which we loaded logs twelve feet long and about a foot and a half in diameter. The elephants pulled the logs to the line. Then the elephants dragged each log to where it needed to be. The elephant diet was as bad as ours, and so were their digestive problems. It didn't matter that I was the doctor; I had to work. One day, I was preparing the bobsled for an elephant, when I heard a rumble coming from his insides. I moved too late. The elephant spattered me with diarrhea. The Japs laughed their heads off. I went straight off into a nearby stream and cleaned myself up.

After Thailand, we were put into several camps. I went once with a party of Australians to a barracks that were quite comfortable. The Japs had asked for electricians, carpenters, and the like to build administrative offices for them. They must have thought they were going to be there forever. Next to our camp was a camp full of Indian prisoners of war. One day I called out to one of them in Hindustani. He saw the Red Cross on my arm, got quite excited, and started waving. One of them asked the Japs if I could go and see one of their chaps. Some of the Indians had been stealing petrol from the Japs, and selling it to the local Chinese. Someone had been smoking a cigarette while they were doing this. It started a fire, startled this chap, who spilled petrol all over himself and got pretty badly burned. I told them he should really be in hospital. I wrote down what they had to get to treat these burns. He got better slowly. He was horribly scarred but got well on the mend.

Next door to us were tired-out or wounded Jap soldiers. They fraternized with us in broken English. Some looked like they were only sixteen. I felt sorry for them because they, too, were far from home. If they had problems, they came to me, and I would treat their sores or whatever they had.

We started getting fragments of news that told us the war was coming to an end. The Japs started supplying us with vitamin pills in order to fatten us up. We were suffering from vitamin deficiency, and I think they were too. How good the pills were I don't know, but they were sort of brownish, and tasted a bit like wheat. They gave us quinine tablets to keep malaria away.

Then our own bombers, either British or American started coming over. They were coming from Christmas Island, I learned later. The Japanese air raid siren would go off in Singapore to the south of the camp. We watched the bombs falling like confetti. We always felt as though they were going to fall on us. The bombs fell on the harbor, which we visited next day. There were tin mines in Malaya, and we had been loading the tin into ships in the harbor. The tin was cast into bricks, and there were piles of these bricks waiting to be loaded. The bombs they dropped on the harbor were incendiary bombs, and they burned so intensely they melted these piles of tin, and the molten metal flowed through the pier and cascaded over the edge of the harbor into the water.

We were sent back to Changi Camp, then to another camp, again with the Australians. In wartime it had never been used much but the Japanese were digging into the hills around it for defensive positions. One day, the Australians came back from digging there. One of them said, "You know, I think it's over."

I said, "Why do you say that?"

He said, "The Indians who were working there with us were all giving us the thumbs up."

Two days later, the Japs told us, "No work today."

Then they moved us back into Changi Camp. After the war ended on 15 August, the British came back to Singapore. A plane came over, and dropped a fellow by parachute. He came down and walked into Changi. He was a big fellow, a Grenadier Guardsman, about six foot three. He disarmed the Japanese guards. He introduced himself as Colonel so and so. The local Japanese commander came out. This Guardsman spoke Japanese.

He said, "I want to see the commandant of this camp. Go and fetch him."

The commandant came along in the back seat of his car with the Japanese flag on the front, which we called the "Bloody Poached Egg." The first thing this young colonel did was pull that flag off and stick the Union Jack in its place! He told the commandant to drive through Singapore where there would be the most exposure, so people could see the Union Jack on the front of the car. It was all very moving, and a good thing after all that time. I think that was the first time I really slept right through the night without having any nightmares, though they recurred after I got home. My wife would have to wake me up. "Terry! You're having a dream about the prisoner of war camp."

I was always glad when she woke me, because the feeling was awful. I remember thinking in the dreams, "Oh! Not again!"

The British made sure we got proper food. They released a lot of New Zealand lambs from the freezers in Singapore, and that fattened us up a bit. I was in pretty good condition considering. I didn't have to do nearly as much physical labor like some of the other poor chaps. I felt a bit guilty about it, but I thought I should keep fit because then I'd be able to look after the other chaps.

I left Singapore for India in October 1945. I went back by sea from Singapore to Madras. I would have liked to get on a train right away to see my wife and family, but they said, "No. You have to be debriefed."

They treated us awfully well. There was a bunch of ladies from the Women's Volunteer Force who fed us with good food. We were housed in these ordinary dwelling houses that had been commandeered. We had comfortable beds to sleep in. They even organized a dance for us, though we were rather rusty dancers. We were there for two days and then we were put on a train and sent home. I saw my parents first, because it was on the way. I stayed with them for a day, and then I went on to join my wife, who was staying with my cousins in Bombay. That was the happiest time of my life, being reunited with my wife. We had our first child, Carol, soon after the war.

They were demobilizing the British military in India. There was not much of a future for us in India after Independence in 1946. I was offered a post in the new Indian Army, but there wasn't much of a future there, either, for former British officers. Sorry to leave India, we went to England in 1947. I joined the Royal Victoria Hospital, specializing in Pathology. In 1963, I accepted a position as Chief Pathologist for a hospital in Bermuda. I worked there for seven years, after which we moved back to England. Eventually, we moved to the United States to be closer to Carol and our grandchildren.

There was a very moving incident near the end of the war, when we were in the camp north of Singapore. There was a little stream that went through the camp, and, one day, we went down to wash our clothes. The Japs came down screaming at us, gathered us shoulder to shoulder, and stood around us. It was a bit worrying, because we knew the war was going against them, and we thought they were going to load us up into trucks, drive us to the beach, and make us walk into the sea, where they would machine-gun us all. They did that with some of the Chinese when Singapore first fell. The trucks came and we got on the trucks. We didn't know what was happening. The trucks drove through Singapore to go to Changi. As we were driving through Singapore, all the Chinese came out to give us the thumbs up. On that day, I remembered that old woman who gave me thumbs up years before when Singapore fell. Now it was over. It was finished. That was a wonderful feeling.

"We Can Say We Shot at the Enemy."

Robert "Boomer" Woomer, Jr.

23rd Naval Construction Battalion (Snug-Tuggers) "Seabees" Company A
Greensburg, Pennsylvania, 1915

"The bombers released their bombs and bracketed a ship. Huge geysers erupted around the ship and we thought that it had actually been hit. Every gun on the island opened up. A formation of four airplanes came over us, but the 105mm's broke it up because the planes risked being trapped in their pattern. They dropped several bombs as they broke up including one that landed in an army barracks nearby killing one soldier. That was the only casualty that day. Of course, with our 20mm we couldn't reach the planes, but we sure shot a lot of rounds at 'em! The gun crew all took turns firing at them. I got my shots in. We can say we shot at the enemy!"

I WAS AT HOME ON SUNDAY evening when I heard about Pearl Harbor. We all knew what was coming, but since I was married, I figured that I might be deferred, but one day I got a draft notice classifying me as 1A. After that, I thought enlisting would give me a choice of service. I tried the Air Corps, but my eyes weren't good enough. The Navy was my next choice. I went to the Navy recruiting office, and I passed all their examinations with flying colors. A fellow in the Navy said to me, "Since you worked for the telephone company, we want you to go into a new outfit called the Construction Battalions. They build bases outside the United States for the Navy. You would fit right in."

I said, "That sounds pretty good to me."

The Construction Battalions were called the Seabees, which comes from the initials CB. I joined them in April 1942, but they didn't call me up until October. I got a farewell party at the telephone company in May, but I was still working through August.

One day my boss asked me, "When the hell are you going?"

I said, "I really don't know. I'm on hold."

The Seabees were brand new at that time. They were still forming the battalions. That's why it took so long for them to call me up. I ended up in the 23rd Naval Construction Battalion. My wife drove me into Pittsburgh to get on a train. We said our good-byes on the platform and I left for Norfolk, Virginia, boot camp, and the war.

We were preparing to go to the Pacific Theater from Oxnard, California, but they changed our orders. We didn't know where we were going to go, until the rest of our battalion arrived. Once they did, we boarded a train for Bremerton, Washington, where we got on a Liberty ship, and headed for Kodiak Island off the Alaskan

Peninsula. Kodiak was a deserted place, except for a few houses. We were stationed in eight-man wood cabins about two miles from an air base. We were assigned to build more cabins, just like the ones we were living in, but they would be for Air Corps personnel. We also put up some warehouses. We got our wood from a nearby lumberyard, but the wood was wet from the snow and ice. Once we got the buildings up and got heat inside them, the wood dried out and warped. A lot of those warehouses had big gaps and bows in the planks. When we weren't building, we drilled and practiced on the rifle range.

After several months on Kodiak we boarded a ship and headed for the island of Attu in the Aleutians. Part of the battalion went to Dutch Harbor and others went to Coal Bay. My company spent two months on Attu building Quonset huts and splicing telephone cables they had buried in the ground. The Navy had outfitted us with waterproof snowsuits, sheepskin coats, pea coats, and wool-lined hats with earflaps that connected under the chin. An Army detachment on the island with us had very poor winter clothing. We got to know some of them, and we gave them about a dozen of our pea coats. The snowsuits were good enough for what we were doing. They had nothing to give us in return except a box of BAR ammo. One Sunday we took the box of ammo out, loaded up the BAR, and shot up the side of a hill across the bay from where we were stationed. We burned out the barrel on that gun because the Army guy had given us only tracer ammunition

While we were shooting up the hill side, there was some real shooting on Attu, where American troops were invading, trying to dislodge the Japanese who had captured the island as part of a diversionary move during the Battle of Midway. Once our combat troops got ashore, the Navy assembled our battalion for Attu. By the time we got there, the island had already been declared secure, but there were still some Japanese who had either escaped or were bypassed by the Army. They sent about forty of us from my company out about a mile from where we were stationed to do our first job, putting up a village of tents for the Army. On the second day of work this army officer came by asking us what we were doing there. We told him, and he went over to talk with the chief.

He said, "You know there are Japanese in this area who are desperate. If they can kill somebody before they are killed they consider it honorable. Worse yet, you guys don't have any rifles here."

We said, "We didn't think that we needed any."

He said, "I just killed a Jap an hour ago. They're all around here and still armed."

We were situated in a valley that had a little hill behind it. The army officer explained to us, "When you come out here fairly early in the morning it's a little foggy, isn't it? They could stay on the side of that hill and you wouldn't see them. Then once the fog lifted, they could kill ninety percent of you before you could do anything about it. Without weapons, how could you guys retaliate?"

The next day, we all carried our weapons and had a lookout posted. About the third or fourth day that we were out there our lookout spotted something, and pointed out some movement in the distance to a couple of the Army guys. One of them asked, "Is that a buddy of yours?"

Our lookout said, "No, we are all here."

The soldiers took off with an officer. Fifteen minutes later we heard shooting. When he came back, he had a Japanese soldier's sword, rifle, helmet, canteen, and all the memorabilia that he could carry. He had killed this Jap, proving his point that there were enemies around that we needed to be watching out for. Fortunately, there were no other incidents. We had finally gotten to see the enemy. Actually, in order for us to see the enemy all we had to do was go to the compound for captured Japanese, but that was far away, and they didn't let us go there anyway.

Attu was a desolate island made up mainly of coral. The weather was pretty steady — always cold. We spent a winter there, during which time we had several hours of daylight. At night, the temperature would drop to five below zero, and during the day the temperature would go up to zero. Basically, I got used to the cold, but I was in a Quonset hut with two fellas from Georgia who never did. We had heat, but these fellas slept in their sleeping bags, plus their blankets.

Before we went into our Quonset huts, we only had tents. It was chilly when we would get up around six, especially since we just had a board floor that stood ten inches off the ground on poles, and the drafts would come up through. One fella, a cook at Headquarters Company, cracked up because of being on the island. They sent him back to the States after they found out he was suicidal and suffering from depression. The isolation didn't seem to bother me because I could make friends easily, and I played a lot of cards.

We had some alcoholics in our outfit, guys forty or fifty years old. I didn't know this until I was in the head one morning and saw this guy with a bottle of Bay Rum shaving lotion shaking it up and taking swigs out of it.

I thought, "Boy, that's really something!"

Then I realized that this was the only fix that he could get, because we had no beer, nor other alcoholic beverages. The only thing some guys had was shaving lotion! One time a transport docked, and two guys bought a bottle of rum for eighty dollars from a sailor. They brought the rum back to the tent and offered us all a drink. After that they sat outside and drank the rest. Occasionally, when we were building the dock, someone would fall into the cold water. The medics would take the person to sick bay and give him a shot of whiskey. Of course, that was for medicinal purposes only. One guy from Texas fell into the water on a regular basis, until the medics got wise to him.

Our regular food was stew for dinner and baked beans for breakfast. We had lots of canned vegetables. One time, one of our tent mates, a truck driver, was transporting fifty-pound cartons of steak reserved for officers to the mess hall. He dropped one carton off at the tent, and we buried it so the steak would stay frozen. We had steak and fried potatoes while the supply lasted. We also fished to supplement our food. I had a buddy who was a fisherman. He said, "Hey, Boomer. Let's go fishing."

We walked across the island for about an hour and a half until we got to this stream that was as clear and as cold as could be. He cast his line in the water and

"He cast his line into the water, and caught two steelhead trout."

caught two steelhead trout. He cleaned the fish, brought it back to the tent and we had fresh fish for dinner that night. I had never eaten fish that delicious in all my life!

We got our nickname, "Snug-Tuggers" while we were on Attu. One day soon after we first arrived, we had a meeting. Our commander told us, "I want to run a tight ship."

So some smart joker remarked after everything was over, "Well, we'll be a snug tug."

We were a small battalion. A tug is a small ship, so that's how we got the name "Snug-Tuggers."

After I helped build quite a few Quonset huts on Attu, I had to man a 20mm anti-aircraft gun, a gun designed to shoot down low-flying, strafing aircraft. It didn't have much range. I'd man that gun every day, and it became monotonous. It was so boring that we played cribbage to pass the time. That's how relaxed we got to be. One day, we came in for a surprise. They assigned my battalion the task of building two docks for six ships we had out in the harbor. We had finished one, and were just beginning to build the second when the air-raid alert sounded. It was a clear day, and Japanese Betty bombers came in at about eight thousand feet. The bombers released their bombs and bracketed a ship. Huge geysers erupted around the ship and we thought that it had actually been hit. Every gun on the island opened up. A formation of four airplanes came over us, but the 105mm's broke it up. They dropped several bombs as they broke up including one that landed in an army barracks nearby, killing one soldier. That was the only casualty that day. Of course, with our 20mm we couldn't reach the planes, but we sure shot a lot of rounds at them! The gun crew all took turns firing at them. I got my shots in. We can say we shot at the enemy!

It looked like the Fourth of July on that island. One ship had 20mm, 40mm and other guns, all of which opened up. A fella down below us with a .50 caliber machine-gun opened up and burned his gun up, he fired so much. Some fellas were so excited they went and got their rifles. They were shooting BARs and M–1s at these planes as they came over. One would have thought we would have had some friendly-fire casualties, but all this shooting was going out over the bay. None of the planes were shot down, that I know of. This all only lasted a few minutes. It seemed like hours. But once the all clear sounded we looked at each other and realized we had just seen the enemy. We weren't as isolated as we thought. After we finished the dock, we got a lot of traffic in and out. They stepped up our gun watches because we were a pretty good target. We had several alerts mostly at night. I guess there were enemy aircraft in the vicinity, but we were not bombed again.

There was an airfield on Attu where B–24's took off looking for submarines. Once I had the whole day free, and I got a ride on one of those bombers. They weren't supposed to do that, but my buddy had a buddy on his plane. I sat in the tail of the plane where there was no heat. We flew over Russia, we were that close, but I didn't see much land because of the cloud cover. During our ride we didn't see the enemy, but I saw a lot of ocean.

I spent thirteen months on Attu. In total I spent eighteen months on the Aleutian Islands. After a while I asked myself, "Am I ever going to get off this rock?"

We held discussions about this. Some men were downright angry about being stuck there and thought their talents would be better served elsewhere, particularly back in the States, which is where we all wanted to go, really. We were certainly in a theater of operations that was pretty much forgotten back home. We got *Stars and Stripes* (twenty or thirty issues at a time), and the occasional movie. We really didn't have too many discipline problems, because there was no place to go. You couldn't go AWOL. We played a lot of Poker. One game had no limit, and the stakes were high. The other games had a limit on the betting. There was also a lot of crap-shooting. Another thing that kept us in good spirits were pin-up girls. Our Quonset huts were filled with pin-up girls. We were all young. I was about twenty-five when I went in. Most of the fellows in my outfit were my age or a little older.

One day they built a small hospital in Attu and brought in some Army nurses. We hadn't seen women for at least ten months. Our eyes were bugging out! We'd be out working, and we'd see them go by in a Jeep. Their living quarters were close by. When we got ready to leave for the States, these nurses came down to say goodbyes to our officers. We were on the deck of our Liberty ship just peering over the railing at the nurses hugging and kissing our officers. The way they were kissing and hugging and fondling each other, we thought, "Wow! Are they allowed to do that?"

We left Attu on 30 December 1943 and headed for California. We ran into a bad storm on the way back, but fortunately we were close to the shoreline. They put all the seamen to work in the mess hall as waiters. They told me that I had to go and work in the mess hall. I carried cups that had to be washed. The floor was already slippery from the coffee and soup that soldiers had spilled. To make matters worse, the ship was going up and down. All of a sudden my feet slipped out from under me and I slid hitting the bulkhead of the ship, splitting my head open just beneath the eyebrow. When I came home, I had a big patch over my eye. I told my wife that I was going to get a Purple Heart. Finally, the captain had our ship go through the Inside Passage because of the storm. I thought to myself as I stood on deck, "Boy, this is beautiful. I'll have to come back here some day."

I've taken that trip about four or five times since. However, I've never returned to the Aleutians. When we got to California we were given thirty-days leave. I came home by train. Ruth was working in the Philadelphia Navy Yard and living in Chester, which is south of Philadelphia. I spent three days in Chester and then I came back to Greensburg because that's where my parents were. My mother was pretty sick at that time. In fact, she died while I was at home on leave. She died on a Tuesday and I was to leave on a Wednesday, so I went to the Red Cross and they got me an extension of seven days. Then I went back to Chester and caught a train out to Port Huemene, California, a big Seabee base. We did more drilling and training there. In July of 1944 we got on a ship and went to Hawaii. I got to see President Roosevelt while we were there. He drove by and we all stood at attention. He got out of the limousine that he was in, waved to us, then got back in and left.

From Hawaii we went to Eniwetok, an atoll in the Pacific. They had a recreational area set up there after the Marines secured the island. Aboard ship, we were only allowed to take saltwater showers on the ship because we had to conserve our fresh water for drinking. One day, we heard that rain showers were coming our way. Everyone stripped, soaped up and went out in the rain. Most of us got rinsed. Some of us did not make it because the rain passed that quickly. Some guys had rigged up this tarpaulin, which collected the rain. Some of the people who didn't get rinsed off stood under the tarpaulin while some guys poured the water on them.

The Navy offered each of us a case of either Coca-Cola or beer, but we had to drink it all before we left the island. We drank gallons of the stuff and, though we weren't supposed to, we took the leftovers with us. As we climbed the rope ladders onto the ship, cans of beer kept falling out of our pockets.

We left Eniwetok and arrived at Guam on D+90. We built a mess hall, and Quonset huts. My company was assigned to build a mess hall for a Marine detachment that ran a radar station. The Marines were issued one case of Coca-Cola a month, but their food was miserable. We invited them to eat with us, because we had good chow. The first night we happened to have ice cream, and one Marine went for five helpings. They all thought it was great. They ate with us every night.

There were still some Japanese holdouts on Guam. They captured a few of them while I was there. They were in a pretty pathetic condition. These holdouts were hungry and they ventured out of the hills to find food and were discovered.

I spent the rest of the war on Guam. One day, they announced over the loudspeakers that the war was over! I had accumulated enough points to go home. I went to San Francisco then to New York. When I got there, the first thing they asked me was, "Would you like to re-enlist?"

I said, "No way."

When I got home there weren't any big parties for me. My mother was dead, and my father became ill with stomach cancer. He lived with Ruth and me for several years and then with my sister, who was a nurse in New Kensington. He was dead two months after moving in with my sister.

I was lucky during the war, I guess. I had a wife and a job to come home to. I didn't need the military life anymore. The war was over.

"Your Son Was A Ball-Turret Gunner."

Robert C. Yowan
Eighth Air Force, 487th Bomb Group, 838th Squadron
West Newton, Pennsylvania, 12 January 1926

"A phosphorus round had hit the turret. I could smell my flesh burning. That odor is still in my mind today. I had no idea how I was going to get out of the turret, or how badly I was hit. Somehow, I succeeded in getting the ball-turret lined up with the fuselage, which it had to be, and I ran the guns in the down position so I could open the door. I ripped my oxygen hose off, and disconnected my throat mike. I came up into the waist of the plane. There had been no response from anyone. I didn't know where the waist gunners were, or the radioman. They should have been there, either there, or right adjacent to me. When we, the survivors, talk about it today, no one is sure who left the plane first. I found out later that the navigator and the bombardier and the flight engineer got out from the front. The fighters that came in at twelve o'clock high killed Kenneth, the pilot, and Howard, the co-pilot. The waist gunner was killed. The radioman was killed. Five of us got out."

MY WORLD WAS A SMALL WORLD. I never left West Newton until I went into the service. There was definite ethnic conflict among the older people in West Newton after the war started. There was a German *Liederkranz* club in town, and those not of German descent avoided it. The Germans went there, and the Slovenians went to the Slovenian Lodge. The younger people didn't get involved so much in that, but they were apprehensive because they didn't know what was coming next, and because they would be the ones called into service. One of my brothers went right in after Pearl Harbor, and I pretty much made up my mind that I would enlist as soon as I turned eighteen, which happened in the middle of my senior year. I immediately left school, but got a diploma *in absentia*. My mother might have objected to my decision, but she had died while I was in first grade. My father and older sister, who had remained at home, had no objection. I think my father was rather proud that his sons were serving his country.

I went to the Pittsburgh Recruiting Station, hoping to get into the Naval Air Corps. I felt it was the place to go. I had an admiration for the Navy fliers who took off from aircraft carriers. Unfortunately, the Navy quotas were full, so I enlisted in the Army Air Force. I entered the service officially on 22 January 1944. The high school had an assembly for those of us going into the service. They gave me a gift and wished me well. My brother and sister drove me to the railroad station in Pittsburgh. That was it. I looked forward to a great adventure.

We picked up our winter clothing at Indiantown Gap, near Harrisburg. After a few days, we headed for Miami Beach, Florida. When we arrived there, it was close to noon and really hot! They made us stand there with our full overcoats on. That was my introduction to Army discipline.

In Florida, everything was in bloom. We had basic training on the beach. We stayed in hotels at the south end of Miami Beach. Today it is called South Beach, one of Miami's most fashionable areas. We couldn't use the elevators, because climbing the stairs was part of our training. We sang as we marched down Miami's streets to the drill area. Our flight liked "Little Liza Jane," and we had a special song for our flight, "Flight Number122." After basic training and a series of psychological and eye-coordination tests, most of us ended up going to gunnery school. Some guys went to pilot training.

I left Florida in March, and went to Kingman, Arizona, some sixty miles from the California border, for Gunnery School. We learned about our weapons, practiced with them, and got familiar with the gun positions on aircraft. We did a lot of shooting with shotguns at clay pigeons, learning how to lead targets. We had a lot of fun with that! We had different colored bullets that would leave marks on the targets. We also had .50 caliber gunnery ranges on the ground, and we had moving targets out in the distance against the mountainside. They dragged the targets along at various speeds, and we fired at them.

Because I was only five-five at the time, I got to be a ball-turret gunner. That's where all the little guys usually ended up. The ball-turret was a dangerous spot, and there was a little bit of the ego or pride in being a ball-turret gunner! So you sort of had this macho thing about being in a dangerous position. There was a poem we recited:

> *Take down that blue service flag, mother.*
> *Replace it with one of pure gold.*
> *Your son was a ball-turret gunner.*
> *He died when he was eighteen-years old.*

A ball-turret was extremely crowded, but it got rather comfortable once I got in there and put the turret in the guns-up position because I would sort of lean back, in a reclining position. The turret was made of plexi-glass, and my first impression was a concern for how well it was attached to the plane. I got into the turret through a small door that you entered from inside the plane. Once I got into the turret, it rotated downward, the entry door was now at my back, and all around me was empty space and plexi-glass. Most of the doors were semi-sprung, and they didn't fit too well. Of course, I did have a single safety belt that went across my back, but, to be honest, I really didn't trust the thing.

The controls were nice. There was a grip for each gun. The ball-turret was electrically-hydraulically driven. I could take the two handgrips and move the turret right or left or straight down, or combine the downward movement with a circular one. There were buttons on the control grips that triggered the guns. The sights had reticules, a light image on a screen. The idea was to try to get a plane in your sights, and then adjust the reticules with foot pedals to frame the plane. Then I had the right range. The manufacturers built ammunition cans into the turret, one near each gun. I did so well with the turret that they asked me to stay on at Gunner School as an instructor, but I was trained for another cause, and I wanted to move on.

After Gunnery School, I entrained for Lincoln, Nebraska, where we got crew assignments. We looped the country, and I got to see places I never thought I would see! We went from Lincoln to Alexandria, Louisiana for crew training. Louisiana was real military country with airborne, armor, Air Corps, and infantry camps everywhere. At Alexandria, we underwent crew training and training missions.

Our pilot was Lieutenant Kenneth Lang; our co-pilot was Lieutenant Howard Miller. Lieutenant Cox was the bombardier. Our navigator was Warrant Officer Sam LaVine, the flight engineer was James Weber, the radio operator was Donald Huck, the waist gunner was Donald Kausrud, the other waist gunner was Donald Boland, the tail-gunner was Charles Haskett, and I was the ball-turret gunner.

We flew most of the time out over the Gulf of Mexico so that the navigators could get some over-water training. Since we were going to fly missions at high altitude the Army put a strong emphasis on the use of the oxygen mask. We'd practice with the masks, and we learned the inherent dangers of having oxygen aboard. Lack of oxygen gave one a false sense of euphoria, and it was a deceptive way to die. Sometimes, an individual's oxygen supply would accidentally disconnect, and he'd move around not knowing it. We learned to keep an eye on each other so that, in case someone's oxygen got disconnected, we'd get him back on it in a hurry.

After three months, we qualified for overseas duty. We returned to Lincoln, where we picked up a brand-new B–17. We flew the northern route in the night, over Labrador, to Wales. It was a scary ride, and cold. Over Greenland there were some high areas, and we had to execute a last-minute maneuver to clear the ground height. That was a new experience for the pilots and everybody else on the plane. After we landed, we went by train to Lavenham, England, where we trained for a bit. At Lavenham we were assigned to the 487th Bomb Group, 838th Squadron.

We flew our first combat mission on 27 November 1944, to the rail yards in Bingen, Germany. It was an easy mission, except for the flak. I was more curious than anything else, even though we could have been hit. I could see these puffs of black smoke above or below us. Apparently, the German gunners didn't have our correct range, at least their initial rounds didn't. The puffs looked harmless. I swung the ball turrets around watching the puffs until it came time to release our bombs. Then I swung around to the bomb bay and watched the bombs drop. I verified their release, and then watched them head for the ground.

When we crossed into enemy territory, we all became more alert. I would scan 360 degrees checking the horizon for enemy fighters. I constantly watched, and I said a lot of prayers during the winter months when it was difficult to see in the distance because there was little contrast. I had to look carefully. I was especially alert coming out of a target, because that was the time we were most likely to come under fighter attack. It was a long way home, and I was really the only protection our plane had in its belly. I feared the fighters more because they had a human element involved, and, of course, they could seek us out and pursue us and adjust to conditions. Flak was fired thousands of feet below us, and the German gunners had problems adjusting for range.

On most missions, by the time we got back to England it was always a pretty long day, twelve hours from the briefing to the return, late in the afternoon. I didn't get out of the turret until the last minute, because I had heard stories of German fighters that attacked returning bombers at their most vulnerable time, during landing. Only during the final minutes before landing would I leave the turret and go into the waist section of the plane. That was for my own safety. The turret lay very close to the runway, and if something happened to the landing gear, I didn't want to be in the turret. After landing we took the internal parts of the guns back to the armorer. Then we went to de-briefing. If nothing special happened on a mission, there wasn't much of a debriefing. Then we all got a shot of whiskey to relax, went to dinner, then back to the Quonset hut that was our barracks to get our mail, write letters, and wait for the next mission. We couldn't give many details in our letters home, but the censors even blacked out things that were non-military. Occasionally, we'd have some USO entertainment. Sometimes we had movies. You might see a movie or do some reading, write letters home and to other people. I bought a bicycle and I was able at least to ride around the base to get a little exercise to relieve tension.

We went a couple times to Marsburg, German, on 30 November and 6 December, to hit a synthetic oil plant. On these occasions, the flak was heavy. We might have developed a false sense of security from our earlier experience. Perhaps, if on an earlier mission we had taken some light damage, we would have had a little more respect for the stuff, but when you go through it and you don't get hit, you feel that you're immune, that you can handle it.

My last mission happened during the Battle of the Bulge in December 1944. It was a bad situation on the ground. In England the weather had been really lousy. We had about what seemed like a week or so of very bad fog. I never saw fog like that before or since in my life. Nothing was flying, and there was a great need to get planes in the air and to get air support and supplies for our ground forces. On Christmas Eve the fog lifted and the weather was beautiful. The 8th Air Force put every available bomber they could in the sky for various missions to support the ground troops. The 487th was chosen to lead the entire 8th Air Force armada that day.

So, we got up very early as usual, went through the routine of going to the mess hall, getting briefed, getting into our planes, and getting them off the ground. On that day, we flew with the 836th Squadron instead of our usual 838th. As a result, there wasn't the usual familiarity among the crews. There were nearly 2,000 bombers in this Armada!

It was awesome! There was nothing in front of us. From the turret, I had my 360-degree panoramic view. Behind us, as far as I could see, was nothing but planes. Unfortunately, we were "Tail-End Charlie," headed for Babenhausen, Germany, an airfield. Our mission was to destroy German aircraft on the ground to keep them from supporting their ground troops. We were up around 26,000 feet. We really couldn't distinguish anything on the ground. As usual, I was sort of scanning around the horizon and looking down underneath. In the distance, I saw a few fighter planes, but assumed that they were our escorts. Then somebody yelled over the intercom, "Bandits at 12 o'clock high!"

I swung the ball around. I didn't see anything at first, and then a German fighter plane passed right down through our formation. I took a few bursts at him as he went by. The next thing I knew I heard the tail gunner call out, "Bandits at six o'clock!"

They were attacking us from behind!

I swung the ball turret around there, into the up position, the guns parallel with the base of the plane. I opened fire on a Focke-Wulf–190. I could see the bursts from his wing guns. The tail-gunner was firing at him, and I was firing at him, but I could only fire when our plane's tail moved up. I couldn't understand why the German kept coming straight in from the rear. It seemed like he was in a vulnerable spot, just coming in at one elevation, straight at us. Whether he felt that there wasn't going to be any response or not, I didn't know.

Then I felt a tremendous crash in the turret. I stunned me, but I managed to yell on the intercom to the waist gunner, "Don! I'm hit!"

Phosphorus round had hit the turret. I could smell my flesh burning. That odor is still in my mind today. I had no idea how I was going to get out of the turret, or how badly I was hit. Somehow, I succeeded in getting the ball-turret lined up with the fuselage, where it had to be, and I ran the guns in the down position so I could open the door. I ripped my oxygen hose off, and disconnected my throat mike. I came up into the waist of the plane. There had been no response from anyone. I didn't know where the waist gunners were, or the radioman. They should have been there, either there, or right adjacent to me. When we, the survivors, talk about it today, no one is sure who left the plane first. I found out later that the navigator and the bombardier and the flight engineer got out from the front. The fighters that came in at twelve o'clock high killed Kenneth, the pilot, and Howard, the co-pilot. The waist gunner was killed. The radioman was killed. Five of us got out. It amazed me that the plane kept horizontal flight. The top-turret gunner told me later that Howard had kept the plane in horizontal flight for a while before he died. The top gunner gave the order to bale out, but neither the tail gunner nor I heard it.

When I came up into the plane I was off of oxygen, and I was getting groggy. Out of the corner of my eye I saw a fire burning in the wing and bomb bay area. We still had a full bomb load! A chest parachute lay near the waist window. I picked it up and tried to clip it onto the rings of my parachute harness, but I didn't have the coordination. I made several attempts. Finally, I got it hooked up. I went to the rear of the plane, to the emergency door. I looked at the door's red handle. I knew that when I pulled it, it would pull the hinges out of the door and the door would blow off. I thought of the parachute. I remembered what I was told, to count to three before pulling the cord so I wouldn't get hung up on the tail. I pulled the door handle. The door blew into the wind. I looked out, and then I dropped. I counted to three and pulled the cord. There was a loud pop, the chute opened, popping occasionally as I drifted with it to the ground.

Suddenly, I hit the ground. My chute, as it turned out, got caught on a tree right on the edge of a woods. It must have broken my fall a little bit before I hit the ground. I lay on the ground looking up at the sky. It was a beautiful day, light clouds floated by. I don't know how long I lay there. Then I heard voices, "American, American!"

"I must be in Germany," I thought. "This is not going to be good for me at all!"

I closed my eyes. The voices got closer. I opened my eyes. People were gathering all around me; some were old, some were children. Someone picked me up, very carefully, and put me on a blanket that they used as a stretcher and carried me into a small village where they took me to a house and laid me on a couch. I don't know how far they had to carry me. The older ladies looked at me and shook their heads as if to say, "How terrible. How young he is."

The little kids were bug-eyed. They didn't know what to make of it. They offered me some, I guess it was cognac, and they offered me something to eat, but I was in no mood for any of that. Some time later an elderly gentlemen came into the house, carrying a black bag. He looked like the pictures Norman Rockwell painted of our early-American family doctors. He had some morphine in the bag, and he gave me a shot. It sedated me, and eased the pain. I stayed in the house for some time. It was late afternoon when a US Army ambulance showed up. In came a GI and his guide, a young Belgian girl. They put me in the ambulance. After a while of bouncing over country roads, I wound up at the 298th Field Hospital in Liege, Belgium. I could not use my right leg at all. Most of the muscle in my right hip and buttock was gone.

We got to the field hospital late at night. It was very dark, and they set my litter down on the ground. German prisoners who acted as my litter bearers startled me. They carried me into the hospital tent. It was very late by the time they operated on me. I woke up in a big ward tent that was crowded with other casualties. The nurses were dressed in battle fatigues, and were wearing steel helmets. Liege was still under attack by German buzz bombs. The hospital lay in what we called "Buzz Bomb Alley." The German V–1s flew until they ran out of fuel, and then they dropped on whatever was down there. I lay in that hospital bed listening to the chug-chug-chug of those jet engines. Then it would get quiet. Then there would be a BOOM! The concussion from the explosion would shake the walls of the tent. Things would tumble off shelves. It was kind of a precarious time for the hospital.

On Christmas Day, the Belgians brought us Christmas cards. They tried to do whatever they could for the wounded, mostly Battle of the Bulge infantry casualties. They even tried to give a special dinner to the patients, but I was so sick I just couldn't eat anything. A fella next to me had been in some kind of armored vehicle, when a shell fragment struck his helmet. He didn't know anymore who he was. There were many amputees. I felt that I was really one of the least wounded. What I didn't know at the time was that my brother was also in Liege with an anti-aircraft outfit.

Eventually, they took me down to the train station, put us on a train and took us all the way to Paris, well behind the lines. They put me in the upper room of a schoolhouse that had been converted into a hospital. There was no elevator, so they had to carry the wounded up the stairs on stretchers. Here, again, they used German POWs for litter bearers. In the course of carrying me up, the litter bearers tilted my stretcher at a dangerous angle. Somebody yelled at them, "*Dummkopf.*"

An officer came to me and gave me the Purple Heart. I was proud to get that.

I was taken from the hospital to Orley Field in Paris and put on some kind of cargo plane bound for the United States. I was still stretcher-bound. By the first part of January, I was back in the States, at Mitchell Field, Long Island. I was under sedation to some extent, but I was becoming more alert to what was around me. I spent a few days there.

The hospital at Mitchell Field was a typical wooden barracks building, very plain. It was a sort of staging area from which patients were distributed to different parts of the country. I had access to a phone, and called my sister. She was shocked when I told her that I had been wounded and where I was. All they had received at home was a telegram that came to my father saying I was missing in action. Oh, it was great talking to them! It was hard for each of us to believe that so much had happened in the year that I had been away.

Then they flew me into Pittsburgh Airport, and I was taken from there by a military ambulance to Butler, Pennsylvania, to Deshon Hospital, a big Army general hospital. When I got to Deshon, I got more intense care. All that they had done so far was replace my dressings quite frequently because of all the drainage from my wound. Fortunately, they had Penicillin, the only miracle drug available then, and they were constantly giving me shots, especially after I had developed Osteomylitis. Then I got Hepatitis, but that wasn't uncommon. They weren't using throwaway needles; they had stainless steel ones which they sterilized and used on the next guy. When I was ready for it, they started physical therapy, at first simply lifting my leg, then progressing to weights. I exercised with those, and gradually got strength back into my leg. I also got skin grafts with skin taken from the lower thigh of my wounded leg. I still have shrapnel in my leg.

During my early treatment, one fella told me that I might never be able to use my leg, but he was wrong. I was nineteen, and I didn't accept the possibility that I would have a permanent disability. I was determined to get up and going. I walked and swam, but I avoided anything where I would bump the wound and mess up the skin graft.

While I was at Deshon, the Germans surrendered. The war in Europe was over. Once I could get around, I got some leaves to come home. I was what could have been called "crippled." I was very bent over, favoring my wound, but I wouldn't use crutches. I know people at home wondered if I would ever be able to walk right again. Finally, I was discharged in November 1945. I entered the University of Pittsburgh in June 1946. In between I just did things around the house, socialized a bit, and got back into the usual hometown routine. I helped with military funerals when they brought bodies back home. In 1952, I married Elizabeth Stahlman, a lady with whom I worked. I spent my post-war career as an engineer. Even though my degree is in Mechanical Engineering, I was probably closer to being an Electrical Engineer or Chemical Engineer.

Sixty years later, I still get together with those of my crew who survived. We never knew what happened to our plane. We all just assumed that, since it was still carrying a full bomb load when it went down, it just exploded and disintegrated. Then, fifty-six years after we jumped from the plane, some relatives of 487th airmen were searching the Internet for information about that day in December 1944. During their research, they discovered snapshots of what turned out to be my B–17. The plane crashed and had been broken into several large sections, one of which was the entire tail. Clearly visible on it was our emblem and the serial number. They also found photos of the wing sections. Belgian civilians had cherished the sections as reminders of the U.S. airmen who died on 24 December 1944 in the air battle above their homes. At one point, however, a farmer used a seventeen-foot wing section as a rain shelter on his farm. In 2000, the 487th Bomb Group Association raised the money to bring that wing section back to the States. Now it's down at Savannah, Georgia, at the Mighty Eighth Air Force Heritage Museum.

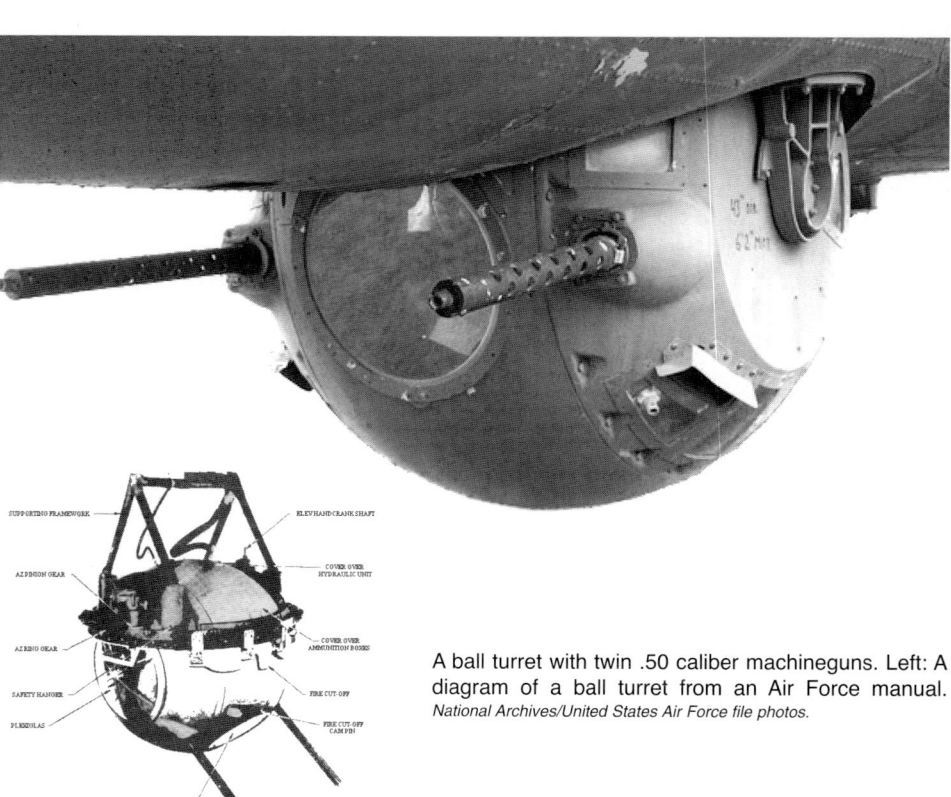

A ball turret with twin .50 caliber machineguns. Left: A diagram of a ball turret from an Air Force manual.
National Archives/United States Air Force file photos.

"We Ate the Rice, Bugs and All."

John M. Zubay

803rd Engineer Battalion (Aviation), Headquarters Company
Philippine Defense Force, Bataan Death March, Camp O'Donnell,
Cabanatuan Prisoner of War Camp, Hirohata Prisoner of War Camp
Leechburg, Pennsylvania September 26, 1919; East Liverpool, Ohio

"Then they interned us at Cabanatuan Number 1, a hellhole of a place. I was there from July 1942 until October 1943. They captured some Filipino guerrillas outside the camp. They cut one guerrilla's head off, and then they hung it over the gate on a piece of rope. It stayed there three days, dripping blood. When we went out on a woodcutting detail, we had to walk underneath that head. One Filipino tried to escape from Cabanatuan. They tied him to the front gate. They left him there for days. Every time the Japs walked by him they kicked and beat him. It was hot and they didn't give him any water. Finally they killed him. Three officers in the camp tried to escape. They caught them, made them dig their own graves and then they shot them. They made sure the whole camp watched that."

I GREW UP in a little coal-mining town. My dad was a coal miner and my older brother was a coal miner, too. I started mining coal myself when I was sixteen-years old. When it came time for me to go into the service, my little brother took my place in the mine.

I graduated high school in 1936. My dad got sick and couldn't mine any more. Anyway, I had nowhere else to go, so it was the mine for me. My older brother put a good word in for me with the boss. He lied to the boss, and said I was twenty-three years old. One day while I was at work the boss came past and said, "Who the bloody hell are you?"

I told him I was Zubay's son.

He looked at me again and said, "Twenty-three my ass!"

Then he walked away. He never said anything about it.

We lived with danger in the mine. I was in some cave-ins, nearly blew myself up once or twice when we were shooting coal and my older brother nearly got crushed when part of the ceiling fell on him. I loaded coal for sixty-four cents a ton. That's how I got paid. All the other work, putting up support beams, laying down tracks for the cars, blasting, that was all dead work. I only got paid for the amount of coal I loaded and if some of it fell off the cars as they were taking it up then that was my tough luck. This was the life of a coal miner. I think it prepared me for things to come when I was a prisoner of war. It toughened me. I worked in that mine until I was drafted in 1941.

My draft number was 256. In the county it wound up being number sixteen. I went to Kittanning, Pennsylvania, for my physical. They classified me as 4F, flat feet. Two weeks later, they called me back. I was 1A! I don't know why they did that. I suppose they needed some cannon fodder. I got on a train at Freeport, a "flag stop." That meant that you had to flag a train to get it to stop and pick you up. I flagged the wrong train. I ended up back in New Kensington. I had to wait there for forty-five minutes until the right train came along to take me to Pittsburgh. They gave me another examination there and that night I got on a train for Fort Meade, Maryland. From Fort Meade I went to Fort Belvoir where I took my basic training. I was independent, so I didn't like the military. I didn't like anyone telling me what to do. I still don't.

At Fort Belvoir, my squad was called the "Drunken Sixth." I was the only one in the squad that didn't drink. Once we went on a twenty-mile hike. The rest of the guys filled their canteens with whiskey. The longer we marched, the drunker they got. After thirteen weeks at Belvoir, they sent me to Whistler Field and the 803rd Engineers. General "Hap" Arnold came around to inspect us. We had lots of pride in ourselves, and everyone got really slicked up. Arnold marched up and down our ranks, but he couldn't find anything wrong. Rather than letting it go at that, he had to say, "Your belts are too long!"

That was chickenshit!

I passed the exam for Engineering School, so they sent me back to Belvoir where I trained on heavy equipment. I got promoted to Private First Class at Belvoir. Then they sent us back to the 803rd for transfer to the West coast. This was September 1941. I ended up at Fort McDowell on Angel Island, right off the coast of California, near San Francisco. One day my platoon was on KP, and a guy broke a dish. The mess sergeant came running over to him yelling, "What's your name, rank and serial number?"

As soon as the rest of us saw that, another guy broke a dish. The sergeant ran over to that guy. Then another guy broke a dish, and so on. We had that mess sergeant running all over the place until he cursed us and threw us all out. You didn't mess with the 803rd!

We left Angel Island on 4 October 1941 on the *President Cleveland* and the *Taft*, and were escorted by the cruiser *Chester*. We didn't know where we were going until just about the time we got there! One guy lit a cigarette when we were leaving port in 'Frisco and they threw him in the brig. No lights were allowed on the ship, not even a cigarette. We hit some rough water. The Navy cooks made us pork and sauerkraut! We were all seasick. Later they gave us ham. It was tainted and sixteen of us got food poisoning. We stopped in Guam, which was a lot closer to Japan than 'Frisco was, and they turned all the lights aboard the ship! That didn't make any sense after the cigarette incident.

We got to the Philippines in nineteen days. We were surprised because rumor had it we were going to Alaska. But we should have known better considering the tropical clothing they issued us. But, then, again, we weren't all that smart, either. We pulled into Pier Seven in Manila. They took us out to near Clark Field where they had tents pitched for us. Filipino kids came running into the camp in the morning saying, "Joe-Joe! Joe-Joe! You wanna puck-puck my sister!"

One of the saddest things I saw after the war when I came back to the Philippines was a little half-American, half-Filipino kid coming up to us and asking, "Are you my Dad? Are you my Dad?" It tore me up, because his dad was probably dead.

Outside our compound in the town of Angeles, there were three bars — the Yankee, the Moonlight and the Star. They were also houses of prostitution. The government ran trucks full of guys into these places. The guys who went knew that I would never go, so they would give me their wallets to keep. One buddy missed his ride back to camp. He came in early in the morning wearing only his shorts. They had rolled him for everything, but I still had his wallet.

We started getting rumors about a Japanese attack. About a week before Pearl Harbor they issued us live ammunition, and ordered us to carry our gas masks at all times. They had us go all around Clark Field with heavy equipment digging trenches and emplacements. On the morning of 7 December we learned that the Japs had attacked Pearl Harbor. We knew this was it. Then, at 12:20 that afternoon, Jap fighters came over Clark Field, strafing. I went out the door of the barracks, and realized that I didn't have my gas mask. I turned around, went back in, and got it. My buddy from Kittanning didn't bother to use the door. He just jumped through a screened window. We headed for the trenches we had dug the week before. We had bolt-action Springfields at the time. I flipped that bolt up and down as fast as I could. I don't think I hit any of those planes. Our anti-aircraft guns didn't do much better. Our Air Force was practically wiped out that first day. We moved off the airfield into a banana grove. The first thing our major made us do was build a bomb shelter just for him. That first night one of our guys thought he saw Jap paratroopers, and he accidentally shot one of our guys. Later, the guy died from his wounds. He was our first casualty. Everybody was afraid and wondered what was going to happen next.

We held on to Clark Field, but the Japs had air superiority. One day they bombed Clark seven times. But as soon as they left, our guys would go out and repair the bomb craters. We stayed there until Christmas Day, and then we started moving down into the Bataan peninsula, building airfields along the way. I said, "All we're doing is building something for the Japs to practice their bombing and strafing on."

When we moved on, the Japs made use of the fields we had built.

The Army cut our rations by half in January. In March, they halved them again. We hoped some relief would come from the States, but after a while we knew we were on our own. We had an officer from Georgia, a real "Cracker." He became another reason I didn't want to stay in the military. On Bataan, he wanted me to shoot this water buffalo so the officers would have meat to eat. The Filipinos relied on them as beasts of burden and for plowing their fields, so we had strict orders not to shoot them. I told him I wouldn't do it, because orders that had come from above him forbade us to shoot the buffalos. That major must have had something on somebody. Everybody knew he had VD, but he kept his rank all through the war.

Except for the airplanes, we hardly saw Jap troops during the battle for Bataan. One time, toward the end on Bataan, they were going to use my outfit as regular infantry. They took us up to a mango grove. We stayed there until dusk, and then they moved us up front, to a position on the crest of a hill. From there we saw Japs moving in the valley below. Our heavy artillery on Corregidor behind us opened up. They walked those shells right through our lines. I heard shrapnel cutting through weeds and trees all around me. I couldn't get close enough to the ground! Our company commander sent a squad out on our left flank and a squad out on our right. I was in the squad that went to the right. As we moved out, a shell from Corregidor landed in front of us. It was a dud. It was a big round, painted orange, maybe an eight-inch shell. It skipped across the jungle floor, rolled past us and went down an embankment. If it had gone off we would have all been killed. We didn't even have sense enough to hit the dirt, it happened so fast.

Nothing came of our patrol. We were called back. The artillery fire continued. And then we were sent back to our bivouac area. The next day we heard about our surrender. I was in my foxhole asleep. My buddy that was with me woke me up. "John! Throw your rifle on the pile. We surrendered," he said.

I couldn't comprehend it. I took the bolt out of my rifle and threw it away. Then I threw my rifle on the pile. We came out of our bivouac area. Jap troops came in by the truckload or riding on tanks. Then I saw something horrible on the road. There were dead Filipinos there, flattened like pancakes. I don't know if they were dead before the Japs got there, or if they had been run over deliberately. Some were in piles, some were all smashed up together. The Japs just kept running them over with their trucks and tanks, like they were nothing.

The Japs gathered us into lines. There was no real order to it. We all just followed suit. I didn't have any contact with our officers at this point. We were getting all mixed together, the Filipinos and us. It was every man for himself. We started marching down the road. Japs would drive by on the backs of trucks, hitting guys at random with their rifle butts. We were near a swamp, and I stopped to fill my canteen. I threw in a couple chlorine tablets to purify the water. It was like drinking Clorox. I went around a bend in the road, and there were dead, bloated Filipinos floating in the same water I had just drunk from. I didn't care. Water was scarce. There were a lot of artesian wells on Bataan, but you took your life in your hands trying to get to them. Some Jap guards would let us get water, some wouldn't. During the march they'd put us out in these open fields for hours with the sun beating down on us. It was hot and miserable. That's when the lack of water hit us. We thought they were going to give us something to eat each time we stopped. But all they said was, "We feed you next town."

For nine days they didn't feed us. Sometimes we stopped near sugar cane fields, and I'd grab a piece of sugar cane to suck on. They parked us one time in a turnip field. We dug those up and ate them. The Filipinos would take their lives in their hands by throwing food to us during the march. Some were beheaded on the spot for helping us. I saw our guys die. If a fella fell by the way side, he'd get shot. If someone tried to help, he got shot. I saw guys drop out of the line and just give up. What got me was we'd march so many kilometers, stop, and then the Japs would have us march back the way we'd just come! That made no sense! The Japs took anything of value.

They took one guy's spectacles because they had gold rims. He was practically blind without his glasses. They took our watches. One Jap took my last four pesos. I was broke after that, but I didn't need money, anyway.

They marched us to Camp O'Donnell, where we stayed from 19 April to 23 April. I was lucky not to have stayed there. A lot of guys died at Camp O'Donnell after the Death March. The Filipinos had guerilla troops in the mountains, and the Japs were going to go in after them. They took the bulk of my outfit and sent us north to serve as pack mules carrying disassembled mountain howitzers. An old Filipino man in front of me carrying a gun part was all bent over. He had Jungle Rot on his hands where flies gathered and bit him. He suffered terribly.

We marched uphill for a long time. The Japs were getting tired carrying their ammunition, so they made us carry the satchels. When the Japs weren't looking, we tipped the satchels over and dumped the ammunition over the mountainside. They lost quite a bit of ammunition that way, and when they figured out what was going on, we suffered some beatings.

We went through a pass in the mountains, and our force split up. The Filipino guerrillas attacked the other force and killed a couple Americans. They cut their ears off, as was their custom. Maybe they thought the Americans were Germans traveling with the Japs. I don't know. The guerrillas blew up a bridge in front of us, blocking our way. At one point, I nearly gave up, I was so sick and exhausted. I just lay down in the middle of the road and said, "Just do what you want with me."

A couple of Japs took pity on me. They gave me medicine. They saw to it that I didn't have to carry heavy loads. That's one of the reasons I'm here today, because of those two fellas. But most of them weren't that way.

After the expedition against the guerrillas, they took us to a place called Bontoc. A lot of us were sick, and a Japanese surgeon helped. He performed two appendectomies and a hernia operation by candlelight on some of our guys. It didn't matter to him if someone was Japanese or American. He was a doctor first. I admired him for that. Two of the guys survived. The third died of infection.

Then they interned us at Cabanatuan Number 1, a hellhole of a place. I was there from July 1942 until October 1943. They captured some Filipino guerrillas outside the camp. They cut one guerrilla's head off, and then they hung it over the gate on a piece of rope. It stayed there three days, dripping blood. When we went out on a woodcutting detail, we had to walk underneath that head. One Filipino tried to escape from Cabanatuan. They tied him to the front gate. They left him there for days. Every time the Japs walked by him they kicked and beat him. It was hot and they didn't give him any water. Finally they killed him. Three officers in the camp tried to escape. They caught them, made them dig their own graves and then they shot them. They made sure the whole camp watched that.

We worked on the camp farm, most of us in bare feet. There were snakes to contend with, but the fire ants were horrible. They crawled all over our legs, biting and stinging. We called our Jap foreman, "Air Raid," because that sonofabitch always hollered, "Air raid! Air raid! Everybody get busy!"

Mostly, we planted rice. We made up a little song about it: "Planting rice is no fun / From early morning to set of sun; / Cannot stand, cannot sit, cannot rest a little bit."

I think the Japs had the idea that we would grow our own food, but I think they got most of it. We didn't see much of it, for sure. We did black market trades through the fence when we could. I bought two pounds of red peppers through the fence once. I don't eat hot peppers, but I ate that whole two pounds. When we did get rice to eat, it would be filled with bugs. "Bug Soup," we called it. But when one is hungry, one is hungry. We ate the rice, bugs and all. What I missed most was bread and milk.

We suffered from malnutrition, dysentery, and bloody stool. We didn't have toilet paper, so I used a copy of *Reader's Digest*, one page at a time, then a half page at a time. Soon, the *Reader's Digest* was gone. Then I started using a leaf from a kind of bamboo plant. All that came out of me was mucous. A buddy helped me by getting me food from somewhere, but I didn't want any, I was so sick. The Japs put me in a hospital for a while. I was lucky, but a lot of guys, guys who were real fighters, weren't so lucky. They died, not because they gave up, but because their bodies couldn't handle it anymore. I recovered from the dysentery, but I got malaria and diphtheria. I became resigned to being sick and hungry.

The Japs allowed only many sick men to stay in camp. Above that number, everyone had to work, sick or not. One time a fella who was sick exchanged his numbered hat with a sergeant, and the sergeant went out and worked in his place. The Japs found out about it, and they dragged the sergeant out into the compound, took a garden hose, stuck it in his mouth, and then turned the water on full blast. If he moved, they beat him.

Living like that day after day, we had to find some humor to keep from going insane, and an American can find humor in any situation. One of our guards wanted to learn English. We taught him how to say his "name" in English, and he was very happy about it. He went around saying to his friends, "Hello. My name is Masturbation!"

In October 1943 they shipped us to Japan. We hit a typhoon in Formosa Straits. Our ship listed so much we almost capsized. The stench below deck was awful. Guys were vomiting in one corner and having diarrhea in the other. They put us in Hirohata prisoner of war camp in Japan. It was outside of Kobe, where there was a big steel mill. We worked in the scrap yard and the rolling mill, but mostly we worked unloading ore from barges. That was tough work. The foreman of our gang was a Korean. We bargained with him that if we loaded up so many cars in one day and got done early he'd take us back to camp. The arrangement worked for a while. Then one day we came back early, and the Japs gave us balls of rice about the size of tennis balls for being good workers. We washed up, ate our rice and then they called us out into the courtyard of the camp. They called out all the numbers of the men in my detail, all except me. They all got beatings for being bad workers. Just an hour before that we got rice balls for being good workers. I guess they found out about our arrangement with the Korean. I don't know how I escaped getting a beating like the rest. The good Lord was watching out for me that day.

Then they fired the Korean and gave us a Jap honcho, a short fella we called "Screamer" because his mouth was going all the time. I had learned enough Japanese just to get me in trouble. I more or less spoke for our group. There were five or six of us. We were working unloading the barges this day and it came time for a break.

I said to the Screamer, "Honcho, the soldiers say we are supposed to take a break."

He said, "No."

I kept after him, and I must have pressed him enough and he agreed to give us a break.

No sooner had we sat down when he said, "*Sanyo*! (Back to work!)"

He came down across my back with club. Without thinking I got up and started chasing him. I guess I lost it. I suddenly realized what I was doing and stopped. I often thought what I would have done if I had caught him. I was worried all day he was going to turn me in, but he didn't for some reason. He just told us to get back to work.

Another time this kid in our detail picked up his shovel and threw it over his shoulder. This Jap honcho standing next to him thought the kid was going to hit him with the shovel. He beat that kid unmercifully. We had to stand there and watch it. That was one of the hardest things; standing back and watching someone get a beating and not being able to do anything about it.

Another time we were working unloading coal from a coal belt onto cars. They had three of us shoveling coal into the chute so it would go down into the hopper. The cars weren't there yet, but the Jap in charge of the shift wanted us to pick up the ore that had fallen around the belt and put it in piles. I said, "No."

He picked up pieces of coke and started throwing them at us. I picked up my shovel and shook it at him. Then I realized what I was doing and stopped. He could have shot me on the spot, but he didn't.

In Japan, our main personal task was to look for food. We ate anything. If it crawled, if it grew, if it swam, if it flew, it didn't matter. Whoever could catch it, it was grist for the mill. I was working on the ore barges and I saw what looked like a nut lying on top of the ore. I picked it up and ate it. It tasted like a maple nut. I'm gazing around and I found a few more of them. I ate them all, and pretty soon I started to feel sick. At the end of the day, they marched us back into camp. I was really feeling sick by that point, and I couldn't wait to lie down. Instead, they decided to give us a little close-order drill outside the camp. They marched us back and forth, and I couldn't take it any more. I fell into a ditch and vomited. For that "transgression," I spent the night in the guardhouse with the guy we called the "Mad Sailor." He had been in the Japanese Navy and his leg was all crippled up. All the guards had these sabers that looked like swords but were made out of wood. He was sitting right across the table from me. He was giving me a lecture in Japanese and he would emphasize a point on top of my head with this wooden sword. After a whole night of lecturing and beatings, they sent me out to work the next day. I was weak, but I had to go. I learned later that what I ate might have been a poisonous castor bean that the Japs were trying to employ in chemical warfare. How those beans got on the ore pile, I never did find out.

At Hirohata they sometimes gave us a loaf of bread about the size of a hoagie bun. One guy broke into the kitchen and stole some of the loaves. The Japs found out, and marched us into the courtyard. It was winter, and they just barged in and hustled everyone out without giving them a chance to get coats. They kept us standing in the cold until someone confessed. Finally, they pinned the theft on one guy. The Japs had fifty-gallon drums that they kept filled with water for fighting fires. They stuck the guy in one, and he stayed in it for a couple hours. It's a wonder he didn't die.

We were all pretty thin and ragged after three years in prison camp. Most of the fellows who got through it were from small towns or were country boys, so they were used to rough times. The city guys often just gave up. They wouldn't eat the rice. I didn't like it any better than they did, but I ate it anyway. We had a saying, "Rice is a very adaptable food. There's nothing you can add to it or take away from it to make it taste any better."

Humor helped us day after day, but the uncertainty got to us. We made up sayings like, "Back to you in '42," or "Mother's door in '44." or "Home alive in '45." It seems like a childish thing today, but doing things like that helped keep our spirits up.

One day, when some American carrier planes came over, we began to realize that the war was not going so well for Japan. Our planes strafed, dive-bombed and rocketed the steel plant across the river from us. There was a two-story building in our camp, and I got to the roof with a couple guys to watch the attack. A fighter flew past us. It was so low that it passed below us. We could look down into the cockpit. Some of the fighters dropped little parachutes and had packs of cigarettes and pilots' notes attached to them. I saved one of the chutes and made an American flag out of it. A couple British and Australian prisoners made Union Jacks and Australian flags out of the parachutes they got.

Then we saw the vapor trials, high in the sky. We didn't really know what they were until the Japs told us. They were B–29's. Now we were sure the war was ending. Whether or not we all survived to the end was another matter. We learned afterwards that the Japs intended to execute us all before we got liberated.

We learned about the Atomic Bomb the day after it was dropped. A few days later, they marched us out to work, then marched us back into camp. It was 15 August 1945. There was no more work after that. On 2 September, we took over the camp. The Japs just handed over their weapons. Some of the guys went looking for a Jap we called "The Bull," but they couldn't find him. He just disappeared. The other guards made themselves scarce. The American Army came in on 9 September. They took us to Yokohama where we were deloused and fed. I was eighty pounds lighter than I was the day I enlisted.

Long after I came home, I was guaranteed one nightmare per night. I could bank on it. Today, they call it Post-Traumatic Stress Syndrome. I also had an intestinal bug.

I couldn't eat fresh fruit. Even today I can't eat apples. I even have trouble with applesauce. I can eat bananas, and I can eat oranges. My wife cuts them up, puts them in a jar with some sugar, let's them sit over night and I can eat them for lunch the next day. I used to go out in the garden before the war, pick up a cucumber, rub the dirt off it and take a bite out of it, skin and all. I didn't think anything had changed after the war. After I got discharged, I came home, went out in the garden, picked up a cucumber, took a bite and immediately got sick. I spoke with a number of doctors, psychiatrists, and neurologists with the VA program. Some of them just looked at me and said, "Well, after all, you're an old man."

And they'd just write me off. One doctor, though, was interested enough in my case, and he helped me.

When people ask me what I did in the war, I tell them, "I got three ocean cruises courtesy of Uncle Sam, and one courtesy of the Empire of Japan. I also got a walking tour of Luzon in the Philippines, courtesy of the Empire of Japan. I really didn't enjoy any of them."

As far as seeking retribution against my captors, I did go to Kittanning after the war to give a deposition against one of the guards at our camp. He had put the garden hose down the sergeant's mouth. He was tried as a war criminal, found guilty, and sentenced to thirty years.

I don't have the nightmares any more, but the other day I got to reading some of the letters I had written to my wife back in 1941 and 1942. I spent a miserable night that night. Things came back to me. Telling my story now might not do me any good, but, down the road, years from now, someone will read it and remember what we went through and learn something. That's all I can hope for.

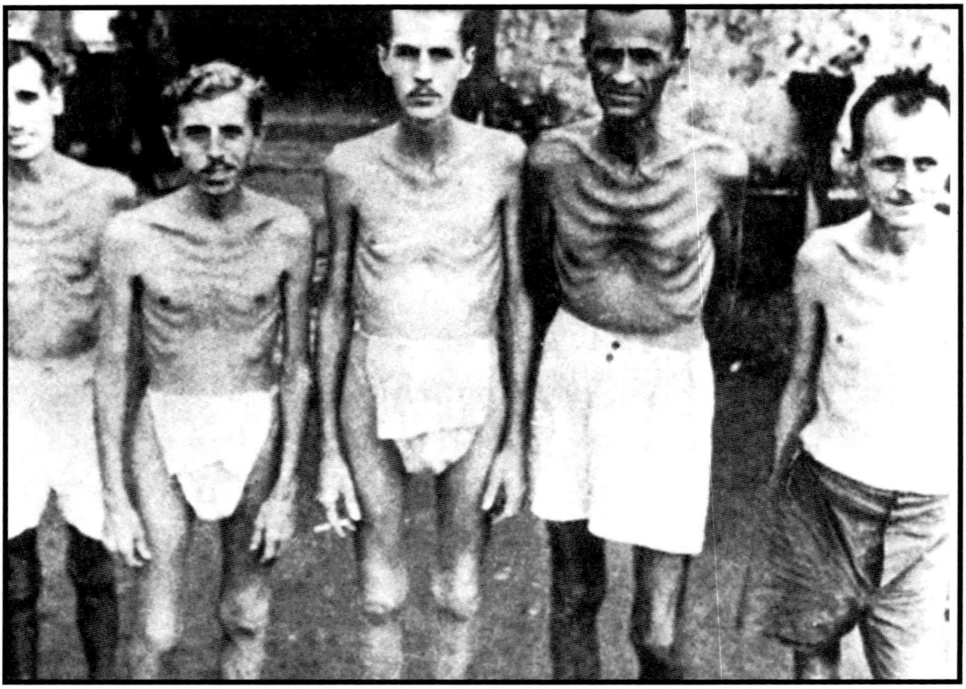

American prisoners of war, Bilibid Prison, Philippines. *National Archives.*

British and Australian POWs on the way to Hellfire Pass on the Thai/Burma railway. *www.hellfirepass.com*

Vintage Maps

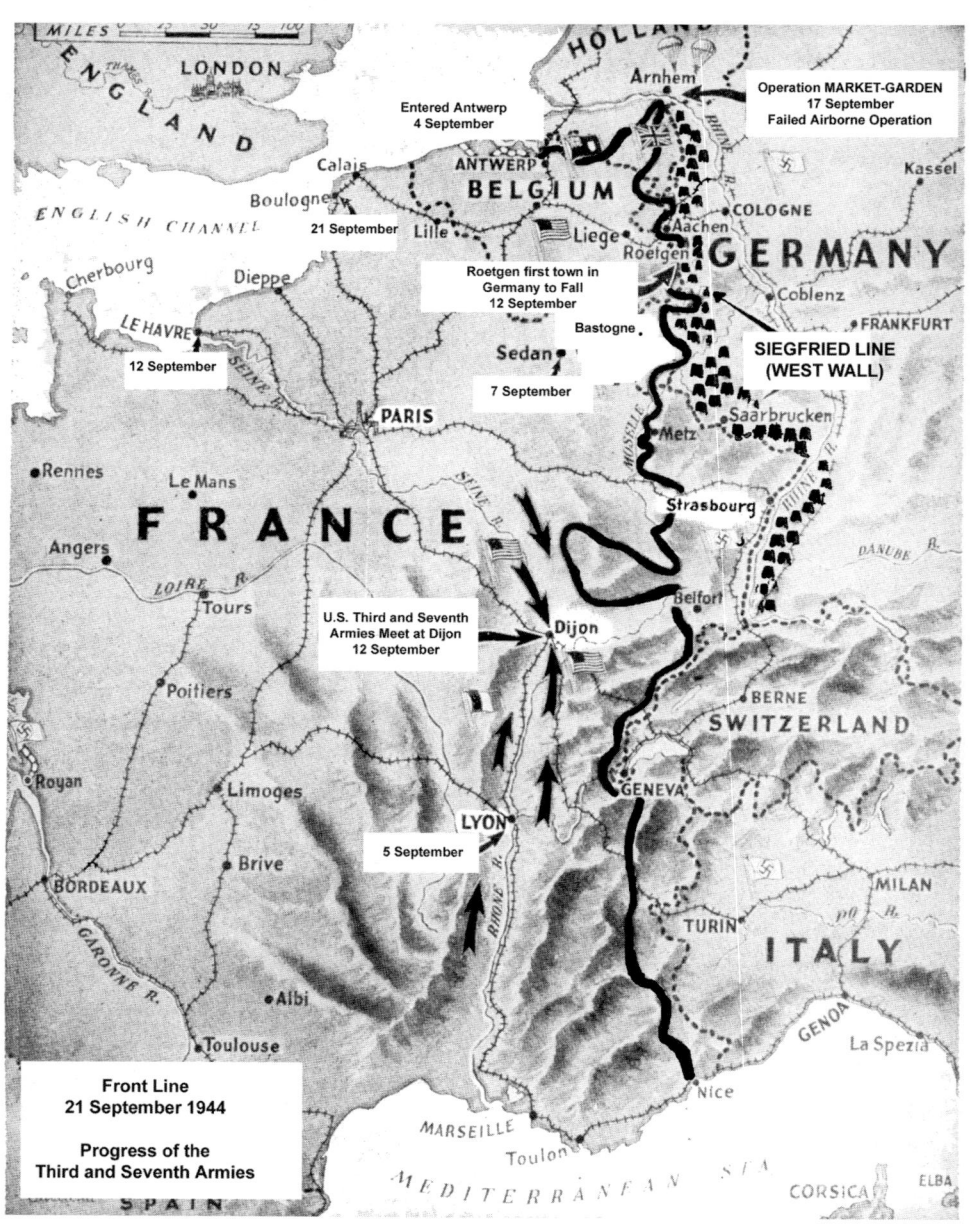

Department of Defense, 1951

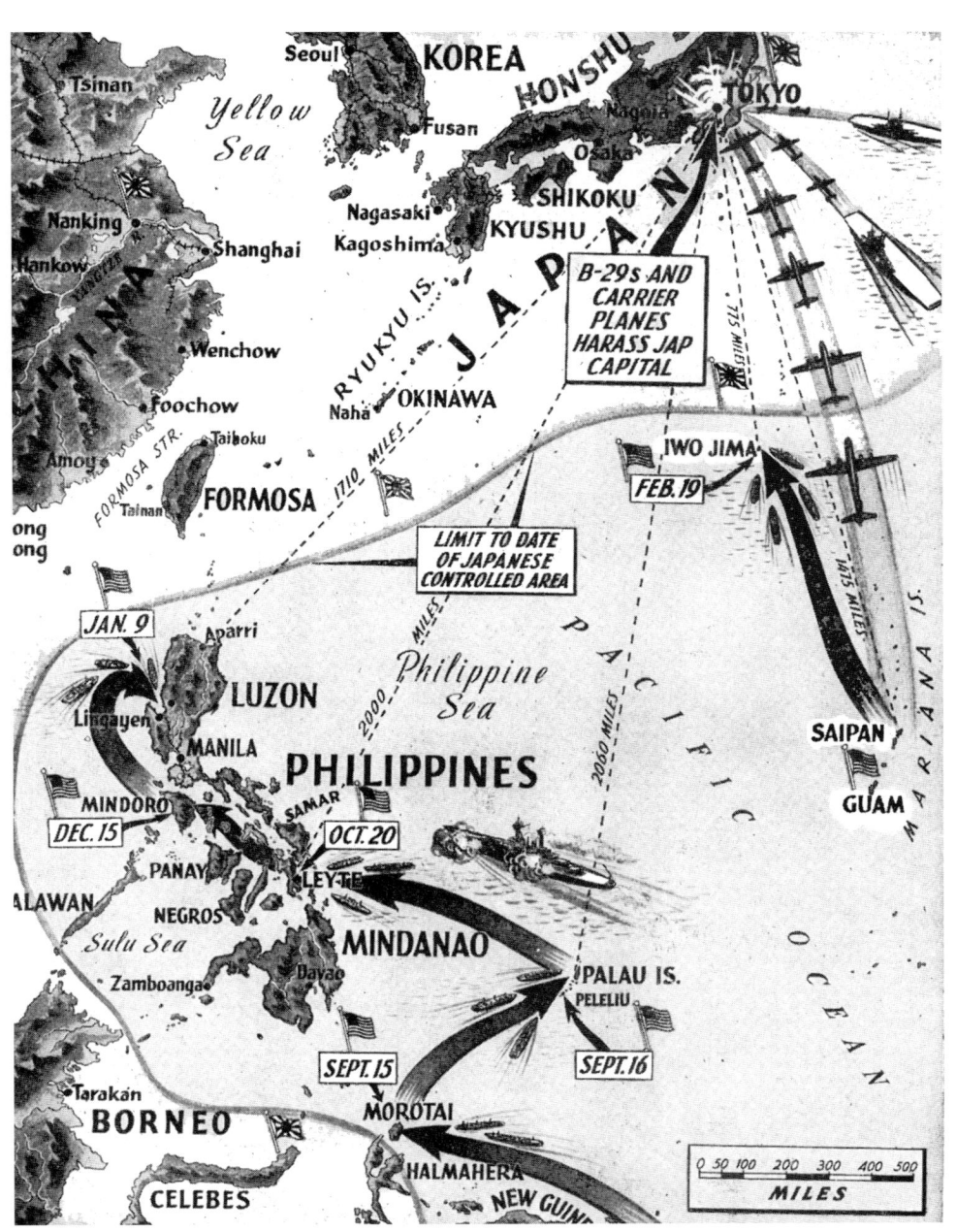

Department of Defense, 1951

Department of Defense, 1951

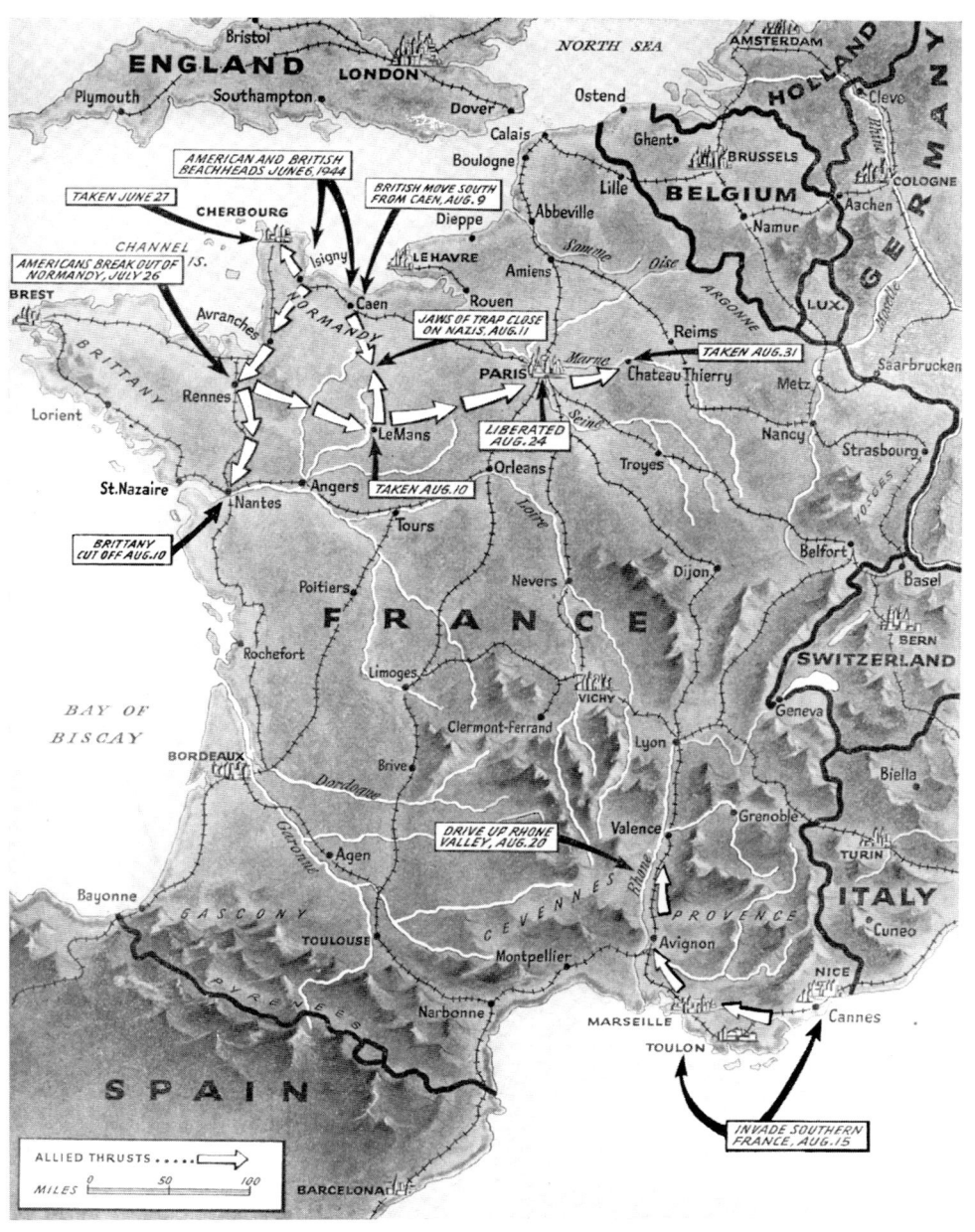

Department of Defense, 1951

Department of Defense, 1951

Department of Defense, 1951

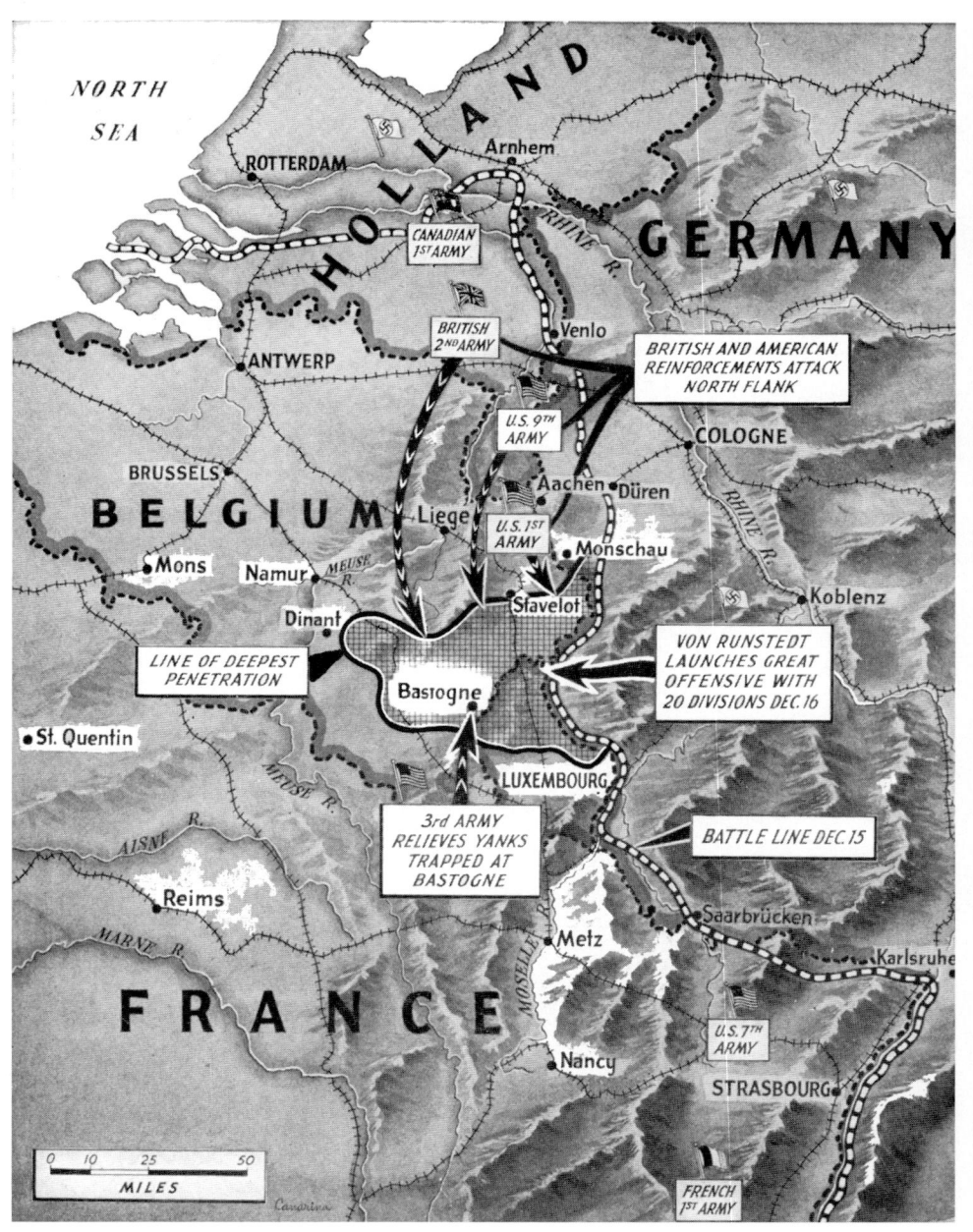

Department of Defense, 1951

Glossary

88: 88mm high velocity German artillery piece used throughout the war. It was a triple threat weapon because it could be used as an anti-aircraft, anti-personnel, or anti-tank cannon.

A–20: Douglas twin-engine attack bomber, the "Havoc." Known to the British as the "Boston."

Aleutian Islands: A remote chain of islands extending from the southwestern Alaskan peninsula. As American possessions they became a center of naval, military, and air strategy in the Pacific, and, in World War II, a station from which the Japanese had hoped to invade the United States. The Japanese also used the Aleutians as to divert attention away from their real objective, Midway Island.

Alsace-Lorraine: This geographic area dividing France from the German frontier has always been a route which invading armies have used in moving from central to western Europe. It was perennially contested between France and Germany, and loyalties among residents within the region were divided between the two countries. A number of Alsatians served with the German army during World War II.

AMTRAC: Amphibian tractor containing Marines that could ferry them from ship to shore, and then continue on dry land, thus providing the troops with protection and better odds against the dangers of amphibious landings.

Anzio: On 22 January 1944, **Operation SHINGLE**, the invasion of the Italian peninsula at Anzio, was launched to bypass the heavily fortified Gustav line to the south of Anzio. Though the defending Germans were caught by surprise, Major General John Lucas delayed further advance until his heavy equipment was landed. Allied troops advanced inland only ten miles until they were stopped by a German counterattack.

AT–11: Beechcraft advanced training aircraft, the "Kansan." *AT–6:* North American advanced training aircraft, the "Texan."

Autobahn: A superhighway constructed in Germany during the Third Reich to facilitate transport of troops and equipment from military fronts to the east and west of Germany. It provided a model for the Pennsylvania Turnpike.

AWOL: Absent Without Leave.

Axis: Germany under Adolf Hitler, Italy under Benito Mussolini, and Japan under wartime premier, Hideki Tojo. The word "Axis" was coined by Mussolini in a speech given on 1 November 1936, in Milan, when he referred to an "axis" around which other countries in Europe could function. Other countries in the "Axis" were Austria, Bulgaria, Hungary, Rumania, and Finland.

Axis Sally: There were two Axis Sally's. Rita Louise Zucca broadcast from Rome, using the title Axis Sally. She was born in New York, but renounced her American citizenship. After the war, Zucca served nine months in an Italian prison. Mildred Elizabeth Sisk (Gillars), an American citizen, broadcast Nazi propaganda to Allied troops from Berlin, Chartres, and towns in the Netherlands. She called herself "Midge at the Mike," but the GIs came to call her "Axis Sally." She was tried for treason in 1949 and given a ten to thirty year sentence. She was paroled in 1961, and died in 1988.

Bailey Bridge: The brainchild of Donald Bailey, an Englishman, the Bailey Bridge consists of ten-foot-long sections of seventeen parts, including trusses, floorbeams, stringers an fittings, not unlike a giant Erector set. Interchangeable parts made rapid construction possible.

***Banzai* charge:** *Banzai* 'May you (we) live ten thousand years' — a Japanese cry of encouragement and patriotic fervor, usually shouted after victory. On the other hand, the *Banzai* charge or attack, preceded by bugle calls and shouts, was a desperate, suicidal, headlong rush into enemy lines. One of the most famous of such attacks occurred on the Tenaru River, Guadalcanal.

BAR (Browning Automatic Rifle): Developed by John Browning during World War I, the BAR became the US Army's principal light-automatic weapon, or squad machinegun in World War II and after. Its official designation was "Rifle, Automatic Caliber .30 Browning M1918A1. It weighed 18.5lb and had a rate of fire of 400rpm, with a muzzle velocity of 2400fps.

Bastogne: A Belgian town which in 1944 was a major regional transportation crossroads. It was defended by the encircled 101st Airborne Division, which held off German attacks for seven days until relieved by General Patton's Third Army. Holding Bastogne was crucial to stopping the German advance toward their objective of Antwerp. The American defense of Bastogne during the German offensive was called a "second Gettysburg" by Winston Churchill in honor of the American defenders.

Battle of the Bulge: The last major German offensive in World War II. It is also known as the Ardennes Offensive and took place in the bitter winter cold from 16 December, 1944 to 25 January 1945. American forces suffered 19,000 dead during the course of the battle, and the Germans 20,000. The battle was so named because of the bulge-like appearance of the front lines when viewed on a map.

Belém: Brazilian city located sixty miles upstream on the Amazon River from the Atlantic Ocean. The airfield there was used as a stop-over on the southern air route to England during WWII. Planes flew from Florida to Belém and across the Atlantic to Dakar, Senegal.

Berchtesgaden: A resort town in the Bavarian Alps, near the Konigssee and Mt. Watzmann. In the mountains nearby, Nazi Party officials constructed homes and other recreational buildings, including Hitler's residence, the Berghof. While the Berghof has since been demolished and all traces of it removed, the Kehlsteinhaus, also known as the Eagle's Nest, still exists nearby as a restaurant atop a mountain peak.

"B" Designation for American Bombers. ***B–17:*** Built by Boeing, the B–17 "Flying Fortress" was a four-engine long-range bomber, with a crew of ten and armament of thirteen .50 caliber machineguns. ***B–24:*** The "Liberator," conceived in January 1939 by Consolidated Aircraft Corporation, was a four-engine long-range bomber and served in all theaters. ***B–25:*** North American twin-engine medium-range bomber, named the "Mitchell," after General Billy Mitchell (1879-1936). 9,984 were built, and they served with distinction in every theater of war. ***B–26:*** Twin-engine bomber built by Martin. The official name was *Marauder*, but one of its nicknames was the "Incredible Prostitute," because the early models had wings so short that it was said that the plane had no visible means of support. ***B–29:*** The Boeing B–29 was designed in 1940 as an eventual replacement for the B–17 and B–24. The first one built made its maiden flight on September 21, 1942. In December 1943 the Army decided not to use the B–29 in the European Theater, thereby permitting the airplane to be sent to the Pacific area where its great range made it particularly suited for the long over-water flight required to attack the Japanese homeland from bases in China.

Bf–109: Popularly the ME–109, the Messerschmitt fighter, manufactured and designed by Professor Willy Emil Messerschmitt (1898–1978).

Black Market: Items in short supply and/or subject to rationing during the war were often hoarded and sold illegally for much more than their normal retail value on the "black market."

Bocage: (see hedgerows).

Bougainville: A Pacific island located east of Papua New Guinea and north of the Solomons Island Group. Both Bougainville and Guadalcanal were scenes of heavy fighting in 1943/44.

Bouncing Betty: Anti-personnel land mines which, when tripped, are propelled into the air about a yard off the ground where a secondary explosion takes place, usually causing death or at least severe injury to the trunk of the human body.

Bradley, General Omar (1893 – 1981). Bradley graduated from West Point in 1915 and was Dwight Eisenhower's classmate, who picked him over more senior officers. He began World War II as a division commander and ended in command of four armies. Under Bradley, the Afrika Korps was defeated in three weeks, the Americans sliced through Sicily, and the Germans were expelled from France in less than four months. His forces fought in the Bulge, captured the Remagen Bridge, and met the Russians on the Elbe River. His caring qualities as a commander earned him the title "GIs' General" from the troops who served under him.

Buchenwald: One of Germany's largest concentration camps, liberated 11 April 1945. Located near the city of Weimar in a beech woods, or *Buchenwald* in German.

Buzz-bomb. The ***V–1.*** Also called "buzz-bombs," "doodlebug" or "putt-putts." These were German vengeance weapons designed to instill terror in the minds of British subjects. Powered by a pulse-jet rocket engine, the V–1 carried only a small payload. The flying bomb was built by the Volkswagen works at Fallersleben. Over 32,000 were constructed. An American equivalent was called the "Doodle Bug." Although militarily insignificant, the V–1 proved to be the precursor to the more advanced *V–2*, which ultimately led to the space race. The V–2 took some twelve years to develop. Forty-six-feet long, the V–2 carried a 2,000 pound warhead. The first V–2 was launched against Paris on 8 September 1944. 1,145 were subsequently launched against London, and another 2,000 against cities in Belgium.

Camp Lucky Strike: One of the "cigarette" camps, all of which were named after famous American cigarette brands. They were located in the vicinity of Le Havre, France, and were used as staging areas for troops arriving and departing from the continent. Other camps included Chesterfield, Pall Mall, Philip Morris, Old Gold, Wings and Herbert Tareyton, among others.

C–47 (see DC–3).

Changi Prison Camp: POW camp, located near Singapore, used to house Allied prisoners of war. Formerly a British Army encampment of barracks, Changi was hurriedly converted to a prison camp in February, 1942, upon surrender of the British garrison to the Japanese at Singapore.

Chetniks/Partniks: Chetniks were members of a Serbian nationalist resistance organization led by Colonel Draja Mihailovic that carried out guerrilla warfare during the German occupation of Yugoslavia in World War II. The Chetniks were collaborators with the Allies, and downed airmen were told to seek them out in case they were shot down over Yugoslavia. Partniks were those, many of them "former" Chetniks, who sympathized with the Germans and the Italians. Airmen were advised to avoid them.

Colmar Pocket: Furious battle near the French city of Colmar, where a large force of Germans trapped in the pocket eventually escaped across the Rhine River into Germany. As such, they were the last significant German force to leave French soil in WWII. Congressional Medal of Honor recipient Audie Murphy earned lasting fame for his one-man stand during the battle of the Colmar Pocket.

Convoy: Ships of various designations (merchantmen and war ships) traveling in a group as added protection against submarine attack. There were fast convoys and slow convoys. Convoys from the Americas to Europe were stalked by groups of German submarines called "Wolfpacks."

Corpsman: U.S. Navy Pharmacist Mates, trained as medics to provide first aid and basic medical treatment to wounded personnel. Thousands of these Navy "corpsmen" served in front-line battle conditions with Marine Corps units.

Cryptographer: Personnel trained to encode allied communications to ensure secrecy, and to decode enemy transmissions.

D-Day: (see OPERATION OVERLORD).

Dachau: A Nazi concentration camp organized near Munich in 1933. By the end of the war, the camp contained 160,000 slave laborers. On 29 April 1945, American troops liberated the camp. Dachau was also a medical research center for the German SS.

DC–3: Douglas "Dakota" or military C–47, nicknamed "Gooney Bird," in the Pacific Theater.

Dengue fever: Flu-like viral disease spread by the bite of infected mosquitoes. Visitors in the tropics are often susceptible to dengue fever.

Depression (Great Depression (1929–1940). A period of worldwide economic failure which followed the stock market crash and panic of 1929.

Dornier: German aircraft manufacturer. "The Flying Pencil" or the Dornier 17 was the most famous of the Dornier bombers to fight in the Battle of Britain in 1940.

DUKW: Amphibious 2 1/2 ton truck that could travel on both land and sea, produced by General Motors Corporation from 1942 to 1945. The name is an acronym for D (year of production); U (body style); K(front wheel drive); W(rear wheel drive).

Dulag(luft): Abbreviations for *Durchganges Lager* 'entrance camp,' or 'transit camp,' for POWs. The suffix *Luft* designates a camp for airmen.

Dutch New Guinea: In March, 1942, Japanese forces began the battle to eliminate a Dutch and Australian force from the western half of New Guinea, to consolidate strategic control over the East Indies. Dutch New Guinea came under Indonesian control in 1963.

Eisenhower, General Dwight David (1890–1969): General of the Army, Supreme Allied Commander of the Allied Expeditionary Forces in Western Europe (from December 1943), and President of the United States (1952 – 1960), Eisenhower had great personal charm and a talent for diplomacy. These qualities made it possible for him to reduce friction among the various Allied nations and commanders, especially during Operation Overlord.

Falaise Gap: Refers to the gap in Allied lines between Argentan and Falaise during the Allied offensive toward Paris. Within the Falaise pocket the German 5th and 7th Panzer Armies were trapped between American and Anglo-Canadian forces, and effectively destroyed as fighting units. But half of the trapped German troops and substantial numbers of armored vehicles managed to escape through the gap. Blame for failure to close the gap is generally attributed by the American military to the lack of aggressive generalship by British Field Marshall Montgomery (see).

Fascism: In the context of the 1930s and 40s, fascism described a form of totalitarian dictatorship. Its modern origins were in Italy, whereby a nation's labor, capital and means of production were controlled by the state in partnership with industries grouped into *fasci*, the ancient Roman symbol for bundles. In Mussolini's Italy, there were twenty-two such *fasci*, or industry sector groupings, ranging from energy to manufacturing to transportation, etc. all under control of the National Council of Corporations, a government agency. The corporations themselves, however, were privately owned. The similarity between the two major fascist powers of the era – Italy and Nazi Germany – is based primarily on the fact that both were totalitarian dictatorships.

FFI: *Forces Francais d'interieur* or French Forces of the Interior. Established in December 1943 to unite all paramilitary forces of the French Resistance, operating in both occupied and Vichy France, under a single military command structure.

Flak: *Fliegerabwehrkanonen* 'anti-aircraft cannon.'

Forty & Eight: Identifies railroad boxcars used by the French in World War I to carry troops to the front. These boxcars, which had a capacity to carry forty men or eight horses, carried a numerical 40&8 symbol on their sidewalls to signify cargo capacity in terms of men or horses. The same nomenclature was used by American troops to identify boxcars during World War II.

Fraternization: A SHAEF policy of non-fraternization with the enemy was intensified during the rapid movements through the Rhineland. The British considered the non-fraternization rule to be an attempt to shun the German people as an expression of disgust against the beastiality of the Nazi regime. Given the gregariousness of the typical American soldier, the rule was almost impossible to enforce.

FW–190: Focke-Wulf–190 was one of the outstanding German fighters of the war. It never achieved the "romantic" stature of the Bf–109, which it was built to succeed.

Geneva Conventions: A series of conventions designed to protect victims of war. The first was signed in 1864. Subsequent conventions were signed in 1899, 1907, 1925 and 1929. The most recent convention was developed by the *Diplomatic Conference for the Establishment of International Conventions for the Protection of Victims of War*, held in Geneva Switzerland in August 1949. The Convention was adopted internationally by its signatories in 1950, with two additional protocols added in 1977.

Gestapo: Abbreviation for the German term *Geheime Staatspolizie,* or Secret State Police.

GI Bill: The Serviceman's Readjustment Bill (also known as the GI Bill of Rights) was enacted in 1944. For veterans of WWII, the act provided unemployment benefits; education assistance in the form of college tuition, along with a monthly stipend for expenses; and low interest loans for homes, farms and small businesses.

GI: A term used throughout World War II to describe anything associated with the US Army. It was generally understood to stand for "Government Issue," but actually came into use when supply clerks listed garbage cans as GI for "galvanized iron." Its most famous connection was to the infantry man himself, "GI Joe," first popularized in print in Lieutenant Dave Berger's comic strip in *Yank* magazine, 17 June 1942, and later in the cartoons of Bill Mauldin, who created the characters Willie and Joe.

Gold Star Mother: Mothers whose sons were killed in action were given a small banner with a gold star to hang in their windows.

Guadalcanal: Part of the Solomon Island Group in the South Pacific. The U.S. invasion of Guadalcanal by the First Marine Division on 7 August 1942 marked the first offensive action by American forces in the war against Japan.

Guam: An island in the North Pacific strategically situated between Hawaii, Japan and the Philippines. Was ceded to the United States by Spain in 1898, taken by the Japanese in 1941, and re-taken by the United States in 1944.

Gung-Ho. Chinese for "work-together." It was the motto of the Marine Corps unit known as Carlson's Raiders in World War II. In modern American English it has come to mean any zealous attitude toward any cause or activity.

Ghurka: Indian troops who fought with the British Army during both world wars in European and Pacific campaigns. Known as fierce fighters who relished hand-to-hand combat at night, where they could employ their famous Kukri knives to kill their enemies in silence.

Hedgerows: Man-made structures formed by the controlled growth of dense shrubbery, trees and other vegetation. Used in the Normandy countryside to define borders between properties, and to control the movement of livestock. They served German defenders well by providing strong defensive positions which blocked offensive fields of fire and were virtually impervious to penetration, even by Sherman tanks. When the Shermans were equipped with hastily devised front-mounted cutting devices, dubbed "rhinoceros," they were finally able to blast through the hedgerows in support of infantry action.

Higgins Boat: Designated LCVP (Landing Craft Vehicle/Personnel), the boats were used to ferry troops and small vehicles from anchored ships to land. The 36-foot long boats were named after their designer, Andrew Higgins, and were made of wood.

Hitler (Youth) *Jugend:* Nazi organization which, in theory, taught National Socialist ideals to German youth. In later practice, the youth in this organization were used in desperation as home defense troops when Allied Forces neared the heart of Germany proper. The group was headed by Baldur von Schirach (1907 – 1974) from 1933 to 1940. *Hitler Jugend* was the designation of the 12th SS Panzer Division which successfully counterattacked the 3rd Canadian Infantry Division at Carpiquet (near Caen) airfield on July 5, 1944. The division was made up of teenagers. Its commander at the time was SS General Kurt Meyer. 90% of the division, formed in June of 1943, was killed or captured in the fighting around Caen.

Hodges, General Courtney H. (1887–1965): Commander of the US First Army from 1944 – 1945. He became one of the best Allied commanders of the war. He flunked out of West Point in his plebe year. He was an expert in infantry tactics and was instrumental in the action at Normandy, the Bulge, Remagen, and the encirclement of the Ruhr. After VE day, he went to the Pacific and participated in the invasion of Okinawa.

Holocaust: The systematic extermination of Jews (including other ethnic groups and other nationalities) by the Nazis.

Hurricane: A British Royal Air Force single-engine fighter manufactured by Hawker Aircraft Ltd. It was the first British fighter to exceed 300 mph. More Hurricanes than Spitfires were employed by the RAF during the Battle of Britain.

Hürtgen Forest: The site of bloody fighting from mid-September 1944 to February 1945. The forest covers about fifty square miles below the city of Aachen on the German/Belgian border.

Iwo Jima: A Pacific island that lies 660 miles south of Japan. The island was invaded by the 4th and 5th Marine Divisions on 19 February 1945 and was secured a few days later at heavy cost in dead and wounded.

Japanese "Zero": Designated by its manufacturer, Mitsubishi, as the A6M2 fighter plane. Upon acceptance by the Navy, the plane was designated as Navy Type 0, Model 11, and became known popularly as the *Rei Sentoki,* which means Zero Fighter. During the first two years of the war, the Zero outclassed American planes in both speed and maneuverability.

Jeep: A small, versatile and highly dependable four-wheel drive reconnaissance and utility vehicle used extensively by the Allies in World War II. The government awarded a contract to Willys Overland Corporation of Toledo, Ohio, in 1941 after a competition with Ford and American Bantam Motors, of Butler, PA, both of whom offered very similar designs. Ford produced the greatest volume of vehicles designated by the military as "GP" vehicles. Other producers besides Willys and Ford included American Bantam, Checker Cab and Chevrolet. Folklore has it that the GP designation stood for "General Purpose," which was pronounced "Jeep" by GIs. Other sources claim that the name derives from Ford's internal designation of GP for the vehicle, which was adopted by the Army as the military designation. According to Ford's service manual for the vehicle, the letter "G" identified the vehicle as produced for the government, and the letter "P" was code for the 80-inch wheelbase. However the name evolved, the Jeep nameplate survives to this day in the form of a vehicle produced by Daimler-Chrysler Corporation.

Ju–88: Manufactured by Junkers, it was the most versatile of German aircraft. Nicknamed the *Schnellbomber* 'fast bomber,' it was designed in 1936.

Kamikaze: "Divine Wind" suicide squadrons organized by the Japanese air force toward the end of World War II. Historically, the term alludes to a typhoon that destroyed a Mongol invasion fleet in 1281. Kamikaze pilots flew their explosive-laden planes into Allied naval vessels.

Kasserine Pass: In February 1943, after the American landings in North Africa during Operation TORCH, German Field Marshall Erwin Rommel (see) counterattacked inexperienced American troops at the Kasserine Pass in Tunisia. The Americans were badly defeated.

Kempetai: The brutal Japanese secret police. The Japanese equivalent of the Nazi *Gestapo*.

Kristallnacht: 9 November 1938. A night of Gestapo-ordered attacks against Jewish businesses throughout Germany. *Kristallnacht,* 'Night of Broken Glass," refers to the shattered glass of countless storefronts in Germany, Austria and the Sudetenland. The night also symbolized the destruction of Jewish life in the Third Reich, and was to serve as a warning to Jews to leave before it was too late.

Kwajalein: An atoll in the Marshall Islands, west central Pacific Ocean, in the Ralik Chain. During World War II the atoll was strongly fortified as a military base by the Japanese. It was taken by American forces in 1944.

LeMay, General Curtis (1906-1990): Commander of Army Air Force Operations in Europe and later in Japan. LeMay was largely credited with developing the tactics used for large-scale bombing raids. After the war, LeMay organized the Strategic Air Command, which was capable of delivering nuclear warheads worldwide.

Liberty Ship: An expendable, mass-produced vessel used during World War II to transport troops and materiel. Henry J. Kaiser (1882–1967), known as the "Father of American Shipbuilding," headed the Liberty Ship project.

Looting (American Troops). Under an April 1945 directive issued by Eisenhower, looting by Allied troops was forbidden. The only booty that might be mailed home consisted of objects that were Nazi in origin: flags, arm bands with swastika emblems, and the like.

LST: (Landing Ship Tank) LSTs were landing craft, especially for use in amphibious operations. LST 779 contributed the flag that was raised at Mount Suribachi on Iwo Jima. Irreverent crewmen called LSTs "Slow Moving Targets." Other Navy designators for landing craft were: LCA (assault), LCC (control), LCF (flak or anti-aircraft), LC(FF) (flotilla flagship), LCI (Infantry), LCI(L) (infantry, large), LCM (mechanized), LCP (personnel), LCR (rubber), LCS (support), LCT (tank), LCT(R) (tank/rocket), LCV (vehicle), LCVP (vehicle/personnel), LSD (dock), LSM (medium), LSM(R) (medium/rocket), LSV (vehicle), LVT (tracked).

Luger: After Georg Luger. This was the standard German service pistol (1908 – 1945). A 9mm semi-automatic of distinctive shape that was popular with German officers in both world wars. It was a popular souvenir among Allied troops and is still much sought after by modern collectors. Despite its popularity, it was not as good as the Walther P–38 which was introduced as its successor in World War II. The working parts of the Luger required extreme machining and were prone to malfunction.

MacArthur, General Douglas (1880–1964): Supreme Commander Southwest Pacific. Placed in command of American troops in the Philippines in July 1941. As the Japanese advanced closer to the American perimeter in Bataan and Corregidor, President Franklin D. Roosevelt ordered MacArthur to leave the Philippines for Australia before the Americans were forced to surrender. MacArthur complied with the orders, earning for himself the nickname "Dugout Doug" from embittered American soldiers left behind. MacArthur was embittered and frustrated by the Allied strategy that gave priority to Europe and forced him to share the Pacific command with Admiral Chester W. Nimitz. As Supreme Commander Southwest Pacific, MacArthur developed the strategy of island hopping in which American forces bypassed and isolated certain Japanese held islands, while attacking others as stepping stones to the Japanese home islands.

Maginot Line: A series of heavily fortified bunkers along the French border named after World War I French Defense Minister André Maginot. The Maginot Line was completely ineffective against the Blitzkrieg tactics of the German army.

Malmedy Massacre: Near the village of Malmedy, Belgium, eighty-six American soldiers captured by the Germans during the Battle of the Bulge were executed by German troops under the command of Col. Joachim Peiper (see). The massacre occurred on 17 December, on the second day of the German attack.

Marianas: Island group in the Pacific containing Saipan, Guam, Tinian.

ME–109: See Bf-109

M–1 Rifle (Garand): .30 Self-loading rifle, considered by Patton to be the best infantry rifle ever produced. It was the only self-loading rifle to be a universal issue to any army in World War II. The Garand could withstand great abuse.

Model, Field Marshall Walter: Commander, German Army Group B, which attacked allied forces in the Battle of the Bulge. Model, together with Field Marshall von Rundstedt, Commander of the Western Front, planned the German attack in the Bulge. Later, Model ordered the surrender of over 300,000 German troops who were trapped in the Ruhr pocket. A dedicated Nazi, Model then committed suicide.

Monte Cassino: A "mountain" that dominated the town of Cassino, northwest of Naples, and site of the historic Benedictine monastery. Monte Cassino had been fortified by the Germans, and the Allied route to Rome was blocked. The Allies responded with a series of heavy artillery and air bombardments that reduced the monastery to a pile of rubble that, ironically, offered the Germans even greater protection. After weeks of fighting the monastery was finally captured, and the road to Rome was open.

Montgomery, Field Marshall Bernard Law (1887–1976): Flamboyant British Field Marshall best known for his campaign across North Africa (after having adapted his predecessor Auchinleck's plans) and the defeat of German General Rommel in the desert at El Alamein. After his victory he blamed Auchinleck and his own staff for all the failures, and gave none of them credit for the successes. Later in the war, "Monty," as he was known, would be roundly criticized for the ill-planned and executed Operation MARKET-GARDEN. Montgomery would not attack unless he had overwhelming superiority. His egoism was notorious, and Eisenhower called him "a thorn in my side." His nemesis was the equally flamboyant American general George S. Patton. At the Falaise Gap, where Allies tried to encircle the bulk of German forces in France, Montgomery's failure to do so resulted in the escape of half of the German troops, allowing them to continue the defense of the Reich. At the time, Montgomery was still giving orders to US troops, even though Bradley should have been doing so, and he would not allow Patton to complete the encirclement. He took a grossly unmerited credit for American success in the Battle of the Bulge and Bastogne. History's hindsight is beginning to show that Montgomery's reputation was markedly less than his real performance.

Nazi. Derisive name coined by Konrad Heiden for members of Adolf Hitler's political party, *Nationalsozialistichen Deutschen Arbeiterparetei*. Original party members were called *Nasos*.

Nebelwerfer: Originally a German device for launching smoke-screen ordnance. It was found to be also suitable for rockets. American troops called the weapon and its projectiles "Screaming Meemies" because of their peculiar sound.

Ninety-Day Wonder: A second lieutenant newly arrived at the front, who had been trained for his rank in only ninety days.

Nuremberg Trials: Trials held in Nuremberg in 1946 that led to the imprisonment or execution of Nazi war criminals.

OA–8: An observation/amphibian plane built by Sikorsky, and in service from 1925-47.

Okinawa: Part of the Ryukyu Island Group, located 400 miles south of the Japanese homeland islands. It was of strategic importance as a staging area for a planned invasion of Japan. The invasion of Okinawa took place on 1 April 1945 and the island was not secured until late June. The bloody battle resulted in 12,000 American dead. Over 100,000 Japanese troops were killed, along with an estimated 100,000 Okinawan civilians. Only 10,000 Japanese troops chose to surrender.

Omaha Beach: The largest of the five Normandy invasion beach sectors, stretching for six miles from Port-en-Bessin to Vierville. Ranging from west to east, Utah and Omaha beaches were assigned to the American Army for the invasion. Gold, Juno and Sword were the responsibility of the British and Canadians.

Operation MARKET GARDEN: Designed to secure bridges behind German lines spanning Holland's rivers, thereby providing access into Germany without need to penetrate the formidable obstacles of the Siegfried Line (see). On 17 September 1944, thousands of British paratroopers were dropped as deep as 100 miles behind German Lines, only to run into stiff resistance at some of the bridges, including the major span at Arnhem. The operation ended with evacuation of remnants of the 1st British Airborne Division from the Arnhem area on 27 September. **Operation OVERLORD**: 6 June 1944. D-Day, when Allied forces invaded Northern France to open a "second front" against the Germans. **Operation COBRA.** Launched at the end of July, Cobra was designed to break out of Allied positions in Normandy. The movement was preceded by a devastating carpet-bombing of German positions by 500 fighter-bombers of the American 9th Air Force, who were followed by 2,000 heavy and medium bombers (B-17s and B-24s). Over 4000 tons of standard and high explosive bombs and napalm pounded the German positions, supplemented by 125,000 rounds of artillery.

Panzer: German word for tanks (armor).

Patton, General George S. (1885–1945). Nicknamed "Old Blood and Guts," Patton commanded the US Third Army in Europe. He died in a postwar auto accident and lies buried in Diekirch, Luxembourg. Patton was one of the first Americans to embrace new theories of armored warfare, in which he later excelled. During service in Sicily in 1943 Patton was involved in an incident which nearly cost him his military career. He impulsively slapped a battle-fatigued soldier, and after the resulting publicity and public apology, he suffered in humiliation until he was assigned a role in the impending invasion of Normandy (1944). He played a key role in maintaining pressure on the Germans through the campaigns of 1944-45 and in the defeat of the German offensive through the Ardennes (Battle of the Bulge).

"P" (Pursuit) American designation for fighter plane: *P-26:* Dubbed the "Peashooter" by pilots, the Boeing P-26 was the first all-metal pursuit plane produced for the Army Air Force, and the last of the open cockpit types. It went into service in 1932 and was replaced by the P-36 in 1938. *P-36:* The P-36, developed from the Curtiss "Hawk" Model 75 originally designed for France, was first produced for the Air Corps in 1938. Obsolescent by 1941, it was relegated to patrol and training duties. *P-38:* Built by Lockheed, the twin-boomed "Lightning" first appeared in 1939. It was called "Fork-tailed Devil" by the Germans. *P-39:* The Bell "Airacobra," a single-seat fighter plane of limited success among the Allies, but much liked by the Russian airmen. The Airacobra was lend-leased to the Soviet Union in massive quantities. *P-40:* One of the Curtiss "Hawk" series, and the principal USAAF fighter plane at the start of World War II. Four of these types were the only fighters that got airborne to confront the Japanese at Pearl Harbor. The plane was used with great success by General Clare Chennault and his American Volunteer Group ("Flying Tigers") in China before the outbreak of the war. *P-47:* The Republic "Thunderbolt," a powerful fighter-bomber nicknamed "The Jug." It was called the *Jagdbomber* or *Jabo* by German infantry and armored troops. *P-51:* The Mustang (first called Apache by the British), designed by the North American company, was a USAAF single-engine fighter, and arguably the best fighter plane in World War II. *P-61:* The Northrup radar equipped twin-engine night fighter successfully used in the Pacific campaign. It was nicknamed the "Black Widow."

P-38 pistol: See Walther.

Pillbox: A fortified bunker, usually made of concrete.

Pontoon Bridge: (See Bailey Bridge).

Ploesti: The site of German oil refineries in Rumania. Ploesti was bombed three times by the USAAF, the first raid being a particular disaster.

Quonset Hut: Pre-fab, single-story steel buildings used throughout World War II by United States forces worldwide. They were recognizable by their half-circle shape and corrugated metal construction and were named after the town of manufacture, Quonset Point, Rhode Island.

Rations (military): The C-Ration was an individual ration for one day in the field, and was developed by the US Army in World War II. The ration contained three cans of meat and vegetables, three cans of crackers, sugar, and some kind of candy. The most famous of military rations was the K-Ration, named after American physiologist Ancel Keyes. These were mainly designed for use by airborne troops. K-Rations consisted of a breakfast box, dinner box, and supper box, each containing concentrates like fortified biscuits, canned meat, malted milk tablets, chewing gum, coffee, sugar, bouillon paste, and lemonade powder.

Red Cross. An international humanitarian agency established in 1865, which provided medical care for military and civilian casualties on *both* sides during World War II. It also oversaw the treatment of POWs. The image of the Red Cross was tainted in the Second World War because it would charge soldiers for nearly everything they wanted. However, this was because the US Army specifically asked them to do this. The Red Cross did provide food parcels for prisoners of war on both sides, free of charge. These parcels were especially looked forward to by Allied prisoners because it was often the only good food they could get. See the prisoner of war experiences of Alexander Robert Nelson and John Slaney.

Remagen Bridge: Located on the Rhine River halfway between Cologne and Koblenz, at the town of Remagen. Known in Germany as the Ludendorff Bridge, it was captured intact by the Allies on 7 March 1945, and used extensively until it collapsed on 17 March. It was the only bridge over the Rhine still standing at that late date in the war, and greatly facilitated offensive action by the Allies.

Ridgeway, General Matthew (1885-1993): Commanded the 82nd Airborne Division on D-Day. Helped plan the airborne operation and jumped with the troops in the invasion drop. In 1951 commanded the 8th Army in Korea, and eventually replaced Douglas MacArthur as Supreme Commander of UN Forces in Korea. Later became Commander in Chief, Far East Command. Upon retirement in 1955, Ridgeway became Chairman of the Board of Trustees of the Mellon Institute for Industrial Research in Pittsburgh, PA.

Roi-Namur: An island in the Marshall Islands Group. Was invaded and secured by US Marines in February 1944, and used as an air base. Nearby islands in the Marshalls include Kwajalein and Eniwetok. Roi-Namur is still in use as a radar and tracking station.

Rommel, Field Marshall Erwin (1891-1944): To the western world, perhaps the most famous and respected of the German generals. He was known as the Desert Fox for his legendary feats as commander of the Afrika Korps during the North African campaign against the British 8th Army. Rommel later planned the system of fortified defenses along the coast of France. He was wounded shortly after the D-Day invasion when his car was strafed by a British Spitfire. Rommel was forced to commit suicide after he was implicated in the July 1944 plot to assassinate Hitler.

ROTC: Reserve Officer's Training Corps.

Ruhr Basin: One of the areas crucial to the plans of Operation OVERLORD. Eisenhower (10 September 1944, SHAEF SGS, Post OVERLORD Planning 381, I) states: "…to break the Siegfried Line and seize crossings over the Rhine …. Once we have the Ruhr and the Saar, we have a strangle hold on two of Germany's main industrial areas, and will have largely destroyed her capacity to wage war.… At the moment and until we have developed the Channel ports and the rail lines therefrom, our supply situation is stretched to the breaking point, and from this standpoint the advance across the Siegfried Line involves a gamble which I am prepared to take in order to take full advantage of the present disorganized state of the

German armies in the West."

Schofield Barracks: Barracks in Hawaii made famous in James Jones' novel *From Here to Eternity* and in its film adaptation starring Burt Lancaster, Frank Sinatra, Montgomery Clift and Ernest Borgnine.

Selective Service. The Selective Service used the lottery system to select draftees. In the Draft of 1940, the first number drawn was 158. Henry L. Stimson drew it from the same bowl that was used in the 1917 draft. After 17 1/2 hours, Lewis B. Hershey drew the last number, which was 2,114. The Draft Classifications were 1A (fit for general service); 1B (fit for limited service); 1C (member of the armed forces); 1D (students fit for service); 1E (students fit for limited service); IIA (deferred for critical civilian work); IIIA (deferred due to dependents); IVA (already served in the military); IVB (deferred by law, i.e., draft officials); IVC (alien); IVD (ministers); IVE (conscientious objector); IVF (physically, mentally or morally unfit).

SHAEF: Supreme Headquarters Allied Expeditionary Force.

Sherman Tank: The M4 Sherman was the most prolific Allied tank. Unusually rugged and dependable, it carried a 75mm cannon and a crew of five.

Siegfried Line: (West Wall): Concrete barriers emplaced to prohibit the movement of armored vehicles through a certain area, so named because they resembled teeth. Employed mostly along the beach or the Siegfried Line on Germany's western defenses. It ran from Switzerland to Belgium, and was nine-miles deep in places. A song popular among the invading Allies had the line, "We'll hang out our washing on the Siegfried Line."

Sikh: Sikh troops have long been associated with the British Army, dating back to the 19th Century when Sikhs, a minority in India, sided with British forces in 1857 when the Indian Army revolted against British authority. Sikhs joined the British Army in large numbers during the First World War, and fought again on the British side during World War II, most notably in Burma, preventing the Japanese from invading India and moving on to Calcutta. The British military consider Sikh troops to be among the finest soldiers in the world.

SPAM: The brand name for a canned chopped-pork product introduced by the Hormel Company in 1937. SPAM was the ideal product for military use, since it was high in protein, had a long shelf life and required no refrigeration.

SS *Schutzstaffel*: The SS began as a personal guard unit for Adolf Hitler, and came under the control of Reich Leader Heinrich Himmler. It was touted as an elite unit, the members of which manifested the Aryan ideal. In the latter role, it particularly attracted the support of physicians, especially those interested in racial superiority and genetic manipulation. The SS assumed control over all police forces in Germany by the late 1930s. Himmler supposedly modeled the SS after the Jesuits, with the idea of sworn allegiance and obedience, to Hitler alone, cemented by sacred oath. Himmler also made use of ancient Germanic myth and ritual in SS indoctrination and initiation ceremonies. The SS was divided into a number of units: the SD (*Sicherheitsdienst* "Security Service"); The Office of Race and Settlement; The WVHA

(*Wirtschafts-und Verwaltungshauptamt* "Office of Economics and Development), the branch which administered the concentration camps; and the *Waffen-SS* (the armed or military branch), which rivaled the regular *Wehrmacht* "Army" in power and influence. One of its first units was the *Leibstandarte SS Adolf Hitler*, Hitler's personal body guard. SS units were much involved in the *Einsatzgruppen* atrocities which occurred in Poland and Russia, earlier in the war. The *Totenkopfverbände* "Death's Head Units" (whose uniform symbol was a skull and crossbones), were a special unit of concentration camp guards, under the command of SS Brigadier General Theodor Eicke, the first commandant of Dachau after 1934, and Inspector of Concentration Camps. The highest rank in the SS, corresponding to Field Marshall or General of the Army, was *Reichsführer*, and was reserved for Heinrich Himmler.

Spitfire: Legendary British fighter plane, perhaps the most romanticized aircraft of World War II. The Spitfire is said to have won the Battle of Britain.

Springfield Rifle: Springfield M–1903 0.30in (7.62mm) rifle. Standard US infantry rifle until the introduction of the M-1 (Garand).

Stage Door Canteen (Hollywood Canteen): American servicemen had their morale boosted with the opportunity to mingle with Hollywood stars and other entertainment celebrities. *Stage Door Canteen* (1943), a film directed by Frank Borzage to support the Allied war effort, shows the lives of service men on leave in the city. Countless celebrities from Shakespearean actress Dame Judith Anderson to comedian Harpo Marx appear in the film.

Stalag: *Stammlager* 'common stock." German POW camp for enlisted men. *Stalagluft* usually held airmen, though this was not always the case.

Suribachi: The promontory on Iwo Jima where United States Marines raised the American flag. There were two raisings; one spontaneous, and the other posed. The posed raising was immortalized in a photograph by Joe Rosenthal.

Tenaru River: The Battle of the Tenaru River (Alligator Creek), Guadalcanal, 21–22 August 1942. A series of Japanese *Banzai* attacks led by Col. Kiyono Ichiki against Marine defenders. Private Albert Schmid, despite having been blinded, earned the Navy Cross during the battle for manning a machinegun after the gunner had been killed. Schmid was assisted by his comrade, Lee Diamond. Together they broke up several of the attacks. Ichiki committed suicide after failing to breach the Marine lines. John Garfield portrays Schmid in Warner Brothers' film *Pride of the Marines*.

Typhoon: British fighter/bomber with top speed well in excess of 300 mph, manufactured by Hawker Aircraft Ltd. Placed in service in September 1941. Type IB, adapted for ground operations support in 1944, carried eight airborne rockets, in addition to machine-guns and cannon.

USAFI: United States Armed Forces Institute. Offered service personnel during WWII and the Korean War the opportunity to take correspondence courses for high school equivalency and college credits.

USO: United Services Organization, a group providing entertainment to troops and other military personnel. The biggest names in American entertainment participated in USO shows, the most active and popular being Bob Hope and his entourage.

Tiger Tank: Popularly known as the German King Tiger Tank; officially designated the PzKpfw VI. This 68-ton behemoth was the largest tank deployed by either side during World War II. Armament was the 88 mm cannon. The Tiger was capable of speeds up to 24 mph, but was limited in range due to excessive fuel consumption.

U-Boat: Derives from the German word for submarine, namely *"unterseeboot."* All U-Boats were designated with the letter "U" followed by an identifying number.

Utah Beach: The westernmost of the three invasion beaches assigned to American forces on D-Day. The Utah Beach invasion zone was three miles wide and included the inland objectives of Carentan, St. Mere-Eglise, and the seaport of Cherbourg at the tip of the Cotentin peninsula.

V-E Day: Victory-in-Europe Day, 8 May 1945, the day the Allied Forces accepted Germany's unconditional surrender.

V-J Day: Victory-over-Japan Day. This date is either 15 August 1945, the day Japan agreed to surrender, or 2 September 1945, the day General Douglas MacArthur accepted the surrender document on behalf of the Allied Forces aboard the *U.S.S. Missouri* in Tokyo Bay.

von Runstedt, Field Marshall Gerd (1875–1953). von Runstedt developed the breakthrough offensive into France in 1940, and the attack in the Ukraine in 1941. von Runstedt was called from forced retirement in order to participate in the 1939 invasion of Poland. In June 1944, he was again forced to retire for his views that the war should be ended, and was briefly arrested for alleged complicity in the July 1944 bomb plot against Hitler. Again reinstated, he commanded the German armies during the Battle of the Bulge. Regarded by many Allied personnel as a perfect professional who had none of the excesses of some of Hitler's military cronies, von Runstedt was nevertheless considered for trial as a war criminal.

WACS. Women's Army Corps established 30 September 1943.

Walther (P–38): Pistol developed by the Walther Waffenfabrik of Zella Mehlis, Germany. It was intended to replace the Luger as a standard German sidearm.

Autographs and Notes